King's Pawn

The summons of Christ our Lord, the eternal King, goes forth to all:
"It is my will to conquer the whole world . . .
and thus to enter into the glory of my Father.
Whoever wishes to join me in this enterprise
must be willing to labor with me,
following me in suffering,
and thus following me in glory."

Those who wish to give greater proof of their love
and to distinguish themselves in the service of the eternal King will
not only offer themselves entirely for the work
but will act against worldly love
and make offerings of greater value.

From the Spiritual Exercises of Saint Ignatius of Loyola

King's Pawn

The Memoirs of George H. Dunne, S. J.

A Campion Book

Loyola University Press

Chicago

Loyola University Press
3441 North Ashland Avenue
Chicago, Illinois 60657

Library of Congress Cataloging in Publication Data

Dunne, George H. (George Harold), 1905-
    Kings's pawn: the memoirs of George H. Dunne.
    p.   cm.
    Includes index.
    ISBN 0-8294-0637-9
    1. Dunne, George H. (George Harold), 1905-   2. Jesuits-
-Biography.   I. Title.
BX4705.D879A3   1990
271'.5302--dc20   90-36734
[B]   CIP

Dedication

For Mary Isabel, sister *sans pareille*

Contents

Foreword

When the publishers sent me, out of the blue, the type-script of Fr. George Dunne's 800-page manuscript and asked me to draft within two weeks an introduction to the book, I was truly grateful for the invitation but, frankly, felt that I was being asked to do the impossible. Intimidated by the sheer bulk of the manuscript, I thought it most unlikely that I would be able to read it from cover-to-cover in time to meet what struck me as being an impossibly tight deadline. Accordingly, since I am reluctant, on principle, to review a book of any length that I have not been able to read in its entirety, I was tempted to decline the publisher's invitation with thanks, while hoping that he would generously permit me to keep the manuscript with the understanding, of course, that after I had finished reading it from cover-to-cover, I would look for an opportunity to review it in my weekly syndicated column or in some other appropriate forum.

Be that as it may, my initial concern about the length of the manuscript was completely unfounded. The fact is that once I had begun to read it, I was hooked and couldn't put it down. As it turned out, I managed to finish reading it within a few days in five consecutive four-hour sittings, and I enjoyed every minute of it.

This is by way of saying in shorthand that it is one of the most impressive and most gripping sets of memoirs I have read in recent years. In my judgment, it is a minor classic. I am pleased to recommend it enthusiastically, but, in doing so, I must stipulate that I am not competent to adjudicate all of the many personal conflicts, whether in or out of the Society of Jesus, in which Father Dunne has been involved during this long and multifaceted career and about which he has outspokenly stated his own position in what promises to be the most controversial book of its kind published in recent years. All I can say, as a sympathetic outside observer and long-time friend and admirer of Father Dunne, is that, in my opinion, it would be unfair to him to interpret his frankness and outspokenness as a peevish attempt on his part to even scores, so to speak, or to do his critics in. To be sure, he writes very pointedly without fear or favor, but, to his credit, he does so as a man of solid faith, with a wry sense of humor and with no trace of personal rancor or vindictiveness.

I have been around long enough and have been close enough to the ecclesiastical establishment to suspect that, had his book been written in its present form and style twenty-five or even fifteen years ago, it might not have been cleared for publication by his in-house Jesuit censors and probably would not have been issued under the imprint of a Jesuit-sponsored publisher. The fact that both his censors and his publisher are now comfortable with the book is good news—a sign that we are becoming a more tolerant and open-minded people and a more mature Church. In this respect I fully agree with Father Dunne when he says that "the Church is far more damaged by the suppression of truth than by its frank admission" and that "furthermore, the attempt to suppress the truth is an exercise in futility."

I do not wish to leave the mistaken impression, of course, that Father Dunne's book deals only or even mainly with his conflicts with ecclesiastical authority in and out of the Society. His gracefully crafted story, related here in vivid and engrossing detail, covers an extraordinary mix of diverse assignments and apostolates in many different climes and cultures from California to China, to St. Louis, Chicago, and Washington, D.C., to Rome, Switzerland, and Brazil, and finally back to China again on two occasions in recent years. I found it a fascinating and inspiring story.

Father Dunne himself, in looking back at the age of eighty-five on the highlights of his busy life, modestly concludes that he can see "little of lasting accomplishment." His story, he says, "is largely a record of failure and frustration which contrasts sharply with the achievements of most of my contemporaries." I am sure that I am not the only reader of his absorbing memoirs who will strongly disagree with him in this regard. In my judgment, few American priests of this century can match his combination of talents. He has excelled as a teacher and lecturer, a journalist and essayist of genuine distinction, a successful playwright, a pioneer civil rights activist, a champion of democratic trade unionism in the movie industry, a director of Peace Corps training projects in Ethiopia and Brazil, the first director of an innovative (but, alas, ill-fated) Geneva-based ecumenical project concerned with international economic development and world peace, a parish priest, an overseas director of American university students living in Switzerland, etc. In all, a most impressive record.

The title of Father Dunne's memoirs, *King's Pawn*, suggests that, more often than not, he took up these diverse assignments unexpectedly, on very short notice, and almost by happenstance as a pawn in "the game of chess which is life." His readiness to roll gracefully with the punches and to adapt, almost overnight, to such a wide variety of assignments, and to do so without indulging in self-pity speaks well for the depth of his lifetime commitment as a religious; and his ability to carry them out with professional competence of a high order says to this reviewer that his life has been a great success. I would add only that I, for one, literally stand in awe of his ability in his eighty-fifth year to tell his story in such engrossing detail and with such enviable clarity and literary grace. From this point of view alone, his book is a veritable *tour de force*. Again, I recommend it very highly. In my judgment, it is a significant contribution in the field of twentieth-century American Church history.

Rev. Msgr. George G. Higgins, Adjunct Lecturer
Department of Theology
The Catholic University of America

Acknowledgments

I owe thanks to Jack Izzo, S.J., whose genteel and persistent urging got me started, thanks to Peter Fleming, S.J., and to Len Hilts for their early attention to the manuscript, and special thanks to Paul Locatelli, S.J., whose benign harassment kept me chained to the workbench until I had got it done. Thanks too to my editor, Edward W. Schmidt, S.J., who together with expertise brought to his task a personal interest that made working with him a delight. Thanks to the publishers of *Commonweal* and *America* for permission to use articles of mine whose copyright belongs to them. And last, but far from least, thanks to all my Jesuit confreres, the tall and the short, the stout and the lean, *compagnons de la route*, who have made the pilgrimage a memorable one.

Introduction

When it was first proposed that I write my autobiography, I did not think the suggestion could be serious. My life hardly seemed worth recording. It has not been a record of brilliant achievement, but rather of many failures. When it is finished there will be little to indicate that I passed this way; a book, some articles in library files which few will ever see, but which might win me the modest immortality of an occasional reference in a scholarly footnote. This is not the kind of life that offers material for autobiographies.

It may be, on the other hand, that every life, however undistinguished, deserves to be recorded. Perhaps anyone who has lived beyond the allotted three score and ten has something to say. Possibly from my own career, compounded largely of frustrations and defeats, there are certain conclusions to be drawn of general interest. Reflection upon my experiences may generate ideas or lead to observations worth noting.

This is not a Book of Confessions. It does not contain an account of my sins, which have been many; that book has already been written by the Recording Angel and filed away, I am afraid, for future reference. I will not attempt to give a full account of my life, but only of those episodes from which conclusions of a more than personal nature can be drawn. Little or no mention is made of many, notably family and friends, who have enriched my life. From this it is not to be concluded that I cherish less their memory nor value less what they have meant to me.

Life is like a chess game, in which each move shuts the door upon a variety of future possibilities and at the same time opens the door upon an incalculable number of potential developments. One decision, sometimes made without thought of the future, may determine the whole course of one's life. Karma, the Hindus call it, the mystery of human destiny, with which Thornton Wilder concerned himself in *The Bridge of San Luis Rey*. What forces or factors, what influences, what decisions and whose, determined the course of my life?

A Jesuit provincial superior once said, not anticipating that his remark would be reported to me, "George Dunne could have gone far in the Society of Jesus, if he had used his head." His reference was to my resistance to the effort of the president of St. Louis University, who was also my immediate superior at the time, to impose racial segregation upon the students. This decision, in this case my own, had, according to a man in a position to know, radically changed the whole course of my life, determining there and then that instead of "going far" in the Society of Jesus I would go nowhere. What other decisions, my own and those of others, have similarly affected my life?

Timothy Manning, then still a young auxiliary bishop of Los Angeles, once remarked to a group of priests, not foreseeing that one of them would carry his word to me the very next day, that "Fr. George Dunne has the makings of another Martin Luther." This was obviously grossly to underestimate the genius of Luther and greatly to exaggerate my talents. Making all due allowances for the hyperbole, what were the influences in my life which ruled out the possibility of my following the path of Martin Luther and made Timothy Manning a poor prophet?

The late John Farrow, writer and motion picture director, was not pleased by some of my activities. According to a story in Ebony magazine, he was reassured, probably by his friend and my immediate superior, Fr. Edward Whelan, S.J., president of Loyola University in Los Angeles, that he would not have to worry about me much longer because within a few months I was to be sent back to China. What factors and whose decision determined, to the disappointment of both John Farrow and Edward Whelan, that I would not return to China? And where would I be now had I returned?

The ordinarily phlegmatic Waldemar Gurian, learned scholar and author, in a burst of enthusiasm uncharacteristic of his Teutonic temperament, once hailed me in a letter to my provincial (which my provincial never mentioned to me) as an American Henri de Lubac and Hans Urs von Balthasar. I do not recall which of my articles was chiefly responsible for eliciting such high praise; in any case, Gurian's estimate was as wide of the mark as had been Timothy Manning's. Again allowing for the hyperbole, if I possessed talents justifying a hope that I would make a substantial contribution to American Catholic thought, what prevented me from doing so? Whether or not one believes with Shakespeare that "there's a divinity that shapes our ends, rough-hew them how we will," there is fascination in the mysterious play of forces that determine the course of every human life.

One

Origins

I should start by telling where I came from. That is easy. I came from St. Louis, where I first appeared on March 11, 1905. The question is how I got to St. Louis. It is unfortunate that few of those who migrated to America and built a nation preserved family genealogical records. I have always been sadly conscious of the void in my knowledge of our family history.

One day in San Gimignano, a medieval town in Italy between Florence and Siena famous for its many towers, a medieval status symbol, I stood looking at what was once the monastery where Fra Girolamo Savonarola began his tempestuous career. It is now a state penitentiary. A small Italian boy watched me.

"Where do you live?" I asked him.

"Here," he replied, nodding toward the ancient two-storied house behind him.

"How long have you lived here?"

"Five hundred years" was his matter-of-fact reply.

He could not have imagined how I envied him this continuity with the past, these roots so deeply planted. His family probably listened to the first fiery sermons that Savonarola preached in the monastery church across the street. They may have stood in front of the house, where the boy stood now, and watched the bold monk as he rode off on his mule, bound for Florence, where he would later die on the scaffold, his body burned at the spot marked today by a plaque in the great piazza.

I am much less envious of that Italian boy today, because I know much more about my roots now than I did then, thanks to Len Hilts. A prolific writer of books and articles, Hilts is a grandnephew of Finley Peter Dunne, America's famous satirist of

"Dooley Letter" fame. His grandmother Katherine was Finley Peter's sister. He has traced the Dunne family back to the early middle ages. The Dunnes did not easily accept the yoke. Perhaps it is in the genes. "The Dunne priests," writes Hilts, "traditional Irishmen that they were, ignored the rule of celibacy issued by Rome and continued to marry for centuries. They passed pastorates and bishop's hats from father to son for generations, in accordance with an Irish custom dating back to the sixth century."[1]

My great-grandfather Patrick Dunne and his wife, Amelia Malone, with their seven boys and three girls, in the summer of 1825 left their home in the town of Stradbally, Queen's County (it now bears the Gallic name of Leix County), and sailed from Cork for Chatham, New Brunswick. Here, according to Elmer Davis in his biography of Finley Peter Dunne, they joined friends and relatives who had preceded them.

Tragedy was not slow to follow. On September 20, 1825, a month after their arrival, they lost the oldest girl, seventeen-year-old Bridget, perhaps as a consequence of the rigors of the ocean voyage. In October the Great Miramichi Fire destroyed four million acres of timber, killed more than 160 persons and laid waste to Chatham and Newcastle. On February 2, 1826, the second-oldest son followed his sister in death; this was John, nineteen years old, probably a victim of the disease which ravaged the area after the fire. Their tombstone, which they share with their father, who was to die on September 20, 1839, is still to be seen in the churchyard of Saint Patrick's in South Nelson, seven miles from Chatham.

Five of the boys became skilled shipbuilders, learning their craft at the Cunard Line shipyard in Chatham. The sixth son, Dennis, became a priest and later the first vicar general of the Chicago diocese. Mary, the older of the two surviving daughters, married Matthew Riordan, a native of Kinsale in County Cork, like her brothers a shipbuilder. Two of their children were to have distinguished careers as churchmen: Patrick William Riordan, as the archbishop of San Francisco (1883-1914), and Daniel J. Riordan, as chancellor of the Archdiocese of Chicago and pastor of Saint Elizabeth Parish.

Meanwhile Edward, next to youngest of the Dunne boys, had been carrying on a courtship with Mary Finn. Whatever the special difficulties caused by the fact that he lived on the mainland and she, an only child, on Prince Edward Island, where she had grown up, he overcame them, fortunately for me—for he was to become my grandfather and she my grandmother. One day in 1846, all the Dunnes crossed the waters to participate in the nuptial Mass in Saint Patrick Church of Edward, aged twenty-one, and Mary, aged fifteen, and to join in the festivities which followed.

With economic conditions in decline in New Brunswick, the Cunard shipyards having failed, thoughts began to turn to the United States and especially to the booming town of Chicago. From a population of 50 in 1830 it was fast approaching 30,000 and becoming an important center of transportation for railroads, stagecoaches, and steamboats. After much discussion the family decided to move to Chicago and, being expert ship's carpenters all, to do so by a boat of their own construction capable of carrying fourteen or fifteen people. By mid May 1848, the boat, a three-master, was completed and ready for launching, recaulking and the final touches. Before the month was out they set sail for Chicago by way of the St. Lawrence River and the Great Lakes. En route they picked up Dennis at Quebec, where he had completed his studies for the priesthood.[2]

They did not immediately establish their home in Chicago, because a cholera plague was raging in the area; instead, with the exception of Dennis and the Riordans, they moved on to Dodge County , Wisconsin, where their other sister, Elizabeth, and her husband, William Dowling, offered them the hospitality of their farm.

In Chicago, Dennis was assigned by the bishop, James Oliver Van de Velde, to minister to the many small, largely Irish-Catholic communities which had grown up during the construction of the Illinois and Michigan Canal between Chicago and Ottawa, some seventy miles distant.

The dispersal did not last long. Within a few years the cholera danger had passed. In 1854 Bishop Van de Velde died. His successor, Bp. Anthony O'Regan, in the same year called Dennis Dunne back to Chicago and named him pastor of the second oldest church in Chicago, Saint Patrick's, at the corner of Adams and Desplaines.[3] The others soon followed. Romance had flowered during their Wisconsin days. Peter, who at forty-five years of age was thought by his siblings to be a confirmed bachelor, had fallen in love with and married a vivacious Irish girl, Ellen Finley, like himself an immigrant and twenty-five years his junior.

My father, Michael, was a hotel man, associated with John Burroughs Drake, whose Drake Hotel on the Near North Side remains today one of Chicago's more elegant hotels. Mine was a

Chicago family; father, mother, three older brothers, and a younger sister were all born in the Windy City. During the early years of the marriage my father was manager of the Chicago Beach Hotel, a waterfront hotel near the University of Chicago. My two oldest brothers spent much of their early boyhood there. During the St. Louis World's Fair, however, he was managing the then-famous Planters' House. That is how I chanced to be born in St. Louis on March 11, 1905. The family went back to Chicago when I was three months old.

Almost forty years later I returned as a faculty member of St. Louis University. But my second stay was not much longer than the first. After less than eight months, my short and happy life as a professor in the newly established Institute of Social Sciences at St. Louis University ended abruptly when I was summarily dismissed by the president of the university and ordered to return to California.

Two

Destiny

We moved to California in 1912, following the death of my father that same year. His death was quite unexpected inasmuch as he had always enjoyed robust health. It was ludicrous in the sense that it was caused by an ailment which today would be classified as minor. He had gone to Minneapolis to reorganize and to sell the Revere Hotel. He developed hemorrhoids. The doctor ordered an operation. Reluctant to undergo surgery at a distance from the family, he postponed the operation until he finished his business and returned to Chicago. He delayed too long.

The only clear image I retain of my father is as he appeared upon arriving home. We lived just off the Midway near the University of Chicago on a street then called Rosalie Court, now named Harper Avenue, after the first president of the university. I happened to be on the front porch, and I distinctly remember his face, deathly pale, as he slowly climbed the front steps. He was operated on that same day by a famous surgeon, Dr. Charles Murphy, but died in the operating room. It was Palm Sunday, April 1, 1912.

A few months later our mother herded her five children, the oldest of whom was thirteen, onto the train and headed for California. Only a year earlier my father had declined an invitation to take over managing the Del Monte Hotel in beautiful Monterey, California, because mother was reluctant to leave Chicago and her many friends and relatives for the strange, friendless and distant land of California.

Two decisions thus drastically altered the destiny of many people: her decision not to move to Monterey, his decision to postpone surgery. They affected his destiny, hers, that of each of the children, and also, to a greater or lesser degree, the destiny of all those whose lives would later impinge upon our own. What direction would the lives of each of us have taken had we gone to Monterey in 1911? Or had my father recovered in 1912? What schools would we have attended, what friends made, what careers chosen, what marriages contracted, what children generated? Thus the game of chess which is life.

California was a distant land in 1912. It took us six days to get there. The Pullmans were still lighted with gas, and the conductor—or perhaps it was the porter—would go around in the evening lighting the gas jets. I shared an upper berth with one of my brothers, two years older and smarter than I. He assigned me the outer half of the berth, and one night, as the train rounded a sharp curve in the Rockies, I tumbled out, landed face down in the aisle and bloodied my nose. I spent the rest of the night in the lower berth with my mother. Ever since, when traveling by train, I have loved to prop myself up in the berth at night and gaze out at the darkened, mystery-filled countryside moving by the window.

Los Angeles—1912

Los Angeles was a small, pleasant town in 1912. I remember the miles upon miles of beautiful orange groves which reached almost into the city. Most of them have long since disappeared and with them much of the beauty of Southern California. It would have been impossible to find smog even in the dictionary.

The corner of Vermont and Santa Barbara avenues—the latter is now Martin Luther King Boulevard—was on the southwestern edge of town; both were dirt roads beyond there. The maiden King sisters, who became life-long friends of my mother, still lived with their mother in the small ranch house in which they had been born and from which, armed with shotguns, they had more than once driven off marauding bandits. Later, as the city developed, their land would make them wealthy, and their wealth would support many charitable institutions.

Western Avenue did not exist. What is now Crenshaw Boulevard was a cow path through agricultural land. The upper-middle-class Baldwin Hills residential area, now already past its prime, was then part of a huge ranch over which hundreds of horses roamed. Where the Los Angeles Coliseum now stands was a one-mile race track and stables. During our first several years in Los Angeles we lived in a flat on Vermont Avenue, just south of Santa Barbara Avenue, where the pavement ended.

What induced mother to move to this outpost of civilization after a year earlier vetoing a move to a much more developed part of California was, I believe, the desire to escape from the city where everything was associated with the memory of my father. They must have loved each other very much. His name was Michael Damian, but because he disliked the nickname Mike his friends always called him M.D.; and that is how mother always referred to him. There was nothing saccharine in her comments about him, but from the anecdotes she told us of their life together there emerged the picture of an attractive man whom she admired, respected, and deeply loved and who had returned her love. She had been engaged to another man when she met him, on summer vacation on Mackinac Island, where he was the manager of the Grand Hotel. The other man, she liked impishly to tell us, had afterwards become a millionaire. But mother had no regrets.

She did, however, have memories, and she wanted not to be reminded at every turn of all that she had lost with my father's death. Earlier that year one of her four younger sisters had moved with her husband to Orange, California, and mother decided to follow her.

It could not have been an easy decision, and it was vigorously opposed by my father's family, especially by his mother, a strong-willed matriarch who had borne fifteen children and who would live to be eighty-eight. The Dunnes had roots in Chicago. Three generations in a city as young as Chicago in 1912 made you one of the old families. That is why grandmother Dunne could see neither rhyme nor reason in mother's decision to take her five children away from the protecting circle of so many relatives and friends who could help her with the new burdens thrust upon her by the sudden interposition of death. But well-intentioned help can easily become unconscious domination. Mother, no less strong-willed than her mother-in-law, was determined to raise her own children.

We had a maid, Mabel Waite, who had been with us for several years. Mabel insisted upon accompanying us to California. She was of invaluable help for several years until she left us to go to San Diego, where she married and raised her own family.

In Los Angeles, mother, inexperienced in business, made some bad real estate investments. She tried operating an ice cream parlor, but there was no future in that, at least not in 1912 in the sparsely settled area around Fortieth and Vermont. So she left the store in charge of Mabel and enrolled as a student in the Teachers' College. Armed with her teacher's certificate, she supported, raised, and educated her brood on the less-than-handsome salary then paid by the Los Angeles school system.

For some years mother taught school in Highland Park, on the opposite side of the city from where we lived. It involved some three hours of travel every day on the street car, an early morning departure, a late afternoon return. My second-oldest brother, Marshall, prepared the evening meals. As a consequence he became an expert cook, something mother never was.

Her experiences and observations during those years of daily streetcar journeys to and from school furnished her with an almost inexhaustible fund of stories, in most of which the joke was on her. When she was past seventy and visiting me in Chicago, she kept a group of sophisticated University of Chicago students in a state of high hilarity for several hours recounting some of her adventures.

I recall one story she especially delighted to tell. Waiting at her Second Street and Broadway transfer point, she noticed a little Japanese boy standing on the corner. Thinking it would gladden his lonely heart in this strange land to hear some words in his native tongue she approached him and, in her best Japanese, said, "Ee kaga deska." He looked up, scowled, and, in his best American, replied "Go to hell!" She discovered then what most Californians would not learn for many years and some have yet to learn, that the naturalized or second-generation Japanese or Chinese is no less an American than any other citizen of the land.

While she was still teaching in Highland Park and I was in high school, I participated in a small nonecumenical riot that rocked the Highland Park community and made headlines in the *Los Angeles Times*. A speaker, sponsored by Protestant church groups, appeared in Los Angeles claiming to be a former Catholic monk and titillating his audiences with tales of the shocking things that he said went on in monasteries. It was in the old-fashioned Maria Monk tradition, and his audiences loved it. He was a fraud. Investigation proved that the monastery in northern Ireland to which he claimed to have belonged did not exist.

Some of us students at Loyola High School had heard him speak, and we decided to challenge him and expose the fraudulent nature of his charges. The star debater in the school was Bill Rains, who had an aplomb and a mature speaking style beyond his years. The plot called for us to attend the next lecture. At an appropriate moment Bill Rains, with the rest of us lending moral support by our presence, was to interrupt the speaker and engage him in debate.

It turned out that the next appearance of the alleged ex-monk took place in a Protestant church near mother's school. The minister's daughter was in mother's class as were a number of other students whose families belonged to the church. When we arrived, some two dozen strong, the rather small bungalow-style church was already well filled. No seats remaining, we crowded into the back and stood surrounding our champion.

The reputed ex-monk appeared, dressed in a priest's cassock. He was a husky, handsome man in his early thirties. He launched into his speech. As he proceeded, each of his spicy tales endorsed by a cry of "Amen" chanted in chorus by the congregation, we waited for Bill Rains to intervene. Before his untimely death some years later, Bill would become a highly successful trial lawyer, but that night in Highland Park he had cold feet. He ignored our pleading looks and gestures.

One of our group, a nephew of federal judge Paul MacCormack, had arrived ahead of our main body and found himself an aisle seat well down in front. Out of patience both with Rains and with the speaker, he suddenly cried out, "You are a liar!"

The speaker stepped off his platform, strode down the aisle, and took a wild swing at MacCormack, who successfully ducked the blow. We poured out from the back of the church and down the aisle after the monk, who took refuge behind a phalanx of men who leaped to their feet and formed a line of defense to meet our charge. The battle was on!

Although the screaming of women in the congregation created an impressive background sound, it actually was not much of a battle. There was a good deal of pushing and shoving, but jammed into the narrow aisle we did not have much punching room. I found myself by ill chance in the front line of the charge and became the target of some of the few blows thrown.

Not a great deal of damage was done. In the thrust and counterthrust of the two contending armies, the door of the church was knocked off its hinges; an electric light was smashed. Someone got to a phone and called the police. When two uniformed officers arrived on the scene the donnybrook ended. Their remarkably low-keyed approach might serve as a model to police today. They quietly and good-naturedly advised us to disperse and go home. And we did, merciless in our comments about Bill Rains, but secretly delighted that his dereliction had led to so exciting an adventure.

The next morning the *Los Angeles Times* headlined its story "Sinn Fein Hoodlums Riot in Church." The Sinn Fein connection was less than tenuous, but it would have made grandfather Higgins proud.

Mother arrived at her school the next morning to find it humming with excitement. Her students, some of whose parents had been in the congregation the previous night, gave her lurid descriptions of the riotous scenes. Not suspecting that her son had been one of the hoodlums, she deplored the rioting but suggested that it be seen in the perspective of the religious intolerance which had provoked it. That night she told us about the excitement and the discussions with her students. I told her that I had been there. I think she was amused and perhaps a little bit proud. Although she was wholly without racial or religious bigotry herself, she was thankful for her Catholic faith and proud to be Irish.

When a quarter of a century later the American Jewish Committee at its Civic Awards Dinner honored me with a citation for my services in promoting better community relations, the Highland Park incident was not among the services mentioned. Perhaps it might have been appropriately included, for as a result the ex-monk disappeared from Southern California. His disappearance helped relieve interfaith tensions in the community.

I entered Loyola High School in 1918 and was not at all happy about it. My three brothers attended Manual Arts public high school. Some of my grammar school friends had registered there and so had I. From our backyard I could climb up the back of the Manual Arts grandstand. I knew all their football stars by sight and by name. Some of them belonged to my two oldest brothers' "gang."

Only a few days before the school term was to begin, a Jesuit scholastic, Eugene Ivancovich, with a list of parochial school graduates in his pocket, called upon my mother. He persuaded her to send me to the Jesuit high school, about to begin its second year of existence on what was then Sixteenth Street, now called Venice Boulevard. At that time Sixteenth Street was really not a street at all but a right-of-way for the Pacific Electric Railway, whose big, clumsy red cars passed that way en route to Venice and Santa Monica Beach.

As I climbed the front steps at Loyola High School that September morning in 1918, the first person I met and the second Jesuit I ever met—Gene Ivancovich had been the first—was the redoubtable Zacheus J. Maher, S.J., who was destined to have a large impact on the course of my life. I was to be one of the disappointments of his life. He was to be one of the disappointments of mine. So the disillusionment was mutual. Much water would flow under many bridges, however, before that happened.

Father Maher was then principal of the high school and in the early stages of his career. He would later serve terms as president of the University of Santa Clara, president of Loyola University, provincial head of the California Province of the Jesuit order, and assistant to the superior general of the order in Rome, representing all the American provinces. During the war years, because of the difficulty of communicating freely with Rome, he made his headquarters in Poughkeepsie, New York. It was during these years, when with broad powers delegated to him by the general of the order he was virtually head of all the Jesuits in the United States, that our long friendship, begun that first day of high school in 1918, came to a shattering end.

Because I did not expect to be able to go to college—few boys did seventy years ago—I enrolled in the commercial course which the Jesuits had just introduced and which, ill-starred from the start, was destined not to last beyond that first year. Most of those in the class had failed the classical course and were repeating the first year of high school. Apparently the Jesuits had established the commercial course especially for them. Latin had proved beyond their reach. Bookkeeping was substituted. The teacher was a frail young man, once a seminarian, I believe, who was utterly unable to cope with the ruffians who kept the class in a constant undisciplined uproar.

One day one of the ringleaders notched a slip of cardboard in his pen and, when the teacher turned to the blackboard, hurled it like a dart, not aiming to impale him, I trust, but trying to come close. A roar rose from the class, the door flew open and an irate Zach Maher confronted the suddenly silent mob. The pen still quivered in the door in which it had imbedded itself. When the culprit would not identify himself Father Maher threatened to keep the entire class there until someone pointed out the guilty party.

I should have suspected then that he and I would eventually come to a parting of the ways. I thought the culprit should have identified himself. Perhaps it is for the same reason that, although I believe in the Fifth Amendment, I have never been able to muster up a strong feeling of solidarity with those who invoke its protection. I feel that we should be willing to answer for our actions and convictions. On the other hand, informers are a low species of animal; and I thought it extremely bad policy for one engaged in character formation—one of the chief ends of Jesuit education—to induce young boys by threat of punishment to turn informer. Happily, Father Maher's efforts failed. At six o'clock, when his own dinner was on the table, I imagine, he gave up the contest of wills and dismissed us.

I did not remain in this turbulent class more than a few weeks. Realizing that the prospects of learning anything were very dim, I bade farewell to a commercial career and transferred to the traditional academic course of the Jesuits which is best described as college preparatory.

I spent eight years at Loyola, four in high school and four in college. The college, which in 1929 would move to its present campus at Playa Del Rey and become a university, might be called in current terminology a microschool. High school, college, and Jesuit living quarters all occupied a single building. Space destined eventually to be reconverted into classrooms had been partitioned into cubicles to provide makeshift rooms for the Jesuits. One or two of them lived in classroom clothes closets. My freshman college class in 1922 numbered perhaps forty students. In 1926 ten of us were awarded our bachelor of arts degrees, the largest graduating class to that date.

Our relations with the Jesuits were close and informal. There was always a good deal of bantering about the small-town aspects of Los Angeles. The Jesuits were without exception natives of the city by the Golden Gate, with the contempt for the provincial town in Southern California characteristic of all San Franciscans. Los Angeles had not yet supplied any recruits to the Jesuit order. Although a half dozen or more Loyola High School graduates would precede me, I would be the first graduate of the college to enter the Society of Jesus.

The junior and senior years were especially enjoyable. Since we numbered only ten and met around a large table, every class was in the nature of an informal group discussion. Often enough the discussion had little connection with the academic subject. This was especially true of the course conducted by Fr. George Golden Fox, of beloved memory.

Father Fox began class every morning, after lowering his 250 pounds into his chair, by running a hand over his bald pate, heaving a ponderous sigh, and announcing, "I'm so-o-o tired!" It was never difficult to divert him from his subject, scholastic philosophy, to a discussion of the theater, current motion pictures, and Hollywood personalities.

He was an aficionado of the theater. As a boy he had haunted the theaters of San Francisco. He would have been a fine actor; he had the most expressive face and hands of anyone I have known. Instead, he became a Jesuit. But he never lost his love of the theater and always directed the dramatic presentations of the school with which he was associated. Edmund Lowe learned to act under his coaching at Santa Clara University.

He was well known, widely loved, and frequently consulted by the motion-picture celebrities of the day. Many an evening saw a heavily veiled Mabel Normand emerge from her chauffeured limousine and enter the building, in search, no doubt, of an answer to the problems of her tormented life. Father Fox loved to talk about the stars and could always find a word to say in their defense or in extenuation of their faults.

His defense of Marion Davies has always seemed to me a classic of charity. Marion, as everyone knew, shared bed, room and board with William Randolph Hearst, who was separated but not divorced from Mrs. Hearst. One Christmas season when I was at the perfume counter in Robinson's Department Store buying a modest present for the current girl friend, I was surprised to find myself alongside youthful, freckle-faced Marion and Hearst, whose equine face surmounting the high starched collar was unmistakable and who looked more like her father than her lover. Hearst, who did everything on a lavish scale, bought her a bottle of perfume the size of a giant thermos bottle, and my own modest purchase shrank to nothingness.

His extenuation of Marion Davies was typical of the way Father Fox rose to the defense of the stars in our classroom discussions. In response to an unkind comment about Marion, Father Fox, his expressive face looking as afflicted as that of a basset hound, remarked reproachfully, "I wouldn't be too critical of Marion, boys; after all, she has been faithful to Mr. Hearst for many years."

I last saw Father Fox before I sailed for China in 1932. He still looked like Friar Tuck, still wheezed, still dipped his cigarettes into a medicinal fluid that was supposed to make them less aggravating to his emphysema, and was still tired. God's rest to a loveable man.

And rest to his great friend, Fr. James Taylor—"Calamity James," Father Fox always called him. He was a handsome, grey-haired man, whose naturally aristocratic air was enhanced by the opera cape which he always wore on campus. The two of them were constantly dueling with each other in a bantering exchange which had evidently been going on ever since they had traveled together in Europe years before. We could easily divert Father Taylor from his subject at least momentarily by reporting an amusing anecdote Father Fox had told us about him during the previous hour. He was not so easily detoured as Father Fox, however, and after a few moments of scornful rebuttal he would bring us back to the subject he taught, which was dynamic psychology.

One feature of Loyola College in the early twenties which would scandalize educators today, including Jesuit educators, was the admissions policy of its evening law school, established in 1920. Not only did it accept high school graduates, a not uncommon practice at the time, but it allowed students who were attending the liberal arts college in the morning to attend the law school in the evening. At the end of four years, it conferred upon the survivors at the same commencement a bachelor of arts and a bachelor of laws degree.

I had originally intended to attend liberal arts college for two years and then enter law school, for my ambition, since dropping the commercial course in first year high school, had been to become a lawyer. When I discovered that many of my classmates were combining morning college and evening law school, I felt I was being cheated. At the beginning of the second semester I enrolled in the law school as well.

To add to the seeming absurdity of this as an educational experience, I worked in the afternoons. I had worked since my first day in high school, during the first two years in a fruit-and-vegetable store whose Japanese owner Harry, his wife, and little boy became fast friends. They sometimes took me to a Japanese restaurant for sukiyaki. During idle hours in the store Harry, a university graduate, and I had long discussions, often about the irrationality of racial prejudice. In the following years I held a variety of jobs; for a brief period—patience being in short supply—I was even a piano teacher.

Publisher-Editor

During my last two years of college, in partnership with a former high school classmate, Edward O'Connor, I was editor and copublisher of a weekly community newspaper; during one wild period, we had three papers. Community newspapers, which have developed into major enterprises, were then in their infancy. There were only four or five in Los Angeles, one of them being the *West Jefferson Press*, which Ed and I published. I gathered the news, wrote and edited, for which Ed had no talent. He, a born salesman, handled the advertising sales, for which I had no talent. I had briefly tried selling hardwood flooring to builders and had learned that salesmanship was not my gift.

Ed O'Connor and I successfully ran the *West Jefferson Press* during two action-filled, exciting, and sometimes exhausting years. When Los Angeles adopted a new charter which substituted the ward system for the former citywide election of councilmen, our newspaper acquired a certain political leverage, and we leaped into the electoral fray with more enthusiasm than prudence. We did not look carefully before we leaped. We backed the wrong man. Our candidate, John Topham, came in second in a field of eight; but unlike a horse race, politics does not pay off for second place. I think we had backed our man chiefly because he got to us first. The eventual winner, "Cupid" Sparks, who had acquired his nickname as head of the Los Angeles County Marriage License Bureau, came to solicit our support the day after we had announced for Topham.

As we watched returns at election headquarters we had the satisfaction of knowing that our man had carried every precinct reached by the *West Jefferson Press*, but had been swamped in the rest of the ward. We learned a lot about politics and profited handsomely from the advertising which companies supporting Topham bought in our newspaper, at double the regular rates. Most of them were construction or supply companies, which like to have friends in government.

During all of this time I was attending college in the morning and law school at night. In retrospect it seems impossible; but I managed to get good grades in college and more than my share of gold medals for academic excellence in law school. When I decided to enter the Society of Jesus, Ed O'Connor and I sold the newspaper.

The dean of the law school was "Bulldog Joe" Ford. Early in his career Ford had locked horns with the noted trial lawyer Clarence Darrow, who, in a famous trial, had defended the MacNamara brothers, who had dynamited the *Los Angeles Times* building. Darrow himself was then brought to trial on the charge of attempting to suborn a juror in the MacNamara case. Darrow conducted this own defense, in the course of which he dubbed Ford, whose underslung jaw matched his tenacity as a cross-examiner, "Bulldog Joe." The nickname stuck.

When Ford learned at the opening of the fall term in 1926 that I had abandoned law to join the Jesuits, he wrote an angry letter to the provincial urging that I be dismissed from the novitiate and sent back to law school. He was evidently convinced that I was more qualified for law than for the priesthood. He may well have been right.

Three

Come, Follow Me

My decision to enter the Society of Jesus and study for the priesthood came as a surprise to my family and friends, and to the Jesuits. It was the result of an entirely unexpected manifestation to me of God's will; it was so unmistakable that I was unable to ignore it, although I tried, and so imperative that, although I fought it bitterly, in the end I was forced to surrender. That is how it seemed to me then. That is how it seems to me now, over sixty years later.

Those who do not believe in God, or who do not believe that he intervenes in human affairs or that he concerns himself with human destinies, will have to find some other explanation. Perhaps a psychiatrist, analyzing the evidence of my life to this point, can find an entirely natural explanation of why, when approaching the end of my senior year in college, I suddenly renounced all the ambitions I had nurtured for many years and entered upon a career which to me represented the abandonment of everything appealing in life.

For my part, the experience was so real and so overwhelming that I am convinced I was in direct contact with the supernatural. This is one reason the God Is Dead school of thought made no impression upon me. I saw nothing new in their arguments, most of which seem to say only that we really have no idea of the nature of God. We had arrived at this conclusion in one of our round-table discussions in college very early on in our course in theodicy.

In any case, far more than any of Saint Thomas's Five Proofs for the Existence of God, of which at least four are of doubtful probative value, my experience has made me impervious to doubt.

21

I know that God exists, although I know little else about him, because I have experienced him. Faith may be dying, but not God.

I do not know why he would bother himself with me. There is no achievement in my life, nothing in my record to suggest why he would wish me to become a priest instead of a lawyer. If he had some special purpose in mind, I have long since disappointed him.

It is difficult, I admit, to believe that God has a concern about every human being. Yet, if he is concerned about me, he must be equally concerned about everyone else. This is a mystery which forever haunts me. In Buddhist temples in Tokyo years ago I watched devout men and women at their prayers. In Asmara in Ethiopia I observed devout Moslems performing their devotions. All were communicating with God, called by other names and sought through different symbols than those to which I am accustomed.

I look at my fellow passengers on a flight from Miami to Belem, or from Athens to Rome. I look at the people around me on a crowded bus as we careen madly through the streets of Rio de Janeiro. I look at the tens of thousands of wildly screaming fans at a football game in Maracana Stadium. I look at the hordes of men, women, and children swarming in the *barrios* of Fortaleza, strangers all to me and mostly to each other. Each is an individual with a personal history, a personal destiny; each has a small circle of friends and acquaintances.

I scan the faces of people who pass me in the street. Each morning in Rio de Janeiro I watch people of all ages, all shades of color, from nearly all walks of life, as they visit a chapel at the church of Nossa Senhora do Carme da Lapa to light a candle and pray to a saint or to Christ. I am awed in the presence of this mystery of human destiny. To say that each of this myriad of human beings is an object of God's concern is a staggering proposition. Yet we have Christ's word for it.

Our difficulty in believing this is undoubtedly due to the fact that we really have no positive concept of the nature of God. Having no real idea of what he is, we tend to think of him in anthropomorphic terms. We think of God as we might of the head of the personnel department in some large corporation, surrounded by filing cabinets filled with the curriculum vitae of each of the employees which he must keep up to date with the details of their every activity. This kind of an image reduces the notion of divine providence to a patent absurdity. The fact is that we have no concept of the nature of God, and there is nothing in our experience which can help us understand what he is. Whenever we think about him in images drawn from our experience, as we are obliged to do, we are in danger of forming an erroneous and misleading concept.

We know some things God is not: a golden calf, an old grey-bearded man sitting on a cloud in the sky. We can make a few other negative statements about him, that he is not finite, not change-able, although we really have only the foggiest idea of what that means. But nobody really knows any more about his nature than that it exists. That, if the Old Testament is to be believed, is all that God ever told us about himself: that he is and that that is what he is. "I am who I am."

There is a hymn attributed to Saint Gregory of Nazianzus which in my judgment says all that can be said about God. I quote it in French because that is the language of my breviary and because it says it better than I can say it in English: *L'au delà de tout—n'est-pas là tout ce qu'on peut dire de toi?* A rough, prosaic translation might be: "The beyond-all-else: isn't that all one can say of you?"

This seems to make arguments about the nature of God, some of which have led to schisms, to violence, and to bloodshed, rather meaningless. It would greatly simplify the task of theologians if the entire dogmatic statement about God were reduced to the simple affirmation that he exists and that he has revealed himself to us chiefly in the person of Jesus Christ. This would still leave room for dissent, inasmuch as there are many who do not accept the divinity of Christ; but it would narrow the area of disagreement to the essentials. Perhaps, because of the venerable position it occupies in Christian theology, a statement that he exists in three persons might be added, provided that it were understood that nobody really knows what that means.

This is one of our peculiarities. We begin by affirming that certain dogmas of the faith are mysteries, which means that they cannot be understood or explained—the Trinity, the Real Presence; we then proceed to try to understand and to explain them. I find it much easier to believe in the Trinity, not knowing what it really means, than to understand the learned theories that have been spun about it. Nor have all the learned treatises on how Christ is present in the Eucharist, all the discussions of accident, substance, transubtantiation, added anything to my understanding of this incomprehensible mystery, much less to my faith in it.

The difficulty of believing, it seems to me, is greatly dimin-ished as science reveals to us that in the final analysis matter is simply a form of energy. But I still would not expect science, any more than theology, to explain the inexplicable. Faith in the mystery is simply a matter of taking Christ's word for it because, as Peter pointed out when challenged to make a choice, there really is no choice. "To whom would we go, Lord; thou hast the words of eternal life."

A learned French Dominican, père de Moidrey, who was for twenty-one years the editor of *La Vie Intellectuelle*, once remarked to me, "Christ, the Blessed Sacrament, the Mass, the Holy Virgin—all the rest is flummery."[1] He expressed what I have long felt.

He would not have wanted to be understood in a literal sense, nor would I; certainly not everything else is window dressing. But there are essentials upon which my faith is centered; the rest is peripheral. I do not disbelieve the rest or reject it. But my faith is not grounded in it, nor does the validity of my faith depend upon it. My faith is, I hope, less vulnerable for that reason. Modern scriptural and theological scholarship may chip away as much as it likes without disturbing me. The Church may abandon positions she has long defended without shaking my faith, as long as the core remains. Without that—God and his Christ—I would agree with Sartre that life is an absurdity. I do not think it is an absurdity.

Some find it difficult to believe in God because of the wretchedness in the world. I recognize the problem, for I have seen the wretchedness. On the other hand, having seen the wonders of the world and the myriad mysteries of life, I find it more difficult to disbelieve. The birth of a misshapen child is difficult to understand in a providential universe. The birth of a perfectly formed child is impossible to understand in a godless universe. To believe that this and all the other marvels which fill the world are the result of chance requires an act of faith greater than I am capable of mustering. I am by nature too skeptical and incredulous to accept an atheistic view of the universe. I do not know who God is or what he is or by what name, if any, he should be called. But I know that he is. I have experienced him.

Undoubtedly some priestly vocations result from strong parental influence, though there are probably as many cases of parental opposition as of encouragement. My mother had a strong faith and was always a devout and observant Catholic. She was in no sense of the word a pious devotee. She never discussed the priesthood with me. I am not aware of any family influences upon me at all. The priests in the Dunne family did not influence me. They were only names to me.

The subject of vocation was usually raised in during the annual student retreat, but only once in my eight years at Loyola was the question put to me personally. The questioner was Fr. Henry Welch, whom we irreverently called Holy Joe. We all knew that sooner or later we would each be cornered and asked the same question. My turn came one night when we met as I was entering and he was leaving the school building.

"What are you planning to do in life, my son?"

"I intend to be a lawyer."

"Don't you think it would be better as a priest to plead for souls at the bar of God's justice than to defend clients in a court of law?" I made a noncommittal reply and went my way.

There was nothing in my personal life to suggest an inclination in that direction. Many youngsters feel an attraction to the priesthood when serving as altar boys, but I had never become one. Not until I was a Jesuit novice did I learn to serve Mass.

I was not especially religious. I had the faith. I attended Mass on Sunday and occasionally, after going to confession, received holy communion. My Sunday Mass attendance barely met the requirements of ecclesiastical law. During the last two years I always arose Sunday mornings too late to attend Mass in our parish church and regularly assisted at the noon services at Saint Vincent's, halfway downtown, never arriving before the reading of the Gospel.

In my personal behavior, if I was no worse, I was no better than my companions. We committed all the follies typical of our age and of that age. Fortunately we did not have LSD or marijuana. But we had bootleg whiskey, always easy to obtain during Prohibition. One of our favorite suppliers was a police officer who had cases of whiskey stacked to the ceiling in the kitchen of his apartment.

There were parties at The Ship, a nightclub in Venice Beach, and at The Plantation in Culver City, where the management, tipped off by a phone call from the federal agents that they were on their way, would send the waiters around to warn the clientele. Everyone would place their bottles of liquor out of sight on the floor beneath the table. A few minutes later the feds would appear— easy to identify, because like detectives in television thrillers they never removed their felt hats; they would saunter through the club, find no liquor, and, having earned their fee, leave. As soon as they disappeared the liquor reappeared. One night I bumped into Jack Dempsey on the dance floor; it was better than an autograph.

I do not pretend that we were the golden youth of the Roaring Twenties. We had neither the money, nor the leisure, nor the sophistication of the characters who people F. Scott Fitzgerald's novels. We were not as wild as some of this may sound. Our opportunities were limited by lack of time, so our excesses were occasional, not habitual. Still, they were frequent enough to establish that there was nothing in the pattern of my life which pointed to the altar.

As I entered the last months of college I had a decision to make. It was not about my career, because it was long settled that I was to be a lawyer. But since I had started freshman law in the second semester and had been prevented by my newspaper work from following the Thursday night classes, I had some courses yet to take before qualifying for my law degree. The newspaper business was interesting, and Ed O'Connor and I saw that the community newspaper business might develop into a major enterprise. I could complete my law courses at Loyola, take up the practice of law, and combine it with newspaper publishing. On the other hand, though I had earned good grades in law school, I was not satisfied. I considered applying for a scholarship at Harvard Law School and doing it over again from the beginning.

The problem became complicated with the interposition of romance. I was a member of the college debating team. The previous year we had traveled to San Francisco to meet the team from Saint Ignatius College, now the University of San Francisco. We defended Gen. Billy Mitchell, who had been court-martialed for his advocacy of the thesis that air power would make battleships obsolete in wars of the future. We lost the debate, to home-town judges we maintained, and I lost my heart to one of Father Fox's nieces.

Father Fox, our debating team coach, had arranged dinner for us at his sister's home the evening of our arrival. We went reluctantly, agreeing that we would make our excuses as early as possible, since we hoped to do a bit of San Francisco on our own. It was a superb Italian dinner, prepared by Father Fox himself. This was a specialty of his, and he loved to demonstrate his art. Besides having a talent for Italian cooking, he had several attractive nieces, and they had friends who came in after dinner. We saw some of San Francisco, but not on our own.

We returned the next night, after the debate. We danced the Charleston until 3 o'clock in the morning, a beaming Father Fox looking on from the sidelines. When we piled into Tom Haddock's Cadillac and set out in a driving rain on the long return trip to Los

Angeles, I had been badly smitten by Kay Hanley, the youngest of the nieces. During the months that followed we corresponded, and I felt keenly every mile that separated Los Angeles from San Francisco. Sixty years ago, 450 miles was a continent away.

This was the situation when I began to face the problem of the future. A third alternative had been added to the original two. Should I remain with the newspaper and finish my legal studies at Loyola? Should I go to Harvard? Or should I enroll at Bolt Hall, the University of California law school in Berkeley, only a ferryboat ride away from Kay?

Although in general my religious observance was casual, I had remained faithful to one habit formed in childhood. I rarely retired at night without kneeling down and saying a few prayers. I began to include in my night prayers a petition for light to decide which alternative I should choose. The strange experience which followed is not easily described.

One night as I started to repeat this petition it was as though a blank wall suddenly descended between me and each of the three choices I was debating. I was cut off from them, unable to reach them. I rose to my feet, puzzled. The same experience was repeated night after night. The few other prayers I was accustomed to say went smoothly, but the moment I turned to this theme the wall descended.

I changed my approach. I modified my petition to a request for light to see which of the alternatives God wished me to choose. For several nights things went smoothly. Then the experience repeated itself. Again the wall descended, blocking me off from the objects of my prayer, which were really the objects of my desire. This happened night after night. I was able to pray for anything else, but not for this.

One might infer from this description that I was spending hours at prayer. This was not the case. I was not then nor since adept at prayer. The experiences I am describing took place in the space of a few minutes.

After many repetitions of this frustrating experience, I one night abandoned any reference to the three alternatives or to my own inclinations and simply asked to know what God wished me to do. It was then that suddenly and from nowhere there appeared—emerging through the wall as though breaking out of a fog—the idea of the priesthood.

It was terrifying. It was farthest from my mind and farthest from my desires. I scrambled to my feet, wondering "where did that awful thought come from?"

From then on it became a desperate contest. The harder I tried to concentrate upon Kay, or Harvard, or the newspaper, the more insistent became the voice of the intruder. Many nights I abruptly broke off; many nights I omitted prayer entirely. It was like a battle to resist temptation, and it settled into a grim struggle. When I recall it I think of the wrestling match between Jacob and the Angel, the biblical myth which was perhaps intended to describe the struggle of a man against his fate, destiny, conscience, or God. I argued that it was out of the question, that it was impossible, that I could not give up all that I had my heart set upon.

After a long and bitter contest I surrendered. One night I simply said, "If that's what you want, then give me the grace to do it." The argument was over. When I rose to my feet I was satisfied that this was what God was asking of me, that this was what I had to do, and that I could do it. I have never doubted since.

In the darkest hours, and they have been many, it has never entered my mind to turn back. I have thought of leaving the Jesuit order and in 1958 actually initiated steps to do so, but I have never for a moment contemplated leaving the priesthood.

I have had two especially difficult periods. The darkest years were from 1929 to 1932, when I was studying philosophy at Mt. St. Michael's near Spokane, Washington. Along with serious study there was much play and good companionship; but, unknown to my companions, these were years of deep depression for me. Perhaps, unknown to me, they were having the same experience.

The depression was part of the battle of celibacy. Celibacy is not a normal life for any human being. It can be supported only if sustained by strong supernatural motivation, and even then it remains always a struggle.

The struggle is not simply to resist what are called temptations against chastity, to drive from the mind aberrant images, to subdue the surge of passion. It is a much deeper struggle against the intolerable sense of isolation and loneliness which is an inseparable part of the celibate's life. The companionship of a group of men sharing the same ideal alleviates the sense of aloneness, but does not banish it. Men, except as golf or fishing partners and drinking companions, are poor substitutes for a wife and children and family hearth. No one who cannot learn to live with loneliness should enter the priesthood.

It would have been easy to escape then and to return to the study of law—and to Kay, who was still unmarried and uncommitted. I was not yet a priest. But it never entered my mind.

The explanation lies in the experience which led to my initial decision, which I have attempted to describe. I was not drawn to the priesthood, as perhaps some are, by the notion that it is an attractive, rewarding, and on the whole not too difficult career. When I surrendered after bitter resistance I had no illusions. The invitation to the priesthood came to me not as a *billet doux*—a "love letter"—but as a stern call to take up a cross and follow Christ. It was a call to renunciation which echoes Christ's harsh warning: "He who loves mother, father, wife more than me is not worthy of me." I knew from the beginning what I was being asked to give up, and the nature of my experience was such that I was and have remained convinced that the call came not from me but from God.

Experts in the subject maintain that a vocation to the priesthood requires three elements: a disposition to embrace this career, the moral and intellectual qualities required to follow it, and acceptance by the appropriate ecclesiastical authorities. An experience like mine, resulting in a profound conviction that Christ had unmistakably manifested his will, is not a prerequisite. I would argue, though, that unless a candidate for the priesthood understands from the beginning what he is renouncing and that the very nature of the life he is choosing is renunciation, he is on insecure ground.

One might infer from these observations that the priestly life is necessarily an unhappy one and that over the portal of every seminary should be a sign: "All ye who enter here abandon hope of happiness." This is not at all the case. The happiness available to the celibate priest, however, is by its nature paradoxical. It is a derivative of the renunciation of happiness as the primary goal in life. It is the satisfaction of having given up all things for Christ. There is a sense of fulfillment in the very struggle against oneself, in the self-discipline required to meet the severe demands, even in the humble renewal of the struggle following temporary defeats. *Agere contra*—"act against [natural inclination]"—is a sound ascetical principle.

The satisfactions found in this principle are not easily understood in this permissive age. Those who have battled their way to the top of Mount Everest, fighting to overcome pain, numbing cold, physical exhaustion, the ever-present threat of sudden death, for the satisfaction of standing finally upon the summit, will understand. The secret of the happiness which they realize in this seemingly mad enterprise is not simply that they have conquered a mountain, a rather futile feat, but that in conquering the mountain they have conquered themselves. This is the essential nature of the happiness available to the priest. Added to it, to be sure, are the minor satisfactions peculiar to his work: the satisfactions of the priest-scholar in his research, of the priest-teacher in his students, of the priest-missionary in his evangelical work, of the priest-pastor, of the priest-chaplain, etc.

The nature of this happiness is, however, quite different from the sense of fulfillment found in a woman's arms or from the satisfaction of sharing with her the tasks and rewards of raising the children they have together created, building a fortress against the loneliness which is at the heart of human existence. Anyone who chooses the priesthood should understand this.

I am unalterably opposed to so-called apostolic schools and junior seminaries. The saddest sight I have ever seen was in one of the hill towns near Rome. Two dozen or more boys, the oldest of whom could not have been more than twelve years old, walked two-by-two in a column headed by a young priest. Each of them was dressed in a black cassock reaching to his shoe tops; and each wore the absurd shovel hat that is part of the clerical garb in Italy, which could have been designed only by a bitterly anticlerical caricaturist. At an age when they should have been running wildly through the fields, or splashing in a swimming hole, or romping through the streets, or carving their initials and a girl's on a tree trunk, they were being marched soberly through the streets like little doll priests on their afternoon outing. This practice of taking little boys out of the world and sheltering them in the hothouse of seminary life in the hope of cultivating a few priestly vocations is a crime comparable with the barbarous custom of castrating choir boys to preserve the purity of their tenor voices.

Christ said, "Suffer little children to come unto me." But he never said to children, "Go, sell what you have and give it to the poor and come, follow me." That was to grown men who knew what they were doing.

It is argued that these boys will know what they are doing before they make their final commitment. But it is doubtful that anyone who has lived the sheltered life of the seminary since he was twelve really understands, at twenty-four, what he is giving up or that this renunciation is the very nature of his commitment. When five or ten or twenty years later he falls in love with a woman, he will argue that he cannot be held to a commitment which he made without understanding its full import.

This was the argument of a priest whom I hired to teach Portuguese to Peace Corps trainees and who fell in love with one of them. Because of the longer course of Jesuit studies, he was thirty when he was ordained, so one might suspect some rationalization in his argument. Nevertheless, in view of the fact that he had entered apostolic school at the age of twelve, who could gainsay him? His very affirmation—"God cannot wish me to be unhappy"—revealed that he had never really understood the nature of the happiness available to the celibate.

Ordination does not change a man's nature. Nor does the wearing of a cassock or even the tonsure insensitize him to the attractiveness of the other sex. Nor, oddly enough, do they necessarily make him unappealing to a woman. This is why the devices that ecclesiastical authorities used to protect a priest's virtue—the odd clerical garb, the tonsure, the shovel hat—have been by and large ineffective. They have indeed served to set him apart, thus limiting the area of his effectiveness, but they have not guaranteed him immunity to a woman's charms.

Any priest can fall in love. The only ones who can feel secure against this possibility are those who have no contact with women. In the modern world few priests can isolate themselves from such contact by living, like the ancient saint Simon Stylites, on top of a pillar or protected by cloistered monastic walls. This is not a Book of Confessions, but I would be lacking in honesty if I did not admit that it had happened to me; this was the other tormented period of my life.

Under John XXIII and Paul VI, the Church followed the more humane and realistic policy of restoring to the lay state a priest who felt unable to continue the lonely struggle. The priest whom I mentioned above asked me if I would have asked for laicization had the humane policy existed at the time that I was in the throes of this obsession which haunts every waking hour of the mind and from which there is no escape except flight, for which there is no cure except the healing passage of time. I had told him I could sympathize with what he was suffering, because I had been there. But my answer to his question was no. I had renounced the lay state with full knowledge of what this entailed, because I was deeply convinced that this was what God had asked of me. He, of course, could argue that his case was different.

To return to my own story, I have never been accustomed to seek advice, but have always made my own decisions. This has been a lifelong failing which I do not recommend and cannot explain. It is not so much a reluctance to turn to others for advice; it simply does not occur to me.

So I told no one of the strange struggle I had been engaged in. Father Fox was the first one I told about my decision. Finding him seated next to me at our senior class dinner, on a sudden impulse I told him I had decided to join the Jesuits. He was quite astonished. Unfortunately, he told others, and before I had informed my mother word had reached her. Understandably, she was deeply hurt and in tears that she had not been the first to be told.

My two oldest brothers were married by then. Before making a decision I should have discussed it with my other brother and my sister, who would be the only ones left with mother after my departure. The only explanation I can give for my failure to talk with them is that the very nature of the experience which had led to my decision seemed to resolve itself into a lone struggle between me and God.

I left for the Jesuit novitiate at Los Gatos, California, in mid July 1926. I stopped first in San Francisco. Kay and I went to a movie and held hands. I tried to explain to her why I was doing what I did not want to do but was convinced I had to do. She said she understood. She visited me once in the novitiate, on the regular once-a-month Sunday afternoon visitors' day. I was grateful that she did not come again.

Four

To China and Back

My decision to ask to be sent to China was another example of my habit of making my own decisions without seeking the benefit of advice. It was also a consequence of the way in which my vocation had come to me.

Once I surrendered to what seemed to me a clear manifestation that I was destined for the priesthood, I chose the Jesuits rather than the diocesan clergy. I anticipated that as a Jesuit I would be engaged chiefly in teaching. I knew that there were Jesuits in Alaska; however, despite my eight years at Loyola, I was unaware that the Society of Jesus was not only a teaching order but also one of the principal missionary orders in the Catholic Church.

I passed the first three years of my life as a Jesuit at Los Gatos. For the first two, I was a novice, being familiarized with the routine of religious community life and initiated into the mysteries of the spiritual life. The third year I was a junior, studying the humanities and rhetoric. At Los Gatos I learned that each province of the order maintained one or more foreign missions and that the Alaska mission was assigned to the California Province. I do not recall, however, that the idea of becoming a missionary suggested itself to me.

Philosophy study at Mt. St. Michael's followed. Here some of the scholastics—as young Jesuits studying for the priesthood are called—devoted a few of their Sunday free hours to teaching catechism in poorer sections of Spokane. Early in my first year I took over one of these centers. The economic level of the neighborhood is indicated by its name—Dogtown. It lay behind the railroad yards in Hillyard, within walking distance of Mt. St. Michael's. Paul

O'Brien, a classmate, accepted my invitation to join in this little apostolate.

Every Sunday we gathered together a dozen or more children, played games with them and taught them catechism. A Japanese family, the Iwatas, lived quite near Mt. St. Michael's. We got to know the children, who began to walk to Dogtown with us.

In time, the Iwatas moved to Hangman's Creek, far on the other side of Spokane, where Mr. Iwata had leased land for truck gardening, and they begged us to follow them. Mr. Iwata converted a small bunkhouse into a meeting place. A zealous young Catholic couple who were friends of all the Japanese in Spokane arranged teams to drive us to Hangman's Creek. Some seven or eight Japanese families lived in the area, and the Iwata children recruited all of them for our mission. Later Paul and I persuaded the bishop of Spokane, without too much argument, to give us $250 to buy a second-hand Ford. This simplified our transportation.

After these children, with the permission of their parents, had been baptized and received into the Church, Mr. Iwata built an altar for us in the bunkhouse. From then on we brought a priest with us from the Mount to celebrate Mass each Sunday.

When the two oldest Iwata boys finished grammar school, we obtained scholarships for them at Gonzaga High School, where they also completed their college studies. Both of them fought in World War II in the famous Nisei regiment, which won more decorations than any other unit of the American armies. One of them, now a retired chemical engineer, lives in Baltimore. The other, an executive with an importing firm, lives in Seattle, where he built a lovely home for his mother and father, both of whom lived into their nineties. Last Christmas they sent me a beautiful photograph of all the Iwatas—seventy in all—gathered for a family reunion at Tom's Seattle home. The day when we first stopped to talk to the children while passing their place on the way to Dogtown was one of those chess moves which had far-reaching consequences in their lives.

Paul O'Brien and I were associated in many activities during our three years at Mt. St. Michael's. We also volunteered for the China mission and went to China together. Our association had all the earmarks of a very close friendship. He may have guessed this years ago, but if not he will be surprised to learn—should he read these lines—that our friendship had its origin in an antagonism which I felt for him and which, I suspect, was mutual. Of all my companions in those early years as a Jesuit, he was the only one who rubbed me the wrong way.

My annoyance was not rational; so I decided I had to overcome it. The way to overcome it was not to avoid the irritant, but to come to grips with it through maximum exposure and to subject the emotional response to the control of reason. That is why as soon as I inherited the catechetical station in Dogtown I invited Paul to join me. When I had initiated steps to be assigned to China I told him what I was up to and suggested, if he were interested, that he do the same. It seemed to me that it would be a kind of marvelous ascetical joke to play upon my recalcitrant nature sentencing it to a lifelong association which would force it either to overcome itself or to continue to suffer annoyance.

A reader, especially Paul himself, is entitled to ask whether this conflict was ever resolved. It was, and out of the struggle to dominate my irrational reaction a sincere, genuine friendship developed which was the more solid because it had to be constructed laboriously and painfully and was not the product of natural affinity.

This does not mean that Paul was no longer able to annoy me. I recall an occasion towards the end of our first year in China. After several months in Hsuchou, a city north of Nanking, we returned to Shanghai by boat, landing at half past four in the morning. The trams were not yet running. Paul controlled the purse. Never one to take liberties with poverty, he refused to hire rickshaws but said we would walk the four or five miles to our home at Zikawei, on the far edge of the French Concession. In a cold fury I hailed a rickshaw and had myself taken to the house on Avenue Joffre where several California Jesuits ran a small high school for boys. I borrowed coppers to pay the rickshaw man. I think, however, my anger in this case was something other than an irrational reaction arising from personal antagonism.

I do not know what modern psychology would have to say about all of this. To me it seemed the logical application of the *agere contra* principle that is central to the asceticism of Saint Ignatius that we learned in the novitiate. I suspect that this runs counter to some modern psychological theories which hold that natural impulses should be freely indulged, not resisted. I think the ancient principle is still valid. At least irrational impulses or rational impulses which cannot be indulged without spiritual or psychological damage need to be brought under control. This self-discipline is acquired not by avoiding the challenge but by deliberately confronting it and coming to grips with it.

That is how it seemed and still seems to me. I make only one exception. For the man (or woman) who falls in love or becomes infatuated with a woman (or man) in circumstances which rule out the possibility of marriage there is only one way to free himself (or herself) from the toils. That is flight. This is one case in which confrontation, coming to grips, is foolhardy and flight is not cowardice, but wisdom. If flight is impossible, he (or she) will either succumb or continue to struggle amid torment.

My decision to ask for assignment to China developed out of this same philosophy and was a consequence of the dark struggle of my years at Mt. St. Michael's. Because of the way in which my vocation had come to me, my response to this conflict was a conviction that I should commit myself more deeply, rather than abandon the battlefield.

In the normal course of events it was almost certain that after philosophy studies I would be assigned to Loyola University in Los Angeles. Fr. Zacheus Maher, then president of the university, had given me to understand that he expected to have me on the faculty. I had every reason to expect that later, as a priest, I would spend a good part of my life in Los Angeles, where I had family and many friends. It was a pleasing prospect, and I could think of no way to make a deeper commitment than to renounce all of that and bury myself for life in an obscure Chinese village.

In 1929 the California Province had been divided. The newly created Oregon Province, embracing Oregon, Washington, Idaho, and Montana, had been assigned the Alaska mission. California was to develop a mission in China and in 1929 sent several priests to initiate the work.

The California provincial, Fr. Joseph Piet, was due to finish his six-year term of office in 1931. I wrote to him and told him I wished to volunteer for the China mission, but that I was afraid if I waited to complete my third year at the Mount my chances of being assigned there were nil. It was my guess that Father Maher would be his successor as provincial; inasmuch as Father Maher had made it clear to me that he thought my future was at Loyola University and because he did not have Father Piet's personal interest in developing the China mission, it was highly unlikely that he would let me go.

Father Piet had several brothers who were priests working in foreign missions; one of them, a Jesuit of the Province of Paris, worked in Shanghai. He himself had come from France as a young man to work in the Rocky Mountain Indian missions. He was mission minded. So I proposed that he send me to China at the end of my second year of philosophy, while he was still provincial, arguing that I could complete my third year in the French Jesuit house at Zikawei. He agreed to the proposal, but said that it would have to be approved by the general of the order in Rome.

At this point I told Paul O'Brien what I was doing. He wrote to Father Piet asking that the same disposition be made of him. Some weeks later Father Piet informed us that the general wished us to finish our third year at Mt. St. Michael's, but that he was assigning us forthwith to the China mission, ruling out the danger that Father Piet's successor would decide otherwise.

Father Maher did succeed Father Piet the next year and was unhappy to discover that I had been assigned to China. The situation was complicated by the tragic death of my oldest brother, Francis (Fran), on November 11, 1931. He was killed in a collision while driving to Los Angeles from his home in Manhattan Beach, leaving his wife and a three-year-old daughter. It was a crushing blow to mother. Fran was the most extroverted of her children and, I think, in many respects her favorite son. The night before his death he had organized a family surprise birthday party for her with much song, laughter, and dancing.

Father Piet had not thought this should affect the decision to send me to China. Father Maher did, but he was hesitant to ask the general to reconsider out of fear that he might be rationalizing his desire to send me to Loyola University.

I was fully sensitive to the added pain my going to China would cause mother. On the other hand, if that were the sacrifice God was asking of her and of me, I did not want to refuse it. The conviction that God has designs upon our lives does not always simplify the decision-making process. More often it complicates it.

It is easier to know what we want than what God wants. In 1926 I had known very well what I wanted, and in that instance it had seemed to me that God had made very clear what he wanted. It had also seemed that up to this point I was following a road he had marked out for me. Now, however, I was not sure.

I took refuge in the Jesuit teaching on obedience, which, following Saint Ignatius, maintains that the will of God is manifested to us through the decisions of superiors. I have serious reservations about this doctrine, except when qualified by a strict exegesis. In this situation, however, I fell back upon it and waited for Father Maher to reach a decision.

Father Maher changed his mind several times, and in the end the decision was made by mother. Without a word to me she wrote to Father Maher expressing her desire that the decision the general had already made not be changed out of consideration for her. This must have cost her dearly, inasmuch as she did not expect to see me again once I left for China; but it was in keeping with the pattern of her life. We sailed for China in mid August 1932.

China Years

The plan was that the California Jesuits in China—we numbered fewer than a dozen, only five of whom were already priests—would serve an apprenticeship under the French Jesuits of the Province of Paris, who were in charge of one of the largest foreign mission areas in China. When the Americans grew enough in number and experience they would take over a section of the vast territory under the French and develop it as an independent mission. Meantime the priests in the group established a small high school in Shanghai.

Shanghai, with numerous churches, schools, and hospitals and a flourishing university, was one of the two largest Catholic centers in China. The other was Peking. The Catholic Church had been established in both cities since the first decade of the seventeenth century.

The mission was centered at the village of Zikawei, just outside the French Concession. Zikawei was the ancestral home of Hsu Kuang-ch'i, the most illustrious convert in the history of the Chinese Church. A learned scholar, he had helped Matteo Ricci, the Jesuit pioneer, translate his apologetic and scientific writings into Chinese; after Ricci died in 1610, Hsu Kuang-ch'i remained an invaluable collaborator of the other Jesuits in Peking. At the time of his death in 1633, he was a member of the Nei K'o—the Imperial State Council—the highest political post in the empire.

A cathedral-sized church, an observatory and meteorological station, a major seminary, boys' and girls' high schools and grammar schools, a boys' orphanage whose beautiful wood carvings and a girls' orphanage whose exquisite silk embroideries enjoyed international reputation, a flourishing publishing house staffed by graduates of the orphanage who had learned their trade there, a school of theology in which Jesuits of more than a dozen nationalities completed their preparation for the priesthood—all of this made Zikawei a fitting monument to Hsu Kuang-ch'i, whose tomb in 1933, the tercentenary of his death, lay behind the major seminary. It was in Zikawei that I spent my four years in China.

Those were happy years. Occasionally, when from my room I would hear the Chinese youngsters in the grammar school across the compound burst out of their classrooms for a recess with a shout, I would see a cheering crowd in the Coliseum at home—the grass, the football teams—and feel a pang of nostalgia. Or when on our monthly excursion days a group of us picnicked on bread, cheese, and wine at the juncture of the Whangpoo and the Yangtze rivers and an American ship steamed by, headed down towards the open sea, I had a glimpse of the Golden Gate and thought of all the people at home, and a shadow passed by. But it always passed by. Although I often thought about and prayed for those at home, chiefly my mother and sister, I was satisfied that I was doing what I had to do and what God wanted me to do. And I was happy. The cloud under which I had lived at Mt. St. Michael's had lifted.

Our first year was devoted entirely to studying the Chinese language. Paul O'Brien, three French Jesuit scholastics and I were initiated into the mysteries of Chinese by Fr. Pasquale d'Elia, S.J., a dour but learned sinologist. He was later called to Rome to occupy the chair of sinology at the Gregorian University and at the University of Rome. In Rome he completed his monumental work of scholarship, the *Fonti Ricciane*, an edition of the writings of Matteo Ricci; there I was to see him again in 1959.

At the end of our first year Paul was sent to teach in the young Gonzaga High School. I had expected the same assignment, but to my surprise was notified by the French superior that I was immediately to begin my theology studies. This meant that I would be ordained two years sooner than I had anticipated.

Before the end of my first year in China, I wrote a letter to Zacheus Maher which was to have far-reaching and unforeseen consequences. At that time Mao Tse-tung and his Communist partisans were bottled up in south-central China, surrounded by Chiang Kai-shek's Kuomintang troops. On the surface they seemed to offer no real threat. But one did not need to be long in China to detect that beneath the surface, as a consequence of the poverty, misery, and ignorance of the masses, the corruption and reactionism of Kuomintang politicians and war lords, the feudalistic structures of society, all the preconditions of revolution were already in place.

In my letter I stated my opinion that unless something were done to develop a new breed of dynamic and democratic Chinese leaders capable of replacing the old, outworn economic, social, and political structures with wholly new structures which could make life meaningful for the masses, China within thirty years would be in the hands of the Communists. That would have seemed to many in 1932 a foolhardy prediction. History has borne it out. Thanks to Japanese aggression leading to the Marco Polo Bridge incident in June 1937 and the war which followed, the timetable was shortened. Seventeen years later China was in Communist hands.

Nanking Institute

My letter to Father Maher suggested that all the American Jesuit provinces combine forces to establish a leadership-training institute in Nanking, then the capital city. A group of men recruited from all the American provinces, each with a doctorate in his special field, would staff the institute. Specially qualified students attending the national university would be invited to live at the institute, where, besides their regular courses, they would receive intensive specialized tutoring. The objective would be to develop a group of highly qualified leaders dedicated to democratic ideals in the areas essential to China's development: economics, politics, sociology, education, technology, etc.

Father Maher's reply surprised me, as my letter must have surprised him. Through a remarkable coincidence, at almost the same time my letter arrived, he had been notified by the general of the order in Rome that, at the request of Pope Pius XI, he was instructing all the American provincials to take steps to establish some such joint undertaking in China.

Some years later I learned the origin of the pope's request. Msgr. Celso Costantini, later a cardinal, had been apostolic delegate to China during the 1920s. Costantini was a perceptive and forward-looking man. Among other merits, he saw the importance of cultural accommodation at a time when most missionaries still confounded Christianity with European cultural forms. Costantini had evidently analyzed the Chinese reality in the same way I had and had reached the same conclusion. When he was recalled to Rome to head the Congregation for the Propagation of the Faith he had persuaded the pope of the importance of training leaders. In 1926, this pope had already demonstrated his interest in China by his consecration of the first Chinese bishops in modern times.

Costantini evidently felt, as I did, that Americans were best suited for the undertaking. I argued that the Chinese were more favorably disposed towards Americans and the United States than towards Europeans and Europe. This may no longer be true, but it was at that time. The Opium War, the unequal treaties, the French abuse of the protectorate of the Catholic missions to extort humiliating concessions from China had left a residue of bitterness from which Americans were exempt. The United States had taken full advantage of the unequal treaties, but Americans seemed to be held less to account than others in the thinking of the average Chinese.

Because of my initiative, I became by a kind of tacit understanding the spokesman and liaison for the Nanking project. I submitted to Father Maher more concrete and detailed suggestions. In my first communication with him on the subject I stated my opinion that time was of the essence. The Nanking Institute could not wait until men like Paul O'Brien and I and others of our generation had finished their theology studies and the graduate studies needed to prepare them for this specialized work. Men of our generation should, indeed, be started on the road which would prepare them to join the staff in the future, but the training of a new generation of Chinese leaders who might offer China a third choice between the doomed bankruptcy of the Kuomintang and the crushing totalitarianism of communism could not wait until we had been trained to train leaders. I therefore urged that each of the American provinces assign to the institute a man who had already completed his graduate studies and established his qualifications so that the work could begin without delay.

During the next three years I served as the channel through which Father Maher and later his successor sought information or suggestions. The French superiors also developed a habit of looking to me to keep them informed. When Abp. Mario Zanin, Costantini's successor as apostolic delegate, wrote from Peking asking what the American Jesuits planned to do in Nanking, the bishop of Shanghai, Auguste Haouisée, asked me to supply the information. I wrote a précis in French, English and Latin to cover all contingencies and Bishop Haouisée forwarded it to Peking.

This document figured in a curious incident several years later, which I shall describe further on. At the time my précis actually was a case of wishful thinking. It described what I hoped the American Jesuits were planning to do. As I discovered shortly after my return to the United States, they were not really planning to do anything.

This was the second service I performed for the apostolic delegate. The first had been shortly after his arrival in China.

Unlike a papal nuncio, an apostolic delegate is not accredited to the government of the country to which he is assigned. He has no diplomatic status. He functions as a liaison between the pope and the hierarchy. There had been a papal nuncio appointed to China in the seventeenth century, the first Chinese Dominican priest. But during the Rites Controversy, a dispute over the theology and methods of missionary work in the seventeenth century, diplomatic relations between the Holy See and Imperial China had been severed; and they had never been reestablished. Consequently, the newly arrived apostolic delegate did not expect to be recognized by the Chinese government.

Great was his surprise and great the excitement in his entourage when word reached him at Zikawei, where he was a guest of the Jesuits, that the elderly President Lin Shen would receive him in formal audience in Nanking the following day. The reception was to follow the protocol of a presentation of credentials, and the archbishop would be expected to make a speech in English.

Someone had to be found to write this speech. The archbishop's secretary, a young priest then in the initial stages of a career in the diplomatic service of the Vatican, appealed for help to the French superior, who sent him to me. He told me what was wanted and impressed upon me the grave importance of my task. This would be the first time since the seventeenth century that the head of a Chinese government officially received a representative of the Holy See; it might lead—as indeed it did—to the establishment of formal diplomatic relations.

I wrote the speech. The secretary, whose name was Ildebrando Antoniutti, presented me with a lovely Chinese silken scroll as a token of the delegate's gratitude, not however until he had insisted that I must never reveal my authorship. It must never be known that so historic a document had been written, not by the archbishop himself or another highly placed official in the ecclesiastical diplomatic bureaucracy, but by a lowly Jesuit student of theology. I have kept faith until now, but it cannot now harm the relations of China and the Holy See to let my secret out. Perhaps in some future century a scholar who discovers this document in whatever archives it lies may immortalize me in a footnote.

Antoniutti himself went far after leaving my room that day with my speech in his pocket. He turned up years later as apostolic delegate to Canada, where he seems to have played a key role in the removal of the progressive Abp. Joseph Charbonneau of

Montreal, whose support of the laboring class was displeasing to powerful industrialists. Later he was papal nuncio to Franco's Spain. Later still, raised to the cardinalate by John XXIII, he headed, until his death, one of the congregations in Rome where he added strength to the extreme conservative wing of the college of cardinals.

Fateful Moves

Like most of my confreres, I had come to China expecting to spend my life among the rural and village poor. My role in developing the Nanking Institute made it likely that I would be assigned to this work instead. Some of my American confreres thought this was essential; and this conviction of theirs, as a result of a well-intentioned intrigue with altogether unexpected results, led to my recall from China and changed the course of my life.

The theological school at Zikawei belonged to the French Jesuits of the Province of Paris, but it had an international character. All the Jesuit missions in China sent their scholastics there for their theology studies. There were thirteen nationality groups in the community, the two largest contingents being the Spaniards and the Chinese. Mandarin Chinese and French were the official languages of the house.

The rector was a volatile, high-spirited Breton, brimming with energy, père Yves Henry. At the very beginning of my first year in theology, perhaps because I had good rapport with all the nationality groups in this highly diversified community, he appointed me beadle—a kind of top sergeant—of all the theologians. I held this job for nearly three years. Each morning I met with him for a briefing session, and out of these daily contacts I developed a deep admiration for him.

Some of the Americans and some of the Europeans were not particularly fond of Father Henry. I think it was his impetuosity and the emphatic and positive manner in which he asserted his strongly held opinions that annoyed them. I enjoyed his impetuosity and quickly discovered that his habit of immediately adopting a position did not preclude further debate. He loved an argument, especially a loud one. Our arguments, which I sometimes won and often lost, always ended in the same way when, roaring with laughter, he would give me a hearty embrace and say, "Ah, mon bon cher George, vous êtes un ace!"—Ah, George, my good man, you are an ace. The first time or two he called me that I was startled; in French, it sounded as though he were calling me an ass.

He was, in my judgment, one of the few truly great men I have known. Thirty years later, as a token of my respect, I dedicated to him and to Bp. Auguste Haouisée my book *Generation of Giants*, the story of the first hundred years of Jesuit work in China in the sixteenth and seventeenth centuries.

When the French had agreed to the request of the general of the order to establish a theologate at Zikawei to serve all the missions in China, they had stipulated that, because of the many needs of their own mission and their limited personnel, they could not staff the faculty by themselves. The faculty had been recruited from other provinces. None of them had made his theological studies in China; most had been sent directly from Europe to teach theology.

This caused problems. They imposed upon us the same kind of regime to which they had been accustomed in Europe—days filled with classroom lectures, each a full fifty minutes long, leaving little time for independent study. They were not disposed to make any concessions either to special difficulties like the fierce summer heat or to the special needs peculiar to pursuing the study of theology in China. The most important special need was to keep up our Chinese language studies.

At the end of my first year of theology I drew up a proposed schedule, reducing both the number and the length of classroom lectures and organizing them in such a way as to leave solid blocks of time, rather than short intervals, for theology and language study. Throughout the second year, with the full support of père Henry, I fought to overcome the resistance of the dean and his faculty consultors. In the end a compromise was reached and some modifications were made.

As a consequence of this struggle, which had evidently been reported to him, the general of the order decided that a faculty should be developed out of graduates of the Zikawei theologate who, having made their studies in China, would better understand the special needs there. So he authorized the superior of the mission, père Pierre LeFebvre, to draft a number of Zikawei students for this purpose.

Père Henry told me of this development and informed me that he and LeFebvre had decided that I was to be the first draftee. He stated that upon my fourth year of theology at Zikawei I would be sent to Europe for two years of graduate work and then return to join the faculty. He prefaced his remarks by saying that he and the superior of the mission were fully aware of the sacrifice they were asking of me. They knew that I had not come to China to become a professor of theology. By anticipating my objection he had robbed me of any basis of argument. I replied that I appreciated their understanding and for that reason would not dispute their decision. We embraced and again I was told that I was an ace, pronounced as usual with its broad *a*.

Some of my fellow Californians were highly displeased when they learned of this development. Unbeknownst to me they began to search for ways to snatch me from my fate and save me for the projected Nanking Institute. Ringleader of the plot was Paul O'Brien.

I had had some health problems in China. Asthmatic attacks obliged me to spend a good part of each night throughout the summer and into the fall sitting up in bed or hunched over my desk inhaling some kind of prescribed medicinal fumes. A condition of chronic diarrhea defied both medicinal and dietary treatment. Periodically I was obliged to spend a few days in the small infirmary which the French Jesuits maintained in downtown Shanghai for the treatment of their men.

One of the collateral benefits of these occasional infirmary stays was that I several times served Mass for Fr. Pierre Teilhard de Chardin, who was then living in Tientsin. Not until the posthumous publication of his books would he become a figure known to the general public. He was, however, well known to French intellectuals, and his studies of the *homo sinanthropus pekinensis* fossils—Peking man—had made him an international figure in scientific circles. He was a hero to all the French Jesuit scholastics at Zikawei, if not to the faculty, which had misgivings about his ideas. Whenever he passed through Shanghai on his frequent journeys, he stayed at the downtown house in which the infirmary was located. Thus on several occasions I had the good fortune to meet him.

It was the state of my health which suggested to Paul O'Brien a way to defeat the designs of the French superiors. He wrote to Fr. Francis Seeliger, who had succeeded Fr. Zacheus Maher as California provincial, and also to Maher himself, now in Rome as assistant for American affairs to the general of the order, arguing the importance of preserving me for the Nanking Institute and outlining a plot to sabotage the French program. Through Maher in Rome, Seeliger would obtain authorization from the general to call me home on the pretext of my allegedly precarious health. I would complete my theology in the States and could later be sent back to China, but I would be detoured around the French and assigned directly to Nanking.

Many years later, as he was clearing out his desk in the Philippines before moving to Vietnam to take charge of the Jesuit novitiate near Saigon, Paul O'Brien came upon his original draft of what he accurately called this "fateful letter." He sent it to me as a souvenir. In his covering letter he said he still thought he had been right. Perhaps he was. Who can judge the rightness or wrongness of such decisions? He acted in good faith and with good intentions. He could not have anticipated that his action would result not only in the defeat of the French plans in my regard, but in the termination of my China career. What happened as a result was apparently part of my destiny. He moved queen's knight, and a thousand unforeseen consequences followed.

I had been kept in complete ignorance of the conspiracy, and so the order to return to the States came as a thunderclap on a cloudless, sunny day. It was a Sunday early in April. When I came out of the dining room following the midday dinner, there was a note in my napkin box telling me that père LeFebvre wished to see me immediately in his room.

"Is your provincial concerned about your health?" he asked me.

"Not as far as I know," I replied. "I have never mentioned my health to him, nor has he ever made any reference to it. Why?"

He handed me a cablegram. "General orders Dunne home immediately. (signed) Seeliger."

I was stunned. "But why?"

He shrugged his shoulders and shook his head. He did not know. He had thought perhaps I had informed the provincial of my health problems. I was not preoccupied with the question of my health. He and père Henry had been far more concerned than I.

Their solicitude was almost embarrassing. On the theory that a change of climate would be beneficial they were planning to have me spend the summer in Japan following my ordination to the priesthood, which was less than two months away. I had no reason to involve the California provincial in the problem.

We wondered if some catastrophe of singular proportions could have befallen my mother. It would have had to be a more than ordinary tragedy, because it was not Jesuit policy in those days to recall men from the foreign missions because of parental illness or death. I urged him to cable Seeliger and ask what the reasons were. He was unwilling to do so. He did not want to seem to be questioning the California provincial's judgment or challenging his authority. He had learned that the Americans, in their relations with the French, were often extremely sensitive and had to be handled with great tact. This kind of provincialism did not happen to be one of my many faults, which is why the French superiors had chosen me as a channel of communication in the matter of the Nanking Institute. Unlike some of the Americans, I liked the French, including the cynical, sharp, acid-tongued Parisians.

At this time Fr. Leo McGreal was the director of Gonzaga High School and as such the unofficial spokesman for the California Jesuits. I asked père LeFebvre if he would interpose any objection to Father McGreal's sending a cable of inquiry. He said he would not.

I took a crosstown bus to Gonzaga High School, which had moved to a new campus in the International Settlement. McGreal refused to send the cablegram. He remained smilingly obdurate in the face of all my arguments.

"It's an order," he said. "When you get an order to go some place, you just go; that's all. It's very simple."

"But this is not an order to go down to the corner and buy a loaf of bread. This is an order to cross the Pacific Ocean, to go halfway around the world, and it might all be a mistake. It can't do any harm to make sure." In those days it did not mean a one-day flight by air but a three-week voyage by sea.

He smiled and shook his head. Afterwards, of course, I learned that he was in on the conspiracy and knew exactly why I was being summoned home. There had not been any chance of persuading him to send the cablegram.

The superior interpreted "immediately" to mean the first boat out of Shanghai. The Japanese liner *Chichibu Maru*, sister ship of the Asama Maru, on which we had sailed out of San Francisco Bay four years before, had a sailing date ten days later. The superior suggested I make a quick trip to Nanking in the interval. The other California theologians undertook to pack my trunk. They included, as I discovered when the trunk was opened by the customs officer in San Francisco, a chamber pot bearing a tag which identified it as a rare piece of Ming pottery.

Fr. Francis Farmer was a onetime Protestant evangelical missionary from Georgia. Following the death in China of his wife and their child, he had become a Catholic, joined the French

Jesuits, studied theology, and returned to China as a priest. He was now the pastor of Sacred Heart Church in the Hongkew section of Shanghai. He invited the small group of California Jesuits—my departure would reduce their number to thirteen— to a farewell dinner. They accompanied me afterwards to the docks, a few blocks away, and waved farewell as the *Chichibu Maru* slipped her moorings and headed down the Whangpoo. I watched the Shanghai skyline fade into memory.

Many times during the years that followed, until I finally realized and accepted the fact that I would not return to China, I resolved that the first thing I would do upon setting foot upon Chinese soil would be to kneel down and kiss the ground. I little dreamed that night as we turned into the Yangtze River that I was leaving China forever.

Return to the States

It was a long and lonely trip back across the Pacific. I was puzzled, entirely in the dark. I do not know how many of the Californians were privy to Paul O'Brien's plot, but I suspect that all of them were. They kept their secret well, and as I racked my brain in search of an explanation during the homeward voyage not even a faint suspicion of the truth crossed my mind.

Father Seeliger, the provincial, and Paul O'Brien's father were waiting to greet me on the dock in San Francisco. Seeliger was evidently hoping I would totter down the gangplank, a wan, trembling ghost of a man, visible justification of the conspiracy. "When I looked up and saw you in the beret," he afterwards told me, "my heart sank. I felt you really could not be very ill."

I was wearing a French beret, a headpiece to which I am partial. It is difficult to follow Seeliger's logic and to understand why the wearing of a beret belied reports of the poor state of my health. Perhaps it gave me a jaunty air.

He did not then tell me why I had been recalled but, after reassuring me that nothing untoward had happened to my mother, instructed me to see him the next day. Then he left me with Mr. O'Brien, who took me to his home to dine with Paul's charming mother and three lovely sisters.

The next day the provincial revealed the plot. I was shocked and angered. I was not angry because I had been brought home. Humanly speaking, there was obviously much to be grateful for.

I would have an unexpected reunion with mother, who was home alone now; my sister, the last to leave, had married while I was in China and was living in Chicago. And I was ordained two months later in the mission church at Santa Clara University with mother present as well as my sister and her husband, who had driven from Chicago, my two brothers and their families, and the O'Briens.

But I was angry out of a sense of loyalty to the French Jesuit superiors, who I thought had been shamefully treated. I had always found them uniformly endowed with sensitivity, thoughtfulness, *délicatesse*, in their relations with the men under their command.

Père Henry had learned of the death of my brother Fran some months prior to my coming to China. He never failed, several weeks prior to the anniversary of Fran's death each year, to give me a simple gift—a Chinese scroll, a piece of embroidered silk—to send to mother with a message of renewed sympathy and the assurance that on November 11, the anniversary date, he would offer his Mass for her and my brother.

Such thoughtfulness was not reserved for me. It extended to all. Every member of his community of well over one hundred men would receive on his feast day a warm personal note and an assurance that he had been especially remembered that morning at Mass. These are typical examples of the personal concern which, in my experience, characterized the French superiors.

In the matter of my own health they could not have been more solicitous. For superiors in California suddenly in a curt cablegram to order my return upon the ground of health, without any consultation or inquiry, was a brutal and undeserved insult. It implied that the French superiors were negligent in fulfilling their obligation to take reasonable care of the health of the Americans entrusted to them. Nothing could have been farther from the truth.

I said all of these things and more in a strong letter of protest which I wrote to Zacheus Maher in Rome. Much later I learned in greater detail the role he had played in my recall. When Seeliger's request for authorization to bring me home arrived in Rome, the general of the order, Fr. Wlodimir Ledochowski, was in Naples. This was a small detail, in itself trivial, which was a key factor in all that followed. Had he been in Rome he would certainly have refused Seeliger's request, and I would have remained in China. When leaving for Naples, however, he had authorized Father Maher to handle any American problems that arose during his absence. Maher took advantage of this delegated authority to instruct Seeliger to recall me in the general's name.

Actually the general knew nothing about it. When he learned about it, I was later told, "he had rapped Father Maher's knuckles." Maher was probably still smarting from his reprimand when he received my angry letter. It added salt to his wounds and probably was the beginning of the end of our long friendship.

Beginning of an End

Some weeks after my return, all of the American provincials met in Los Angeles for their annual conference. Father Seeliger brought me into the meeting to argue the cause of the Nanking Institute. Before I had been talking five minutes I realized that I was championing a lost cause. I was speaking to an indifferent and, in some instances, hostile audience. None of them, other than Seeliger, had any interest in China. While perhaps willing to contribute a modest sum of money, it was plain that none of them, other than Seeliger, had any intention—Pius XI or no Pius XI—of contributing any of their highly trained men to Nanking. The interest and concern of each of these men stopped at the border of the province which he governed. What happened in China or to China was a matter of complete indifference to them.

Today, when what has happened in China has become a matter of gravest concern to every American, their indifference is edged with irony. In fairness it must be admitted that they probably reflected the general American attitude towards China in 1936. On the other hand, one would expect a less provincial attitude among leaders in the Church which claims a universal mission. Unfortunately, men or women of global vision are scarce. Each one revolves within a little kingdom—the pastor interested only in the parish, the bishop in the diocese, the principal in the high school, the president in the university, the provincial in the province. When I left the conference room that day I think I knew that the Nanking Institute was doomed.

The institute would not have saved China. We did not have the thirty years I had estimated. With the war, the Sino-Japanese phase of which began the next year, the accelerated pace of history overran our hopes.

But in 1936, nobody knew that this would happen. Without the war, during which they immeasurably strengthened their position, the Communists were still several decades away from power. Nobody knew that better than Stalin, who had no faith in Mao's revolution. There would still have been time.

In less than thirty years, Mao Tse-tung, a high school teacher, and a half dozen close associates would change the course of history, completely alter the structure of Chinese society and threaten to shake the foundations of the world. No one who knows Mao's history is inclined to minimize what even a few dedicated leaders can accomplish. However, the political science department at the University of Detroit, the economics department at Fordham University, the sociology department at St. Louis University—these were the kind of enterprise that interested the American provincials. Not a leadership training institute in far-off China.

Two other experiences illustrate the same provincialism. One of them was indeed curious.

John Gaffney, a friend since high school days, was one of those with whom I was to be ordained to the priesthood. A few days after my return, I was at Alma College, our theology school. John asked me to go for a walk one evening after supper. During our stroll through the redwoods, he told me that there was a strange story circulating about the alleged reasons for my recall from China which, as an old friend, he did not want to believe but thought I should know about.

The source of the story, he said, was Fr. Frank Sheerin, generally regarded as the most learned member of the theological faculty. Gaffney was only one of several whom Sheerin had told that I had been brought back from China to be dismissed from the Society of Jesus. According to Sheerin, I had conceived the Nanking Institute and proposed it to my Jesuit superiors. They had rejected the proposal. I had thereupon, without their sanction, gone over their heads and outside the Society and had taken the proposal to the apostolic delegate, who in turn had sold the idea to the pope. The pope then had imposed it upon the Society, specifically the American Jesuits. In view of their previous rejection of the proposal, superiors regarded my action as brazen defiance of their known wishes. I had in consequence been brought home and was about to be dismissed from the Society of Jesus.

It was a breath-taking, indeed dizzying, plot. The image it creates of me manipulating the pope and his staff to achieve my ends is flattering and, although laughable, could have damaged the prospects of the Nanking Institute.

After consulting Father Hageman, the spiritual director of the community, I confronted Father Sheerin. I told him that his story was sheer fantasy and damaging to my reputation, explained the history of the Nanking project, and insisted upon a retraction. Father Sheerin, who was standing, book in hand, before his desk when I entered his room and remained standing throughout my visit, to my astonishment quite coolly refused, saying that he had the story from the highest authority in the province. This could only mean Father Seeliger himself.

The plot thickening, I confronted Seeliger, who happened to be visiting Alma that same evening. He was greatly embarrassed and said that Father Sheerin had misinterpreted certain of his remarks and that the misunderstanding was related to the fact that Father Sheerin, whose whole world revolved around the University of San Francisco, bitterly resented sending some of the more promising young men off to China instead of to San Francisco. He asked me to leave the matter to him. He would straighten Father Sheerin out.

I do not know what were the remarks of Seeliger that Sheerin had misinterpreted. Probably to escape the sharp edge of Sheerin's tongue, he told him that not he but I should be blamed for our being saddled with the Nanking Institute. Perhaps he mentioned the précis I had written for the apostolic delegate, without mentioning—perhaps he did not know—that I had written it at the request of the Jesuit bishop of Shanghai. Perhaps this gave rise to Father Sheerin's remarkable story. This, however, is speculation on my part.

My second experience with provincialism involved a suggestion from the general in Rome to Father Seeliger that I visit all the Jesuit scholasticates—schools for Jesuits in their years of training—in the country to develop interest in the Nanking Institute. I spent two weeks at Mt. St. Michael's in Spokane during the Christmas season, giving several conferences. Interest was great, and dozens of scholastics from the Oregon and California provinces came to see me privately to discuss the project.

As I was leaving the Mount, the Oregon provincial, Fr. Walter Fitzgerald, later bishop of Alaska, arrived for his annual visitation. Angry to discover among the Oregon scholastics a lively interest in the Nanking Institute, he wrote a strong protest to Rome, charging that I had been proselytizing his scholastics. The general decided that the same kind of reaction could be anticipated on the part of the other provincials and canceled my tour.

This was the point at which the Nanking Institute as I had conceived it, and evidently as Cardinal Costantini and Pope Pius XI had conceived it, died. It was decided that I should remain in the United States to study for a doctorate. Paul O'Brien would be brought home the next year to finish his theology and obtain a doctorate. Albert O'Hara and John O'Farrell would return after their theology studies for the same purpose. We would return to China equipped with graduate degrees and found the Nanking Institute. But instead of a cooperative undertaking of all the American provinces, it would be simply a project of the California mission in China.

Alma College, located in the hills near Los Gatos, California, followed a different rotation of courses from that at Zikawei, and the theological treatises which I had not yet studied were not being taught that year. So Father Seeliger concluded that there was no need for me to spend the year in the theologate. He assigned me instead to the Loyola High School community in Los Angeles and instructed me to complete privately my fourth year of theology, which in the Jesuit order followed ordination. It was a gracious gesture on his part. It enabled me to spend a good deal of time with my mother, who was still teaching school. As often as possible I dined with her in the evening.

For the final year of my formal Jesuit training—it is called the "third probation," or "tertianship"—I was at Port Townsend, Washington; this was 1937-38. Very early in my year there, word reached me of the Marco Polo Bridge clash between Japanese and Chinese troops. It was June 21, 1937, and it marked the beginning of a tragic sequence of events that would change the course of history in the Far East.

I followed the day-to-day events that year with difficulty. During tertianship, we were not given newspapers. But on Sunday morning walks, several of us usually picked one up at a crossroads tavern and caught up with the news. The cook had a radio and usually passed on to me any especially dramatic news from China. Through this channel, for example, I learned about the bombing of a United States gunboat, the Panay, in a Japanese air attack.

It must have been during the summer of 1938 that I almost punched a newspaper reporter, Fred Williams, in the nose. I was spending a few days at the University of San Francisco. Paul O'Brien, back from China and finishing theology studies at Alma, was also there. Following lunch one day, Fr. Harold Ring, the rector and president, entered the recreation room and announced to the forty or fifty Jesuits there that Fred Williams, recently returned from China, was in his office and would like to describe the Far Eastern situation to them.

Fred Williams was related by marriage to one of the Jesuits and had friendly contacts with many others. He had spent a month in Japanese-occupied China on a conducted tour ostensibly sponsored by the Japanese steamship company Nippon Yushen Kaisha. I was sure he was a paid propagandist for the Japanese military regime. He was unaware that two of us in the room had spent some years in China and had firsthand knowledge of the Chinese reality.

Feeling secure, he spun a fantastic web of historical untruths as I listened in growing anger. The substance of his story was that Chiang Kai-shek was really a Communist. The Japanese invasion of China was not aggression. It was an act of liberation, a crusade to free China and the rest of the Far East from the tyranny of communism. As such it deserved the full support of every American. Williams found it particularly difficult to understand that any Catholics could fail to support the Japanese cause and assured us that the California Jesuits in Shanghai, with whom he had lunched, fully agreed with his analysis.

At this point, imitating Paul MacCormack on the occasion of our youthful donnybrook in Highland Park, I informed him that he was a liar. In my suitcase was a letter I had received only a few days before from the California Jesuits in Shanghai asking me if there were not some way I could unmask this charlatan whose mendacities, reported back to Shanghai, were damaging them in the eyes of the Chinese.

I was not a partisan of Chiang Kai-shek. On the contrary, I was of the opinion then and since that his failure to purge the Kuomintang of the corruption rampant among its politicians and to identify himself with the masses of the people was largely responsible for creating a climate propitious to the development of communism. But to call him a Communist was patently absurd.

Equally absurd was the claim that the Japanese attack upon China was a blow to communism. On the contrary, it would help communism emerge from the war, whenever it ended, in a far stronger position. I said all these things to Mr. Williams and charged him with being a paid propagandist of the Japanese, which he indignantly denied.

"How much time have you spent in China?" I asked.

"A month."

"How much Chinese history do you know? Never mind the last 4,000 years. How much history of the last 30 years do you know?"

"I know about the kidnapping of Chiang Kai-shek."

At the climax of the stormy session I marched across the room and shook my finger in his face. "Williams," I said, "I am leaving this room, because if I stayed here three more minutes I would punch you in the nose!" And I stormed out trembling with anger. It was not a very noble exit line, nor one that reflected the spirit of the Gospels. But I found it impossible to sit quietly by and witness the truth being cynically manipulated to justify a policy which would bring incalculable suffering to millions of human beings. Paul O'Brien followed me to my room and tried to cool me down.

Williams was invited afterwards by the pastor of the Jesuit church in Santa Barbara to speak to his parishioners. He was invited by Fr. Edward Whelan, the superior of Loyola High School in Los Angeles, to address the student body. I had lived an entire year in Whelan's community following my return from China without being asked to address his students.

This has been a curious phenomenon of modern history, the readiness of so many people to sponsor any cause which claims to be anti-Communist, to endorse any leader who raises the anti-Communist banner. Throughout the thirties, neither Hitler nor Mussolini ever lacked sympathizers in the democracies ready to defend them, in the face of their worst atrocities, upon the ground that they were enemies of communism. Communist control of eastern Europe was largely the handiwork of these two men. Communist control of China owes a great debt of gratitude to the Japanese militarists who unleashed the war in 1937.

Several years later, when the United States was at war, I chanced to be in Washington, D.C., when a federal jury brought in its verdict in a case involving a number of unregistered agents of foreign governments. Among those found guilty was Fred Williams. He had been for some years on the payroll of the Imperial Japanese Government, which paid him $250 a month for his services. I copied the item from the *Washington Post* and mailed it without comment to Father Whelan and to one or two others who had charged me with making a rash and uncharitable accusation when I had insisted that Williams was in the pay of the Japanese.

Five

Return to Chicago

I n fall 1938, I began graduate studies at the University of Chicago in the field of international relations. I had chosen the University of Chicago, among other reasons, for the practical one that my uncle, Msgr. Dennis Dunne, was pastor of Holy Cross Parish, a ten-minute walk from the campus; he had agreed to supply me with room and board in exchange for a minimal amount of assistance to the church.

One of the first things I did in Chicago was to visit the house where we had been living when my father died. Another was to visit the house in which my mother had been born and raised and All Saints Church, in which she had been married. I met the doorman at the Chicago Beach Hotel who had started to work when my father was the manager and when my mother, in the early years of marriage, lived there. He had nostalgic remembrances of them both.

It took me two or three years more than it should have to get my doctorate at the university. I got involved in many things other than studies, chiefly in young people and their problems.

There was no Catholic chaplain at the university. Card. George Mundelein nurtured a deep prejudice against the school. He did not approve of any priest enrolling there. I was the only priest on campus. My uncle, who had been his secretary and consultor for many years, had persuaded him to make an exception for me. Mundelein believed, as some Illinois state legislators did, that the University of Chicago was a hotbed of communism and an enemy of the faith. I saw very little evidence of communism. Out of curiosity I attended several Communist-student-sponsored receptions and found only a handful of young people at them.

There was, on the other hand, considerable interest in Catholicism. This was in part the result of the Hutchins-Adler Great
Books course, which had made Thomism almost as hot a campus
subject as Vietnam would be in the 1960s. I recall a lecture by
Mortimer Adler on the existence of God which drew a standing-
room-only crowd to a large auditorium. It was a brilliant display
of dialectical subtlety, although when, at the end of an hour and
a half spent defining terms, he came to the actual proof it suddenly
seemed to me that he had missed the point of Saint Thomas's
argument, apparently assuming that the validity of the argument
from sufficient reason depended upon the impossibility of an
infinite process.

I did not make the mistake of challenging his reasoning.
Several years later in another matter I did, however, and learned
that one disagrees with philosophers at the risk of losing their
friendship. Adler and I had been good friends. In 1943, when I was
living in the woods in Michigan writing my doctoral thesis, he sent
me the manuscript of his forthcoming book, *How To Think About
War and Peace*, and asked for a criticism. I took him at his word,
the more freely since I had heard him say that the true philosopher
always welcomes criticism.

I wrote a critique in which I was not sparing of praise—
"written in your usual brilliant style...customary incisive
analyses...penetrating insights, etc." However, I pointed out that,
in my judgment, his main thesis was vitiated by two logical errors.
Adler argued that state sovereignty was of two kinds, external and
internal. Wars arose out of the claim of states to exercise external
sovereignty and could therefore be eliminated only by the universal renunciation of external sovereignty. On the basis of this
reasoning he charged that Benedict XV was guilty of upholding a
system of world anarchy because his famous peace proposals of
1916 had not included a demand for the abolition of all forms of
external sovereignty.

His error, I thought, was in not recognizing a distinction
between relative and absolute external sovereignty. The latter is
the claim of states to the right to resort to force of arms in order
to impose their will when all other means of settling disputes had
failed. This is the claim which must be renounced to guarantee—
at least in the theoretical world of the philosopher—the elimination of war. Limited external sovereignty could continue to be
exercised without threat to peace. Inasmuch as Benedict XV had
urged a renunciation of the former claim he could not fairly be
called an anarchist.

I had mailed my critique to Adler when I received an almost frantic note from Dr. Waldemar Gurian at the University of Notre Dame, to whom Adler had also sent a copy of his manuscript. Gurian urged upon me the importance of preventing Adler from committing this grievous error. It comforted me when I received Adler's sarcastic reply to know that a man of Gurian's intellectual prowess agreed with me. Adler's reply to my criticism was entitled "Explication of an Axiom," which seemed a neat way of telling me that I was oblivious to the obvious. Our mutual friend, Dr. Jerome G. Kerwin, in whose cottage I was living, told me, much amused, that Adler had shown my criticism to Robert Hutchins, president of the university, and was piqued when Hutchins told him he thought it was "pretty good." When the book appeared I was gratified to note that Adler had made several small changes in the text and added a footnote which represented at least partial, if grudging, concessions to my point of view.

For some time a coolness existed between us. On several occasions when I met him on the Chicago campus he was quite distant. On the first of these, I was crossing the quadrangle, and he was engaged in conversation; he favored me with a bare nod of recognition as I passed. However, time healed the wound, and one night when he saw me dining in the Southmoor Hotel he crossed to my table and shook hands with almost as much warmth as in the days before I discovered that philosophers are not as happy to be criticized as they pretend.

As in any university, Catholic or secular, Chicago had many Catholic students who were indifferent to or had abandoned their faith. There was also a group of extremely active and intelligent Catholics who came together in the Calvert Club, sponsored by Dr. Jerome G. Kerwin, professor of political science. Some of them had been converted to the faith as a result of their reading of the Great Books. One of these, Winston Ashley, had been the brilliant leader of a Trotskyite group on campus. He later entered the Dominican Order and is now a professor of theology and, as Fr. Benedict Ashley, O.P., one of the leading lights of the Aquinas Institute of St. Louis. Janet Kalven, Mortimer Adler's secretary and teaching assistant, became, and is still, a member of The Grail. I was bemused to note that Adler makes no mention of any of them in his autobiography.

Mrs. Frank Lillie, the wife of the dean emeritus of the biology department and one-time president of the American Academy of Science, had a farm, called Childerley, northwest of Chicago. She placed it at the disposition of the Calvert Club for weekends of spiritual, liturgical, and intellectual activity. Some of the simple liturgical practices observed at Childerley, such as an offertory procession, were considered daringly avant garde forty-five years ago.

On the intellectual side, these weekends usually provided stimulating discussion with a guest speaker. One of the liveliest was the weekend that Louis Budenz was our guest. He was a Communist then and defended communism with as much vigor as he would later, after quitting the editorship of the *Daily Worker* and the Communist Party, attack it.

Mrs. Lillie was herself an unusual person. A member of the wealthy Crane family, she had as a young woman been associated with Jane Addams at Hull House. She had become first a convert to Anglicanism, and during that period she built the lovely little chapel at Childerley. Later, influenced by Baron Von Hugel, the English layman who was a central figure in the modernist movement early in the century, she entered the Roman Catholic Church, receiving instructions from the learned French Jesuit, Léonce de Grandmaison. Neither her husband nor any of her children, all of them brilliant scientists, shared her faith, but all respected it. When lecturing at the University of Chicago, Jacques Maritain was always a guest in the Lillie home. It was there I met him and admired his simplicity, modesty, and humility. He seemed always more interested in listening—and with respect—to the opinions of others, including university students, than in expressing his own.

The lack of a Catholic chaplain at the university made it inevitable that I found myself filling that role. I gave over much of my time during the first two years to activities which belonged to a chaplain's office. I did not see how I could refuse to respond to an obvious need. This situation was remedied following the death of Cardinal Mundelein; Cardinal Samuel Stritch, not sharing his predecessor's prejudice, appointed a full-time chaplain, Fr. Joseph Connerton, and dropped the ban on priests or nuns studying at the university.

One of the first to take advantage of the lifting of the ban was Paul Reinert, S.J., who also lived in my uncle's rectory while studying for a doctorate in education. He later served with distinction for more than twenty years as the president of St. Louis University.

An undergraduate student who became a Catholic at this time and would later succeed Connerton as chaplain of the university was Rollins Lambert. He first became interested in Catholicism out of curiosity aroused by a Catholic missal he had come across while browsing in the library stacks. He sought information from Dr. Kerwin, who sent him to me. He later joined the Calvert group, took instructions and was baptized. The liturgical reforms of Vatican II were still far in the future, and so while Father Connerton carried out the rites in Latin, I stood by and read them in English, a daring thing to do in those days!

After receiving his degree, Rollins entered Mundelein Seminary and was the first black priest ordained in the Archdiocese of Chicago in modern times. His highly intelligent and quite articulate mother, who at the time had strong Marxist convictions, was reconciled with great difficulty to his entering the Church and even more to his becoming a priest. In later years, when she was living in Los Angeles, she and I became good friends. Rollins himself, after serving as pastor of Saint James Parish, where Patrick Riordan and Patrick Dunne were listed among his predecessors, spent several years as Catholic chaplain at the university, and was then put in charge of African affairs at the National Conference of Catholic bishops in Washington, where he served with distinction for many years. Card. Joseph Bernardin recalled him to Chicago and appointed him to an archdiocesan office. In 1988 he visited me in my present retreat at Loyola Marymount University in Los Angeles. His mother, approaching her hundredth year, is as mentally alert as ever.

Another of my activities in Chicago illustrates the sweeping change in Catholic attitudes since Vatican II. In my first years in Chicago I was one of only two priests in the archdiocese engaged in the program of the National Conference of Christians and Jews. This consisted in meetings at which a rabbi, a minister, and a priest appeared together on the platform. After brief talks by each of them, the audience was invited to ask questions. Under the rules of the game anything in the nature of theological debate or controversy was ruled out. The objective was simply to demonstrate that, much as they disagreed in questions of theology, it should be possible for Jew, Protestant, and Catholic to live together amicably and to cooperate as citizens in building a better community.

Only one such meeting, of the many in which I took part, produced any surprises. One night the Protestant side was represented by a Unitarian minister. His gothic church near the University of Chicago, complete with choir stalls, baptismal font, pulpit, even sanctuary lamp, resembled a Catholic church in every detail. In the question period someone in the audience put this question to the rabbi: "You stated, rabbi, that although you three disagreed about many things, you agreed about certain basic things. What are some of these basic things you agree about?"

"Well, to begin with," replied the rabbi, "we all believe in God."

"I take issue with that," broke in the Unitarian minister, looking more like a priest than I did, in his black clerical suit, his clerical collar, his handsome head crowned with snow-white hair. "Some of us Unitarians do not believe in God."

Usually, however, the meetings provided no such surprises. If they did not aim to produce spectacular results, they certainly could work no harm and possibly achieved a small amount of good. They were certainly no threat to the integrity of the Catholic faith. This seems obvious, but so narrow was the prevalent attitude, so stubborn the determination to preserve the ghettolike structure of Catholic life in America that many bishops would not permit priests to participate in these innocent manifestations of goodwill.

Chicago was one such diocese. In desperation, Stella Conselbaum, of the National Conference of Christians and Jews, was obliged repeatedly to turn for help to me and to Fr. Edward V. Cardinal, a Viatorian priest who taught history at Loyola University. Not belonging to the archdiocese, he felt no compunction about ignoring the chancery office. Neither did I, but eventually I too was subjected to the ban. The chancery office complained to the Chicago Jesuit provincial, who complained to the California Jesuit provincial, who ordered me to cease and desist from all collaboration with the National Conference of Christians and Jews.

Shortly after the war I had another experience with this closed mentality. I was returning to California from the East. While stopping in Chicago for several days, I was asked by Rabbi Finkelstein of the New York Jewish Theological Seminary if I would join Marshall Field, Jr., as a speaker at an interfaith meeting. We would each address the subject "The Moral Bases of Post-war Rehabilitation." I telephoned California to ask permission to delay my return for this purpose. The California provincial agreed, but specified that I must clear with the Chicago chancery office. I telephoned the chancellor of the diocese, Msgr. John B. Fitzgerald, and explained the nature of my request. He said he would have to check with the vicar general.

For many years, first as chancellor and then as vicar general, the power in the chancery office was Msgr. George Casey. Fitzgerald called him either on another phone or on some interoffice system but neglected to cover the phone to which I was connected. So I was privy to the whole shocking conversation which followed.

"Who is this Dunne?" asked Casey, after the nature of my request had been explained. I resisted an impulse to break in to say, "He is the grandnephew of one of your predecessors, the first vicar general of the Chicago diocese."

Instead Monsignor Fitzgerald replied, "He's that nephew of Dinny Dunne's who was at the University of Chicago a few years ago."

"Ask him if any ministers or rabbis are speaking on the program."

Fitzgerald came back on my line and put the question to me. He then repeated to Casey my reply that Marshall Field, Jr., and I were to be the only speakers. The meeting was to be chaired by a rabbi.

"Tell him no," said the vicar general. "If there are any ministers or rabbis present he cannot take part."

Today, with interfaith meetings and interfaith religious services, with priests and prelates joining Protestant ministers to commemorate the 450th anniversary of Martin Luther's nailing his ninety-five theses to the cathedral door, it is difficult to believe that so short a time ago the official climate within the Church was so stifling—not only in the ecumenical area, but in every area of Catholic life.

The first meetings of the National Catholic Liturgical Conference, in which I participated with a few dozen other people, were almost clandestine and conspiratorial. There was opposition to including on the agenda a discussion of introducing the vernacular even on a minor scale in administering the sacraments. It was feared, not without reason, that such a discussion would brand the conference as a dangerous organization in the eyes of the hierarchy. A thoroughly cowed clergy, afraid to express an opinion on any subject or move in any direction or undertake any initiative for fear of incurring official displeasure, lived with one eye cocked in the direction of the chancery office. This was the pre-Johannine Church.

Dr. Harley Farnsworth MacNair, who had taught for many years at Saint John's University in Shanghai, was my thesis adviser. Because I was a Jesuit, he was anxious that I do a doctoral thesis on the origins of the Jesuit mission in China in the sixteenth century. I was reluctant to undertake this because I thought it would be difficult to find sufficient material in this country for such a study.

Frank Rouleau, S.J., a California Jesuit who had studied theology at Zikawei with me, was now a member of the faculty there. The archives and library at Zikawei contained a great deal of material. He agreed to microfilm it for me. After months of correspondence, I received a letter from him on December 6, 1941, informing me that the microfilming equipment had arrived and been set up and that a team of his Jesuit students was ready to start microfilming. Within a matter of weeks, he said, I could expect to receive the first of a steady stream of microfilms. The next afternoon I was listening to the radio; the program was suddenly interrupted by the shocking announcement of the Japanese attack upon Pearl Harbor. It was the end, among many other more important things, of my carefully constructed plan.

That same afternoon I wrote to the California provincial, still Father Seeliger, pointing out that because I belonged to the China mission where so many of my friends and confreres were now isolated, I felt I had a greater personal involvement than others in the war. I asked to be allowed to enlist as chaplain. He replied immediately that he had already assigned four others as chaplains, but I would be the next to go. A few days later, however, he wrote again saying that he had changed his mind. He wished me to remain at the university until I had obtained my doctorate.

Dr. MacNair was unwilling to permit me to abandon the Jesuit history in favor of another subject. I began the search for material within the United States. It took some time, but I located a surprising amount, especially at Yale University, the New York Public Library, and the Library of Congress. When I was ready to begin writing the thesis I left the rectory and, availing myself of the generous hospitality of Dr. Kerwin, installed myself in his vacation cottage north of Benton Harbor, Michigan, miles from the nearest community. Alone in the woods, except for weekends when Dr. Kerwin and some guests usually joined me, I was well insulated from the distracting interests which in Chicago made concentration difficult. As long as I could stand my own cooking, it was an ideal place in which to write.

I was scarcely embarked upon the task when Seeliger's successor as provincial, Joseph King, S.J., informed me that he wished me to direct the annual eight-day retreat of the Jesuit theology students at Alma, California, next July. I asked to be excused. After Pearl Harbor changed my arrangements, I had spent a year and a half searching for and accumulating material. I was reluctant, now that I was getting under way on the final stage of the journey, to interrupt my work to prepare and direct the retreat. The provincial insisted.

His insistence is evidence that despite my objections to the manner of my recall from China I still held a high rating in the account books of my superiors. To be asked to direct the theologians' retreat was a mark of confidence. The fact that I had not yet taken my last vows—I was scheduled to take them on August 15 of that same summer of 1943—was an even clearer indication that I was still thought to have a promising future. As it turned out, his insistence had as far-reaching and unanticipated consequences for my future as had Paul O'Brien's scheme to snatch me from the hands of the French.

Six

A Retreat of Consequence

I began the retreat at Alma with considerable diffidence. The themes I stressed were evidently revolutionary then, though I did not think of them as such; today they are commonplace. Their effect was evidenced by the behavior of the theologians on the morning the retreat ended, the feast day of Saint Ignatius of Loyola, the founder of the Jesuit order. As I entered the dining room where they were already at breakfast, the young men broke into applause. It was an unprecedented, but entirely orderly, demonstration of approval.

Several days later I called upon the provincial. He told me that he was replying to a large number of letters he had received from theologians expressing enthusiasm for the retreat.

"What pleases me most," he remarked in words which I have never forgotten, "is that these letters come from men of sound judgment."

Following the retreat I went to Los Angeles, where together with Albert O'Hara, S.J., I pronounced my final vows as a Jesuit in Blessed Sacrament Church. There I received congratulatory letters from many of the scholastics at Alma who took the occasion to express again their appreciation of the retreat. Five of them—all of whom celebrated their golden jubilee as Jesuits three years ago—said that the retreat had saved their vocations. One of these, who later would spend several years in a Communist jail in China, thanked me for having given new meaning to his vocation. He remarked that after failing to find satisfaction in any of the stages of Jesuit training he had finally concluded, now that he was in the last stage of preparation, that the ministry of the priesthood did not offer the meaningful kind of life he wanted to live. The retreat, he said, had given him a new insight, and his vocation had taken on a new meaning.

These reactions left me in a state of slight euphoria as I returned to Chicago by train, and I had the feeling that I would like to give the same retreat in every Jesuit house of studies in the country. Hardly had I settled down to work again in the woods of Michigan when the roof of euphoria fell in with a thunderous crash. A letter from Zacheus Maher landed with the weight of a safe dropped from the Empire State Building.

He began by saying that, in view of the high opinion he had held of me over the years, he found it difficult to believe the report he had received about my retreat. He described its effect upon the scholastics as utterly disruptive. "Even the best of them had been knocked off stride," he wrote, leaving one to suppose that the worst of them had been totally ruined. He then made a series of accusations, some entirely untrue, others grotesque distortions of the truth. He concluded by saying that he was reserving judgment until he heard from me.

I should have known that this assurance was not to be taken seriously. The tone of the letter was a sign that he had already made his judgment. Zacheus Maher, a man of many virtues and considerable talent, had a major fault. He was deeply pessimistic about human nature, and especially about the nature of Jesuits under his command. He was predisposed to believe the worst about them. An indictment was equivalent to a conviction. Not only was a man guilty until proven innocent, but his peculiar rules of evidence ruled out as irrelevant and immaterial any testimony that contradicted the bill of particulars. The only thing acceptable was an admission of guilt. I have described him elsewhere as "a man often in error, but never in doubt."

Maher's description of the effect of the retreat upon the theologians created an impression of a community in turmoil or open rebellion. Before replying to his letter I wrote to the spiritual father of the Alma community, Edward Hageman, S.J., a man in a better position than anyone else to know what the effect of the retreat had been upon the scholastics. I listed the charges made by Maher and asked what had happened since I left Alma to give rise to them.

It was the custom for a spiritual father to have an informal chat with each member of the community from time to time, to find out how he was getting on, to offer help with his problems. Father Hageman finished his round of interviews and sounded out all of the theologians about the retreat. Then he reported to me that he had found no evidence to support Maher's charges. There was nothing at all to suggest a community in disarray or men "thrown off stride."

Although Father Hageman's inquiry did not uncover them, I knew that there were some dissenting voices. Approval of the retreat, though general, was not unanimous. I had been told during the retreat that several of the retreatants who were hard-core anti-Semites and pro-Francoites were displeased. This had only further convinced me that I was on target.

Hageman had attended most of my conferences, so he was astonished at the charges. He added that, having observed the salutary effect of the retreat, he had been inspired to revise his own retreat notes. The retreat he was accustomed to give, he wrote, was more oriented towards problems affecting the relations of the individual retreatant with God; he was rewriting his notes to introduce more of the social content of Christianity. Coming from a man far more experienced than I in retreat direction, I thought this was strong endorsement.

Armed with this report I sat down to reply to Father Maher. I discussed each accusation and presented the contradictory evidence: the testimony of the provincial in our conversation several days after the retreat, the testimony of letters from theologians, the testimony of the spiritual father of the community. It was a mistake. His curt reply made it plain that, despite what he had said about reserving judgment until he had heard from me, he did not wish a discussion of the case but a confession of guilt. He said that had I admitted my error and promised not to repeat it he would have felt there was some hope for me; but in view of my refusal to recognize my guilt, he saw little hope. He would, however, in his charity pray for me. On this somewhat off-key note he declared the case closed.

What was scandalous in my retreat? The first charge was that I had not followed the Spiritual Exercises of Saint Ignatius, but had substituted instead a series of "brilliant talks on social subjects." There was no foundation for the first part of the accusation. Upon leaving for California I had borrowed from Paul Reinert the schedule of meditations from one of the retreats he had made as a theologian. I followed this schedule faithfully.

The clue to what was different about the retreat is found in Father Hageman's comparison of his own retreat to mine. The Exercises have been criticized for encouraging an excessively individualistic spirituality. The fault is not with the Exercises but with retreat directors who interpret them according to their own egocentric inclinations. The Exercises are a broad framework within which there is ample room for every message that can be drawn from the Gospels. In my reflections upon such subjects as, for example, the Sermon on the Mount or the two great commandments, I had talked about poverty, peace, war, not in the abstract but in the concrete. I talked about anti-Semitism, Hitler's holocaust, racial segregation, the rat-infested tenements in New York, the exploitation of migrant farm workers, the Spanish Civil War, the anguish of the world's poor, and similar subjects.

This was the basis of the second half of the charge, that I had substituted talks on social subjects for the Spiritual Exercises. Schooled as they had been, I suppose it was difficult for Father Maher and his informer to see that these subjects were far more relevant to the love of our neighbor than were discussions about backbiting or rash judgment.

Who in 1943, with millions of Jews dying in gas chambers, could speak about love of neighbor without talking about the evil of anti-Semitism? My remarks were not a sociological lecture, but a cry of anguish: anguish for the suffering Jews and anguish for complacent Christians who could look on flint-faced and stone-hearted, unmoved by the suffering of these people who were Christ's people; anguish too for people like Father Maher who could not see that the Gospels, and therefore the Exercises of Saint Ignatius, had something to say about this subject.

Granting that the Exercises are concerned rather with improving the retreatant's soul than with the reformation of society, it seemed to me evident that the state of a Jesuit's soul is determined far more by his attitude toward the Jew, the Negro, the dispossessed than by the number of unkindly thoughts he has each day about his fellow monks. In one's underlying attitudes is to be found the meaning of the parable of the Good Samaritan. And in those attitudes, not in small, everyday lapses, is to be found the true measure of his love for God which, according to Saint James, is measured by his love for his neighbor. Apparently there existed a chasm between Father Maher's thinking and my own, for in his judgment, to discuss these themes was to substitute sociology for the Exercises. "Such subjects," his letter had stated, "have no place in the Spiritual Exercises."

Today, the subjects I touched upon would be accepted as commonplace in a retreat. Younger Jesuits would find it incredible that my performance was regarded as scandalous. I am afraid today no applause would follow me as I crossed the floor of the dining room to my place at breakfast, not because applause is considered out of place in Jesuit dining rooms—this too has become commonplace—but because the theologians would not find anything out of the ordinary meriting applause. This too is a measure of how great have been the changes not only within the Jesuit order but within the Church as a whole since John XXIII breathed upon the Church and restored her to life.

I was also accused of having "criticized superiors." The basis of this was a conference on the principles of good government. In sketching the profile of an ideal superior I had clearly in mind certain traits of French superiors whom I had known in China. It could have been considered a "criticism of superiors" only by someone with a guilty conscience.

Counting as heavily against me as anything else was the applause which had greeted my entrance to the dining room. "This may seem a small thing to you," wrote Father Maher, "but it is a straw which shows the way the wind is blowing. Such worldly demonstrations have no place in our communities."

The idea of what was proper in our communities had become distorted over the years, just as Saint Ignatius himself has often been misunderstood and his public image falsified by his own followers. My master of novices, for example, who had no ear and no taste for music, described Ignatius as a man who regarded music as an appropriate interest for women but not for men. This had not helped me feel sympathetic towards the saint.

I thought of the master of novices years later, when I learned that Saint Ignatius not only loved music but played a musical instrument. And I thought of Zach Maher when I learned that Saint Ignatius, to revive the drooping spirits of his retreatant at the end of the first week of the Exercises, had leaped to his feet and thrown himself into a wild Basque dance of his youth. It seemed incredible to me at the time of the retreat, and it seems incredible to me now, that applause was regarded as conclusive proof of the evil effects of the retreat.

Over twenty years later, as we sat down to lunch in that same dining room, I was introduced to the community, as had become the custom with every visitor. And the theologians, as was also the custom by then, responded with applause. "Worldly demonstrations," I thought to myself, "have evidently got the upper hand."

In my reply to Father Maher I said that I was altogether astonished that he felt it scandalous that the scholastics had responded with enthusiasm rather than, as was often the case, with boredom and had resorted to a custom observed the world over to register their approval. I added, not very diplomatically, that I was sure Fr. Yves Henry, my rector at Zikawei, would have been delighted if, at the conclusion of the annual retreat, the theologians had demonstrated their pleasure in this same way. He would have been even more delighted if, in addition to the polite hand clapping, they had pounded the tables and rattled the dishes, as is a common custom in European communities.

Who was Father Maher's informer? By his own admission there was only one, and Maher had warned me not to try to identify him. I had no particular desire to do so. However, Father Maher himself had made it difficult not to identify him without even trying. "This has been reported to me," he had written, "by a man in whom I have every confidence, whom I have known for many years and with whom I have lived in community."

There were only two present at Alma whom this description fit. Though the retreat was primarily for the theology students, several older Jesuits had also made it. One of these fit the description, but he had come to my room the last day of the retreat to tell me that he could not stay for the concluding meditation. He had to return that evening to his community in San Francisco; but he did not wish to leave without telling me how much he had enjoyed the retreat.

"The first day," he said, "I was not quite sure where you were leading us, but after that I liked every bit of it. I thought the fourth day, with your conference on superiors, was the high point; but I liked it all and wanted to tell you this before leaving."

That would seem to rule him out, but some years later I was told by Fr. John McGloin that the same evening in the San Francisco Jesuit community he had expressed to his supper companions concern over what was happening to the younger generation and gave as an example the "un-Ignatian retreat that young Father Dunne gave at Alma."

How to explain the contradiction between this attitude and the unsolicited approval he had expressed to me a few hours earlier, I do not know. Perhaps his derogatory remark originated in nothing more than a rather common inclination of an older generation to keep the younger men in their place. In any case, he was not a witness to the "worldly demonstration" staged by the scholastics when I entered the dining room on the Feast of Saint Ignatius.

One who had witnessed it and who, given his rigidly orthodox cast of mind, undoubtedly disapproved was Fr. Louis Rudolph, the rector of the community. He also perfectly fit Maher's description of a man in whom he had every confidence, whom he had known many years and with whom he had lived in community. Rudolph, commonly referred to as Rudy, was a pious man, firmly committed to the established order in which *nihil est innovandum*—nothing new. I had a minor clash with him midway through the retreat that should have tipped me off that he was not pleased with it.

During the retreat I had made several observations about the liturgy, its importance, its relationship to the spiritual life. And I had described some of the things we had done during the student weekend retreats at Childerley, including the dialogue Mass, in which the congregation, instead of only the altar boys, would respond to the prayers of the priest and join him in some of the ordinary prayers. It became standard in time but was not common forty-five years ago.

One of the scholastics asked if they might have a dialogue Mass during the retreat. I said I thought it a fine idea and would propose it to the rector, who customarily celebrated the community Mass. In the event that he, because he was not accustomed to saying the prayers in unison with the community, felt insecure about it, I was sure he would allow me to say the Mass in his stead.

After lunch that day I broached the subject. Father Rudolph was seated opposite me across the large round table in the fathers' recreation room, only his biretta appearing above the daily newspaper behind which he was hidden. (Father Rudolph was rarely seen without his biretta; one of the wags among the scholastics maintained that he had a rubber biretta which he wore when taking a shower.) I explained the request and asked permission to have a community Mass one day before the end of the retreat. Not until I had finished my explanation and request did he appear from behind the newspaper long enough to say firmly, "No, Father!" and then disappear again behind the paper.

I was jolted both at the refusal and at the curtness of the reply. Thinking he had not understood, I explained in greater detail what had led to the request, my observations about the liturgy, my experiences at the University of Chicago, the developing interest everywhere in the Church. I repeated my request. Once more he emerged from behind the newspaper and said, "No, Father!"

"Why not?" I asked, becoming irritated by these monosyllabic rebuffs.

"The former provincial did not approve of it," he answered, this time without emerging from behind the newspaper.

It seemed a remarkable reason. A dialogue Mass was not to be allowed because the former—not the present—provincial was not in favor of it.

"Does the *former* provincial know," I asked ironically, "that the present general of the order, Father Ledochowski, in two letters to the whole Society not only recommended, but urged, that we introduce the dialogue Mass into our schools and colleges?"

"Yes, Father," he replied, again without lowering the newspaper. That was the end of the dialogue and of the dialogue Mass.

Following the recreation period Father Hageman accompanied me to my room which was next to his. "You have witnessed, George," he said, "what is wrong with Father Rudolph's mode of governance. Nothing is ever discussed. Every request is answered with a yes or a no. I don't think you should accept this. You should appeal to the provincial. If I phone him for an appointment this afternoon will you keep it?"

I agreed and drove that afternoon to San Jose. En route, however, I said to myself: "Father Rudolph is here all year long. I am here only eight days and then am gone. I don't want to cause trouble for him with the provincial and then go blithely on my way." Arrived in San Jose, I did not mention my little conflict with Rudolph, but pretended I had come seeking information about arrangements for my final vows.

None of the things I said during the retreat would have surprised Fr. Yves Henry, although he might have disagreed—and loudly—with some of them. It has always been a source of deep gratification to me to know that until he died in Hong Kong at the age of eighty-two, almost thirty years after I bade him good-by in Shanghai, his opinion of me never changed nor did the later conflicts which marked my career diminish his confidence.

I make no judgment of the men involved in this episode, or in any of the other episodes of my life. I remember them all each morning in my Mass. They acted according to their honest convictions and in tune with the temper of the time. I am not judging, but reporting facts and the interesting way in which lives interact upon one another, shaping the course of human destinies. I do not find it difficult to believe that behind the interaction there is a divine providence, not in the sense that God plots or even desires all the moves and countermoves, but that he is able to fit the consequences to which they lead into a master scheme. This belief makes many things easier to accept.

Seven

In and Out of St. Louis

T he Alma retreat and its deeply disturbing aftermath occasioned a long delay; afterwards, I resumed work on my
doctoral thesis. I finished it the following year and successfully defended it before a panel of professors, including the
distinguished professor of international law, Dr. Quincy Wright,
my friend Dr. Jerome Kerwin, and, of course, Dr. Harley Farnsworth MacNair. I was awarded a doctor of philosophy degree in
international relations in the spring of 1944.

That I failed to achieve this goal two or three years sooner was
due in part to the outbreak of the war, which disrupted my
research, but mainly, as I have remarked, to my becoming
involved in all the concerns of Catholic students. I must in honesty
admit too that I formed personal friendships which absorbed a lot
of my time and were scarcely compatible with my main purpose in
being there.

This delay in completing my doctorate turned out to be a
major factor in determining my destiny. I was still writing my
thesis when Bp. Yu Pin, later a cardinal, asked Fr. Zach Maher for
my services as his secretary; Maher was now the general's
assistant for America. Yu Pin, bishop of Nanking, was the most
visible member of the Chinese hierarchy. He was of Manchu
origin, a tall, solidly built, handsome man of superior intelligence.
I had met him at Zikawei at a national conference of Catholic
Action, of which he was the head. During the war years he
maintained a residence in Washington, D.C., and spent a good
deal of time in the United States making friends and mobilizing
support for Chiang Kai-shek and the Kuomintang.

When Loyola University in Chicago conferred upon him an honorary degree, he wrote to ask that I meet him at the convocation. I did so and that evening accompanied him on a tour of Chinatown. The two of us visited almost every shop in the area and chatted with dozens of Chinese Chicagoans. An interesting feature of these encounters was that the only means of communication between Yu Pin and the Chicago Chinese was English. He could not understand their Cantonese nor they his mandarin. Prior to World War II, practically all Chinese residents in the United States were of Cantonese origin. Although their written language is the same, their spoken language is quite different from the national language, *Kuo-yu*, known to foreigners as *mandarin* because under the empire it was the language used by officials, or mandarins.

It was some time after our Chicago encounter that Yu Pin asked that I be assigned to him as secretary, but this was not possible because I had not yet finished my doctorate. Paul O'Brien, on the other hand, had completed his graduate studies and was available.

Paul had begun graduate studies in Buddhism at the University of California while completing his fourth year of theology at Alma College. Twice a week he commuted from Alma to spend the day at Berkeley. After finishing theology, he was able to devote full time to Buddhism and two years later obtained his doctorate. It was a brilliant performance. He joined Yu Pin in Washington and remained with him until the end of the war in 1945.

As for me, once I finished my degree in 1944, the question of what and where next was quickly resolved. The war ruled out my immediate return to China. But the American provincials had decided to establish at St. Louis University an Institute of Social Science, the main purpose of which was to develop a Catholic response to the social problems of the day and to make Jesuits aware of the same. According to the agreement each American province was to assign one man to the faculty and two to the student body. My provincial, Joseph King, notified me that he was naming me as California's contribution to the faculty.

I reported to St. Louis in September 1944, where I quickly discovered that the agreement had been largely ignored. The I.S.S. faculty consisted of two Jesuits. The New England Province had contributed Fr. James Burke, who held a doctorate in constitutional law from Harvard. He and I constituted the faculty, while Fr. Leo Brown of St. Louis, who held a doctorate in economics from Harvard, acted as liaison with the university. Father Burke did not feel at ease in the St. Louis Jesuit community. I can still see him pacing up and down my room, snapping his fingers in a gesture of annoyance, while complaining, "In my own province I am considered an important man; here they pay no attention to me." At the end of the first semester he resigned and returned to New England, where he became prefect of studies for the province.

For the I.S.S. student body, the Oregon Province sent two scholastics, Richard Twohy, who would later be president of Gonzaga University, and his classmate, Mike Toulouse, a colorful and loveable character who boasted descent from Gypsy origins. A scholastic from the New York Province joined them. Besides these three, several regular university students followed the courses which I taught. Two of these, one of them now a nun, still correspond with me.

My first trouble at St. Louis arose in November. Fr. Eugene P. Murphy, S.J., director of the Sacred Heart radio program, asked me to deliver the homily on one of the broadcasts. This program, aimed especially at shut-ins at the time, consisted of a half hour of hymns, prayers, organ music, and a six-minute homily, for which Father Murphy depended upon St. Louis University Jesuits. I agreed to do so.

He asked me to speak on the eleventh chapter of the Acts of the Apostles, which includes the admonition of Saint Peter, in the version I had, "Thou shalt call no man common or unclean." It seemed to me evident that this was a condemnation of racial segregation. That is precisely what is evil about racial segregation: it brands as common or unclean every member of a particular group regardless of one's merits as an individual. It denies one of the most fundamental of human rights, the right to recognition of one's dignity as a human person. The incompatibility of segregation with this message of Christ was the subject of my little homily; within its given limit of six minutes, it obviously could not have been an earth shaking polemic.

Seven years ago, I was overjoyed upon reading a scholarly article by James W. Reites, S.J., entitled "Saint Ignatius of Loyola and the Jews."[1] My joy was twofold. For one thing, the article established that I had interpreted Saint Peter's vision in the Acts of the Apostles just as Saint Ignatius had. Second, it greatly enhanced my admiration for Saint Ignatius, which had always fallen short of what one would expect of a Jesuit.

The reason was that early in my Jesuit life I had learned that a rule in our Constitutions banned acceptance into the order of anyone of Jewish ancestry. Since Saint Ignatius was the principal author of the Constitutions I presumed that he was responsible for this nasty relic of the fierce anti-Semitism that raged in Europe in the sixteenth century, and nowhere more than in Spain.

This puzzled me, because Saint Ignatius's good friend and successor as superior general of the Society, Fr. James Laynez, was of Jewish descent. It was not until I read the fruit of Father Reites's research that I learned that Saint Ignatius was not anti-Semitic, but quite the contrary. Saint Ignatius consistently, adamantly, courageously, and under insistent pressure from kings, princes, prelates, nobles, and some of his own Jesuit followers refused to the end of his life to include such a provision in the Constitutions or to permit such a policy in the Society.

In the raging anti-Semitic fever of the age, the Jesuits were in fact, during Ignatius's lifetime, the only major religious order in Spain that refused to accept ethnic origin as pertinent to its admission policy. The cardinal archbishop of Toledo, primate of Spain, restricted the ministry of all priests who had made the Spiritual Exercises and forbade Jesuits to do any ministry, even to celebrate Mass, within his jurisdiction as long as Saint Ignatius refused to accept for his order the so-called *limpieza de sangre*—purity of blood—statute which he had imposed upon his archdiocese.

Saint Ignatius's reaction was a calm refusal. "It is not to be thought of," he wrote to a friend in 1552; "it will be enough for him [the archbishop] to mind his own business."

The Spanish provincial, Antonio Araoz, related to Ignatius by marriage, urged acceptance of the *limpieza de sangre* policy. For ten years, until Ignatius died, Araoz kept up a barrage of argumentative letters. And Ignatius insisted to the end that racial or ethnic origins could not be permitted to have anything to do with admission to the Society.

The theological basis of his position was quite clear—the mind of Christ as revealed in the eleventh chapter of the Acts of the Apostles. Unaware of it at the time, I understood the text just as Ignatius had.

Ignatius's first two successors, Laynez and Francis Borgia, resisted with equal firmness. But the fifth general congregation, while Claudio Aquaviva was general, thumbed its nose at Saint Ignatius, yielded to the importunities of its anti-Semites, and introduced this infamous rule. In 1608, Pedro Ribadeneira, one of those closest to Ignatius from the earliest days of the Society, wrote a strongly-worded protest to Aquaviva, "In my opinion, there is no matter in the whole Institute, nothing whatever, more characteristic of Ignatius and more according to his mind." The rule stood.

Though subjected to so many dispensations as to be in effect void, it remained, to the everlasting shame of the Jesuits, on the books until expunged in 1946 following the horrors of the Holocaust.

It is quite common among Jesuits to refer to "the mind of Saint Ignatius." In 1944, though, I was ignorant of the facts later unearthed by Father Reites and so did not know Ignatius's mind. Had I been able to face what happened next with Saint Ignatius at my side, things might have proceeded quite differently.

The morning after my homily, I was summoned by Fr. Patrick Holloran, president of the university and rector of the Jesuit community, to appear without delay in his office and to bring with me a copy of the homily. He spent long minutes studying the less than two pages of text. Finally abandoning his search for something in the text he could make an issue of, he asked me, "Why did you speak on this subject?"

"Because," I replied, "Father Murphy asked me to speak on the eleventh chapter of the Acts of the Apostles, and that is the message of the eleventh chapter of the Acts of the Apostles. Why do you ask?"

He answered that he had received angry telephone calls protesting my talk and especially an angry call from the vicar general of the archdiocese.

My talk was neither demagogic nor polemical, simply a condemnation of racial segregation wherever practiced across the land, north as well as south. It did not single out St. Louis or Missouri for blame. In fact, the Sacred Heart program was not a local St. Louis program. Father Murphy had explained to me that, although originating in the St. Louis studio, it was broadcast nationally over a large number of stations. I actually do not believe that I gave a thought to St. Louis during the short six minutes of my homily.

This vicar general who protested was Msgr. John Cody later to be archbishop of New Orleans and later still the highly controversial cardinal archbishop of Chicago. It should be noted that, curiously enough, whatever the merits of the other charges leveled at him in Chicago—and they were many—his record both there and in New Orleans vis-à-vis racial questions seems to have been above reproach. If he did indeed protest my homily, he must have later experienced a personal conversion, perhaps influenced by Abp. Joseph E. Ritter,

Joseph Ritter became archbishop of St. Louis in 1946, succeeding Abp. John Glennon. Glennon had gone to Rome in the spring of 1946 to receive the long-desired red hat of a cardinal. He did not have long to enjoy whatever satisfaction it gave him. He died in Ireland en route home. Eight months later Rome named as his successor Joseph E. Ritter, the archbishop of Indianapolis.

Ritter had previously been bishop of Evansville, Indiana, where he had left no doubt about his position on racial segregation. When a group of white parishioners threatened rebellion in the face of his order desegregating a parish school, he had quietly informed them that if they persisted he would simply put their church under interdict, close their school and remove the pastor and assistant priests.[2]

John Cody was probably also influenced by the example of his predecessor in New Orleans, Abp. Joseph Rummel. Ritter and Rummel were among the few members of the American hierarchy who refused to make any deals when it came to applying the values of the Gospel to the question of the rights of Negroes, within or without the Church.[3] Or it could have been that, in his protest to Holloran, Cody was expressing not his own convictions, but, as is often the case with ecclesiastical careerists not anxious to jeopardize their future, what he knew to be the view of his superior, Archbishop Glennon. For Glennon was a notorious segregationist, or, as Fr. Claude Heithaus, S.J., described him—not to put too fine a point on it—"an obdurate race bigot." Fr. William Markoe, S.J., who as pastor of Saint Elizabeth's black parish had dealt with him for years, said quite simply that he suffered from "negrophobia."

At the time of my homily, which was less than two months after I arrived in St. Louis, I was entirely ignorant of Glennon's views or policies on racial segregation. With the experience of later years I would not have naively assumed that because he was a bishop he accepted the teachings and spirit of the Gospel or necessarily of the pope. But that morning I knew nothing of Glennon except that he had built over the years a truly magnificent cathedral. I had never met him.

I asked Father Holloran what fault he found with the homily. He replied that it "could be interpreted as an attack upon the archbishop."

In view of my ignorance as just described, this was an absurd non sequitur. The following year, after my hasty departure from

St. Louis, I learned how far the reverberations of such a non sequitur can reach. Fr. Hugh Duce, a former president of Loyola University in Los Angeles, told me that the California provincial had been warned, "He goes about attacking archbishops; for God's sake, don't let him talk in San Francisco." The relations between the Jesuits in San Francisco and Abp. John J. Mitty were tense at the time.

In a sense, I had arrived in St. Louis an innocent abroad. I was ignorant of many things that had occurred affecting the question of racial segregation in the schools. In fact I only learned of them more than forty years later when, in the course of writing these memoirs, I obtained a number of enlightening documents from the archives of the Missouri Province.

Missouri had been a slave state; it was still a segregated state. Schools were segregated, Catholic as well as public. St. Louis University, like every university in the state, had traditionally refused to admit black students. But during and immediately after World War II, some consciences began to stir. A group of Catholics, lay and clerical, petitioned the archbishop to desegregate the parochial schools. He refused. The increasingly persuasive efforts of the desegregationists were confronted by the unyielding obduracy of the archbishop. Among the most active of the desegregationists were three Jesuit priests: Bill Markoe, his brother John ("Cap") Markoe, and Claude Heithaus.

A number of dramatic incidents occurred during the effort to convert the archbishop, none more dramatic than a meeting between him and Mrs. Jane Kaiser, the mother of a boy who had been refused admission to his parochial school because he was a Negro. Few would have suspected the boy's race from the appearance of his classically beautiful mother, who would have passed for caucasian in any milieu. One of those who did not suspect it was the archbishop. When she appeared at his residence by appointment to ask for an explanation of his refusal to admit black children into his white parochial schools, he assumed that she was simply another one of the misguided white women active in the desegregation group. He launched into the stereotypical tirade against Negroes: they were lazy, dishonest, unclean, intellectually inferior, rapists. They started fights, made it unsafe to get on a streetcar, pushed whites around, already got much more than they deserved; and—always the clinching argument—he added that mingling in school would lead to the ultimate horror of miscegenation. Having completed his catalogue of Negro aberrations, he asked her why it should matter to her. She replied, as the walls collapsed upon him who had always denied that he was a racist, "Evidently Your Grace does not understand. I am a Negro mother whose son has been denied entrance to our parochial school."

A furious archbishop felt himself trapped. He roughly showed her out the door, where Fr. Cap Markoe awaited her in the car. At Father Heithaus's suggestion, Mrs. Kaiser wrote a detailed account of the incident to the apostolic delegate, listing in five pages every demeaning comment Glennon had made about Negroes in general. I cannot confirm it, but I strongly suspect that when the choice of Glennon's successor was being considered several years later, Mrs. Kaiser's report was among the documents carefully considered. Within a year of his arrival in St. Louis, Archbishop Ritter had desegregated every Catholic school in St Louis.

Back during the school year 1942–43, Fr. Peter A. Brooks, S.J., the Missouri provincial, had initiated the move to integrate the university. A seven-man committee consisting of long-time St. Louis residents was asked to study the question. At their first meeting they approved four votes to three the request of the dean of the medical school to integrate his school. This apparently so surprised the dean that he withdrew his request, not considering a majority of one mandatory.

Meantime Patrick Holloran, S.J., had become president of the university. Father Brooks recommended that he pursue the matter further. His manner of doing so was a peculiar one indeed. It was clear that integration was a subject in which he had little interest and no moral concern. He wrote to many friends of the university soliciting their opinion. At the same time he reassured them that, should the bars be dropped, he did not think more than twenty would be able to pass the entrance exams over the next twenty years—no more than one a year! A reflection of Holloran's view that all Negroes are stupid.

To his great surprise, no doubt, only one of those who responded to his letter was opposed to integration. The St. Louis Post-Despatch, on January 27, 1944, editorially praised St. Louis University for moving towards the solution of what was obviously a moral problem while the University of Missouri spun legal cobwebs.

On Friday morning, February 11, 1944, Father Heithaus was scheduled to deliver the sermon at the student Mass. He spoke on racial segregation. According to his own testimony, he put the sermon through twenty drafts and submitted it to the judgment of three of the most highly respected Jesuits on the faculty.

It was a masterful presentation, rationally and unemotionally argued. Among more theological issues it posed the practical question: if Muslims and Hindus are allowed to attend the university, why are black Catholics excluded? In conclusion he invited all those willing to do so to rise and join him in a pledge to do nothing in the future to injure a black person. The response of the congregation of more than a thousand, mostly students, was unanimous.

The text of the sermon was published that day in the student newspaper, of which Heithaus was the faculty moderator. The *St. Louis Post-Despatch* praised it and complimented the university for its leadership. From that day, Heithaus became the central figure of the campus movement for integration.

Father Holloran was not pleased by Heithaus's sermon and wrote him a note the same day to tell him so, while at the same time recognizing that until then he had much appreciated his cooperation and efficiency. Zach Maher was later to pontificate that "Father Heithaus was ill-advised and erred in giving that chapel talk, and in publishing it."[4] Others, however, including such nationally known Jesuits as Dan Lord and John LaFarge, and others like Eric Johnson, president of the United States Chamber of Commerce, praised him for his effective leadership. The president of the St. Louis Catholic Clergy Conference on Race, at the request of its membership, described "the profound effect for good" his sermon had had upon the Negroes of St. Louis. Fr. William B. Faherty, archivist of the Jesuits' Missouri Province, thinks it should be included among great American sermons. I fully agree.

As a canonically exempt religious order, the Jesuits were not obliged to have the archbishop's approval to integrate the university. It would no doubt have been the better part of valor, but the lesser part of discretion to do so without consulting him. On the afternoon of February 15, Father Holloran went to see the archbishop to discuss the question. For reasons that are not clear, he took Father Heithaus with him. This resulted in another of the more dramatic incidents of the period: an eyeball-to-eyeball confrontation between the archbishop and Heithaus while Holloran sat silently on the sidelines.

Many months later, Heithaus wrote a detailed report to Fr. Joseph P. Zuercher, who had succeeded Father Brooks as provincial.[5] Using the sermon as a launching pad, the archbishop released a bombardment of charges, listed under twenty-two headings. Heithaus, no wimp, refused to be browbeaten and responded without equivocation to the articles of indictment in which, according to Heithaus, "the archbishop displayed...none of that Olympian serenity and witty persiflage which is said to characterize his public conversations." It seems to have been a donnybrook. When Father Maher wrote to Father Zuercher after the event, he described Heithaus's replies as a failure "to speak to one's Superior with great reverence."[6] My view is that the reverend archbishop got all the reverence he deserved.

After dismissing Heithaus, the archbishop had a private discussion with Holloran. No record exists of what was said, but on the way home Holloran informed Heithaus that he had obtained archiepiscopal approval for integration. But he also said that he agreed totally with the archbishop's views as expressed to Heithaus and in conclusion forbade Heithaus in future talks to discuss the racial issue.

Holloran continued to waffle. A meeting of deans and regents of the university was held to discuss integration. What happened is shrouded in ignorance. No vote was taken, and the minutes were shredded. Norman Cothran, a senior at Saint Joseph's High School and a Negro, was informed by Holloran that his application for admission could not be acted upon at the time. Holloran was no doubt being pressured by bigots of all levels, among them, painful as it is to admit, rabid segregationists from his own community; these even included a professor of ethics and the head of the department of religion! And he lacked the moral fiber to take a principled position based on the Gospel.

The Cothran incident finally settled matters. Notified by the sister superior of the school that Norman Cothran attended, Fr. Bill Markoe and Father Heithaus took the matter up with the provincial. He in turn submitted it to Father Maher, who wrote a letter urging the admission of all properly qualified students to all Jesuit schools.[7] On April 25, 1944, Father Holloran announced the end of racial segregation at St. Louis University.[8]

This was the background of the situation when I arrived at St. Louis in the late summer of 1944. As I said before, when I delivered my radio homily on segregation I was totally ignorant of this history. I very much doubt that knowledge of the situation would have changed the content of my homily. I was preaching on an assigned text of the Gospel, and that text condemned racial segregation. But my ignorance of the background does explain why I was so surprised and shocked by Father Holloran's reaction. It also explains—but hardly excuses—his anger.

Father Holloran ended our meeting by forbidding me in any future talks I might give in St. Louis to mention the subject of race. Upon arriving back in my room I recalled that I was committed to give a talk on race several weeks hence to the men's club of the wealthiest synagogue in St. Louis; its president, who had asked me to give the talk, was the president of the American Car Foundry Company. I phoned Father Holloran, reminded him of the injunction he had just laid upon me, told him of this commitment, and asked his pleasure. I should say that at the time Father Holloran was engaged in a drive to raise $2,000,000 for the university, a meager sum now, but a substantial one in 1944. He replied, "It is all right for you to give this talk to this group." I add as a footnote that following my talk the president of the club presented me with a check for the university in the amount of several thousand dollars.

I obeyed Father Holloran's injunction, but I appealed to Father Maher. I sent him a copy of my homily, pointing out that it contained nothing that was not a statement of Catholic doctrine. I argued that, while I recognized the right of a superior not to permit me to preach, I questioned his right, if I were authorized to preach, to forbid me to teach a specific Catholic doctrine, such as the sin of racial segregation. Father Maher replied that he was coming to St. Louis in the near future, when we would discuss the matter.

Forty years later, with documents from the Missouri archives, I learned that on January 4, 1945, Maher had written a letter to Zuercher highly critical of Holloran: "The thread of his thought in several instances is surprising and the way he handled phases of the situation is not always what I had expected of him. I regret his first approach to the problem."[9]

When he met with me three months later, he completely contradicted what he had said in this letter and supported Holloran fully. His chief argument was "George, we cannot take positions on social subjects which run counter to the positions held by the society in which we live."

Recalling how often, dating all the way back to my high school days, I had heard Father Maher boast "A Jesuit is a man of principle," I remarked, "I thought that was what we were supposed to do when those positions contradicted the teaching of Christ."

I asked him if he agreed with Pope Pius XI that Negroes had equal rights in the Church and must know that they had equal rights; never one to contradict a pope, he replied, "Yes, of course, but what do you mean by equal?"

I replied, "By equal I mean equal, and cannot conceive of unequal equalities." There was nothing more to say and nothing more to be said. It was the end of our conversation and the end of a friendship of almost thirty years' duration.

Father Maher had built an impressive career upon the reputation of being a "man of principle." Through boyhood and beyond, I had looked on admiringly. Now when the crunch came the statue had turned to clay. "We cannot take positions contrary to those of the society in which we live." I had seen the emperor without clothes and he knew it. In the years that followed, on the few occasions when we met, he never looked me in the eye and avoided all conversation.

Apart from the one to the Jewish men's club, I did not mention race in any talks I gave during the few months I remained in St. Louis. I discussed the subject in the classes I taught, but that was quite another matter.

That was my first unpleasant experience in St. Louis. A second one, more serious, ended in my expulsion. I arrived at the university at the same time as integration. Consequently I was an observer from the start. There were sixty-one black students enrolled my first semester there. The experience was a total success. The black students shared in everything: classrooms, library, cafeteria, gymnasium, swimming pool, and all kinds of extracurricular activities without any friction.

This was a success largely due to the moral ascendancy of Fr. Claude Heithaus. He had convinced the students that segregation was wrong. By profession an archeologist with a doctorate from the University of London and a specialist in ancient Roman coins, he was an unlikely leader in this kind of issue. He was a tall man, six-foot-two, slender, intensely serious. It was the sincerity, depth and firmness of his convictions that probably accounted for his influence upon the students.

So successful had desegregation proved that *Life* magazine sent a team of photographers to shoot scenes of racial mixing on campus for a feature story. St. Louis was the first, and then still the only, university in Missouri to admit Negro students. It was rightly thought that its example could prove to be a major breakthrough in the battle against segregation. The Supreme Court's landmark *Brown v. Board of Education* decision was still ten years in the offing.

Some efforts have been made to cosmeticize Father Holloran's role. A few years later, after Holloran had finished his term as president, he was presented with an honorary degree; the citation included among his accomplishments the admission of black students to the university. I recall remarking in an article at the time that this must have caused great hilarity in heaven at least among the black angels. The plain fact was that he and several of his closest friends and advisers in the community were racists. There is no other word for it. Consider the following evidence.

I have referred to the letter of inquiry which he mailed to some friends of the university. One of them was Vincent P. Ring, president of the previous year's retreat league—which itself says something of significance. (A tag line keeps knocking around in my head, something about "there is no place in the Spiritual Exercises for the social teachings of the Church.") Ring's reply, which he circulated among his friends, gives his encapsulated analysis of the Negro:

> He has a great distaste for hard work or personal application. He regards money as something to be spent. His new leaders DEMAND rights instead of undertaking to win respect. . .The admixture of Negroes presents a further host of problems for which answers will be difficult to secure. . .race riots. . .in the near future. . .guards are posted at our armory to protect our guns and munitions stored in anticipation of such riots. . .[10]

The source of this arrogant racist nonsense—the president of a retreat association—is less surprising than the response it drew from Father Holloran:

> Thank you most sincerely for sending me back your card. . .but incomparably more grateful am I for the excellent letter which you took the time to write to me.
> Between the two of us your statement of the case is absolutely identical with my convictions in the matter. Again and again I have said to individuals who have been urging this point on me: there are many, many things that we can give to the Negroes, and we are doing it; but there is one thing that you can give to no one and that is self-respect. . .[11]

Even in formally announcing the integration of the university on May 16, 1944, Holloran larded his address with expressions taken from the vocabulary of gradualism; and he reassured jittery friends that beyond admission to the academic life of the university there would be no further integration—"identity," he called it—in other areas of student life.

Even the usually cautious Father LaFarge complained to Father Maher:

> It would be vastly better if he had never spoken at all. . .the phrases he uses: e.g. "evolution not revolution," are stock phrases which, though they sound well to the inexperienced, are in fact commonplaces in the propaganda of the advocates of "white supremacy," and generally recognized as such by Negroes.[12]

The commencement address drew the line at what it called "academic equality." There was to be no integration beyond that:

> In the wider and less well-defined field of social relationships, contacts, and activities, we do not approve, nor shall we attempt to enforce, identity between white and colored students. We do not intend to ape the mistakes of Communists who, after a futile adventure into the field of utter leveling, have now reverted to a structure of society [segregation] which human nature and common sense would have told them are requirements of civilized, harmonious and prosperous social relations.[13]

I think I may be excused for refusing to accept the cosmeticization of Patrick Holloran. He told Heithaus he fully agreed with Glennon. He told Ring that their views were absolutely identical. He assured his commencement audience that there would be no mingling outside the classroom.

It is evident that Holloran was not pleased with the success of desegregation. No doubt he was being encouraged by the little coterie of close Jesuit friends in the community who shared his unhappiness and his resentment of Father Heithaus. And he was receiving mail from white parents raising the specter of miscegenation.[14]

A major student ball was scheduled for April 13, 1945, in the Jefferson Hotel, and the old hobgoblins were already on hand. There has always been something amusing in this old red herring which assumes that once the bars are lowered white girls in droves will throw themselves into the arms of black boys. The underlying assumption is neither flattering to white girls nor complimentary to white boys. And quite insulting to black girls!

Suddenly Holloran resolved to reintroduce segregation on the campus. He ordered the student council to pass a resolution forbidding Negro students to participate in extracurricular activities. This covered about everything but the classroom: gymnasium, swimming pool, basketball court, theater (there was a play in rehearsal at the time with a mixed cast), and, of course, social events such as the upcoming ball.

In return for Holloran's assurance that he would integrate the university, Heithaus for nearly a year had abstained from any public discussion of the race question. With Holloran's flagrant violation of his promise, Heithaus was released from his commitment and published in the *University News*, March 16, 1945, a masterly statement of the moral principles involved in the racial problem. Entitled "Why Not Christian Cannibalism?" it was unemotional, logical, satirical, and unanswerable; and to Holloran and his friends it was infuriating.

The student council refused to pass the requested resolution; Father Heithaus was its moderator and moral counselor. Failing to persuade Heithaus to change his position, Holloran used every kind of pressure within his reach as president to force the council to bend to his will. There followed two or three weeks of mounting tension on campus.

This was before 1968, of course, and students were far more vulnerable to intimidation on the part of the father president of a Jesuit university than they are today. Eventually Holloran succeeded in getting the student council by a one-vote margin to pass his resolution. He then ordered black students dropped from the cast of the play. The director of the play was the minister of the Jesuit community, an administrator for physical, nonspiritual concerns. He was a kindly and thoughtful man, and he must have found this an extremely painful order.

The dance at the Jefferson Hotel became the next issue. Through a friend in the police department, Cap Markoe learned that Holloran had arranged for a police detail to be on hand to throw out any black students who might attempt to enter the dance. As moderator of the student newspaper, Father Heithaus refused to clear publicity for the dance for publication. Holloran ordered him to do so; Heithaus refused. He was convinced that to exclude black students upon racial grounds was immoral; by approving the publicity, he would be cooperating in sin, and his conscience forbade it. He offered to resign so that the rector could appoint someone else, of whom there were quite a number, who had no such qualms of conscience, who would in fact be delighted. Holloran replied, "Jesuits don't resign." He then asked Holloran to fire him and appoint another. Holloran refused.

Following this, Fr. Henri Renard, one of the most distinguished and cultured men in the community, a former professor of metaphysics at the Gregorian University in Rome and then professor in the Jesuit scholasticate at St. Louis University, went to Holloran and told him: "I am Father Heithaus's confessor. You may not agree with him. I may not agree with him. But I must tell you that he is absolutely sincere in his conviction that to do what you want him to do would be to commit a sin. Consequently, if you do this you will be responsible for forcing him to commit a sin." Father Renard himself recounted this shocking incident to me.

Even more shocking to me, who have always considered Heithaus one of the most principled Jesuits I have known, was the revelation that Father Zuercher, the provincial superior, with the unanimous approval of his consultors, had recommended to Zacheus Maher "that Father Heithaus be strenuously urged to leave the Society unless higher Superiors judge that his conduct calls for dismissal." Maher had the good sense to realize that such dismissal lacked canonical support, adding, "personally I feel that it would be a mistake even to 'urge him strenuously to leave the Society.' If you as provincial wish to do so on your own responsibility, that would be within your rights."[15]

And most shocking is the divulgence by the handwritten minutes of this same consultors' meeting that the question raised by Father Renard about Heithaus's conscience had been submitted for resolution to the theologians at Saint Mary's, the theology school of the Missouri Province.

What was to resolve? Throughout their history the Jesuits have been accused of giving superiors, by the principle of "blind obedience," the power to require sinful actions of their subjects. We have denied this without qualification. This denial rests upon two fundamental principles of Catholic moral doctrine: (1) everyone is obliged to follow the dictates of one's honestly formed conscience, even though erroneous; (2) no one can be obliged to act against one's honestly formed conscience, even though erroneous. The appeal to the Saint Mary's theologians, implicitly challenging these propositions, in effect tore down the entire system of defense of Jesuit obedience.

There may indeed have been an examinable question here about who belonged in the Society and who did not, but it did not concern Heithaus.

Holloran continued his effort to force Heithaus to act against his conscience. About four o'clock one afternoon, Heithaus stopped in my room to tell me that he had just been summoned to the rector's office. About fifteen minutes later he stopped by again looking pale and shaken. He told me that he and Holloran had danced the same pirouette: command to publicize the dance; the plea that conscience prevented compliance. But a new step was introduced. Holloran informed him that because of his refusal a public penance—a *dicitur culpa*—would be imposed upon him that evening at supper. Correspondence in the archives between Zuercher and Maher pretends that the reason for the imposition of the culpa was the publication of the "Christian Cannibalism" article. This contradicts what Holloran told Heithaus at the time, that it was because of his refusal to approve publicity in the university newspaper for the segregated dance.

Culpas were quite common in religious life in my younger days. Novices were always asking permission to recite a culpa. The format was quite simple. One knelt in the dining room and, after the community said grace and sat down, recited a simple formula of contrition for a fault committed during the day: an act of impatience on the ball field, a violation of a rule.

A *dicitur culpa* was something else again. It was imposed by the superior only for what was deemed a serious fault. It was not recited by the culprit but read out from the pulpit by the minister of the house while the accused knelt in a penitential attitude before the community. At least that is the way both Heithaus and I expected it would be performed. I had never witnessed one.

The scholastics in St. Louis formed a separate community but shared the dining room with the university community. I am only guessing, but I would estimate the number at supper that evening at over three hundred. Father Holloran occupied the first place at one of two head tables; Fr. Thomas Sheehy, superior of the scholastics, occupied the same position at the second. By sheer chance, I was next to Father Sheehy; also by chance, Father Heithaus was at the same table as I, four or five places down on the other side.

The procedure was not as I had expected. Following the grace, everyone except Heithaus sat down. He remained standing, holding his biretta in his hand. Not the father minister, but the scholastic reader of the day read out the culpa, which charged him with having "ignored the known wishes of his superiors" and ordered him to make three days of retreat in penance. I noted that he had not been charged with disobedience. I wondered why the minister had not read the charge. Probably because his sympathies were entirely with Heithaus.

The ritual as described seems simple enough. Nevertheless, I was infuriated. I thought this an outrageous humiliation of a man of noble character, mature years, and Christlike dignity. Holloran sat there, arms akimbo, sleeves pulled up to his elbows, and—it seemed to me—gloating; the thought entered my mind that I should cross the few feet to where he sat, pick up the large soup tureen, and dump its contents over his head. I did not do so, but have sometimes regretted it. It would have made a significant statement and was no more than he deserved. I also conceived at that moment a horror of the power of office which enables a man to inflict humiliation of this sort upon a man incomparably his superior and felt that if offered to me I would flee to the ends of the earth before accepting it.

Following the meal and the customary thanksgiving prayer, the community turned towards the exit. As I followed Father Sheehy around our table, again by sheer chance, I came alongside Father Heithaus, following the others on his side of the table. With my left hand I squeezed his right hand and said quietly, "It's an honor to know you." It was not a public demonstration, but a minor gesture of moral support. It would have been appropriate as a gesture of supportive charity had he committed a grievous crime and accepted with such dignity the public scolding. It could not even have been noticed except by four or five Jesuits immediately following. All the rest of the community, turned towards the exit, had their backs to me. I shall later point out what incredible and grotesque transmogrification was effected upon the basis of this innocent gesture to calumniate me in Jesuit circles and elsewhere throughout the United States.

Father Heithaus was expelled from the university, sent to Saint Mary's, Kansas, to make his imposed retreat, and from there went to serve as assistant army chaplain at Fort Riley. He later spent some years at Marquette University in Milwaukee. He ultimately returned to St. Louis, where he died in 1972, having developed the Saint Stanislaus Museum of Jesuit History and, with the help of his brother William, having established a foundation for its support.

I visited Heithaus once after his return to St. Louis. It was some twenty years after the events of 1945. He was utterly without bitterness. I do not recall that we talked much about the affair or that Holloran's name was even mentioned. I went over to the church to say Mass. There are a great many Masses said every day on the numerous side altars in both the upper and the lower church. The sacristy was swarming with neatly cassocked and well-behaved altar boys waiting to serve Mass. Fifty percent of them were black boys.

What was my role in these events? It was minimal compared to that of Father Heithaus. I was new at the university; other than the handful of students in my classes, a few student leaders who knew me, and a few members of Dan Lord's sodality staff, I had no constituency. Father Heithaus, on the other hand, was student council and newspaper moderator and had a long affiliation with the school and so, especially after his famous sermon denouncing segregation, had a university-wide constituency.

Those who knew me knew my views, to be sure. This included the Jesuits of the scholastic and university communities, and most of them agreed with my views, though they were more reticent in expressing them. I also met almost daily with Father Heithaus and frequently with Fr. Bill Markoe and his brother Fr. John Markoe, called "Cap"; throughout their Jesuit careers, the brothers had been intrepid champions of the emancipation of the blacks from the trammels of segregation.

Cap Markoe was a West Point graduate, where he had been a fellow student and much beloved companion of those who later became the commanding generals of the American forces in World War II. During the Italian campaign they had requested the Missouri provincial to release Cap to serve as chief chaplain of the American forces. The provincial refused. Cap, a star athlete at West Point, was a man of powerful physique and normally of extreme gentleness. He also had a lifelong struggle with demon rum, a struggle in which he usually, though not always, prevailed.

One night in 1916, while serving with the rank of captain in the American army on the Mexican border, in a scene reminiscent of an old time Western, he "cleaned out" a bar in a row provoked, it gives me pleasure to recall, by the anti-Mexican bigotry of some American soldiers. For this he was court-martialed out of the army. He later entered the Society. Cap was the most loving and loveable man I have ever known. In my opinion and in that of others who knew him and his exquisite charity, he was a saint.

With the departure of Father Heithaus, I undertook the only positive action for which I can claim credit in this imbroglio. I wrote a letter to Father Zuercher, the Missouri provincial; this was a rather commonplace action. A recent examination reminded me that it was not, however, a commonplace letter.

My letter was a bit lengthy—eight pages. And it was highly emotional. I described the situation on campus, including the presence of *Life* and *Time* reporters, and noted the devastating effect upon the university and of the Jesuits if Holloran were permitted to carry through his plans. Imagine the effect of pictures appearing in *Life* of Jesuit students being thrown out of the dance by request of the Jesuit president. I argued, of course, the incompatibility of racial segregation with Christian teaching. I added that if Father Holloran were permitted to introduce his policy of racial segregation I would have a problem of conscience. I had been brought to St. Louis to teach Catholic social doctrines. I would find it difficult to continue to teach in an institution whose policy was in direct contradiction to that doctrine.

Before sending the letter I showed it to three of the most distinguished Jesuits in St. Louis: Fr. Henri Renard, Fr. Thomas Davitt, professor of ethics, and the widely beloved octogenarian, Fr. Laurence "Pop" Kenny. Known as "Father St. Louis University" because of his longtime dedication, he was confessor to most of the community and to many diocesan priests.

All three urged me to send the letter. Father Kenney wanted me to add a statement to the effect that if the provincial failed to act I would carry the matter to the apostolic delegate. He also urged me to crop the sentence about a difficulty I might have in continuing to teach at St. Louis. "They will latch on to that," he said with acute prescience, "to get rid of you." I did not follow his advice, but sent the letter as it stood.

A lull of some days followed, during which the provincial met with his consultors to discuss the case. I had to go to Chicago to conduct the funeral services for an uncle. Just as I was leaving, Fr. Paul Reinert told me the result—still a secret—of the provincial consultation. Father Reinert was at this time the dean of the college of liberal arts; he was destined to succeed Holloran and to preside for more than twenty years over the university's destinies. According to Father Reinert, the provincial, in accordance with the recommendations of the consultors, had ordered Holloran to abandon his entire segregation program. The arrangements with the police had been canceled and all other arrangements annulled.

I left for Chicago feeling very relieved that the battle had been won and anticipating the prompt return of Father Heithaus. I returned two days later, arriving at the university around 8 A.M. As I came down the corridor, I heard my phone number ring, and I picked up the corridor phone. It was Father Holloran. He ordered me to come immediately to his office. I told him that I had just arrived from Chicago and had not yet said Mass. "As soon as you have said Mass, come to my office," he said.

When I entered his office, without a word he handed me an envelope across his desk. I asked what it was. "That," he replied, "is a railroad ticket and a reservation on the four o'clock train for California this afternoon." That gave me around six hours to arrange my departure for the western rim of the continent. Besides my regular classes, I had scheduled three public lectures in St. Louis over the next four weeks and one in Chicago—the latter to a gathering of rabbis, ministers, and priests on the subject of Christianity and racial segregation.

I asked the reason for this astonishing action. He replied, "You wrote a letter to the provincial in which you said you would find it difficult to continue teaching here; consequently, he is sending you back to your province."

"No," I replied, "I told the provincial that if you were permitted to establish a policy of segregation in the university, I would have a difficulty. But I have been told that by order of the provincial you have been directed to abandon your segregation policy. Consequently, I have no difficulty whatever teaching here."

"Well, anyway," he said impatiently, "the provincial orders you back to your province, and there is your ticket."

I went upstairs, phoned Father Zuercher, and asked for an explanation. He said that in view of my letter he had phoned my provincial, Fr. Joseph King, who had said to send me home. I pointed out, as I had to Holloran, that my problem had been very clearly defined. "If racial segregation as envisaged were introduced, I would be forced to leave. Segregation was not being introduced. Consequently the difficulty no longer existed."

Admitting that he could not answer this, he shifted the blame to the California provincial: "Your provincial said to send you home." He denied, however, that he was responsible for the precipitous nature of the dismissal.

I then phoned my provincial in California and asked him for an explanation. "All I know about it," he said, "is that Father Zuercher phoned me and said that he was sending you home."

I did not take the four o'clock train for California. I had persuaded Father King that the failure to observe my Chicago engagement would have far-reaching repercussions. He authorized me to stay in Chicago until I had given my lecture. I was then to report in San Jose, the provincial headquarters.

As word spread, a constant stream of visitors, Jesuits and non-Jesuits, converged upon my room, some to commiserate, some to congratulate. I felt congratulations were in order. Both Heithaus and I had been thrown out, but the Negro students remained. I had no time to pack more than a suitcase for my Chicago trip. Several scholastics volunteered to pack my trunk and books and ship them after me to San Jose. I cashed my railroad ticket in for a ticket to Chicago. That evening the California and Oregon province Jesuits took me to dinner at Yogi Berra's Steak House. From there we converged upon the railroad station in the teeming rain. "Even the heavens are weeping," I quipped.

This was the first time I had been fired out of a religious community without so much as time to adjust my trousers, as it were, but I did not feel as though I had suffered a defeat. On the contrary. There were wounds—and they would endure for the rest of my life and of Heithaus's life—but they seemed of small moment.

The minutes of the consultors' meeting which I have cited contain quite an effective ego-deflator. Holloran had evidently never forgiven me my little homily about segregation, and he intended to fire me at the end of the academic year. He was at this meeting, and one of the consultors asked him if he would prefer to get rid of me immediately. "No," replied Holloran, putting me in my proper place, "no good will come, no harm averted. He is rather inconsequential." He could wait until the end of the academic year.

That was not the end of it. They then turned to a discussion of the reasons for which they think Heithaus "unworthy of the Society" following which "after long and prayerful consideration Father Provincial and Consultors agree that we recommend that Father Heithaus be urged strongly to ask for his release from the Society, unless higher superiors judge that his conduct calls for dismissal." Having thus "prayerfully" disposed of Heithaus they returned to a discussion of my case, specifically of my letter to the provincial. Having misquoted me as saying that in view of the circumstances I could not carry on, they agreed "that Father Dunne should be relieved of his duties and sent back to his Province, thus respecting his conscience." In view of their brutal lack of concern for Heithaus's conscience, their delicate concern for mine, which they no doubt deliberately misread, is touching.

The brutal experience of these days had, nevertheless, robbed some of the savor from the scriptural paean "quam bonum et iucundum habitare fratres in unum"—how good and happy for brothers to live as one. In Chicago I took refuge at the University Club to await my scheduled lecture.

Meanwhile, Fr. Wilfred Parsons, former editor of the Jesuit *America* magazine and at this time superior of Carroll House in Washington, had read in the newspapers of my expulsion from St. Louis. He telephoned his successor, Fr. John LaFarge, and urged him to appoint me to the staff of *America.*

LaFarge made a special trip from New York to see me—at least he said he did. We met at the University Club. He told me of Father Parsons's demarche and explained why, much as he would like to act upon it, he did not think it would be "prudent" to do so for the moment. "If I were to do so now," he said, "it would look as if I were championing your cause against the superiors who have removed you. So we shall wait until the heat is off and then bring you to *America.*"

Actually I do not think LaFarge had any intention then or later of bringing me to *America.* Twenty-two years later, in 1967, in Rio de Janeiro, I received a letter from Fr. Thurston Davis, then editor of *America,* inviting me to join his staff. In reply I said that I would be delighted. I then described my meeting with Father LaFarge in the Chicago University Club long ago and added: "Thurston, you have given me the perfect ending for my autobiography. I shall tell about this meeting with LaFarge and conclude: 'Twenty-two years later the word came. The heat is off! Come to *America!*'"

Father LaFarge is almost universally admired for his lifelong efforts to improve the lot of the black American. I share that admiration, but with a few reservations. He was always careful not to challenge authority, which is to say power. I above cited a letter of his to Zacheus Maher, dated June 7, 1945, which is typical. It concerns Holloran's commencement address, described above, and a letter Heithaus had written to the provincial criticizing it. Evidently the provincial had shared the letter with LaFarge.

LaFarge's letter begins by saying that "the tone of Father Heithaus's letter is indefensible" and criticizes the style. He then affirms that "Father Holloran's good intentions deserve sympathy. He is wrestling with a tough situation and trying manfully to make what seems to him a wise and just distinction." Having thus disassociated himself from Heithaus and assured the authorities of his loyalty, he proceeds to point out in Holloran's address the same faults to which Heithaus had called attention. Although he admits that many things Heithaus had said were true, it is clear that he has little sympathy for the man himself. I was a friend and admirer of LaFarge. I preferred Heithaus.

This is vintage LaFarge, a man of many virtues, of which one of the most notable was "prudence." In another letter, he had referred to the "serious heresy of racism." It would seem clear that he agreed with Heithaus, for this was the very thesis of the latter's article on "Christian Cannibalism." Yet he found this a shocking article.

LaFarge was not one to challenge the establishment directly. "There is a recognized way of going about these matters," he wrote, "a series of steps to be taken, of means to be used." These were the LaFarge means, quiet collaboration in Catholic interracial councils, discreet conversation, which generated a certain amount of goodwill but left the apartheid picture pretty much unchanged and, above all, rocked no boats. Because these means seemed inadequate "to men like Heithaus and others," LaFarge concluded that they lacked "a clear idea of methods of racial reform." I suspect that I was included among the others.

Father LaFarge's prudential penchant for reassuring the conservatives once resulted in a situation which he must have found extremely embarrassing. In 1943 he published a book, *The Race Question and the Negro*. After correctly stating that the Church did not forbid racial intermarriage he listed the "grave reasons" arguing against it, from which he concluded that where present they "amount to a moral prohibition of such a practice." In 1948, in a landmark decision in the case of *Perez v. Sharp*,[16] argued by my friend and college mate, Daniel G. Marshall, the California Supreme Court in a 4 to 3 decision declared unconstitutional the state law forbidding such marriages. In his dissenting opinion Justice J. Shenk quoted at some length from LaFarge's book. Fortunately for LaFarge's reputation as an apostle of racial justice, the majority of the court was not persuaded.

It is fair to say that the ultimate desegregation of all Catholic institutions in St. Louis accomplished by Archbishop Ritter began with Heithaus's famous sermon, deplored by Zacheus Maher as a "serious mistake." And I think his "Christian Cannibalism" article, deplored by LaFarge, makes the point more clearly than anything

John LaFarge ever wrote. Heithaus had indeed, "a clear idea of methods of racial reform," although not those dear to LaFarge.

Following my Chicago lecture I departed for California. In Los Angeles I found a change of orders awaiting me. Fr. Leo Simpson, the provincial's secretary directed me to go not to San Jose but to Santa Barbara. Long afterward I learned that the reason for this change was the ridiculous warning sent to King that I go about "attacking archbishops." San Jose was in the Archdiocese of San Francisco, where the Jesuits were having problems with Archbishop Mitty; Santa Barbara was in the Archdiocese of Los Angeles.

Shortly after my arrival, evidence began to reach me that a broad campaign of calumny had been mounted against me in St. Louis. Apparently those in charge were aware that were I to carry the case to Rome they were on weak ground. To expel a man from a community, from a university faculty, and from a province for the "crime" of having appealed to the provincial may have been without precedent in the four-hundred-year history of the Society. They evidently thought I might, as I had the right, demand canonical proceedings. So they built up a case on calumny.

The first indication of this that reached me came in the form of a newspaper clipping from the *St. Louis Star-Times* dated April 20, 1945. The story was headlined: "Two Quit S.L.U. Faculty; Race Issue Denied." After reporting Heithaus's and my departure, the story continued: "While Father Holloran said he did not care to air in public the reasons behind the withdrawal, he stated that a report that the two faculty members left because of disagreement with him over the Negro problem was 'extremely contrary to fact.'"

This, of course, was a flat lie. Heithaus's "withdrawal" was related only to the segregation question. The only reason Holloran or Zuercher gave me for my "withdrawal" was the letter I had written to the latter, and this had nothing to do with anything except the race question at the university. Holloran's delicate reluctance to air the matter in public left people to wonder, as some no doubt did, if I had been caught in some act of sexual misconduct or rape. These are the kind of things one ordinarily thinks of when one speaks of reasons too delicate to mention.

"According to one report," said the story, "the question of admitting Negroes to the annual student conclave formal prom at Hotel Jefferson last Friday came to the fore. Father Holloran, the report said, was opposed to admitting Negroes and instructed the hotel management not to admit them, and to have asked for a police detail. Several Negro couples did appear without incident. Father Holloran told the *Star-Times* –'I never said a word to Hotel Jefferson, never, never.' He denied he had opposed the admission of Negroes to the prom."

After this first manipulation of mendacity, they—Holloran and his cohesive little group of friends and advisers—went on to fabricate a totally false story of a supposed dramatic act of defiance on my part which was alleged as the reason for my expulsion. I first learned of this story in a letter from a friend, Dr. Frank McMahon, a professor of philosophy at the University of Notre Dame. He had just published a book, entitled *A Catholic Looks at the World*, in which he mentioned the desegregation of St. Louis University and praised the Jesuits for this courageous step forward. The book was already set up in galleys and about to go to press when he read in the newspapers of the expulsion of Heithaus and myself. It being too late to change the text, he added a footnote in which he said, "It is likewise regrettable that when two Jesuit Fathers, Rev. George H. Dunne, S.J., and Claude H. Heithaus, S.J., professors at St. Louis University, sought to apply fully Christian principle to the treatment of the Negro in that institution, their connection with the University was forthwith severed by the authorities."

This footnote merited for him a letter which he sent to me for comment. Its author was the pastor of Saint Ignatius Church on Chicago's North Side. He took Dr. McMahon sternly to task for what he called his grievous breach of charity towards Father Holloran. He asserted that our expulsion had nothing to do with the race question and added:

> While Father Heithaus was kneeling in the middle of the dining room floor undergoing a public penance for flagrant disobedience, Father Dunne rose from his place at table, stalked across the floor and stood shaking Father Heithaus by the hand in a shocking public display of defiance of authority of the rector, Father Holloran. What makes the offense of Father Dunne even more grievous is the fact that he is not even a member of the Missouri province, but was a guest from another province.

This is the story, fabricated out of whole cloth, which traveled through every one of the American provinces and more than forty years later was still on occasion being repeated. I have twice encountered it in recent years, once at a Jesuit meeting at Weston

College in Cambridge and again on a visit to Georgetown University. In both these instances the Jesuits who questioned me were of the recent generation to whom my supposed act made me a kind of folk hero. I was sorry to have to disillusion them.

I wrote to the Chicago pastor informing him that the story, which he had obviously heard from someone else, was false and suggesting that an apology and retraction were in order. I received no reply. Nor did Dr. McMahon receive a correction.

A curious detail, which might be of interest to extrasensory-perception people: when Father Heithaus informed me that a *dicitur culpa* was to be administered to him that evening, thinking, as he did, that it would be read out by the minister with Heithaus kneeling in the middle of the floor, I had the definite thought of doing exactly what the fabricated story accused me of doing. Someone must have read my mind, since I never mentioned the idea either to Father Heithaus or to anyone else. Whether, had the culpa been administered as I had expected, I would have carried out the thought, I have no way of knowing. I probably would have lacked the courage, as I had lacked the courage to turn the soup tureen upside down on Holloran's head.

Among those who contributed to the promulgation of the calumny against me was my own provincial, Fr. Joseph King. When I first accused him of this he denied it. I then confronted him with the source of my information, a member of the faculty of theology at Alma College, who had told me that Father King had narrated the supposed incident to him in the presence of several other fathers and had cited it as the reason for my expulsion from St. Louis. Thus confronted, he acknowledged that he had heard the story and had repeated it to "a few people," but when visiting St. Louis he had learned from others that the story was not true and so he had not repeated it. He seemed to think that this excused both his calumny and his lying about it.

Twelve years later I learned from Fr. Carroll O'Sullivan, then the provincial, that continuing his effort to build a case against me, Holloran had made other charges against me to Fr. King. O'Sullivan gave me a list of them. They were all puerile and all false. I shall discuss these further on.[17]

At the time of the St. Louis incident, Fr. Leo Robinson, S.J., was provincial of the Oregon Province. He was the youngest and reputed to be the most progressive and open-minded of the American provincials. Among the provincials he had major responsibility for the Institute of Social Science. Following my expulsion from

St. Louis he remarked to a group of Oregon Jesuits, "If George Dunne had used his head, he could have gone places in the Society." His remark was promptly reported to me by several people. I was astonished, it never having occurred to me that one should wish to go places in the Society—least of all for a price.

I awaited, rather patiently, the opportunity to discuss the St. Louis experience with the provincial. I assumed that in view of the circumstances any provincial worth his salt would wish at the first opportunity to hear my version of the affair.

One morning in Santa Barbara I answered the phone. It was Fr. Edward Whelan, S.J., calling from Los Angeles. He asked me to tell Father Leahy, the pastor, that the provincial would arrive on the morning train and spend the day in Santa Barbara. Leahy was manifestly unhappy. He was planning to take a day off for the first time in two months and spend it in Los Angeles. With no thought in mind except to salvage his day off, I said: "Why don't you go to Los Angeles. I am sure the provincial is stopping here to see me about the St. Louis affair." He did not think he could very well do so. The provincial would expect him to be on hand. I said no more about it.

I awaited a summons from the provincial in my room. I was disappointed, but not surprised, that it did not come before lunch time, figuring that he was occupied with Leahy. During lunch he ignored me. After lunch he disappeared. After allowing a decent interval I knocked at his door. There was no answer. I repeated the process from time to time, until around four o'clock Br. Peter O'Brien informed me that after lunch the provincial had gone out with Father Leahy. They did not return until supper time. By now I had decided that he was staying all night. That he could go through Santa Barbara without discussing St. Louis never crossed my mind. Following supper I had to go to the church to conduct the Sacred Heart Novena. When I returned to the rectory there was no sign of him. Around ten o'clock I heard Leahy enter the side door directly below my window. I went down and asked where the provincial was. He told me that he was on the train en route to San Francisco. The two of them had spent the afternoon and evening visiting friends.

I had a volcanic eruption the violence of which I think frightened Leahy. Until now I had not lost my "cool" over the events of St. Louis. Nothing Holloran had done upset me the way this behavior on the part of King did.

Leahy somewhat apologetically remarked that he was probably in part to blame because he "jokingly" remarked that I had said he was coming to Santa Barbara to see me, not him. King had angrily replied that if I thought I was as important as that, he would teach me a lesson by not speaking to me at all. To have corrected the provincial's misunderstanding would have obliged Leahy to admit that he had been complaining about the ruination of his day off. This he was reluctant to do. So he let it stand.

In my fury I wrote a scorching letter to King telling him in no uncertain terms what I thought of him and that I considered him totally unfit for the office of provincial. Two days later I wrote him an apology for the intemperate nature of my remarks but repeated that his action was inexplicable and inexcusable.

After my departure from St. Louis, one of my students—the same who over forty years later never fails to write every year—wrote, "Most particularly I want to thank you for two big things: The knowledge that you'll always hold on to the important things and keep them first and not let the builders of buildings break you inside, and the two words 'intellectual honesty'—I'll make these words haunt me." And she has. And I think these are fitting words with which to close the story of the St. Louis caper.

E- and Devaluation

One of the methods employed by the Jesuits to establish a pool of those who may be expected "to go places in the Society" is to inquire into the fitness of individuals to hold the office of superior. This is done by periodically sending to a number of individuals who are presumed to be in a position to express a well-founded judgment a questionnaire concerning the aptitude of an individual to govern. Prior to my return to the United States from China I am confident that I would have won high marks on such inquiries. I am aware of the regard in which my superiors in China—notably Bishop Haouisée, Father LeFebvre, and Father Henry—held me and of the warm relations I enjoyed with my peers of all nationalities.

The Alma retreat in 1943 marked the high point. With the conclusion drawn from that, everything shifted suddenly into downgrade. Zach Maher's final word had made that clear. Because I refused humbly to confess myself blameworthy of charges of which I was innocent, I was guilty in his eyes and beyond redemption. With this tortuous sally in logic, he closed the book on my future in the Society.

Although the Alma retreat marked the watershed, the descent had probably begun before this. There was first of all my strong protest to Father Maher over the tactics employed to withdraw me from the jurisdiction of the French Jesuits. I had regarded this as a defense of my superiors, who in Shanghai were the French. Maher probably regarded himself and Seeliger as my superiors, and they were the objects under attack. He was not one easily to brook criticism. Nor would the fact that Father Ledochowski, the superior general of the Society, agreed with me and severely reprimanded Maher for recalling me from China have rendered him more amenable. It is probably safe to say that this prepared the way for and made easier the subsequent repudiation of his ancient friendship of which nothing was left but the promise that in his "charity" he would pray for me.

There had also been a rather stormy conflict with Father Seeliger. Many of my fellow Jesuits have told me over the years that as their novice master, Father Seeliger had been in the habit of holding Paul O'Brien and myself up to them as role models. This high opinion of me suffered a rude test in an incident which occurred the year after my ordination to the priesthood.

I spent this year, as I have explained above, at Loyola High School in Los Angeles. Father Seeliger, now the provincial, came for his annual community visitation. One day one of the six or seven scholastics who belonged to the community came to see me in obvious distress. He had been ordered by the provincial, he said, to write a formal request to be released from his vows and from the Society. He was in what would normally have been his final year of regency—the period of teaching before theology—and would have begun his theological studies the following year. Seeliger had told him, he said, that if he did not request his papers of dismissal, he would not be sent on to theology, but left perpetually in regency. It was quite clear that the man had no wish to leave the Society, nor did there seem to be any obvious reason justifying his dismissal. Had there been, the provincial could quite simply have dismissed him.

The only instance of misconduct cited against him by the provincial, he said, was that he occasionally attended the cinema without permission. It is true that, in those earlier days, permission was required. In fact, however, it was a rule observed more often in the breach than otherwise and no oftener by this man than by his peers.

It seemed obvious to me that the provincial was acting on the recommendation of Father Whelan, the rector of the high school, and that it was a matter of clash of personalities. The two could not have been less alike. Whelan was a bouncy person, gushing with personality, overflowing with energy. The other man slouched about, never expending any more energy than the minimum required, probably a constant source of annoyance to Whelan. He did the job required of him, taught a passable class of Latin, and did the required community exercises. In short, it seemed to me that Whelan wanted to get rid of him because he did not like him. I thought the tactics amounted to a form of blackmail, and I doubted that the constitutions of the Society provided shelter for such. I was not too familiar with the constitutions, not yet having made my third year of probation—"tertianship," we call it—when they are a principal object of study. In the absence of Whelan himself I consulted Fr. Jerry Flynn, who assured me that this was the case.

That night, following the community prayers at 9 P.M., I knocked at Father Seeliger's door. There ensued a firestorm. I cannot now recall, after all these years, along what lines the discussion developed. I pleaded the cause of the scholastic, arguing the absence of any solid reason for his dismissal. Father Seeliger was visibly taken aback by my intervention in a matter which he undoubtedly thought none of my business. Perhaps in a sense it was not. It was certainly unusual for a newly ordained priest directly to challenge the judgment of his provincial superior. However, I was not a schoolboy. Furthermore, I instinctively react against injustice. In this instance, the victim had asked me for help; that left me with no choice. That is how I saw it. Father Seeliger saw it differently. He was angry. I was persistent. The discussion, which became a debate, lasted until nearly midnight. Finally, Father Seeliger denied that he had told the scholastic that he would never be sent on to theology.

"In that case, it is simply a misunderstanding," I said. "He thinks he either writes for his papers or remains perpetually a scholastic. Let me go call him. You can put him straight and that is the end of the affair."

I had touched a flame to the powder keg. "Father Dunne, if you think you can sit in judgment on your superior," he cried, "you don't know the Society of Jesus."

"Father Seeliger, if I can't speak on behalf of a fellow Jesuit whose vocation is threatened, then I *don't* know the Society of Jesus."

I suppose I was sitting in judgment of my superior, although that had not occurred to me. In any event, we had reached the end of the interchange. I knelt down and asked for his blessing. He refused it and waved me off. He left the house early the next morning, so upset, according to Father Whelan, who had returned during the night, that he had been unable to sleep. No doubt he carried with him a revised image of the young Jesuit he had formerly offered his novices as a role model.

This revised image appeared the following year when, in the course of my tertianship at Port Townsend, Washington, I viewed my *speculum*. During his third year of probation each tertian received from the provincial a speculum—in Latin, a "mirror," a picture of oneself—compiled by the provincial on the basis of reports and varied sources of information. I thought Father Seeliger extravagant in his fault finding; I did not recognize myself in my speculum. I cannot now recall all his complaints in detail, but they were a fairly exhaustive list of human failings. And he made the curious observation that he had found no negative judgments in his files and had based his conclusions upon his own personal observations.

Much of the sting was taken out by the genial observations of Fr. Joseph Piet, the tertian master, who read the speculum to me. (This was the same Father Piet who as provincial had sent me to China.) He began by remarking that the document was filled with contradictions. He then proceeded, in his wry fashion, to call them to my attention. "It says here that you are thus and so, and down here it says that you are so and so. Now you cannot be thus and so and so and so at the same time. That is a contradiction." Thus he proceeded to analyze the entire document until, arriving at the end, the speculum lay shattered in fragmented shards and he and I were wreathed in smiles.

I cannot close this account without remarking that, if I did not emerge from it unscathed, the confrontation was not without its positive effect. The scholastic concerned heard nothing more about asking for his dismissal and in due and proper course was notified to report for his theology studies. Several years ago he celebrated his golden jubilee as a member of the Society of Jesus. All is well that ends well.

Eight

Post Bellum

I was still in Santa Barbara in August 1945, when the bomb fell, first on Hiroshima and then on Nagasaki, and the emperor of Japan declared the end of Japanese resistance. The war was over! Cars raced through the streets of Santa Barbara. Sirens screamed. Whistles blew. Bells rang. I rang the bells of Our Lady of Sorrows Church so violently that the ropes broke. We were not celebrating the unspeakable horrors upon which we had not reflected, but the end of the war. Years later, on a visit to Hiroshima, I spent several stricken hours in the museum which keeps alive the memory of those horrors and recalled with shame the role I had played of joyous bell-ringer in Santa Barbara. No doubt it was right to celebrate the end of the war. But a tolling, rather than mad ringing, would have better suited the occasion.

The China Question

The end of the war meant that the way to China was open again. Paul O'Brien was sent back, but I did not return, except for two trips as a transient visitor thirty years later. Not constantly, but frequently over the years, this singular fact has weighed heavily upon me, especially during the years when several of my confreres, whose decision to volunteer for the China mission I had influenced considerably, were suffering in Chinese Communist prison cells.

Had I put my hand to the plough and then turned back? The evidence is that this was not the case. The failure to return to

China was not the result of any decision of mine. Still, I bear some responsibility for not returning, since this resulted from actions of mine. How much, I shall have to leave to the determination of God.

During the war, I had fully expected to return to China as soon as the cannons fell silent. True, I had been concerned about demanding of my mother the sacrifice of seeing me off a second time, especially under now totally changed circumstances. My summary expulsion from St. Louis had been a severe shock to her. The high esteem in which she held all Jesuits, especially Fr. Zacheus Maher, made it difficult for her to understand how this could have happened without some very serious misbehavior on my part. I had sailed in 1932 as a kind of favored protégé of whom he expected great things. I would be sailing in these latter days under the fulmination of his excommunication as one bereft of hope who could expect no more than the charity—his word—of his prayers.

During this brief family crisis my sister, Isabel Higgins, was a splendid support. Supported by my Jesuit confreres at Loyola University, especially the younger generation, she had won mother to my side, where she remained during the seven years of life that were left to her. I was sure she would make the sacrifice of my second departure with the same courage she had displayed four-teen years earlier.

With this assurance, while the war was still raging, I wrote Father King from Santa Barbara that spring of 1945 asking in strongest terms to return to China without delay. A rumor had reached me that he was planning to transfer me to Loyola University in Los Angeles for the following academic year.

Assignment to a teaching position at Loyola had an ominous ring of permanence that harmonized ill with the street vendors' cries in Shanghai or Nanking. With the war still unsettled it was, of course, not possible to return to Japanese-occupied areas; but a Catholic priest, Father Ryan, who was working in Chungking, the provisional capital, with the United Nations Relief and Reha-bilitation Administration (the UNRRA), had invited me to join him.

I presented this proposal to the provincial, arguing that marking time at Loyola for a year or more would be a waste of time in terms of my future career. In Chungking I would be in a Chinese cultural and linguistic environment where every waking moment would help prepare me for the future and enable me to contribute something to the present needs of the people with whom I had chosen to spend my life.

I do not think I could have pleaded a stronger case. The provincial did not reply. But some time after this, Paul O'Brien told me that the provincial had the impression I did not wish to return to China. Quite recently the archivist of the California Province sent me a photocopy of a note addressed by Father King to Father O'Brien saying exactly that: "I have the impression George Dunne does not want to return to China. He never talks about it." This was a rather bizarre observation inasmuch as I had not had the opportunity to talk to him about China or anything else since leaving St. Louis. Not until September would I have a personal encounter with him. My letter urging that I be allowed to go to Chungking makes his observation to O'Brien unintelligible.

I now wrote to him, told him what Paul had told me and said that I wished to make my position absolutely clear. I wished to ask him nothing. I wished neither to return to China, nor did I wish not to return to China. I accepted whatever decision the superior— himself—should make. That was my understanding of Ignatian indifference. In 1931–32 I had practiced little of it. Now I would have a go at it.

Following this, in what was not exactly a reply to either of my letters, he wrote me that he had notified Paul O'Brien to latch on with UNRRA and that I would be available to go with him. O'Brien was to make arrangements. Two months later I had a letter from Paul telling me that, to his surprise, his mother had informed him that she had heard that he was to return to China with UNRRA and that I was to go with him. This was the first he had heard of it; he had never received the directives mentioned above. He immediately went to San Jose to see the provincial.

Paul reported to me that King's mind was still not clear to him. His understanding was that King, capitalizing upon my idea but changing the principals, wished him to go to China now with UNRRA and *perhaps* send for me later. It was evident from his talk, said Paul laughing, that King would not loose me in China with UNRRA without Paul there to keep an eye on me. I told Paul frankly that I would prefer not to go in those circumstances. I resented the implication that I had to be tied to anyone's apron strings, even his.

This seems not to fit my recent profession of Ignatian indifference, evidently too fragile a reed to withstand the blow which I felt when Paul apparently accepted an image of me which I should have expected him forcefully to resist. I mark from this moment not a renunciation of China but an end to any efforts on my part to lobby for my return. Ignatian indifference began to be replaced by something more akin to the famous principle of the Chinese sage Lao Tse: *wu wei erh chih*— imperfectly translated "Govern by doing nothing" or "Act by doing nothing."

Twice that summer at Santa Barbara I was notified that the provincial wished me to move to Loyola in Los Angeles. He set no date but specified "as soon as convenient to Father Leahy," the pastor where I was. I decided that it would be convenient for Father Leahy for me to move to Loyola as soon as I had seen Father King, who sooner or later would have to pass through Santa Barbara. This time I would waylay him.

At last, five months after leaving St. Louis, I saw him. The meeting lasted three hours. I wrote an account of it to Fr. John B. McGloin, S.J.,[1] which can be summarized in its own words: "It was fruitless except that it forced him to sit down and at last look me in the face."[2]

There were other unpleasantries that summer. While still in St. Louis I had, with the provincial's permission, accepted an invitation to lecture at both the Chicago and the New York Summer Schools of Catholic Action in the summer of 1945. When I left St. Louis in haste, I had my books and all my notes, gathered over some years, shipped to San Jose, as King had ordered. I have explained above that King changed my traveling orders to Santa Barbara. When I received an inquiry from Marian Prendergast, Fr. Dan Lord's secretary, about whether I would be able to keep my engagement to teach at the summer school, I wrote to Fr. Leo Simpson, King's secretary. Explaining that I needed my books and notes to prepare the lectures, I asked him kindly to send them to me. He replied that he had not seen them but presumed they had arrived because he had seen a rather substantial bill for their transportation. A few days later he wrote again that the provincial, stating that the cost of shipping them to Santa Barbara was too great, ordered me to cancel the engagements in New York and Chicago.

Good-by, not au revoir

I said good-by to Paul O'Brien in mid October. Not without considerable self-mastery and difficulty over a period of years— perhaps more difficult for him—we had managed to forge a firm and authentic friendship. It never occurred to me that this marked the end of what I had expected to be a life-long association. Paul had just seen the provincial. The war now ended, he could now return to China without recourse to UNRRA, and the provincial told him to sail at the earliest opportunity. Paul also told me in confidence, since he was not supposed to release the news until he was back in China, that he had been appointed superior of a new California mission to be established independent of the French Jesuits.

I do not know why—perhaps to confirm my estimation of how far I had fallen from grace—he added that the provincial and the consultors had stated that "not for a moment would they consent to your being appointed one of the consultors of the mission of China."[3]

I no more ambitioned being a consultor than I did being a rickshaw puller. But it gave a rather dramatic picture of how far I had fallen. I had left Shanghai with the friendship and fullest confidence of my superiors. I have a rather thick dossier of letters exchanged during my years at Zikawei between Bishop Haouisée, the superior Fr. Pierre LeFebvre, the rector Fr. Yves Henry, the two provincials, Fathers Maher and Seeliger, and me dealing chiefly with the plans for the Nanking Institute but also with other sensitive problems relating to future relations between the California Province and the French mission. The importance attached by Father Ledochowski, the superior general, to the Nanking Institute is indicated in words addressed to me, which I quoted in a letter to the provincial: "[The institute] could have the widest possible influence in the vast region of China."[4]

Evidently the "indispensable," the "inspiration of all the young men at Zikawei"—Paul O'Brien had so described me in his fateful letters of 1936 urging my recall from China—like Humpty-Dumpty had taken a great fall, with far less chance that his pieces would be put together again.

Proposed Visit to USSR

I received a note from Father King, postmarked October 31, informing me that Paul would sail from Seattle on November 1, which meant that he had gone before the letter reached me. He added that I should take steps to obtain a passport and arrange my return to China. That same day—karma? destiny? providence? chance? chess?—I had forwarded to King a telegram from

Bp. Bernard J. Sheil asking me to give a series of lectures in Chicago during December on racial segregation. One does not lightly refuse episcopal requests. China was temporarily shelved.

I gave seven lectures in Chicago and saw again many of the friends I had made during my years at the university. From Chicago I went to Washington to visit the Georgetown School of Foreign Service and its founder, Fr. Edmund Walsh, S.J., with the Nanking Institute in mind. While there I paid a courtesy call with unforeseen results upon John Hazard, a young friend and former professor of mine at the University of Chicago; freshly returned from the USSR with a degree in Soviet law from the University of Moscow, he had taught a course at Chicago in the Soviet form of government. John was currently with the State Department and would later go on to a long and distinguished career with the Center for Russian Studies at Columbia University. I called upon him in his office in Foggy Bottom with no purpose in mind but to renew what had been a pleasant acquaintance.

In the course of our conversation, I asked him on an impulse, "What do you think my chances would be of visiting the Soviet Union?"

"Nil," he replied. "First, because you are a Catholic priest, and worse still, a Jesuit"

"What do you think would happen if I were to go to their embassy and ask?"

Actually the idea had not occurred to me until then, but I was deeply interested in the Soviet Union. The history of Russia and its politics, both before and after 1917, had been one of the five major areas that constituted my doctoral program at Chicago. Its importance to the future of China was self-evident.

"It's an interesting idea. I'm sure the diplomatic wires to Moscow would be hot that night with messages about the mysterious visit of a Vatican emissary. Why don't you try it, just for fun?"

"I think I will—just for fun."

"If you do, the man to see is not the ambassador, but Ivan Gromov, head of the cultural relations department, who also directs all espionage activities in this country. He is a hard party man from Moscow, and more important than the ambassador." (Some years later, during the trial of Elizabeth Bentley, accused of espionage for the USSR, I noted in the press that Ivan Gromov, since returned to Russia, was alleged to have been her control.)

The next morning found me hailing a cab. The wartime regulation about cab-sharing was still in effect, and there were already two occupants when I climbed in. When I announced to the cabbie that my destination was the Soviet Embassy, both heads jerked in my direction as though on a string, and four eyes stared curiously at me.

I told the man who answered the door of the stately old Washington mansion which was then the Soviet Embassy that I wished to see Mr. Ivan Gromov. He ushered me across a large reception room, apparently once a ballroom, and lodged me in a small, windowless office. Within a few minutes a handsome, husky young man, whom I judged to be in his mid thirties, entered. I asked if he were Mr. Gromov. He replied that he was Yuri Brusilov, Mr. Gromov's assistant, and had been sent to ask what I wanted. Thus began a conversation of more than two hours, which I, and evidently he, found quite interesting. Several times I apologized for taking so much of his time and offered to leave, but he insisted I stay.

Mr. Brusilov was a man of keen intelligence. He spoke English remarkably well, considering that he had been in this country only eight months. His accent was minimal. He occasionally had to search a bit for the word he wanted—that was the only weakness I noticed. He had an impressive knowledge of details of American realities. He complained that, despite the fact that the United States and the Soviet Union were allies in the great struggle against Nazism, the *Chicago Tribune* throughout the war remained hostile to the USSR. "How do you explain that?" he demanded. I tried to answer by minimizing the influence of Colonel McCormick's newspaper. It was a fragile argument, as he exposed by citing the exact circulation figures of the *Tribune*, by far the largest newspaper in the Midwest.

Our conversation ranged widely, even at one point entering the field of theology. Shortly before leaving St. Louis I had written an article analyzing the possibility of peaceful coexistence with the Soviet Union following the war and the merits of a United Nations organization. It was published in the *Historical Bulletin*, a St. Louis University quarterly, and attracted wide and mostly favorable attention, being republished in many newspapers across the country and inserted in the *Congressional Record*. There was at the time—on the eve of the San Francisco conference which was to give birth to the United Nations—a strong wave of opinion which regarded war with Russia as both inevitable and desirable and membership in a United Nations as folly. The attention my article attracted in such circles was anything but favorable, approaching rather the apoplectic. I recall that William F. Buckley, Jr., in the early postnatal period of his career as spear-carrier for the extreme right, devoted to me and the article the vitriol of one of his columns in the *Brooklyn Tablet.*

I had brought a copy of this article with me and presented it to Mr. Brusilov. He promised to read it later, but meantime glanced through it. His eyes fell upon a passage in which I had written that one of the chief errors of Marxism was that it ignored the fact of original sin. With a slightly puzzled look he asked, "What is this that you call original sin?"

Probably for the first time in its history the walls of the Soviet Embassy echoed with a brief discourse on original sin. I explained the concepts of original justice, grace, fallen nature, etc., and argued that the evils and injustices in the world, which we recognized and deplored no less than the Marxists, were due not, as they thought, to the private ownership of the means of production but to original sin. These evils would not disappear with the abolition of private ownership, but only as sin is overcome by grace. Mr. Brusilov's verdict upon my little theological fling was, "Ah! That is very interesting; yes, very interesting."

Mr. Brusilov was quite at ease, was good-natured, and had a good sense of humor. He lost his composure only once, and what occasioned it was, I thought, quite significant in the light of certain future political events. Throughout our discussion, it was evident that he did not wish to say, "No, you may not visit the USSR." So he attempted to dispose of my request by persuading me that, under present circumstances, I really would not want to go. He argued, for example, that they did not then have any university for foreign students. I had an answer to all of his dissuasive arguments; I told him, for example, that by desiring to study the Soviet Union I did not mean academic study in a classroom. I simply meant to observe, travel about, talk to people, see how they lived, etc.

At last he presented what he evidently thought would clinch the case: "You must understand that for four or five years we have been engaged in a total war, the whole nation, all our resources concentrated on the war effort. For this reason, but only for this reason, we have not been able for the time being to give attention to what you call consumer goods. So, for this reason—all the nation concentrated on the war—today you would not find in Russia a standard of living to which you are accustomed. It would be hard."

"Oh!" I lightly dismissed his concern, "That would not bother me. I have lived in China."

He exploded. "Do not," he shouted, pounding the desk with his fist, "Do not compare our living standards! Do not compare our living standards to China!"

He was furious. Gradually his rage sputtered out as I murmured my excuses. It was a reminder that throughout history little love has been lost between the Russians and the Chinese. More than a decade later, a rift occurred between Chairman Mao and Premier Khrushchev, who pulled all the Russian advisers and engineers—together with their blueprints—out of China. This was greeted with skepticism by many Americans, who regarded it as a charade, a hoax set up to fool the non-Communist world. The monolithic character of communism, they thought, ruled out any possibility of genuine division. Not even the subsequent border incidents along the Amur River convinced all the skeptics. I had no difficulty accepting its authenticity. I remembered the rage of Yuri Brusilov.

Finally, having failed to dissuade me, he told me that the question of visiting the Soviet Union fell within the jurisdiction of the consulate rather than of the embassy. The next day I went to the consulate. It was quite a different experience. The consulate offices were at the head of a narrow flight of stairs on the second floor of a drab red-brick building. While waiting for the consul general, I tried to engage the secretary, an attractive blond Russian, in conversation.

"I am sorry," she said in perfectly accented English, "I do not speak English."

The consul general was an entirely different type from Yuri Brusilov. He looked like the average American's caricature of a communist—small of stature, cold, humorless, dead-eyed. Shaking his hand was like picking up a dead fish. He disposed of me quickly. Learning that I was from California, he told me I would have to take my inquiry to the Russian consulate in San Francisco.

In New York, I told Father LaFarge of my demarche. He was quite interested and offered, should I manage to get a Russian visa, to send me as a correspondent for *America*. He also promised to put in a word in favor of the project with Fr. Zach Maher.

Before leaving Washington I had telephoned the Polish Embassy, hoping to speak with Oscar Lange, who had recently been named the first postwar Polish ambassador to the United States, but he was in Poland. After I arrived back in California, I wrote to him, telling of my interest in visiting the Soviet Union and asking that he use his influence in my behalf.

Lange was one of the world's leading statistical economists; he and I had become friends at the University of Chicago, where he was a tenured professor. While at St. Louis University I had organized a series of lectures by distinguished scholars, and Lange was one of the participants. On that occasion he had lectured not on economics but on the political prospects in Poland as the war approached its end.

Lange was not a Communist. He had once been a socialist, but during his years in the United States he had developed a different perspective. He had become convinced of the possibility of a viable third way, neither socialist nor capitalist. As the problems of reconstructing a new Poland arose out of the ruins of war, Lange was asked to serve as its ambassador to the United States. He replied to my letter, telling me why he had agreed to do so: "Though it involved great personal sacrifices on my part, I considered it my duty to accept because of the strategic significance of Poland in international relations which may decide about peace and war." Among the sacrifices was the renunciation of his American citizenship, which he valued highly.

He added an interesting bit of confidential information: "You may be interested to know that one of the persons who most contributed towards persuading me to accept the post was Bp. Bernard J. Sheil."

The struggle between the forces represented by the London-based Polish government in exile and those represented by the Lublin-based government set up by the Russians had not yet been finally resolved. Knowing Lange, Bishop Sheil undoubtedly and correctly thought that his influence would be a moderating one.

As far as my proposed trip to Russia was concerned, he pointed out that he could do nothing in his capacity as ambassador, but should the occasion arise privately he would be glad to make inquiries. He added:

> I wonder whether either in connection with your trip to Russia or, if that trip should not materialize, independently of it, you would be interested in making a trip to Poland. The problem of the new Poland and the relations of the Catholic Church toward the social and political changes going on there are really fascinating and deserve the attention of a sympathetic observer and student like you.[5]

In view of the developing situation in Poland, I thought the opportunity not one to be lost. The return to China, already on hold for ten years, could be kept on hold for a few more months. I informed Mr. Lange that I would ask my religious superiors for permission to accept his invitation. He wrote back, "I think that as correspondent of *America* you would be most welcome and that there could be no better choice for that post than yourself."[6] He added that I should get the proper permissions and credentials and then apply to him for a visa. He would then inform his government about my visit and give me letters of introduction and arrange contacts with the different Catholic circles in Poland.

Father Whelan, the rector at Loyola University in Los Angeles, agreed that it was a great opportunity to shed light upon the Polish reality and said that he would urge its approval upon the provincial. He returned some days later from a meeting of the provincial's consultors, of whom he was one, to tell me with an air of disappointment that despite his best efforts he had been unable to persuade the provincial. The provincial notified me that my request was denied with the *unanimous* agreement of the consultors. I did not bother to ask Father Whelan how he reconciled the two statements. I appealed the decision to Norbert de Boynes, S.J., vicar general and acting head of the Society in Rome. Not surprisingly, the response was negative. My last word from Oscar Lange was an expression of regret, which he concluded with the pointed remark, "You can now see for yourself that there are two sides to the iron curtain."[7]

Father Simpson had apprised me of the negative decision from Rome. To this he added that the provincial wished me now to take the necessary steps to return to China. On the heels of this directive came word from the provincial to the effect that Simpson had exceeded his instructions; he was canceling the order to return to China.

There was probably considerable uncertainty at the time about what to do with me, as evidenced by the conflicting orders. Had it not been for the war I should, of course, have gone back posthaste after completing my studies. But the retreat at Alma and then the St. Louis episode raised doubts about me that had never been raised before. There were those who earnestly wished me back in China. But doubts grew as what were considered my trouble-making activities increased. Would I cause more trouble here or in China? This is the conclusion I reach after painstaking examination of my recollections, the not inconsiderable files of correspondence, and a few pieces from the province archives made available to me. Writing from Vietnam more than a quarter of a century later, Paul O'Brien was to confirm this conclusion.

In the intervening years Paul had a distinguished career in the Far East. He returned to China in 1945 as superior of the California Jesuits, who accepted responsibility for the Yangchow area from the French Jesuits. The city of Yangchow, on the Grand Canal, was an ancient metropolis which Marco Polo had once governed by appointment of the emperor.

With the Communist triumph in 1950 and the imprisonment and expulsion of foreign missionaries, O'Brien was given the job of relocating Jesuit missionaries as they emerged from the mainland. He reassigned them to Taiwan, where they were joined by missionaries of other orders and by Chinese bishops, priests, nuns, and seminarians, thus laying the foundations of the flourishing Taiwanese Church of today. After this, he was named rector of the Jesuit theologate, which had been moved from Zikawei to Baguio in the Philippines. Some years later he was appointed rector of the Jesuit novitiate in Vietnam near Saigon. From there he moved to Thailand to serve as superior of the Jesuits in that country. Although relieved of the office of superior, he remains active, engaged chiefly in directing the Spiritual Exercises of Saint Ignatius. Most of this activity is centered in Chiang Mai, Thailand, where he lives, but he frequently travels to direct retreats in other parts of Southeast Asia.

While cleaning out his desk as he prepared to move from Vietnam to Thailand, Paul came upon the original draft of what he called his fateful letters to Fathers Seeliger and Maher, outlining his plan to snatch me from the hands of the French; this was the plan that had resulted in my recall from China and had changed the entire course of my life. He sent it to me in Switzerland, where I was then living, correctly surmising that, although the damage had been done some forty years earlier, I would be interested in seeing the fatal instrument employed.

At the same time he told me why superiors had not sent me back to China. I had acquired the reputation, he said, of being a gadfly who was prone to express himself forthrightly on controversial subjects. They were afraid that in China I might air my critical appraisals of Chiang Kai-shek and the Kuomintang, bringing down upon both Church and Jesuits the wrath of the Generalissimo. This accounts for the moves that came next, first to Phelan

Park and then to Phoenix, for the final inhumation of my China career.

There is in the California Province archives a curious note that King addressed to O'Brien which only recently came to my hands. It says, "George Dunne thinks if he returns to China he might cause trouble for the Church and Society with Chiang Kai-shek." This was an invention. I can say without hesitancy that such a thought never crossed my mind.

It is true enough that I was and am critical of Chiang, a hard-headed autocrat—"peanut-head" was the rude epithet habitually applied to him by Gen. Joseph Stilwell, American commander of Chinese troops in Southeast Asia, one of the most brilliant and frustrated American generals in World War II.[8] Chiang's reaction-ary policies alienated the masses and made the ultimate triumph of the Communists inevitable. In the early years of the Sino-Japa-nese War, there occurred a spontaneous upsurge of grass-roots democracy. Millions of Chinese carried on their backs the machin-ery of entire factories which they set up again in the interior, far from the reach of Japanese armies. Whole student bodies and their faculties, carrying libraries with them, walked from as far north as Peking to as far south as Kweilin. Literacy movements were organized on a vast scale.

If Chiang Kai-shek had put himself at the head of this phenomenal movement of grass-roots democracy, he would have emerged as a hero of the first magnitude. But Chiang never understood democracy, least of all popular democracy. The auto-crat is always suspicious of anything that smacks of a popular movement. Chiang turned his back upon this movement and for support looked instead to the notoriously corrupt and reactionary Chen brothers and their followers, known as the C-C clique. The result was the alienation of the masses. Chiang was left with the support of those who profited from the regime and those who found communism ideologically unacceptable. It would be an error to say that the masses embraced communism. It would be true to say that they were not disposed by any sense of loyalty to resist its advance. Mao Tse-tung and his cohorts found the road to power paved by the alienating policies of their enemies.

Although I was indeed critical of Chiang Kai-shek, the notion that I would trumpet my views, causing a crisis in the relations of the Church with the Generalissimo, is the stuff of which fairy tales are made. In any event, within five years the Communist takeover rendered the question moot in mainland China.

I was not at the time familiar with the contents of Paul O'Brien's fateful letter of February 15, 1936, in which he argued that I was "irreplaceable." I was aware, however, of the extraordinary measures, involving the intervention of the provincial and of Father Maher, acting as surrogate for the superior general, which bespoke the high importance attached to my exercising leadership in the Nanking project. If I had then been considered "irreplaceable," I was now regarded by my California superiors as a loose cannon.

Perhaps I should have protested loud and clear. But who can say? Possibly this was God's convoluted way of saying that my destiny was not, as I had thought, China.

The Loyola phase of my career was to be quite short, two to three years, but probably the most productive—some would say the most controversial—of my life. Today Mayor Tom Bradley, a black, is serving his fifth term of office in Los Angeles. Black men and women appear regularly on television as news announcers, sportscasters, stars of theater and of sports, business executives, beauty contest contestants. It is a different world. Although there remain long roads to travel, rivers to cross, and mountains to climb before full justice is achieved, much has been accomplished. It is difficult today to imagine what yesterday was like.

I recall my shock as I beheld on my first trip through the South the sign For Whites Only—on restrooms, in bus depots and train stations, eateries, hotels, theaters, virtually everywhere. And in the North, if the signs were absent, the reality was not. Segregation existed in every major city, a constant humiliation to every black man, woman, and child, an implicit denial of their human dignity.

With four or five others, I once called upon the general manager of the Los Angeles Angels, the local baseball team, to protest its refusal to employ black players. Jackie Robinson and Branch Rickey had not yet appeared on the horizon.

Lynchings of black men—and in one particularly nauseous case, of a black boy—were still not uncommon occurrences. The days of Martin Luther King, Jr., and of the Freedom Riders still lay far in the future.

With the social evil of racism ubiquitous and manifest, I had to identify myself with the struggle against segregation. To me it was a cancer gnawing at the vitals of this nation which it would in time destroy if it were not excised. From its very founding our nation had proclaimed its belief in the equality of all; countless Fourth of July orations by innumerable Fourth of July orators had reaffirmed this belief in all the years since. Yet from our beginnings we contradicted this noble principle, first by the institution of slavery and subsequently by the institution of segregation. This contradiction between professed ideals and actual behavior is a form of schizophrenia which if not resolved must ultimately destroy the national personality.

This issue became the preoccupation of my life. By spoken and written word I waged an unceasing battle against the evil of racism. I cannot now even estimate the number of rallies and meetings I addressed, alone and sometimes with others.

Several times I shared the platform with Lena Horne, a greatly gifted artist and extraordinary human being, and listened, deeply moved, as she recounted her experiences with racial discrimination. One experience she did not relate at any of these public gatherings, but shared with me at a private meeting in her apartment.

The occasion was a documentary interracial play which I had written, entitled *Trial by Fire*. She had read the script and wished to talk to me about it. Actually she wanted to play the leading female role but was prevented from doing so by the terms of her contract with Metro-Goldwyn-Mayer.

In those days blacks were limited to stereotyped roles like that of Step-n-fetchit or Rochester, Jack Benny's front man. Lena Horne was no more black in color than Norma Shearer. She was nevertheless of the same race as Rochester. Her contract therefore stipulated that she was not to accept any dramatic roles, lest damage be done to the myth that Afro-Americans, even beautiful ones such as Lena Horne obviously was, were by nature an inferior breed. In the course of our conversation she described her first day at MGM. She had been asked to visit the studio to discuss the terms of her contract. As was the custom, a luncheon meeting had been arranged. She was seated next to Louis B. Mayer, head of MGM. During the luncheon she suddenly felt the Titan's fingers crawling up her leg under the table cloth and beneath her dress.

"I'm sorry, Mr. Mayer," she coolly remarked, "but I don't sleep with white men." The fingers fell from her leg, like a giant spider from a cliff. She had made her point, even though her words were not literally true. Actually present with me when she told this story was her future husband, the musical director of MGM, a white man.

I might add as a footnote to this story that several years later Louis B. Mayer was an honorary pallbearer at the funeral of

Abp. John J. Cantwell, of the Roman Catholic Archdiocese of Los Angeles.

The Jesuits at Loyola University at this time, in addition to their teaching, were usually sent on weekends to assist in a local parish, hearing Saturday confessions, saying Mass and preaching on Sunday. The subject of my Sunday homily, not always but often, was racial discrimination. I recall one Sunday preaching in a church on Santa Monica Boulevard, discussing South Africa and predicting that within a half a century, unless the vicious suppression of blacks ended, that country would explode in a revolutionary violence which would claim among its victims innocent as well as guilty. As I write these lines—less than a half century later—South Africa struggles with change; may change come peacefully.

It is unlikely that every pastor in whose church I preached was pleased by my performance. That the chancery office was not was suggested when, following a speech I had delivered to an enthusiastic crowd of 15,000 people at an anti-Ku Klux Klan rally in the Olympic Auditorium, I was summoned to appear at the chancellor's office for an interview. The chancellor was Timothy J. Manning, destined to become cardinal archbishop; he retired in 1985 after a distinguished career as head of the Los Angeles archdiocese. At the time he was an auxiliary bishop, the youngest bishop in the United States.

My previous relations with him had been cordial. I had in fact been told that he admired my articles which had appeared chiefly in *Commonweal* and *America* magazines. That was back when, as a young monsignor, he was secretary to the archbishop, John J.Cantwell. Now that he was a bishop—he seemed to call attention to the fact by fingering the pectoral cross as he spoke—he saw things from a different vantage point.

Over several weeks, a series of ugly racial incidents which bore the imprint of the Klan had disturbed the peace of Southern California. Fiery crosses had been burned on the front lawn of black families who had moved into a white neighborhood, and in one case of a white family which had sold its property to blacks. Two synagogues had been desecrated with anti-Semitic and KKK graffiti, and sacred scrolls stolen. An organization which called itself Mobilization for Democracy called for a mass rally of protest. More than 15,000 persons responded.

The audience represented a good cross section of the community—gentiles and Jews, Protestants and Catholics. Undoubtedly there were a few Communists in the audience, possibly several hundred. But the overwhelming majority were simply citizens concerned about the preservation of American democratic ideals threatened by KKK terrorism. The chairman of the meeting was Robert Kenny, the attorney general of California; Edmund "Pat" Brown, future governor of the state and father of another future governor, was one of the speakers. Still another was Lena Horne.

There was not a subversive word uttered that night. There was a great deal said about human dignity, about inalienable rights, about justice, about charity, about fair play, about the brotherhood of man. The audience responded with enthusiasm. My speech, in which I spoke of the "obscene spectacle of a groveling people worshiping the whiteness of their own skin," brought the 15,000 people to their feet in a standing ovation. I came away with the exalted feeling that such a demonstration and manifestation of the dynamism of democratic ideals inevitably arouses.

The next morning, a friend whom I had first known when he was a student at the University of Chicago but who was at the time both a staff member of the National Labor Relations Board for Southern California and a student at Loyola University's School of Law phoned to say, "Hail, to the man who brings Aristotle to the masses."

Subsequently, two reports—one of four pages, the other of nineteen—were mailed upon stationery marked Confidential to the Chancery Office, to my superior, Father Whelan, and to certain parish priests. These reports purported to describe the meeting in detail. They caused me a great deal of trouble, including the summons by Bishop Manning, who wanted an explanation of my presence at this allegedly subversive meeting.

The author of these documents, I discovered, was the chief of the private police force of a large industrial plant notorious for its antiunion labor policy. His thinking and consequently his reports were obviously controlled by two assumptions that reflected his bias: labor unions are "Red" and foreigners are "Reds."

His two reports on the meeting astounded me. It was impossible to recognize in his description the meeting in which I had participated. Yet, curiously, apart from minor details, his report of the facts was substantially accurate. How did he manage to paint a wholly deceptive picture without deviating materially from the facts? By a very simple technique: in the first paragraph of his initial report he stated as a categorical fact the assumption that the 15,000 people assembled in the Olympic Auditorium were "a subversive group." After that assumption, the most innocent details acquired a sinister and conspiratorial flavor. For instance: "8:45 P.M. people begin to arrive in the hall. . .8:45, Father Dunne arrives and takes his place on the platform. . .8:45, there are small groups of people clustered in the vestibule. . .8:50, some people are going out, some coming in. . ."

The conspiratorial atmosphere has been established. The unwary reader, who may have witnessed exactly the same details at the Olympic fights, at wrestling matches, at political conventions, at business conventions, at Rotary Club conventions, at Shriners' meetings, now begins to sense something sinister in all these goings on. A simple act like stepping outside for a smoke or leaving the balcony to hunt for the restroom becomes a significant detail in the mosaic of conspiracy. The groups of people gathered in the vestibule—probably making dates for bowling the next night—become furtive, shadowy figures discussing in sibilant whispers the plan for dynamiting City Hall.

So when Father Dunne called upon the churches and the labor unions to spearhead the "fight for democracy," clearly he was urging his listeners to pour out into the streets to man the barricades. Since Father Dunne is manifestly "an absolute subverter of the American way of life," his very virtues become vices. "He is clear, direct and intelligent in his presentation;" and "he does not use notes, nor read his speeches." This "gives the listener the impression that he is convinced of what he is saying. At no time does his audience lose the trend of his thoughts." For these very reasons, "Father Dunne becomes more dangerous."

Such propaganda operates subtly. Once the supposition of subversive conspiracy is accepted, the very fact that Father Dunne speaks with sincerity proves that he is insincere; the fact that he speaks with conviction proves he is cunning.

Then there is the master touch. "Father Dunne speaks with a slight accent." Ah-ha! South Side Chicago with a heavy coating of Los Angeles, flavored with Chinese and French? More probably Jewish or Russian. In any event—foreign! The last doubt about his subversive character disappears!

It is sad and deeply disturbing that otherwise intelligent people—Bishop Manning was an intelligent man—are easily beguiled by such blatant propaganda. That they are is substantiated by the whole history of the McCarthy era. The key, of course, is the almost obsessive fear of communism peculiar to Americans. To suggest that someone is a Communist, or associates with Communists, or is sympathetic to them is an extraordinarily effective way of condemning the accused and of mobilizing support for the accuser.

Senator McCarthy understood this well and employed the technique to win wide support among all classes of society. Several years later, when I lived in Phoenix, an otherwise intelligent monsignor told me he could not understand why I was against McCarthy. "After all," he said, "he is against communism, isn't he?"

"Which does not justify his use of innuendo, insinuation, and deceit to destroy the reputations of innocent people and organizations," I replied.

I said the same thing to Senator McCarthy himself. This too was when I lived in Phoenix. The senator phoned me one night at the rectory of Saint Francis Xavier Church. He was evidently visiting Phoenix friends who had given him my phone number. His slurred speech suggested that he had been drinking more than was good for him. He wanted to know why I was against him. I replied as I had to the monsignor and added the comment that the end does not justify the means. This elicited a hearty belly laugh from McCarthy. "Every time somebody tells me that," he said, "I think of a story."

He then proceeded to tell a joke involving two Irishmen. I have forgotten the joke, but its point was to demonstrate the absurdity of the theory that the end does not justify the means. This was evidently an ethical doctrine outside his ken. I hung up the phone feeling sorry for McCarthy; a few months later he was dead of excessive drink.

I do not recall the details of my discussion with Bishop Manning. I endeavored to dissuade him of the idea that the meeting was subversive and to convince him that, on the contrary, it defended ideals to which he himself was thoroughly committed. I doubt that I cleared either the meeting or myself of all suspicion.

Some months later, speaking at a dinner gathering of fifteen or twenty priests which followed confirmation services in a parish in the Watts area, the bishop remarked that I had the makings of another Martin Luther. Early the next morning one of the priests present, a member of the White Fathers missionary order, drove out to Loyola to inform me of the bishop's remark. Although not meant to be complimentary, it was in fact the most flattering, if absurd, thing ever said about me.

My crusading against racism was not limited to the question of the segregation of blacks. It included other forms of racism, such as the shabby treatment of Hispanics, the shameful herding of thousands of decent, law-abiding Japanese into concentration camps during the war, and anti-Semitism as one of the most virulent and abiding kinds of racism. Because of my activities in this area, the local chapter of the American Jewish Congress awarded me a citation for distinguished leadership, and after my expulsion from Los Angeles in 1947, the Southland Jewish Organization brought me back to receive an award at a dinner where the actor Howard da Silva served as master of ceremonies.

These activities involved another speaking engagement at the Olympic Auditorium, an engagement I was fated not to keep. This time an international rather than a local event sparked a rally of protest; it was the exodus of thousands of Jews, survivors of the Holocaust, from Europe to the Promised Land. Great Britain was still the mandated ruler of Palestine and did not welcome this influx. The British began to intercept and disembark the Jews on Cyprus and there intern them in improvised prison camps. The barbed-wire enclosures were a grisly reminder of the horrors from which they had so recently been liberated.

A committee of local citizens, headed by a conservative Republican, sponsored a protest rally. I was asked to be one of two speakers; the other was to be B. C. Crum, who had been sent to Palestine by Pres. Harry Truman to investigate and report on the situation. I replied that I was not sufficiently acquainted with the political situation to speak on that subject, but that I would be glad to speak on anti-Semitism. The committee accepted this; Mr. Crum would deal with the political situation.

The morning before the rally I found an unsigned note under my door. It read, "John Farrow wishes to speak to you. Call him at such-and-such a number." I carried the note into the Jesuit recreation room, where several members of the community were engrossed in the morning newspaper. Showing the note to Fr. Victor White, I asked if he recognized the handwriting. "That's Father Rector's handwriting," he said.

Father Rector Whelan happened to be there, so I turned and asked what John Farrow wanted to talk to me about. "It's about that meeting you were going to address tomorrow night. You must not speak there. John Farrow says that meeting is sponsored by all the left-wing elements in Los Angeles."

"What Farrow says is untrue," I replied. "Of course there will be some left-wing people there, but it is by no means a left-wing meeting. The chairman of the meeting is Judge Ben Rosenthal, a leading Republican and a leader in this community. Farrow is simply doing a job for the British Embassy."

"Well, you must not give that speech. Take a plane to Chicago. Tell them you were called out of town."

"If you say I must not speak at this meeting, I won't speak at the meeting; but I will not lie about it. I have not been called out of town. I will tell them the simple truth, that I have been forbidden by my superior to appear." This is what I did.

The organizing committee was dismayed. They had already published a half-page ad in the daily newspapers publicizing the rally, and it listed me as one of the two speakers. The committee called upon Bishop McGucken, the other auxiliary of the archdiocese, who, because of the age and poor health of Archbishop Cantwell, was effectively in charge. McGucken told the committee that he did not object to my speaking at the rally, but that the matter was not of his concern. It concerned the Jesuits, specifically my superior and me. The committee then contacted Father Whelan but was unable to persuade him to withdraw his ban. He agreed, however, that I might send a telegram to be read at the rally.

I sent a telegram of some five hundred words. After an opening statement of regret that I was unable to address the meeting, the telegram consisted of a long quotation from an essay of Charles Peguy on anti-Semitism. It was read by Eddie Cantor with not altogether happy results, according to my mother and sister, who were in the audience. Peguy has a unique style, difficult even in the original French. His sentences often lack verbs, and he frequently repeats his ideas, merely rearranging the order of words. Eddie Cantor, a master of musical comedy, song, and dance, found himself stumbling over the unaccustomed rhythms and verbal involutions of Peguy's literary style. It fell short of a stellar performance.

A word about John Farrow, a multitalented writer, actor, director and producer in Hollywood and good friend of Father Whelan. I had first met him in 1936, when Father Whelan, then rector of Loyola High School, introduced him with characteristic excitement to the Jesuit community gathered for evening recreation. I suspect, though I do not know, that Whelan had been instrumental in arranging through Archbishop Cantwell the nullification of Farrow's previous marriage, making it possible for him to marry the actress Maureen O'Sullivan. This would explain why

Farrow dedicated to Archbishop Cantwell a popular history of the popes which he authored and why the latter arranged with the Holy See to have him named a Knight of Saint Silvester.

More than 20 years later I read in the Italian magazine *Oggi* an interview with Mia Farrow, John's daughter, in which she complained that when she was growing up her home was "always filled with Jesuits." This was no doubt an exaggeration, but it probably reflected the frequency with which Father Whelan, with one or another of his Jesuit colleagues, was a guest. In the same interview Mia Farrow stated that her father could never make up his mind whether he was a Casanova or the father of a family, thus seeming to add some weight to what Howard da Silva had once told me, that Farrow "was the most licentious man in Hollywood."

Farrow was a native of Australia and had served in the royal navy. Whether he was still a British subject or a naturalized American citizen I did not know, but I was sure his intervention had been motivated by his British connections. This was confirmed when, in compliance with Whelan's orders, I phoned him.

"Oh, yes," he said when I asked him what he wished to talk to me about, "it's about that meeting where you are speaking tonight."

"I am not speaking at that meeting," I said. "Thanks to your intervention, I have been ordered by Father Whelan to withdraw."

"Oh, I am sorry about that. Such was not my intention at all. I merely wished to suggest that you meet with the British consul to discuss over a cup of tea the situation in Palestine."

As I suspected, he was merely doing a job for His Majesty's government.

The Problem of Censors

During this period I contributed quite a number of articles to *Commonweal* and *America*, chiefly to the former. There was a reason for this preference. *Commonweal* was a journal founded and staffed by Catholic laymen and laywomen. In a Church strongly reflecting a clerical cast, lay initiatives were looked upon with suspicion. *Commonweal* received little support from priestly, much less episcopal, quarters.

Long before Vatican Council II, I disagreed with the tendency to identify the Church with its clerical component. I was persuaded, as the Council would later declare, that the Church was the people of God and that the sheep were no less important that the shepherds. I felt that lay initiatives should be encouraged, not discouraged, so I elected to write for *Commonweal* in preference to the Jesuit journal *America.*

There was an advantage in writing for *America,* which was authorized to censor its own articles. Articles that Jesuits wrote for other journals had first to be submitted to the provincial superior, who would in turn farm them out to censors of his own choosing, whose identity remained unknown to the author. This would not have been an intolerable system had the censors scrupulously observed the rules, which established criteria of fairness, impartiality, promptness, and objectivity. In my experience, that was not always the case.

Often the censor, protected by his shield of anonymity, would shove the manuscript into a desk drawer and forget about it for months. When he finally got around to reading it he would often base his decision not upon the article's doctrinal or factual soundness, but upon his own debatable opinions. A weapon ready at hand to condemn an article was to label it "imprudent." Whatever was "controversial" was imprudent. Whatever challenged generally accepted institutions or practices was "controversial." This severely limited the range of opinions which could pass safely through the censorial process.

While still in St. Louis I had once given a lecture on anti-Semitism at Webster Grove College. It was well received, and Fr. Dan Lord offered to publish it. I sent it to the provincial for censorship. The manuscript came back several months later with the judgments of the three censors. One said flat out that it could not be published. One said its publication would be imprudent. The third said it could be published provided I made the eight typed pages of changes that he enclosed! These changes gutted the article and gave credence to all the popular anti-Semitic myths of the day.

I took my case to the provincial, still Joe King. I prudently avoided basing my argument upon the question of fairness, impartiality, or objectivity of the censors, but argued that the tardiness with which they attended to their duties made it impossible to write articles dealing with matters of current interest. By the time their decision reached the author his article was outdated. I asked therefore to be allowed to ask two members of my own community to censor whatever article I might wish to publish. Not without surprise did I receive the provincial's reply agreeing to my request. Some years later, Father King apparently forgot that he had authorized this procedure: a colleague told me that he had overheard King saying that I was in the habit of publishing articles without submitting them for the customary censorship.

The first article I wrote under this new dispensation was "The Sin of Segregation." It appeared in *Commonweal* and reappeared many times in other journals and in an anthology published by *Commonweal* of the best writing to appear in its columns over the years. Several years ago Edward S. Skillin, publisher of *Commonweal*, noted that "The Sin of Segregation" had been reprinted more often than any other article ever to appear in *Commonweal*. Yet I am sure that, had it been submitted to the ordinary mode of censorship, it would never have seen the light of day. Actually it barely survived the less rigorous form of censorship which I had devised with consent of the provincial.

I had given the manuscript for censorship to two men in the community. I had selected these two because they seemed to be devout and observant religious. I assumed that, as good Christians, they would agree with my thesis. My illusion was quickly shattered when one of the two, Fr. Arthur Spearman, returned the manuscript with a note stating that it could not be published. The great advantage of my system of censorship over the old was that, knowing who my censors were, I was able to confront Father Spearman. I demanded that he point out any doctrinal error; he could not do so. I demanded that he show where my reasoning was at fault; he could not do so. Nevertheless, he continued to insist that the article should not be published. His only argument was that its publication would be imprudent.

Behind his pious facade I sensed the lurking presence of a racist attitude which felt challenged in its central belief that blacks are by nature an inferior race. I refused to bow before this idol. Our argument was spirited, and in the end an angry Father Spearman told me to do what I wished. My other censor, Fr. John Collins, had given unreserved approval to publication. So now that Spearman had in effect withdrawn his veto, I sent the manuscript off to *Commonweal*.

Its publication marked a milestone in the struggle for complete emancipation of the blacks. It was the first time anyone had bluntly labeled segregation sinful. Fr. John LaFarge, for example, who was properly recognized for his efforts in support of the black people in this country, had argued in favor of desegregation, but always upon the ground of expediency. A "prudent" man, he stopped short of calling segregation what he privately admitted it was—heresy. I argued that segregation was not only an offense against democracy, it was also an offense against God.

Today, outside of racist circles, this proposition is generally accepted. This was not the case in 1945, when "The Sin of Segregation" first appeared. Thomas H. Clancy, S.J., former provincial of the New Orleans Province, recognized this in an article written in 1979: "When George Dunne wrote his epoch-making article on the sin of segregation in 1945, it was remarked that he enjoyed a distinction possessed by only a few moralists in history, that of discovering a new sin."[9]

One wonders how many other potentially epoch-making articles never saw the light of day because they were aborted by the system of censorship then in vogue. Because my provincial's permission, probably granted in a moment of distraction, enabled me to operate outside this system, I was able for several years to publish a number of articles on controversial subjects.

Perhaps the most controversial of these was entitled "Socialism and socialism." It argued the thesis that "there is no insurmountable obstacle to peaceful relations between Catholicism and socialism. If both sides would abandon their deeply entrenched ideological dogmas, the socialists that religion and socialism are by their nature antithetical, the Christians that the public ownership of the means of production is irreconcilable with the faith, peaceful co-existence would be possible."

Both socialists and Catholics disagreed. Indalecio Prieto, the exiled head of the Socialist Party of Spain, took issue with me in a lengthy article published in Mexico City's *Excelsior*. Norman Thomas, the universally respected leader of the Socialist Party in the United States, disagreed more mildly in a letter to *Commonweal*; we met later at lunch in New York and amiably discussed our differences. And, of course, Pius XI had said in *Quadragesimo Anno* that "no Catholic can be a true Socialist."

Despite this impressive array of dissenting voices I continued to hold to my opinion, the basic reason for which I had put in these words:

Socialism has embraced two different things: a philosophy about man and society, and a program for the economic reorganization of society to assure a just distribution of this world's goods. The philosophy was not essential to the program, nor was the program a logical derivative of the philosophy. Many socialist movements of non-Marxist inspiration were innocent of the philosophy. But modern Socialism, scientific as distinguished from utopian, has been Marxist. It is a tragedy that founders of this, the most influential socialism, insisted that philosophy and program were inseparable.[10]

When Pius XI affirmed an incompatibility between Catholicism and "true" socialism, he was making no distinction between program and philosophy. He was in fact implicitly accepting the thesis of Marxist dogmatists, that true socialism cannot separate the two. There is nevertheless an implicit recognition that such a distinction is possible in his remark in the same encyclical that socialist "programs often strikingly approach the just demands of Christian social reformers."

John XXIII, in *Pacem in Terris*, goes much further, insisting not only upon the possibility but upon the necessity of making such a distinction:

> It must be borne in mind that false philosophical teachings regarding the nature, origin and destiny of the universe and man cannot be identified with historical movements that have economic, social, cultural or political ends, not even when these movements have originated from those teachings and have drawn and still draw inspiration from them. . .Who can deny that those movements, in so far as they conform to the dictates of right reason and are interpreters of the lawful aspirations of the human person, contain elements that are positive and deserving of approval?

John XXIII's carefully constructed statement was an affirmation, many years after its publication, of the validity of the thesis I had defended in "Socialism and socialism."

Not everyone had disagreed with me. My article was published in France in *La Vie Intellectuelle*, whose editor, père de Moidrey, O.P., a hero of the French Resistance, had been saved from death in a Nazi prison by the timely arrival of American troops in 1945; later, on a trip to the United States, he came to Phoenix to visit me.

Trial by Fire

Another article I wrote during this period resulted in my launching myself in the sea of play-writing. It was entitled "The Short Case" and came about in this way.

One night I attended a meeting of the Catholic Interracial Council, a small group of concerned and dedicated Catholics who met from time to time in the home of Dr. Julia Metcalfe. The founder and president, Daniel G. Marshall, an attorney and old college mate of mine, and Ted Le Berthon, activist Catholic and newspaper columnist, reported on the shocking tragedy of a young black couple and their two lovely children who had been burned to death in their newly built home in the town of Fontana, east of Los Angeles; their family name was Short. A bomb had been set to go off as they entered the house after an evening shopping trip. The district attorney whitewashed the case, declaring what was obviously a terrorist outrage an accident.

At the conclusion of his report Dan Marshall remarked, "Mrs. Short's sister is here tonight and perhaps will say a few words to us." An attractive young woman arose to tell us about the tragic fate of her sister. I was struck as by a hammer blow. The young woman was no more black than I was, or Lena Horne was. I was staggered by the thought that her own sister had been burned to death, presumably because she was "black." I returned home and before the night was out had written an account of the tragedy and the ensuing whitewash. I called it simply "The Short Case."

Its publication in *Commonweal* elicited an angry reply from the district attorney of San Bernardino County reaffirming that it was a mere accident, denying that it was a whitewash and charging me with libeling him.

Dan Marshall and I went to Fontana and San Bernardino. After visiting the grim site of the Short home, reduced to ashes, we went to the courthouse, where we asked to see the court records of the case. The sheriff tried to persuade us that there was nothing there that would interest us. We were not dissuaded. Speaking as a lawyer, Dan pointed out that the court records were public property and that under the law we were entitled to receive copies upon demand. With obvious reluctance he turned over the records to us. They supplied shocking evidence that a crime had indeed been whitewashed.

Armed with the evidence, I wrote another article for *Commonweal*, entitled "Trial by Fire," which repeated with supporting documentation my original accusation. The district attorney was not heard from again.

Meanwhile I had been saying morning Mass at Mount Saint Mary's College. The mother superior, Sr. Marie de Lourdes, was also a professor of drama and theater. One morning she told me that she had wept upon reading "The Short Case" and had been unable to sleep all night. "Why don't you write a play about it?" she asked.

I protested that I was not a playwright. For some days she repeated her challenge, arguing that the tragedy had all the elements of drama. Under her goading I finally took several volumes out of the library containing the best plays of a couple of successive years in the 1940s. After reading them, I said to myself, "That doesn't seem to be such a difficult thing to do." I shut myself up with a typewriter and in three days wrote the play *Trial by Fire*.

Sr. Marie de Lourdes showed my manuscript to Emmet Lavery, well-known playwright, scenarist, and president of the Hollywood Screen Writers Guild. In a dinner meeting at his home, at which Anthony Quinn was a fellow guest, Mr. Lavery called my attention to the fact that my play violated a fundamental Aristotelian principle of dramatic art—it lacked unity. The first act told the story of the family's move to Fontana to escape the black ghetto of Los Angeles; then the family and hence the leading characters died. For the rest of the play, an entirely new set of characters took over and told the story of the official whitewash. At Lavery's suggestion I rewrote the play employing the flashback technique. Using two stages, the play moved from a courtroom scene, where a witness under questioning by the district attorney testified to what happened, to stage two, where what had in fact happened was enacted. The contrast between the two added immeasurably to the dramatic tension, so much so that frequently during productions of the play someone in the audience, swept to the emotional edge, would cry out in protest at the brutal injustice revealed.

Trial by Fire was produced by the Catholic Theater Guild at the Wilshire Ebell Theatre. This first production received highly favorable reviews from the critics. One of the first reviews praised, among other things, the audacity with which the author had dared dramatize an interracial marriage. In fact, the subject of interracial marriage did not enter into the play at all. It happened, however, that the actress who played the leading female role while racially black was pigmentally white. The critic's mistake underlined the utter folly of racial discrimination based on race or color.

Over several years, *Trial by Fire* was staged before many audiences in such cities as New York, Chicago, Omaha, Phoenix, and Los Angeles. In New York it was staged at the off-Broadway Blackfriars Theatre. In translation, it saw both theater and radio productions in Czechoslovakia. Like the first production, all the later ones received favorable reviews.

When *Trial by Fire* came to the experimental theater in the famed Pasadena Playhouse, I suddenly found the notorious Sen. Jack Tenney, like a hound dog, on my trail. Tenney, onetime secretary of the musicians' union, had got himself elected to the California state senate. Finding little gold in the hills where he had formerly roamed with far leftists, he had shifted to the far right, where he became a professional hunter of witches. With his California Un-American Activities Committee, he made like a Joe McCarthy in miniature.

Tenney phoned me and urged me to take *Trial by Fire* off the boards. It was, he said, "Communist propaganda." I am afraid my reply was less than genteel. Later I found myself listed among the alleged subversives in one of his annual reports published by the State of California at tax-payers' expense. According to Tenney I had been nominated for the presidency of some subversive organization of which I had never heard.

Trial by Fire was not received with open arms by the administrative heads of the Pasadena Playhouse. They refused it entry to the main theater, fearing that its interracial character might not sit well with a certain wealthy Pasadena spinster who was one of their chief financial supporters. On the staff was Marcella Cisney, who later went on to a long and distinguished career as head of drama first at the University of Denver and then at the University of Michigan in Ann Arbor. Despite official misgivings, she chose to do *Trial by Fire* in the experimental theater, which she controlled. She directed it herself and despite cramped quarters did a brilliant job. Every night after the performance, as was the custom if the author were available, I answered questions from the audience.

One night a good friend of mine, Dr. Roy Thomas, and his wife attended. Dr. Thomas was a brilliant physician and surgeon, as well as an accomplished pianist. He had paid his way through Columbia University and medical school performing with his own orchestra. Later, while doing research at a London institute for cancer, he supported himself and his family by playing in England and on the continent.

Dr. Thomas had once accompanied me to Immaculate Heart College, where we addressed the student body. Dr. Thomas was black. He was handsome and articulate and spoke with a slight Oxonian accent which he had acquired during his years in

England. He first mesmerized the student body with his charm and then, seating himself at the piano, sent them into ecstatic raptures with his musical skills.

On this night at the Pasadena Playhouse, during the question period, someone in the audience questioned whether racial segregation was really a serious problem, asserting that she did not see evidence of it in Pasadena. Dr. Thomas asked if he might reply. He told us that he had arrived at the playhouse that evening without having had time to take his supper. After checking the curtain time with me, he and his wife had gone to a small and quite drab hamburger place less than a block away. They were refused service. The idea of this distinguished and accomplished man and his elegant wife being publicly insulted by the proprietor of a cheap hamburger joint sent the blood racing to my head.

I asked Dr. Thomas if he would return with me the following night to the same restaurant. "If he refuses to serve you we will file legal charges," I said. Even in those days the law forbade, under pain of an automatic fine, refusal by a house catering to the public to accommodate anyone because of race or color. Dr. Thomas was naturally reluctant to take part in a demonstration of this kind, but several black members of the cast offered to accompany me.

The next evening when, with my friends, I entered the restaurant in full clerical armor, Roman collar and all, the place was jammed. Word had spread during the day of our intentions. Word had also reached the proprietor who met us as we entered and, bowing and scraping, ushered us to a table and insisted upon waiting on us himself. There were no fireworks. The expectant crowd was probably disappointed, but a point had been made.

Among those who saw *Trial by Fire* at the Pasadena Playhouse was the noted poet Langston Hughes. He wrote a lengthy and laudatory review of the play for the *Chicago Defender*, to which he regularly contributed a column. Later, when *Trial by Fire* played in Chicago, he saw it again and wrote a second and equally warm review.

Charlie Chaplin

Following its run at the Pasadena Playhouse *Trial by Fire* was staged in Hollywood in a theater on Sunset Boulevard near Vine by Frank Scully, well known writer and author of "Scully's Scrapbook," a regular feature of *Variety*. This production occasioned an encounter with Charlie Chaplin. Years later, in the June 2, 1972, issue of *Commonweal*, I related this episode in detail. I borrow freely from that account here.

The night before our opening, Charlie Chaplin appeared at the dress rehearsal. He came no doubt at the suggestion of Herb Sorrell, head of the Conference of Studio Unions, which in 1946–47 had waged an epic, if losing, battle for the survival of democratic trade unionism in Hollywood. They had faced the combined power of the major producers allied with the International Alliance of Theatrical and Stage Employees (IATSE), still carrying the rancid odor of its history of control by the Chicago crime syndicate.

Chaplin was at the time at the nadir of public esteem. In the witch-hunting atmosphere of the time, his undisguised sympathy for left-wing causes had made him a favorite whipping boy of the red-baiters. In addition, thanks largely to the efforts of Joe Scott, he had acquired the public image of a moral monster, a seducer of innocent young girls who aspired to movie stardom.

As far back as my memory ran, Joe Scott had been Mr. Catholic of Southern California. High-pitched, raspy-voiced, loud, and eloquent orator of the old school, he was a man of strong, un-diluted, and simple loyalties: to the Catholic Church, to Irish independence, to the Red, White, and Blue, to the Republican Party—he was one of the nominators of Herbert Hoover at the party's 1928 convention—and to the principles of old-fashioned morality.

As a boy I had often thrilled to his denunciations of persecution of the Church in Mexico, to his paeans of praise on patriotic feast days of America, land of the free and home of the brave. As a high school student I had marched through the downtown streets from the old ramshackle Los Angeles railroad station to the baseball park then located at Washington Boulevard and Grand Avenue, in a parade honoring Eamon de Valera, recently escaped from a British jail. I had listened with a lump in my throat and tears of righteous rage in my eyes as Joe Scott, from a platform erected at the pitcher's mound and with Mr. de Valera at his side, called down the wrath of heaven upon the British Empire and the *Los Angeles Times*. In those days the *Times* had a markedly anti-Catholic and anti-Irish bias, and Scott had carried on a long-standing feud with its publisher. On his office wall hung a framed photograph of a check which he had collected from the *Times* in payment of a judgment awarded in one of several legal battles he had fought with the newspaper. Forty years later I met with Mr. de

Valera in his Dublin office and reminded him of this incident. He had not forgotten.

Those were the early twenties. By the late forties, the perspective had changed. So had the issues and enemies. As a conservative Republican Joe Scott was not in sympathy with labor unions or with their occasional strikes. As a superpatriot and a militantly loyal Catholic, he was an uncompromising foe of communism. He was easily persuaded that the striking Conference of Studio Unions in Hollywood in 1946–47 was run by Communists and that I, who publicly supported them, was their tool. He wrote to my acting provincial, Hugh Duce—the incumbent, Joe King, was out of the country at the time—denouncing me in the abrasive terms which were a part of his eloquence and demanding that my activities be limited to hearing confessions of Mexican-Americans in the historic Plaza Church where Scott himself—it was one of his many admirable virtues—daily attended Mass and received the Eucharist. "That was what he was ordained for," he said, a questionable canonical assumption.

Charlie Chaplin had become another object of Joe Scott's holy anger. In spite of a long and highly remunerative career in the United States, Chaplin had never become a citizen. This offended the patriotic sensibilities of Scott and of other superpatriots who could not understand why a man who had made a fortune here would not become a citizen. Not to become an American was to be anti-American. There was no middle ground. Furthermore, although not politically active, Chaplin had made no secret of his sympathy for left-wing causes. When Chaplin became involved in a paternity suit, the fat was in the fire.

With the exception of Irish independence, which was no longer an issue, all of Scott's basic loyalties felt challenged. And they combined to trap him into a most discreditable episode in a career often distinguished by many virtues, laudable deeds, and the defense of worthy causes. He was determined to pillory Chaplin by any means, fair or foul. The means chosen were foul.

My reference to Scott's loyalty to principles of old-fashioned morality was not meant disparagingly. I subscribe generally to the same principles. Among them is a warning—a point overlooked by Scott and many others in the Chaplin case—about judging others lest we ourselves be judged. In a world where the Sixth Commandment was honored in the breach more than in the observance, there is no evidence that Chaplin's private sex life was any more aberrant than that of a great many others. Furthermore, the area of private sexual behavior would seem to be one which, more than any other, is reserved to God's judgment, not human judgment, and has no place for stone-throwers.

The question of paternity is, of course, another matter, for it involves responsibility for one's child. The issue here, however, hinges upon a question of truth. And here the truth was, and Scott knew it, that the child was not Chaplin's.

The name of the girl is unimportant. She has long since faded from history. Like many other girls before, and many since, she had come to Hollywood equipped with little talent, moderate good looks, and a consuming ambition to become a movie star. She was prepared to use whatever purchasing power her sex afforded her to foot the bill. When stardom did not materialize she charged Chaplin with being the father of her child. When blood tests established that Chaplin could not possibly have fathered her child, her lawyer, a leading member of the Los Angeles bar, honorably withdrew from the case, refusing to carry it further.

At this juncture, Scott, determined that Chaplin not be let off the hook, offered his services. Because the rules of evidence in California had not caught up with medical science, blood tests were not at that time accepted as proof of non-paternity. The only possible conclusion from the medical data was that at the same time that the young lady was engaged in seductive play with Chaplin, she had been bedding down with another man who fathered her child.

The evident fact did not deter Scott, nor did the archaic state of the rules of evidence prevent his calling upon all the considerable resources of his courtroom eloquence to elicit the sympathies of the jury for a poor, innocent American girl shamelessly seduced and tossed aside by the un-American, Communist-sympathizing moral monster who was Charlie Chaplin. It was a sordid performance. And it won the case. Chaplin was defeated. So were truth and justice.

There is nothing in the record to suggest that Scott felt that he had compromised his integrity. Perhaps he reasoned—after all, like Mark Anthony, he was an honorable man—that regardless of the falsity of this particular charge, Chaplin, given all the other things said about him, had got what was coming to him. That, after all, is the definition of justice! To each, one's due!

These episodes, not directly related to my meeting with Chaplin, are pieces of the mosaic; they help establish the moral ecology of the time.

What impressed me about Chaplin when I met him at the dress rehearsal was his simplicity. If, thanks to the prevailing hysteria of the McCarthy era and to the paternity suit, he was less esteemed than formerly, he was no less famed. His lofty place in the pantheon of the entertainment arts, as artist and particularly as incomparable mime, was secure. But there was no hint of this in his easy, informal and friendly manner with me and with the cast. He was totally without affectation. There was no hint of the Hollywood star *grande manière*.

He sat next to me during the rehearsal and from time to time quietly made suggestions about various bits of stage business. Afterwards, with the cast gathered about him, he was both serious and at times hilariously funny. To make a point about the enormous size of the stage in the Hollywood Bowl he improvised bits of pantomime which showed why he was the greatest mime in the world. He was Jascha Heifetz, world-famous violinist, acknowledging the applause of the audience in the Hollywood Bowl. That was the scene which he then acted out without a word, without a sound, but with such consummate artistry that we were transported to the Bowl, heard the music, joined the applause, howled with laughter.

He began, standing in center aisle, by sawing away furiously left-handed, which he was, upon an imaginary violin, bringing the concerto to a close. Solemn bows, center, left, right, center as the applause thunders up from the audience. Then the exit as the applause pursues him across the stage, the enormous size of which came to life as Chaplin marched briskly up, down, up, down, and up the aisle before disappearing into the wings. The applause thunders on and he reappears. Again the long march to reach center stage, down, up, down, up, and down. Again the solemn bows, center, left, right, center. Again the exit and the long march up, down, up, down, up, and off, as the applause rolls on. . .

As described it sounds prosaic. As mimed by Chaplin, it was outrageously funny. Remembering it forty years later I find myself laughing. It was an unforgettable demonstration of Chaplin's genius for creating out of next to nothing a universe of comic fantasy with a touch of his unequaled gift for pantomime.

To make another point, this time in an effort to persuade me to eliminate from the play some stage business to which I was tenaciously attached, he improvised a dramatic bit. When I returned to Hollywood with my play, remembering the support I had given them during a strike, the set designers' union designed and the carpenters' union built a magnificent set for *Trial by Fire*. The main feature was a lovely California bungalow mounted on a platform on rollers. On the back side of the platform was a replica of the house, but blackened and shattered as by an explosion and fire. At a dramatic point of the play, as a neighbor woman is on the stand testifying to the tragic event upon which the story centers, the lights fade out. Out of the darkness a loud explosion startles the audience, red lights flash, a siren shrills while stagehands swing the platform around on its rollers. When a few moments later the lights gradually come upon main stage the lovely redwood bungalow is gone. In its place stands the stark and twisted outlines of a home blasted by racial hatred.

I was proud of that scene. Chaplin argued that it should go. It was melodrama, not drama. "I don't know anything about religion," he said. "I don't know anything about politics. But there's one thing I know more about than any man in this country"—he spoke not boastfully, but quietly stating a fact — "and that's the theater. The theater is sheer magic. Let me show you. Imagine an empty stage. Dim lights. It is night. Suddenly the shrill ringing of a telephone on stage shatters the silence. A door slams open stage right. A man enters briskly and hurries across stage to the telephone. . ."

And Chaplin acted it out. He grabbed up the phone: (Staccato) "Hello—yes—when? where? right—yes—OK—on my way."

"He hangs up the phone, rushes off stage. The door slams. Silence. Curtain. You see?" Chaplin resumed the lesson. "The audience has been shown nothing. They don't know what has happened. But their imaginations, fired by the dramatic intensity, have taken over. They are sitting on the edge of their seats. Magic. That's the theater. In your play, don't show the audience the horrors of the scene. That's melodrama. Let the audience participate, not just look on like spectators at a fire. The dialogue of your courtroom scene is good enough to fire the imagination. Let the audience take off from that and recreate, relive in their own imaginations the horrors. Let the magic of the theater work." Chaplin won the argument. Sadly, I cut out the explosion, the flashing lights, the siren, the blasted bungalow. But every future performance of *Trial by Fire* which I witnessed, in Hollywood or elsewhere, proved to me how right Chaplin was.

Chaplin considered *Trial by Fire* a very good play. One scene involving an FBI agent he labeled a great scene. He insisted that

I was a born playwright. Again appealing to his knowledge of the theater, he said: "Playwrights are born, not made. Even the business of getting people on and off stage properly requires a special gift. If you are not born with it, you cannot acquire it. You were born with it." It is, of course, not impossible that these kindly evaluations have something to do with the warmth of the memories I have retained of Chaplin over the years.

After we left the theater Chaplin took me, Herb Sorrell, and Flo Contini, the secretary of the Conference of Studio Unions, to the Players' Club for a bite to eat and more conversation. He drove his own car, an unpretentious model. At the Players' Club we spent a good part of what was left of the night in serious conversation, in the course of which we touched upon almost every reproach that had been directed at him.

The first thing that struck me was that in his brief reference to the paternity case he had nothing to say in criticism of Joe Scott. It seemed remarkable restraint on the part of a man who had been held up to public scorn and scathing tongue-lashing.

Chaplin talked about a plot he had in mind for his next production. It was still in the early stages of development in his mind. Some years later I saw it on the screen; it was *Limelight*. There was a brief scene in which mention is made of God. Chaplin had talked about this scene, repeating what he had said earlier in the evening about not knowing anything about religion. How could he have been expected to? The circumstances of his life, the environment into which he had been born and in which he had grown up had not included religious influences. He made a point which is at least arguable. He had not asked to be born. He had not chosen the circumstances of his birth and upbringing. He therefore found it difficult to accept that he was accountable for the consequences.

He discussed quite frankly his attitude on the subject of American citizenship. Chaplin considered himself a citizen of the world. "I have been in nearly every country," he remarked. "And I have found people everywhere regardless of color, race, or nationality to be pretty much the same, all human beings with the same desires, the same impulses. I feel a bond with all of them. If I were to take citizenship anywhere it would be here. This is where I have made my home. This is where I have made my career and my money. I am grateful to America." The superpatriots would no doubt have been surprised had they been listening. "But the swearing of allegiance to one country seems to me a rejection of all the other people in the world. And this I cannot bring myself to do."

Perhaps today, when more and more people accept the concept of the world as a planetary village, when there is increased awareness of the unity of humankind and a concern about the mistrust, suspicion, and hatred that flourish behind walls, Chaplin's essentially humane and universal attitude would be better understood. He was no more anti-American than he was anti-British. He refused to be anti-anybody.

He said little about Oona O'Neill, to whom he had only recently been married, but what he did say was significant both as an evaluation of the reasons for his previous marital failures and as prophetic insight. His marriage to a young woman more than thirty years his junior had, of course, been added to the evidence in the dossier of the "moral ogre." He spoke fondly of his young wife and with quiet confidence that theirs was a union destined to endure. He was confident of this because, he said, "Thank God, she has absolutely no theatrical ambitions, no interest whatever in a stage or screen career." More than a quarter of a century of successful married life attests to the soundness of his judgment—and of hers.

Chaplin spoke a good deal that night about his nostalgia for the premechanical age and in doing so unwittingly brought to light, I think, the roots of his sympathy for the Soviet Union. He spoke with genuine feeling about the horse-and-buggy days, about how he missed the splendid sight of handsomely groomed and richly caparisoned horses and shining carriages and the bracing fragrance of fresh horse droppings on city streets.

Chaplin was against not so much capitalism as the mechanical age. That was quite plainly what *Modern Times* is all about. He was against the process of mechanization which had driven the horses and buggies off the streets and replaced them with noisy automobiles, had exchanged the piquant odors of a horse-drawn civilization for the choking fumes of a motorized world. He was against the dehumanization and pauperization of people and their environment. It was only coincidentally—because it was responsible for these developments—that capitalism attracted his animus. And because communism also rejected the system, he felt that he had something in common with the attempt of the Soviet Union to construct a society on other principles.

These are not things Chaplin said, but conclusions suggested to me by what he did say about the mechanical age. If my speculation is correct the flaw in his reasoning is obvious. The Soviet Union is indeed opposed to capitalism but by no means to mechanization—quite the contrary. And, as the crushing of

Hungary in 1957 and of the Czechoslovakian experiment in 1968 showed, prior to Gorbachev it was not interested in efforts to combine humanization with mechanization. However, as Chaplin had said, he knew nothing about politics. His orientation had been determined not by ideology so much as by a feeling for humanity and for the attractions of a simpler world not dominated by the machine. Perhaps here too, when grave doubts about the validity of life in an increasingly technologized world assail more and more people, he would be judged more sympathetically.

Highly significant was his reply to a question put to him by Flo Contini. "Mr. Chaplin," she asked, "have you ever visited the Soviet Union?"

"No," he replied. The Soviet Union was one of the few countries he had not visited.

"Why not?"

"Because," he said, "I am afraid I might be disillusioned."

To me that said everything that needed to be said about the nature of Chaplin's interest in communism and the Soviet Union. It grew out of an act of hope that there was an alternative to the dehumanizing kind of society organized under capitalistic auspices which threatened human values, and it issued in an act of faith that the Soviet experiment contained the promise of an alternative. If he lost that faith what would be left of hope? And so he refused to run the risk.

I shared his hope, and still do, but not his faith. Nevertheless, it did not seem to me then, nor does it now, that Chaplin deserved abuse because of it. It was simply the fragile faith of a man clinging desperately to the possibility of a less tawdry world than the one we know. Is that so evil?

Chaplin told us that night that he badly wanted to visit Europe, but he was afraid that once he was out of the country his reentry permit might be revoked. He had made inquiries of the State Department and had been assured that there was no danger of this. He could leave the country without fear of being denied readmission. Despite this, he still hesitated, uncertain how much he could rely upon this assurance. Several years later he sailed for England. His ship was hardly out of sight of the Statue of Liberty when his reentry permit was revoked by the Attorney General of the United States. His misgivings had been well founded. It was a shameful deed and another sordid episode in the story of Charlie Chaplin.

It was near dawn when we left the Players' Club. That night Chaplin brought his charming young wife to the opening of *Trial by Fire*. My last and one of my warmest memories of Charlie Chaplin is the simple and gracious courtesy with which he treated my mother, to whom I presented him after the performance. He could not have shown her more respect had she been a queen— which of course she was.

Although I was never to see Chaplin again, during the last ten years of his life I lived less than an hour's drive from his home in Vevey, Switzerland, where he settled after being barred from the United States. Whenever en route to Lausanne I drove down the steep, circuitous highway that passed near his chalet and looked down upon the sparkling waters of Lac Leman and across to the magnificent panorama of snow-clad Alpine peaks leaning against azure skies, I said to myself, "Chaplin got the better of the deal." The loss—and the shame—were America's.

Nine

Immorality in Hollywood

A s I have indicated, my stay in Los Angeles was destined to be of relatively short duration. It climaxed in and was terminated by my involvement in the major strike in the Hollywood motion picture industry of 1946–47.[1] On one side, in collusion with the producers, was the larger and older of two Hollywood labor organizations, the International Alliance of Theatrical and Stage Employees, commonly known by its acronym IATSE. On the other was a group of striking unions banded together in the Conference of Studio Unions, or CSU.

The IATSE, an honest union prior to 1934, had been taken over in that year by the Chicago crime syndicate, headed by Frank Nitti (known as "the Enforcer"), who had succeeded Al Capone when the latter was sent to Alcatraz, the federal prison in San Francisco Bay, for income tax violations. The takeover was easily effected at the June meeting of the International in Louisville, Kentucky. With mobsters already in control of the large New York, New Jersey, and Chicago delegations, the election of their man as president presented no problem; their man was George E. Browne, business manager of Local 2 in Chicago. Browne then appointed Willie Bioff, a convicted pimp and until now small-time hoodlum, as his representative in Hollywood, center of the motion picture industry. Bioff sent two hit men with violin cases under their arms into a meeting of the Hollywood local to announce the takeover of their union. There was no resistance. The members knew what the violin cases contained, and they had read of the Saint Valentine's Day Massacre in Chicago. They dispersed quietly and went home.

Bioff and Browne then met in New York with Nick Schenck, representing all the Hollywood producers, and worked out a deal whereby each of the producers would pay an annual fee of $250,000 in return for immunity from bothersome demands from the working men and women whose toil and skill were largely responsible for the prosperity the industry enjoyed. The purpose of the agreement was "to insure that the number of employees would not be increased, that wages [of employees] would not be increased, and that strikes of the employees would not be called," according to Judge John W. Kern, who presided over the Nitti Tax Hearings, held in Chicago September 27 to October 4, 1948.[2] It was, in other words, a conspiracy between Hollywood producers and the Chicago crime syndicate to sell the interests of the worker down the river.

This conspiracy, constituting one of the more sordid chapters in the history of management-labor relations in America, continued until 1941. In that year the federal government sent George E. Browne and Willie Bioff, convicted of extortion, to the federal penitentiary.[3]

In 1937 a new figure had appeared on the Hollywood labor scene. Herb Sorrell, whose flattened nose witnessed to an early and not too successful boxing career, led a successful strike of the painters' union against the combined forces of the producers and IATSE. Sorrell was a rare phenomenon in the moral miasma of Hollywood management-labor relations: a man of honesty and integrity. Members of small, unorganized, and therefore highly exploited groups, such as Disney's cartoonists, turned to him for help. Soon there appeared in Hollywood a new group of affiliated unions centered on the carpenters' and painters' unions and headed by Herb Sorrell. It was known as the Conference of Studio Unions, and it became a symbol in Hollywood of democratic and honest trade unionism. By 1945 some nine unions, representing nine to ten thousand workers in the industry, had joined the conference.

I had been asked by Ed Skillin, editor of *Commonweal*, to do an article on the Hollywood labor situation. I began by interviewing Daniel Marshall, a close friend since our college days together. Dan had been counsel for the Hollywood local of the IATSE prior to its takeover by Willie Bioff, at which point he refused to continue to represent the union.[4] Participating in the interview was Carey MacWilliams, lawyer and writer on California social and political problems, who would later serve for many years as editor of the journal *Nation.*

After this I called upon both Herb Sorrell and Roy Brewer, who had succeeded Willie Bioff as the IATSE man in Hollywood, to ask their respective views of the labor situation. I found Sorrell optimistic. Unaware that at the very moment Brewer and the producers were meeting secretly to agree on a strategy for the destruction of the CSU, he predicted a period of peace. In stark contrast was the attitude of Brewer. "The CSU cannot exist together with the IATSE in Hollywood," he said. "It has got to be destroyed." Unlike Sorrell, as one of the principal figures involved in the conspiracy, Brewer was fully aware of what was going on behind the scenes.

What was going on was a series of hush-hush meetings between Roy Brewer and the producers to plot the destruction of the CSU.[5] The strategy agreed upon was to force the CSU members out on strike and to lock them out by relying upon strikebreakers supplied by the IATSE. A pretext had been found in the ambiguous wording of a phrase in the decision of a three-man committee appointed by William Green, president of the American Federation of Labor, to define jurisdictional lines in Hollywood with a view to eliminating this fruitful source of conflict between the many craft unions in the industry.[6]

The flawed wording in their decision occurred where they attempted to define the respective jurisdictions of the carpenters' union and the IATSE; they awarded "all trim and millwork on sets and stages" to the carpenters and "the erection of sets on stages" to the IATSE. The ambiguity lay in the phrase "erection of sets on stages." All construction work of sets on stages had always belonged to the carpenters' union. Now the "erection of sets" would be turned over to a hitherto unheard of and hastily created IATSE "set erectors" union.

At a meeting on September 20, attended by representatives of Columbia, Goldwyn, MGM, Paramount, Republic, Fox, Universal, Warner Brothers, Roach, and Technicolor, a September 23 deadline was established. "By 9:00 A.M. Monday clear out all carpenters and then clear out all painters, following which proceed to take on IA men to do the work."[7]

Everything proceeded on schedule on September 23. The carpenters and painters were "cleared out." Inevitably, they set up picket lines. Inevitably, the other CSU union members refused to cross the picket lines. The well-laid plans of the smoothly working team of producers and IATSE leaders had borne fruit; they now had their strike. Actually, it was a lockout, but by a subtle bit of alchemy they had transmuted it into a strike. Called by whatever name, the results were the same.

What followed is history: the history of thousands of men and women, many of whom had invested as much as a quarter of a century in their studio jobs, thrown out of work; the history of these same men and women fighting to save their jobs, their homes, their future; the history of their picket lines being forcibly broken; the history of hundreds being rounded up by the police, notably by the notorious "Red Squad," thrown into jail and herded into courtrooms where they were tried like cattle in batches of twenty to forty on the charge of disturbing the peace. To those who witnessed them, these trials were travesties of justice.

In one of them I testified as a character witness for some of the defendants. The testimony of a character witness is limited to stating how long he has known the person and whether the person has a good reputation in the community. After I had testified, the judge, notorious in the legal community for the bias with which he presided, took over my cross-examination. The following interesting exchange took place:

Judge: On such and such a date did you not give a talk on the radio at the Wilshire Ebell Theatre on behalf of the Conference of Studio Unions?

Dunne: No, I did not.

Judge: Yes, you did.

Dunne: No, I did not.

Judge: (angrily and shouting) I remind you that you are under oath! (At this juncture one of the defense lawyers vigorously protested the judge's assumption of the role of prosecutor. After threatening to hold him in contempt of court, the judge returned to me.)

Judge: I repeat my question. Did you not on such an such a date give a talk on radio at the Wilshire Ebell Theatre on behalf of the Conference of Studio Unions?

Dunne: I repeat my answer. No, I did not. I have spoken more than once on the radio in support of the Conference of Studio Unions. I have never spoken on the radio at the Wilshire Ebell Theatre and on the date given by you I did not speak there or anywhere on behalf of the Conference of Studio Unions or anybody else!

Flustered and angry, the judge dismissed me from the stand. At the conclusion of the trial the jury acquitted all the defendants.

How did I get deeply involved in this? Some weeks after the beginning of the strike, I was one of several dozen guests at a gathering of people interested in the social problems of the day. Our host was a brilliant black lawyer who was later to serve as a member of Thurgood Marshall's legal team which in 1954 successfully argued *Browne v. The Board of Education*, the history-making case which destroyed the legal basis of segregation in the schools of the nation. In the course of the evening one of the other guests mentioned to me that the morale of many CSU members was at a low ebb; they were discouraged by weeks of marching on the picket lines and the apparent lack of public support. He asked me if I would be willing to appear at their weekly strike meeting and speak a word of encouragement. I told him that, inasmuch as I was convinced of the justice of their cause, I would be glad to do so, provided that Herb Sorrell did not object. He agreed to clear the matter with Sorrell, and the next day phoned me to report that the latter had no objection.

The following Sunday night I appeared at the Hollywood American Legion Stadium, the local boxing arena, climbed into the ring, and assured the striking members of the CSU of the justice of their cause. During the months that followed I appeared almost every Sunday night to assure them of my support.

On one such occasion Herb Sorrell did not appear. Answering a phone call to his home, his wife said that he had left for the stadium at his usual time. A pall of apprehension settled over the meeting. The headlines of the following day disclosed that the apprehension had been well founded. En route to the meeting, Sorrell had been kidnapped at gunpoint by three mafia-type hoodlums, forced into their car, driven into the San Bernardino mountains, pistol-whipped, and left for dead in the sagebrush. Regaining consciousness, he had crawled some fifty yards to the highway, where he was picked up by a passing motorist and driven to the hospital in San Bernardino. The following Sunday he appeared at the strike meeting, his bandaged head a reminder of the allegedly severed ties with the Chicago crime syndicate. The IATSE leadership and the producers denied any connection with the affair. They even suggested that Sorrell had inflicted the head wounds and black eyes upon himself!

A major factor in keeping the studios running was the Teamsters' union, which transported hundreds of strikebreakers through the picket lines. The head of the Teamsters' local in Hollywood was Joe Tuohy. When the question was put to the members of the local, they voted to observe the picket lines. When later interrogated under oath, Tuohy evaded answering a question as to whether, as reported, the vote had been unanimous. He admitted, however, that "the opinion [of the members] probably was in the majority to not haul those people through the picket lines."[8]

Tuohy simply ignored the views of the members and ordered them to break the picket lines. It was reported that he even imported Teamster business agents from outside locals to run the buses when members of his local refused. When later questioned about this under oath, Tuohy developed a convenient lapse of memory.

Enter Ronald Reagan

The only international labor leader to endorse Ronald Reagan for election and again for reelection to the presidency was Frank Fitzsimmons, the head of the Teamsters, whose late leader, Jackie Presser, was spared trial on felony charges thanks to the benign neglect of Reagan's Justice Department. Reagan's honeymoon with the Teamsters' union has had a long life. It began in Hollywood.

My own acquaintance with Ronald Reagan also began and ended in Hollywood. In one of my Sunday night appearances at a strike meeting I made the statement that the strike would be settled within twenty-four hours if the actors and actresses would refuse to cross the picket lines. It was possible for the IATSE to find scabs to replace the painters, carpenters, and other CSU craftspeople. It was not possible to finds scabs to replace the actors and actresses.

Although the Italians, especially Federico Fellini, had shown that it could be done, the Hollywood star system was not geared to making movies with nonprofessionals. One could not pick up surrogate Clark Gables or Ingrid Bergmans on the street. Without the actors and actresses the studios could not operate. If they refused to cross the picket lines the producers could not make movies. The studios would close. The flow of money would cease. Though this seems obvious now, until that time no one had focused the spotlight upon the key role played by the Screen Actors' Guild, whose president at the time was Ronald Reagan. That he himself was quite aware of this was evidenced by the immediacy of his reaction.

Accompanied by Jane Wyman, his wife at the time, and by George Murphy, like himself a Hollywood actor of mediocre talent, Reagan came to see me at Loyola University. They arrived about nine o'clock in the evening. I presume, although I no longer recall, that the meeting had been arranged by telephone. It is unlikely that they would have dropped in at the university unannounced. I recall that Reagan was by far the most articulate of the three, that Murphy contributed little beyond a sheepish and apologetic smile, and that Jane Wyman, the only one of the three who in my estimation had any genuine acting ability, had nothing to say. Perhaps she had been brought along on the not implausible theory that I would be more susceptible to her unquestionable charms than to those of her husband—or to his questionable arguments.

This meeting was supposed to persuade me that I was being hoodwinked by the Communists. Then, as now, Reagan was convinced that behind every activity with which he disagreed lurked a Communist. He and Murphy, he said, had gone to Indianapolis to interview the three members of the labor committee, the meaning of whose decision was the issue of the strike. According to Reagan they had come down firmly on the side of the producers and of the IATSE. From this Reagan concluded that the CSU did not have a leg to stand on. This was not a labor dispute. It was a Communist conspiracy, first to disrupt and then to take control of the motion picture industry. I was being used by the Communists.

That there were active Communists in Hollywood during these years is beyond doubt. There were probably Communists in every union, including Reagan's Screen Actors' Guild. There were Communists in the CSU. There were Communists in the IATSE. I had been told by its own business agent that the union with the

largest number of Communists in its membership was the cos-
tume designers' union, which belonged to the IATSE, not the CSU.
But communism was not the issue here. The Red Menace was
manifestly a red herring, employed repeatedly by Reagan and the
producers whom he served to cloud the issue and to deceive the
public.

As for Reagan and Murphy's trip to Indianapolis, I later visited
there myself and interviewed William C. Birthright, one of the
committee members. The other two were away at the time. He flatly
contradicted Reagan's account. Later, testifying under oath at the
congressional hearing which Congressman Kearns held in Los
Angeles, all three again flatly contradicted Reagan's version of
their position.

The lawyer for the congressional committee brought up the
moves of the producers' labor-relations man, Pat Casey,[9] in transferring from the carpenters to the IATSE the erection of sets on
stages—the heart of the controversy. He asked William Doherty
whether Casey "was carrying out the thought that you had in mind
when you wrote this original decision."

Doherty replied, "The answer is definitely that he was not
carrying out the thought that we had in mind."

Then the same question was asked of Felix Knight, who
replied, "He was not carrying out my thought, Mr. Counsel."

When the same question was put to William Birthright, he
answered, "Absolutely not."[10] So much for Reagan's account of
what these same three men had supposedly told him Indianapolis.

I happened to be sitting next to Reagan in the federal
courtroom as these three men under oath flatly contradicted what
he had alleged to be their position. I glanced quizzically at him. He
was staring stonily ahead, the winning smile, which in his later
political career would seduce millions of Americans into taking
leave of their senses, notably absent.

It was close to midnight, as I recall, when our meeting at
Loyola ended. As Reagan and his companions took their leave, I
thought to myself, "This is a dangerous man." I do not know now
exactly what I had in mind. I was certainly not thinking of his
future political career. Farthest from my thought was the idea that
either he or Murphy had a future in politics. But he was very
articulate. He had considerable personal charm. He had a remarkable facility in presenting what is false in the guise of truth. A
combination of these three qualities in one person spells danger.

Reagan's Version

Reagan has himself written an account of our meeting. It is vintage Reagan—a melange of truth, half or partial truth, and untruth. His account appears in an autobiographical piece entitled, "Where's the Rest of Me?"

> Father Dunne took to the air waves and blasted the SAG [Screen Actors' Guild] and all opponents of the CSU eloquently and with vigor. The papers reported also that he appeared on the platform at CSU rallies. George Murphy and I decided he must be the victim of a snow job. We knew he had never been exposed to the Guild side of the controversy, and he was saying some pretty harsh things about us. We called and asked if we could see him, and then went down to the university one evening armed with our records. We were a little taken aback when he introduced us to his lawyer, and coldly informed us that he had asked his lawyer to sit in on our meeting. It was a short meeting. The next night he was back on radio kicking our brains out. But not for long; someone else began to teach political science and he was on the other side of the country.[11]

The text calls for some editing. My recollection of the meeting differs substantially from Reagan's description. He does not mention that, besides George Murphy, Jane Wyman was also present. His statement that they came "armed with our records" sounds impressive, but it is also false. They carried no records.

Why they should have been taken aback by the presence of my lawyer is not clear; in any case, I did not then or later have a lawyer. My recollection is that I met Reagan and his companions alone. And though my immediate reaction upon reading this text was to brand it a lie, my friend Dan Marshall was a lawyer and, as I have indicated, had formerly represented the IATSE; it is possible that he participated in the meeting. I do not recall this to have been the case. When I call up from my memory the details of the meeting I see myself, Reagan, Wyman, and Murphy seated in the parlor of the Jesuit residence at Loyola University; I do not see Dan Marshall.

Neither do I recall that it was, as Reagan says, a short meeting. They arrived around nine o'clock and left around midnight. The dialogue, which was amicable enough, was limited almost entirely to Reagan and me, and it ended where it had begun, in complete disagreement. His statement that I was back on the radio the next night is a typical Reagan rhetorical flourish not to be measured by any strict standard of exactitude. The same is true of his remark that I soon found myself "on the other side of the country." True enough, before long I was out of Los Angeles, but a dozen or more years were to pass before I would find myself "on the other side of the country."

Some day someone will make a study of the extraordinary way in which as the "Teflon president" he repeatedly and *successfully* distorted, misrepresented, inverted, and manhandled the truth. By successfully, I mean without any apparent damage to the favorable image in which his admirers hold him. He is the beneficiary of that bizarre American phenomenon, the hysterical adulation of Hollywood movie stars.

It is probably too much to say that Reagan is a liar. A liar knows that he is lying. It probably never occurs to Reagan that he is lying. He believes his own untruths. He lives in a world of fantasy which becomes for him reality.[12]

Proposals of Arbitration

With the CSU members forced out of the studios, the strategic goal of the producers and the IATSE was clear: to keep them out until the cumulative misery of months of unemployment took its toll. They were not interested in a peaceful settlement of the dispute. Repeated attempts by disinterested parties to bring the opposing parties together to arbitrate their differences always met the same response: Herb Sorrell and the Conference of Studio Unions accepted the proposal; the IATSE simply ignored it. The producers piously expressed their solicitude, agreed that arbitration offered the only feasible solution, but regretted that they could not interfere in a dispute that was solely a union matter. This, for example, was the response to a message sent to the producers and the unions involved by an interfaith committee of eight leading representatives of the Jewish, Protestant, and Catholic clergy.

Later on, when their pretense that they were not party to the dispute grew a little thin, the producers tried a new angle. To the proposals that the issues be arbitrated they replied that arbitration, while theoretically ideal, was practically useless because of the dictatorial powers of "Big Bill" Hutcheson, international president of the carpenters' union, who could order the carpenters' local to refuse to abide by any decision he did not like.

On March 9, 1947, at a crowded mass meeting in a downtown auditorium, I proposed an arbitration scheme which, while demanding sweeping concessions from the CSU, cut the ground from under the objection raised by the producers. It challenged the CSU to agree in advance to accept all the decisions of an arbitrator and to agree that, in the event Hutcheson refused to abide by such decisions, the other CSU unions would not support the carpenters in any action they might take.

What were the reactions? Walsh and Brewer of the IATSE predictably ignored the proposal. Herb Sorrell and the CSU, with the approval of its strike committee, immediately accepted it. The producers? Within a few hours of receiving a telegram announcing the proposals and the CSU acceptance, they attempted to bring pressure to bear upon me through my superiors to prevent me from pursuing the proposal any further.

The Archbishop's Peace Move

Less than two weeks later, on March 21, 1947, *The Tidings*, the official organ of the Archdiocese of Los Angeles, published over the signature of Abp. John J. Cantwell a report prepared by Rev. John Devlin, the archbishop's liaison with the film industry, and Rev. Thomas Coogan, Ph.D., the archdiocesan expert on labor relations. The report presented the conclusions they had reached after an investigation of the Hollywood labor conflict. After reviewing the history of the dispute, it stated, among other things, that the strike could be settled if all the parties got together in a determined effort to end it, that the producers had taken a most negative attitude by doing little to settle the dispute, and that the strike issues could not be beclouded with cries of communism and radicalism if a settlement was to be accomplished.

The report then made concrete proposals for setting up arbitration machinery to settle the issues, including a challenge to the CSU to agree "to refuse to support the carpenters if Mr. Hutcheson refuses to abide by any further jurisdictional decisions."

When I arrived at the strike meeting the following Sunday night I brought with me a copy of *The Tidings*. I began my remarks by saying that I did not represent the Catholic Church, that the statements I had made in my frequent appearances before them represented only my personal opinion. "The only one who speaks authoritatively for the Catholic Church in Los Angeles," I said, "is Abp. John J. Cantwell. He has now officially stated the position of the Church in Los Angeles on the strike." I then read the archbishop's statement. Quite understandably it elicited an enthusiastic ovation.

The next day I was summoned to the chancery office by the young auxiliary bishop, Timothy Manning. He had been told that I had marched down the aisle at the Hollywood American Legion Stadium triumphantly waving a copy of *The Tidings* above my head. This was false. I made no triumphant entry of the Stadium. I carried *The Tidings* in my pocket, from which I removed it only to read the archbishop's statement. I had the impression that the bishop was skeptical of my disclaimer, preferring his informer's word to mine.

He then proceeded to admonish me with some severity that I did not speak for the Catholic Church and that the only one who spoke for the Catholic Church in the Los Angeles archdiocese was the archbishop! At this point I began to feel that I was wandering with Alice in Wonderland. I tried to assure him that not only did I recognize the archbishop's unique authority and that I spoke only for myself, but that this in fact had been the precise burden of my remarks the previous evening at the stadium. He was not impressed and dismissed me with the distinct feeling that I was being censured, but with a quite indistinct understanding of what I was being censured for. For reading the archbishop's statement? For proclaiming his unique authority as spokesman for the Church in Los Angeles? For being on the same side as the archbishop in my interpretation of the Hollywood strike?

Archbishop Cantwell later made an effort to effect a settlement of the strike. As the congressional hearing, which I shall later describe, was drawing to a close in late August 1947, he invited the three disputing parties to meet with his representative, Msgr. Thomas O'Dwyer, on Labor Day. Herb Sorrell and other CSU leaders attended the meeting, as did Roy Brewer for the IATSE; the producers were conspicuous by their absence. When the congressional hearings resumed the next day, Pat Casey dropped the bombshell that Victor Clarke, an agent of the producers, had taken extensive notes of their secret negotiations; the producers' insult to the archbishop, it was speculated, prompted Casey's revelation.

Trip to Washington

All of the unions involved, both those of the IATSE and those of the CSU, belonged to the American Federation of Labor. Every local effort to effect a settlement having been stone-walled, the strike committee of the CSU asked me to undertake a mission to Washington to try to persuade William Green, president of the AFL, to intervene. Herb Sorrell did not favor this strategy. Knowing Bill Green's character, he doubted that he could be persuaded to take any effective action. As usual, however, he accepted the majority opinion of the committee.

With the permission of my provincial, I took the train to Washington, where my meeting with Bill Green confirmed Herb Sorrell's prescience. It was a waste of time. Green proved to be a mean-spirited old man whose whining complaints about all the trouble his unions gave him were more appropriate to a union-busting industrial mogul than to the head of the American Federation of Labor. He could not be persuaded to arbitrate the issues which had split the Hollywood AFL unions into two warring camps.

Word reached me in Washington that the House Committee on Labor and Education, which had planned to look into the Hollywood labor situation, now intended to turn the investigation over to the House Un-American Activities Committee. The chairman of the committee was Congressman Fred A. Hartley, of the Taft-Hartley Labor Bill. In an extended and friendly meeting with him and several other members of the committee, I argued that this would be a serious mistake. It would result in nothing but an orgy of red-baiting and witch-hunting. The issue in Hollywood was a labor issue, not communism. If any congressional committee were to investigate, it should be the Labor Committee, not the Un-American Activities Committee. My arguments proved convincing, and they decided to keep the investigation in their own hands.

Congressional Hearing

In August 1947, Congressman Carroll D. Kearns, a member of the House Committee on Education and Labor, arrived in Los Angeles under the committee's mandate to investigate the Hollywood labor conflict. He conducted daily hearings in the Federal Building throughout August and into early September. The chief counsel for the committee was a Mr. Irving G. McCann, who handled the questioning of witnesses. Also on hand was the chief counsel for the AFL, Mr. Joseph A. Padway, and the lawyers for the IATSE, George Breslin and Michael Luddy.

I was subpoenaed to testify and spent an entire day on the witness stand. Cross-examination by Breslin and Luddy, IATSE counsel, was a cumbersome process since the rules of procedure obliged them to submit their questions in writing through McCann. I caused some embarrassment to Michael Luddy when I revealed that he had attempted to pressure my religious superior into forbidding me to continue my efforts to bring about a settlement of the strike. The revelation, which formed part of the story carried in the evening newspaper of the day, was probably equally embarrassing to Father Whelan.

That evening in the Jesuits' recreation room at Loyola University I listened to the radio newscast, which carried a recording of perhaps fifteen minutes of my testimony. In conclusion it carried a statement made by Congressman Kearns thanking me for my testimony and praising its balance and objectivity. Listening with me was Fr. Joseph O'Brien, professor of canon law at the Jesuit theologate in Alma, California, who was visiting in the house. After the program he remarked that he was pleased that he had chanced to hear it because, having heard rumors and reports about my activities in connection with the Hollywood strike, he had had some misgivings. Now, having listened to my own account and to Congressman Kearns's note of appreciation, his mind was at ease. This minor incident is interesting in light of my later relations with Father O'Brien, which I shall describe further on.

Removal from Los Angeles

Shortly after this, Fr. Joseph King, the provincial, came to Loyola for his annual visitation. I had the most agreeable meeting with him since the St. Louis episode over two years earlier. He had no fault to find, and when I asked him directly if he had any criticisms or complaints he replied in the negative. He told me that he had an appointment to see Bishop McGucken and so I bowed myself out with the satisfied feeling that I had been restored to the good graces of superiors.

The bubble was soon to burst. Before the week was out I was notified of my expulsion from Los Angeles. The notification was as unexpected and as brutal as my summary expulsion from St.

Louis. It came in the form of a brief letter from King's secretary, Fr. Leo Simpson, which was at once brutal, pious and funny. Dated August 31, 1947, it reads:

> Dear Father Dunne, P.C. [Pax Christi],
> The Provincial is at Santa Clara making his retreat. He called me last night and told me to write to you and tell you that he spoke with Fr. William Finnegan of Los Gatos. Father Finnegan will gladly take you at Los Gatos. The Provincial wishes you to go to Los Gatos to work on your thesis and get it done. He directs you to go there right away.
>   This is going to be a test of your obedience, I think. But I am sure that after all these years in Religion, you see the need we have of bowing to the will of God, as made known to us by our Superiors. We will never have God's blessing on us, nor be at peace, until we bring ourselves to make our surrender.

Bill Finnegan, rector of the novitiate at Los Gatos, was a one-time classmate of mine. I had not been aware, though, of any need to find someone who would take me, gladly or not. I had even been assured, just a few days earlier, that I had a clean slate with the provincial. So these orders came as a bolt from the blue.

The shock was so great that I did not notice at the time, but only now upon rereading the letter over forty years later, how funny it is. The funniness is in the sentence, "The Provincial wishes you to go to Los Gatos to work on your thesis and get it done." This was August 1947. I had got my thesis done in January 1944, defended it in February or March, and was awarded my doctorate in the spring of the same year. Evidently the channel through which the will of God was made known to me was malfunctioning.

What had happened was that Bishop McGucken, yielding to pressure from the producers and from the "prominent Catholic layman" George Breslin, had asked King to remove me from the archdiocese. King had not defended my cause four years earlier in the face of Zach Maher's condemnation of my retreat at Alma or, for that matter, in the St. Louis affair. He did not defend me now.

Two years later I was playing golf one day at the Phoenix Country Club in Arizona with Fr. Bill Hanley, one of God's noblemen. After holing out on the eighth hole, I noticed Eddie Mannix, the general manager of MGM, and Clark Gable coming down the eighth fairway behind us. I asked Bill to wait a minute. Mannix and Gable, after holing out, headed for the ninth tee.

Mannix, walking with head down, almost collided with me as I awaited him on the pathway. Looking up he asked with surprise, "What are you doing here?"

"Thanks to you," I replied, "I am living here in Phoenix."

Mannix laughed. "Well," he said, "You were getting in our way in Hollywood. We had to get you out of there." Unneeded confirmation of the role of the producers in my abrupt departure!

They may have been aided in their effort to enlist Bishop McGucken's assistance by a particularly nasty attack upon me by the syndicated columnist Victor Riesel which appeared in the *Los Angeles Times*. It appeared the morning of the day I was to take the stand at Congressman Kearns's hearings, timed perfectly to discredit my testimony by questioning my credibility as a witness.

Riesel's weapon was a familiar one during the McCarthy era, and one not unfamiliar today—the specter of communism. Riesel compared me unfavorably to several other Catholic priests active in labor relations. Unlike them, he said, I habitually consorted with Communists. As a conspicuous example he cited my appearance at a CSU strike meeting on the same platform with Vincent Toledano, whom he described as a notorious Mexican Communist labor leader.

Toledano, head of the largest Mexican labor organization, was the Mexican counterpart of Bill Green, head of the American Federation of Labor. Unlike Bill Green, he was admittedly left-wing in his politics. It was also bruited about that he was a Communist, though this allegation had never been proved. Toledano was also the official Mexican labor delegate to the International Labor Office (ILO), headquartered in Geneva.

The ILO, originally an agency of the League of Nations, was now an agency of the United Nations. Each member country was represented by a three-member delegation representing industry, labor, and government. Toledano had come to Los Angeles to participate in an ILO conference of the delegations from all oil-producing countries.

The Los Angeles Chamber of Commerce honored the delegation with an elaborate luncheon at the Biltmore Hotel attended by four or five hundred prominent Angelenos, among whom I had been included. Several dozen or more leaders of the industrial and business community shared the speaker's table and platform with Vincent Toledano. A day or two later I received a phone call from a member of the CSU staff, who told me that Toledano had agreed to appear at the strike meeting the following Sunday; he thought

I should be informed in case I would not care to appear on the same platform. I thanked him for his courtesy and said that I would think about it.

There was in fact little to think about. I did not know whether or not Toledano was a Communist, but it made no difference if he was. I had been appearing regularly at CSU meetings, and my appearance the following Sunday night could not possibly be regarded as an endorsement of Toledano or of his political views. On the other hand, to absent myself because of his presence could raise serious doubts about the sincerity and depth of my commitment to the justice of the CSU cause. It would be sheer folly to concede to Toledano the power to determine what sort of posture I should adopt and what kind of image I should project. To abandon every cause which is "tainted" by Communist support is to yield the entire field of social justice to the Communists and confirm the widely held view of the Church as an ally of the forces of reaction. I should add that Bishop McGucken was fully aware of my views on this subject, for I had written him a lengthy exposition of the same.

The following Sunday night I appeared at the American Legion Stadium as usual. In a brief speech, Toledano assured the CSU of the moral support of Mexican labor, following which I made my customary pitch in support of the justice of their cause. This is the incident seized upon by Victor Riesel and blown up into an utterly false picture of my alleged consorting with Communists.

I found it particularly repellent that Riesel would draw a picture of me that he knew was false. We had had a lengthy exchange of views about the Hollywood situation, and he knew exactly my position and the nature of my activities. While I was stopping over in New York after my Washington meeting, mentioned above, Fr. Ben Masse, the labor editor of *America* magazine, remarked to me that the *New York Post* columnist Victor Riesel did not agree with me. I was aware of the fact and said that I would gladly meet with Riesel to discuss the matter.

Riesel and I met the following morning at breakfast in the Biltmore Hotel. It quickly became apparent why Riesel differed with me. The source of all his information was Judge Matthew Levy, chief counsel of the IATSE.

Prior to becoming a judge, Matthew Levy had been a lawyer for Local 306 in New York. This was the local controlled by the notorious "Lucky" Luciano. Testifying at the Nitti tax hearings and describing a mobster meeting in Riverside, Illinois, Willie Bioff had said, "Nitti instructed Buchalter to contact Luciano when he got to New York, and convey his message to him, for Luciano to see to it that Local 306 of New York was carried for Browne."

Note that the Buchalter mentioned was the head of Murder, Inc. Note too that Judge Levy appeared before the delegates at the 1940 convention of the IATSE to add his meed of praise to the tributes to George Browne: "I appreciate with you, the modesty, earnestness, effectiveness, and devotion to the cause of the Alliance which characterize your International President George E. Browne. The growth of this Alliance is a living monument to the leadership of modest, earnest, effective, devoted George E. Browne." Unfortunately for Levy's credibility as a witness, Browne's subsequent full confession at the Nitti tax hearings revealed the full facts about the unspeakably corrupt "leadership of modest, earnest, effective, devoted George E. Browne."[13]

Riesel's view of the Hollywood labor situation was based entirely upon what he had been told by Levy. When he and I parted after two hours of friendly enough conversation, I did not presume to have won him over; but I thought, upon the perhaps naive assumption that he was an honest reporter, that I had given him more than enough reasons to reexamine his point of view. So the appearance of his vicious column, heavily loaded with insinuations and innuendos, seemed to me a particularly nasty blow below the belt.

That it was an effective bit of calumny was evidenced by the many letters I received from old friends, including Jesuits, from all parts of the country expressing surprise and concern that I had strayed from the straight and narrow. To what extent it contributed to Bishop McGucken's decision to have me removed from the archdiocese I do not know. I am sure, however, that it was called to his attention by those who, like Eddie Mannix, were determined to get me out of Los Angeles.

The prospect of living in the novitiate was less than exciting. When I had been a novice, our novice master, Fr. Tom Meagher, had told us that in case a priest were to take up residence at the novitiate without any apparent assignment we should pray for him because he probably was on his way out of the Society either by way of dismissal or by way of request. I wrote to King, mentioning this and remarking that every time I passed a novice I would be conscious that he was saying Hail Marys for my soul. While I should no doubt be grateful, I would in fact find this embarrassing. I therefore asked his permission to take up residence instead at Phelan Park, which served as the province summer camp.

Permission being granted, I moved in with three other inmates of what we called our DP camp. They proved congenial companions. One was Cy Kavanagh, a philosophy professor and congenital gadfly, in the face of whose caustic wit the average superior was defenseless. Another was Armand Robidoux, who claimed to be the only Jesuit in the California Province who could prove that he was sane—in virtue of a certificate of discharge which he held from Agnew's State Mental Hospital. The third was amiable Art Falvey, who was not really an inmate of the camp but was in dire need of a rest from his heroic and almost solitary efforts to inculcate a social conscience into his high school students; he had been relieved of his teaching responsibilities and sent to take charge of Phelan Park.

Had the thought occurred to me to appeal my order of dismissal from Los Angeles, I would have dismissed it as an exercise in futility. Though Simpson's brief letter had not mentioned it, I learned that King had acted in response to a request from Bishop McGucken that I be moved out of the archdiocese. However, shortly after my arrival at Phelan Park I received a letter from the superior general in Rome, Fr. John Baptist Janssens, which said that he had received so many letters from Jesuits in Los Angeles protesting my removal that he had concluded that my transfer was not a routine change of status. He therefore ordered me to send him a complete account of the affair.

Among those who had protested to Rome were Clinton Albertson, Charles Cooney, and Daniel McGloin, all Jesuit contemporaries of mine. I was aware of this because they had informed me of their demarche; who the others were, I do not know. Among the documents sent me a few months ago by John McGloin, S.J., was a copy of the letter his brother Dan sent to Father Janssens. Dated September 17, 1947, it was an eloquent protest several pages in length, from which I briefly quote:

> The students of the University who have come to be very enthusiastic about him will see in his absence from the faculty not only a great loss to Loyola University, but they will suspect and resent the cause of his removal. And the thousands of little people, the "poor of Christ" whose lives Father Dunne has brightened with hope and gladdened with assurance of Christ's love for them, will be saddened.

Noting that "many other Jesuits of this Province" shared his concern, Dan asked the superior general to investigate.

Dan's letter was an eloquent testimony to his friendship and generosity. Together with that of others it effectively moved the superior general to make an inquiry. In response to his orders I wrote a detailed account of the events which had transformed my image in the eyes of superiors from that of a highly regarded and promising young man into that of a suspect troublemaker. The account, which ran to forty or more pages, was accompanied by an almost equally copious dossier of supportive documentation, consisting of correspondence, articles, and clippings. I doubt that the general read it. Far more important things had prior claim upon his time.

One might suppose that, in the ordinary course of administrative events, he would have delegated his American assistant to read and evaluate my report. Perhaps he did, though several years later when I met the assistant, Fr. Vincent McCormick, in Phoenix, where I was then stationed, it quickly became evident that he had never read either the letter or its documentation. It also became evident on that occasion that, without having met me or heard from me, he had diagnosed what was wrong with me. He did not tell me, but he confided to Jim Deasy, my immediate superior at the time, that I was suffering from something called "intellectual pride." Some years later Jim passed the word on to me.

Ten

Hibernation

P helan Park was the property of Noel Sullivan, a nephew
and heir of James Phelan, onetime mayor of San Francisco and United States senator from California. A talented
musician, he also was a patron of the arts and a personal friend
of the leading black artists of the country, who were often his
guests in his Carmel Valley home. A devout Catholic, he had built
for the Carmelite nuns a beautiful convent on the shores of Monterey Bay. A friend of the Jesuits, he had offered them the use of
the twenty or more partially wooded acres of Phelan Park as a
summer vacation spot. This beautifully located property looked
out from the oceanfront bluffs a mile or two north of Santa Cruz
at an abandoned lighthouse across the road and upon the
sparkling waters of the bay beyond.

Despite its beauty, the Jesuit scholastics did not particularly
appreciate Phelan Park as a vacation spot. This was because the
several weeks they spent there each summer coincided with the
foggy season, and the tents which housed them provided no
protection against the heavy coastal fogs that moved in every night
leaving them thoroughly drenched by morning. My months there
were, on the contrary, free of fog, and I was able thoroughly to
appreciate the beauty of the place, the sun-drenched days and
star-filled nights. I enjoyed long walks along the beach accompanied by the three dogs, of varied breed, who were our companions
and in whom, in light of recent experiences, I was inclined to see
my best friends. At night I enjoyed the crashing of waves on the
shore below and the mournful barking of seals, who at any hour
day or night lolled about a huge rock which thrust itself up from
the sea a few yards off shore. For some reason their mournful

intonation evoked in me the same feeling of nostalgic loneliness that a distant train whistle calling through the night had evoked in me as a child.

In a word, I enjoyed my stay at Phelan Park and felt that I would be content to spend the rest of my life there. I was not isolated. There was companionship and repartee at mealtimes with my fellow "displaced persons." And every Thursday, a group of young Jesuits came down from Alma College, our theology school some twenty miles to the north, to enjoy their weekly holiday at Phelan Park. Noel Sullivan, who became a warm and cherished friend, often drove up from Carmel.

Once and often twice a week, Fr. Joe O'Brien drove down from Alma for a visit. Out of many hours of conversation developed what I thought was a warm friendship. On the day he was named rector of the Alma community he made a special trip because he wanted me "to be the first to have the news." That marked the high point of our friendship, and in retrospect I would have to say the end point as well. After a brief stint as rector he became provincial, and during his six years of office I was separated from him by a wall of ice. His attitude towards me did a 180-degree turn. What seemed and still seems strange was the sudden shift from warmth to deep cold without explanation. I was unaware of what had provoked this change. When Zacheus J. Maher had abruptly ended a friendship of many years' standing, I knew upon what shoals my ship had foundered. In the case of Joe O'Brien, I did not have a clue. I probably should have asked him, but for some reason I did not have the heart for it.

This unpleasant development lay in the future. For the present I was enjoying the peaceful life of Phelan Park, where I sometimes mused over the unexpected turns my life had taken since I had watched from the deck of the *Chichibu Maru* the lights of Shanghai recede in the distance. Contrary to what the title of this chapter suggests, it was not in truth a hibernation. During my months there I accomplished a fair amount of writing. I also made several sorties.

The first of these was a brief return to Los Angeles to attend a dinner organized by the Southland Jewish Organization to honor me for my contributions to racial and religious understanding; I mentioned it above. The actor Howard da Silva, he who had informed me of John Farrow's assurance that I would soon be shipped back to China, was a gracious toastmaster. My mother and sister, who were guests, were touched by the display of friendship and esteem. I was deeply moved.

Brief Encounter

My second sortie from Phelan Park took me to New York for the opening of my play, *Trial by Fire*, at the Blackfriars Theatre. It also led to my first encounter with the far-reaching power of Abp. James McIntyre, at the time chancellor of the New York archdiocese and destined to become the cardinal archbishop of Los Angeles.

Shortly before this, my friend Dan Marshall had written a letter on his legal stationery to the *New York Post* calling attention to the libelous character of Victor Riesel's column that I mentioned above and demanding a retraction. Not by calculation but by sheer coincidence, the letter and I arrived in New York at about the same time. I was given a quick look behind the scenes at how power brokers of the ecclesiastical and business worlds operate in the Big Apple.

I was staying, as I usually did when visiting New York, at *America* House. When I arose the morning after my arrival I found a message directing me to phone Fr. Francis McQuade, the New York provincial. It was marked urgent. A manifestly distraught McQuade answered my call. The chain of events was clear. The *New York Post* had wasted no time. Upon receiving Dan Marshall's letter they had immediately communicated with the archbishop, requesting that he call me off. McIntyre had in turn called McQuade and ordered him to muzzle me. McQuade, fearful of archiepiscopal wrath, ordered me to notify the Post that I was withdrawing the request for a retraction. All of this had been accomplished within twenty-four hours of my arrival.

"You have no idea of all the trouble I have with a certain place," said McQuade with quavering voice, "caused by Jesuits from other provinces who have no understanding of the special situation in New York." The certain place was, of course, the chancery office, and it is starkly revealing of the miasma of fear distilled by McIntyre that McQuade was evidently reluctant even to utter his name over the phone. Hence he became a "certain place."

I called McQuade's attention to the fact that Riesel's column had inflicted serious damage to my reputation and suggested that, as a fellow Jesuit, he should be concerned about that. He said that he would take care of my reputation by posting a corrective notice on the bulletin boards of Jesuit houses in New York. This was, of course, a puerile idea that would have meant nothing even had he implemented it, which he did not. Readers of Riesel's column did not read Jesuit bulletin boards.

Actually I had no intention of suing the *New York Post* for libel. Dan and I both hoped that the threat of such an action, implied but not expressed in his letter, would elicit the retraction demanded. McIntyre's swift intervention freed the management of the Post from threat and took care of any retraction.

A week or so later I had a rather poignant experience which did nothing to improve my opinion of Archbishop McIntyre. Fr. George Ford, pastor of Corpus Christi Church, the parish church of Columbia University, was one of the more prominent and respected Catholic priests in the metropolitan area. It was to him that Thomas Merton had first come for direction when he found himself being drawn towards the Catholic faith. His friends and admirers extended far beyond the Catholic Church itself and included a wide range of clergy and laity of all faiths. It was this ecumenical aspect of his life that annoyed McIntyre. Ford found himself constantly harried and harassed for participating in meetings with Protestant and Jewish clergy. Finally, during a temporary absence of Cardinal Spellman from the archdiocese, McIntyre carried persecution to its extreme by removing Father Ford from his position as pastor of Corpus Christi. Fortunately, upon his return Cardinal Spellman restored Ford to his post.

I had met Father Ford through a mutual friend, Bernice Fitz-Gibbon, ranked by *Fortune* magazine as one of the outstanding professional women of the country. As advertising manager of Macy's she had coined the famous slogan "It's Smart To Be Thrifty" and as manager at Gimbel's, which she was when we became friends, the equally famed slogan "Nobody But Nobody Undersells Gimbel's."

Father Ford asked me to have lunch with him. We met, as I recall, at the Astor Hotel, in a dining room crowded with prominent New Yorkers. And he recounted to me, in tears, the bitter story of his harassment by the chancellor of the diocese. The spectacle of this distinguished and beloved priest of mature years weeping at the recollection of all that he had suffered at the hands of Archbishop McIntyre was profoundly moving. One can easily understand why, when McIntyre was named archbishop of Los Angeles in 1948, the New York clergy dubbed the train which carried him westward away from New York, the "Freedom Train."

Blackfriars Theatre

Blackfriars Theatre on West 57th Street was the creation of two Dominican priests, Urban Nagle and Tom Carey, both long associated with the effort to develop a national Catholic theater movement. Since its opening in October 1941 it had established a solid reputation. It usually scheduled four productions a year. *Trial by Fire* was its second production of the 1947–48 season, opening shortly after Christmas. It was not directed by Dennis Gurney, the regular director, but at his own request by Albert McCleery, the head of Fordham University's drama department and future director of NBC's "Theatre of the Air."

I arrived in New York for the dress rehearsal and found that with opening-night only twenty-four hours away a crisis had developed. The previous day McCleery had replaced the actor who played the important part of the district attorney with an actor in whose talents he had more confidence. To me this seemed highly risky, but McCleery was not overly concerned. He told me that the actor in question was a quick reader and had spent the entire night learning his lines and the stage business; McCleery was confident that he would measure up. Nevertheless, I awaited the curtain rise that night with trepidation. I feared it was too much to ask that anyone learn one's lines on twenty-four hours' notice and join a cast that had been in rehearsal for several weeks.

My fears proved unfounded. Faced with such emergencies actors of proven ability rise to the challenge. This is a tradition in the theater. The replacement, whose name I no longer recall, did a creditable job. The few rough spots which appeared at the dress rehearsal were ironed out before the opening-night performance, which went off brilliantly.

Following the time-honored ritual in the world of theater, I repaired after the performance with Fathers Nagle and Carey and with McCleery and most of the cast to a neighboring restaurant on Columbus Circle where, over sandwiches and coffee, we awaited the first edition of the morning papers. With their arrival nervous tension evanesced and the coffee klatch became a joyous celebration. Without exception the reviews were highly favorable. The only disappointment was that some of the critics, including Brooks Atkinson of the New York Times, had not covered *Trial by Fire*. Their absence on opening-night was not, however, unexpected. Urban Nagle was a man of many gifts, but diplomacy was not one of them. His freely expressed opinion of critics who had given a low rating to one or another of his productions had not endeared him to them. In retaliation some of them were boycotting the Blackfriars Theatre.

Father Nagle has written with wit and charm the history of Blackfriars Theatre and of its productions.[1] I quote here some of what he says of *Trial by Fire*:

> The second production of the season—and our twenty-fifth in New York—was a biting "documentary" about race prejudice. Fr. George H. Dunne, S.J., champion of democratic civil rights and an enemy of the "sin of segregation," was justifiably incensed at the murder of a Negro family who had dared build a home in a part of rural California where the best people still worship the whiteness of their skins. He protested in magazine articles and lectures—not that the dead be brought back to life—but that the land of freedom would not insist that this murder was an accident, because he hoped that others with illusions might have grounds for hope. The articles did little more than most articles do, so he wrote a kind of play—more like the living newspaper—with emotional overtones and called it *Trial by Fire*. . .
>
> This play had been done first in Los Angeles, and, although it received an enthusiastic press, we weren't so sure that it would fare so well in New York where the original story received little notice. But we were gratified by a large and warmly applauding group of reviewers. It was a novel presentation and had a good cast and the newspapers unanimously acknowledged the fact. Albert McCleery, Fordham's director, came down to do the staging and got acclamation from all. . .
>
> In spite of this extremely gratifying press, audiences weren't as large as for many plays which fared badly with the reviewers. Perhaps some of this falling off was due to the fact that our opening followed closely upon the Christmas season. . .I think the answer to the question which suggests itself is that it wasn't particularly good entertainment. It was rather the cause of an examination of conscience—a soul-searing experience. People want to be entertained and not jolted to the core of their being. They don't want to stir up sleeping fears and, in this case, the fear at the heart of almost everyone is that he has been at fault.

Father Nagle's analysis is undoubtedly correct. Max Gordon, one of the leading producers in New York, came twice to see *Trial by Fire* and took Mr. McCleery out to dinner to discuss moving the play to Broadway. He wished to do so, but had doubts about whether it would succeed commercially. In the end he decided it was too risky. No doubt he was right. *Trial by Fire* was meant not to entertain but to do violence to one's smug complacency about self and about society. It was, as Nagle says, "a soul-searing experience"; or, as the *Catholic Worker* put it, "This is not a play; it is a nightmare." This was half right. It was a play. But it was also a nightmare. I have seen it dozens of times in different productions—in Los Angeles, New York, Chicago, Phoenix, Pasadena, Hollywood—and I have never seen it without tears. It was not designed for the commercial theater. It was not made to make money—I always refused to accept royalties for it. It was made to change hearts.

It was the custom at Blackfriars to have a cast party following the curtain fall on closing night. Gathered on stage the members of the cast entertained each other with songs, dances, or whatever the spirit prompted. A young woman who had been in charge of the lighting contributed her bit. With tears in her voice she said that she did not want to sing or dance but simply to say a few words. She explained that she was from Georgia, where she had been raised with all of the prejudices that this play was about. When she had learned, after accepting the job of running the light-effects board, that there were black people in the cast, her impulse, conditioned by a lifetime of prejudice, had been to quit. But she had been so anxious for the backstage experience that she stayed on. *Trial by Fire* had made her realize for the first time in her life the vicious nature of racial bigotry. She promised us that never again would she consciously yield to it.

While in New York I called, as was my habit, upon Ed Skillin and the editorial staff of *Commonweal*. Paul Blanshard had recently published a series of three articles in the Nation. This was the beginning of many articles and books which would win him fame akin to that of Robert Ingersoll as the leading American critic of the Catholic Church. I asked Ed Skillin and his associates if they thought I might attempt to reply. Because there was an element of truth in most of Blanshard's charges, they were skeptical about the possibility of writing an effective response. It is not easy to separate wheat from chaff.

Despite this appraisal, upon my return to Phelan Park I undertook to write a reply. Upon its completion I sent it to Joe O'Brien at Alma College for censorship. Without undue delay he returned it, noting that he had transmitted it to the provincial, who had approved its publication. I was annoyed by this, annoyed that O'Brien had on his own initiative placed in jeopardy the special arrangement under which I had been successfully publishing. I had asked him to read it, not to turn it over to the provincial. I did not want anything that might lead to the provincial's revoking the permission he had given me to select my own censors. As it turned out, it was O'Brien himself who several years later, as provincial, ended my privileged arrangement by ordering me to submit to him any articles I might write.

Who Is My Neighbor?

I shall abandon chronology for the moment to describe how this change came about. Living in Phoenix at the time, I was alerted by Los Angeles friends to an especially revolting incident of racial bigotry which had occurred in a neighborhood I knew well. It was an upper-middle-class area of comfortable homes and well-tended lawns and tree-shaded streets. A considerable number of its residents were professional people. They were also exclusively white, until one day a black family moved in, adding a bit of color to the scene. The man of the family was, like many of his neighbors, a successful attorney. His wife was well educated and attractive. Their children were well mannered. But tocsins were sounded. Ugly threats were made. People gathered to form what with incredible irony they called the Good Neighbors Protective Association. The purpose of the Good Neighbors was to drive the new neighbors out of the neighborhood.

One morning the woman of the house, answering the doorbell, found on the doorstep what looked like a neatly wrapped box of candy. She brought the box in, untied the ribbons, removed the wrapper, and opened the box to find within a dead rat!

Shortly after this the family went away for the weekend. They returned on Sunday evening to discover that another of their neighbors had inserted the garden hose through the mail drop in their front door, turned the water on, and left it running during the two nights and two days of their absence. The rugs were ruined, the hardwood floors irreparably damaged.

Not all the neighbors were villains; not all had joined the Good Neighbors Protective Association. One who had not joined decided to launch a countermove. She invited the neighbors to a tea party in her home, honoring and welcoming the new family into the neighborhood. Among those she invited was the pastor of the Catholic parish church, since she thought that his example would carry some weight at least with the neighbors who belonged to Transfiguration Parish. It did, but not as she had hoped. The pastor curtly rejected the invitation, choosing to play the role of the priest in the Gospel parable about the Good Samaritan who had passed by the bruised and beaten victim without so much as a glance of pity.

I wrote this story with a minimum of commentary, letting the brutal facts speak for themselves. *Commonweal* published it under the title "And Who Is My Neighbor?" Two enraged members of the parish who had sons enrolled at Loyola High School telephoned Frank Harrington, S.J., the superior of the school, and, citing my article, told him that if that was the sort of stuff taught by Loyola they would remove their sons forthwith from the school and Jesuit influence. Harrington tranquilized them, probably assuring them that the views expressed in the article represented only my thinking, not that of the Jesuits. I hate to think that he was possibly right.

Harrington then brought the matter to the attention of the provincial, Joe O'Brien, complaining that my published views posed a threat to our schools. O'Brien took prompt action. I received a note sternly ordering me in the future to submit to him anything I might write for publication. This, of course, put a heavy restraint upon any inclination I had to write. I still had access to *America*, which as a Jesuit publication had the privilege of itself censoring any article it chose to publish. But I had developed a special bond with *Commonweal*, and to sever it was painful.

My friendship with Father Harrington was unaffected by this incident. Neither of us ever referred to it. His problem was one which often confronts those heading a Catholic institution which depends to a large extent upon maintaining good public relations with the Catholic public. In such a position it is easy to forget that the first priority is to maintain the Gospel values and that the teaching of "the sort of stuff" found in my article—the same sort of stuff taught by the parable of the Good Samaritan—is indeed the sole excuse for the existence of any Jesuit school. I regret this confusion of priorities but understand the pressures which are responsible.

Phyllis Sits Tight

While still at Phelan Park I wrote another play, which I entitled
Phyllis Sits Tight. Like *Trial by Fire*, it was an interracial play and
also a documentary. Unlike the other, it was not a tragedy, but a
farce in three acts. I had heard of the incident upon which it was
based in the home of the former singer-actress-congresswoman
Helen Gahagan Douglas. Mrs. Douglas was a friend of mine.
Earlier, on a visit to Washington, I had lunched with her in the
congressional dining room, after which she had accompanied me
to the visitors' galleries in both the Senate and the House, where
like a visitor to the zoo I watched the antics of Senator Bilbo and
Congressman Rankin, both notorious racists from the South.

On this occasion Mrs. Douglas had invited me to her home in
Hollywood, where she lived with her husband, actor Melvyn
Douglas. There I was to meet a Southern woman of a distinguished
family, who, contrary to what one would expect in the South of that
time, was an active leader in the antisegregationist Southern
Conference on Human Welfare. Despite her prominence, her
name after all these years has faded into the mists of memory. In
any event, as we awaited the arrival of other guests, she narrated
an incident that had occurred in Atlanta.

It involved the recently established Fair Employment Practices Commission. A young staff member was sent to Atlanta to
open a regional office. Among others he hired as a secretary a
young black woman who was attractive, intelligent, and educated.
No one objected to his hiring her, but when she ventured to visit
the For Whites Only women's restroom, the only restroom for
women in the building, all hell broke loose. The young FEPC man
from Washington found himself beleaguered by protest commit-
tees representing women employed in other offices in the building,
by the Daughters of the Confederacy, and by the Chamber of
Commerce. Fed by inflammatory editorials in the local press the
storm developed into a major crisis. Before the potentially explosive situation was defused, it had involved the intervention of
Eleanor Roosevelt and through her of President Roosevelt himself.
At the conclusion of the narrative I remarked, "That has the makings of a very funny play."

At Phelan Park, with time on my hands, with additions and
interventions of my own, I built on the basis of these facts what I

think was a very amusing farce in three acts and five scenes. Because the humor was a bit on the scatological side I never tried to have it produced. I did, on a number of occasions, read it with friends who found it quite amusing. The nearest I came to staging it was with one of the nine Peace Corps training programs I directed at Georgetown University in the early 1960s. In one of the programs was a young married couple, both of whom had degrees in drama, one from Carnegie Tech and the other from the Royal Academy in London. They put together a cast, gathered the props, and directed a walk-through version of the play, each cast member with script in hand. The audience, chiefly other trainees and staff members, thought it hilarious. If they did not roll in the aisles, they rocked the small theater with laughter.

I have sometimes regretted that despite the slightly scatological nature of some of the lines I never attempted to produce it. *Trial by Fire*, by revealing the tragic consequences of segregationist attitudes, was an effective instrument of consciousness raising. *Phyllis Sits Tight*, by pillorying the ridiculous aspects of segregation and laughing it out of court, might have proved no less effective.

Saint Jan

A surprising telephone call from Chicago signaled the end of the pleasant interlude at Phelan Park. The call came from an actress, Jan Sterling, who was starring in a play called *John Loves Mary*. She was in the early stages of a career which would later flower into stardom in motion pictures and in television and in marriage to the actor Paul Douglas. She wanted me to come to Chicago at her expense.

The circumstances were these. *Trial by Fire* had been produced in the spring of 1948 at the Sheil Social Center on Chicago's South Side. Miss Sterling had seen it and had been deeply moved. Somehow she heard of the Summer School of Catholic Action, which met every summer in a different major city. For two weeks hundreds of high school and college students listened to lectures, participated in discussion groups, and debated social subjects. In 1948 it was to meet in Chicago. Miss Sterling contacted Fr. Martin Carrabine, S.J., who was organizing the program, and easily persuaded him to include at her expense *Trial by Fire*. She then managed to locate me and called to insist that I be on hand after each performance to give a talk and conduct a discussion on the evil of segregation. With the provincial's permission, I did so. The results, I think, fully justified Jan Sterling's faith in the educational value of the play.

I do not know whether Jan Sterling was a Catholic. I did not ask her. Unlike the priest at Transfiguration Parish and some of his parishioners, she knew who her neighbor was. If I were in charge of the process of canonization, I would declare her a saint.

We decided to do a special performance of the play for public and private school teachers. *John Loves Mary* was finishing its Chicago run and moving on to another city. This meant that Jan Sterling would be lost to us. At this point Bp. Bernard J. Sheil filled the breach. With his financial support we rented the Wabash Theatre in the Loop, made changes in two supporting roles, and, after two weeks of rehearsals, gave a Saturday afternoon performance to a standing-room-only audience of school teachers and principals. Before curtain rise Bishop Sheil appeared on stage and announced our readiness to present the play for any organization for expenses only, the sponsoring group being allowed to keep the profits. On this basis *Trial by Fire* played two or three times a week for more than a year in Chicago and its environs.

I stayed on to see this project well launched on its way. The first to take advantage of the offer was Mundelein College, a women's college contiguous to Loyola University on the North Side. On the first night an incident occurred which illustrated poignantly how varied are the ways in which racial discrimination wounds the human spirit. Shortly before curtain rise one of the cast, a young man, asked me if he had time to run down to the corner for a sandwich. He had come straight from work and had not had time to grab a bite. I did not think of it again until, following the performance, I was going with some of the cast for coffee and a late snack. I asked him if he had got his sandwich. When he replied in the negative I immediately bristled and proposed repeating what I had done on the occasion of the Pasadena Playhouse.[2] But he said, no, he had not been refused service. Instead, when he arrived at the drugstore lunch counter, his courage had failed him. He did not enter.

"Perhaps I would have been served," he said, "but, Father, when all of your life you have never known when entering a place whether you would be served or refused service, a time comes

when you cannot again face even the possibility of being humili-
ated because you are black. That time came for me tonight. I could
not risk it."

I thought, with sorrow and with anger, of the innumerable and
grievous wounds inflicted daily upon sensitive souls by the cruel
contempt of racial segregation.

The Glacier Priest

One afternoon during my extended stay in Chicago, while visiting
the Sheil Social Center on the South Side, I had a surprising phone
call. It was from Fr. Bernie Hubbard, S.J., the noted "Glacier
Priest." He was calling from California. How he managed to track
me down to the Sheil Social Center I cannot imagine. I was staying
at the Morrison Hotel, but I had not left word there as to my
whereabouts. But Bernie Hubbard had ways of getting what he
wanted.

Bernie Hubbard's fame rested chiefly upon his filmed explorations of Alaskan glaciers, but he had expanded the horizons of
his interest and had made interesting films of his travels in several
other countries. He wished to add a sound track to these films and,
while I was still at Phelan Park, asked me to write the commentary.
As an inducement he promised to give me a recording machine and
several other things, a new typewriter among them, if I recall.

As many Alaskan missionaries could testify, Bernie Hubbard's
path through Alaska was strewn with unkept promises. It was his
way of getting what he wanted. I was aware of this, and so did not
take his promises seriously. He was a man, nevertheless, of great
charm. I was glad to help him. With borrowed projector and tape
recorder I watched his films and wrote the commentaries and sent
them off. I received no acknowledgment. I knew from Alaskan
missionaries that this was vintage Bernie Hubbard, so I was not
surprised. I had not heard from him again until he ran me down
at the Sheil Social Center. "George, this is Bernie," said the voice
from California. "I called to tell you those commentaries you wrote
were great. I recorded them on a sound track and everybody thinks
they are wonderful."

"Thanks, Bernie," I said, "What is it you want?"

What he wanted was that I write a similar sound track for a
film on Japan which he had just completed. He would airmail the
film to me so that I could get started without delay. The Sheil Social

Center had both a projector and a tape recorder. I love Japan. The film, like all of Bernie Hubbard's films, was well done. I enjoyed doing the commentary, which I completed in a couple of days and airmailed, with the film, back to him. As expected, I did not hear from him again, but assume that it reached him.

Almost ten years later I was convalescing in the Santa Clara University infirmary. I listened with sadness, but with fond memories, to the heavy breathing of Bernie Hubbard, dying in a room across the corridor. He had been a great human being, who could charm blackbirds out of the trees.

Ghostwriter for a Bishop

During these weeks in Chicago I became a ghostwriter for Bishop Sheil, producing several important speeches for him. This was not difficult since we saw eye to eye on most subjects. Bishop Sheil was without a doubt the most progressive member of the American hierarchy. He was a strong supporter of labor. His forthright support of the workers in the packinghouse strike of 1939 had not endeared him to the Armours and Cudahys. His opposition to all forms of racial discrimination was reminiscent of the nineteenth-century leadership of Archbishop Ireland. He gave strong support to the revolutionary social reformer and innovator Saul Alinsky, who had achieved the impossible in creating a viable union out of the multiple ethnic and religious groups that made up the stockyards neighborhoods; Alinsky would later write Sheil's biography. Sheil was best known nationally for his Catholic Youth Organization (CYO), which provided thousands of young people, especially underprivileged, with opportunities to engage in a broad range of sports.

With all this, he was never given his own diocese, but remained until the end an auxiliary bishop in Chicago. The reason was perhaps in part that his social activism made the predominantly conservative strata of the hierarchy nervous. Probably more important, however, was the undeniable fact that, unfortunately, he was a poor administrator. Eventually, the activities of the CYO on a national scale created financial problems which were beyond his means to solve. When I was ghostwriting speeches for him, however, he was still riding the crest of the wave.

One day my sister phoned me from Los Angeles; a Jesuit friend had told her that he had heard a report that the provincial intended to assign me to our parish in Phoenix. I had received no orders to this effect and so ignored it. Perhaps two weeks later I received a discourteous letter from Joe O'Brien, who had replaced King as provincial, angrily demanding to know why I had not reported to Phoenix; he said that the pastor there, Fr. Jim Deasy, was short-handed and impatiently awaiting my long-deferred arrival. I replied that the only indication that I was to go to Phoenix had been an idle rumor handed on to me by my sister. "Since I am not accustomed to accept assignments from my family," I wrote, "I ignored the rumor."

Bishop Sheil telephoned the provincial, informed him that I was engaged in some important speech-writing for him, and asked that my stay be extended two or three weeks. Provincials do not refuse bishops easily, so permission was granted. This allowed me, as I have recounted, to witness the launching of *Trial by Fire* at Mundelein College. Following this, I returned to Phelan Park, where I gathered up my few belongings and headed for Phoenix, and a new stage of my career.

Eleven

Phoenix Years

I was to spend nine years in Phoenix, where, thanks to the generosity of Mrs. Frank Brophy, the Jesuits had had a high school, a residence for the Jesuit faculty, and a beautiful chapel which served as parish church. But in the depression years of the early 1930s, after only a few years of operation, they had been unable to make both ends meet and had evacuated, turning the thirty acres and the buildings over to Bp. Daniel Gercke. At his request, a few of them had remained to direct Saint Francis Xavier Parish. They lived for many years in the garage, converted into a residence of sorts. Shortly before my arrival they had moved into a new rectory. The B.V.M. nuns—Sisters of Charity of the Blessed Virgin Mary—had been brought in by Bishop Gercke to staff a girls' high school and a parochial grammar school; and they occupied the former Jesuit residence.

My transition from a DP camp to what was, in effect, exile in Arizona, a far cry from China, was made easier by the presence of Jim Deasy as pastor. He and I had entered the Jesuits the same year. He had served with distinction as chaplain with the marines during World War II, when he had won fame as one of the subjects of Ripley's *Believe It or Not* cartoons. A Japanese shell burst had buried him alive on the beach of Iwo Jima, but his hand, protruding from the sands, had called attention to his plight and led to his rescue.

Jim Deasy was first-rate both as superior and as pastor. Unlike some, he took no particular relish in exercising authority. He did not demand of others more than he gave himself. As pastor he was much beloved by the parishioners, especially by the children. I can still see him, cassock flying, as he ran across the playground pursued by flocks of laughing, screaming boys and girls. He had, unfortunately, the bad habit of denigrating himself in letters to the provincial, questioning whether he measured up to the requirements of the job. Several times I warned him that one day the provincial would seize upon these totally unwarranted protestations of unfitness as a pretext to replace him with one of his cronies. This, of course, is what happened. Although no announcement was made of his departure, word leaked out, and when Jim arrived at the Phoenix airport hundreds of parishioners were on hand to see him off. It was a singular tribute.

The affectionate esteem in which the people held him contrasted sharply with the provincial's attitude. When Jim arrived in California he learned that Joe O'Brien, in a monumental error of judgment, had assigned him to the novitiate at Los Gatos to serve as spiritual director to the juniors, young Jesuits in the first years after taking their religious vows. It would be impossible to conceive of a more inappropriate assignment. It showed a complete ignorance of, or perhaps indifference to, the man he was dealing with. Jim Deasy, a man of intense nervous energy, needed always to be busily engaged. Sitting quietly in his room in the rustic quiet of Los Gatos, awaiting the occasional visit of a young Jesuit in search of spiritual advice, would have driven him up the wall. He was aware of this, as was anyone who knew him. Quite understandably he balked. O'Brien, typically, washed his hands of him.

In a number of phone calls from Phoenix to men in California in positions of leadership I argued with some vehemence that one did not sit idly by while a man of Deasy's merits and services was lost to the Society. Among his recent services had been persuading Bishop Gercke to give back to the Jesuits, in return for their reopening Brophy Preparatory School, all of the original buildings and half of the acreage which they had abandoned to him. This was no mean feat of diplomacy. Bishops are not naturally inclined to give away valuable properties. A new high school was built for the girls and a convent for the nuns, who turned back to the Jesuits their old residence. Brophy was reopened and today is one of the most flourishing high schools in the state.

Fr. Ed Whelan, a compassionate man, shared my view of the folly of doing nothing. He visited Jim Deasy, who was living at his sister's home in Glendale. Fr. Neil O'Mara, superior of the retreat house in Los Altos, another compassionate man as well as classmate and fellow chaplain during the war, invited Deasy to join his community. I hope he did not think it necessary to consult O'Brien, who, in any case, did not interpose a veto.

The crisis was resolved, and Jim Deasy continued for many years his active life of dedicated ministry in the Society, for the last eight years while fighting with extraordinary courage the ravages of a cancer which has subjected him to several major operations and to the loss of an eye. I list him, along with Pedro Arrupe, former superior general of the Society, and Yves Henry, my rector at Zikawei in China, as one of the truly great men I have known during the sixty-three years I have spent to date in the Society of Jesus.

Another who greatly eased the transition was Fr. Bill Hanley, a friend *sans pareille*, who initiated me into the ineffable delights of golf. I registered 137 strokes for the eighteen holes on my first attempt. But before I left Phoenix nine years later, by dint of dedication and repetitive effort, I had brought my score down to the low 80s, and on one glorious occasion to a 2-over-par 74. Bill and I wore a hole through a carpet in the living room of the rectory practicing our golf swing during evening recreation. Thanks to his coaching I became a real fan. The first time I broke 85, I sent Bill a telegram to announce the event. This was in the mid 1950s, and by then he had, to my great regret, been recalled to California.

Frank Cullen Brophy

I made many precious friends during my Phoenix years. Perhaps the most difficult to account for was my friendship with Frank Cullen Brophy, for apart from religion there were few things we agreed on. Frank was a grand-nephew of Card. Paul Cullen of Dublin, who had played an important role in organizing support for the definition of papal infallibility at Vatican Council I. It was Frank's mother who had brought the Jesuits to Phoenix and presented them with both land and buildings for Brophy Prep. His father had been a pioneer tradesman and cattle rancher in Arizona. Frank, a Yale graduate, was president of the Bank of Douglas (later the Arizona Bank) and, when I knew him, of the Arizona Bankers' Association. He was quite conservative politically, becoming in the years that followed my departure from Phoenix, through his friendship with Robert Welch, a member of the National Council of the John Birch Society. Obviously we did not see eye to eye. Yet we always remained warm friends.

Frank wrote a good deal, and he wrote well. Everything he wrote he sent to me for my appraisal. Invariably I praised the literary style and took issue with the content. And invariably he solicited my opinion of his next production.

One year the American Bankers' Association held its annual convention in Los Angeles; and immediately following, the Arizona bankers sponsored a two-day symposium of their own. Frank Brophy asked me to be one of the speakers. My paper was a straight-from-the-shoulder lecture to the bankers on their obligation, as members of the privileged class, to pay for their privileges by contributing generously to the common good. Frank was delighted. Nor did the bankers seem to take offense, for they published this rather hard-hitting talk in its entirety in the daily newspaper of the American Bankers' Association, published in New York.

This led to an invitation the following year to address the national convention in Des Moines, Iowa. When I arrived at the hotel where the convention was being held, I found a picket line in place. The hotel employees were on strike. As a matter of principle I do not cross picket lines. I contacted the head of the local union who graciously removed the picket lines for the duration of my stay. I was thus able to deliver my speech. It made much less impact than the previous talk in Arizona. This was, I think, because I had been scheduled as the last speaker on a week-long program. Sen. Robert Taft, who had been jobbed out of the Republican nomination for the presidency by the promoters of Gen. Dwight Eisenhower, had preceded me. The delegates were weary after a week of speeches and anxious to start for home. Many of them had already done so. I did not blame them.

Another with whom Frank Brophy maintained a warm friendship, in seeming contradiction to his conservative convictions, was Amman Hennacy. Amman was a radical of long standing. He had spent the years of World War I in the federal penitentiary at Leavenworth as a conscientious objector. The only reading material allowed him during his years of incarceration was the Bible. This resulted in a familiarity with religious tradition but not in a religious conversion. That would come many years later as a result of his becoming a devotee of Dorothy Day. Amman was in a sense a nomad. He had two daughters, highly talented college graduates. They and their mother, who generally shared Amman's convictions, tired of traipsing about the country after him. The marriage had ended, but not their friendship. Amman continued his traipsing, but alone.

When I knew him Amman was living in Phoenix. Every Sunday morning he sold copies of the *Catholic Worker* outside Brophy Chapel. During the week he worked for farmers in the area to earn his living. He also waged a continuing and successful battle with the Internal Revenue Service.

Amman refused to pay taxes. Among other things, taxes were used to manufacture death-dealing armaments, including—worst of all—nuclear weapons. As a matter of conscience Amman refused to contribute, in however modest a fashion, to this monstrous enterprise. The IRS, on the other hand, was determined that Amman should pay his taxes, however modest. From time to time an agent would come out from Washington armed with authority to garnishee his wages. The strategy invariably failed, because there were no wages to garnishee. Amman always arranged to collect his wages in advance. The farmers for whom he worked were glad to cooperate with him in thwarting the agent; this was partially, no doubt, because the IRS does not inspire empathy in many people, but chiefly because, although they did not share his radical notions, the farmers liked him as a person. It was difficult not to, despite his rather bizarre appearance, because he exuded the spirit of benevolence. He was one of the few persons I have known who genuinely loved his enemies no less than his friends.

In August every year, commemorating the terrible tragedy of Hiroshima, Amman fasted for nine days; and on each of those days he picketed the post office from morning to night. He took only water, without which he could not have survived in the intense heat when the temperature often reached 110 degrees. It was a heroic one-man demonstration against the atomic bomb. And every day of the demonstration Frank Brophy made a point of stopping by the post office for a friendly chat. They made an odd couple, the neatly groomed president of the Bank of Arizona and the single-toothed, long-haired radical engaged in an amiable tête-à-tête in front of the Phoenix post office. Some years later, persuaded by Dorothy Day that he did not have to look like a radical to be one, Amman cut his hair and got a set of false teeth.

Perhaps Frank Brophy was not as conservative as he seemed. Bill Mahoney, a leading Arizona Democrat and John Kennedy's Ambassador to Ghana, once said to him: "Frank, you are not a conservative. You are simply against the government."

And Frank replied, "Maybe you are right." That would have been part of his Irish heritage too.

Another facet of his character was his sense of responsibility and respect for the dignity of those in his employ. Ben Kenji

Nakasato was a Japanese who served as family chef for a quarter of a century. When Ben died, it seemed natural to Frank that he should be buried with the honors due a member of the family. Frank asked me if I would prepare a dignified service. Relying upon scriptural texts chiefly from the Old Testament, prayers, and a homily, I put together a liturgy which I conducted in the chapel of the mortuary. Frank and his sons served as the pallbearers.

More than thirty years later I returned to Phoenix for the marriage of Frank Cullen Brophy, Jr, and Anna Andreini, a woman of exceptional beauty, intelligence, and accomplishment. I was living in Switzerland, but they insisted that I fly to Phoenix at their expense to preside at their wedding. Both had been married before, and their daughters were beautiful bridesmaids at the wedding. They had themselves written the liturgy, which the bishop approved, and incorporated some of the beauty of the Jewish liturgy. Anna's father had been Jewish.

Anna, who was from New Jersey, was a liberal activist. She had marched in the South with Martin Luther King, as had I. She had raised several million dollars for Cesar Chavez and had helped him in the badly needed reorganization of his United Farm Workers. I told her I never thought any son of Frank Brophy, Sr., would marry a friend of Cesar Chavez. She replied that Frank, Jr., was a "closet liberal." Frank would later, teasingly, describe Anna as "radical chic." At the wedding Cesar Chavez and his wife brought the offertory gifts to the altar. A dozen or more of his staff had driven over from Bakersfield in the union bus for the wedding and reception which followed at the Phoenix Country Club.

Before the ceremony I chatted with Sallie Brophy, widow of Frank, Sr., beloved by all who knew her, and with Gladys Robinson, the Brophy housekeeper for more than fifty years, a black woman of quiet dignity. Their relationship was that of two old friends, which indeed they were, rather than that of employer and employee.

Several years later at Sallie's own funeral, for which I returned again to Phoenix, I saw further evidence of this unusual employer-employee relationship in the large number of ranch hands who on their own initiative came to Phoenix from the Brophy cattle ranch in southern Arizona to pay their last respects to one who was more a friend than a boss.

My last encounter with Frank Brophy took place on the eve of my final departure from Phoenix after nine years at Saint Francis Xavier. It occasioned a bit of rude behavior on my part and an angry exchange with Claire Booth Luce.

Claire Booth Luce

I had met Mrs. Luce some months previously, when I received a surprise telephone call from her inviting me to play a round of golf and to have lunch at her Phoenix home. I was less surprised than might have been expected, since I realized that the suggestion that she make my acquaintance had undoubtedly come from our mutual friend, John Courtney Murray, S.J.

The Luce home was a part of the Biltmore Estates and was located on the eighteenth fairway of the golf course. I arrived there on the appointed day at about nine o'clock in the morning to find everything on hold as a consequence of a totally unforeseen event. President Eisenhower had chosen that day to have his ileitis attack, which had landed him in Walter Reed Hospital.

Mrs. Luce was naturally entirely preoccupied with the news of Ike's illness. I found her sitting in the sunshine on the patio, a telephone at her side. She managed to create the impression of a person who had taken over the management of the country.

"I just phoned Nixon," she said to me. "Dick," I said, "you have got to attend that meeting in Paris two weeks from now. Never mind what others advise. That meeting must go on, and you must attend." Her reference was to a summit meeting in which Eisenhower was scheduled to participate.

"I phoned Knowland and I said, 'See to it that Nixon understands that the Paris meeting must not be abandoned.'" Knowland, the Oakland publisher, was senator from California and leader of the Senate Republicans. She had also phoned Joe Martin, Republican leader in the House, and told him what to do.

There could, of course, be no question of golf. She ordered the younger of her two secretaries to take her place on the course. We left her, sitting in the sunshine, phone in hand, exuding an aura of power as she rallied the people in Washington and across the land to save the country—and the world. She might have said, as would Alexander Haig, Jr., on a later occasion of presidential crisis, "I'm in charge here!" I had the feeling, as I headed for the first tee with the charming young lady who was to be my golfing partner for the day, that Mrs. Luce was relishing every minute of it.

My next experience with Claire Booth Luce was also as a recipient of her hospitality. Fr. John Courtney Murray, who with characteristic delicacy was accustomed to spend several days with her every year at the anniversary of the tragic death of her daughter and only child, killed in an automobile accident near

Stanford University, was her house guest. He and I had just finished eighteen holes of golf and were enjoying a preluncheon scotch and soda in his room, which looked out upon the swimming pool area. Suddenly we were startled by the shrill screams of Mrs. Luce. One of her miniature French poodles had tumbled or jumped into the swimming pool, and its mistress, on her knees at the pool's edge, was screaming for help. The poodle, which like any canine could swim from the day it was born, was happily paddling towards the edge, as servants came running from the house to be sent back for bath towels, while Father Murray and I, not reacting with gallantry to the challenge of the occasion, looked on, bemused, scotch in hand.

During the excellent luncheon which followed, Mrs. Luce fed tidbits accompanied by expressions of endearment to the poodle, which lay swathed in bath towels in a basket at her feet. She also carried on a dialogue with Father Murray on the nature of justice according to the metaphysics of Aristotle. Although I recognize and react spontaneously to situations of injustice, I lack competence to discuss the metaphysics of its opposite virtue. I was therefore a respectful listener to the discussion to which I contributed nothing.

I was later invited by Mrs. Luce to have lunch followed by a game of golf with her husband, who had not been present on the two previous occasions. I have no doubt that Henry Luce was a brilliant man. The testimony of many who have known him and the evidence of the enormously successful publishing empire which he built from virtually nothing attest to this. It must be said, however, that none of this brilliance was in evidence at our meeting. During the luncheon which preceded our game of golf he was dour, grumpy, and uncommunicative.

Henry Luce had been born of missionary parents in China and had spent his early years there. He was a strong supporter of Chiang Kai-shek, and the Kuomintang. As an interesting footnote, I digress to remark that eight years earlier, on the very day that Mao Tse-tung and his Communist armies occupied Nanking while Chiang Kai-shek fled to Canton and thence to Taiwan, I was trudging along the road leading into the Biltmore Estates. I stepped off the road as a chauffeured limousine passed. And I looked up to see sitting in the back seat the enormously rich T. V. Soong, at various times foreign minister and secretary of the treasury of China, brother-in-law of Chiang Kai-shek, and member of the Soong dynasty. The sight of T. V. Soong entering the most luxurious resort in Phoenix as the Communist armies were entering the capital of China offered food for sober reflection.

Because of our mutual interest in the subject, I thought that Luce and I could have an interesting discussion about China, a discussion made more interesting by the fact that I disagreed almost totally with his interpretation of events and with the China policy for which he ardently lobbied through the columns of *Time*. This, however, proved not to be the case. After several futile efforts to engage him in conversation I gave up and for the most part talked with the agreeable young lady who had been my earlier golf partner. Luce, for his part, confined his remarks to angry complaints about the Biltmore management, which insisted that, while he could use his own electric golf cart, he was obliged also to hire one of the regular caddies. He thought this altogether unfair, and he did not tire of saying so. Evidently Henry, like Claire, was interested in the subject of justice, but, like myself, in its concrete application rather than, like his wife, in its abstract nature.

During the golf game that followed lunch, Luce remained sullen and uncommunicative. While the unwanted caddy drove the cart in blissful ease, Luce and I strode the fairways wrapped in a cocoon of silence. Not until we were well along on the back nine did he suddenly emerge. It happened on a two-hundred-yard, par-three hole, where my drive wound up on the edge of the green. I then by lucky chance sank a forty-foot putt. At this Luce raced across the green with a loud cry to seize and shake my hand. It was the only sign of animation he showed during the round, and I was as astonished by it as I was by my birdie.

It is possible, of course, that his sullen mood arose out of a suspicion that he had been maneuvered into making the acquaintance of a priest whom he had no desire to meet and who would wish to talk about Catholicism. If that were the case, I could have reassured him that I had not the slightest interest in discussing religion with him, although I might have enjoyed a debate about China.

My last, and rather pyrotechnical, meeting with Claire Booth Luce was as a dinner guest in the home of Frank Brophy. The principal guest of the evening was Mrs. Luce. Others present, besides Frank and Sallie Brophy, were Blake Brophy, one of their four sons, his bride and her parents, Fr. James Deasy, S.J., former pastor of Saint Francis Xavier, and one of Mrs. Luce's two secretaries. The fireworks did not begin until, after a pleasant dinner, we had moved to the living room, where Mrs. Luce took charge of the conversation.

She began by launching into an implausible anti-Roosevelt tale designed to show that he was a Communist sympathizer. She claimed that on a visit to the Detroit rectory of Fr. Charles E. Coughlin, the famed "Radio Priest," she had been shown a photocopy of a check for $10,000 signed by Roosevelt and made out to Vincent Toledano, the Mexican labor leader.

The story was totally implausible. Had Father Coughlin possessed an authentic photocopy of such a check, given his notorious and virulent hatred for Franklin Roosevelt, he would certainly have published it far and wide, instead of saving it for covert display to Claire Booth Luce.

I was not surprised by the anti-Roosevelt character of her remarks, since her animosity towards FDR was as well known as Coughlin's. I was, however, surprised that she would stoop to so low a level of McCarthyite tactics in order to vent her hatred.

Having disposed of Roosevelt, she launched into a viciously anti-Semitic diatribe. The tale she told ranked with the infamous Protocols of Sion both for its viciousness and its patent absurdity. According to Mrs. Luce, there existed a relatively small group of wealthy Jews who met once a year in the greatest secrecy and planned the strategy of world Jewry for the future. Every major evil that had occurred in the political, economic, and social areas, dating back at least to the overthrow of the tsarist regime in Russia in 1917, the breakup of the Austro-Hungarian Empire—which breakup she deplored—and continuing through World War II and its aftermath, had been planned at and was the result of these meetings. She did not disclose how she had penetrated the secrecy of these meetings.

While inwardly seething, I listened for some time in stunned incredulity to her anti-Semitic absurdities, which one would hardly expect from a woman of the reputed intelligence of Claire Booth Luce. Meanwhile, Frank Brophy, who was wholly innocent of anti-Semitism but like many others not insusceptible to the glamour of famous women, had been nodding in apparent agreement with her every statement.

Finally, my reserves of self-control eventually exhausted, I intervened. "Frank," I said, "why do you agree with all of this nonsense? Simply because it comes from Claire Booth Luce?"

The temperature of the room dropped sharply. Mrs. Luce's monologue came to an abrupt end and was followed by a sharp exchange between the lady and myself. A few minutes later, accompanied by her secretary, she took her leave.

We all accompanied her outside, where she managed to have the last word. Arrived at her car, she turned around with a regal air and called to the group gathered at the front door, "Tell Father Dunne that at least I am not anticlerical."

Some years later a Jesuit colleague of mine who had been admitted to her circle of friends in Honolulu asked if she remembered me. "Oh, Father Tom," she replied, "I meet *so many people*, I can hardly remember them all." That may indeed be the case, but I have some doubts. I do not think Claire Booth Luce was so accustomed to having her views rudely challenged as easily to forget me.

At the time of this confrontation John Courtney Murray, who a few days earlier had slipped a spinal disk while playing golf with me, was confined to Saint Joseph's Hospital. Since I was leaving Phoenix the next day, I wrote him, describing the incident and saying how shocked I had been to hear such vulgar anti-Semitism coming from Claire Booth Luce. In reply he wrote: "You have seen one facet of a multifaceted woman. You have seen the facet which I call—and she is aware of this—the 'from rags to bitches' side."

No doubt I had been rude to Frank Brophy, inasmuch as I was his guest. He did not permit this to affect our friendship. If I had been rude to Claire Booth Luce I do not regret it. She deserved it. Unlike Wilfred Sheed and many others, I am not counted among her admirers.

Several years later I was hospitalized in Rome, recuperating from abdominal surgery. During his visits to monitor my recovery my physician and I discovered that we shared a mutual acquaintance and a mutual lack of esteem for Claire Booth Luce. As physician for the American Embassy he had been summoned to the bedside of Ambassador Claire Booth Luce while headlines carried the electrifying news around the world that the Communists had poisoned her by mixing arsenic or cyanide into the paint used to redecorate her quarters in the embassy. According to the doctor there was no poison in her system. In fact, he said, she was not ill at all. This alleged Communist assassination plot was no less a figment of her imagination than the conspiracy of rich Jews to control the world. Mrs. Luce was bored with her ambassadorial duties. Instead of quietly resigning, she wished to go out while screaming headlines and glaring spotlights made her the cynosure of world attention. Hence the alleged Communist conspiracy.

I have been severe with Mrs. Luce. I am sure, however, that the attractive facets of her multifaceted character, observed by John Courtney Murray and her other friends but invisible to me, will not have been overlooked by whoever registers these things for the next life and will have received a rich reward. Such has been the burden of my orisons. May she rest in peace.

Parish Vicar

The tale of my adventures with Claire Booth Luce has carried me far forward to the very end of my nine years in Phoenix. For the larger part those years were spent in the satisfying but not particularly newsworthy duties of an assistant parish priest: saying Mass, hearing confessions, teaching catechism to fourth grade children and a course in ethics to the senior high school girls, conducting the mixed parish choir and a boys' choir, directing the ladies' sodality, serving as part-time chaplain to the Veterans Administration Hospital.

Outside these normal parochial activities I became involved in the struggle for racial justice. When I arrived, Phoenix was totally segregated, as was all of Arizona. Schools, hotels, theaters, restaurants, residential areas were all segregated. The only exception was the Catholic parochial school system. Bishop Gercke refused to permit segregation in the schools or churches of his diocese.

My contribution to the desegregation of Phoenix was minor. Besides sermons and speeches, it consisted chiefly in collaboration with the efforts of a group of public-minded citizens headed by a young lawyer, William P. Mahoney, Jr., one of the leaders of the Democratic Party in Arizona; Pres. John Kennedy would later name him ambassador to Ghana. His wife, Alice, was a niece of Noel Sullivan, mentioned above.[1] I recall going with Mahoney and others as a committee to call on Barry Goldwater, then the head of the city council and as such mayor of the city, to argue for desegregation of the airport restaurant, which fell under the jurisdiction of municipal authorities.

With the support of these people and the help of a group of young people interested in the theater, I produced Trial by Fire. It was well received, although I cannot say to what extent it influenced public opinion. However, the speaker of the Arizona State Assembly, known as an intransigent segregationist, attended a performance at the invitation of a mutual friend. Some claimed afterward to notice a softening in his hard-line attitude on the subject.

One day Margaret Bourke-White, the famous photographer, arrived in Phoenix to take my picture. Doubleday-Doran, the publishing house, was preparing a book about the Jesuits in *America*. One of its objectives was to show the diversity of activities in which Jesuits were engaged, which it would do chiefly with photographs accompanied by an explanatory text, to be written by Fr. John LaFarge. I had been chosen for inclusion because of my activities in the field of racial justice.

Margaret Bourke-White spent the entire day with me as we moved about Phoenix. She took not one but seemingly hundreds of pictures. This was her method of operation and probably accounted for her reputation as one of the great photographers of our time. Few, if any, of her pictures were formally posed. She accompanied her subject and repeatedly snapped off pictures—often at an unexpected moment—as he or she engaged in normal activities. From the dozens or hundreds of shots, she made her final selection. In my case, two were selected for inclusion in the Doubleday-Doran book.

A revealing incident—amusing, in a sense—occurred in connection with my antiracist activities. I was asked to join a Jewish rabbi in a discussion of racial discrimination. The discussion took place in the Westward Ho Hotel, then the leading downtown hotel in Phoenix. The next morning a small article describing the meeting and discussion appeared in the *Phoenix Republic*. Within forty-eight hours I received a letter from Bishop Gercke in Tucson sternly reprimanding me. He was angry, but not because I had spoken against racial discrimination; as I have said above, Bishop Gercke was an antisegregationist. He was displeased because I had appeared on the same platform with a Jewish rabbi. This, he said, was in violation of Pope Pius XII's mandate governing the participation of priests in dialogue with non-Catholic clergy.

Bishop Gercke was completely wrong. The mandate of Pius XII, narrow though it was, concerned sharing in activities of a religious or theological nature. By no stretch of the imagination could it be interpreted to cover a discussion with a rabbi about civil rights or the evil of segregation.

What is revealing about the incident is the insight it affords into the narrowness which characterized ecclesiastical thinking in pre-Vatican II days. Not every American bishop would have interpreted Pius XII's mandate the way Gercke did, but few of them did not share the circumscribed point of view which it represented. Ecumenism was a dirty word. In 1968 I was present when Pope Paul VI visited the World Council of Churches in Geneva and in the chapel there participated in a prayer service with Orthodox clergy and Protestant pastors of numerous denominations. I wondered what thoughts passed through the mind of the Swiss theologian, Card. Charles Journet, a member of the papal entourage, who before Vatican II had hurled fiery bolts at the idea of ecumenism and the World Council of Churches.

I should say that at my final departure from Phoenix Bishop Gercke, a good and kindly man, wrote me a warm note of thanks for the contributions he said I had made to the diocese during my stay.

The Blanshard Debate

The most noteworthy event of the Phoenix years was my debate under the auspices of the Harvard Law School Forum with Paul Blanshard, who had won considerable fame by his unsparing attacks on the Catholic Church. He had begun his assault with three articles published in the *Nation*. As recounted above, I had replied in a single article, published in *Commonweal*. Blanshard subsequently extended his offensive with eight articles carried by the *Nation*, and these he expanded into a book, *American Freedom and Catholic Power*, which enjoyed a long stay on the nonfiction best-seller list.

My initial response had been favorably received. As a consequence, the editor of *America* asked me to write a series of articles in answer to Blanshard's book. The seven articles which resulted appeared in *America* between June 4 and July 30, 1949, and were subsequently published in a brochure entitled *Religion and American Democracy*.

Some time the following year—I no longer recall the date—I received a phone call from Cambridge, Massachusetts. The director of the Harvard Law School Forum was on the line. He informed me that Paul Blanshard had accepted an invitation to speak at the forum. The objection had been raised that fairness required that someone representing the opposing side should also be invited. He wanted to know if I was willing to appear at the forum to debate Mr. Blanshard.

I was confronted with a dilemma. On the one hand I had no desire whatever to debate with Paul Blanshard. He was, as his articles and book showed, an intelligent and clever man. He was an ordained minister in the Congregational Church, although I do not believe he exercised any ministry. He was also a lawyer. By appointment of Mayor Fiorello La Guardia, he had held the chief supervisory position over New York's hospitals and other institutions of health. While serving in this capacity, he would say later in the course of our debate, he first learned that according to the Catholic Church's teaching on abortion, if a choice had to be made the life of the child must always be preferred to that of the mother (not an exact statement of the teaching). He was so horrified by this shocking discovery, he was to say, that opposition to the Catholic Church became the chief purpose of his life. He was a formidable opponent whom I had no desire to engage in public debate.

On the other hand, were I to refuse, it would appear that Catholics were afraid to confront Blanshard and thus tend to confirm his views. I thought, however, that I had in canon law a shield against being impaled on either horn of this dilemma. To undertake a debate of this kind in defense of the Church required the permission of the bishop of the place. Not within living memory had any bishop granted such permission. Their unwillingness to do so was well grounded. Like Richard Nixon in his debate with John Kennedy, the priest might do poorly, in which case not only he but the cause he represented would suffer defeat.

Confident that I had in canon law a sure escape hatch I replied rather smugly, "I would be glad to debate Mr. Blanshard, but, of course, you would have to have the bishop's authorization for me to do so."

I was taken utterly aback by his response, "We have already taken care of that. Bishop Wright has approved." Bp. John Wright was auxiliary to Card. Richard Cushing, archbishop of Boston. Momentarily stunned, I quickly regrouped and fell back upon a secondary line of defense.

"Oh, he has? Well, I will still have to have the permission of my Jesuit provincial. I'll call him and let you know."

Although my confidence had been badly shaken by Bishop Wright's betrayal, I still hoped that the provincial would save me. Given his not particularly benevolent attitude towards me, I thought it unlikely that he would assent. Again I suffered a rude awakening.

When I had explained the nature of the Harvard invitation, Father O'Brien, probably thinking, as I had, that the likelihood of episcopal sanction was nil, remarked, "Of course you would have to obtain permission from the bishop."

"They have already obtained it," I said.

"In that case," he replied, "I do not object." The last possible door of escape slammed shut in my face.

The invitation arrived at an especially bad time. There were but a few weeks remaining before the scheduled date of the debate. The Conference of Studio Unions, which had been crushed in the lengthy strike I have described earlier, had filed suit against the producers and the IATSE union for damages. Representing the conference was Robert Kenney, formerly attorney general of California; he had asked me to write the background history of the strike for his use in the courtroom. I was busy writing what would become my brochure entitled *Hollywood Labor Dispute: A Study In Immorality*. Because of the importance which Kenney attached to this material for use in the litigation and because of my own bonds with the conference, bonds forged in the fires of conflict, I continued to devote all my spare time to the completion of this task.

Consequently, when I climbed aboard the Santa Fe Chief in Flagstaff, Arizona, I had made no real preparation for the debate with Blanshard. Actually it did not seem to me that there was a great deal I could do in the way of preparation. My assignment was to defend the Church. Blanshard had the affirmative side, I the negative. I had to wait to see what affirmations he made. I could hardly prepare a defense until I knew the nature of the attack. As the Santa Fe Chief clickety-clacked its way across the great American midlands, holed up in my roomette, I reread Blanshard's *American Freedom and Catholic Power*. This would have to serve as my preparation. I had long had the habit of speaking extempore. This I proposed to do in the present instance, replying to Blanshard's arguments as he made them.

One thing that had given me some concern was Pope Pius IX's famous Syllabus of Errors. Although he had not exploited this in his book, I felt sure that Blanshard would not fail to bring it up. It lay like a bomb in my path waiting to be detonated. In his Syllabus Pius IX had managed to anathematize practically every value cherished in the modern, democratic world. Ever since the promulgation of the Syllabus, those Catholic apologists who were not of a feudal cast of mind were driven to their wit's end in an attempt to defend it. The fact is that it is indefensible. It can be explained, but not defended.

The explanation lies in the psychological odyssey of Pius IX. Early in his career he had been of so liberal a bent that Cavour and other leaders of the Italian *risorgimento* had seriously considered naming him, once unity had been achieved, president of the fledgling Italian Republic. However, the doctrinal and political excesses committed in the name of democracy both in Italy and in other European countries eroded his progressive inclinations. The last stage of his journey from center to far right was precipitated by the assassination in November 1848 in Rome of his friend and faithful servitor, Count Pellegrino Rossi, the civil governor of the Papal States. Henceforth, everything of a liberal or democratic coloration was anathema to Pius IX.

I had written to John Courtney Murray, S.J., asking him to meet me at America House in New York. Here he and several members of the editorial staff discussed with me the forthcoming debate with Blanshard; but neither he nor they were able to offer an answer to the problem of how to handle the Syllabus of Errors. I decided, if the issue were raised, to forgo all evasive tactics and meet it head-on by stating that the Syllabus of Errors was itself an error, that it was not an infallible document but represented the understandably biased views of Pius IX and that probably few American Catholics, of those who were familiar with its contents, agreed with its strictures.

As it turned out, I had been needlessly concerned. Blanshard did not mention the Syllabus of Errors. Perhaps he was unaware of its existence, although that is hard to believe, since it was common grist for the anti-Catholic polemicist mill.

From my meeting with John Courtney Murray I learned that I was the second choice of the Harvard Law School Forum. They had quite understandably first approached Murray. Although far more qualified than I, he had refused their invitation. He had offered to appear on a later forum program to reply to Blanshard, but not to engage him in debate on the same program. He was undoubtedly right. A debate of this kind is extremely difficult. As I had stated in *Religion and American Democracy*: "A paragraph, a sentence, even a phrase suffices to make an accusation. A book may be required to refute it. To make a charge it is enough to say that the Catholic doctrine on a specific moral problem is based on nothing but 'arbitrary theological formulas.' [The quoted phrase is from Blanshard.] To refute the charge adequately would require a comprehensive discussion of the precise nature of the Catholic doctrine, its history, the sources and principles of Catholic moral theology." In a half hour of debate Blanshard could make a dozen or more charges. It would be surprising if the respondent could adequately reply to three or four of them. John Courtney Murray was aware of this and wisely refused to fall into the trap. I had entrapped myself by blithely agreeing to debate if the bishop approved, thus learning, not for the first time, the folly of putting one's fate in the hands of a bishop!

It should not be concluded from this that I approached the debate in fear and trembling. I did not. In the opinion of many whose views I respected, I had answered Blanshard's arguments satisfactorily in my series of *America* articles; and I saw no reason to fear that I could not do so in public debate.

I arrived in Boston the day before the debate and discovered that it had aroused intense interest. It was to be held in the largest available auditorium in Cambridge, that of the Cambridge High and Latin School, and the demand for tickets outstripped the supply.

The evening of the debate got off to a bad start. A journalist friend in Hollywood had asked me to procure tickets for her niece and her niece's husband, who lived in Boston. In return they asked for what they said was the privilege of driving me to the place of encounter. A dinner had been scheduled in the Harvard Faculty Club preceding the debate. I was staying in the Jesuit community at Boston College High School, and I waited in the lobby there with ever-growing nervousness as the hour when my friends were supposed to pick me up arrived, passed, and moved inexorably on, guaranteeing that I would be late for the dinner. Finally, as I was about to call a taxi, they arrived, a good half hour late, apologetic but not excessively so.

At the Harvard Faculty Club, the officers of the Harvard Law School Forum with Mr. Blanshard and other guests awaited our tardy arrival. It was my first meeting with Blanshard. During the dinner, which got under way without further delay, he and I were seated opposite each other at the long refectory-style table. Our other tablemates, as I recall, were student officers of the forum. The conversation was light and pleasant. Blanshard, wiser than I, declined the proffered wine, remarking with sly pleasantry that

Jesuits were reputed to be formidable adversaries and he had to keep a clear head for the encounter. I, less wise, and my nerves not yet settled after the long wait to be picked up, took a second glass.

After the dinner we walked to the auditorium, where we found several hundred people trying in vain to gain admission. Reports of a sellout had not been exaggerated. Every seat was occupied, with standees crowding the back and both side aisles and perhaps two hundred more people occupying folding chairs that had been set up on the stage behind the podium.

The student president of the forum escorted Blanshard and me to the stage. We were seated at a table stage right but would speak from a podium center stage. The president explained that we would each have twenty-five minutes for our main presentations and would be given a three-minute warning signal. We would each have ten minutes for rebuttal, followed by questions from the audience. Having explained the ground rules the president turned the meeting over to the chairman. I have long since forgotten his name, but I shall never forget the maladroitness of his performance.

The role of the chair at a debate is to announce the subject, to define the rules if necessary, and to introduce the debaters, a matter of several minutes. Our chairman spoke for twenty-seven minutes, two more than the twenty-five minutes allotted to each debater. His entire speech was in effect an endorsement of Blanshard's position. Typical was his comment, "I have read Mr. Blanshard's well-documented book and Father Dunne's impassioned reply." This was quite clearly a vote for Blanshard; it was also proof positive that while he may have read Blanshard's book he certainly had not read my reply. If there was anything my reply was not, it was not impassioned. I had in fact received a letter from the editor who had published Blanshard's articles in the *Nation* complimenting me precisely on the unimpassioned character of my reply.

The chairman also devoted considerable time to warning me that I should not drag the subject of communism into the debate. It was a curious performance, perhaps reflecting a persuasion peculiar to the Harvard academe that every Catholic priest was a Joe McCarthy in miniature. It had never crossed my mind that Paul Blanshard was a Communist or that, if he were, that had anything to do with this evening's debate; our subject was not communism but Catholicism and Blanshard's dismal and unjust view of the same. If the chairman had indeed read my brochure he would have known that I nowhere raised the specter of communism. He was evidently hung up on the subject.

Arrangements had been made for a Boston radio station to broadcast the debate beginning with the rebuttal segment. This called for another introduction by the chairman, this time to the radio audience; and once again—I still had not mentioned communism in my presentation—he warned "Father Dunne against introducing communism into the discussion."

I found him insufferable. I had been told that he was a member of the philosophy faculty. I was strongly tempted to advise anyone in the listening audience who might be thinking of coming to Harvard to study philosophy to go instead to Yale, where Blanshard's brother was a professor of philosophy.

Blanshard, an intelligent and articulate speaker, delivered a well-prepared indictment of the Catholic Church. I was prepared with pencil and pad to jot down the various charges and answer them one by one. Within minutes, realizing it was impossible to reply to all the charges, I abandoned both pencil and strategy. Instead I decided to impugn all of Blanshard's arguments by establishing through examples from his book that he was in fact a religious bigot and that everything he said must be seen in that perspective. Whatever time was left following this general indictment of his credibility I would devote to answering two or three of his more serious charges.

Perhaps most effective was a passage I read from my *Religion and American Democracy*. It was a little anti-Semitic tract I had composed in the style employed by Blanshard throughout his book:

> The American Jewish people have done their best to join the rest of America, but the rabbis have never been assimilated. They are still fundamentally Eastern European or Near Asian in their spirit and directives.
>
> It would be a mistake to judge the power of the Jewish community in terms of numbers only. Even a minority bloc in the population can make a tremendous impression if it is closely knit.
> The Jewish synagogue is an important item in the technique of denominational display. The synagogue is usually a big synagogue and usually an oversized synagogue. . . The big synagogue in the American community is the Exhibit A of rabbinical power, and the Jewish people have accepted it as their symbol of success even when it is heavily mortgaged.

The observer of any Jewish religious ceremony is impressed by its foreign character. Even the names of their feast days emphasize their foreign provenance: Rosh Hadesh, Rosh Hashanah, Yom Kippur, Hanukkah, Lag Beomer, Shavuot. They are celebrated with elaborate ceremonies in the synagogues, with impressive pageantry and a great many chants sung by a be-shawled cantor and be-shawled choral assistants. These chants sound strange to ears accustomed to the traditional American melodies of Cole Porter or even, though he is a Jew, of Irving Berlin.

These feasts and their ceremonial pageantry, commemorating events that happened thousands of years ago in a remote and foreign part of the world, annoy and disturb non-Jewish Americans, who are likely to ask: "Is not such religious observance of servility to the historic memories of the Chosen Race utterly contrary to the American tradition? What good American cares about the Bar Kokhba Revolt, sixty years after the destruction of the temple in Jerusalem? How did this Asiatic posturing ever get to the United States?"

I then went on to say, "Every one of these obviously anti-Semitic allegations I have lifted from Mr. Blanshard's book. . ." At this point, Blanshard leaped to his feet and began to protest in indignation that he had never written such anti-Semitic slurs. Unfortunately, I did not hear his outcry or observe that he had risen to his feet, and without pause went on to say, "only changing the Catholic context into a Jewish context, Catholic people into Jewish people, priest into rabbi, church into synagogue, Catholic ceremonies into Jewish ceremonies."

At this Blanshard's outcry faded out, and he subsided into his chair. It was only after the debate that a member of the audience informed me of this incident, which had entirely escaped my attention. Later, listening to the recording of the debate, I clearly heard Blanshard's cry of protest. Had I heard it at the time I would have paused until he had completed his disclaimer, which proved my point, that Blanshard was so biased that even he recognized the prejudicial nature of his testimony when it was put into a Jewish rather than a Catholic context. In any case, although his intervention had escaped my notice I do not think the audience missed it.

At the conclusion of the debate several hundred people filed up on the stage to shake my hand. Among them was Erwin Griswold, dean of Harvard Law School, who would later serve as Solicitor General of the United States. I remarked to him that I was

afraid I had spent too much time discussing Blanshard's prejudice, since this had prevented me from replying to more than a few
of his specific charges. Dean Griswold did not agree. Speaking as
a lawyer he said that this had been the most effective argument
possible, since it undercut Blanshard's credibility as a witness,
thus calling into question the validity of all of his arguments.

Besides the antics of the chairman there was another feature
of the debate which I found unpleasant. A hard core of what might
be called dyed-in-the-wool Blanshardites occupied the first several rows. Throughout Blanshard's speech they audibly marked
their agreement with each of his arguments, somewhat like a
Baptist congregation stamping each of the pastor's declarations
with an "Amen!" I did not mind that, though I found it somewhat
amusing. But throughout my own speech they responded to my
every argument with a quite audible murmur of disapproval.
When one of my arguments brought a burst of applause from a
segment of the audience, I remarked, "That's *my* claque." The
innuendo was not lost upon the audience, which, after a moment's
hesitation—and excepting the die-hards in the front rows—broke
out in general applause mixed with laughter. That may have been
the beginning of a certain empathy which became noticeable as
the evening wore on.

I have often been asked, "Who won the debate?" My answer is
that I do not think anyone wins a debate of this kind in the sense
of convincing the audience that one is right and one's opponent
wrong. On the other hand, one can lose a debate of this kind by
losing the sympathy of the audience.

The question period, during which the audience addressed
questions to both of us, but chiefly to me, ran on much beyond the
original time limit. When the chairman finally announced that
janitorial requirements necessitated that we vacate the auditorium and declared the debate ended, I turned to shake Blanshard's
hand. Ignoring my hand, he uttered a brusque "good night" and
strode briskly off stage. A reception had been scheduled afterwards, again in the faculty club. Attendance was large, but
Blanshard did not appear. I drew the inference that he was not
pleased with the outcome of the debate.

Some time after my return to Arizona I received a letter from
the Harvard Law School student who had chief responsibility for
organizing the debate. Giving his own evaluation, he wrote, "As
you yourself must have remarked, at the beginning the volume of
audience applause showed that most of the people were on

Blanshard's side; but in the course of the evening a notable change took place, so that by the end the favor had shifted to you." I had indeed remarked this change. I attributed it not to my own performance, which I thought rather poor—the next day I thought of any number of brilliant things I could have said, but did not think to say—but to the fact that Blanshard had alienated a considerable part of the audience. This was confirmed by many of the hundreds of letters I later received. One of the more interesting was from a man who said that he had been an ordained minister in the Congregational Church—Blanshard's church. He had been so offended by Blanshard's tactics that he renounced the ministry, left the Congregational Church and joined the Anglican! I suppose that could be registered as a partial victory. He had, after all, come half way over.

The day after the debate I went to the offices of the Harvard Law School Forum to collect my check for expenses. Word spread that I was there. Soon the entire staff had gathered. For more than two hours they plied me with questions about my faith and the reasons for it, and about the Catholic Church and its practices and policies. It was lively, amiable and the most pleasant experience of my visit to Boston.

That morning I had had another experience which confirmed what has often been said to be a characteristic of the New England mentality, including that of Jesuits there. I was lodged with the Jesuits of Boston College High School. I arose a bit late and after saying Mass went to the dining room. There were ten or twelve Jesuit priests having a late breakfast. I took a seat at the end of the same table. The others ignored me. No one introduced himself or asked my name. They went on with their conversation. I did not listen to what they were saying, but was quickly absorbed in my own thoughts, thinking of the previous evening's events and especially of all the brilliant and clever things I could have said but did not.

Suddenly through my reverie I heard my own name. I quickly pricked up my ears in time to hear one of the Jesuits ask, "Well, who is this guy Dunne?"

To this another replied, "Oh, I don't know; he's some fellow from out West some place." To the New Englander, anything west of Niagara Falls is unexplored Indian country.

I was now fully alert, as I realized they were discussing the debate of the night before. The principal speaker had evidently listened to the broadcast and was recounting to the others what Blanshard had said and what I had said. I was afraid that at any moment one of them would say something like "That fellow Dunne is a damn fool," then discover who I was, to our mutual embarrassment.

The potentially dangerous situation was defused with the arrival of another latecomer. He took the seat opposite me, and as he sat down I extended my hand in greeting and loudly said, "My name is Dunne, father, what is yours?" Every head turned sharply in my direction as dead silence fell upon the table. There was no further discussion of the Blanshard-Dunne debate. Each one finished his breakfast and took his departure in silence, in what rightly or wrongly has been said to be typical New England behavior, still ignoring the "fellow from out West some place."

My own naiveté caused a near disaster after my departure for that West. At the conclusion of the debate the Harvard student in charge had asked me for a copy of my manuscript. The Harvard Forum intended to publish the proceedings in brochure form. I did not have a manuscript. As was my bad habit in those years, I had spoken off the cuff. I had noticed, however, the presence on stage of a stenotypist who, I was told, was transcribing the debate for *Time* magazine. I suggested that Harvard ask *Time* for a copy of the transcript. I had always assumed that courtroom reporters had to produce errorless transcripts. Because the man from *Time* had employed a stenotype machine such as that used by courtroom reporters, I had naively presumed that he would produce a faithful record of my remarks. Consequently, I had not bothered to demand to see the transcript before publication.

When I received a copy of the brochure a week or two later, I was horrified by what purported to be my contribution to the debate. It was a nightmarish distortion. In some places, by the omission or addition of a negative, it had me saying the exact opposite of what I had said. Other places had me talking gibberish. Fortunately, I had asked the Harvard people to arrange to record the debate and had brought a copy of the recording back with me. I wired Harvard demanding that distribution of the brochure be immediately halted until my corrections were received. I then sat down at my typewriter with a recorder at my side and the brochure open on my desk. The recording was perfectly clear and was irrefutable evidence of how badly botched the transcript was. The *Time* stenotypist had evidently been listening with one ear and half a brain.

I sent a copy of the recording and eight single-spaced typewritten pages of corrections to Harvard with the demand that the brochure be corrected and reprinted. The Harvard people did so, but with bad grace, evidenced in their refusal to correct the last page or two of the brochure. The last several minutes of the question period had, for some reason, not been recorded. Because I could not produce the irrefutable evidence of a recording, they refused to correct the gibberish of the last page, which still has me talking like an illiterate buffoon.

Ever since this experience I have read *Time* magazine with considerable skepticism.

Defensor Fidei

Some were surprised that I should have entered the lists in defense of the Church. The *Nation*, which had first published Blanshard's articles, carried in its issue of September 22, 1951, a profile entitled "Father Dunne: A Study in Faith," by free-lance writer Joseph Stocker; it began:

> It was to be anticipated that someone would strike out in defense of the Roman Catholic Church against the onslaught delivered by Paul Blanshard in his widely read book "*American Freedom* and *Catholic Power*". . .but nobody could have foreseen the quality of sublime paradox which characterized the defense. For a man who had himself suffered at the hands of the church came forward as its foremost defender in the Blanshard controversy—voluntarily and inspired by a massive faith. . ."It's a matter of faith," he explains. "Either I believe in the things the church stands for or I don't. If I don't there's no sense in remaining a Catholic. If I do believe in these things, they don't cease to be true because of the action of the Catholic hierarchy." Among the most important of "these things," in Dunne's view, are the principles for which he fought at St. Louis and Los Angeles—the rights of minorities and labor. Before the outbreak of the Blanshard controversy Dunne was renowned in Catholic circles chiefly for his unflagging defense of those rights. . .
>
> Dunne believes that it is he who represents "authentic Catholic thought" and not the members of the hierarchy who have buffeted him around. To his way of thinking they represent "various social pressures." He dismisses them as "ministers of mediocrity who consistently sacrifice truth and justice to expediency." He has been accused by his superiors of being "imprudent" in his crusades. "What do they mean by imprudence," he asks, and replies, "They mean anything that

steps on the toes of someone who is important." His faith, however, remains unyielding. By way of analogy he says: "If I'm firmly convinced of the truth of democracy in our political order, I don't lose faith because there may be people in office like Senator McCarthy who stand for things totally undemocratic. It's the same with the church. I don't lose faith—stay in and remain faithful to the true principles of the church. To me one of the chief missions of the church is to witness to truth and charity, regardless of whose toes are stepped on. Every time that principle is betrayed, the church is betrayed."

Stocker did not misquote me. I am reminded of the words of an elderly monsignor many years ago in Evansville, Indiana. I was on a lecture tour of medium-sized middle American cities, which began in Paducah, Kentucky, and ended in Omaha, Nebraska. Over dinner in his rectory, the monsignor recited a litany of the troubles he had had with his bishop. In conclusion he remarked, "What a joke! A lot of damn fools trying to run a divine institution." It's not exactly a joke, but it's something to keep in mind. My difficulty has not been with the Church but sometimes with people who are trying to run the Church—and the Society of Jesus.

Theatrics

Among my duties in Phoenix was that of director of the parish ladies' sodality. Back in 1926 one of the reasons which had prompted me to opt for the Jesuits rather than the diocesan priesthood, probably reflecting a strain of male chauvinism, was that I could not see myself devoting a considerable part of my life to the Altar and Rosary Society, as it seemed to me the parish priest was obliged to do. Now, over twenty years later, I found myself entrusted with the ladies' sodality.

As it turned out, my earlier misgivings were unfounded. The ladies and I actually had a lot of fun together, partly due to the fact that I did not run a very orthodox ship. When Fr. Joe Howard, the province's over-all director of sodalities, departed after his annual visitation, he wore a worried look. The chief concern of a sodality is with the spiritual life of its members. Father Howard, I think, had difficulty understanding how such things as square dances, farces, Gay Nineties revues, and musical comedies fitted into the rule. I cannot claim that the spiritual life of the ladies flourished during my incumbency, but neither do I think it suffered grievous damage. We had many a joyous moment as we walked together through this vale of tears. And I have many golden memories.

The first of these memories are associated with a one-act farce I wrote and directed entitled *Hagnet*, a satire on the very popular *Dragnet*. In an inversion of the medieval custom, all the roles, male and female, were played by ladies of the sodality. The audience, which by chance included Frank Scully, found it very funny. Scully, theater critic, humorist, author, whose column "Scully's Scrapbook" was a regular feature in *Variety*, happened to be passing through Phoenix on a vacation trip with his family. An old friend, who had coproduced my *Trial by Fire* in Hollywood, he came to see *Hagnet*. He gave it a generous review in "Scully's Scrapbook."

The following year the ladies and I undertook a more ambitious project. I wrote a full-scale musical comedy entitled *Virtue Well Rewarded; or, She Got What Was Coming To Him*. It was fashioned somewhat along the lines of *The Drunkard*, a farce that had run in Los Angeles for many years: the mortgaged homestead, the innocent maiden, her widowed mother, the naive swain, the mustachioed villain with lust in his eye and the mortgage in his pocket, etc. Unlike *The Drunkard*, however, *Virtue Well Rewarded* was a musical.

Most of the songs I borrowed from the extensive repertoire of popular melodies of the Gay Nineties, of the "She's Only a Bird in a Gilded Cage" variety. Three of them I wrote myself. Added to this were the famed quartet from *Rigoletto* and a smidge of Gilbert and Sullivan, for both of which I wrote new lyrics. It was quite a musical smorgasbord. I was flattered to overhear a young woman in the audience say to her escort, "The best songs are the ones he wrote himself." This was obviously a wild exaggeration, but a potent ego booster.

In the first act we had a Greek chorus, which at one point metamorphosed into the Shakespearean witches of Macbeth and in the second act into real, red-blooded American chorus girls who executed, among other dances, a rousing version of the cancan. In retrospect, perhaps Father Howard had reason for his misgivings.

This cast was made up of men and women. The part of the love-sick swain was expertly sung by Jim Powers, a brilliant young lawyer recently graduated from Harvard Law School. (His future law partner, William Rehnquist, is now Chief Justice of the United States Supreme Court.) Jim recently wrote me, some thirty years later, that he was no longer able to reach B flat below high C.

Taking a tip from *The Drunkard*, we encouraged the audience to cheer the hero and hiss the villain, which they did with great gusto.

Remembering *Hagnet* of the previous year, Frank Scully made a special trip from Hollywood to catch *Virtue Well Rewarded*. His review in *Variety* was headlined "Most Hilarious Musical Meller in the History of Show Biz!" He also wrote a piece about me and my extracurricular theatrical activities for the quarterly of the National Catholic Theatre Guild.

Yielding to popular demand, the ladies' sodality decided upon a second production. I rewrote the text, creating a role for a talented young singer, Mary Cavanagh, who had not been available earlier on. This required plot modifications and new songs. Together with Marian Pressendo, who as in previous performances sang the lead, we now had not one but two beautiful sopranos.

We did a number of performances in the large, barrack-like restaurant-theater we rented at a resort on the outskirts of Phoenix. They all played to SRO audiences, which indicated by the ovation they gave the cast that they agreed with Frank Scully's review. *Virtue Well Rewarded* would have made good material for any amateur choral group, including other sodalities, though other sodality directors might not agree. In any case, I did not attempt to promote it.

Still, it did have one more production. Fr. Walter Schmidt, S.J., the founder and director of a youth club in Santa Clara, had seen the Phoenix production. He asked permission to use *Virtue* for the operetta his youth group produced each year, a permission I gladly granted. It was produced at Santa Clara in 1958. I had by then been transferred to Santa Clara University and was able to enjoy the "musical meller" as a member of the audience. It proved no less hilarious when done by a youth club than when done by a ladies' sodality.

Not everyone shared Frank Scully's appreciation of my theatrical activities. One who took a dimmer view was Card. James Francis McIntyre of Los Angeles, late of New York. It was the custom of the National Catholic Theatre Guild to present two plays at its annual national conference. In the summer 1949, the conference was scheduled to be held at Immaculate Heart College in Los Angeles. One of the plays it chose for presentation was *Trial by Fire*. Bp. Bernard Sheil had offered at his own expense to bring the Chicago cast of *Trial by Fire* to Los Angeles. I had been asked and had agreed, as part of the week-long program, to give a lecture on the role of the theater as an agent of social change. An elaborate and beautiful program had been printed at considerable expense. At this point, Joe Rice, head of the Los Angeles unit of the Catholic Theatre Guild and organizer of the conference, sent a copy of the program to the chancery office. Word came back in the form of a thunderbolt, "His Eminence, Cardinal McIntyre, wants neither Father Dunne nor his play in his diocese."

The beautiful program was shredded. New and simpler programs were printed omitting mention of Father Dunne and his play. Father Dunne was furious and wrote a scorching letter to the chancellor of the Los Angeles archdiocese, Msgr. Benjamin Hawkes, telling him so. What angered me was not my banning or that of the play. It was the insult to Bishop Sheil and above all the uncalled-for blow to all the members of the Chicago cast. Most of them were young working people or students, few of whom had ever set foot outside Chicago. For a year they had been performing *Trial by Fire* several nights a week, at considerable sacrifice; they performed because they believed in what *Trial by Fire* had to say. They did not expect to be paid, but they had for months been looking forward to the trip to California and to Hollywood as to a dream. To smash that dream out of spite for me was the action of a mean-spirited and insensitive man. I asked the chancellor to communicate my views to His Eminence. I am sure he did.

McIntyre was not only mean spirited and insensitive. He was also appallingly ignorant. One of the first things he had done after his arrival in Los Angeles was to order the dissolution of the Catholic Interracial Council, which had been established and nurtured by Daniel G. Marshall, Dr. Julia Metcalfe, and a handful of the most devoted Catholics in the city. According to McIntyre, there was no racial problem in Los Angeles and hence no need for the council. Shades of Watts!

Both these actions were manifest abuses of power. If they were not peculiar to McIntyre, they were typical of him.

Cold Front

My years in Phoenix saw no improvement in my relations with Fr. Joe O'Brien, the provincial. On the occasion of his official visitation of the community I was informed that I was not obliged to see him; the pastor brought me this news. If I had something to say to him, he was at my service; otherwise, I was excused. That was that. If he had nothing to say to me, I had nothing to say to him. I had no desire to joust with windmills. Our relationship was over.

Many years later he was living in retirement and in poor health at the former novitiate in Los Gatos, California. Every year when visiting the States from Switzerland, where I was living, I made a point of going there to see my old friend and colleague, Bill Hanley, likewise in his declining years. On these occasions I met and exchanged friendly greetings with Joe O'Brien. We never discussed the past, and he carried with him to the grave the secret of what had caused the dissolution of a once warm friendship. In nostalgic moments I sometimes recall an amusing scene which brings to mind those friendly years.

It was at Phelan Park. We had a young male German shepherd. Noel Sullivan had a German shepherd bitch in heat. He brought her up from his Carmel Valley home. We put the two of them together in an enclosure. The scene, which unfortunately was not photographed, was of Joe O'Brien, Noel Sullivan, and myself crouched on our haunches eagerly peering through an opening to observe what was taking place within. Nothing was. The bitch was willing, but our boy was not interested. After giving him all the time in the world, we finally gave up and rose to our feet, laughing at our disappointment. Joe O'Brien returned to Alma, where he was soon to become rector, then provincial, then former friend. Noel Sullivan took his frustrated bitch back to Carmel. I was left with my excessively celibate canine, upon whom I looked with reproachful eyes. Happier days!

My relations with my provincial superior did not show any marked improvement when Carroll O'Sullivan succeeded Joe O'Brien. This was surprising because, as with O'Brien, we had once been quite good friends, and I had never had any conflict with him. Perhaps each retiring provincial passes on to his successor his evaluation of his subjects. That would explain why O'Brien, successor to King, suddenly switched from friend to—the only word that comes to mind is *foe*. It would also explain the drop in temperature of which I became aware with the first request I made of O'Sullivan following his accession to office.

I was quite content in Phoenix. I enjoyed parish work—and golf as well. The ladies of the sodality—Alice Mulligan, feisty mother of ten and inexhaustible source of sometimes randy jokes; Betty Abraham, with whom I would have fallen in love had I been free to do so; Norine Samuelson, indefatigable friend; Ollie McKone;

and so many others too numerous to mention—we were partners in fun and innocent frolics as well as piety and prayer. I had no desire to leave Phoenix. Nevertheless, it seemed evident that I was marking time, that whatever knowledge and skills I had acquired were not being put to use.

My doctoral thesis had been a study of the Jesuits in China in the sixteenth and seventeenth centuries, at the end of the Ming and the beginning of the Ch'ing dynasties. Because the war had walled off access to the archives, I had been forced to rely upon secondary sources. The director of the University of Chicago Press had expressed interest, but I was not interested in publishing it in that condition. Now, ten years later, the war was over and the barriers were down.

I wrote to Carroll O'Sullivan, pointing out that I was marking time in Phoenix, if not exactly wasting it; and I asked permission to go to Rome, where, with access to the Vatican and, more important, the Jesuit archives, I could rewrite and publish my study of the Jesuits in China. Comparing what I was doing in Phoenix with what I would be doing in Rome, I thought it an eminently reasonable request, particularly in the light of the Ignatian principle expressed in the motto *ad majorem Dei gloriam*—for God's greater glory. The answer was an unembellished negative. Superiors are, to be sure, not obliged to give reasons for their sometimes bizarre decisions, but to brush someone off with a simple negative does not foster confidence or friendly feelings.

When Father O'Sullivan came to Phoenix for his first official visitation as provincial, I went to see him, only to discover that, like O'Brien, he really had nothing to say to me. He expressed no complaints, made no criticisms, found no faults, registered no disapproval—or approval. He simply had nothing to say. He was willing to listen, but not to discuss. I felt as though I was in the bottom of a well talking to myself. The monologue soon limped to a halt and I escaped into the real world.

Tailed by the FBI

Following the transfer of Bill Hanley from Phoenix, I took over his responsibilities as part-time chaplain of the Veterans Administration Hospital. These consisted in saying Mass on Sundays for a small congregation of perhaps a dozen people, visiting the patients, bringing communion to those who wished it, and administering the last sacraments to the dying.

As part-time chaplain I received part-time pay, amounting, if information recently supplied me by the FBI is correct, to less than five dollars a week. I did not think so paltry a sum entitled the government to order me about like a marine in boot camp. Consequently, when a telegram arrived ordering me to appear at VA headquarters in Washington the following Tuesday, I replied that I was occupied that day and would appear two weeks hence. The next week a second telegram countermanded the first. I was puzzled by this strange business but dismissed it from my mind.

Two months later the chief of VA chaplains arrived in Phoenix in the course of a visitation of VA hospitals across the country. He was a Catholic monsignor, a former military chaplain. He told me what accounted for the conflicting orders. The FBI had notified the Veterans Administration that it had information that I had consorted with Communists in Hollywood, from which it concluded that I was a security risk who should not be employed by a government agency such as the Veterans Administration. This led to the first telegram, asking me to appear in Washington to answer to these charges. After some inquiries of his own, the chief of chaplains had persuaded the Veterans Administration that the charges were unfounded. The matter was dropped; and the second telegram was sent canceling the order to appear in Washington.

Now I was indeed angry: first with myself for not having obeyed the first telegram; second with a sneaky informer who, from behind a screen of anonymity, had smeared my reputation; and third with the FBI, which in the spirit of the McCarthy era allowed itself to be used as an agent of character assassination. I asked Carroll O'Sullivan for permission to go to Washington to clear my name. I naively thought that he would be as angry as I was at the besmirching of the reputation of one of his subjects. I thought that he would not only permit me but would order me to take the first plane to Washington. Instead he denied me the permission.

Some months ago I sent Carroll a copy of the pages of these memoirs giving my version of the St. Louis University caper. In thanking me he remarked, "I have never doubted your integrity." I took this with a bit of salt. Actually I think Carroll in those days really believed that I was a crypto-Communist or at least a comsymp. Today, however, long after he has abandoned the burdens of office and with the two of us well along the path of old age, when we meet it is in the renewed friendship of our youth. Probably he genuinely believes that he never doubted my integrity.

Ronald Reagan—Informer?

Who was the FBI informer? Some months ago I read in the *Los Angeles Times* that the White House had acknowledged that during the 1940s Ronald Reagan and his wife had served as informers for the FBI, supplying "confidential information on suspected communist activities of their Hollywood colleagues"; this confirmed reports published in the *New York Times*. At the same time Ronald Reagan's older brother, Neil, was a paid informer for the FBI. His demeaning service consisted in hiding in the shrubbery and noting for the FBI the license plate numbers of cars parked near a home in which a number of people were meeting, any gathering of people other than certified right-wingers being, by FBI definition, subversive.

As I indicated above, from my first meeting with Ronald Reagan I have regarded him as a dangerous man.[2] Although not a colleague, I was an acquaintance. In his interview with me, which I have described above, it was clear that he believed, or pretended to believe, that the CSU unions I was supporting in the Hollywood labor war were Communist controlled. It seemed plausible that I might have been one of those he informed upon. I was curious to find out. Urged on by my religious superior, Fr. Paul Locatelli, I wrote to the FBI demanding, under the Freedom of Information Act, that they send me copies of whatever information they had about me in their files.

They cannot, under that act, refuse to respond. They can, however, stall. Due largely to the persistence of Father Locatelli, who enlisted the aid of a lawyer and two congressmen of his acquaintance, the requested documents were eventually forthcoming. They were a block-buster—in size.[3]

I had expected six or seven pages. Instead I received two bulky packages containing almost five hundred pages, the fruit of what the FBI terms a "full field investigation," which involved the FBI offices in Chicago, Phoenix, New York, Sacramento, Milwaukee, St. Louis, San Francisco, Seattle, Salt Lake City, Los Angeles, and Washington. Four copies of the reports submitted by each of these agencies were carried "by special messenger" on February 26, 1953, from J. Edgar Hoover to James E. Hatcher, Chief of the Investigation Division of the U. S. Civil Service Commission.

It was a tremendous ego-booster when I thought of the money, time, and number of people engaged over a period of years in this absurd effort to find any shred of evidence questioning my loyalty to this country. But when I thought of how many homes could have been built for the homeless or how great a contribution could have been made to the rebuilding of Nagasaki or Hiroshima by the expenditure of these same resources, I ceased to laugh.

Over a period of years the FBI had evidently shadowed my every move, recorded my every statement. Every speech I made had been covered, whether from the steps of the city hall, the stage of the Hollywood Bowl, the Olympic Auditorium, a Baptist church, a union hall, the American Legion Stadium, or a dozen other places. Every time my name appeared in the press, the item was clipped and sent to the FBI. *Trial by Fire* receives considerable attention, much of it obviously emanating from the contemptible Jack Tenney, California state senator, whose despicable activities as head of the state's microimitation of the House Un-American Activities Committee I have already mentioned.[4]

Not all of the items that found their way into the FBI report are negative. One newspaper story about *Trial by Fire* (the name of the paper does not appear on the clipping), after an accurate description of the play, remarks: "Father Dunne is counted one of the most out-spoken critics of the American race-caste system. His indictment of compulsory racial segregation, based on moral and political principles and an intensive study of its evil social effects, originally published in *Commonweal* and widely reprinted, is regarded as authoritative."

One thing that exceedingly annoyed Mr. Hoover was the difficulty of confirming the authenticity of my signature. Repeatedly a document bearing what purported to be my signature was sent to the FBI laboratory for verification, and repeatedly the answer came back as on February 17, 1953:

> Results of examination:
> No conclusion was reached as to whether the signature "Fr. George H. Dunne" appearing on specimen Qc1 was written by George H. Dunne, whose known handwriting is designated as K2, because the questioned signature is too distorted to warrant an opinion one way or another.

Evidently someone was taking liberties with my signature, because that which appears on specimen Qc1 is obviously not my signature, which is naturally "distorted," but never like this.

What conclusion the FBI drew from this mass of material, if any, I do not know. But on February 26, 1953, J. Edgar Hoover sent a memo to James Hatcher, together with the reports of ten of his field offices; the top right-hand corner of the memo has a notation, the meaning of which arouses my curiosity:

Closing Full Field
Disloyal #3.

It is impossible to determine from these documents whether Ronald Reagan and his brother were among the informers who supplied the FBI with information and misinformation about me, because the names of all informers are blacked out, as are the names of all the "special agents" who prepared the reports of the field offices. Blacking out the names of their informers is permitted the FBI under the terms of the Freedom of Information Act.

I often met with the other members of the Catholic Interracial Council at the home of Dr. Julia Metcalfe. I occasionally met at one of several other homes with like-minded citizens to discuss the Equal Rights to Employment Act, or incidents of police or sheriff brutality to blacks and hispanics on the east side, or problems engendered by the Ku Klux Klan and other racists, or other problems of civic concern. If Neil Reagan was skulking in the bushes outside any of these homes, I hope it was a damp and chilly night. If his younger brother Ronnie was huddled alongside him, I hope it rained torrentially.

Also blacked out extensively are whole paragraphs and entire pages, probably concealing what I would consider most relevant and most damning to the FBI. Not blacked out are three documents which, taken alone, give sufficient insight into my views to have satisfied the ends of their inquiry, without resorting to the expenses of a "full field investigation":

1) My entire testimony before Congressman Kearns's one-man subcommittee of the House Committee on Education and Labor.[5] I was on the stand an entire day; my testimony fills fifty pages of the FBI report.

2) An interview with me by a team of special agents. I had forgotten this incident. It was probably conducted at Loyola University in Los Angeles, where I resided. Covering nineteen pages, it is a fairly accurate, if rhetorically flawed, description of my views on such subjects as communism, democracy, racial discrimination against Negroes, anti-Semitism, exploitation of labor, participation in meetings sponsored by Communist front organizations, etc.

3) A letter I wrote to the National Labor Relations Board. There are several copies of it in the FBI papers sent to me, but on none of them is the date decipherable. It was written in defense of Mike Komaroff, one of the three staff members of the Southern California office of the NLRB, all of whom were close friends of mine. Mike's loyalty had been impugned by the FBI upon the theory of guilt by association. In concluding a vigorous defence I remarked:

> It is possible that I have sat at table with Communists. . .as it is possible that I have sat at table with adulterers, masturbators, wife-beaters and drunkards, which does not make me a Communist or an adulterer or a masturbator or a wife-beater or a drunkard. Nor does it make me a sympathizer with communism, adultery, masturbation, wife-beating or drunkenness. . .
>
> I think it is time that Mr. J. Edgar Hoover looked into the activities of his underlings who are subverting every American concept of justice. . .

Saga of Emmet McLaughlin, O.F.M.

One of the best-known people in Phoenix, when I arrived there in 1948, was Fr. Emmet McLaughlin, O.F.M. The respect and admiration which he enjoyed were due to his extraordinary achievements for the poorer segments of the south side.

Emmet belonged to the Franciscan community at Saint Mary's Church in downtown Phoenix, but his main apostolate was among the residents of the near south side, many of whom were blacks and Hispanics. Here he said Mass every Sunday, attended to their spiritual needs, and concerned himself increasingly with their temporal problems. He also succeeded to a remarkable extent in awakening the consciousness of the entire Phoenix community to the existence and the needs of the poor in their midst. With the invaluable help of Eleanor Roosevelt he persuaded the federal government to finance an extensive public housing project on the south side. His crowning achievement was to build, again with government financial support, a hospital serving especially the poor.

My Jesuit confrere at Saint Francis Xavier, Bill Hanley, had known Emmet since childhood in San Francisco, where their families were close friends. He introduced me to Emmet shortly after I arrived in Phoenix. Out of our mutuality of interests a warm friendship was born, and on my not infrequent visits to the hospital I never failed to stop in his office for a visit. As a result of our conversations I became aware before most people in Phoenix that Emmet was having trouble with his Franciscan superiors.

According to his probably biased account, they had never been really interested in what he was doing. Knowing something of human nature and of the realities of life in a religious community, I would not be inclined easily to dismiss his allegation that the prominence he had reached in Phoenix had not equally pleased all of his brothers. On the other hand, his superiors were increasingly of the opinion that he was becoming so absorbed in the material and temporal aspects of his ministry as to lose sight of and interest in the spiritual.

Their concern was not without reason. Although Emmet was not administrator of the extensive public housing project he had established, he did maintain a quasi-supervisory interest in its operation. More important, he was the administrator of the hospital; this, as anyone familiar with hospitals knows, is a full-time job. Emmet had little time left for what might be called priestly ministry. One sign of this, noted by his superiors, was that Emmet no longer said Sunday Mass in the chapel which had been the starting point of his south side ministry. He had handed this responsibility over to one of his Franciscan brothers from Saint Mary's.

Emmet argued that administering the hospital was a priestly ministry; but to his superiors, sitting behind a desk and directing the complex affairs of a large hospital is not the same thing as ministering to the sick. Their concern about Emmet increased as he appeared less frequently in his Franciscan community at Saint Mary's. They feared that he was distancing himself more and more from the religious life to which he had committed himself. They decided to move him away from Phoenix, which had become, in their eyes, not only the scene of Emmet's exceptional achievements for the poor but also a growing threat to his vocation as a priest and as a Franciscan.

When I left Phoenix to give a lecture in Sacramento, I was aware that the tension between Emmet and his superiors had reached the crisis point. Emmet was unwilling to quit Phoenix. This was understandable. He had become one of its most prominent citizens. Extensive housing developments and a large hospital were impressive reminders of his accomplishments. The number of his friends and admirers was legion. To abandon all of this at a superior's command would have required an act of obedience little short of heroic.

On the other hand, his superiors were convinced that at stake was fidelity to his vocation. I sympathized with Emmet, but I understood the concerns of his superiors. I hoped an understanding could be reached which would not uproot Emmet.

The morning after my lecture in Sacramento I learned that I had hoped in vain. The *Sacramento Bee* carried in a front page story Emmet's announcement that he was leaving the Franciscan order and "the active ministry of the Catholic priesthood."

Upon my return to Phoenix I went immediately to see Emmet. We met in his hospital office and discussed his situation at length. I attempted to persuade him to accept his superior's orders and to leave Phoenix. The substance of my argument was that he had accomplished his work in Phoenix. Neither the housing developments nor the hospital would disappear with his departure. Through them, even though absent, he would continue to serve the poor in Phoenix. At the same time he could repeat elsewhere what he had accomplished here.

Emmet's answer to my argument was "that might be true if they were assigning me somewhere else; but they are assigning me to Spokane." I gathered from this that Spokane served as a kind of Franciscan Siberia, where troublesome subjects could be sent to be seen and not heard, much as Joe O'Brien had sent me to Phoenix, I think, or—due allowance being made for the difference in the persons involved—as his Parisian superiors had sent Fr. Teilhard de Chardin to faraway China. Unlike Teilhard, whose heroic obedience stood the test of years, Emmet refused to go. In the years that followed he became increasingly bitter, not only towards the Franciscan order but towards the Church. After his marriage to the medical librarian of his hospital, he instructed her that, in the event he should, on the point of dying, ask for a priest, she should ignore his request.

I continued to drop by his office whenever I was in the hospital. Some years later, after Emmet had divorced and remarried, I received a telephone message from his wife that he wished to see me at the hospital. I had read in the newspaper that he had recently suffered a heart attack. Thinking that he might not have enjoined his second wife from calling a priest and that faced with death he might wish to be reconciled to the Church, I hurried to the hospital. I found Emmet recovered from his heart attack, in seemingly good health and apparently not thinking about death or reconciliation. A patient in the maternity ward, young, unmarried, and pregnant, was having a problem deciding what to do with her baby. She was a Catholic. Emmet advised her to consult a priest and had his wife call me for that purpose. I was sorry that reconciliation had not motivated my summons; but I was happy to find Emmet in good health and was pleased that, despite his personal bitterness, he would still turn to the Church when the spiritual needs of those he served required it.

Emmet died in the late 1960s or early 1970s—I do not recall the exact date. I was living in Switzerland at the time. His former Franciscan superior wrote me that he had been reconciled with the Church and at his own request received the sacraments on his deathbed. Emmet had a younger brother, also a Franciscan priest, whose death preceded Emmet's by several years. Perhaps his memory played a role in bringing to a happy ending a generous, fruitful, and yet tormented life.

Ice Follies

In early summer 1957, I received orders from the provincial transferring me to Santa Clara University. I had mixed feelings about quitting Phoenix. Leaving behind the pastor, Dan Kelleher, would cause me no pain. He was no doubt as happy to see me go— I suspect he had urged it upon the provincial—as I was to bid him adios. But during my nine years there, I had made many friends, and saying good-by to friends is a wrenching experience. I have found myself deeply moved watching people who are total strangers to me taking leave of each other at the airport or the railroad station. Similarly, although this is peculiar to my later years, I find it an emotionally trying experience to say a funeral Mass even when the deceased is unknown to me. Separation is a cruel experience, which is why, I suppose, the traditional Irish wake is designed to postpone facing its reality. I have often said to myself and sometimes to others, at some moment of departure, "My life seems to be a succession of good-bys." That in fact is the life of a Jesuit, almost by definition. So I prepared for another turning point in my life—departure from Phoenix. The date was set at July 5.

The teen club of the parish had planned an ice-skating party for the eve of my departure. Ice skating in Phoenix on July 4 with the temperature standing at 110 degrees seems a bizarre idea. But an indoor rink with artificial ice, the first of its kind in Phoenix, had recently opened just a few blocks from the church. The teenagers invited me to join them in a kind of farewell party. I accepted, with almost fatal consequences. The last time I had been on ice skates was some eighteen years before, on Chicago's Midway.

On my rented skates I ventured boldly, if awkwardly, onto the ice amidst the crowd of joyous teenagers, boys and girls. With each tour of the rink my confidence grew, as I maneuvered the turns, crossing right skate over left, with increasing ease. On one of my turns I spotted a little girl, perhaps eight or nine years old, standing alone on the sidelines. She was equipped with double-runner skates. I skated over and asked her if she would like to skate with me. Hands joined in approved skater fashion, we had happily managed several tours of the rink, when disaster struck. I describe what happened not from memory, of which I have none, but from what witnesses told me afterwards.

One of the teenage boys suddenly veered in front of me and in doing so tripped me up. Probably because I was holding the little girl's hands, I had no control of my fall and landed with exceptional force. I came to in the emergency room of Saint Joseph's Hospital, whither I had been brought by ambulance. I was hazily aware of the doctor who was putting the last of fourteen stitches in my forehead. I heard him tell my several Jesuit confreres, of whose presence I was also dimly aware, that when he finished the stitching they could take me home.

As he continued stitching, he asked me questions about the accident. I could not answer them, because I had no idea what had happened or where it had happened. This, he would later tell me, gave him pause. Concluding that the injury might be more serious than he had thought, he canceled the permission to take me home and arranged to keep me in the hospital for further examination.

This decision was one of those chess moves of far-reaching consequences of which I wrote early on in these memoirs. Some weeks later the doctor, with admirable candor, told me that he had almost committed a grievous error that night which would have cost my life. Had he permitted me to be taken home, I would certainly have died. In this case, of course, many of the events described in the rest of these memoirs would never have occured, the others would have taken place without me. This, to be sure, would little affect the history of the world, but it would have written a different conclusion to my personal history and would have altered the histories of those who have lived in these events with me. Thus the game of chess, which is life.

The doctor had assumed that the abrasions on my forehead were the only injuries I had sustained. He had noticed that a certain amount of blood had accumulated in my left ear but had thought the abrasions accounted for this. The fact that I had no recollection of what had happened gave him second thoughts, and fortunately, for both of us, he decided to put me on hold.

The next morning a specialist examined my ear and determined that the eardrum had been completely knocked out and that the blood had flowed, not from the forehead, but from inside the head! A neurosurgeon was called, who quickly established that I had suffered a basal skull fracture, which, I was told, is the most serious kind. Knowing this I was content to stay in the hospital, where I remained for a full month, flat on my back and motionless for most of that time.

The second day, Betty Abraham, of the ladies' sodality and *Virtue Well Rewarded*, who had been at the rink with her teenage daughter, visited me and gave me an eyewitness account of what had happened. She told me that I had been a horrible sight to behold, lying in a pool of blood, my face turned purple. She also stooped over and gave me a chaste, sisterly kiss. Although it was chaste and sisterly, I felt that the skull fracture had been a small price to pay.

I asked Betty what had happened to my little skating partner. She did not know. She undoubtedly was terrified by what must have been a traumatic experience and in the future did not need a mother's warning never to skate with a stranger!

Upon my discharge from the hospital the neurosurgeon told me that I must remain in Phoenix for a year for regular checkups. He also said that during the year "you may listen to the radio, watch television, but DON'T THINK!"—an injunction impossible to observe unless one excludes daydreaming from the category of thought.

The neurosurgeon's order that I remain in Phoenix did not sit well with Dan Kelleher. He had been within twenty-four hours of seeing the last of me and did not relish the idea of having me around for another year. He reacted somewhat like the California Angels, who in 1986, with two outs in the ninth inning, had been within one strike of the World Series, when Dave Henderson of the Red Sox drove the ball over the center-field fence. Kelleher made no effort to disguise the bitterness of his disappointment nor to conceal his efforts to persuade superiors to countermand the doctor's orders.

The problem was solved by Frank Harrington, the superior of the Jesuits in the rectory as well as those in Brophy Prep, and therefore Kelleher's boss. Frank authorized me to move into a house on North Central Avenue that belonged to the parish. It had been given to the parish by an executive of the Del Webb corporation as a tax write-off. A next-door, but occasional, neighbor was Dizzy Dean of baseball fame. A near neighbor was Frank Brophy. The house was used for parish committee meetings or small social affairs. I had used it for the rehearsals of *Virtue Well Rewarded*. It now became my convalescent home.

Here, with regular visits to the neurosurgeon, I spent six tranquil months. They cannot be called uneventful months, because it was during this period that I had the encounters with Claire Booth Luce narrated above.

With the advent of the new year, although I still suffered an occasional stab of pain in the area of the fracture and sometimes took a sudden lunge or forward stagger when walking, the neurosurgeon decided that I had improved enough to justify releasing me on parole. I could go to Santa Clara, but must continue for six more months to observe the "don't think" injunction.

Twelve

Back in the Mainstream

My return to California spelled, in a sense, my reentry into the mainstream of Jesuit life after nine years of exile in Arizona, admittedly enjoyable, but exile nonetheless. The reentry did not occur immediately, because the first six months were spent in almost total idleness. I was still on parole. My only assigned duty was a weekly visit to hear the confessions of the nuns at the nearby Carmelite convent, whose foundress and current prioress was a sister of my friend Noel Sullivan. Another weekly activity, not prescribed, was a game of golf at the Olympic Club in San Francisco with two of my Jesuit colleagues, Walter Schmidt and Lou Bannan. If golf was not prescribed neither was it proscribed, my neurosurgeon evidently not agreeing with those who regard it as a thinking man's game.

With the end of July 1958, several events signaled my formal entry into the mainstream. My medical parole ended; I was allowed to think again. Herman Hauck, S.J., was succeeded as president of Santa Clara University by Patrick Donohoe, S.J. For the approaching fall semester I was to be resident prefect of the second-floor students in McLaughlin Hall and professor of constitutional law. Santa Clara was not then coeducational, so all my students were men. My academic load was light, because the medicos had recommended what the Chinese would call a *man-man-ti*—take it easy—approach to renewed intellectual activity.

I enjoyed teaching again. My relations with the students were good. I looked forward to spending the rest of my life at Santa Clara, growing old as a benign Mr. Chips. This was not to be the case. As in St. Louis and in Los Angeles, I was destined to have a short, if happy, life at Santa Clara that would end in conflict with the establishment. First, however, I had another brush with death.

It was early in the semester. The day was beautiful, and I never felt better. Following my class I enjoyed a good lunch and then went to my room, where I began to read my breviary. Suddenly, although I did not feel ill in any way, waves of weakness began to pass over me. I went into my bedroom and lay down until they ceased. I returned to my office and resumed the breviary, only to have the experience repeat itself. This happened several times.

Thinking a walk might help, I went out; but before I had gone very far, sitting down on the curbstone several times to regain my strength, I returned to McLaughlin and took the elevator to the second floor. While ascending, for the first time I felt nauseated and at the same time an urgent need to get to the bathroom as quickly as possible. A mad rush down the corridor got me there just in time, as my innards seemed to pour out with explosive violence. It was a hemorrhage from a bleeding ulcer, which I did not know I had. I managed to make it to my phone, called the infirmary and told the nurse that I had had a hemorrhage. The nurse arrived posthaste, having already been in touch with the university doctor, who had told her to call an ambulance and take me to the hospital.

Two Jesuits arrived on her heels. I was vaguely aware of their presence but could follow the argument which immediately broke out between them. One of them wanted to hear my confession, undoubtedly a good idea, but wholly inappropriate to the circumstances. I was as incapable of compiling a catalogue of my sins as I was of reciting the multiplication table. The other one prevailed and, dispensing with confession, administered what were then called the last rites, or the sacrament of extreme unction.

The ambulance arrived. I was carried on a stretcher downstairs and through a crowd of students, attracted by the screaming siren, to whom I gave the V-for-victory sign. This was my second ride in an ambulance. The first time I had been unconscious. This time I was semiconscious and rather enjoyed the wild dash through the streets with shrieking siren sweeping everything out of our path.

Arrived in the emergency room, I had little consciousness left. But I had enough left to hear, as from a great distance, the nurse crying to the doctor in tones of desperation, "I can't find a vein." The doctor took over and soon the first of the fourteen blood transfusions which I was to receive over the next few days was flowing.

I have very fine veins. They have been a perennial problem for nurses trying to insert a needle. Some years ago, following a heart attack, I had to have a monthly blood test. The nurse, wearied of the incessant search for a vein that would work, solved the problem by pricking a finger and squeezing out the blood she needed. Fortunately we have five fingers on each hand.

It had been a close call. My sister and her husband flew up from Los Angeles the first night and stayed for more than a week, until I was pronounced out of danger and taken off intensive care. This was her second flight; the first had been to Phoenix, occasioned by my skull fracture. One of the positive results of the two episodes was that she overcame her fear of flying and has since become a seasoned world traveler.

I spent a month in the hospital, followed by several weeks in the university infirmary. It was shortly after I returned to work that the next conflict with authority, to which I seemed to be predestined, began to develop.

Storm Warnings

My relations with Pat Donohoe, president of Santa Clara, had until then left nothing to be desired. I had known him since my days in St. Louis, when, as a scholastic about to embark on graduate studies in political science, he had written me for advice. I recommended Harvard over St. Louis, in considerable part because of the presence on Harvard's faculty of Dr. Charles McIlwain, a renowned specialist in the political theory of the Middle Ages. St. Louis University, on the other hand, did not have a particularly distinguished faculty of political science. It was later that Dr. Kurt von Schuschnigg, the pre-Hitler chancellor of Austria, and Fr. Charles McCoy would bring a certain luster to the department. Donohoe went to Harvard. He did not finish there, however, but after two years transferred to St. Louis.

Pat Donohoe was an extremely intelligent man. He was also a very able teacher and motivator, much admired by his students. He was a first-rate university president, as the years of his administration, 1958 to 1968, were to prove. Not the least of his accomplishments was the transformation of Santa Clara, against the opposition of many hard-line traditionalists, into a coeducational institution. The greatly enhanced academic status of Santa Clara, to which others contributed, to be sure, and the impressive number of new buildings which arose during his presidency testify to his many admirable qualities. With all his positive qualities he had, like most of us, his faults.

One of these, as I was to learn to my cost, was vindictiveness and a readiness to use others, including his friends, as instruments to achieve his sometimes less than noble ends. He also had a stubborn determination to achieve those ends. Whether this was a virtue or not depended, of course, upon the nature of his ends in any given case.

In addition to my duties as professor and prefect, Pat Donohoe named me moderator of the law school, supposedly because I had studied law. I think that this office, formerly known as regent, was peculiar to Jesuit universities. Its apparent purpose was to maintain a Jesuit presence in a school whose dean was usually a layman. My job description specified that I was to have no authority in the premises, but was to act solely in an advisory capacity both to the academic vice-president and to the dean. As things developed I began to suspect that my real role was to spy upon the dean, Warren McKenney, for the president. I consulted Fr. Alexis ("Bocci") Mei, the academic vice-president, who confirmed my suspicions.

As Bocci told the history, two years before, when Pat Donohoe was still a faculty member, three of his former students had poisoned his mind against the dean. These students, who had become his personal friends and who had later matriculated in the law school, charged McKenney, among other things, with incompetence both as dean and as professor and with drinking on the job. Pat accepted their stories at face value and urged Herman Hauck, the president, to fire the dean. Hauck refused to act upon the unsubstantiated charges. Pat appealed to the provincial, who directed Hauck to conduct an inquiry. Hauck then asked a man who was a judge of the Superior Court in San Jose, a graduate of Santa Clara's law school, to investigate the charges and to render a decision. The judge conducted regular hearings in which he questioned the student informants, other students, the dean himself and all whose testimony was relevant. At the end of the investigation, he rendered a decision that not only found the dean innocent but added that the university owed him an apology. Pat did not take kindly to this rebuff, and now that he had replaced Hauck as president, illustrating the stubborn determination to achieve his ends which I mentioned above, he was determined to use his powers to fire the dean. I was expected to gather the evidence with which he could justify his action.

There was one bizarre and, because of its epilogue, amusing incident in his effort to use me to prove his case against the dean. One of the charges was that the dean was biased against certain students; as proof, he was alleged to have unfairly failed a student in his course on evidence. The president sent the student to me with his examination paper as graded by the dean, with orders that I should reevaluate it. Such a procedure was extraordinary, and besides, more than thirty years had passed since I had studied law. But upon the president's insistence I put my misgivings aside and, pretending that I was a professor of evidence, evaluated the examination paper, grading each answer on a scale of one to five. The result was in the neighborhood of 72. The dean had given the student a 68. The difference was obviously not enough to justify overruling the dean. Grading examination papers in subjects other than mathematics being a matter of judgment, one could justify either a barely passing or a barely failing grade. One could not establish a case of prejudice or favoritism on so narrow a basis.

The amusing epilogue is this: some eleven years later a young man appeared in my office at the World Council of Churches in Geneva, Switzerland. He wished to go to confession. That taken care of, we had a pleasant chat. He was staying at the Interconti-nental Hotel, a few blocks away. He identified himself as the student whose paper on evidence I had reviewed. Knowing my whereabouts and being in the vicinity he had come to thank me for having refused to raise his grade to a passing mark. As a result, he had decided to abandon a career in law, had gone into the in-vestment business instead, and was already, in his early thirties, a millionaire. We had a good laugh together about the unexpected consequences in the game of chess which is life. He had been one of Pat's informers.

Early on, Pat had told me that he was disappointed in the earlier investigation into the dean and that he expected me to look into the man's merits from within the law school. In the months that followed, with the interlude of my hospitalization, I made a detailed and painstaking examination of the state of mind of the students vis-à-vis the Santa Clara law school, its faculty, and especially its dean. Father Donohoe maintained that ninety percent of the students regarded McKenney as thoroughly incom-petent, both as teacher and as dean; the evidence I gathered established beyond any doubt that this was not the case. On the contrary, only an insignificant minority thought the dean incom-petent.

I wrote a fifteen-page report giving facts and figures from which I concluded that nothing I had learned from the students and nothing that I had observed myself supported the charge of serious incompetence on the part of Dean McKenney. "If the Administration feels that it is unable or unwilling to give its full support to the dean," I wrote, "then I think it should frankly tell him so and ask him to resign." The dean had assured me that in these circumstances he was ready to do so. But Pat was determined to fire him even upon manufactured charges.

On the morning of April 11, 1959, I put my report in campus mail.[1] At 2 P.M. that same day Father Donohoe telephoned me. He had not yet seen my report. He informed me that he had arranged a meeting for 4:15 P.M. with the consultors, some of the trustees, and the attorney for the university, who would question some students about the law school situation. He told me he "had to call this meeting," though he did not say why. He had arranged this without consulting me or notifying me, while I was still making the investigation and writing the report he had assigned me. He told me that I should attend this meeting "to ask any questions and make any statement" I desired. I assured him I would be there but said that I wished he would read my report before the meeting. He replied that he would do so immediately.

Less than an hour later he telephoned me again. When I answered the phone he said, without any preliminaries: "I have read your report. I gather from it you don't want to attend the meeting this afternoon. So you are excused." With heavy sarcasm he added "thanks" and hung up the phone.

The meeting from which I had been excluded was held that afternoon. The students who had been summoned as witnesses were warned to reveal nothing of what transpired, but such secrets cannot be kept long. Before the day was out the dean had been told of it by one of the students; others had discussed it with Audie Morris, S.J., the only Jesuit member of the law faculty. Fifteen students had testified, eight from the third year, where opposition to the dean was centered, and four each from the first and second years.

The star-chamber proceedings were a farce. The students who had been summoned to testify had been handpicked. Not one faculty member was asked his opinion. Judge Edwin A. Owens, who had served for twenty-three years as dean and was still an active member of the faculty and respected member of the bench, was not consulted. He was shocked and hurt when he learned what had been done.

In a letter of April 26 to the provincial I warned of the possible consequences of Donohoe's actions. If he were to fire McKenney, the latter would take his case to the American Association of Law Schools. Donohoe, I predicted, would be called before its governing board to defend his action. I pointed out that "the procedures followed here violate basic principles of legal ethics and of due process of law. A lawyer who attempted to suppress evidence and to counterfeit a case in this fashion would be subject to reprehension, if not to outright disbarment. It is shocking that these students, whom we are supposed to be training to become creditable members of the bar, have been induced by the Administration itself to participate in a kind of process that does violence to even minimal standards of legal ethics." In view of this, I said, it was quite possible that the American Association of Law Schools would strike Santa Clara from its list of accredited law schools.[2]

After mailing this letter I left for Los Angeles to attend the ordination of a nephew. During my brief absence Donohoe finally satisfied his almost pathological hatred. He notified McKenney that he was being dismissed for reasons of incompetence. Upon my return I found the law school in chaos. There had been a fist fight in the lobby between one of the students who had testified in the hearing and another student who, outraged by the proceedings, had posted a notice on the bulletin board charging that the malcontents had at last had their way. For this he had been summarily dismissed from the university by Fr. James Sweeters, the prefect of discipline.

On May 8, Fr. Wilfred Crowley, as emissary for Father Donohoe, came to see me. He said that Father Donohoe had heard that I was planning to show my report to outsiders, in particular to the newspapers and to the American Association of Law Schools. He also had heard that I had shown it to McKenney. He ordered me, through Crowley, to turn over to him all copies of the report in my possession. He was wrong on all counts. I did not plan to show the report to anyone, nor had I shown it to McKenney, though I think he had every right to see it.

Word reached me later that McKenney did indeed have a copy. I wrote to him to inquire about it, and he wrote back on September 12 from the University of Texas, where he had accepted a position as executive assistant to the director of the Law-Science Institute and Academy of America.

McKenney admitted that he had a copy, but he assured me that I was not responsible: "I took a copy without you knowing it and had a copy made for myself." I do not know how he obtained the copy, perhaps from the typist or perhaps from my office. In any case, I do not blame him. He had a right to know what conclusions I had reached.

I fully agree with his justification of his action: "Father, after all my trials and tribulations at Santa Clara, the only thing that I have for my own protection is your report. . . .So I took the report, the only evidence that I had to substantiate all that I have said for all these years. I took it for the protection of myself and my family."[3]

In concluding his letter, after expressing sympathy for Father Mei, "who unfortunately was caught in the middle of the mess," he assured me of his prayers and those of his family "for always."

That was the end of the affair for Warren McKenney and for me, but not for Santa Clara. As I had predicted, Father Donohoe was obliged to appear before the governing board of the Association of American Law Schools. He succeeded in dissuading them from striking Santa Clara from the roll of approved law schools, as I had predicted they would, but at the cost of accepting an imposed constitution granting the law school a degree of autonomy that made it virtually independent of the central administration of the university.

Three Strikes and Out

At the end of my report I had asked to be relieved of my job as moderator of the law school. I need not have bothered. Father Donohoe went me one better: he dismissed me from the university. There is a phrase for this in football—being sacked. This was the third time I had been sacked. Notification came in the form of a note from the provincial informing me that he was transferring me to the University of San Francisco. Pat Donohoe had not only rid himself of McKenney, he had persuaded the provincial to rid him of me.

In the two previous instances, St. Louis and Los Angeles, I had accepted the bruises as part of the game. But to be sacked because I was unwilling to be used as an instrument in the furtherance of Pat Donohoe's obsession seemed to me what the Irish call a bit much of a much. Adding to this was the fact that the provincial, who had been fully informed of the facts and who later would tell me that he did not see how I could have written any other report or behaved otherwise than I had, would so easily lend himself to the achievement of Pat's goals. "Three times is out," I said to myself. It began to seem clear to me that there was a fundamental incompatibility between myself and the mode of governance of the Society of Jesus. I began to think not of leaving the Society, but of temporary exclaustration, that is, a two-year leave of absence during which to reflect upon whether or not I was suited to the Society or it to me.

The straw that broke this camel's back was a phone call from Fr. John F. X. Connolly that reached me in Santa Barbara. Father Connolly was president of the University of San Francisco. "George," he said, "we are delighted to have you with us at USF; I am going to name you a student counselor." I am sure he had the best intentions in the world, but to me it was the end of the line. The only student counselors I had known were alcoholics. This is not to say that they were not good men and good priests. On the contrary, despite the illness from which they suffered, they had done a great deal of good and, in at least two cases, were admired and respected by all who knew them. It seemed to be the practice in those days to make them student counselors, the theory evidently being that in that post the absences, sometimes of several weeks, occasioned by their periodic binges, would be less disruptive than if they were absent from the classroom. I hasten to add that this is neither the theory nor the practice today. The office of campus ministry, which has supplanted that of student counselor, is one of top priority to which only highly qualified men and women are appointed. That was not the case yesterday.

I was not an alcoholic. Nevertheless, confinement to the office of student counselor seemed clearly to be just that—a confinement. I was to be kept out of the classroom. I knew from my experience in St. Louis and in Los Angeles that I was an effective teacher. A student poll at Santa Clara had ranked me among their best professors. I would have to have been an idiot not to see in the assignment as student counselor a declaration of lack of confidence.

This may have been a prudent decision taken to avoid a firestorm with Fr. Ray Feeley, the university's long-time prefect of studies. Back in 1945, the *Brooklyn Tablet*, in those days of the extreme right, had published some letters commenting upon my *St. Louis Bulletin* article upon postwar possibilities in Soviet-American relations, and it had mistakenly identified me as a member of the University of San Francisco faculty. Father Feeley, militant anti-Communist crusader and author of numerous Red Menace pamphlets, had written to the *Tablet* declaring that

"Father Dunne is not now and, as long as I am here, never will be a member of the University of San Francisco faculty." Father Feeley was still there and still a force with which the president had to reckon. That I could understand; but I could not accept my relegation to the dump heap without justifying reasons. I wrote to the provincial requesting exclaustration.

We met on August 29 in his office in San Francisco. He expressed shock and surprise at my request. He could not understand what reasons I could have. I was mildly surprised at this, because I thought the reasons were manifold and manifest. He told me that he had spent the two previous days reading my dossier from the province archives. As the fruit of his study he listed faults which had been attributed to me. Eight of them were manifestly the handiwork of Father Holloran from my St. Louis days. Most of them were concerned with trivialities, and all of them were false. I was said, for example, not to have turned in my mail to be censored before mailing, not to have attended our common praying of litanies, frequently to have dined out.

A more serious charge of Holloran's is an example of hermeneutics gone mad. He alleged that in the radio talk which first incurred his wrath I had made a "subtle attack" upon St. Louis's Cardinal Glennon by a "sly reference to the purple." I was talking about the dignity of each individual, and I said, "Whether we wear the princely purple or the rough garb of a peasant, we all possess the same human nature." This was the subtle attack upon Glennon, and this was the origin of the report that I went about "attacking archbishops."[4]

The fact is that I gave that radio talk more than six months before Glennon was named a cardinal, thus becoming a "prince of the Church." The violence done to the most ordinary canons of exegesis, to say nothing of Saint Ignatius's admonition always to put the best possible interpretation upon a text, suggests how desperate Holloran was to build a case against me and how little of substance he had to build upon.

Other allegations which O'Sullivan said he had found in the dossier were cut from the same cloth as these. In a letter to him dated September 14, 1959, after stating "my reaction to these allegations was one of profound sadness that a man's reputation and standing in the Society could be destroyed on the basis of so paltry and unsubstantial a record," I examined each of them in detail.[5]

The Society of Jesus has a rule to which I directed O'Sullivan's attention: "Let superiors not easily believe informers, but investigate every case; first of all hearing the accused and giving him an opportunity to defend himself; and if he is found to be innocent, let the informer be reprehended or punished according to the gravity of the case."[6] Blame for bad government cannot be laid upon the rules of the Society of Jesus, but upon their nonobservance. By ignoring all five injunctions of this rule, a pejorative image of me had been created and by now was firmly established in the official folklore of the province.

I concluded: "Only a few weeks ago a Jesuit priest who has known me since before I entered the Society. . .and who was speaking without any idea that I had asked for exclaustration, said to me: 'You may as well face it, George; among those who have power in this province and have had power for many years now, you are a *persona non grata*.' I am, I think, now facing it. *Persona non grata* means 'not wanted.' All these years I have tried to accept this sense of repudiation in the spirit of the 11th Rule [of the Summary of the Jesuit Constitutions],[7] but I am afraid rebellion was only suppressed into the subconscious. I am now asking to be freed from what has become intolerable to me. Let me simply say that I lack the virtue longer to accept the situation."

O'Sullivan had suggested that superiors had found me difficult to deal with. I disputed this. Two cases in particular, both involving Father Whelan, make my point. They both illustrate the difficulty I had in dealing with him rather than any difficulty he had in dealing with me.

In May 1947, with the explicit sanction of both Father Whelan and Bishop Manning, I had given the first of a series of radio talks on social problems. I received more than three hundred letters from listeners praising this talk. The following week I prepared a second talk. It dealt with the proposed Taft-Hartley labor bill and consisted largely of quotations from *Quadragesimo Anno* and various other Catholic authorities, including Abp. Robert Lucey, Bp. Bernard Sheil, and Bp. Francis Haas. After reading the manuscript Father Whelan told me that I could not deliver this speech. He also told me that he did not wish me to continue these weekly radio talks. He said that I would have to have the bishop's permission. I reminded him that I had the bishop's permission, and he said he did not think the bishop approved.

I notified the director of the program that I would not be able to continue the broadcasts. My failure to appear on the air that week led to hundreds of letters to the radio station and to me. Shortly thereafter Father Whelan came to my room and informed me that the director of the program was in his office; the director had asked why I had quit the program, and he, Father Whelan, had told him he did not know why!

That afternoon I had a talk with Whelan. I told him it was impossible for me to operate this way; if he disapproved of my activities he should say so clearly, and I would obey. He replied that he did not disapprove, but that he knew that the bishop disapproved. "Then the Bishop should say that he disapproves," I said; "then I will know where I stand, and when I am asked to speak I can simply reply that I cannot do so because my Bishop does not approve."

Whelan said that I should not say this. When I asked him what I was to say, he replied that I could say that I was too busy. I said that this was an untruth and concluded by saying that I thought I should see Bishop Manning. Whelan agreed.

I met with Bishop Manning and asked him what charges or complaints, if any, the chancery office had against me. He said that I had "built up a mass following" in the community but did not say what was wrong about this. He complained that I had spoken in support of the Fair Employment Practices Act but failed to note that Abp. John Cantwell had endorsed the act.[8] He said that I had set myself up as the "sole authority in the archdiocese on labor matters" but did not document the charge. Finally, he repeated a complaint he had made over the phone many months earlier, that I had been "imprudent" in sending a telegram to the Hollywood producers proposing terms for a settlement of the strike; but he did not refer to what I had told him then, that my superior, Father Whelan, had approved both my sending the telegram and its text.

At the conclusion of our not particularly enlightening discussion I asked if he wished me to check with him before I took a position on any issue or engaged in any activity. He replied that he did not. "The situation is what it has always been," he said. "Provided you have the approval of your superior, that is all that is necessary."

I reported back to Father Whelan, who said that despite the bishop's assurance that he did not disapprove of my activities he knew that in fact the bishop did disapprove. I remarked that this seemed to me an extraordinary situation, with the bishop saying one thing to him and the contrary to me. He made no comment. Between this time and my sudden removal from Los Angeles the following September I engaged in no public activity of any kind, with the single exception of my testimony under subpoena at the congressional hearing.

The second incident that illustrates my difficulty with Father Whelan occurred when Daniel Marshall, president of the Catholic Interracial Council, wrote to Whelan suggesting that Loyola University sponsor a series of lectures on the evil of racial prejudice. Pope Pius XI had expressed the wish for such a conference to the rectors of Catholic universities throughout the world. Father Whelan thought it a good idea and suggested that Mr. Marshall meet with me, that we draw up a tentative program and submit the same to him.

We submitted a detailed program with a list of lecturers whom we proposed to invite. We suggested that the program be held in conjunction with the summer school at Loyola University. Father Whelan went over the program with us point by point and approved it with apparent enthusiasm. I contacted the proposed lecturers, all of whom accepted the invitation. I then turned the program over to Fr. William McIntosh, director of the summer school. The programs were printed and delivered.

Fr. Arthur Spearman, S.J., who was bitterly opposed to everything I did and who had told nuns in teaching communities that they should not allow me to address their students, had been trying to find out from Father McIntosh's secretary the nature of the program. Two days after the printed programs arrived on campus Father Whelan came to my room. He showed me a note written to him by Msgr. Patrick Dignan, superintendent of arch-diocesan schools; the note said, "I have been informed that the Institute to be conducted by Father Dunne at Loyola University this summer is unfit for nuns."

Father Whelan immediately canceled the program, and I had the embarrassing task of notifying all the lecturers. I told Father Whelan that, inasmuch as my reputation was at stake, I should see Monsignor Dignan and demand to know what in the program was "unfit for nuns." He agreed but insisted that he see Dignan first. He did, and upon his return he reported that Dignan said that the subject matter of the institute did not "properly belong in the academic program of a university." Whelan then directed me to tell Dignan that he had canceled the program before receiving Dignan's note, because that was what he had told Dignan! Offered this Hobson's choice, I chose not to see Dignan.

Three weeks later at Loyola's commencement, Father Whelan conferred an honorary degree upon Monsignor Dignan. The speaker at the ceremony was Mr. William Jeffers, retired railroad president and well-known laissez-faire capitalist. His speech, in which he branded Jefferson's "all men are created equal" a "silly doctrine," exhorted the Loyola students to resolve to make a million dollars, which he termed the goal of education and of life. Most of the Jesuits and many of the students thought this had been arranged to publicly repudiate my ideals; and Fr. Hugh Duce, acting provincial at the time, later confirmed that this was indeed the case.

During my conference with Carroll O'Sullivan, he disclosed that it had been reported to the provincial that I was "losing friends for Loyola." That may well have been true. There is evidence, however, that I was also winning friends. Among the documents which I sent to Father General with my report of 1947 was a thirteen-page miscellany of quotations from letters which I received during my two years of activity in Los Angeles. These letters came from lawyers, doctors, executives, union leaders, rank-and-file union members, rabbis, priests, religious, Jewish, Protestant, and Catholic lay people, and a member of the Catholic hierarchy. Abp. Robert Lucey of San Antonio wrote, "Upon reading your article ["The Sin of Segregation"] I felt like throwing my hat in the air for joy. . ."

These many letters and testimonies written to me put the complaints and concerns of my Jesuit and episcopal superiors in a different context. I can, nevertheless, understand their concerns better today than I did then. They had institutions and dioceses to maintain and enhance. These were their main concern. It was a matter of first importance that they maintain good relations with men and women of weight and wealth in the community. That this sometimes required compromises with truth and Catholic social teaching they could rationalize and probably did so with a good conscience. My concern was with truth, justice, and the social implications of the Gospel. This did not require that I cultivate the Joe Scotts, George Breslins, Frank Dohertys, or Frank Montgomerys of the community. It is clear to me today, as it was not then, that I was indeed a problem for superiors and that they did not know how to handle it. This is probably what they meant when, according to Carroll O'Sullivan, they told the provincial that they found it impossible to talk to me.

They could have handled it by a simple order. I am not disobedient. On the few occasions—and they are all recounted in these memoirs—when a superior has ordered me to abandon a project, I have obeyed, which is not to say that I agreed that his decision was correct. The difficulty was, I think, that they were reluctant to give orders for which they were unwilling to assume responsibility.

The root of the problem was an almost diametric difference between their way of thinking and mine. Basically, it is the difference between Zacheus Maher's conviction that social problems had no place in the Spiritual Exercises, which is to say in the preaching of the Gospels, and my conviction, expressed by the 1971 Synod of Bishops, that they form "a constituent dimension of the preaching of the Gospel." It is the difference between his claim that we cannot oppose the social institutions accepted by the society in which we live and my position, also confirmed by the same Synod of Bishops, that "participation in the transformation of the world" is also part of that same dimension. (None of these observations apply to the Santa Clara episode; in that case I was simply caught between the determination of a vindictive man to have his way and my own, I suppose equally stubborn, resolve not to be used as an agent in the service of his vindictiveness.)

The most extreme example of the gulf that separated their way of thinking from mine came in a reprimand from Joe King when he was provincial. He sent me a clipping from the union newspaper of the Conference of Studio Unions and expressed shock and displeasure. The article which had shocked him was a letter I had written to Herb Sorrell, president of the CSU, after a profile of Sorrell that I had written, entitled "Peace in Jail," appeared in *Commonweal*:

> I have received a couple of letters about my article in the *Commonweal* which I thought you would be interested in knowing about. One is from a Jesuit scholastic in San Francisco. He is not yet ordained but is studying for the priesthood. He writes: "Please convey my sympathies to Mr. Sorrell and, if you think he will understand, tell him that I am offering my Masses, prayers, communions, beads and good works every day this week for him and his people and that I shall continue to offer my prayers and good works every Monday from now on until I hear that they are out of trouble." The other is from a woman in New York named Regina Brady. She is a saintly woman who makes a practice of spending from midnight to 3 A.M. every morning in the presence of the Blessed Sacrament in her parish church. She writes: "Please tell Mr. Sorrell that I am offering my vigil tonight for him and his intentions." I thought that you would be pleased to know that people like these are on your side.

King was willing to excuse the publication of this letter only upon the assumption that "it is possible you did not intend this letter to be seen by anyone but Mr. Sorrell." King deplored "the publication of these more intimate practices and details of our Catholic life." One would think that the "intimate practices and details of our Catholic life" were obscenities to be concealed from prying eyes.

The division between my way of thinking and that of superiors seemed absolute. Divorce for reasons of incompatibility seemed the only answer. Many of my friends and confreres urged other solutions.

Bocci Mei wrote that Fr. Arby Lemieux, president of Seattle University and a close friend since novitiate days, was most anxious to have me on his faculty. He added: "I have always admired you not merely for your talents, but for your admirable qualities of heart and character. You have been a great source of edification to me and to many others for your patience and acceptance of the many severe trials that have come your way. I am sure there would be general rejoicing among your friends in the Province who are many indeed, if you should decide to remain in the Society."

Four days later I received a letter from Arby Lemieux confirming Bocci's information: "We—both the community and myself— would love to have you join us. We feel that you could contribute a great deal to our faculty."

Fr. Taylor McGuigan, Seattle University faculty member and another old friend, wrote: "George, I do not know how to say it but this will be a happy happy house if you come here. The young Fathers who made your retreat at Alma and knew you at Phelan Park are as interested as your old friends."

I also heard from Fr. John Rea Bradstreet, a close friend since eighth grade, when we played baseball against each other, he for Saint Vincent's and I for Saint Cecilia's. He wrote a long letter, eloquently urging me to reconsider: "Expressions like 'Tamquam de manu Dei [as from God's hand],' 'God's Providence rules the world,' 'You can't outdo God in generosity,' 'God draws straight with crooked lines' are still true, no matter how stale and trite they may sound. . .For a man who has consistently been forthright and unafraid, uncompromising in principle and conviction, you now show a strange inconsistency: surrender. I'm not saying that you haven't had cause. I'm not saying that you shouldn't be tired and weary and disgusted—all I'm trying to say is that more is expected from you than from the rest of us. Your past proves it."

Brad was, of course, right; I was being inconsistent. The Jesuit rules hold up an ideal for those making progress in the spiritual life: they should "wish to suffer abuse, injustice, false accusation and to be considered and treated as fools (without, however, giving occasion for such treatment), their whole desire being to resemble and in some way imitate our Creator and Lord Jesus Christ."[9] I had, in return for a favor granted, knelt down one night not long before the Alma retreat and earnestly prayed that this ideal be realized in me.

I had expected the contradictions, if they came, to come from outside, not from within the Church and within the Society. That was the surprise. Nevertheless, I got what I had asked for and had no reason to complain. "Ask and you shall receive." I had learned long ago, in the prayer that ended in my vocation to the priesthood, that one does not always get what one expected. But in this case I got what I had asked for and was, as Brad would have said, "chickening out." One does not play games with God.

I do not now remember why I did not accept the kind invitation of Arby Lemieux to join the faculty of Seattle University. Possibly because of developments which occurred before the invitation arrived. I had received under date of August 19, 1959, a letter from Bp. Charles F. Buddy of San Diego certifying "his willingness to accept you, pending the required permission of your Very Reverend Provincial and an indult from the Holy See. . .A cordial welcome awaits you in San Diego."

In a letter dated September 10, Father General Janssens wrote me asking that I delay ("Quare in nomine Domini tuam reverentiam instanter rogo ut paululum expectet") further action to give him time to reflect upon my request ("donec rem coram Deo profundius meditari possim"). Subsequently, he ordered Carroll O'Sullivan to send me directly to Rome to discuss the matter with him. I was in Santa Barbara when I received these orders from O'Sullivan, together with a check to cover travel expenses. These developments occurred shortly before I received Arby Lemieux's letter inviting me to Seattle and may explain my failure to respond to it.

I went to San Diego to tell Bishop Buddy about my orders to go to Rome. He was quite understanding, while repeating that I would always be welcome in San Diego.

While I was in the bishop's office I received a telephone call from Washington, D.C., from Fr. Edward ("Doc") Bunn, S.J., president of Georgetown University. I do not know how he had managed to run me down. One of Doc Bunn's closest Jesuit friends was Fr. Bill Dunne, S.J., former president of the University of San Francisco and then in residence at Georgetown. Doc Bunn was looking for a dean for Georgetown's School of Foreign Service. Bill Dunne told him of my present travail and recommended me for the job; characteristically, Doc was ready to ride to the rescue. He told me of his problem and asked me to come to Washington to discuss the deanship. I replied that I couldn't because I was under orders to fly directly to Rome. He suggested a stopover in Washington. Undoubtedly interpreting my orders too literally, I said that I did not think I could. Eventually, as I shall later narrate, I did end up at Georgetown, though not as dean; there, in a later stage of my life, Doc would join Bill Dunne as one of my closest friends.

Brad was completely right in arguing that exclaustration was not the solution to my problems. Nevertheless, in choosing it I had moved king's pawn into a position from which unforeseeable consequences followed. When I took off for Rome on October 24, 1959, from the Los Angeles International Airport, although I did not know it, another phase of my life had ended and a new and less turbulent phase had begun. I was headed in new directions.

Thirteen

The Eternal City and Beyond

I was met at Rome's Leonardo da Vinci Airport by an old friend and pinochle partner from China days, Frank Rouleau, S.J. More than twenty years had passed since we had waved good-by, he on the quay at Shanghai, I on the deck of the *Chichibu Maru* as it nosed out into the crowded waters of the Whangpoo River and headed for the Yangtze-chiang and the open sea. Neither of us, who had expected to spend the balance of our lives associated in the work of the Nanking Institute, had any idea, as the shore line receded from my view and the *Chichibu Maru* from his, that destiny had radically different things in store.

Frank, a highly-intelligent and first-rate scholar, had spent the war years with the other American Jesuits interned by the Japanese occupants in the Jesuit house at Zikawei, where he was professor of ecclesiastical and China-mission history. After the Communist conquest of China in 1950, he had moved to Rome, where he was assigned to the Istituto Storico—the historical institute—engaged in archival research on the history of the Jesuit missions in China.

I was initially lodged in the Istituto Storico on the Via dei Penitenzieri, adjacent to the Jesuit curia, the international headquarters of the order. The first discovery I made about Rome was that it can get very cold! And the fall of 1959 was exceptionally cold, and wet as well. The room to which I had been assigned, the only one available, was on the ground floor. A high stone wall just outside the window blocked out all direct sun and virtually all light. The stone floor contributed to the impression that I was living in a medieval dungeon.

Actually, there *was* a subterranean dungeon in the house—no longer in use, I am glad to report. For in the seventeenth century this had been one of the houses of the famed and powerful Barberini family, whose coat of arms, easily recognized by the three bees prominently displayed, is still to be seen on its walls, as it is seen everywhere in Rome. The whole city owes much of its sculpted beauty to Pope Urban VIII, a Barberini. Thanks to the patronage of their powerful uncle, the nephews of Urban VIII amassed enormous wealth. And like him they spent much of it on art and literature. The Barberini library was surpassed only by the Vatican library itself. The principal Barberini palace was built near the Quattro Fontane on the slope of the Quirinal by Bernini, the famed architect of Saint Peter's Piazza.

None of these past glories, however, made my gloomy room any warmer. Nor did the newspapers which I laid both under and over the mattress. The result was that I contracted a very heavy cold and lost no time in buying a sweater and some clothing heavier than what I had brought from California.

Another discovery I made was that the rush to get to Rome had been unnecessary. I could well have stopped in Washington to see Father Bunn. It was a case, as in the army, of "hurry up and wait." Four weeks passed before I was summoned to my meeting with Father General. I did not mind this delay, for I made good use of it to familiarize myself with the inexhaustible historical and artistic treasures of Rome.

Fr. John Baptist Janssens, the superior general, received me graciously. He was quite sympathetic. Unlike Carroll O'Sullivan, he had no difficulty understanding what had moved me to ask for exclaustration, but he asked me to reconsider in the light of the eleventh rule of the summary of the Constitutions, with its principle of imitating Christ in suffering. I was by now so enamored of Rome that I had no desire to hurry things to a conclusion. Furthermore, here in the same house were the archives to which I had so long wanted access. I asked Father General for permission to remain in Rome to document and rewrite my thesis on the history of the early Jesuits in China; meanwhile I would reconsider my request for exclaustration. Without hesitation he granted my request. Another interesting move in the game of life: I had asked permission to go to Rome to make use of the archives, and had been refused. I asked for exclaustration. This brought me to Rome and to the archives. God writing straight with crooked lines?

The room I had been given was unsuitable for permanent occupancy, so I was assigned a room on the top floor of the Curia.

I was to remain, nevertheless, a member of the Istituto Storico community, where I would take my meals. This was no problem. A bridge, perhaps fifty feet long, led from the top floor of the Curia to the hill in back, once the site of one of Nero's palaces, whence there was access to the Istituto. The Istituto Storico, as its name suggests, housed a group of Jesuit historians, many of them specialists in the history of the Jesuit foreign missions; here these scholars were editing and publishing the historical documents found in the archives, each one with his special field of interest.

One of the most attractive was Fr. Georg Schurhammer, who was nearing the completion of his monumental definitive biography of Saint Francis Xavier. In his early eighties, he was always cheerful and always lively. He went up the stairs two steps at a time, rarely walked, usually half ran. He was at his desk at three every morning—a quite extraordinary man who had evidently reincarnated the energy of Xavier.

Father Rouleau was engaged in his China research, as I have said. Another American, Fr. Ernest Burrus, who had studied philosophy with me at Mt. St. Michael's, was a specialist in the early Jesuit missions in Mexico. Another, Fr. Emil Schmidt, who had commanded a German submarine during the war, now sailed the more tranquil seas of historical research. An accomplished pianist, he supplied the accompaniment at our community Christmas party, when each nationality group was expected to contribute to the entertainment. I contributed for the Americans, announcing my number as an old American Christmas carol, but actually singing in Italian a very popular song of the day entitled "Piove"—"It's Raining"— the lyrics of which I had rewritten. Since there had been few days without rain that fall my satirical bit elicited much merriment.

Actually there were two communities in the Istituto; besides the historians, the Jesuit staff of Vatican Radio also lived there. Between the two, quite a number of nationalities were represented. As with the international community at Zikawei, I felt completely at home and warmly welcomed.

I also felt entirely at home in the spartan surroundings of my room in the Curia. The rooms which now composed the top floor had not been part of the original structure. They had been added on to accommodate transient visitors, and were extremely limited in size and in furnishings. My room was just large enough to accommodate an army-type cot, a small desk, two straight-backed chairs, a wash stand, slop bucket, and water pitcher. Two hooks on the wall substituted for a clothes closet. Down the corridor was a bathroom and a rather questionable shower which usually gave forth only a thin stream. I was, nevertheless, quite comfortable and content. I did my own laundry, using the slop bucket for a wash tub and, in true Italian fashion, hanging the sox, shirts, and shorts out the window to dry.

For some reason, I have always been fond of the simple and the old, which is probably why, with its glitter and glamor, American society is not my favorite society. This too is probably why I was so fond of China and am so fond of Europe. I once remarked that I did not have much to ask of God; all I asked was that I be allowed to live for a thousand years and to live each of those years in a different Italian village, hanging my laundry out the window, drinking *vino rosso*, and arguing politics with fellow villagers by the fountain in the village square as the sun went down painting the western skies. That does not seem too much to ask of a God to whom a thousand years are as a day.

Settled in my Curia room I wrote to the warehouse in Santa Clara where I had stored my trunk, asking that it be shipped to Rome. A copy of my doctoral thesis was in the trunk, and until it arrived I was free to continue my explorations of Rome. From them resulted an article entitled "This Is Rome," published in *Commonweal*, December 25, 1959.

Its subject was the numberless memories of history which echo from every nook and corner of this wonder-filled city. Among these were memories evoked by the massive Castel Sant'Angelo. Built by the Emperor Hadrian to serve as his tomb, it had through the ages been the scene of an extraordinary pageantry of history. In the dungeons of this tomb-fortress-castle had been imprisoned and here died Fr. Lorenzo Ricci, the superior general of the Society of Jesus when it was suppressed by the harried Pope Clement XIV. Thinking of this as I gazed upon her from my window, I wondered, as I wrote in the article, "what thoughts must have passed through the mind of Clement XIV as he looked from his window at the Castel Sant'Angelo, where for two years in a cold, dismal dungeon of stone Ricci languished, deprived of Mass and sacraments. Poor Ganganelli! I stood by his tomb the other day in the Church of the Apostles, hard by the Gregorian University and around the corner from what was once the convent of the Conventual Franciscans of which he was regent before he was pope. I said not one, but two Hail Marys, for the repose of his soul."

A Conventual Franciscan in New York, Peter Fehlner, took umbrage at my reference to Clement XIV, whom he defended in an angry letter, almost as long as my article, published in the February 19, 1960, issue of *Commonweal*. The same issue carried my brief reply:

> I think Father Fehlner is right about the sacraments. What I should have said is that Ricci was not allowed to say Mass and was subjected to other rigors of such severity as to be indeed, as Father Fehlner says, incredible; incredible, but true. The unimpeachable sources Father Fehlner asks for are the letters and reports of some of those chiefly responsible. They are in the once secret, now available, archives, especially of the Vatican, of Florence and of Naples. The citations can easily be found in the works of the historians Father Fehlner complains about.
>
> Beyond this I fail to see that Father Fehlner has any quarrel with me. My article said none of the things about which he complains. I expressed no opinion and passed no judgment on Clement XIV. I said two things about him:
>
> 1) I wondered what he thought when he looked at the Castel Sant'Angelo. I did not venture to guess what he thought; but surely it does him no honor to suppose, as Father Fehlner seems to, that he had no thoughts on the subject, that once the deed was done he dismissed it from his mind.
>
> 2) I said "poor Ganganelli." Ganganelli is not an epithet. It is his name. As one may say "wise Pecci," one must say "poor Ganganelli." Whether one agrees with Father Fehlner or with the historians there is nothing else to say. It is exactly what Saint Alphonsus Liguori said. "I don't know what else to say," he wrote in a letter of July 23, 1774, "but poor Pope!" That is what I said.
>
> I am afraid that Father Fehlner has simply used my rhapsody about Rome as an occasion to indulge in polemics. His quarrel is not with me, but with the historians with whom he disagrees.

This was not the end of the affair. Shortly thereafter I was summoned to the office of the American Assistant, Fr. Vincent McCormick. My previous encounter with him on his visit to Arizona had left me with an impression which was not to be enhanced by the present meeting. When I entered the room, he exclaimed in anguished tones, eyes directed heavenward, "How *could* you, Father? How *could* you?"

Not having a clue as to the reason for my summons, I asked, "How could I what?"

In the same anguished tones as before he exclaimed, "'Poor Ganganelli!' How could you, Father?"

"Ganganelli was his name," I replied.

As McCormick, with his long residence in Rome, surely knew, it is quite customary in Rome to refer to the pope by his family name. One does not, to be sure, so address him, but one often refers to him in this fashion. Pius XII's name was Pacelli, and he was accustomed to answering the phone by saying, "Pacelli speaking." John XXIII was the Roncalli pope; Clement XIV, the Ganganelli pope.

Ignoring my reply, McCormick resumed his lament: "Our holy father, Saint Ignatius, would *never* have permitted himself to speak in this way of the pope," he said.

"What do you think our holy father, Saint Ignatius, would have said about Father Ricci being imprisoned and starved to death in the Castel Sant'Angelo?" I asked. He had no answer, so I left him with the same anguished look with which he had greeted me.

I had visited the dungeons of the Castel Sant'Angelo. I had also recently read in a biography of Card. Alessandro Farnese the documented proof that with the express approval of Clement XIV the governor of the fortress had put Father Ricci on half rations. From my window I could see not only the Castel Sant'Angelo, in which Ricci had slowly starved to death, but also the church from which he had been buried. All in all, I thought that in saying two Hail Marys for the soul of the Ganganelli pope I had been rather generous. Nor was McCormick's scandal a matter of much concern to me.

During the period of waiting for my trunk to arrive I wrote another article which I think was one of the best I have written. It was never published. The curial censors evidently thought it revived memories better forgotten. The article was about Via Giulia, the first straight street in Rome. It dates from the pontificate of Alexander VI (1492–1503) and is named—according to one explanation—after the most beautiful woman in Rome, Giulia la Bella, who was his last mistress. It takes its rise across the Tiber from the Castel Sant'Angelo, off the present-day Corso Vittorio Emanuele, and ends only a mile away at the Palazzo Farnese, which today quarters the French Embassy. To stroll that mile, as I did countless times during my Roman days, is to relive an extraordinarily rich history featuring sinners and saints.

At the very beginning of the street is the church to which Saint Philip Neri used to come every morning to say Mass, walking from his convent near the end of Via Giulia. This was the Florentine quarter of Rome, filled with the shops and studios of craftsmen and goldsmiths from Florence. Among them the greatest goldsmith of all, the flamboyant and superb artist Benvenuto Cellini, who once escaped from imprisonment in the Castel Sant'Angelo by letting himself down with ropes; breaking his leg in a final fall when the ropes proved too short, he crawled a half mile to take sanctuary in a church which stands on what is today the Via della Conciliazione.

Every palazzo on Via Giulia claims a piece of history. In one, Cardinal Pecci stayed with friends when he came to Rome to attend the conclave which elected him pope; he took the name Leo XIII. Much of that history I recounted in my article. The richest part of the history is associated with the last hundred yards or so before the street ends with the Palazzo Farnese and the Campo dei Fiore, where the brilliant but erratic Giordano Bruno was burned at the stake in 1600 and where Queen Christina of Sweden, "one of the wittiest and most intelligent women of her age," maintained a modest apartment after her conversion to the Roman Catholic faith in 1654 and her abdication of the throne in the royal hall at Uppsala, until she installed herself in the palace Cardinal Riario built on the Lungara in Rome.

Here is the famed English College, to which young Englishmen come to study for the priesthood today as in the days of Elizabeth I, but with their days less haunted by the hope or specter of martyrdom. Here came Edmund Campion en route from Czechoslovakia back to England and a martyr's death; his brilliance as an Oxford student had won the admiration of a still youthful Elizabeth. The morning he was to leave for England he crossed the cobblestoned Via Giulia to the convent where lived Saint Philip Neri to ask his blessing and to bid him adieu.

A few steps further on is the small Spanish church built to care for the burgeoning community of Spaniards who flocked to Rome during the pontificates of their countrymen Calixtus III and his nephew Alexander VI. Both Saint Ignatius Loyola and Saint Francis Xavier preached in this church. As they stood in the pulpit, out of the corner of their eye they could see the tomb of Alexander VI, which lies in the alcove of the first side altar to the right as one enters the church and which no doubt reminded them, as it does us, that the Church of Christ is composed of sinners as well as saints. Above his tomb, joining over four centuries of history, is the tomb of Alfonso XIII, grandfather of Juan Carlos, today's reigning king of Spain.

There is a certain poignancy in finding the tomb of Alexander VI here. For no more than a stone's throw away is the Palazzo Farnese, where Giulia la Bella lived with her older brother Alessandro Farnese, whom Alexander VI had named a cardinal, and where she often entertained her close friend, Alexander's daughter, Lucrezia Borgia.

These, of course, are historical details from what might be called the underside of life on the Via Giulia, which the censors did not wish exposed to the light of day. I understand their thinking but do not agree with it. The Church is far more damaged by the suppression of truth than by its frank admission. Furthermore, the attempt to suppress the truth is an exercise in futility. And to pretend that her history has been unblemished by sin is to caricature the Church, denying her human dimension, which is her sinful dimension. What is left is a parody, as would be the Gospels if the evangelists out of concern to preserve an unblemished image had scissored out the story of Peter's denial, Magdalene's failings, Judas's betrayal.

Alexander himself is, to my way of thinking, a symbol of hope. Sinner though he was and knew himself to be, he held fast to his faith; and when stricken with fever in 1503, he died shriven and—if what the Church teaches and the Gospels say means anything—forgiven. That gives hope to the rest of us, sinners all.

John XXIII

I was in Rome during the pontificate of John XXIII. Although the process of ecclesiastical de-Stalinization has not gone as far as one might wish, the liberating influence of John XXIII remains one of the remarkable phenomena of the age. There are those who would like you to think of John XXIII as a not very bright man endowed with a kind of saintly simplicity. Behind that genuine simplicity was in fact a very astute man, an accomplished historian, a skilled diplomat.

One afternoon I witnessed a wonderful scene which dramatically and unforgettably symbolized both his spirit and its electrifying effect. I was accustomed to interrupt my research with a one- or two-hour prowl about Rome. This day I chanced to wander into Piazza S. Ignazio, upon which fronts the Jesuit church of the same name attached to the historic Roman College, now a public high school. Many of the most illustrious members of the Society of

Jesus were students or professors here, Saint Aloysius Gonzaga, Saint Stanislaus Kostka, Saint Robert Bellarmine, Matteo Ricci, and a host of others. It is one of the largest churches in Rome.

I was surprised this afternoon to find the piazza crowded and asked someone the reason. "The pope is inside speaking to all the seminarians of Rome," I was told. I joined the crowd. A sudden bustle and movement of Vatican guards and functionaries signaled the end of the meeting. The great doors of the church swung open. The pope emerged, smiling broadly, surrounded by his entourage of solemn cardinals and a flock of fussing, fluttering monsignori. He descended the steps of the church towards his waiting limousine. A squad of motorcycle carabinieri fired up their machines ready to escort him back to the Vatican.

Apparently on a sudden impulse, the pope, upon reaching the bottom of the steps, ignored the open door of his car and the monsignor who waited to hand him in, turned to his left, and marched off down Via del Seminario, the ancient and narrow Roman street which leads to the Pantheon, leaving the cardinals, monsignori, guards, and functionaries frozen with astonishment. After a moment of stunned surprise in the piazza, the crowd went wild with delight. Leaving the panic-stricken prelates in their wake, shouting, cheering, singing, waving, even dancing, they poured into the narrow Via del Seminario after the stocky figure of John XXIII, who, grinning with delight, was stomping along alone. In a moment he was surrounded, and one could see only his bobbing head as he strode along in the midst of the delirious mob.

It was an extraordinary and beautiful sight. I am sure that among the cheering mass of Italians were old-fashioned anticlericals, socialists, and even Communists. John XXIII's simple, spontaneous gesture, ignoring old restraints, bursting through ancient barriers, breaking new ground, had sparked an instant response from all.

My first close-up view of John XXIII had been from a small balcony high on the interior wall of Saint Peter's. From here Vatican Radio broadcast descriptions of papal ceremonies. Fr. Tom O'Donnell, S.J., of the Irish Province, handled the English-language broadcasts. He asked me to substitute for him one afternoon at a public papal audience. (The large audience hall now used did not yet exist.) A papal audience is an exciting event, but to have to attend one every week, as the pope does, must become rather a bore. I noticed, as the speeches of presentation of the numerous nationality groups dragged on, John kept jiggling his foot, not only betraying his impatience but also revealing what a thoroughly genuine human being he was.

This was not my only experience on Vatican Radio. On several occasions Tom O'Donnell asked me to substitute for him on his regular broadcast, a commentary related to events of the day. One of these occasions—it was my last experience as a Vatican Radio commentator—was shortly before the 1960 presidential elections in the United States. Abp. James Davis of San Juan, Puerto Rico, had committed the monumental gaffe of instructing his people that they were not to vote for Governor Muñoz in the upcoming gubernatorial elections because of his acceptance of contraception as an instrument of population control. This naturally had revived all the old Protestant fears, more or less put to rest by John Kennedy in his pivotal campaign speech in Houston, of the pope occupying the White House with a Catholic president. Without referring explicitly to the incident, I took the occasion to discuss the separation of Church and state as practiced in the United States. I defended it both as policy and as doctrine.

It should be recalled that John Courtney Murray was still under ban. Seminarians were still being taught that separation of Church and state was at best the lesser of two evils, acceptable only where Catholics were in a minority. Vatican II, which would abandon positions historically and philosophically untenable, as Murray had brilliantly demonstrated, and would put its seal of approval on freedom of religion, was still in the future. It is understandable that my commentary sent minor tremors through the establishment. I was quietly advised that it was imprudent to express such ideas over Vatican Radio.

Archbishop Davis and I were friends. As a priest he had belonged to the diocese of Tucson-Phoenix in Arizona. He had been named archbishop of San Juan because he was American and spoke Spanish fluently. Besides, if some of his former confreres in the Tucson diocese were to be believed, Bp. Daniel J. Gercke, who recommended him for the post, was happy to be rid of him. Also, robed and mitred, he had a very commanding episcopal presence. He frequently visited the Tucson diocese, where, if one were to believe the gossip of the same former confreres, he hoped one day to succeed Bishop Gercke. It was there that I made his acquaintance. I recall playing golf with him one summer day; neither robed nor mitred but garbed only in a pair of shorts and golf shoes, he nevertheless managed to preserve the episcopal character of his presence by wearing his bishop's ring. Since he could not be described as svelte, he cut a bizarre figure.

On a visit to Puerto Rico several years after the ill-advised election instruction, I had dinner with Archbishop Davis. I questioned him about the famous gaffe which had almost cost Kennedy the election. Somewhat self-conscious about it, he was not disposed to defend it.

Rest and Healing

The ulcer which had almost done me in at Santa Clara became active again in Rome. It manifested itself oddly enough through acute chest pains that forced me to lie down until they passed away. I thought the heart was to blame; but Prof. Erich Budzislawski, the doctor to whom our infirmarian, Brother Rodriguez, referred me, suspected that an ulcer was the culprit. He sent me to a radiologist, whose X-rays confirmed the diagnosis and located the ulcer. I was impressed by this because in California, following the nearly-fatal hemorrhage, X-rays taken by several radiologists over a period of months had failed to reveal the offender. The doctor explained to me that this was not surprising, because ulcers are not a permanent feature of the abdominal landscape. They come and go. Mine evidently had come and, after dealing me a nearly-lethal blow, had gone its way. I did not question this explanation. Nevertheless, I found the performance of the Italian pathologist impressive in view of the common American illusion that Americans are superior to non-Americans in all fields calling for expertise.

In any case, my ulcer had evidently returned again, seeking new adventures. Dr. Budzislawski decided first to try dietary measures. He put me on a spartan regime, both dinner and supper being limited to a bowl of liquidy rice. I offset the gnawing effect of this upon my vitals by procuring a small hot plate and a pot in which to boil water. Every afternoon during my walk I bought two eggs and a small loaf of bread, and upon my return prepared a private feast.

Eventually the doctor resorted to more drastic methods. He put me in the hospital of S. Stefano Rotondo for a month. The hospital bore the name of the ancient Roman basilica which was its neighbor. It was operated by the nuns of the Little Company of Mary, or—as they were more familiarly known from the color of their habit—the Blue Sisters. All the sisters at S. Stefano were, with one exception, from Ireland; the exception was Sister Augustine, an American nun, whose cousin Gene Patrick was an old friend of mine from the University of Chicago days. In the room directly below mine the noted Harvard philosopher George Santayana had lived out his days, tenderly cared for by the Blue Sisters.

If S. Stefano and the sisters who ran it left nothing to be desired, the same cannot be said of the milk diet to which Dr. Budzislawski's orders restricted me. From childhood I have despised milk as the Christian Temperance Society despises alcohol. It may be assumed that I looked with dour countenance upon the approach every hour of a glass of milk. After two weeks boiled eggs were added, not hourly but twice a day; I welcomed them as if they were caviar. At the end of a month the symptoms indicated and X-rays confirmed that the ulcer, however battered and bruised, was still hanging in there. Dr. Budzislawski recommended surgery. The surgery would be performed by the chief surgical team of the hospital.

This led to a chorus of advice from many sides, the common theme of which was "Don't let these Italians touch you." Even the minister of the Curia, Fr. Bernard Hall, urged me to go to London for the operation. I asked Sister Augustine what she thought of the "Don't let these Italians touch you" refrain.

"If you had asked me that a year ago when I first came here from America, I probably would have said the same thing," she replied. "But for more than a year I have watched these surgeons perform, and, in my opinion, they are as skilled and as competent as any surgeons in the world." And so the team of four who performed the gastrectomy, which passed without incident, proved to be. A few days after my operation John Kennedy was elected president of the United States; in the wee hours of the morning I listened on my transistor radio to the election returns.

Following my release from the hospital I spent two months of convalescence in Fiesole on the hills above Florence. Here the Blue Sisters maintained a home for their own aged but, with the hospitality which they had brought from their native land, also for other elderly people, for convalescents, and even for occasional tourists in search of a *pensione*. With all the beauty of Florence laid out at my feet and all its art treasures within the reach of a short bus ride, I was grateful to all the factors which had unwittingly conspired to bring me here: to Pat Donohoe, Carroll O'Sullivan, a request for exclaustration, a bleeding ulcer, and the Blue Sisters. Like all of Florence, even the house, built in 1428 by Cosimo de' Medici, "Il Vecchio," was rich in history.

Part of that history was its service from 1870 to 1897 as the Jesuit Curia, the nerve center of the order's worldwide activity. Forced out of Rome by the *risorgimento*, three successive Jesuit generals, Pieter Beckx, Anton Anderledy, and Luis Martin, lived here. The dining room in which the Blue Sisters served me my meals, with its breath-taking view of the whole city of Florence, had been their office. In 1897, tempers having cooled and the original Curia restored, Martin moved back to Rome. The other two are buried in Fiesole, where I visited their tombs in the small but neatly tended cemetery.

Time for Decision

At some point during these months Vincent McCormick, S.J., passed out of my life. He was succeeded as assistant to the general for the United States by Fr. Harold Small of the Oregon Province. Nothing could have pleased me more. Harold Small and I had been ordained together, had made tertianship together, and were old friends. He read, as I am sure McCormick had never done, my documented report sent to Father General more than a decade before. He was shocked by the account.

The decision about my request for exclaustration had yet to be taken. Bishop Buddy of San Diego had been in touch with me and had assured me that the welcome mat was still out should I decide to go through with it. Father Bunn had been in touch with Father Small and still wanted me at Georgetown. He had meantime found a dean for the School of Foreign Service, but he wanted me as his assistant for international programs. My sister, Isabel Higgins, had always been a strong supporter. In this case, although she would support any decision I made, I could sense in reading between the lines of her letters that she hoped I would remain a Jesuit. I think that subconsciously I had already decided to do so. I was very happy with the Society of Jesus as I experienced her in Rome, as I had been happy with the Society of Jesus I knew in China. With the rewriting of my book nearing completion I had to make a definite decision, as I had promised Father Janssens to do.

Before doing so, I had a few things to take care of. Before I left Villa S. Girolamo one of the Irish nuns, an old family friend of Eamon de Valera, had insisted I visit him and had written to advise him of my coming. I flew to Dublin, where President de Valera received me most graciously in his office in the presidential mansion in Peacock Park. He remembered very clearly his visit to Los Angeles in the early 1920s. We reminisced nostalgically. I remembered him as tall and slender. I found him, forty years later, still tall and straight, but no longer the gaunt figure he had cut then. When I departed he insisted, although nearly blind, upon accompanying me to the door.

From Dublin I flew to Paris, whose historical and artistic riches must make it one of the favorite cities in the world for anyone who has ever been there. It is certainly one of the most beautiful cities in the world. I stayed in the Jesuit house on rue de Grenelle, the usual stopping place for Jesuits in transit. I was there on April 17, 1961, when, listening to a television newscast, I heard with dismay of the Bay of Pigs invasion of Cuba. I was dismayed because I knew it was doomed to failure. The idea that it would be accompanied by a massive uprising of the people in support of the invasion was the product of the appalling ignorance of the realities and of the muddle-headed thinking that has characterized so much of American policy towards Latin America.

From Paris I went to Lourdes. This was a little out of character, because normally I am skeptical about alleged apparitions. The legend of Fatima leaves me unconvinced. Lourdes, however, is in a category by itself. There is *something* there, something more than natural. During the three days that I spent there I felt myself irresistibly drawn back to the shrine time and time again. I sensed something supernatural in the ambiance. That sounds like a contradiction. Can one sense the supernatural? I do not know; I leave the answer to theologians. What I do know is that I sensed a presence, something over and above and beyond what the eye sees or the ear hears. The only other place I have ever had a somewhat similar experience was at Assisi, where Saint Francis was born, where he lived, and where he lies buried.

In any case, when I left Lourdes the decision had been made. I wrote to Bishop Buddy, who accepted the decision with the same graciousness with which he had offered sanctuary. I informed Harold Small and asked him to tell the general that I was prepared to go wherever he chose to assign me, even back to Santa Clara or to San Francisco—as a student counselor!

Meantime I had completed my work of revision. The former director of the University of Chicago Press, who fifteen years earlier had been interested in publishing my thesis, was now with the University of Michigan Press, whose board of directors was not interested in what the Jesuits were doing in China in the sixteenth or seventeenth centuries. He had therefore brought the manuscript to the attention of Emily Schossberger, director of the University of Notre Dame Press. She was interested, and in due course sent me a contract for the publication of *Generation of Giants*, the title I had chosen for the reincarnation of what had originated as my doctoral thesis.

I was informed by Harold Small that Father General had decided to assign me to Georgetown University. "I won't last two months there," I said.

"Why not?" he asked.

"You know my position on racial discrimination," I replied. "Georgetown has a reputation as a segregated institution, and Doc Bunn as a segregationist. Within two months there will be a head-on collision."

"Georgetown is no longer segregated, and I don't think you will have trouble with Doc Bunn," he replied, proving himself a prophet.

The day I left Rome, as Harold saw me off at the front door, he told me that I was the first Jesuit in history who had wept upon leaving the Curia. He exaggerated a bit. I did not actually weep, though there were tears in my eyes. The tears, however, were not because I was leaving the Curia—though I had been perfectly happy there in my tiny cubbyhole on the roof—but because I was leaving Rome.

I had booked passage on the *Leonardo da Vinci*, which was sailing from Genoa. I intended, however, first to make a grand farewell tour of Europe, and then board the ship at Gibraltar.

The tour began with a trip to Berlin which, thanks to General Eisenhower's decision to let the Russians take the city, remained an isolated island surrounded by East Germany. I was there in June 1961. I expressed my impressions in an article that appeared in the August 26 issue of *America*. There have been many changes in the more than a quarter of a century which has passed since then—dramatic changes recently—but in 1961 the passage from West to East Berlin was, as I described it, "a passage from light to shadow, from life to death." I understood what Nikita Khrushchev meant when he said that West Berlin was a chicken bone stuck in his throat. "How can he permit this confrontation in a communist heartland," I wrote, "between this small island in which men are free to make their choices and which throbs with the pulse of life worth living, and the city where death walks through the streets because freedom has died?"

A month later, as if in answer to my question, the Wall went up. I had by then left Berlin, flying out to Hanover and thence by train to Paris for my second visit in two months. From Paris I took the express—I think it was called the Blue Express—destination Madrid, not anticipating the rather remarkable coincidence which would occur en route.

When I was at Loyola University in Los Angeles in 1946, I had taught a course on the state in Catholic thought, using as text a book bearing the same title. Its author was a distinguished German scholar, Heinrich Rommen, who was one of the founders of the Christian Democratic movement in Europe. Rommen had quit Germany for the United States and, after teaching political science for some years at Saint Thomas College in St. Paul, had become a member of the faculty of Georgetown University. I had long admired his thinking and looked forward to meeting him.

There were few, if any, empty seats on the express when we pulled out of the Paris station. My compartment had its full complement of six passengers. I had a middle seat. The occupant of the window seat on my left was a man somewhat beyond middle age, of average appearance. The six occupants of the compartment were evidently all strangers, and this being France, not Italy, they all minded their own business, reading or dreaming or watching the French countryside flow by as the train sped southward. There was no conversation. It was well on into the afternoon and we were approaching the Spanish border, when the man on my left took a *Saturday Evening Post* out of his bag, affording me a conversational opener. I asked if he spoke English. He did, fluently, with a slight Germanic accent. In response to my questions he informed me that he was a savant, that he was going to Madrid to address a learned congress, and that he was a professor at Georgetown University in the United States.

"What a remarkable coincidence," I exclaimed. "I am on my way now to Washington to join the staff of Georgetown."

I finally got around to asking his name. "Heinrich Rommen," he said, and I almost fell off my seat!

We were soon at the Spanish border, where we had to change trains, and so had little time to extend our acquaintance. However, I would soon join him at Georgetown, where we became and remained good friends until his death a few years later. The rest of the tour passed without incident.

In Madrid I stayed in the Jesuit professed house and accustomed myself to the Spanish way of life: sleep late, go to bed late, eat late; dinner at 2 P.M., tea at 5 P.M., supper at 10 P.M. I saw my first bullfight and did not like it. The Hemingway mystique was lost on me. I went a second time and still did not like it. My sympathies were entirely with the bull. In one of the fights the bull obviously had no desire to fight. To make his point he managed to half jump, half scramble over the wooden wall that separates the bullring from the grandstand. He simply wanted to go home. I felt like cheering, whereas everyone else was whistling—the European bronx cheer. To its *aficionados* bullfighting is an art form. I did not understand the art of tauromachy and so failed to appreciate it. In its favor one might say that, unlike what takes place daily in the Kansas City or Omaha stockyards, here the bull is given a chance to give as good as he gets. In one of the fights which I witnessed he succeeded in doing so, and a badly gored matador was carried off the ring on a stretcher.

In Toledo I admired the wonderful paintings of El Greco in the sacristy of the cathedral. In Seville, while visiting the tomb of Christopher Columbus, I spotted a young man wearing a cassock. Assuming he was a Spanish seminarian, I engaged him in conversation, asking questions about the history of this ancient and beautiful cathedral. I put my questions in Italian, and he answered in Spanish, which I understood but did not speak. After some five minutes of bilingual conversation I learned that he was an American Jesuit scholastic who was studying theology in Spain and that he belonged to my own province of California! We had a good laugh and switched to English.

The grand tour ended at Gibraltar, where I boarded the *Leonardo da Vinci.* The purser handed me a stack of mail which had been delivered to the ship before its departure from Genoa. The first letter I opened, from Jim Deasy, cast a pall over the end of my tour and the beginning of my journey home. It brought the sad news of the death of Fr. George Feeney, pastor of Saint Theresa Church in Phoenix and a close friend and golfing partner during my years in that city. A true devotee of golf, he had been killed instantly on the golf course when his golf cart overturned and struck his head.

It was impossible to dismiss this shocking news from my mind during the otherwise pleasant ocean voyage to New York and the beginning of a new phase of my life. I shared my cabin with a young and genial Maltese Jesuit priest, and he and two other Maltese priests who were table companions prevented gloom from settling in. *Que sera sera!*

Fourteen

Georgetown Interlude

Notre Dame and Danielou

Upon arrival in New York I spent about four hours sitting by my trunk in the customs warehouse waiting for an official finally to get around to examining its contents. In later years I would pass many times through customs in many countries of the world, both east and west. In terms of efficiency the United States, in my experience, is far the worst of the lot.

Before settling in at Georgetown I spent the month of July at Notre Dame doing the final editing of my book, *Generation of Giants*. Emily Schossberger, the director of the Notre Dame Press, was of invaluable help, suggesting the elimination of considerable superfluous material. The book was published in the fall of 1961. It was awarded a special honorable mention by the Catholic Historical Association. It also was the Catholic book of the month and the Maryknoll book of the month. A second printing was issued within three months. By arrangement with Notre Dame Press, Longmans and Green published another edition in England.

During my month at Notre Dame I made the acquaintance of Jean Danielou, S.J., who was lecturing in the summer school. Danielou was an internationally known theologian, especially renowned for his scholarly studies of the church fathers. There were several dozen young Jesuits studying at Notre Dame that summer, many of them attracted by his course. On the Feast of Saint Ignatius, July 31, we all joined for dinner in an off-campus restaurant. I sat next to Danielou. He was an affable and interesting dinner companion.

Danielou, like Henri de Lubac, S.J., with whom he was associated, had been known and admired as one of the more open-

261

minded of modern theologians. In his later years he veered markedly to the right—as would de Lubac. When he was named a cardinal by Paul VI, some students staged a mild protest in the chapel of the Institut Catholique in Paris. A few years after this I filed, from Geneva, where I was living, a protest of my own.

I had read in the journal *Information Catholique* a talk which he had delivered over Vatican Radio. It amounted to a severe castigation of the general superiors of all major orders, who were meeting in Rome at that very time under the chairmanship of Fr. Pedro Arrupe, the general of the Jesuits. Far-reaching changes had taken place in the Church since Vatican II. These changes were for the most part forward-looking and a result of John XXIII's desire to bring the Church up to date. Some of the side effects, such as the considerable fall off in priestly and religious vocations, were matters of concern. Danielou, however, deplored the new aspects of the Church, particularly inveighing against the failure of priests and seminarians to wear at all times the traditional soutane. For these changes, which he lamented, he blamed what he called the permissiveness and laxity of major religious superiors. I thought it an uncalled-for slap in the face, especially for Father Arrupe, in my judgment the best superior general we have had since Saint Ignatius Loyola and certainly since the restoration of the Society in 1814. Arrupe, as Danielou's superior, had agreed to Paul VI's request to release him from obedience to the Society in order to become a cardinal.

I wrote to him from Geneva:

> Dear Jean:
> I have just read your inappropriate remarks over Vatican Radio. Permit me to give you some brotherly advice: Make your own the self-admonition of the psalmist (Ps. 38): "I shall put a gag in my mouth."

Danielou died a few months after this in somber and tragic circumstances. I greatly regretted his death, but not the message I had sent to him. John Paul II would later name Henri de Lubac as his successor in the College of Cardinals.

Doc Bunn and Georgetown

In mid August I checked into Georgetown. It was my first meeting with Fr. Edward "Doc" Bunn. (Stories differ on the origin of the nickname by which he was known to all his friends, who were legion and of whom I quickly became one.) He was a man of small stature, feisty, utterly without pretense and utterly without fear. In contrast to some of the superiors I had dealt with in California, he was entirely candid, and one could be candid with him in return. He had an exceptional achievement to his credit, of which he was understandably proud. He had once gone to the mat with the archbishop of the diocese, in defiance of the superior general, of Zach Maher, the American assistant to the general, and of his own provincial, and had won!

Before becoming president of Georgetown, he had been president of Loyola College in Baltimore. Among his old Baltimore friends was an elderly woman of considerable wealth. As her health worsened Father Bunn often called upon her, as a priest and friend, to comfort her. When, following her death, her will was divulged, it appeared that, while leaving a substantial share to the diocese, she had also left a substantial portion to Loyola College. Abp. Michael J. Curley, who had expected to get the whole kit and caboodle, accused Father Bunn of taking advantage of the infirm woman's enfeebled state of mind to influence her to change her will. He threatened to sue. Panic seized in turn the provincial, the assistant, the general. One does not go to court to dispute an archbishop.

Doc Bunn was ordered by all three echelons of superiors to retire meekly and leave the field uncontested to Archbishop Curley. He refused. It was a matter of principle with him; his honor was at stake. While superiors held their breath he locked horns with the archbishop, who brought suit to break the will, as he had threatened. The headline-making case—"Archbishop Sues Priest To Break Will!"—was heard by a jury. Doc Bunn testified at length and calmly withstood a grueling cross-examination. After hearing all of the testimony and examining all of the evidence, the jury completely vindicated Doc Bunn and upheld the will.

The bells of victory would ring out in Doc's soul as long as he lived. And rightly so. His honor had been vindicated, his judgment confirmed. To make everything perfect, Archbishop Curley proved a good loser. He took his lumps like a man.

Before coming to Georgetown I had heard it said that Father Bunn was a racist. In one sense he was, but in a more important sense he was not. Racial prejudice was part of his heritage. Two of his uncles had been generals in the Confederate army. The feeling that black people are somehow inferior and are not to be associated with had been inbred in him by his mother. His father had died when he was but an infant and his sister not yet born.

I once overheard him, surrounded by a half dozen Jesuits, telling how his mother had one time given him a memorable thrashing as a nine-year-old. To help his widowed mother in the not easy task of supporting her little family, he sold newspapers in the afternoon. One afternoon he went into a saloon to sell his papers. When he came home he mentioned this to his mother, who promptly gave him the thrashing of his life—not, he said, because he had gone into a saloon but because he had gone into a saloon where they served blacks as well as whites. This kind of a lesson is calculated to make a lasting impression. It is not surprising that he grew up with certain discriminatory feelings deeply rooted.

Doc Bunn freely admitted that he had such feelings. Again, I once overheard him say that when he shook hands with a black person his toes curled within his shoes. Having these feelings, he could be said to be a racist. But he did not succumb to these feelings. He knew they were not rational, and he did not yield to them. He controlled them and did not permit them to affect his policy or his behavior. During the years I was his assistant I never saw him betray any sign of whatever racist feelings lay beneath the surface.

I remember one occasion on which I subjected him to particularly close scrutiny. It was an elegant ball which brought together faculty, alumni, and students in celebration of Georgetown's 175th anniversary in one of Washington's more fashionable hotels. Father Bunn stood in a reception line to greet the guests as they arrived. Since I was in charge of the ball as director of the anniversary year, I was in a position to keep a sharp eye out. I watched Father Bunn as he greeted and shook hands with the guests with all the Baltimorean courtesy and charm which was distinctive of him. He showed no less warmth, no less courtesy, no less charm when the guest was black than when he or she was white. I said to myself, "If his toes are curling within his shoes, he has established total domination over his inbred racial prejudices." Who could ask for anything more?

Georgetown University itself had for a long period been a segregated institution, as were other Church institutions. The split in religious institutional thinking showed up in a rather widely read novel, whose villains were religious policies of the

Maryland region. The heroes of the story were the scarcely disguised Frs. Wilfred Parsons and John LaFarge, both of whom have appeared in these memoirs.[1]

Georgetown's record in this respect, although regrettable, is not surprising. From its origins until rather recent years Georgetown was very much a Southern institution. At the outbreak of the Civil War—or, as Southerners prefer to call it, the War Between the States—the large majority of the student body were young men from the South. More Georgetown students fought and more died in the Confederate armies than in the Union armies. As a reminder of her bipartisan heritage, Georgetown's school colors, chosen after the war, are blue and grey. It is not realistic to expect those who could not see that slavery was wrong to see that segregation was wrong. Hence segragation persisted as part of Georgetown's legacy. It was Doc Bunn who put an end to it.

It is an anomaly of Georgetown's history that one of her most notable presidents in the post-Civil War period, Fr. Patrick Healy, was of Afro-American lineage. His mother was the house slave of an Irishman become Southern plantation owner, who married her and fathered, among others, Patrick, the future Jesuit president of Georgetown University, as well as James, a future Roman Catholic bishop of Portland, Maine. A daughter, Eliza, joined the sisters of the Congregation of Notre Dame as Sr. Mary Magdalen, eventually becoming the general superior of the order.

Harold Small had been right; I had no trouble with Doc Bunn. He raised no objection when on August 28, 1963, I joined with large numbers of students who participated in the march on Washington that ended in the Mall before the Lincoln Memorial, where Martin Luther King delivered his inspirational and deeply moving "I Have a Dream" speech. In fact, Doc arranged to have the university food service hand each student a packaged lunch as they passed out the front gate to join the march.

Peace Corps

I did have trouble getting my bearings at Georgetown. Doc Bunn told me that I was to be his assistant for international programs, but he did not define what that meant, leaving it for me to find out myself. As I nosed about in search of something to do I discovered that for everything that seemed to have an international aspect there was a Jesuit who regarded it as his special domain. At the first sign that I was in the vicinity he tended to react like a male seal in mating time to another bull approaching his territory. I learned quickly to withdraw before I found myself engaged in mortal combat and to look for virgin territory. The Peace Corps was such.

At that time the Peace Corps policy was to farm its training programs out to universities across the land. Georgetown was not one of them. I wrote to Sargent Shriver, the director of the Peace Corps, and expressed astonishment at this. The most important part of the training program was language. Georgetown had one of the best language and linguistics schools in the country. Located right under the nose, as it were, of the Peace Corps head offices, it would take a special effort to overlook her.

Sargent Shriver asked Georgetown to form a consortium with the other six universities in the area for training purposes. Every week for six or more weeks I met with a representative of American, George Washington, Johns Hopkins, Howard, Catholic, and Maryland and two representatives of the Peace Corps to work out the form of the consortium. We named a vice-president of Howard University secretary of the consortium, and American University supplied him with an office. The Peace Corps then gave us twelve training projects to dole out among ourselves. The largest of them called for more than three hundred trainees with destination Ethiopia. It was in fact the largest group the Peace Corps had ever or would ever undertake to train. Because Georgetown was the only university in the consortium that had enough housing space to accomodate so large a crowd I was asked to take the Ethiopia program in lieu of two smaller programs for which I had expressed a preference. These I turned over to Howard University, which gladly ceded Ethiopia to me.

I named Howard Geer, a young instructor in geography who was also assistant director of the summer school, as my assistant. We worked out the details of the program and established a budget. Then Howard and I, along with Fr. Joseph Cohalan, the university treasurer, negotiated the budget item by item with a Peace Corps team whose tough stance was a reassurance to the American taxpayers that their money was not being tossed away. In the end the budget agreed upon was slightly over $250,000.

The Ethiopian volunteers were destined to teach in schools of that country, and in those early years the Peace Corps training program lasted only eight weeks. In those eight weeks we were supposed to teach the trainees the Amharic language, to which we devoted five hours of class each day, plus thirteen different subjects, including several varieties of crafts, such as tinsmithing, which among them they would be expected to teach in Ethiopia. Add to this lectures in Ethiopian history, religion, and social customs, plus soccer and several rugged weekends of hiking and camping out in wilderness areas, and one may well conclude that we had a rather crowded schedule. For the faculty I recruited not only from Georgetown and other universities in the consortium but, because of the crafts components, from trade schools in the Washington area.

The language was a problem. Amharic, the language of the ruling group in Ethiopia, was not taught anywhere in the United States. I managed to locate in Ethiopia a young man with a master's degree in linguistics and flew him over to direct the language program. By sheer happenstance it turned out that he had earned his degree at Georgetown. Through the Ethiopian Embassy I located twenty-five Ethiopians who were studying at various universities in the United States and who were glad to earn some money teaching their language. Not everyone is a good teacher of one's own language. A few of the twenty-five proved to be excellent teachers; some were satisfactory; and some were virtually useless. But this is about all one can expect out of putting together a teaching faculty in this haphazard fashion.

We began the program with a dinner at which I introduced all the faculty members and consortium representatives to the trainees. Sargent Shriver arrived late and slipped in, unnoticed by me, to take his place at the speaker's table. When someone called my attention to his presence, I apologized for not having a brass band to meet him. Harrison Wofford, assistant director of the Peace Corps and principal speaker of the evening, was visibly not amused.

Wofford was a bright young Harvard law school product who had made his mark as a member of the Kennedy campaign team by suggesting that Kennedy telephone Coretta King to express his sympathy when her husband, Martin Luther King, was in prison for his civil rights activities in Alabama. I thought this a rather obvious suggestion to make, but for some reason it was regarded as brilliant; and it assured Wofford of a position in the new administration. He was named assistant to Sargent Shriver, the founding director of the Peace Corps. It was the logical place for him. He and his wife, after traveling extensively in India, had written a book on that country which revealed a keen sensitivity to the problems of the underdeveloped world.

Ethiopia was Harrison Wofford's pet project. He had conducted the negotiations with Emperor Haile Selassie to establish
the program, and he intended to accompany the group as field director. Consequently, he took an excessive interest in the training,
frequently sending orders through the half dozen or so aides who
were daily on campus; the effect was generally to disrupt the
program. This was a common tendency of the Peace Corps in those
days. To my mind the Peace Corps, after contracting with a
university to train a group of volunteers, should have left the job
to the professionals and stayed out of sight. Harvard University
would eventually refuse to accept any more training missions
because of this kind of interference.

Balancing his many talents, Harrison Wofford was utterly
humorless and took himself very seriously. He had communicated
this attitude to his worshipful aides. When on occasion I treated
his directives with less than reverential respect, they were shocked.

The first day of training was a day of total confusion. I had
named Howard Geer my assistant because the dean of the
summer school had told me that Howard had a geographer's
familiarity with the campus and its facilities, knowing the number, location, and availability of every classroom. The first morning, group after group arrived at its assigned classroom to find it
already occupied by some other group. Soon the Peace Corps office
was crowded with trainees milling about demanding to know
where they should be. I locked Geer in his office, cut off his phone,
and told him not to come out until he had untangled the mess and
got his classroom map straightened out. I told the trainees, tongue
in cheek, that the confusion was planned as part of their training.
It would prepare them to deal with the confusion they would
encounter when they arrived in Ethiopia.

From then on, the program proceeded with few serious
problems, apart from the annoyances caused by what I suspect
was Harrison Wofford's compulsion to impress upon the trainees
that he would be their boss in Ethiopia. We did have one minor
crisis when a lecturer on Ethiopian mores discussed at some
length sex and the danger of contracting venereal disease. The
language teachers were not at the lecture, but one of the trainees
could not wait to give one of them her version of what had been
said. The language teachers rose in revolt. Their honor as Ethiopians had been impugned. They threatened to strike unless a
public apology was forthcoming. I met with them and managed to
put the remarks in context and the incident in perspective. The
bomb was defused, and all were friends again.

In the last week of the program we had the selection process—it was called selecting out or in. There was a psychiatrist or psychologist on every training staff, and it was he or she who presided. All members of the staff participated in examining the suitability of each of the trainees. A general consensus on each candidate was usually reached, but the psychiatrist had the decisive word.

To be selected out was usually a painful experience. One of the young women in the Ethiopian program who had her heart set upon going lay on the floor of my office in tears and pounded her fists in protest, thereby proving that the psychiatrist had read her well. The contrary was true, however, in the case of another young woman who was selected in. On the way from the airport into Addis Ababa with other trainees, the view from the bus as it passed through the muddy lanes and hovels on the outskirts of the city so traumatized her that she completely broke down and had to be flown back home before the week was out, accompanied by one of Wofford's aides.

In accordance with Peace Corps policy, all the trainees, now become volunteers, were permitted at the end of training to go home for a visit before reporting on an assigned date and time at Idlewild (now Kennedy) Airport for the flight to Ethiopia. The Peace Corps was to have all the tickets made out and delivered to me by the final day, when I would calmly distribute them to the 273 volunteers who had survived the selection process. Departure morning arrived. All the volunteers were gathered in the auditorium of the Foreign Service School, some of them scheduled to fly out of National Airport in less than two hours, and I had no tickets. A telephone call to Peace Corps headquarters disclosed that, through a bureaucratic mistake, the tickets were only then being frantically made out. As they were issued, in order of the departure times from Washington, they were rushed in batches by taxi to Georgetown. As they arrived I passed them out to their owners, whom I then shoved into the taxi and headed to the airport. Meanwhile, I assured those who still waited for their own tickets with increasing nervousness that our program had been perfectly consistent. "It began," I said, "in total confusion, and it is ending in utter chaos." And I again assured them that it had all been planned to prepare them for the bureaucratic frustrations which they would encounter in their future.

A few weeks later I went to New York to see them off on their great adventure. I had become quite close to them during the training, an experience which was repeated in all nine training programs I was charged with during my years at Georgetown. Ten years later they held a reunion at Georgetown and urged me to attend. Unfortunately, I was unable to leave Switzerland at the time, but I did send them a motion picture which I had taken in Ethiopia. This, they wrote me, was a main feature of their reunion.

Ethiopia and Haile Selassie

The motion picture resulted from an unexpected visit I was able to make to Ethiopia several months after seeing the volunteers off at Idlewild Airport. Fr. Dan Power, an old Georgetown hand, had been a chaplain in the army during the war. The colonel currently in command of the United States base in Asmara, Ethiopia, was a close friend of his. The colonel was not a Catholic, but he greatly admired Dan, whom he asked to come to Asmara during the Christmas season to minister to the Catholic soldiers in his command. They had the services of a Maltese priest in the area, but the colonel argued that they would like the chance to receive the sacraments from a fellow American. He had arranged for Dan to go on an army flight. Dan, who did not particularly care to go, generously asked me to take his place.

I took an army flight to Asmara, stopping for several days in Athens, where I almost froze to death while visiting the Parthenon with a tourist group. Greece on occasion can be and on that day was bitterly cold, a frigid wind blowing in off the Aegean. Some distance below the crest I had spotted on a roadside lunch wagon a sign advertising Metaxa brandy. At the risk of leaving my appreciation of the Parthenon forever incomplete, I abandoned the group and headed down the road for the lunch wagon and a generous glass of Greek brandy. It was a question of survival.

The base at Asmara was one of the army's two most important communication centers in the world, as the forest of antennas in the area testified. I was told that no matter where President Kennedy was, he could always be reached within half a minute from here. I was also told that every message that went out over the air from the Soviet Union was monitored from here; and from here every rocket launched from the Soviet Union was traced, the tracing instruments locking onto its path even before those of the Soviets did. This explains why the benevolent friendship of Haile Selassie was of such importance to American policy makers and

why they worried so much about his succession. His only surviving son and apparent heir was a far-from-impressive man in
middle life.

When I was there the emperor still seemed secure on his
throne, and the United States government was missing no opportunity to curry his favor. A minor such gesture was an invitation
to dine at the American base. At Haile Selassie's request, an
American style picnic—rather elaborate to be sure—was prepared
and long tables set up outdoors. After a parade through the downtown streets of Asmara, the emperor arrived at the army base,
where he was received with all the military honors. I was introduced to him, and a military photographer took my picture
shaking his hand. He also took my picture standing next to the
emperor's Rolls Royce, probably as close to a Rolls Royce as I had
ever been.

The following year, when I was back in Washington, the
government made a more serious effort to please Haile Selassie.
One day I had a phone call from the State Department informing
me that he was coming to Washington and asking if Georgetown
would be willing to confer an honorary degree upon him in the
course of his visit. I submitted the question to Doc Bunn, whose
reply was negative. He had a thing about letting the university or
its academic degrees be used as instruments of governmental
policy. The State Department was shocked by the refusal and
begged me to explain to Father Bunn the vital importance of the
army base at Asmara to our strategic position in the world and
therefore of cultivating the friendship of Haile Selassie. I did so,
still with negative results. Only after the State Department had
figuratively on bended knees for the third time begged for a degree
for the emperor and I had returned for the third time to the charge,
did Doc Bunn reluctantly agree.

I arranged a presentation ceremony with appropriate speeches
for the presidential reception room, known as the Hall of Cardinals. Among the guests were a number of distinguished people,
but the most important of all was Fr. Lucien Motte, a French-
Canadian Jesuit whom I had asked to come down from Montreal.
I had learned of him when in Ethiopia.

When Haile Selassie had returned to Ethiopia after the Italian
invaders were driven out during World War II, he wanted the
Jesuits to establish a high school and a university. Because his
own education had been in French, he wanted the Jesuits to be

bilingual in English and French. Hence he had turned to the French-Canadian Jesuits with his request. They had responded to his complete satisfaction, developing two excellent institutions in Addis Ababa. During the years, the superior of the French-Canadian Jesuit community, Father Motte, had become an intimate friend in whom the emperor confided and to whom he frequently turned for advice. Shortly before my visit to Ethiopia the superior had been forced by ill health to return to Canada.

When Haile Selassie stepped out of his limousine at the foot of the stairs leading into Healy Hall and found his old friend Father Motte waiting to greet him, he was visibly moved and delighted. The State Department had reason to be satisfied. However, as often with the best-laid plans of mice and men, all the efforts to assure the future by building upon the friendship of Haile Selassie eventually came to naught. Not too many years had passed when a military coup overthrew the emperor, slew most of his relatives, who had monopolized the power and most of the land, and installed a Marxist regime. The emperor's son, who was out of the country at the time, renounced the throne. The "vitally important" American communications center at Asmara folded its tents and disappeared into the night.

But when I was in Ethiopia, the communications center and the army base supporting it were alive and thriving. One of the officers, near retirement age but having no desire to retire, was a major who seemed never to have grown up. His particular delight was to lead a squad of thirty or so men out into the desert on what could be called not a search-and-destroy but a search-and-find mission. His explanation was that there was always a possibility— I don't think it had ever happened—that an army flyer might have to bail out somewhere over Ethiopia, in which case it would be up to him and his men to find and rescue him. The purpose of these periodic forays into the desert was to keep his team on its toes, ready at any instant to dash to the rescue. A chance visitor to the base gave him an excuse to ask the base commander's authorization to organize such a patrol. I was delighted to cooperate.

We set off one morning in about a dozen jeeps, two to a jeep, except that I was third man in the last jeep in the column. The major, who led the column, was in exuberant spirits. I suspect he fantasized that he was leading a cavalry patrol against the Indians in the Wild West. His men had mixed feelings. Some no doubt enjoyed the safari; others did not especially mind. But at least one bitterly hated it. This was the driver of my jeep, Sergeant McQuaid. I have an extraordinary propensity to forget names, but I shall never forget his.

I never knew whether he was simply an old-fashioned anti-clerical or whether he resented having to leave the comforts of the base and the allurements of Asmara for a week of roughing it in the desert and held me responsible for this—perhaps a combination of both. In any case, it quickly became evident that he was determined to make things as uncomfortable as possible for me.

The first misadventure was not long in coming. We were but a few miles out of Asmara when a herdsman began to lead a couple of dozen long-horned Ethiopian cattle across the road ahead of our jeep. It was obvious that if McQuaid took his foot off the accelerator for a moment all would be across the road with no damage done, but if he did not do so he was going to hit one of them.

McQuaid continued at a steady pace. "You're going to hit him!" I shouted. No sooner said than done. The jeep struck the last beast in line squarely, lifted him from his feet, and dropped him. He scrambled to three feet and hobbled off, his fourth leg dangling helplessly from a shattered hip.

Without a flicker of expression McQuaid picked up his microphone and tonelessly radioed the major at the head of the column, "animal encountered." The major ordered the column to halt and sped back to investigate. In Ethiopia cattle are a most precious possession. To kill one is a very serious offense. It took considerable effort on the part of the major to calm the distraught herdsman and to satisfy him that the American army would compensate generously for the loss. McQuaid meanwhile waited expressionless.

A few miles farther on, we came to the end of the asphalt road. From here on, we would be traveling for seven days on dirt roads or on no road at all, but on camel paths through the desert. The major radioed orders to each driver to remain seventy-five yards behind the preceding jeep to give the dust a chance to dissipate. McQuaid ignored the order and for seven days remained only a dozen yards behind the preceding jeep, assuring that we would be almost constantly in clouds of dust.

The worst was when we had to cross wadis. Here for hundreds of years camels had been crossing and had churned the sand into a fine powder. Every time a jeep plunged into the wadi and up the other side, it stirred up a cloud of dust as thick as smoke. All the other jeeps waited until the dust had settled before plunging into the wadi. Not McQuaid. Invariably he poised our jeep on the edge, and the moment the preceding jeep mounted the other side, he hurtled down into the boiling caldron of suffocating dust. I covered my mouth and nose with a handkerchief, which offered minimal protection.

McQuaid and I became locked in a grim struggle that would endure for seven days. It was evident that he was trying to break me and being some thirty years younger and considerably huskier was confident that he could do it. I was determined that, though I died of asphyxiation, he would not get a whimper, a protest or a complaint out of me. Before we settled into our battle without quarter, it had become evident that he did not intend to speak to me or to reply to any question. So for seven days any remarks I made were addressed to the young corporal who occupied the seat next to the driver. He was a pleasant young man, caught in a crossfire. He wished to be agreeable to me but without incurring the wrath of his sergeant.

The first evening we pitched camp on a riverbank about ten miles from the Sudan border. Crocodiles, only their heads visible above the surface, cruised down the middle of the stream as we bathed close to shore. I was ready to grab my clothes and run should one of them suddenly turn in our direction. That night we dined on gazelle, shot that afternoon by one of the men from his jeep. Delicious is the only word to describe it. During the night we heard the strange howling of hyenas as they feasted on the remains which had been left just outside the perimeter of the camp.

Suddenly I awoke to the voice of Pres. John F. Kennedy. He was giving his State of the Union address to Congress, and the radioman, the only navy man on the team, had picked it up. I later wrote to Kennedy, whom I had met during his first term in the House of Representatives, telling him of this remarkable experience, lying under the brilliant star-studded African skies near the Sudan border, listening to the president speaking to the assembled Congress of the United States. He wrote a gracious reply, typed to be sure by his secretary, but to which he had added a personal note in his own handwriting.

A special added value of the safari was that in the course of the week we passed through eight or nine villages or small towns in which Peace Corps volunteers who had trained with me at

Georgetown were stationed. The major always called a halt long enough to permit a more than brief reunion. I would later see them again, and most of the others, in a reunion in Addis Ababa.

The morning of the fourth day the major announced that we were going to an area where the largest elephants in the world were found. He said that we would arrive there in late afternoon in time to see them as they arrived at their accustomed watering hole. At midday he called a halt and before we started out again announced a change in plans. He had been studying his maps and had spotted a dry riverbed which led to our target area. We would abandon the road and follow this shortcut. The major was in his element as we headed down the sandy riverbed. I think he saw a redskin behind every tree and in a distant village a kidnapped maiden waiting to be rescued. It was great fun. Unfortunately the major had made one oversight. One or another of the jeeps repeatedly sank into the loose sand of the river bottom. Over and over again the column had to stop and wait while soldiers dug a jeep out of the sand. Instead of a short cut, the river route turned out to be a long way there. We arrived at our destination long after dark. The elephants had long since drunk their fill and gone their way. They had, nevertheless, left their traces. If we did not see the elephants, we saw their droppings, which were sufficiently impressive to persuade me that they probably were the largest elephants in the world.

Not many miles before reaching home on the afternoon of the seventh day, we had a close brush with disaster. We were back on the asphalt road leading into Asmara, and the column of jeeps was passing a rickety old truck. Just as McQuaid started to pass, the truck driver, thinking the entire column had passed, swerved to the right, forcing our jeep off the road. Had this happened a quarter of a mile sooner we would have dropped several thousand feet, because for many miles the road skirted the edge of breath-takingly sheer precipices. Fortunately here we were only forced off onto the sandy shoulder. McQuaid wrestled the jeep back onto the road and as he passed the truck, which had veered again to the left, hurled a stream of obscenities at the frightened truck driver. It was the first sound he had uttered since his "animal encountered" announcement seven days before. I almost cheered.

When we arrived back at the army base, the tough Sergeant McQuaid was exhausted. He was not only bushed, he was beaten. I on the other hand never felt better in my life, and never in my life have I had a greater sense of triumph. As I peeled off the army fatigues and the dust-saturated shorts and climbed into the bath tub, I felt like singing a song of victory.

Georgetown Anniversary

In the five years which followed at Georgetown I directed nine Peace Corps training programs. However, except for the last two, for Brazil in 1965 and 1966, I exercised only a general supervisory control, leaving the day-to-day direction to Dr. Jesse Mann of the philosophy department. This was because throughout 1963 and 1964 most of my time was taken up with organizing and directing the university's 175h anniversary year program. Doc Bunn had appointed me to this job just before I left for Ethiopia.

In October 1962, he had called a meeting of all the Jesuits in the community to announce and discuss the forthcoming anniversary program, for which he had put aside a nest egg of $200,000. He said that he would shortly name a director but gave no indication of who this might be. When a few weeks later he called me to his office and told me that I was the one, I was thunderstruck and unbelieving. Perhaps I should have been forewarned of the possibility by a gracious letter he had written me on August 30. It began:

> Dear George,
> Perhaps this letter, with the Gold Seal of Georgetown, may give some inkling of my deep appreciation and gratitude for the magnificent leadership you have displayed in the Peace Corps achievement. . .

It continued at considerable length in the same vein. It hangs today, framed, on my wall.

Despite Father Bunn's appreciation of my accomplishment with the Peace Corps training program, I thought his new decision was a mistake. I had never been associated with a university anniversary program and knew nothing about running one. But more important, I was not a member of the Maryland Province and especially was not an old Georgetown hand.

Georgetown Jesuits in those days regarded their university as unique among American Jesuit institutions—a kind of member of the Ivy League—and themselves as a sort of core elite. In a sense they had reason for their attitude. Georgetown was the oldest Catholic university in the country. It had been established in 1789 by John Carroll, the first bishop of the United States, several months before the adoption of the Constitution of the United States. It was therefore older than the United States itself. True enough, it had started as a small academy, but it had before long achieved the status of a university, chartered by the Congress itself. A touch of snobbishness was understandable and could easily be forgiven. I was a total outsider only recently brought in from the outlands. I was sure that my appointment to conduct Georgetown's anniversary-year program would outrage feelings. I argued this with Doc Bunn. I tried to persuade him to put Fr. Gerald Yates in charge.

Gerry Yates had more of a sense of elitism than anyone else in the community. It showed quite clearly. He made no attempt to disguise his disdain even for Doc Bunn himself. After all, he was a Yale man. The most Doc could claim was a Fordham connection. What could be said for me, who did not have even an East Coast connection? My appointment would strike him as absolutely outrageous. On the other hand, despite his snobbishness, he was a good professsor of government, respected by the students and with an undeniably wide acquaintance among the alumni nation-wide. I strongly argued the case that he should be director of the anniversary. Doc was not to be persuaded and dismissed the argument with the short but conclusive remark, "I cannot work with that man."

I sought the help of Fr. William Dunne, a fellow member of the California Province. Bill had served as president of the University of San Francisco. He was now a consultant for Catholic women's colleges with offices in Washington and had been living for several years at Georgetown. He was probably Doc Bunn's closest Jesuit friend. Bill agreed that it was a mistake to appoint me; as he put it, "If I had named a man from another province to direct our centenary at San Francisco, the community would have howled for my head." He promised to reason with Doc. If he could not change Doc's mind, nobody could. As it turned out, nobody could. Doc was adamant. As Archbishop Curley had found out, Doc Bunn was a stubborn man.

The first expression of outrage was amusing enough. One evening, shortly after Bill Dunne's failed mission, Fr. Joe Haller knocked at my door. Joe had become university treasurer follow-ing the sudden death in May 1963 of Father Cohalan, who had helped me negotiate the Peace Corps budget. Upon entering my room he said without ado, "George, I have nothing against you personally; but I want you to know that of all the damn fool things Doc Bunn has ever done, naming you director of the 175th anniversary-year program is far the worst."

Inasmuch as I was inclined to agree with him, though I did not know what other damn fool things Doc had done, I took no offense.

Instead I laughed and told him that he was undoubtedly right. Joe and I remained good friends.

It was at this point that I took off for Ethiopia. When I returned I discovered that Doc Bunn had given Prof. Riley Hughes a leave of absence from his teaching obligations in the English department and made him assistant director. He was to prove a congenial and effective working partner.

We set up offices in one half of a two-story house that the university owned just outside the main gate of the campus. The other half was occupied by a family. We found ourselves immediately involved in difficulties with the Georgetown housing restrictions. The house was a so-called federal house, that is, dating from the late eighteenth century and having a certain historical value. It was forbidden to use federal houses for anything but the residential purposes for which they were originally intended. After considerable discussion we managed to persuade the civic authorities to permit us to maintain our offices there upon condition that we vacate the premises the very day that the anniversary ended, which would be December 3, 1964.

Gerry Yates was not long in putting himself on record. One evening the family sharing the house with us was entertaining guests, among them Father Yates. I happened to be in my office, working late. Apparently not realizing that the walls were thin, or not knowing that I was in my office, or not caring, he declaimed loudly and at length about Doc Bunn's stupidity in appointing me to direct the anniversary program. I could not but hear every word. Evidently I was going to have to move carefully to defuse the lurking explosives.

I resolved to make myself as inconspicuous as possible. I organized the many programs that filled the fourteen months of celebration, but only once did I appear on stage. That was when Edmund "Pat" Brown, governor of California, spoke to an overflow crowd in Gaston Hall. I had spoken from the same platform with Brown at an anti-Ku Klux Klan rally in Los Angeles when he was district attorney in San Francisco.[2] He would have been surprised had I not introduced him. In doing so I praised his courage in speaking on that earlier occasion. He in return told the Georgetown crowd that the speech I had given then was the greatest he had ever heard. I did not argue with him.

Brown's Georgetown speech, on the Pacific as a future concern of American policy, was the object of considerable interest in Washington political circles. For Brown was being considered as a candidate for the vice-presidency on Lyndon Johnson's ticket in the 1964 elections. The choice in the end fell upon Sen. Hubert Humphrey, unfortunately for him; had Humphrey not carried the heavy burden of association with Johnson's Vietnam involvement, he might well have been elected president in 1968.

On the positive side, I resolved to make judicious use of the special anniversary-year medals I had decided to have cast. Father Bunn presented the first of these, given for meritorious service, at one of the first events on the anniversary calendar, a lavish dinner for the entire faculty and their spouses. Its recipient was Fr. Gerald Yates. The strategy worked. I heard no more outbursts.

I had two secretaries at the beginning. I had hired the first one after we formed the Peace Corps training consortium. The secretary to the dean of the School of Foreign Service had told me that she had a younger sister out in San Antonio who would come at the drop of a hat. And Yola arrived on the first plane, almost before the hat dropped, ready to go.

Freckle-faced Yola, who was always laughing when she was not smiling, was a delightful eighteen- or nineteen-year-old. She had been born in Manila in a Japanese internment camp where her mother, a highly cultivated Mexican citizen, and her father, an American engineer, had been interned during the war. Yola was sufficiently skilled in shorthand, but she could not spell. Through the three years Yola was with me she never typed a letter which I did not have to correct and have her retype. But it was impossible to fire her. She was simply too nice a girl, who lived in perpetual sunshine and banished gloom by her very presence.

She thought her spelling and other mistakes were enormously funny. She once booked me on a flight to Atlantic City, where I was scheduled to deliver a speech to the National Council of Catholic Men. To my surprise, the plane made a stopover at Philadelphia, and I just reached the conference at the moment scheduled for my speech to begin. When I arrived back at Georgetown prepared to be angry with her she utterly disarmed me by laughing uproariously as I described my mad dash from the airport.

Yola frankly confessed that she had come to Washington to find a husband by whom she wanted to have a lot of babies. She left me when she found that husband, by whom she has had a lot of babies. Every Christmas since, I have received their photograph, together with Al, the husband she found, and Yola, still laughing.

The other secretary, Theresa Oehman, was a much more mature woman and highly skilled professional. She had been one of John Kennedy's secretaries who accompanied him on his campaign and was present at Hyannis Port on election night. Afterwards she had joined Robert Kennedy's staff. Her marriage had been a rather late one for both her and her husband, from whom she was separated; her husband was a legislative assistant to Robert Kennedy. Doc Bunn, who had performed the wedding ceremony, had asked her to join my staff as secretary. She was invaluable. Theresa did the serious work while Yola banished gloom. Both were important.

The anniversary year, which proved to be one of the most exciting years in Georgetown's history, began on a note of unplanned merriment. A bit of research had led to the discovery that the colors of the family escutcheon of Charles Carroll were red, black, and gold. Since John Carroll, the founder of Georgetown, was a cousin of Charles, I chose these as the anniversary-year colors because they were more dramatic than the rather pallid blue and gold of his own episcopal escutcheon. I had a flag manufactured to be flown from the campus flagpole every morning. The first morning it broke out on a gale of laughter. The red and gold on a background of black looked for all the world like a pirate's flag and evoked images of Long John Silver. I lost no time in having it redesigned, making red and gold the dominant colors.

The year began with a couple of special dinners. One was an alumni dinner at the Waldorf Astoria Hotel in New York, at which Vice-president Lyndon Johnson was the speaker. And at a dinner on campus for the faculty and their spouses, the president of Barnard College was the speaker. But the formal and dramatic opening of the celebration on October 19 was a truly historic event; for the first time in history a pope spoke directly on television to the United States.

The idea had first been broached sometime during the summer. Telstar had just gone into operation. Fr. Dan Power asked me if I thought it were possible to arrange a papal speech. I got in touch with Fr. Tom O'Donnell of Vatican Radio, who reported that it might be within the realm of possibility. Lengthy negotiations followed. It was necessary to get the approval of AT&T, which owned Telstar, to use the satellite. This involved considerable correspondence with the president of the company, who was persuaded of the historic significance of the occasion and generously consented. Then it was necessary to persuade one of the major networks to carry the program. This proved not so difficult; NBC agreed to carry it on the "Today Show." More complicated were the arrangements between an NBC crew in Rome and the Vatican. This required repeated phone calls to Tom O'Donnell in Rome. At last everything seemed in place.

On campus we installed a huge screen in the gymnasium and ran in special cables to carry the "Today Show." The plan was to have a full student body and cap-and-gowned faculty process at 7 A.M. from Healy Hall to the gymnasium, followed by the telecast and a solemn high Mass.

October 19 was the feast of the Jesuit North American Martyrs. Fearful that the pope might be diverted into a homily on the martyrs and forget to mention Georgetown, I wrote a speech for him. It did not fail to mention Jean de Brebeuf and his companions, but I focused on Georgetown, and I sent it posthaste to the Vatican.

A few days before the great day I telephoned the NBC people in Rome and told them to send their team out to the Vatican, which was expecting them, to set up their equipment. The next day— disaster! NBC called from Rome to tell me that they had gone to the Vatican, where nobody seemed to know anything about it!

Frantic phone calls followed. The first was an unsuccessful effort to reach Father O'Donnell. Then a call to Fr. Harold Small, American assistant to the Jesuit general, revealed that O'Donnell had gone to Ireland, evidently without telling anyone who in the Vatican was in charge of our telecast. Through calls to Ireland we learned that O'Donnell was touring the country with his sister. The Irish police put out an all-points bulletin. That evening as he drove with his sister into Roscommon he was spotted by a policeman, who brought him to the police station and told him to phone Rome. O'Donnell told Small that the contact in the Vatican for our broadcast was Msgr. Paul C. Marcinkus, the man who some twenty years later as Archbishop Marcinkus, head of the Vatican Bank, would achieve a certain notoriety. I passed the word to the NBC people in Rome. They contacted Marcinkus, and the panic subsided.

On the morning of October 19, everything went off without a hitch. Father Power, who had gone to New York, phoned me at 5 A.M. from the NBC studio and reported that the screening had come in perfectly. At 8 A.M. the bigger-than-life figure of Paul VI seated before a microphone in the Vatican, with Marcinkus and Small standing in the background, appeared on the screen in McDonough Gymnasium. It was a historic moment and a deeply moving one. He did not use my ghostwritten speech, but my fears proved groundless. He paid his respects to the American martyrs in passing, but his entire discourse was directed to Georgetown and to its faculty, alumni, and students. Some hours later Doc Bunn dropped into my office to tell me it had been the greatest day in his life. Some years later, on the occasion of my first meeting with Paul VI, I asked if he remembered. He did. "I'm the one who organized that event," I told him, not without a touch of vanity. The pope smiled.

There was a danger that everything that followed would seem anticlimactic. Still, we managed during the ensuing months to maintain a high level of interest through a series of events that featured an impressive number of distinguished persons as lecturers or participants. Among the most impressive was Barbara Ward, Lady Jackson, the noted British economist, who lectured to an enthusiastic and overflowing crowd. She had given me an advance copy of her text, which she completely ignored, speaking ex tempore and brilliantly for a full hour. As I was to tell her some years later in Rome, she always brought tears to my eyes, so poignantly did she speak of poverty in the third world.

One memorable conference dealt with poverty in America. Msgr. George G. Higgins, a friend since his student days at Catholic University, had suggested the idea. I had in mind organizing a conference on collective bargaining and had asked him for suggestions. "A quarter of a century ago," he said, "collective bargaining was a largely unplowed field. Not today. Why don't you plow a new field, poverty, for example?"

In 1962, Michael Harrington had written about poverty in America, but the subject had not yet aroused much attention. I invited ten panelists, experts all, to spend a full day debating the subject and seeking answers to the problem. The conference aroused wide interest in Washington, and a capacity crowd filled Gaston Hall throughout the day. I do not think it is an exaggeration to credit the Johnson administration's War on Poverty in considerable part to the inspiration of this conference.

The panel that day included Harrington, but the star attraction was Gunnar Myrdal, the noted Swedish sociologist, author of a classic work on segregation in the United States. I had learned by chance that Myrdal was in the United States and had caught him by phone in New York as he was about to fly home to Sweden. And I persuaded him to come back from Sweden to take part in our program. It is a measure of the man and of the depth of his dedication to the cause that, having made a brilliant contribution to the symposium, he absolutely refused to accept a penny more than the exact price of his airplane ticket.

Probably the least successful of our enterprises was a concert of electronic music, which had only recently begun to attract attention. Time had run a feature article on the subject; and the pioneer in electronic music, featured in the article, accepted my invitation to come over from Germany and give a demonstration of his art. It attracted a respectable audience. What they thought of it I cannot say. To my ears, it sounded like all the demons in a boiler factory had been let loose. Every once in a while the artist or his single assistant would arise from his chair, cross the stage, and add to the general confusion of noise by striking a tremendous blow upon a large temple gong. If the fault lay in my lack of education, I was in good company. For the following morning Paul Hume, music critic of the *Washington Post*, gave it a review which was both devastating and amusing.

Paul Hume, who besides being music critic for the *Post* had for many years been director of Georgetown's glee club, figured personally in another of our programs which skirted disaster. I had commissioned a special concerto composed by an artist proposed by Hume. It was to be performed by Washington's National Symphony Orchestra together with the Georgetown glee club under Hume's direction. The members of the glee club assured me that they would take care of selling the tickets. I failed to monitor them and was aghast when only a few days before the performance I learned that they had done virtually nothing.

The prospect of the National Symphony Orchestra performing what was in fact a very good concerto—I had heard it in rehearsal—before a sparse audience in Constitution Hall was terrifying. The only hope was to "paper the house." For the next three days I was on the phone from morning to night calling every religious house, male and female, and every school in the area offering them gratis as many tickets as they would take. They no doubt thought me extraordinarily generous. They did not know they were saving me from catastrophe. I was unable to attend myself. Card. Franz Koenig of Vienna, one of the luminaries of Vatican Council II, was arriving that night to give a lecture the following evening, and I had to meet him at the airport. But reports assured me that Constitution Hall, while not crowded, was reasonably occupied by an appreciative audience.

Apart from the electronic-music travesty, and perhaps there were some who liked that, the anniversary year featured a series of events that brought distinction to the university. There is recognition of this in the citation which accompanied the conferring upon Riley Hughes and myself of the John Carroll Medal of Merit, Georgetown's most prestigious award.[3] I recently received letters independent of each other from two people who were there. One is a Jesuit professor of theology. The other, a graduate student then, is now a lay vice-president of the university. They both were writing with reference to the university's bicentennial celebration, already in the planning stage. Both of them credit the 175th anniversary program with a large measure of credit for the high level of academics and the excellent reputation that Georgetown enjoys today. They both made the identical argument: the efforts of the university to live up to the image created by the 175th anniversary year have resulted in the Georgetown of today. This thought had never occurred to me, but upon reflection I think there may be a grain of truth in it.

It is true that I had a rather high concept of the values a university should represent, particularly in celebrating an anniversary of its existence. This explains my anger when the board of directors, in those days all Jesuits, added to the list of distinguished men and women whom I had recommended for honorary degrees an undistinguished congressman from New Jersey whose only claim to the university's recognition was that he headed the subcommittee of the House which controlled grants to universities. No doubt the motivation for conferring honorary degrees is sometimes the hope of getting something in return. I was willing to accept this as legitimate in ordinary circumstances; but it seemed to me altogether out of place in an anniversary year, which should speak only to the highest ideals represented by the institution. It is possible, to be sure, for a congressman from New Jersey to merit an honorary degree; but the mere fact of being a congressman from New Jersey does not of itself merit this honor. His name on the program, among the truly distinguished honorees, looked tawdry and manifestly mercenary. It did not add luster and meaning to the anniversary theme: wisdom and discovery for a dynamic world.

I wrote an angry letter about this to Doc Bunn. In his absence his assistant, Fr. Gerard Campbell, who was being groomed to succeed him at the end of the anniversary year, wrote me a stern reprimand telling me in effect that decisions of the board of directors were none of my business. He was undoubtedly right. But on the day of convocation I still thought the congressman looked like a gate-crasher.

Grand Finale

From the outset I had planned to end the anniversary year with a grand finale. The concluding day had been set for December 3, 1964. I planned to precede this with a three-day symposium bringing together some of the world's distinguished theologians and philosophers to discuss the subject "Man and Freedom." This would conclude with a speech on freedom by John F. Kennedy, President of the United States, upon whom the university would confer an honorary degree; a solemn high Mass would follow, sung, for the first time in the United States, in English. President Kennedy had agreed to speak and I was well into the further planning when the never-to-be-forgotten-day of November 22, 1963, dawned.

I was attending a luncheon in honor of the former president of Colombia, who was to lecture that night in Gaston Hall. We were nearing dessert when a waiter informed Edward Martin, the Assistant Secretary of State for Latin American Affairs, that his office wanted him to phone immediately. He left the dining room, then returned in a few minutes, white and shaken, to announce, "The president has been shot." That was the end of the luncheon and of much else besides, including Camelot.

The evening lecture was postponed. I went to my office and turned on the television, and I was still sitting there when the next day dawned. Like most Americans, I was in shock. Three days later I was brought back to reality as I watched on television the unforgettable scene of little John-John at the foot of the steps at Saint Matthew's Cathedral saluting his father's flag-draped bier as the funeral procession prepared to move off. I left my office and walked over the Key Bridge across the Potomac River and on to Arlington Cemetery, where I arrived in time to hear from the slopes above the raspy voice of Cardinal Cushing reciting the graveside prayers. The world had not come to an end. But an era had.

I had to try to put the pieces together. I proposed to Doc Bunn and the board of directors that the concluding convocation be made a memorial to the late president, upon whom we would confer posthumously the honorary degree. The proposal was accepted, although not without considerable persuasive effort. Pres. Lyndon Johnson agreed to speak. Robert Kennedy agreed to accept the degree in his brother's name.

Gradually I managed to assemble a panel of distinguished theologians of different churches. The most notable of the Roman

Catholic participants were Karl Rahner, Hans Küng, and John Courtney Murray, all of whom emerged from Vatican II with worldwide reputations.

Karl Rahner, who was generally recognized as one of the three or four leading theologians in the world, proved difficult to snare. He first refused, pleading the inadequacy of his English. I answered by assuring him he could speak in German, which we would have simultaneously translated into English. I also invited his older brother Hugo Rahner, a distinguished Church historian. His age and the precarious state of his health prevented Hugo from accepting.

Hans Küng was a brilliant Swiss theologian who had first sprung into world notice at the Council. He had not yet incurred the displeasure of Roman authorities. He proved at Georgetown to be a charismatic personality with particular appeal to young people.

John Courtney Murray was, of course, chiefly noted for having developed over the years—against stubborn and powerful opposition—the thesis on religious freedom which was adopted by Vatican Council II as a statement of the Catholic position, overturning the contrary position on Church and state long maintained by Rome.

I had never thought of a theological-philosophical symposium as a spectator sport. Consequently I had originally thought of the simultaneous-translation room in the School of Foreign Service as an ideal site; it could seat perhaps 150 people in addition to the lecturers and discussants. But I had egregiously underestimated the interest which Vatican Council II had stimulated both in the subjects treated there and in the personalities who had played leading roles. There was early evidence of this in the overflow crowds that packed Gaston Hall for lectures by Cardinals Leo Suenens, Franz Koenig, and Bernard Alfrink, three of the leading lights of the Council; but I had failed to read the signs of the times. As demand for tickets poured in, it was evident that the simultaneous-translation room was woefully inadequate. I shifted the site to Gaston Hall, which would accomodate six to seven hundred. This was soon overwhelmed by the rising tide of demand. I moved the site to McDonough Gymnasium which could hold several thousand. The demand continued to surge, surpassing all expectations. In the end, in addition to a full house in the gymnasium, another full house occupied Gaston Hall, to which the lectures and discussions were carried by cable. It must have been the largest audience ever to turn out in the United States to listen to theologians.

In the course of the year I had accompanied Paul Hume and the Georgetown glee club to Puerto Rico, where, besides a public concert, they performed for Pablo Casals in his home and received in return the rare privilege of a private recital by the great master of the violoncello. My purpose was to invite the artist to play at Georgetown. He had once performed in the White House for President and Mrs. Kennedy, and I hoped to persuade him to do the same at our December 3 convocation. This was not a realistic hope; December in Washington was no place for a man ninety years old. Although his age and frail health ruled out a personal appearance, Casals offered to make a special recording to be played during the convocation. And he later recorded the same two pieces he had played in the White House. When the recording was played at the convocation one could have heard a pin drop. It was a profoundly moving moment.

The Robert Kennedy Crisis

The convocation was only a few days off when a threat developed from a totally unexpected quarter. Robert Kennedy had, as I have mentioned, agreed to accept the honorary degree in his brother's name. When my secretary, who had once been Robert Kennedy's secretary, phoned his office in New York to confirm such details as his arrival time, she was informed that he did not intend to arrive at all! I found this incredible. I took the phone. Kennedy himself, his secretary said, was not in his office and was unreachable. I talked to one of his aides, who reaffirmed that Kennedy did not intend to appear at the convocation. I explained that Georgetown University was honoring Pres. John F. Kennedy and that Sen. Robert Kennedy had agreed to accept the degree in his brother's name. He said that the senator was aware of this but had changed his mind! To say that I was thunderstruck is an understatement.

I managed to reach his wife, Ethel Kennedy, at her home in Virginia. Our conversation was highly charged. She confirmed that he did not intend to appear. She was fully aware that he had promised to do so and that the intention was to honor his brother, but saw nothing censurable in his decision to opt out without bothering to inform me. When I asked if she realized the difficult position this put me in, she asked angrily: "What of my husband?

Do you expect him to sit there on the same platform with that man?" The cat was out of the bag. That man was Pres. Lyndon Johnson.

I had heard reports that Robert Kennedy, together with some members of the so-called Irish mafia, harbored unfriendly feelings towards Lyndon Johnson; but Washington abounds with rumors and reports. Here was rumor confirmed; and it was evidently not merely unfriendly feelings, but the most bitter hostility. He had agreed to accept his brother's honorary degree not knowing that Johnson was to be on hand. When he learned that this was the case he reneged, unwilling to share the platform with his brother's successor.

I found myself three days before the convocation with no one to whom the president of the university could present the honorary degree. Ethyl Kennedy was of no help. When I asked, perhaps sarcastically, if she had any suggestions, she said no and ended our conversation. Eunice Kennedy salvaged the situation. I reached her through her husband, Sargent Shriver. As soon as I explained what had happened, she graciously agreed to appear at the convocation and to accept the degree in her brother's name.

President Lyndon Johnson

The day before the convocation a team of Secret Service agents explored the campus thoroughly and went through the gymnasium with a finetooth comb, examining every board and beam from top to bottom. The memory of Dallas was still green—or red.

More than three hundred universities from all over the world had accepted the invitation to be represented. I arranged for the representatives to report to Harbin Hall, a dormitory, where each one would find the appropriate academic gown with name attached. From there they were to advance in academic procession to the gymnasium some two hundred yards distant.

The morning of the convocation it was raining cats and dogs. Fortunately, I had hired a fleet of buses to transport everyone after the convocation to downtown Washington, where a dinner was to conclude the day and the anniversary year. But anticipating the possibility of rain, I had the buses on hand early and was thus able to drive the more than three hundred cap-and-gowned delegates from Harbin Hall to the gymnasium. In the spacious vestibule the academic procession assembled according to institutional seniority. Here I asked Doc Bunn to hold them until President Johnson arrived.

I had been informed by one of the Secret Service agents that the president had been delayed by a dental problem but that the presidential party, with which he was in touch by walkie-talkie, had left the White House and was now on the way. Fr. Brian McGrath, the academic vice-president, meanwhile took it upon himself to set the procession in motion. I did not object too much to this, provided the program itself was not started before the arrival of the president.

I had a special reason for this, besides the fact that to start the ceremony without the president would be a gross violation of protocol and even of ordinary manners—a not subtle rebuke to the president for being late. The special reason was that I had found a beautiful prayer for the Congress of the United States, composed by John Carroll, first bishop of the United States and founder of Georgetown University. It made a uniquely suitable invocation for this occasion, a celebration of the 175th anniversary of the university in the presence of the head of the government of the United States. Consequently, as soon as everyone was in place I went out on stage and told Brian McGrath, who was to read John Carroll's prayer, that the president would arrive in a few minutes and that he should await his arrival. I had just been told by the Secret Service agent that the presidential party was crossing Wisconsin and M streets, which meant arrival within two or three minutes.

The president was to enter by a side door which led almost directly on to the stage. I had hardly left the stage to return to the side of the Secret Service agent when I heard McGrath's voice. I turned in stupefaction. Sure enough, there he was at the podium reading John Carroll's prayer for the Congress of the United States. This prayer, to be sure, was meant for God, but it was also meant for the ears of the president of the United States, and I had carefully planned the affair so that it would reach them. When the president entered and the orchestra struck up "Hail to the Chief," the prayer was already concluded and its significance lost.

It was understood that President Johnson would not stay for the solemn Mass which was to follow. I noted his departure with particular interest. Before leaving he crossed the stage and warmly embraced Eunice Kennedy Shriver.

The rain had ended, and the sun shone. When we emerged from the Mass I saw the university delegates, de-capped and de-gowned, loaded onto the buses and headed for the concluding dinner at the Sheraton. I did not accompany them. All the details, including seating, were arranged, and a team of students was trained to see that everything went off without a hitch. Dr. Riley Hughes represented the two of us at the dinner. I took the rest of our team, three secretaries and a publicist, to celebrate with a champagne dinner at a well-known—and expensive—French restaurant at the corner of Wisconsin and M.

The anniversary year was over. The red, gold, and black flag was hauled down. The records were turned over to the archives. The offices were vacated, and the federal house was restored to residential use. Doc Bunn, by now the university chancellor, told me to take a vacation. I went to Puerto Rico.

We Shall Overcome

There was a world outside of Georgetown, and even with my anniversary duties I remained part of it. Among the important events in that world, the long struggle for freedom led by Martin Luther King, Jr., which began in Montgomery, Alabama, on December 1, 1955, when Rosa Parks refused to yield her seat on the bus to a white man, returned to Montgomery on March 25, 1965, with the culmination of the march from Selma, Alabama. Less than three weeks earlier, a mounted sheriff's posse had charged a column of some five hundred blacks as they marched peacefully out of Selma with Montgomery their goal. With flailing bullwhips and rubber tubes wrapped in barbed wire they broke up the peaceful demonstration with a brutality that shocked the nation. Seventy men and women were hospitalized on this "Bloody Sunday," seventy others treated for their wounds and discharged. Dozens of others nursed their wounds in Brown Chapel, in which they had sought refuge.

On March 21, with the uncertain protection of a federal court order enjoining Alabama authorities from interfering, another column set out from Selma, at one time a center for the auction of slaves. This time they were unmolested, except for verbal abuse, as they marched towards Montgomery, where thousands of sympathizers from all over the land were gathering to join them upon their arrival.

I flew down from Washington with several Georgetown students on the night of March 24. The assembly point was the baseball field of Saint Jude's Catholic Center on the outskirts of

Montgomery, which we reached very early in the morning of Thursday, March 25. It had rained torrentially the previous afternoon, and the field was a sea of mud in which we milled about with thousands of others for several hours while the march got organized. Most had come with groups and carried identifying banners. I found a group from California and with it, to my great delight, an old friend, Bud Ogren, whom I had not seen in almost twenty years. It was he who had phoned me the morning after my speech in Olympic Auditorium to congratulate "the man who brings Aristotle to the masses."[4]

At last we moved out on the march through Montgomery, the first capital of the Confederacy and still capital of the State of Alabama. We did not really march. We walked, eight abreast and at least twenty-five thousand strong. As we moved through the black neighborhoods, the mood was relaxed and cheerful, the people on the sidewalks and porches smiling and friendly. When we entered the white neighborhoods, the mood became more serious. We were entering enemy territory. Overt signs of hostility, however, were few. An occasional epithet. A gang of toughs on a street corner who made obscene gestures as we passed. A young woman watching from a second story office thumbed her nose at one of the Georgetown students who waved to her. To my astonishment, the Georgetown student asked me what the gesture meant. I told him what it meant when I was his age; I assumed it still meant the same.

Clusters of people gathered on every porch; as we moved into the business area, they were crowded at the entrance to every building or looked down from office windows above, watching us go by. There was a sameness to their expressions which struck me. Only after many blocks of marching and seeing hundreds of faces did I realize what it was. It was a mixture of curiosity, puzzlement, and fascination.

Gene Patrick, a friend since University of Chicago days, had lived in Montgomery since being demobilized from the air force at the end of the war; he gave me the key to understanding their expression. They had so convinced themselves that everybody in the civil rights movement was a beatnik, a sex addict, or a Communist that they could not figure us out. There were a few aging beatniks or other fringe elements, but they were inconspicuous, I later wrote in *America*, "among the thousands of average, sensible-

looking Americans—of all colors, classes, ages and professions—
who did not fit the stereotyped image."

My article continued:

> The participation of hundreds of clergymen, priests, minis-
> ters, rabbis and especially nuns, must have added to their
> bewilderment in view of the almost total failure of their own
> clergymen, of whatever affiliation, to give them even an
> elementary understanding of Christ and His Gospel, least of
> all of the meaning of the second commandment, which He said
> was like unto the first. There surely can be no prostitution of
> truth more frightful than that practised by churchmen who
> have perverted their office, their doctrine and their faith into
> an instrument of racism.

A large number of nuns, who in those days still wore a
distinctive religious habit, added a special dimension to the event:

> Those who have found fault with them for their participation,
> and said they should have stayed home to attend to their
> religious duties, have a curious notion of what religion is all
> about. Ralph McGill showed more comprehension of the
> meaning of religion in the glowing tribute he paid to these nuns
> in his column in the Atlanta *Constitution* the day following the
> march. Who can ever forget the perky little nun making the V
> for victory sign to sullen onlookers watching from the side-
> walk; or the smiling reply of another nun to a heckler who
> asked her what she was doing here: "Educating the whites!" I
> suggest that no one in this country has ever done anything
> that reflected more credit upon the Catholic faith than the
> nuns who marched in Montgomery. What they did might even
> atone for the sorry record of silence, compromise, evasion and
> sophistry on the part of so much Christian leadership in the
> United States.

Nowhere during that entire day, except for the many flags
carried by the marchers, did I see the Stars and Stripes. But I saw
the Stars and Bars of the Confederacy everywhere. This flag hung
from residences and office windows. People who watched on the
sidewalk waved it. One man stood boldly in the street, defiantly
waving the flag at us, perhaps feeling like a Barbara Fritchie in re-
verse. National Guardsmen, who had been federalized by President Johnson wore little Confederate flags on their uniforms.

Two weeks before, I had visited Richmond, Virginia, the Confederate capital after Montgomery, with its heroic statues—Robert E. Lee, Stonewall Jackson, Jeb Stuart—and monuments that evoked the past and kept that past alive. I viewed a heroic portrait of Father Ryan, the poet of the Confederacy; he held a folded Confederate flag, and beneath was the title of the poem he had addressed to General Lee at the end of the war, "Furl that Flag!" Lee did furl that flag, but the Deep South did not. For to furl that flag would be to admit that the war was lost, the Cause defeated. So too, to free the blacks from all the servitudes that bound them would be to face the fact of defeat. Refusing to accept defeat allowed the South not to face reality, I wrote; "when the Deep South finally discovers the courage to look reality squarely in the face and to accept the fact that the war was irretrievably lost, she will recover her sanity and the Negro will be set free."[5]

The psychosis of the North is in some regards more tragic than that of the South. Having at enormous cost emancipated the black people from slavery, the North threw away the fruits of victory by subjecting them to the dehumanizing and manifold servitudes of segregation, a symbol only of the idolatry of White Supremacy. The healing of a psychosis is a long process. The process is far from complete, but over the last twenty-three years both North and especially South have made considerable progress.

Our march up Dexter Avenue, up which more than a century before had moved the inaugural parade of Jefferson Davis, ended at the Capitol where he had taken the oath of office as President of the Confederacy. We stood for several hours, arms linked and swaying to its rhythm as we sang, between speeches, some of them too long, "We Shall Overcome." Not surprisingly, Gov. George Wallace refused to emerge to accept our petition demanding recognition of the right to vote for blacks and an end to police brutality. The previous week, Pres. Lyndon Johnson, in a speech which Martin Luther King pronounced "one of the most eloquent, unequiovocal and passionate pleas for human rights ever made by the President of the United States," had presented the voting rights bill to Congress. Today, standing in the flatbed of a trailer, Martin Luther King, Jr., ended a long but inspirational day, the high-water mark of the civil rights movement, with a speech which approached the eloquence of his "I Have a Dream" oration at the Lincoln Memorial two years earlier.

Post Doc Bunn

With Gerard Campbell, who became Georgetown president on December 3, 1964, my status was a bit cloudy. I had been special assistant to Father Bunn for international programs, but there was no indication that his successor wished me to serve in the same capacity. There was in fact considerable uncertainty about what he wished me to do, if anything. Dr. William Manger, a retired veteran of the State Department and professor of Latin American relations, urged that I be charged with organizing the university's Latin American program. Through the anniversary program I had made many important Latin American contacts. My ideas of the many past sins of American foreign policy vis-à-vis Latin America and what should be its future direction coincided with those of Dr. Manger, who was on the verge of retirement. Gerry Campbell did not respond to the suggestion. I returned to the direction of Peace Corps training programs.

In 1965 I was asked to prepare a group of volunteers to develop school lunch programs in Brazil. I made a quick trip to the State of Espirito Santo in Brazil to find out what that meant. I learned that the volunteers would be expected not only to administer lunch programs, for which powdered milk would be supplied by the United States, but also to teach the children in urban and especially rural schools how to grow a variety of vegetables and raise chickens and rabbits.

This was quite a challenge for Georgetown: it was anything but an agricultural school, located in anything but a farming area. At first I thought of bussing the trainees every day across the Potomac into the rural area of Virginia, where they could learn to plant, cultivate, and harvest. This would have been very time-consuming.

Next door to Georgetown was the venerable Visitation College for girls, founded shortly after Georgetown itself. Fronting the college were several acres of unoccupied land. The mother superior graciously consented to my using one of these acres for truck gardening. I had a soil expert from the University of Maryland test this soil to tell me if anything could be grown here, it being largely fill dirt. After testing the soil he reported that if we ran pipes for irrigation purposes through the area and loaded it with manure, we might produce something. I followed his directions, hired two

Father George Dunne directed Georgetown University's 175th anniversary celebration in 1964; here Father Dunne greets Admiral Hyman Rickover, one of the many speakers he brought to Georgetown during the year-long celebration.

In 1966 President Lyndon B. Johnson visited Georgetown to sign a Peace Corps bill in the presence of volunteers in training for service in Brazil; here Father Dunne stands between President Johnson and Father Gerard J. Campbell, S.J., president of Georgetown.

professors from the University of Maryland's agricultural school, one to teach chicken and rabbit raising, the other to teach vegetable growing, and awaited the arrival of the trainees.

The Peace Corps training had been lengthened to twelve weeks. Within that time, our little farm produced an astonishing amount of twenty-six kinds of vegetables. We supplied not only the Georgetown and Visitation communities, but several institutions for the poor. One day I filled several large baskets with water-melon, canteloupe, string beans, tomatoes, corn, and other pro-duce; I drove with several volunteers to Peace Corps headquarters, where I told them to take our crops up to Sargent Shriver's office and tell him they were a gift from the richest farm in Washington, D.C. In terms of the real-estate value of the property on which they were grown, this was no idle boast. In fact it was probably the only farm in Washington, D.C.

Later that year I spent two months in Brazil visiting the Georgetown-trained volunteers. It was evident to me, as it had been on my trip to Ethiopia, that the volunteers were learning more from the people whose lives they shared and with whom they worked than they were contributing. They were learning to under-stand a society different from their own, and in the process to bet-ter understand their own. They were discovering values among the poor in Brazil that were in short supply at home. For most, if not all, it was a great educational experience. They would return home with a less parochial view of the world and with a new perspective upon life, its goals, and its values; they learned a new cultural humility.

Arrupe and the Peace Corps

I was persuaded that Jesuits, especially those in their training period, could profit from the Peace Corps experience. We had a new superior general in Rome, Fr. Pedro Arrupe, elected in May of this year, 1965. He was a man of world experience, a Spanish Basque, educated in Spain, the Netherlands, and the United States, and an educator for a quarter of a century in Japan. He was a survivor of Hiroshima, where he was master of novices the day Armageddon erupted. He gave promise of becoming, as in my judgment he did, the greatest superior general since Saint Igna-tius himself.

Saint Ignatius had devised what he termed *experiments* as part of the training of Jesuits. Novices were to be sent out for a period of weeks or months to make their way on their own from town to town, accepting such hospitality as was offered them, earning their bread as best they could, seeking to be of service wherever they could. In another experiment they were sent to live and work in hospitals, doing the menial tasks and helping care for the sick and dying. Another experiment is called regency. After finishing their philosophy studies but before beginning theology the scholastics spend two or three years in full-time ministry, often teaching in high school or college.

Upon my return from Brazil I wrote to Father Arrupe proposing that scholastics be permitted to volunteer for service with the Peace Corps. I suggested that it could serve as the regency period, arguing that it would be an adaptation to the contemporary world of Saint Ignatius's experiments. Admittedly some vocations would be lost in the process, but better that they be lost now than after ordination to the priesthood. It would have a lasting effect upon the values of those who participated. I very much doubted that a Peace Corps veteran would in later years invite the reactionary head of the Union Pacific Railroad to address the graduating class of a Jesuit university or defend the thesis that we should not challenge the accepted institutions of our society. I concluded with a request that I be permitted to join the Peace Corps as a volunteer.

Within two or three weeks I received Father Arrupe's reply, accepting my proposal and granting my personal request. And I later learned from one Amercan provincial that Arrupe did in fact write to all the American provincials that requests of scholastics for permission to join the Peace Corps should be favorably considered.

What happened? At almost the same time that I received Father Arrupe's reply, opening the possibility of an entirely new career, Abp. Patrick O'Boyle, archbishop of Washington, D.C., had issued an angry and stern letter pontificating that service in the Peace Corps was incompatible with a seminarian's vocation and should be strictly forbidden. Father Arrupe did not wish to appear to be challenging the position of the archbishop. He wrote to me regretfully withdrawing the permission he had granted. He also recalled his directive to the provincials.

A Changing Peace Corps

The following year the Peace Corps asked us to train two separate groups for Brazil, one for another school lunch program, the other to fill teaching positions in Brazilian universities. I directed the former; Dr. Jesse Mann directed the latter.

The Peace Corps was changing. It was developing its own training camps, one in Puerto Rico and one in the Virgin Islands, and was phasing out its reliance upon universities in favor of its own programs. And it was relying more and more upon returned volunteers for training purposes. This obviously made sense. I used a half dozen returned volunteers on my staff in 1966.

Another trend, which made less sense, was to allow the trainees to do their own training, with minimal direction. I spent a week in the Puerto Rico training camp, where one morning I watched a group of trainees teach themselves how to kill a chicken. It had a sadistic aspect to it. We killed chickens at Georgetown too, not a pleasant operation at best, but we did not simply hand the trainees a knife and turn them loose on the chickens. They were first taught by an expert how to use the knife with minimal anguish to the chicken.

Another change seemed to me fundamental and mistaken. Reflecting President Kennedy's thinking, Sargent Shriver had firmly resisted any effort to use the Peace Corps simply as a tool of American foreign policy. Kennedy had envisioned the Peace Corps as an instrument through which Americans, especially young Americans, could contribute their skills to the effort of developing nations to free themselves from the shackles of poverty. No doubt there was a utopian element and a mythical premise to this concept. The myth was that average Americans are equipped with technical or vocational skills that they can communicate to others. The truth is quite otherwise. In most cases, the volunteers had to be taught in twelve weeks of training the skill they were supposed to communicate.

The case of the school lunch program for Brazil exemplifies this. Only one of the trainees who arrived at Georgetown had ever set foot on a farm or raised a rabbit. The same was true of those in the other group who were supposed to fill teaching posts in Brazilian universities. All of them were college graduates. None of them had ever taught.

What was important to the Peace Corps, however, was precisely its utopian and mythical elements. And these did serve

American interests in that they created an image of America far different from the unflattering one that American foreign policy and American behavior had created in most of these host countries in the past.[6] The moment the Peace Corps came to be seen as a tool of the Secretary of State in promoting policy, both its image and its value were gone.

Sargent Shriver was no longer head of the Peace Corps in 1966, and there were indications that his firm resolve was no longer in place. I saw evidence of this in Brazil. It was Peace Corps policy to bring the volunteers together at the end of the first year in the field for a midterm dialogue, a critical examination of accomplishments and of failures. I was present when the Georgetown group of university teachers gathered in Rio de Janeiro for their meeting. I found them disillusioned, unhappy, and, in some cases, bitter.

What had drawn them to the Peace Corps in the first place was its disinterested, non-self-seeking character. What appealed to them was that they would not be an agent of the CIA or of the Secretary of State, but a Good Samaritan with no ulterior motives. They had been told that every program originated at the request of the host country and in response to a need.

Actually, the average villager or peasant assumed that a newly arrived volunteer was a CIA agent. They could not understand why a young American would voluntarily abandon the style of life which they associated with the United States to share their poverty. One of the greatest satisfactions that the volunteers derived from their experience, in my judgement, was to overcome this assumption and satisfy the sceptics that they had indeed come with no other motive than to be of service.

The Georgetown group had gradually discovered that they had been deceived. The program in which they had enlisted had originated not with the Brazilian government but in the United States Embassy. Anti-American sentiment was fairly rampant among Brazilian university students. The United States ambassador had conceived the strategy of planting Americans in the universities, their purpose being to counteract the anti-Americanism of the students. They were not there to fill a need. In Ethiopia there had been no Ethiopians qualified for the teaching posts filled by the Peace Corps volunteers. In Brazil, on the contrary, there were qualified people available. The volunteers discovered that in some cases a professor, one unfriendly to the United States, had been removed to make room for a Peace Corps volunteer. What led to this strategy is that the democratically elected government in Brazil had been overthrown by the military two years earlier; the new military government began close collaboration with the United States Embassy. When the volunteers learned these facts, they were not only disillusioned but felt they were being used.

This was the beginning of a long period of decline in the Peace Corps. During ten years it had seven different directors. The program became undisciplined. Its ideals were contradicted by Vietnam and Watergate. Some host countries thought they saw looming in the background the frightening figure of the CIA. It lost its autonomy under Pres. Richard Nixon, who joined it with other federal organizations under the umbrella of something called *Action*. Its membership declined from over fifteen thousand to barely five thousand. Pres. Jimmy Carter, whose mother had served in the Peace Corps in India, restored its autonomy; but some of Ronald Reagan's operatives came to Washington intending to guillotine the Peace Corps as they intended to guillotine the Department of Education. Their intentions were thwarted by the leadership of Loret Miller Ruppe, who, as director 1981–89, reversed all these negative trends.

Loret, who is both a cousin and a one-time student of mine, revitalized the Peace Corps, restored its ideals, brought back its sheen. *Time* has called her a "managerial whiz," and Sargent Shriver has praised her for leadership that "is imaginative, dedicated, resourceful and wise." The Peace Corps has again become a sign of hope and a symbol of peace. Whether it will continue to rise or again decline remains to be seen. Pres. George Bush has appointed as Loret's successor a Georgia businessman friend of his. George Bush named Loret ambassador to Norway; I am sure that she will serve with distinction but doubt that she will derive as much satisfaction from her job as she has from her Peace Corps service.

Farewell to Georgetown

As I have indicated, with the end of the anniversary year and the retirement of Doc Bunn, my position at Georgetown had become uncertain. I did not have the same relation with Gerry Campbell, his successor, as I had with Doc. After a year and a half, it seemed clear that I was not Gerry's assistant for international programs. What remained was the Peace Corps, which was about to stop contracting with universities to train volunteers. I thought it time to move on.

Fr. Frank Rouleau had spent ten or more years in the Istituto Storico in Rome during which he microfilmed an immense amount of archival material dealing with Jesuit history in China. He had a grandiose plan for a nine-volume history, but in fact, apart from an article for the *Catholic Encyclopedia* on the Chinese Rites Controversy, he had produced very little. For one thing, he was in painfully bad health. As a young man, apparently as a result of rheumatic fever, he had developed a severe curvature of the spine which grew worse over the years until his upper body was virtually parallel to the ground. He also suffered from severe deafness. Besides, he was a perfectionist, always hunting for more footnotes for a text he had yet to write. This was unfortunate because he was an excellent writer.

His health worsening, Rouleau had quit Rome and with his storehouse of microfilms moved to the Jesuit novitiate in Los Gatos, California. I thought of joining Rouleau and, returning to my Chinese studies, help him get his nine-volume history on the production line. Gerry Campbell had no objections. The California provincial approved of the prodigal's return. He also approved of a codicil which I had added to my request, that I return by way of Brazil, the length of my stay there left undefined. I had developed a keen interest in Brazil and had vaguely in mind doing some writing about this fascinating country.

It was painful to leave Georgetown, where I had been very happy and where I had made many good friends, among them many Jesuits, chief of whom was Doc Bunn. The evening before I left, the superior of the community began the supper with grace and then surprised me with a gracious speech expressing regret at my departure and, for the community, thanking me for my contribution to Georgetown, especially in the direction of the anniversary year. At the conclusion of his remarks the entire community, including Joe Haller and Gerry Yates, gave me a standing ovation. It was a deeply moving experience. The next morning, after leaving on the community bulletin board a note of appreciation for all the fond memories I would carry with me, I boarded the plane for Brazil and quietly wept all the way to Belem, hoping other passengers would think I had a bad cold.

Fifteen

Brazil

Once known as Nossa Senhora do Belem—Our Lady of Bethlehem—Belem, Brazil, is the port city of the north, situated where the mighty waters of the Amazon empty into the Atlantic. Today a city of around a million people, it has retained in its old and elegant mansions the flavor of past glories when rubber was king and most of it passed through Belem en route from the Amazon region, where it was produced, to the industrialized world.

More than a thousand miles up the Amazon from Belem is the city of Manaus. In the late nineteenth century and into the twentieth it was the bustling and fabulously wealthy capital of the rubber industry. That is to say, the rubber barons of Manaus were fabulously wealthy. They are said to have lit their cigars with three-figure bank notes. They also built an opera house in miniature, as elegant as any opera house in Europe, but with a seating capacity of about three hundred, just large enough to accommodate them and their families. Obviously, the idea was not to bring a bit of culture to the Indians of the Amazon but to maintain for themselves contact with the culture of Europe. To this end they paid huge fees to the leading singers and thespians of Europe to sail the Atlantic and a thousand miles up the Amazon to entertain them in their tiny jewel of an opera house.

The boom began to taper off around 1910 with the entry into the market of cheaper Malaysian rubber—grown with seeds from the Amazon! And boom became bust when disease attacked the rubber trees in Brazil. The development of synthetic rubber completed the collapse. Today, thanks to the government's effort to develop the entire Amazon region, Manaus is enjoying a new life as a duty-free open port. But in 1967, it was something of a ghost town.

Drawn, I suppose, by the same magnetic force that attracts people to Virginia City, I wanted to see it. I especially wanted to see the opera house, monument to the arrogance and egotism of the rubber barons. I flew there from Belem, farther than from New York to Chicago, overawed by the stupendous spectacle of the Amazon below.

The Amazon is not in the strict sense a river. It is an enormous body of water formed of many rivers and fed by torrential downpours. One description gives some sense of its size:

> By almost every measure, the Amazon is Earth's greatest river. It pours more water into the sea than the next seven biggest candidates together, almost ten times more than the Mississippi. It rivals the Nile in length but carries at least 50 times the volume. Seven of its tributaries are each over a thousand miles long...Its channel is navigable by boat or barge for almost 3,000 miles. If the Amazon flowed through North America, an ocean freighter could sail from Boston to Denver, and the source would lie 1,700 miles beyond that.[1]

The Rio Negro, one of its greatest tributaries, has an outflow greater than any other river in the world except the Amazon itself. At the juncture of the two lies the city of Manaus.

Although the voice of Jenny Lind no longer soars aloft to the loges of the opera house where once glowed the glamour of Manaus high society, it was easy to imagine the jewel it had been in its heyday. It is serving more prosaic purposes now than as a showcase of Europe's famous artists. When I was there a gathering of evangelical missionaries from northern Brazil was meeting. I understand, however, that in the current revival of Manaus, it has been refurbished to something of its old splendor and serves again as the *Teatro Amazonas*.

It proved more difficult to leave Manaus than it had been to arrive. I flew out after three days on an old DC-3, which has often been called the safest plane ever built. I hoped this was true when less than two hours out of Manaus we ran into a truly torrential rainstorm, typical of this region. The DC-3 took a fearsome beating as it struggled bravely and blindly against solid sheets of rain. The rain began to beat its way through tiny cracks in the fuselage. Soon a rivulet was flowing down the aisle, while the steward kept trying without much success to stanch the flow by stuffing bits of paper into the cracks. Eventually the pilot gave up and announced that we would have to return to Manaus. What sounded like sighs of relief from the badly buffeted old DC-3 were probably just creaks and groans as it labored to turn around. Looking out the window one could easily imagine we were in a submarine several fathoms deep. Somehow the pilot managed to get us back to Manaus; I'll never know how. Brazilian pilots are said to be the best in the world. I could believe it.

Planes did not fly in and out of Manaus every day. Nor did there seem to be a fixed schedule of arrivals and departures. I was lodged in a cabin at the airport to await the next plane. It arrived three days later. I spent the interval further exploring the nostalgic reminders of Manaus's past. On the third day a plane of the Cruzeiro do Sol airline flew me back to Belem without incident.

In Belem's quaintly named riverfront marketplace "Ver o Peso"—Keep an Eye on the Scale—I made the acquaintance of a Lebanese who, like many other Lebanese, had spent most of his life in this country; he taught me much about Brazil and its customs. After a daylong boat tour of the myriad waterways which flow through the luxuriant tropical vegetation in the area, I left for Fortaleza, whose bishop, though less widely known, is no less courageous a spokesman for the poor than Dom Helder Camara of Recife, where I visited next.

This was not my first visit to Recife. I had been there the year before with embarrassing consequences. Georgetown University had established a Center for Population Research. As I was about to leave to visit Brazil for Peace Corps purposes, its director asked to see me. He told me that the center would like to establish relations with a kind of satellite operation in that country. He asked me if I would try to find an institution interested in collaborating in the venture. The proposal was that the Brazilian partner send two medical doctors to Georgetown for training in population research. Georgetown would bear all the expenses. Their training concluded, they would return to Brazil to establish a research center to collaborate with the work being done at Georgetown. From his tone I assumed that he was ready to move as soon as he found an institution interested in his proposal. Consequently, as soon as I arrived in Brazil I undertook the search.

I wrote to Dom Helder Camara, archbishop of Recife, outlining the proposal and asking if I might discuss it with him. Dom Helder was known to everyone in Brazil, and his fame was already reaching the outside world. Tiny in size, he was a giant in the eyes of the poor, whose cause he championed as he decried the injustices of a society which condemned them to subhuman existence. He had urged his fellow bishops to renounce the pomp and splendor attached to the episcopacy since renaissance times. And he himself set the example, refusing to accept any title other than "Father," wearing a plain wooden cross instead of the customary golden pectoral cross, substituting a warm Brazilian *abraço* for the genuflection and kissing of the episcopal ring; whenever possible, he rode on the public bus instead of in a private car.

Dom Helder was also a ceaseless spokesman for all the underdeveloped nations, although here his principal concern was for Brazil, for he was an ardent nationalist. Even when he spoke against the United States policy in Vietnam, as he often did, it was to complain that the money being wasted there could have been used in construction in Brazil. He thoroughly disapproved of Brazil's military coup of 1964 and caused a furor in 1965 when he refused to celebrate a public anniversary Mass of thanksgiving for the coup's success.

Inevitably he had been called a Communist, which was nonsense. In an address to the Federal Chamber of Deputies he called for "an end to the false dichotomy capitalism-communism; to disagree with capitalist solutions does not signify an adhesion to communism."

In reply to my letter, Dom Helder sent a telegram agreeing to a meeting and setting a date for the following week. He was not a man to waste time. The day of my arrival in Recife the morning newspaper carried a front-page story announcing the arrival of "a savant from Georgetown University" who was to meet that same evening with the archbishop and a committee from the state medical association to discuss a center for population research. Dom Helder had already arranged everything!

I met with ten or twelve doctors, the president of the Jesuit University in Recife, and Dom Helder himself. I outlined the proposal, which was unanimously endorsed. The Jesuit agreed that his university would serve as the host institution sought by the director of Georgetown's research center. The doctors elected a smaller committee, to be chaired by Dom Helder, to select two qualified doctors from the medical association to go to Georgetown for training. I returned to Rio de Janeiro with a sense of satisfaction of a mission well and speedily accomplished. I immediately wrote to Georgetown to tell the director of the center that everything on the Brazil end had been set up. It only remained for him to let me know when the two trainees should arrive in Georgetown.

The director was evidently blown off his feet by the speed with which things had moved. He replied in a petulant tone that he was not at all prepared to implement the program. It had been merely an idea which he was turning over in his mind about a future possibility. It was my turn to be blown off my feet. He had certainly not given me the impression that he was asking me to find an institution which was willing to collaborate at some future unde-fined time in an idea which he was turning over in his mind in the event that he might eventually decide to transfer the idea from the world of day dreams to the world of reality.

I was stunned. And I was left with the embarrassing task of writing to Dom Helder Camara that all my talk and proposals had been balderdash. I am sure that it did not enhance his view of the United States and Americans. Nor would I have been surprised if he had concluded that the "savant from Georgetown" had been no more than a con artist.

Because of this shocking experience I had no desire on this, my second visit to Recife, to see Dom Helder. I hoped I would not run into him in the street. I did, however, see my fellow Jesuits at the university and others whose apostolate was to the denizens of Recife's miserable slums. After several such visits I wrote a piece called "To Hell and Gone," which *America* published on October 2, 1971, describing in lurid detail the horrors of living in what in Rio de Janeiro are called *favelas*, in Bahia *alogados*, and in Recife *mocambos*—all of them miserable slums.

From Recife I journeyed south to Salvador, where two young American Jesuit priests showed me through the *alogado* where they lived and worked. Its horrors were comparable but not equal to those of Recife, which, I think, holds whatever distinction there is in being the worst of the lot.

Salvador in Bahia, a Brazilian state, is said once to have had 365 churches, one for every day in the year. When I was there in 1967 the number was down to 30. This could indicate a dramatic fall-off in church attendance, but not necessarily. For in old Brazil, the Church was not organized along parish lines; instead, every individual, guild, or group that had the means and the inclination built a church. The supply far out-reached modern demand or need.

In 1966 I had lodged with the Jesuit community at the Pontificia Universidade Católica in Rio de Janeiro. In 1967, the

Jesuit residence being fully occupied, I stayed at the Hotel Florida in downtown Rio. This was the hotel used by Peace Corps volunteers whenever they visited the city. On weekdays I said Mass at the church of the Carmelites some blocks away. On Sundays I said Mass in the Jesuit chapel at the university and stayed to lunch with the community.

I had been in Brazil nine months, during which I had done considerable traveling and a bit of writing, when I decided it was time to move on. I had made arrangements to fly to Porto Alegre and from there by way of Peru to California, when I received a letter from Thurston Davis letter inviting me to join the staff of *America*.[2] I had scarcely replied to this when a phone call from the Jesuit rector of the university informed me that the superior general, Fr. Pedro Arrupe, was trying urgently to reach me from Rome. On its heels came a call from Rome ordering me to report there forthwith. This was followed by a cablegram from Fr. Philip Land, S.J., professor of economics at the Gregorian University, informing me that the general wished to discuss with me my possible appointment as general secretary of a committee to be established in Geneva jointly by the Holy See and the World Council of Churches—"important and prestigious post," he added. These orders, of course, negated Thurston Davis's invitation to join the staff of *America.*

Another unexpected move on the chessboard with far-reaching consequences for my life. At 3 A.M. on the morning of December 3, 1967, I looked down upon the fast-receding lights of Rio de Janeiro as our Varig DC-10 climbed into the sky and set course for Rome.

Sixteen

An Ecumenical Breakthrough

I landed at Leonardo da Vinci Airport early in the evening, and I was met by Fr. Phil Land, S.J. We had known each other for many years. Equipped with a Ph.D. in economics from Columbia University, he had been appointed to the staff of the Institute of Social Order in St. Louis following my hasty departure in 1945. Some years later he had moved to Rome to fill the position of professor of international economics in the Social Science Institute of the Gregorian University. He was also a consultant for the Pontifical Commission Justice and Peace.

As we drove into Rome he explained to me what my summons was all about. For some time the possibility of establishing an ecumenical committee representing jointly the Holy See and the World Council of Churches to deal with problems of development and of peace had been under discussion in what is known as the Mixed Group. The Mixed Group, consisting of some twenty members—half appointed by the Holy See, half by the World Council—had been created after Vatican Council II. Its cochairmen were Bishop (later Cardinal) Jan Willebrands, secretary of the Commission for Christian Unity, and Dr. Eugene Carson Blake, general secretary of the World Council of Churches.

The group met twice a year to examine problems which might be the subject of joint rather than separate action by the parent bodies. It was agreed that problems of development in the third world and problems of peace were of such a nature. There seemed no good reason why the doctrinal differences which separated the Roman Catholic Church from non-Roman churches should prevent them from joining forces to attack these problems of mutual concern. Consequently, the Mixed Group recommended that a

Joint Committee on Society, Development, and Peace be set up in World Council headquarters in Geneva and, upon the insistence of Dr. Blake, that its secretary general be a Roman Catholic.

The central committee of the World Council had already approved the recommendation. Before submitting it to the pope, a search was launched for a secretary general. My name had been suggested by Phil Land. Doc Bunn's opinion had been solicited, and he had been strongly affirmative. Father Arrupe, although he had not yet so informed me, had already decided to bring me to Rome to establish in the Jesuit curia an office for development; but he agreed to release me from this for the ecumenical enterprise.

That evening I met Pedro Arrupe, S.J., the first of many encounters and the beginning of an enduring friendship. The following day in Phil Land's quarters at the Gregorian University, I met Msgr. Joseph Gremillion, the American secretary of the Pontifical Commission Justice and Peace, through whom I would be responsible to the Holy See. It too was the first of many encounters, not all of them pleasant, and the beginning of a sometimes stormy relationship. The next day Phil Land drove me to Assisi to meet the Mixed Group. The group was holding one of its biannual meetings there, and I was to appear to be interviewed.

I already knew Bishop Willebrands. He had visited Georgetown during the anniversary year, and I had lunched with him. I had met Dr. Blake once, but only in passing, also at Georgetown. I responded to their questions and to those of the other members of the group. I told them that I had no special qualifications for the job. True enough, all during my career I had evidenced a concern for justice and for the oppressed; my writings, especially those from Brazil, had shown concern for the poor of the third world. But I had never thought of the poor in terms of development. Even the word was new to me as was, I would discover, much of the technical jargon with which the discussion of developmentalists is larded.

The members of the Mixed Group were living and holding their sessions in the famous Convent of S. Damiano, where the disciples of Saint Francis had carried his body so that Saint Clare might gaze for the last time upon the face of her beloved friend and bid him a last good-by. From there we adjourned to the refectory of the Franciscan fathers, who shared their lunch with us. I sat next to Dr. Blake, which gave us a chance to get better acquainted. Afterwards we took a tour of the great basilica, ending with a visit to the tomb of Saint Francis. I was impressed by the deferential attitude of the World Council representatives, especially that of Dr.

Nissiotis, lay theologian of the Greek Orthodox Church, who knelt at the tomb in reverential prayer for some minutes.

The Mixed Group then reassembled in the convent to decide my fate. I was, of course, not present, but was informed afterwards that they recommended my appointment. Bishop Willebrands committed himself to recommend to Pope Paul VI the establishment of the Joint Committee on Society, Development, and Peace and my appointment as general secretary. Phil Land and I returned to Rome, where I met again with both Father Arrupe and Monsignor Gremillion.

The idea for this committee, which I shall henceforth refer to as Sodepax, the acronym which it was to acquire, originated with Msgr. Joe Gremillion and several others. A couple of years later I was dining with Philip Potter and his wife in their Geneva apartment. Potter was then the head of the World Council's Commission on World Mission and Evangelism, and a few years later he would succeed Dr. Blake as secretary general. "The idea for *Sodepax* was born at this very table," said Philip, "in a discussion between Joe Gremillion, Paul Abrecht, and myself." Dr. Paul Abrecht, head of the department of Church and Society at the World Council, had organized a highly-successful international conference held in Geneva in 1966. Joe Gremillion participated as a Roman Catholic observer. Dining with Potter and Abrecht he had raised the question about the possibility of the Roman Catholic Church joining forces with the World Council in attacking the social problems of society. In the discussion that followed the idea of *Sodepax* was conceived.

According to Gremillion, the idea had developed from a series of meetings, the first held in Geneva in March 1965, to exchange views on the social issues being discussed in Vatican Council II. The first meeting had included Dr. Visser t'Hooft, Dr. Blake's predecessor; Bp. Marcos McGrath, vice-president of the Latin American bishops' council; and Msgr. Charles Moeller, later undersecretary of the Congregation for the Doctrine of the Faith and later still of the Commission for Christian Unity. In any case, to paraphrase Dean Acheson, Gremillion was present at its creation, a fact that later would cause problems for him and for me.

The Pontifical Commission Justice and Peace, the youngest dicastery—or, department—in the Roman Curia, had been created after Vatican II. Gremillion was its first executive secretary. Its president was Card. Maurice Roy of Quebec. Hovering above it, as above all the dicasteries, was the formidable figure of Archbishop (later Cardinal) Giovanni Benelli. In the organizational chart of the Roman Curia he was listed as assistant secretary of state. *De iure*, so he was. *De facto*, his place as Paul VI's right-hand man made him the most powerful man in Rome after the pope himself. Everyone in Rome was aware of this, none more so than Joe Gremillion. From the start he made it clear to me, with emphasis, that the chain of command ran through him to Benelli. Never was I to approach Benelli directly, but only through him.

From Rome I went to Brussels to attend a meeting chaired by Gremillion of representatives of the national commissions on justice and peace. Archbishop Benelli was the centerpiece of the three-day affair and, as I recall, spoke chiefly about the message on peace which the Holy Father intended to deliver to the world on New Year's Day.

From Brussels I went to Geneva, where over several days I met with members of the World Council staff. We discussed practical questions, such as where I would live. The only Jesuit community in Geneva was a lodging for young working people. It was on the other side of town from the World Council and not suitable if I were to be accessible. So Father Arrupe had agreed that I should live in my own apartment, and Mrs. Moya Burton, a gracious English-woman who headed the personnel office, promised to find one for me. We agreed that we should abide by the personnel rules of the World Council, one of which was obligatory retirement at age sixty-five. I was already in my sixty-second year, so it appeared that my term was to be brief. All of these arrangements were conditioned upon papal acceptance of the recommendation submitted by Bishop Willebrands.

I now flew to California to await the pope's decision, arriving at Los Gatos, which had been my ultimate destination, some ten months after leaving Georgetown. It had been a long and circuitous journey. I had spent the first three years of my Jesuit life at Los Gatos and had been quite fond of it. I remember as a novice thinking that I would be quite happy to spend the last years of my life there. When I set out from Georgetown I had this in mind. Now it appeared unlikely that Los Gatos was to be my ultimate destination.

The Birth of Sodepax

On January 28, 1968, the news services carried the story that Pope Paul VI and Dr. Eugene Carson had announced simultaneously from Rome and Geneva the establishment of the Joint Committee on Society, Development, and Peace with offices in the World Council of Churches and the appointment as general secretary of Fr. George H. Dunne, S.J. It was a historic event of some dimensions. Although there had been instances of cooperative actions on many levels, this was the first time since the Protestant Reformation that the Holy See had joined with Protestant and Orthodox Churches in an operationally organic union of this sort. Or, as the prospectus for Sodepax stated: "This marks the first time that the Protestant and Orthodox Churches, which comprise the World Council of Churches, and the Roman Catholic Church have set up an office of world-wide scope over which they share responsibility."

After bidding a fond farewell to Los Gatos and to Frank Rouleau and his treasure of microfilms and my China connection, I joined Cardinal Roy, Dr. Blake, and Monsignor Gremillion in New York in search of funds. We had several agreeable and ultimately successful meetings with Mr. F. X. Sutton of the Ford Foundation, which was eventually to give us a grant of $750,000 over a period of three years, beginning in June 1968. This presupposed that after evaluating the performance of Sodepax during an experimental period of January to June, the two parent bodies would agree to extend its mandate for three years, which they did.

Our meeting with the head of the Rockefeller Foundation was unproductive. He appeared to me arrogant and unresponsive to ideas other than his own. He was not interested in the Sodepax idea and spent a good deal of time describing a splendid project in the development of hybrid seeds being carried out in the Philippines by the Rockefeller Foundation. To this he added a lecture to the effect that problems of development were not the business of the churches.

The prospectus for Sodepax, of which Msgr. Joe Gremillion was the principal author, had originated as a draft statement, which we reviewed when we met with F. X. Sutton. It was elaborated into a twelve-page document of fifty-eight paragraphs and issued in June 1968, followed in September by a nine-page addition containing budgetary supplements.

The stated purpose of Sodepax was to focus attention upon the problems of poverty, especially in the third world, and upon the imperatives of peace. Through the Churches it proposed to quicken the consciences first of Christians and then of all men and women, to their moral responsibility to concern themselves with the issues. To this end the prospectus proposed for the period

1969–1971 a staggering list of programs or projects, chiefly conferences or symposia.[1]

The prospectus was a grandiose vision with little contact with realities. Its grandiosity is enhanced by the realization that from its beginning in January 1968 to January 1969 the entire staff of Sodepax consisted of me and my secretary. But no one can be faulted for dreaming. Moreover, it was not entirely visionary. Had Gremillion's enthusiasm been fully shared by the parent bodies and had sufficient resources been mobilized the dreaming might have been realized. As it was, given its limited resources, its accomplishments were astonishing.

In a certain sense the business of Sodepax had already begun. The Pontifical Commission Justice and Peace and the Church and Society division of the World Council had agreed to begin to organize a world conference on development in expectation that Sodepax would be approved. A steering committee had already done considerable planning. Since Sodepax had been established, it would be my job to take over and carry on from that point.

I arrived in Geneva on February 6, 1968. Mrs. Burton had provided an office and a secretary, Felicity Hart, a pleasant and competent young Englishwoman. For the year that followed, Felicity and I were the staff of Sodepax.

When I arrived in Geneva I had a bad case of flu. But the steering committee that had started planning the conference on development was meeting the next evening in Brussels, so on February 7, flu and all, I flew to Brussels with Paul Abrecht, head of the Church and Society division of the World Council.

We met in the home of Max Kohnstamm with other members of the committee: Barbara Ward, the famed economist; Vittorino Veronese, president of the Banco di Roma and close personal friend of Paul VI; August Vanistendael, Louvain professor and secretary general of International Cooperation for Socio-economic Development; Joe Gremillion; and Phil Land. The subjects to be treated and the list of participants and papers to be prepared had already been pretty much settled; final agreement was reached. It was decided to hold the conference in Beirut, Lebanon, April 21–27. From this point on implementation of the plans, until now the responsibility of Paul Abrecht and Phil Land, was turned over to me.

The next night, unable to land in Geneva because of a blinding snowstorm, Paul and I stayed in Zurich. The following morning I took the train to Geneva. The apartment which Mrs. Burton had found for me was still under construction, so I checked into the Intercontinental Hotel and sent for the house doctor. Sodepax was well and truly launched.

Introduction to World Council

Shortly after this Dr. Blake called a special gathering of the entire World Council staff, some three hundred in all, to whom he introduced Sodepax in the person of its two cochairmen, Max Kohnstamm for the World Council and Joe Gremillion for the Holy See, and me. The cochairmen and Dr. Blake spoke with appropriate seriousness about the historical significance of the occasion. I spoke in a lighter vein.

Every morning on my way to say Mass in Rio de Janeiro, I told them, I passed a young girl on her way to school who always smiled at me. Because young girls, properly taught by their mothers, smile only at benign and harmless-looking old men, I realized that I had entered the Third Age. Consequently I had made arrangements to end my days in the bucolic tranquillity of Los Gatos, when I was suddenly called to assume the responsibilities of *Sodepax*. The only thing I did not like about the World Council, I said, was its obligatory retirement age. Everyone had been extremely kind to me since my arrival, especially several of the young women on the staff who had helped me shop for furniture, sewn curtains for my windows, and so forth. I was afraid, I remarked, that if word of all this feminine solicitude were to reach Rome I would quickly find myself on a plane heading again for the bucolic tranquillity of Los Gatos. When Dr. Blake remarked that he regretted that Mrs. Burton was not present, I interjected to general laughter, "She's probably hanging curtains in my apartment."

These pleasantries initiated a warm relationship with the World Council staff which was to endure to my retirement and beyond, evidenced by messages sent to me almost twenty years later on the golden jubilee of my ordination to the priesthood.

A word about Max Kohnstamm. Highly intelligent and devoutly religious, he had been asked by Dr. Blake to represent the World Council as cochairman of Sodepax. Of Dutch origin, he had had a distinguished career as secretary to Queen Wilhelmina, as director of European affairs in the Foreign Office of the Netherlands, and as secretary of the High Authority of the European Steel and Coal Community. He was presently president of the Institute for European Studies and close collaborator of Jean Monnet as vice-president of the Action Committee for the United States of Europe. He was always a gentleman, and I have only fond memories of him.

Beirut Conference on World Development

As soon as possible I flew to Beirut to make local arrangements for the conference. Gabriel (Gaby) Habib, Beirut resident and active member of the Orthodox Church, was of invaluable help. We chose as the site of the conference a splendid new hotel in the village of Beth-Marie on a summit above Beirut with a magnificent view of the entire city and of the Mediterranean beyond. The tragic days of Lebanon were yet to come. Beirut was still a bustling, prosperous, peaceful, and beautiful city, a crossroads between East and West.

The conference opened as planned on April 21 with seventy-two participants.[2] As in all future Sodepax conferences, we aimed to strike a balance between Roman Catholics and Protestant and Orthodox representatives. The cochairmen, who alternately presided over the plenary sessions, were Jan Tinbergen, a Protestant, and B. T. G. Chidzero, a Catholic. Tinbergen, a member of the Royal Dutch Academy of Sciences, was chairman of the United Nations Development Planning Committee. Several years later he would receive the first Nobel Prize ever awarded for economics. Chidzero, a brilliant graduate of both McGill and Oxford universities, was in charge of the United Nations Development Program in Kenya. After the conference he was named to head the commerce section of the General Agreement on Tariff and Trade (GATT) in Geneva. Because his lovely wife, mother of his three handsome children, was French-Canadian and he was black, he was not allowed to enter Rhodesia, his land of origin, still under white supremacist colonial rule. With the achievement of independence the ban ended. Chidzero and his family were able to return to what is now Zimbabwe, where he serves in Robert Mugabe's government as minister of economics and development.

Eleven major papers were presented at the conference, one of them by Tom Mboya, the most promising young political leader in Kenya. He did not present his paper, entitled "Regional Development with Particular Reference to Africa": as the conference opened we received the shocking word that he had been assassinated in Kenya.

The participants, divided into four working groups, discussed and debated and hammered together reports. These were then examined, revised in plenary sessions, and returned to the working groups for further discussion, until a plenary session could approve and issue a final report. Our secretarial staff was busy far into each night. The participants themselves found no time for daydreaming.

On the fifth day I had everyone gather in front of the hotel for a group photo. As he took his place the ill-fated Charles Sherman remarked to me: "I have taken part in hundreds of conferences of this sort around the world. Never have I been kept so busy. This is the first time since I arrived that I have been outside the hotel!"[3]

On the last day Fr. Henri de Riedmatten objected to a paragraph dealing with the population problem.[4] Although this paragraph carefully avoided advocating contraception, the chairman appointed a small committee, including de Riedmatten, to formulate an acceptable statement. The reformulated paragraph, as accepted by de Riedmatten, was approved at the last plenary session of the conference. Because we had run out of time before the secretaries were able to type the report in final form, Mr. Robert Bowie agreed to stay over for a few days to edit the final revisions into the text.[5] I was then to send this to all the participants for final approval.

This I did. De Riedmatten in reply demanded the excision not only of the paragraph in question but of the entire section entitled "The Demographic Factor," despite the fact that it took no position either for or against the use of contraceptives. Because it represented the consensus of the conference, a consensus in which he had joined, I refused to edit out the paragraphs to which he objected.

The report was published in a brochure of sixty-four pages, first in English under the title *World Development: Challenge to the Churches*, and then in several other languages. The following year it was published by Corpus Books together with all the papers and an introduction by Barbara Ward.[6]

In my introduction to the report I disavowed any intention of committing the churches or of speaking for the churches:

> This Report does not speak for the Churches, nor do the Churches speak through it. The Report is not presented by the Churches as their teaching. Rather it is offered to the Churches—by a Conference of specialists whom the Churches have asked for advice on *economic and technical* aspects of

certain issues of grave interest to them and to all the human family.

The Churches requested this consultation to help in making *their own* judgments on the *doctrinal, moral and ethical* aspects of these issues. It is now left to the Churches, and more specifically to the World Council and the Justice and Peace Commission, to put this Report to use in their own way.

I included a similar disavowal in every one of the introductions I wrote to reports issuing from international conferences organized by Sodepax during the following three years, in the hope of protecting its freedom. If Sodepax made it clear that it did not pretend to speak for the Churches, they would not take umbrage at or wish to control what it said. Or so I thought.

In the same introduction I made it clear that the report did not offer unanimous views and that participants could disassociate themselves from any one opinion: "Not all the participants would accept its every affirmation. Many would wish to add a nuance, to de-emphasize a point, to enlarge on a topic. No participant is therefore answerable for the entirety. . .Nevertheless, the Report does represent the general consensus of competent experts. . ."

I thought these two precisions established clearly the nature of Sodepax reports. In all honesty I must say that during my association with Sodepax only once, and then indirectly, did it come to my attention that Rome—in this case probably the Secretariat of State—was displeased with something said in a Sodepax report and only once did Rome—in this case definitely the Secretariat of State—attempt to control what was said. Both instances occurred in connection with our conference on peace, held in Baden, Austria, which I shall discuss in due course.

Joe Gremillion wrote me on May 9, 1968, to express his appreciation:

> Dear George,
> For all your initiative, patience, perseverance and hard work in preparing for and carrying out the Beirut Conference, I express my deep admiration and warmest gratitude. . .

These words contrast sharply with an attitude which he was later to adopt and which would make my relationship with him a painful one.

Staff Development

In the letter just cited, Monsignor Gremillion also expressed concern that I be supplied with adequate staff. The first step in this direction was taken in March 1969, when Br. Christophe von Wachter of the Taizé community in France was assigned by its founder and prior, Roger Schulz, to come to my aid. Besides his native German, Brother Christophe also spoke Swedish, his mother's native tongue, and with equal fluency both English and French. In addition, he had learned Russian during the three years he had spent as a prisoner of war in the USSR. After his release and return to Germany following the war, he had studied law and served for several years as counsel for the Lutheran bishop of Munich. He later joined the Taizé community, established by the Swiss pastor, Roger Schulz, with the idea of introducing into Protestantism the long-repudiated ideal of monasticism.

We were still looking for an associate secretary. We found him in the person of Dr. Roy Neehall, a second-generation Trinidadian, whose grandparents had emigrated from India to the Caribbean. It had been agreed that the number-two man in Sodepax should be from the third world. Dr. Neehall was an ordained Presbyterian pastor who had made his theological studies in Canada; his wife was Canadian, of Scottish ancestry. They had five young children. Dr. Blake, Monsignor Gremillion, Card. Maurice Roy, and I had interviewed him in New York, where we had gone for a committee meeting to plan a Sodepax conference to be held in Montreal as a follow-up to the Beirut conference. We were impressed by his intelligence and amiability. Dr. Neehall moved his family to Geneva and joined our staff in August 1969.

The following month we were joined by Dr. Charles Elliott, a brilliant addition. He was a young Anglican priest as well as an economist with a degree from Oxford. He had previously done some work in economics for the United Nations in Geneva and, just before joining us, had finished two years teaching at the University of Zambia in Africa. It was a measure of his belief in what Sodepax was attempting to do that he turned down an appointment to the faculty at Oxford to join us. He moved to Geneva, along with his wife, Hilary, and their two children. His arrival completed the permanent four-member Sodepax team, supported by a staff of four secretaries.

While this was our regular staff, we were assisted at various times by the temporary services of others. While I was still alone, Dr. David Ramage, who had been co-opted from the National Council of Churches in New York for temporary service with the World Council, gave a considerable part of his time to assisting me. Upon his return to the United States he assumed major responsibility for the organization of our Montreal conference, which was held May 9–12, 1969, chaired by Maurice F. Strong, president of the Canadian International Development Agency.

Loyola Centennial

In October 1969, I flew to Chicago to deliver the principal address at the centennial convocation of Loyola University and to receive in return an honorary doctorate in humane letters. I was substituting for Fr. Roberto Tucci, S.J., editor of *Civiltà Cattolica.* He had been appointed director of Vatican Radio and found that the duties of his new office would prevent him from honoring his commitment to deliver the centennial address. A phone call from the president of Loyola University apprised me of the problem and asked me to come to the rescue. I spoke on the subject "The Churches Face the World in the 1970s." The chief problems of the seventies, in my view, would be those of nuclear weapons, mass poverty, expanding urbanization, racism, and technology. They were and remained the problems of the eighties and are still with us as we near the nineties.

Japan's Expo '70

In December 1969 I visited Japan to investigate the possibility of including a Sodepax exhibit in the Christian pavilion at the world's fair to be held in Osaka in 1970. En route I stopped for two days in Karachi, Pakistan, where I discussed with Cardinal Archbishop Cardeiro future Sodepax activity in his country. The cardinal, who impressed me as a man of keen intelligence, was highly sympathetic.

In Japan I called first upon the archbishop of Osaka, an elderly but alert and amiable Japanese, who was chairman of the bishops' committee for the fair. He approved of my proposal, but told me that the determination of what went into the pavilion lay in the hands of a three-man committee, the Catholic member of which was Shusaku Endo, one of the leading playwrights and novelists of Japan. One of his most famous novels, translated into English under the title *Silence*, is based upon the apostasy under torture in the early seventeenth century of the superior of the Jesuit vice-province of Japan. When doing research for my book *Generation of Giants* nine years earlier I had read letters written by this superior before his apostasy and preserved in the Roman archives of the Society of Jesus. It was a poignant experience.

I found Mr. Endo an intense and very serious person. He had to be convinced that Sodepax had a place in the Christian pavilion. He did not yield easily to my arguments, but in the end agreed, provided that the arranging of the materials which we would send were left entirely to the Japanese—a reasonable proviso with which I had no difficulty. He also agreed to translate the Sodepax brochure into Japanese.

The Sodepax display, a modest one in keeping with the deliberately designed simplicity of the Christian pavilion, was located next to the Raphael tapestries loaned by the Vatican and dramatically focused attention upon third world poverty. In a letter of May 22, 1970, Mr. In Ha Lee, secretary of the recently established Sodepax of Japan, described it as "the real challenge of the Christian pavilion," which of that date had been visited by 750,000 persons.

South Korea

Following my meeting with Shusaku Endo in December 1969 I flew to Seoul, South Korea. A cousin of mine, Michael Bransfield, M.M., national chaplain of the Young Catholic Workers, had been in Korea for some years. Today, twenty years later, he is still there.[7] Accompanied by Mike and some of the YCW leaders, I met with Card. Stephan Kim, who had proved his courage in more than one tense moment with the government. He thoroughly approved the idea of a Sodepax in South Korea. The vicar general, whom I saw next, was pessimistic about the possibilities of ecumenical cooperation in South Korea. I also had several meetings with Protestant Church leaders.

By the time I left Korea, we had organized a South Korean Sodepax. The chair was Dr. Ryu Hong Ryol, a Catholic. The secretary was Rev. Kwan Suk Kim, general secretary of the

National Council of Churches. One of the three Catholic members of the six-member committee was Monsignor Carroll, the vicar general.

The committee organized a conference, held the following May, of seventy leaders of Church and government to coordinate the activities of social-service agencies, public and private, in the areas of development. Shortly before the conference, in a letter of May 14, 1970, Monsignor Carroll wrote, "So far things have proceeded very well and we have high hopes that the seminar itself will be a success." His hopes were not disappointed, and they contrasted sharply with his earlier skepticism. It was evidence, as would repeatedly emerge from our experience, of how quickly the ecumenical spirit developed and flourished as a result of working together within the framework of Sodepax.

National Programs

The foreword to the report on the Montreal conference describes Sodepax as a "catalytic agent." The Asian record of Sodepax activities gives striking evidence in support of this description. In less than two years, as a result of these activities there developed an extraordinary degree of ecumenical collaboration between Roman Catholic and Protestant churches where formerly such collaboration was either insignificant or, as in Australia, nonexistent. Beyond this, the catalyzing effect of Sodepax activity in a short time created an ecumenical interest in action for development reaching most of Southeast Asia.

It would be tedious to describe these activities in detail. Most of them were conferences following the Beirut format of papers, discussions in working groups, plenary sessions, followed by publication of conclusions and recommendations. And most of them were an "exciting experience," to use the words of Rex Davis of the World Conference describing the Papua–New Guinea program, which consisted of four such consultations held over a month, each in a different part of the country. A mere listing of the countries involved suggests the extent of the area reached: Australia, Hong Kong and Singapore, India, Indonesia, Japan, Korea, Papua–New Guinea.

Most of these were national conferences, concerned chiefly with their own problems; one exception was the conference in Japan, which was regional in character and besides eighty participating delegates involved fifty invited observers representing international agencies and non-Christian religions.

Sodepax activity was by no means restricted to Asia, Europe, and North America. The Sodepax committee of Lesotho as early as January 1970 held its first conference, involving delegates from five countries: Botswana, Lesotho, Malawi, Tanzania, and Zambia. Charles Elliott traveled extensively in Africa and played a key role in organizing a week-long seminar on development at the Limuru Conference Center near Nairobi, Kenya. I participated in an East African conference at the same center. Mother Madeleine Morawska of the Pontifical Commission Justice and Peace and Dr. Madeleine Barot of the World Council, acting as a Sodepax team, discussed the possibility of future activities with both East and West African leaders.

Sodepax made its first forays into Latin America. In the course of several trips Roy Neehall organized small, informal consultations and met with Church leaders in Bolivia, Brazil, Peru, Uruguay, and Venezuela, and participated in a meeting of youth leaders from African, Asian, and Latin American countries. Notable on several accounts was a Sodepax-sponsored conference in Kingston, Jamaica, in October 1970, where was born the Caribbean Council of Churches with the Roman Catholic Church a member. This was the first time in history that Roman Catholic, Anglican, Moravian, Methodist, and Presbyterian churches from all parts of the Caribbean had joined forces and also the first time that all four language areas—Dutch, English, French, and Spanish—had come together in a common enterprise.

It also made its mark for another reason: it declined the invitation of the governor-general to a cocktail reception as a way of protesting the heavy-handed suppression of demonstrators against colonial rule. This made headlines and, I was told, caused some clucking and head shaking in Rome, which regards political statements as falling exclusively within the province of the Secretariat of State.

The picture which emerges from this summary account of Sodepax activities is of an organism very busy worldwide, involving a lot of people, whipping up a storm of cooperative ecumenical work. At a meeting of the Pontifical Commission Justice and Peace in Rome in early 1971, Fr. Jerome Hamer, O.P., characterized the Sodepax record as "très frappant"—astonishing. Hamer at the time was undersecretary of the Secretariat for Christian Unity. He was later named undersecretary of the Congregation for the

Doctrine of the Faith. And shortly thereafter he was made an archbishop by Paul VI and then a cardinal by John Paul II, who at the same time appointed him head of the Congregation for Religious, one of the dicasteries of the Roman Curia. His endorsement carried considerable weight.

International Programs

Several international programs deserve mention. A meeting of theologians to discuss a theological methodology for reflection upon development was brought together by Charles Elliott in the village of Cartigny, near Geneva. It is chiefly notable as the birthplace of liberation theology, which developed out of a paper presented here by Fr. Gustavo Gutierrez.[8]

Dr. Lawrence McMahon, like Dave Ramage loaned to Sodepax through the World Council, organized a consultation on Church, communications, and development. It took place in Driebergen, the Netherlands, with representatives of twenty-three countries; it derived its importance from the fact that the churches own and operate more communications installations around the world than any other single institution or organization.

Monetary reform was the subject of a high-level colloquium that met under Sodepax sponsorship in Geneva in February 1970; a larger group later subjected to critical ecumenical examination the most important of the groundwork done for the second United Nations development decade.

What about Peace?

Most of our attention during these first years was given to getting the word out about the development needs of the third world. We did, nevertheless, devote a major conference to the critical subject of peace, as our mandate prescribed.

This conference was long in incubating, having first been proposed by Mr. Vittorino Veronese at a steering-committee meeting in Rome, May 21–23, 1968. The conference was held in Baden, Austria, April 3–9, 1970. Although such was not the original intention, it turned out to be comparable to the Beirut Conference in terms of size and of the prominence of its participants; and it produced a document on peace, *Peace, the Desperate*

Imperative, as impressive as the Beirut document on development.

One of the operating difficulties at Sodepax was that the names of all Roman Catholic invitees had to be cleared through Joe Gremillion with the Secretary of State. This invariably entailed a long delay. In the present case, when the list was returned I was shocked to discover that two of the most distinguished names had been stricken: that of Card. Bernard Alfrink, primate of Holland and president of Pax Christi, and that of Dom Helder Camara, archbishop of Recife in Brazil, a candidate for the Nobel Peace Prize. It was to me a depressing indication of which way the wind was blowing in Rome.

Shortly before the opening date of April 3, I was surprised to learn that all the Catholic participants had been informed by Rome that they should arrive a day early in order to be briefed by someone from the Secretariat of State on the position they should take on certain key subjects, such as peace, human rights, and violence. This ran counter to my understanding of the nature of Sodepax and its manner of operation. As I said in the introduction to every one of our publications, Sodepax was not an instrument of either the Holy See or of the World Council; it was an ecumenical instrument of both. The Holy See had no need of it to define doctrine or express policy. Nor did the World Council. This was clearly an effort to use it as such.

I knew that the World Council would resent it. I informed Dr. Blake, who was leaving the next day for Rome. He had an appointment with Pope Paul VI, with whom he said he would discuss the matter. He evidently did, and the Holy Father evidently took appropriate action. No more was heard of the proposed briefing session.

These difficulties out of the way, the conference proceeded smoothly. The opening session was addressed by Card. Franz Koenig, archbishop of Vienna, and by Dr. Eugene Carson Blake. It was graced by the presence of Abp. Opilio Rossi, apostolic nuncio to Austria, and of Dr. Chrysostomos Tsiter, the Greek Orthodox metropolitan for Austria. Taking part in the conference were seventy delegates from thirty-nine countries, including six of the socialist countries: USSR, Bulgaria, Czechoslovakia, Romania, Hungary, and the German Democratic Republic.

Predictably, the subject of human rights provoked the most animated debate in both the working groups and the plenary sessions. I had named to chair this group a quiet, self-effacing

African, Marie Savomey, mayor of Lomé, the capital city of Togo, and president of the National Togo Catholic Women's Association. Like a soft-spoken lion tamer she kept firm control of the sometimes spirited debate.

The sticking point was the proposal that an international body be established to monitor the observance of human rights in all countries. The principal objection was voiced by Alexis S. Bouevsky, secretary of the Department of External and Church Relations of the Moscow Patriarchate of the Russian Orthodox Church. He argued that such monitoring would infringe upon national sovereignty. I proposed that Mr. Bouevsky put his argument in writing and that it be published as a dissenting opinion with the proposal itself. This was done. At the conclusion of the conference an appreciative Bouevsky presented me with a bottle of vodka and a volume of beautiful photographs in color of Russian icons. Metropolitan Nicolas Corneanu of the Romanian Orthodox Church likewise presented me with a handsome volume of photographs of Romanian churches and monasteries.

As relaxation from the intensity of the program, I arranged for the participants to be bused one evening to a cellar pub some miles distant. It featured entrance by way of a slide which propelled one through a huge beer barrel onto the floor below. The sight of ecclesiastical dignitaries such as Abp. Angelo Fernandes and Metropolitan Corneanu; jurists such as Louis Ignacio-Pinto, Chief Justice of the Supreme Court of Dahomey and Judge of the International Court of Justice at the Hague, and Sean MacBride, secretary general of the International Commission of Jurists; academicians such as Prof. Elise Boulding of the University of Colorado and Prof. Gerolamo Bassani, president of the Institute of International Studies in Milan; members of government such as Dr. Margaretha A. M. Klompe, Minister of Culture in the Netherlands and member of the Consultative Assembly of the Council of Europe; and many others sliding down through the beer barrel and spilling out on the floor to laughter and applause added greatly to the camaraderie of all. I recommend it as a ritual to be observed at disarmament conferences, summit meetings, and interchurch theological discussions.

Kyoto plus Tokyo

Sodepax did not sponsor the World Conference on Religion and Peace held in Kyoto, the longtime political and still cultural center

Pope Paul VI visited the headquarters of the World Council of Churches in Geneva; with the leaders of the council, Father George Dunne greets the pope.

The planning group for a Sodepax conference in Istanbul in February 1969 met with Patriarch Athenagoros (3d from left, 2d row from bottom); Father Dunne (left, 3d row from bottom) gathered this group from all over the world.

of Japan. I was, however, rather deeply involved, thanks to Bishop (later Cardinal) John Wright of Pittsburgh. The idea for the conference had originated with him and two others. One of these was Dr. Homer Jack, a Protestant minister active in social causes, whom I had known but had not seen for some years. The other was Dr. Dana McLean Greeley, pastor of a Unitarian church in Boston. It was Bishop Wright who, when auxiliary bishop of Boston, had authorized my participation in the debate with Paul Blanshard at Harvard. Evidently remembering me from those days he had asked that I join as consultant a seventeen-member committee that was to meet in Istanbul February 21–23, 1969, to initiate plans.

Before leaving Istanbul we had a pleasant meeting with Patriarch Athenagoras, head of the Greek Orthodox Church. Afterwards he stood with us for a group photograph on the steps leading into his residence. Abp. Angelo Fernandes of New Delhi, a member of the committee, and Nikkyo Niwano are both tall men. Athenagoras towered over them both. I also managed to slip in a visit to the ancient and famous church Hagia Sophia and a visit to the equally famous Blue Mosque.

In the spring of 1970 a much larger committee met in Kyoto to finalize those plans. The conference itself took place October 16–21. There were 212 delegates representing the ten major living religions in the world. They came from every continent and from thirty-nine countries. Other observers and guests numbered 107, and visitors and members of the press added another 700.

I prepared the paper on development and served as rapporteur of the working group which dealt with that subject. It could be said of every Sodepax consultation in which I participated, but because here the broader participation of world religions gives it greater force, I quote the concluding paragraph of my report:

> We conclude with the affirmation that this Conference has itself been a striking demonstration of the fact that the fragmentation of the world by religious differences can be overcome and that the unity of mankind, proclaimed by all religions as an ethical ideal, can be realized as an empirical fact. It casts a little light into the darkness.

Before adjourning, the conference voted to establish on a permanent basis the World Council of Religions for Peace. Abp. Angelo Fernandes was elected president and Dr. Homer Jack secretary-general. He opened international headquarters in the United Nations Plaza in New York.

At the end of the conference Rev. Nikkyo Niwano invited all the delegates to come to Tokyo at his expense to visit the central headquarters of Rissho-Kosei-kai. Niwano was an extraordinary individual. Starting as a simple pushcart peddlar of coal, after a profound religious experience he had founded this modern Buddhist denomination which in little more than thirty years had attracted tens of thousands of devoted followers and great wealth. Niwano himself was a man of enormous but unassuming charm.

Most of us took advantage of his invitation. We took Japan's famous 100-mile-an-hour train to Tokyo, where a fleet of buses delivered us to one of Tokyo's newest hotels, where rooms had been reserved. The following day the same fleet of buses took us to the amazing complex of Rissho-Kosei-kai.

In the temple some five hundred women were chanting Buddhist sutras. This was not an act prepared for us but was a daily act of religious worship. Rissho-Kosei-kai is one of several new Buddhist sects which have emerged in the last half century. While preserving fundamental Buddhist beliefs, it employs in the propagation of its message and the service of its faithful whatever techniques and instruments the modern world makes available. It has its own staff of counselors and its own psychologists to assist those who have marital or other problems. It has its own schools, its own radio and television stations. It has a large hospice for university students, where I would stay on a visit to Japan some fifteen years later. It has its own school of ballet and its own symphony orchestra.

Most impressive is its many-storied central headquarters. Here are the offices of Niwano himself and of the numerous sections and departments, meeting rooms, assembly rooms, dining rooms, and a modern auditorium with a capacity of several thousand. Here we were entertained through what was left of the morning and, following lunch, through the afternoon by a program that held our unflagging interest. Featured were high-quality performances by two ballet groups and a concert by the symphony orchestra, which, unlike Margaret Truman, would have won more than a passing grade from Paul Hume.

The lunch that interrupted the program was on a comparable level of excellence. Preprandials offered a choice of a wide variety of both hard and soft drinks. I had a scotch, and a Buddhist monk from Singapore joined me. A native of Sri Lanka, he had once been, he told me, a brother in a Roman Catholic order called, if my memory serves me, the Order of the Rosary. He had lost his faith, quit the brotherhood, and wandered for some years in the wasteland of atheism. He had undergone a religious experience which culminated in his conversion to Buddhism and finally in his becoming a monk. He now ministered to the spiritual needs of students at the University of Singapore.

Lunch was served buffet-style from a number of booths staffed by lovely kimono-clad girls and offering a wide variety of Asian and western foods. After this gourmet's delight we returned to the auditorium for the second half of the program.

The program reached a high emotional intensity at its conclusion. We were brought up onto the stage. After we were seated on stage a troop of six- or seven-year-old Japanese boys and girls, beautifully and colorfully garbed in kimonos and each carrying a rose, emerged from the wings. A child had been assigned to each of us. After they had presented us with their roses, the choral group and orchestra soared to a crescendo conclusion of a hymn to peace. There was not a dry eye in the house. I thought of Hiroshima and the utter insanity of war.

The Perils of Service

Another "exciting adventure" not part of the Sodepax agenda was a rather bizarre accident that almost terminated my career. It happened at Max Kohnstamm's summer home in Fenffe, Belgium, where, at his invitation, we were holding our officers' meeting at which I obtained approval of the Papua–New Guinea program. The house was quite lovely, but it had some novel features due to its having been reconstructed from an ancient barn.

The first evening of our meeting we were gathered in the parlor after supper. I slipped out with two purposes in mind. One was to phone the parish priest to arrange for the priests in our group to say Mass the next morning. The other was to find the bathroom.

The first purpose accomplished I went prowling about, opening doors in search of the bathroom. The second door I tried opened into total darkness. I stepped forward to find an electric light switch and found myself plunging into an abyss. I had the fleeting impression that I had fallen into a well. Fortunately I had retained a firm grip on the doorknob with my left hand. That jerked me into an upright position. Otherwise I should have landed head first on the concrete floor of what turned out to be the furnace room, and that would have been the end of the short and generally happy life of the first secretary general of Sodepax. The furnace room was equipped not with stairs but with an iron ladder, one of the rungs of which I struck with my thigh during my downward plunge. After partially recovering my breath, I crawled up the ladder and out onto the floor of the room from which I had just precipitously descended. Here one of the secretaries found me some minutes later.

The next morning my leg was a beautiful mosaic in black, blue, yellow, and green. Madame Kohnstamm drove me to the nearest doctor, who dressed the wound, the mark of which is still visible on my thigh. With a branch from the nearby woods I fashioned a makeshift crutch.

Immediately following our meeting in Fenffe I was committed to delivering a paper, "Chemical and Biological Weapons of War," at an international conference being held in Amersfoort, Holland. I holed up in an Amsterdam Hotel for two days, arriving in Amersfoort for the final day. I explained my tardy arrival by saying that I had fallen into the wine cellar. That seemed more interesting than falling into the furnace room and also, as one of the participants pointedly remarked, made my late arrival quite understandable.

Seventeen

Abrasive Encounters

I have several times indicated that my relations with Msgr. Joseph Gremillion left much to be desired. The first abrasion occurred early on. In July 1968, some two months after the Beirut conference, I attended, as did Gremillion, the World Assembly of the World Council of Churches in Uppsala, Sweden. Also present was Curtis Roosevelt, who as a child together with his sister had become familiar to the American public as Buzzy and Sissy, FDR's grandchildren in the White House. He was United Nations staff officer in charge of relations with nongovernmental organizations, known as NGOs; these are organizations to which the United Nations has accorded official recognition entitling them to certain privileges, such as the right to circulate papers presenting their views on questions being debated in the UN.

At Beirut I had given the experts a hearty laugh at my own expense. As I have already indicated, I was unfamiliar with the jargon; thinking NGO an Arab word, I attempted to pronounce it as such instead of as the acronym which it is. Actually *ngo* means "I" in the dialect of Shanghai, but we were not in Shanghai and I joined in the laughter when my mistake was explained.

Roosevelt felt uncomfortable dealing with Msgr. Alberto Giovanetti, the representative of the Holy See at the United Nations. Accustomed to seeing Giovanetti mingling familiarly at social affairs with the other United Nations diplomats, Roosevelt tended to look upon him as representative of the Catholic Church as a state rather than as a religious body with a mission to preach the Gospel. It was not a question of Roosevelt's understanding of the organization of the Church; as a onetime student of the Jesuits, he was quite familiar with the institution. It was simply a question

333

of the nature of the office. He wondered if Rome could not appoint someone else, someone other than its diplomatic representative, to serve as contact person when, as director of NGOs, he wished to deal with questions pertaining directly to religion.

I understood his problem, but I told him that I was neither authorized nor competent to discuss the question. I offered to introduce him to Monsignor Gremillion, who was qualified to advise him. As it turned out, Gremillion had already left Uppsala.

A week or two later Roosevelt appeared in Geneva. He was staying with a member of the World Council staff, a mutual friend, who invited me to lunch. Beyond telling me that he intended to go to Rome, where he hoped to see Monsignor Gremillion, he did not again bring up the problem he had discussed at Uppsala—nor did I.

Some days later I received a phone call from an enraged Joe Gremillion. In a fury, he wanted to know who I thought I was and what I thought I was doing, negotiating with Curtis Roosevelt on so delicate a matter.

He afterwards wrote me a note of apology, admitting that he had overreacted. The outburst should have revealed to me something of the pressures to which Gremillion felt exposed in Rome. Unfortunately I did not draw that conclusion and so was mystified by signs of hostility which continued to appear.

It reached the point where a steering committee or officers' meeting became a painful event. Gremillion's rudeness to me was obvious. Sometimes it was petty. Once, before a dinner which I had arranged in the Intercontinental Hotel in Geneva, I told him that I had made arrangements for him to say Mass, if he wished, at the nearby convent of La Pouponnière. Then, noticing the presence of Father Reuver, staff member of the Justice and Peace commission, I said, laughing, "I forgot, you are a priest too, so that includes you." At this Gremillion remarked, not laughing, "Yes, he's a priest, and he wears his Roman collar too." It was difficult to keep from punching him in the nose. It was none of his business whether I wore a Roman collar or not. In Switzerland no Jesuit, including the provincial, wore the Roman collar, nor, except in rural areas, was it commonly worn by the diocesan clergy.

Father Reuver had joined Gremillion's staff from the shrine of Our Lady of Fatima, where he had been in charge of communications. When he joined the Justice and Peace commission in Rome he brought with him from Fatima his secretary, whom he had converted from Judaism to Catholicism. Several months after the above encounter, after releasing to the press a searing blast charging the Secretary of State with maintaining inquisitorial thought control over the communications media of the Church, Father Reuver suddenly decamped from the Pontifical Commission Justice and Peace and married his secretary. I restrained the impulse to phone Gremillion and ask him if Reuver still wore his Roman collar.

Other incidents were more concussive. After one officers' meeting, Max Kohnstamm took me out to dinner to discuss the problem of me and Gremillion. His explanation was that it was a matter of chemistry. I did not argue the point, although this theory did not seem plausible to me. Others told me the root of the problem was that Joe Gremillion saw in me a threat to himself. At the time I thought this theory bordered on the absurd. Eventually, as I shall later describe, I examined the theory more closely and concluded that in a peculiar sense it provided the only plausible explanation of Joe Gremillion's hostility.

Sodepax Structures

Some problems developed relating to the burgeoning structures under which our modest executive staff was buried. We had a general assembly of some fifty persons which met once a year, a steering committee of twenty-one persons which met twice a year, and an officers' group comprising the two cochairmen plus two or more consultants which met six or more times a year. This was manifestly a top-heavy structure.

A meeting of the general assembly alone cost us some $18,000. Besides the cost, the preparation for meetings of so many groups, especially the writing of numerous papers, required a great amount of staff time. In addition, the number of executives was in short supply for the demands of so many policy-making bodies. There was also an overlapping and a confusion of authority: the general assembly spent much time discussing issues that had already been thoroughly aired by the steering committee, and the steering committee sometimes made decisions which contradicted a policy set by the general assembly.

I proposed replacing this with a single policy-making board consisting of no more than eighteen members and meeting once a year; a steering committee consisting of the two cochairmen—Gremillion and Kohnstamm—plus Fr. Johann Schütte and Mr. C.

I. Itty would meet with the secretariat twice a year and on other occasions as necessary. This proposed streamlining of the Sodepax structure was eventually adopted.

Birth of CCPD

The World Conference of Churches held a major meeting—I have forgotten the date—at Montreux, Switzerland, on the subject of development. I was puzzled because this subject seemed tailored for Sodepax, having been, in fact, the focus of our Beirut meeting. Yet, although there were some dozen Roman Catholic observers, this was not a Sodepax but a World Council initiative, organized by C. I. Itty on orders, I presume, from Dr. Blake. I had difficulty seeing how this conformed to our oft-repeated axiom "We only do separately what we cannot do together."

Understanding dawned when out of this meeting was born a new World Council agency with the title the Commission on the Churches' Participation in Development (CCPD), to be headed by C. I. Itty. This revealed the real purpose of the meeting. Dr. Blake had for some time worried about the fact that the World Council had "no counterpart to the Pontifical Commission Justice and Peace through which Sodepax" was responsible to the Holy See. At my first meeting with him, in Assisi in December 1967, Blake had explained to me that Philip Potter, head of the mission division of the World Council, would be my liaison with him; Potter would later succeed Blake as general secretary. Blake assured me that I had open access to him anytime I wished, but that I should bring any ordinary problems to Philip Potter. Philip and I were and remained warm friends, but I was never aware of any problems that required his intervention.

Dr. Blake came to feel that there was an imbalance in the organizational structures relating Sodepax to its two parent bodies. The Montreux meeting created the appearance of structural equality between the two partners. Henceforth the organizational charts would read Sodepax → PCJP → Secretary of State, on the Roman side, and Sodepax → CCPD → Secretary General, on the World Council side. In fact, it meant that Philip Potter was no longer liaison and that C. I. Itty, whose CCPD offices were on the third floor of the old mansion whose second floor was occupied by Sodepax, would interpret his role as much more than that of a channel of communication.

I recognize bureaucracies as necessary in any organized society, but I am inclined to think that fewer are better. I did not welcome the advent of CCPD with open arms. Besides, I preferred Philip Potter to C. I. Itty. Itty, a lay member of the World Council staff, belonged to an Indian branch of the Orthodox Church which traced its origin to the Apostle Saint Thomas. I had the feeling, which I could not have justified, that he boded ill for Sodepax.

Nemi: General Assembly

The general assembly of June 21–27, 1971, thanks to Father Schütte, was to meet in a house of the Society of the Divine Word in the Alban Hills, some twenty-five miles from Rome. This would mark the beginning of the third and final year of our Sodepax mandate. In view of our record to date no one on the staff had any doubt that the mandate would be renewed. There was, nevertheless, some speculation about whether changes would be made in its form. The subject was discussed at a meeting of the joint working group held at Naples; from this, C. I. Itty and Monsignor Gremillion prepared for the Nemi meeting a paper on the future of Sodepax, presenting the more promising potential models.

This paper reached me a few weeks before the Nemi meeting with instructions from Itty to have copies made for all members of the assembly. It astonished the entire staff, Neehall, Elliott, Christophe, and me, and we unanimously agreed that it spelled the emasculation of Sodepax. It proposed in effect to transmogrify— the word I was to use at Nemi—Sodepax into a subcommittee of Itty's CCPD, in other words, into a subcommittee of the World Council of Churches. It would bear no resemblance to the Sodepax which in the course of two years had established the track record summarized in these pages.

That such a transmogrification would appeal to Itty was not surprising. That it was recommended by Gremillion was difficult to understand. His attitude, to be sure, had grown ambivalent. His high enthusiasm in our early days had been followed by a period in which optimism and hope would give way to pessimism and gloom. This was so marked that once during a committee meeting Father Schütte had taken him severely to task, pointing out that his persistent negativity was bad for staff morale. At the time I was sorely puzzled by his attitude; later I would realize that he had been reacting to pressures hostile to Sodepax in Rome, a subject I shall discuss later.

With my associates, I prepared a staff counterproposal to the Itty-Gremillion proposal, which we argued was in effect destruction of Sodepax. Our main argument was that Sodepax as presently constituted had proved its effectiveness; it should therefore be continued as constituted. I was not concerned with anything like keeping my job; I had already passed the obligatory retirement age which we had agreed to observe and was staying on only until a successor was found or until the Sodepax mandate expired the following year.

At the first session of the Nemi meeting I presented the two papers dealing with the future of Sodepax. That evening the Roman Catholic and the World Council delegates met separately to discuss the papers. The next morning in plenary session the assembly voted unanimously, staff and officers not voting, to reject the Itty-Gremillion proposal and to adopt the staff counterproposal. Fr. Jerome Hamer, arriving late, expressed great surprise when he learned from me the outcome of the vote. Apparently the transmogrification of Sodepax had been thought assured in advance.

Two other problems arose at Nemi, neither of which enhanced my image in the eyes of Joe Gremillion. One had to do with transportation. The other arose from the accouchement of Charles Elliott's wife, Hilary.

Some two weeks before the assembly Linda Graham, Monsignor Gremillion's secretary, drove me to Nemi for a tour of inspection. Among the problems which I settled—or so I thought—was that of transporting delegates from Leonardo da Vinci Airport to Nemi. The rector of the house did not think this would be a problem. One of the brothers of the community, on temporary duty at the S.V.D. house in Rome, would be able to handle it if his superior approved. After my return to Geneva, Linda Graham telephoned me and at the same time wrote to confirm that Father Schütte had taken care of the matter. The transportation was settled.

The first two days of the assembly, when the bulk of the delegates arrived, there was no problem. But several late arrivals were due at various times Monday, the third day, and Tuesday. When I presented the arrival list to our driver on Monday morning, he declined to accept it; he had been loaned only for Saturday and Sunday and now had to return to other duties. Apparently there had been a misunderstanding between Father Schütte and the superior of the Roman house.

I had asked one of the staff secretaries who had come from Geneva to bring along her driving license in case of need. But the thought of driving to and from Leonardo da Vinci amidst a horde of drivers such as she had seen en route to Nemi terrified her. After some years of experience, I view Italian drivers as no worse and probably better than what one sees in urban United States. But there is a prejudice nurtured by Anglo-Saxons that they are wild men. I had no wish to subject lovely Helen Carter to torture.

I broached the subject to Brother Christophe, who loved to attend meetings, but at the look of distress on his face I told him not to mind. I would do it myself. Should problems arise, Roy Neehall, who would have been no less distressed than Christophe to miss the meetings, would be there to deal with them. So, after announcing the result of the ballot on the future of Sodepax and reading my annual report I turned the assembly over to Roy and left on the first of three trips that day to Leonardo da Vinci. As I was leaving the hall, I met Fr. Jerome Hamer, as mentioned above, and informed him of the assembly's decision.

Although he said nothing at the time, Gremillion would later point to my absenting myself in this fashion as evidence of my unfitness for my job. Further evidence was supplied by the case of Hilary Elliott's postpartum fever.

Dr. Charles Elliott was organizing a program of study and action focused upon structural transformation, that is, upon an examination of the economic, social, political, and cultural changes of structure required by development. It promised to be one of our major projects. He proposed to make an in-depth study of the structures related to poverty in the twenty poorest countries in the world, to project the image forward to the year 2000, and to analyze the structural changes that would be necessary to effect a substantial improvement in that image. The project was called Poverty 2000, and this would be the title of the book in which its conclusions were ultimately published by Pantheon Press. In preparing this program Elliott had traveled extensively in Latin America in late 1969 and in Africa in May 1970, establishing a network of collaborators and gathering information from competent people familiar with their own area.

For a meeting such as that of Nemi it would normally have been the responsibility of the secretariat to prepare an agenda for each working group. At the officers' meeting of April 22–23, however, I had been instructed not to prepare an agenda for Group I, whose focus was development; instead, Dr. Elliott would lay before the group his Poverty 2000 project, which then would be subjected to critical examination and debate. I did as I was told, which is to say, nothing.

The third Elliott child arrived safely on the eve of the Nemi opening. Because of this Elliott delayed his arrival until Monday, when it was understood that he would meet with Group I. Another tardy delegate was to arrive on the same plane. I was on hand well before the plane arrived. The other delegate emerged from the passenger runway in due time, but the last passenger to appear had passed by with no sign of Charles Elliott. The other delegate said that he had not seen Elliott on the plane. I delayed a bit hoping that he would turn up, then headed back to Nemi, where I learned that Charles had phoned from Geneva to say that Hilary had developed a postpartum fever and that his place was at her side. We should not therefore expect him at Nemi.

This left working group I without an agenda. I frankly was not greatly concerned. Sir Geoffrey Wilson was chairing the group, which included—besides Gremillion, Kohnstamm, and Phil Land—Maurice Strong, head of development for Canada and future Assistant Secretary General of the United Nations. With their familiarity with the subject I thought they should be able to find enough to talk about. And so they did. With Phil Land serving as rapporteur they produced the customary report at the end of their sessions. Nevertheless, Joe Gremillion would use this contre-temps as further evidence of my unfitness as secretary of Sodepax. I am not sure what he held me responsible for, Hilary's fever or Charles' decision to stay by his stricken wife, or his own and Max Kohnstamm's decision to dispense with a prepared agenda for Group I.

As I emerged from the plenary session on the next-to-last day, Max Kohnstamm drew me aside and, speaking for Gremillion, told me that it had been decided to replace me as general secretary with Father Schütte. Thus did Gremillion exact revenge for the counter-proposal which the assembly had accepted in preference to his and Itty's proposal. I did not mind. As I have indicated, I had passed the age of retirement, and I was delighted that my successor was to be Father Schütte. He was preeminently quali-fied and would add strength on the Roman side. I said this to Kohnstamm. I added, nevertheless, that I did not appreciate the off-the-cuff manner in which I was notified. I later made the same observation to Dr. Blake.

A Rude Exchange

On the concluding day of the Nemi assembly Paul VI received the entire group in the private audience room just outside his apartment. He spoke at some length in praise of the work of Sodepax.

There were seven boxes of documents from the Nemi meeting—papers read, reports submitted, recommendations made—to be transported to Geneva. The railroads were in the throes of labor trouble, so I decided to drive back to Geneva in the car I had rented for our Nemi meeting. Just before I arrived in Locarno in mid afternoon a violent thunderstorm erupted. I took a room in a hotel to wait out the storm and drove down to Geneva the following morning.

Joe Gremillion arrived there before me, met with the Sodepax staff, and informed them of my replacement. He left a note telling me that he had done so without waiting for me because I was presumably wasting time "somewhere up in the Alps." On my way down from "somewhere up in the Alps" I had composed a calypso celebrating the triumph of our counterproposal over the Itty-Gremillion proposal at the cost of my dismissal. Roy Neehall, a gifted baritone and a prolific composer of calypsos, joined me in singing it to the staff. As things turned out it proved to be a pyrrhic victory for us; but at the time we naively thought it had guaranteed that Sodepax would go "onward, upward, forward," a phrase beloved of Joe Gremillion that our staff would occasionally joke about.

As for my replacement, Charles Elliott expressed his views in a sensitive letter of July 9 which I may be excused for treasuring:

Dear George,
The news about the change of leadership in Sodepax has come to me as a considerable surprise. I know how mixed your own feelings will be and I sense that you are deeply hurt by what has happened. As some small crumb of comfort that in some ways comes too late, I would like to take this opportunity of saying how very much I personally have appreciated your style of leadership. I have said many times to Hilary and a few others how I admire and enjoy your ability to give your staff their head, pull them out of their worst confusions and defend them beyond their deserts. For me, an arrogant son of a gun who does not easily brook being bossed, this has been a most happy and creative relationship and one that I shall be very sad to see come to an end—even though I like and respect John Schütte.

In addition, whatever criticisms Kohnstamm and Gremillion may make, I think the test of history will show that your big contribution has been to allay the fears of those, particularly in Geneva and Rome, who thought that Sodepax was going to become a power-grabbing machine which would threaten their own kingdoms. [Note: In fact, as time would tell, my efforts to allay their fears had failed utterly. GHD.] I think we do threaten their kingdoms, but in a much more subtle and Christian way than most of them are capable of appreciating, and for that you are happily responsible.

I am sure Dr Blake would not mind my passing on to you the fact that in this connection he recently and quite seriously dubbed you a saint. It is a pity that we Westerners are so squeamish that we save these encomia for the obituary column.

I do not think Dr. Blake's criteria of sanctity would pass muster with the Congregation for the Causes of Saints. Nor do I think he was steadily of that opinion. Following Nemi, Joe Gremillion, in one of his less-than-gracious moods, told me that Dr. Blake had remarked to him, "If Sodepax continues, Father Dunne must go." Surprised, because I had thought that my esteem for Dr. Blake was reciprocated, I asked him for an explanation. It was interesting.

Dr. Blake's major ambition was to receive the Roman Catholic Church into full membership in the World Council of Churches during his incumbency. The times seemed to nurture his hope. Vatican II and especially its decree on ecumenism had laid the groundwork. The Joint Working Group had established a good record. Pope Paul VI had visited the World Council in 1969, and Dr. Blake maintained friendly relations with the pope. A generally euphoric state of mind prevailed in those years. And Sodepax had enjoyed rather spectacular success. So it is perhaps not surprising that he had high hopes of seeing his ambition realized.

Others raised unrealistic expectations. According to Dr. Blake, he had, to use his own words, been "misled by C. I. Itty and Monsignor Gremillion" at the time of the Montreux conference. They had led him to believe that the Roman Catholic Church would join the newly established Commission on the Churches' Participation in Development and that this would be followed by entry into the World Council of Churches. Our staff counterproposal at Nemi had, in his view, sabotaged the whole scheme. His high hopes of presiding at the entrance into the World Council of the Roman Catholic Church had been dashed, and I was responsible! Hence his remark, made at an angry moment, that "if Sodepax continues, Father Dunne must go." This threw considerable light upon what Joe Gremillion was up to and verified our conviction that he and Itty were trying to turn Sodepax into a subcommittee of CCPD.

It also revealed that Alice was not alone in Wonderland. Anyone who thought that the entry of Rome into the World Council was imminent was living in a fantasy world. As Father Schütte, who knew the temper of Rome as well as anybody, remarked to me, "Serious consideration of that is years away." I would have been tempted to say "light years away." If Rome constantly worried, as it seemed to, about what Sodepax *might* do, it is impossible to imagine how, as a full member, it could abide things the World Council *did* do.

It was after the Nemi meeting that my relations with Joe Gremillion reached their nadir. A letter of mine dated October 9, 1970, refers to "our painful meeting in Rome on the evening of September 18." I cannot recall what brought Roy Neehall and me to Rome in mid September, but it does not really matter. My memory is entirely clear as to what happened. I was having dinner in a Trastevere restaurant with Schütte, Neehall, and Gremillion when the latter with heavy sarcasm remarked, "I understand you object to being replaced."

"Not at all," I replied. "On the contrary, I am pleased to be replaced by Father Schütte. What I object to is not what was done, but the inconsiderate manner in which it was done."

Citing the two contretemps which had occurred at Nemi, he then informed me that I was "unfit to be secretary general of Sodepax." Whereupon I remarked, not angrily but as a matter of fact, "You are a rude bastard."

Gremillion was startled and, I think, jolted to his heels. Father Schütte later told me that he did not blame me, Gremillion's remarks having been totally unwarranted. Roy Neehall was delighted that I had finally struck back.

The following day I encountered Gremillion in the lobby of the hotel. I apologized for my remark. He expressed regret for the incident.

Reprieve

Dr. Blake's anger was short lived. So was the decision taken at Nemi to replace me with Father Schütte. The Secretary of State vetoed it. He wanted Schütte to stay in Rome with the Justice and Peace commission. It was agreed that, instead of replacing me, Schütte would spend two days each month at Sodepax, presumably to keep an eye on me. Schütte told me that there was a feeling among some, which he did not share, that I did not keep a tight enough rein on my staff, specifically on Elliott and Neehall. That I did not keep a tight rein on them is certainly true, as Elliott's letter to me quoted above clearly suggests. That happens to be my conception of leadership. If you put someone on your staff because he has special talents, you give him the freedom to use those talents. Such was the case with Elliott and to a lesser extent with Neehall. I did not know of a single instance in which either of them had abused that freedom. Nor in the year that followed did I observe a single instance in which Father Schütte subjected them to greater restraint than I.

In any case, I was quite happy with the arrangement. Father Schütte and I were warm friends and in total agreement. I was happy to provide him with an office, complete with a lay-back chair in which he could take a snooze of an afternoon, and with secretarial help.

An Analysis of Monsignor Gremillion

In a letter of October 9, 1970, to Monsignor Gremillion I attempted to analyze the reasons for the complete change in his attitude since the halcyon days of Beirut. At that time, in a letter of May 9, 1968, he had expressed "deep admiration and warmest gratitude." Not I, as some had suggested, but Sodepax, I theorized, had become a threat to him.

"You cannot possibly attack Sodepax, your creation, so you attack me who, as secretary of Sodepax, symbolizes the threat. Thus your conscious mind continues to think of yourself as the founding father and staunch supporter of Sodepax, while your subconscious mind works out its insecurities and fears upon me."[1]

In his reply Gremillion did not dispute my theory. On the contrary, he wrote, "There is probably some truth in what you say," under the circumstances a fairly remarkable admission.

Solution of a Puzzle

When I wrote the above letter one key piece was missing; finding that piece later solved the puzzle of Joe Gremillion's shifting attitude. The key piece was the role played by Henri de Riedmatten, O.P., who belonged to an ancient and distinguished family in the Valais, the most Catholic, and conservatively Catholic, canton of Switzerland. The family history was closely related to the history of the Church in the Valais, where in the Middle Ages more than one de Riedmatten had been prince-bishop.

Henri de Riedmatten was a highly intelligent, loyal, hard-working, and, as he would be the first to admit, ultra-ultramontanist. As representative of the Holy See to the United Nations in Geneva, he had served faithfully for many years as Archbishop Benelli's man in Geneva. This relationship to one who was generally considered to be the second most powerful man in the Church made him a formidably influential behind-the-scenes figure in Rome. He was no friend of Sodepax and no friend of ecumenism. Although our personal relations were amiable, I was fully aware of the former; and, although he maintained a friendly facade, the people at the World Council were fully aware of the latter. A single example will illustrate both.

Discussions by a joint Vatican–World Council committee to explore the possibilities of combining Catholic and non-Catholic medical activities in mission countries had been proceeding satisfactorily for some time in Geneva. The Catholic delegation was headed by Fr. Leo Volker, the former superior general of the White Fathers, a missionary order whose interest is centered on Africa. There not being a Protestant way and a Catholic way to treat a fever, there seemed no good reason why resources and facilities could not be combined. Tragically, Father Volker was killed in an auto accident en route to the ecumenical center at Bossey, near Geneva. Archbishop Benelli named de Riedmatten to replace him. The tenor of the negotiations changed immediately. De Riedmatten took a consistently negative position, opposing even Catholic participation in the medical commission of the World Council. In justification of his stand he remarked to my friend Canon Joseph Moerman, who reported it to me, "We don't want another Sodepax!"

The day before the opening of the Nemi meeting in June, I had lunch with Cardinal Willebrands in his apartment just across the street from the Vatican. I had made the appointment for the purpose of warning the cardinal that de Riedmatten was a dangerous man to have in Geneva as the representative of the Holy See precisely because he was inimical both to Sodepax and to the ecumenical movement. The warning was unnecessary. Willebrands was already aware of the fact as he illustrated by narrating the following incident.

In preparation for Pope Paul VI's visit to Geneva in April 1969, Benelli had ordered de Riedmatten to draw up a tentative schedule. The invitation to visit Geneva had, to be sure, issued from the International Labor Office; but Geneva was also the seat of the World Council of Churches. De Riedmatten drew up a schedule for the pope's day in Geneva which completely ignored the World Council. Benelli returned it with orders to revamp it, including a visit to the World Council. De Riedmatten did so, allowing ten minutes for a stop at the World Council. At this point Willebrands, with Benelli's acquiescence, took over and inserted a stop of one hour's duration, which allowed for a private meeting with Dr. Blake, a meeting with ten or twelve staff people in which I was included, a general session at which the pope addressed the entire World Council staff, and a concluding prayer service in the chapel.

As I listened to the cardinal's story I recalled de Riedmatten triumphant on the day of the pope's visit. Sensitive to the fact that Geneva, as the city of John Calvin, was in a sense the capital of Protestantism, Rome had quietly circulated word that as far as possible all signs of triumphalism should be avoided. Specifically, members of the clergy other than the cardinals in the pope's entourage should not wear soutane or religious habit, but a clerical suit. De Riedmatten, who normally wore a clerical suit outside his convent, was conspicuous everywhere throughout the day, resplendent in his full Dominican habit, complete with cape. It was clearly a day of triumph for the Valaisan.

On one other occasion Willebrands made a significant remark to me. It was at the offices of the Pontifical Commission Justice and Peace in the Palazzo San Calisto in Rome, where I made a report on Sodepax activities. Present were Cardinal Willebrands, Dr. Blake, Max Kohnstamm, and the two top officers of the International Humanum Foundation. As we were leaving the room for a coffee break, the cardinal suddenly said to me, "Somebody in the Secretariat of State is hostile to Sodepax, and I intend to ask Archbishop Benelli why." I do not know whether he ever asked Benelli, but I have no doubt that the hostility which he detected was engendered by de Riedmatten, who boasted of it to Canon Joseph Moerman.

Canon Moerman, a Belgian priest of the Bruges diocese, had spent ten years in Africa, five in Belgian Congo and then five in Zaire as director of the Regional Office of Catholic Education for Africa south of the Sahara and Madagascar. He had then been named secretary general of the International Catholic Child Bureau with offices in Geneva. He resided in the residence conducted by the Sisters of Providence where I was accustomed to say Mass. We usually breakfasted together and had become close friends.

I was due to leave Sodepax. The project of naming Father Schütte as my replacement having foundered, the question of a successor was extant. In response to my urging, Canon Moerman expressed a willingness to accept the appointment, if offered. A highly intelligent and gifted man who spoke fluent Flemish, French, German, English, and Italian and who was ecumenically oriented, he was admirably qualified. I recommended him to Cardinal Willebrands and Dr. Blake. He was interviewed by the joint working group, who unanimously agreed that he was an excellent choice. Everyone was stunned when Archbishop Benelli vetoed his nomination.

At the time Canon Moerman thought the train had been derailed by a young monsignor now in the Secretariat of State with whom he had clashed some years earlier in Zaire. De Riedmatten would set the record straight. In recognition of his services and talents and, no doubt, of his unquestioning loyalty, de Riedmatten had been appointed by Benelli as general secretary of Cor Unum, the latest addition to the bureaucracy of the Roman Curia. Cor Unum—the name means "one heart"—was, of course, the creation of the Holy Father. De facto, its architect was Archbishop Benelli.

On the eve of his departure from Geneva to assume his new office, de Riedmatten told Moerman that he should be glad that his nomination had been vetoed because Rome was preparing drastically to trim the wings of Sodepax. And he boasted—he was proud of it—that it was he who had convinced the authorities in Rome that Sodepax "was becoming more important than the Pontifical Commission Justice and Peace."

There is the answer to the question Cardinal Willebrands was going to ask Archbishop Benelli. And there is the missing piece of the puzzle, the explanation of how Joe Gremillion came to see in me, who symbolized Sodepax, the specter of a threat to him.

Mushakoji Joins the Team

At the Sodepax conference on peace held in Baden, Austria, a brilliant paper by Kinhide Mushakoji had impressed everyone. Mushakoji was the director of the Institute of Graduate Studies in International Relations at the Jesuit Sophia University in Tokyo. At the Nemi meeting of the Sodepax general assembly, of which he was a member, he was persuaded by Gremillion and Kohnstamm to take a year's sabbatical from his post at Sophia and to join the Sodepax staff in Geneva. His responsibility would be to develop the peace component of our program and specifically to follow up the recommendations of the Baden conference.

Mushakoji's name was submitted to Archbishop Benelli for approval. That this was standard procedure made it no less aggravating. Six months later, despite several inquiries on my part, no decision had been made. In Tokyo Mushakoji was becoming increasingly exasperated. He had arranged with the university to grant him the sabbatical, and he had to make arrangements to rent his home during his absence, because he intended to bring his family with him. The possibility that approval would not be forthcoming was slight. Mushakoji belonged to a distinguished family; his father had held ambassadorial rank in Japan's prewar diplomatic service. He was a devout Catholic and a member of the committee of the Pontifical Commission Justice and Peace. Nevertheless, Mushakoji could not be blamed for fretting. After all, who would have expected the veto of Canon Moerman?

Eventually approval came, and I cabled Tokyo. Mushakoji and his family arrived in Geneva in May 1971. In accordance with a Baden recommendation, steps had already been taken to organize an international conference of women to examine their role in peace-making. In February I met in Geneva with a committee of women to begin formulating plans. With his arrival Mushakoji took my place and completed plans for a highly-successful conference which was held in Ceylon, now Sri Lanka. During the months that followed, Mushakoji was an invaluable member of the Sodepax staff.

Signs of the Times

Sodepax's three-year mandate was to expire in July 1971, which would also mark the end of my service as secretary general.

Neither I nor any member of the staff, however, expected this to mark the end of Sodepax. There had been the surprising Itty-Gremillion memo which proposed a future for Sodepax which was equivalent to no future, but the general assembly had rejected this unanimously. There would later be the revelation by Henri de Riedmatten of his own subversive activities in Rome. There had also been a disquieting report, emanating again from de Riedmatten, that Fr. Jerome Hamer, O.P., (today Cardinal Hamer) had remarked that "Sodepax had taken a wrong turn, and practically speaking had no future." I had written to Hamer on August 2, 1971; reminding him that I had heard him describe the Sodepax record as "astonishing", I asked for an explanation.[2]

Upon receiving my letter Father Hamer immediately telephoned from Rome. Obviously upset, he denied emphatically that he had made the remark attributed to him and repeated the high value he placed upon the work of Sodepax. I dismissed the report as someone's self-serving gossip.

Other criticisms were insignificant. On one occasion Dr. Blake told me that some of the World Council staff people were displeased about some features of our operation. We arranged a meeting with our staff at which they could air their complaints. Only two criticisms surfaced. One, that we had too much money, was motivated not by concern for evangelical poverty, but by simple envy. The other was Paul Abrecht's complaint that, at the rate Sodepax was going, there would not be anything left for the department of Church and Society, of which he was director, to do.

I thought this confirmation that we were moving in the right direction.

Planning for Sodepax's Future

Had there been any doubt about the future of Sodepax it would have been dissipated by its record of accomplishment, witnessed by ourselves and verified by numerous testimonials. Most impressive was the testimonial of the Justice and Peace commission itself. The Secretariat of State, unlike the World Council, had not yet committed itself to the renewal of the Sodepax mandate. Before doing so it directed the Pontifical Commission Justice and Peace to evaluate the performance of Sodepax to date.

The evaluation made was based upon a thorough, extensive, and probing inquiry. Opinions were sought, not merely in Rome and Geneva, but in every region in Australia, India, Indonesia,

Southeast Asia, Japan, Korea, Africa, Europe, South and North America where Sodepax had been active. The final evaluation, issued in the Spring of 1971 and running to some fifty pages, was overwhelmingly positive. It mentioned a few minor faults, some of which had already been corrected, others of which could easily be handled, but it expressed no reservation about the value of what had been done and the importance of continuing Sodepax.

That minor changes might be made in the structure of Sodepax I accepted. But that it would continue substantially intact I had not the slightest doubt. Two facts prove this. One is that I recommended Canon Moerman as my successor. This I would never have done had I the faintest premonition that the Sodepax which he would inherit would, as de Riedmatten predicted, have had its wings clipped. The other probative fact is that I strongly opposed the establishment by Fr. William Ryan, S.J., of a Center of Concern in Washington, D.C.

Bill Ryan, a future provincial of the English-speaking Canadian province, was a brilliant Jesuit with a doctorate in international economics from Harvard. I had proposed him as my successor, but Father Arrupe refused to release him from his commitment to occupy a chair of economics at the Gregorian University. Later, however, he did release him to establish the Center of Concern in Washington, the purpose of which was to research the problems of peace and development and to bring the fruits of that research to the consciousness and conscience of the public. As described in a prospectus that Bill Ryan wrote, the Center of Concern seemed to me an exact duplicate of Sodepax, minus its ecumenical dimension.

In extensive correspondence with Bill and with Fr. Vincent O'Keefe, S.J., American assistant to Father Arrupe in Rome, I vigorously opposed the project. I argued that the center for research already existed, with the added virtue of being a wholly ecumenical enterprise. The resources, both in money and in men, which would go into the Center of Concern would be better invested in Sodepax. What was needed was not another center of research, but a strengthening of the existing ecumenical one. The need on the national level was for centers to get the fruit of that research to the grassroots.

The fruit of Sodepax research in less than three years was already quite extensive. Without including the results of the many national conferences, Sodepax in Geneva had produced ten volumes containing the findings of international conferences held under its auspices.[3]

My argument was sound, but it was based upon the erroneous assumption that the future of Sodepax was secure. Fortunately I lost the argument. The Center of Concern was established and has successfully carried on not only research but also the task of bringing the fruits of its research to the grassroots, at least in the United States.

That I had opposed this initiative, opposed it with vigor, is proof positive of my confidence in the future; and my staff fully shared this confidence. Throughout the last year of our mandate we carried on as before. And upon the assumption that the mandate would be continued Elliott, Neehall, and Christophe prepared a thirty-nine-page prospectus for the years 1972–1974.

In general I approved of the prospectus, which promised that the next period of Sodepax history would be as exciting and productive as the first. I expressed reservations, however, about some of its features and particularly about its most radical proposal. The prospectus spoke about the ideal of Sodepax that it identify itself with the marginal peoples of the world and about the fact that despite all its real concern many failed to see Sodepax as an instrument of the underprivileged and the powerless. It was a question of helping the image reflect the reality.

To remedy this the three-year prospectus proposed moving Sodepax out of Geneva and into the third world. It argued that in Geneva we were living in one of the wealthiest cities in the world and identified with the bureaucracy of the World Council and, more distantly, that of the Roman Curia. This affected our image.

While the idea of moving into the third world was attractive, I was convinced that Sodepax had to maintain a presence in the World Council. I also felt sure that their proposal would be unacceptable to both Rome and Geneva. Nor did I think that its location in Geneva precluded it from acting effectively as an agent of the poor. Perhaps the general secretary could remain in Geneva while the staff was located in the third world; this was not a very practical arrangement, but it could be discussed.

Despite these reservations I thought the staff had every right to argue their proposal. So did Father Schütte. He suggested that they present it to Dr. Blake. He did not think, however, that I should accompany them, lest Dr. Blake suspect that the proposal had originated with me and was, in fact, a Roman Catholic plot to move Sodepax away from the World Council!

The trio returned from their meeting, which had not lasted long, rather shaken. Dr. Blake, they reported, had flown into a rage at the proposal to leave Geneva and had refused even to discuss it. He was especially irate at their reference to the World Council as a bureaucracy, which, of course, it is, as is the Roman Curia.

Why had I not quashed the proposal? Dr. Blake wanted to know. I explained to him that I believed in collegiality not simply as a principle of papal and episcopal relations but as a principle of management in general.

An officers' meeting held at Bossey, July 6–8, 1971, proposed some needed modifications to the Sodepax structure. On July 8 the officers were joined by several members of the executive staff of the World Council, notably Dr. Blake and Paul Abrecht, and on the Roman side by Fr. Jerome Hamer, O.P., and Bp. Torrella Cascante, former auxiliary bishop of Barcelona, recently brought to the Roman Curia as vice-president of the Justice and Peace commission. The purpose was to consider questions relating to the future structure, programs, and financing of Sodepax.

The structural reform mentioned in the preceding paragraph was approved. With respect to the renewal of the Sodepax mandate the minutes of the meeting state:

> The first three-year experimental period of Sodepax ends this year and approval is sought from the WCC and the PCJP to continue with the next three year program. *World Council of Churches*: Dr. Blake reaffirmed the commitment of the WCC to continuing Sodepax's program. *Pontifical Commission Justice and Peace*: Bp. Torrella Cascante said that while official confirmation still had to be given, all indications were that there is unanimity that Sodepax should be continued.

At the same time the bishop

> called attention to a problem which arises out of the fact that the Secretariat [Sodepax], as is normal and to be expected, develops its own elan and initiative while at the same time it is responsible to the two constituting bodies. It is important that an effort be made to solve this problem. If present structures are inadequate, then a more suitable vehicle should be sought.

The Bishop did not further elucidate the nature of the problem to which he referred.

Father Hamer echoed this same concern, asking "whether Sodepax in carrying out its delegated mandate of education for development was to act as a separate entity or as a coordinator for the two constituting bodies."

I had heard this concern before and, innocent abroad, I had never understood it. It was usually expressed in terms of a warning that Sodepax must not become "a tertium quid." Only the day before at the officers' meeting I had asked the question, which was not answered, "Why not a tertium quid? and a quartum and quintum quid?" My view was the more quids the merrier if, as was demonstrably the case with Sodepax, they added momentum to the ecumenical movement.

The problem was contrived. That Sodepax developed its own initiative in no way prevented it from being responsible to its constituting bodies. Sodepax had never done anything independently of them. It could not have done so had it wished. Our officers, who represented and were responsible to the constituting bodies, could at any time veto any proposal we made, as they had in fact at this meeting vetoed the proposal to move out of Geneva.

I realize now that the real concern, veiled by these euphemisms, was that which Henri de Riedmatten had carried to Rome—that Sodepax was becoming more important than the Pontifical Commission Justice and Peace. This was undoubtedly true, and for a reason very well stated by Charles Elliott in the prospectus:

> The record simply confirms what many have long maintained: that an ecumenical pooling of effort by the Roman Catholic, Protestant and Orthodox Churches multiplies the effectiveness of each. To this extent the whole is more than the sum of the parts. The hidden potentialities of each component are multiplied by the dynamism of the spirit of ecumenical action. It is in this sense that the Sodepax formula has proved an astonishingly powerful tool under God for getting the churches moving at a pace and in directions to which they have not hitherto been accustomed.

In every Sodepax initiative we had experienced what Elliott called "the dynamism of the spirit of ecumenical action." That element was missing from any unilateral undertaking of the PCJP or of the WCC. Furthermore, there is no question that world opinion would be more interested in a program in which the Roman Catholic Church was equally involved with the Protestant and Orthodox churches. It seemed obvious to me that every success of Sodepax reflected credit upon both parent bodies, the Holy See and the World Council of Churches. Far from diminishing the image of the Holy See, each successful program of Sodepax enhanced it, showing that it really was concerned about the victims of poverty and of war. The inability to realize this is a form of myopia particularly endemic in Rome but not entirely absent from Geneva.

Not unrelated to this myopia is the overweening preoccupation with "preserving our own identity." This is a major preoccupation not only of Rome but of the more than three hundred churches which hold membership in the World Council. The history of the World Council confirms this. During the half century or more of its existence the number of separate churches belonging to the World Council has not diminished but has greatly increased. To be sure, their interecclesial relations have greatly improved. They pray together, socialize, join in common projects, and together lament the divisions which rend the Christian fabric. But each one is preoccupied with preserving its own identity.

I do not say that one should forget or abandon one's identity, but as long as it remains the major preoccupation it is a road block on the way of ecumenism. I take the ultimate goal of the ecumenical movement to be the gathering of all the separate flocks into one fold. This is compatible with the retention of a certain degree of identity, as the existence within the Catholic fold of a large number of autonomous ritual churches proves, such as the Maronite, the Ukrainian, and others. But as long as the first concern is one's own identity we will remain, while lamenting the fact, several, not one. Better to serve the ecumenical end than the warning that we must preserve our identity is what had been the Sodepax ideal: Let us do separately only what we cannot do together.

Eighteen

Irish Sea of Troubles

At the end of the Sodepax officers' meeting in Bossey in early July 1971, Max Kohnstamm informed me that they had set October 1 as the date of my retirement as secretary general of Sodepax. They hoped by then to have official Vatican confirmation of the renewal of the mandate and to have found my successor.

Before this date arrived a phone call from Dublin began what was to be my last mission for Sodepax. It came from Sean McBride, holder of more dignities than it is convenient to list—among them both the Nobel Peace Prize and the Lenin Peace Prize—who wondered if Sodepax could not offer its services to the riven communities of Northern Ireland. Fr. Michael Hurley, S.J., probably the most active ecumenist in Ireland, was also on the Dublin phone. He suggested that I meet in Belfast with Mr. G. B. Newe to discuss possibilities. Father Schütte happened to be in my office when the call came. He agreed that we should respond.

Mr. Newe was a *rara avis* in Northern Ireland, a Roman Catholic highly esteemed by both his own and the Protestant communities. His acceptance at the hands of Queen Elizabeth of an Order of Merit of the British Empire had in no wise diminished his standing among his fellow Catholics. A few weeks after I met him he accepted appointment as a minister of state in the government of Northern Ireland, again without forfeiting the esteem of the Catholic community. His role was to interpret to the prime minister the "various elements of thought in the Catholic community." For more than twenty years Mr. Newe had been the secretary of the Northern Ireland Council of Social Service and in that capacity had served all the people without regard to religious or political views. This accounts for his hold upon their affections.

I flew to Belfast, which resembled a city in a war zone. On every hand was bleak devastation: bombed out buildings, piles of rubble, barbed wire, and graffiti. The troubles had begun on August 5, 1968, with a peaceful civil rights demonstration by Catholics to protest inequities in housing. The violence began the following November with an attack by mobs of Paisleyites—followers of Ian Paisley—upon another demonstration by 15,000 Catholics in Derry. Increasing violence led to the calling in of British troops on August 14, 1969. The Irish Republican Army (IRA) did not enter aggressively into action until February 6, 1971.[1] Nevertheless, the city already was a landscape of ruins.

Oddly, it seemed to me, one of the favorite targets was the pub. The taxi driver nodded to heap after heap of rubble as we passed and remarked, sadly I thought, "that was a pub." Up until this first visit of mine—many more would follow during the next three months—more than sixty pubs had been bombed. The temperance society might have approved, but I thought it rather odd behavior by the Irish.

Mr. Newe arranged for me to meet with a small group of Roman Catholic, Presbyterian, Methodist, and Church of Ireland (Anglican) clergymen to discuss what, if anything, might be done. Aware of the sensitivity of the Irish to outside ingression in their affairs, I assured them that I did not come with any solution to the problem of Northern Ireland. That, I said, was an Irish problem and could be solved only by the Irish themselves. I came only to offer the help of Sodepax in any effort which they themselves might devise. Reassured, they launched into a frank exchange of views which lasted the entire afternoon. They agreed that to bridge the gap between the Roman Catholic and Protestant clergy would be a major contribution to reconciliation.

I was aware of this aspect of the problem. In Geneva I had known a young Presbyterian pastor from Northern Ireland who had told me of his own experience. As a student at Queen's University he and a Roman Catholic fellow student had been good friends. After completing their university studies the two had entered the seminary, he to become a Presbyterian pastor, his friend a Roman Catholic priest. Some years later the two were assigned to the same town, he pastor of the Presbyterian church, his friend vicar at the Catholic church. But were he, while walking down the street, to see his longtime friend approaching, he would cross to the opposite side to avoid encountering him. For if it were bruited about that he had been seen conversing in a friendly manner with a Catholic priest, he would lose a large part of his congregation and even risk losing his parish. In the Presbyterian Church the congregation selects—and deselects—its pastor.

I would later meet another Presbyterian pastor, much older, who told me that he kept affixed to his fireplace a list, which he kept up to date, of all the pastors who had lost their jobs because of what their congregations judged excessively friendly attitudes towards Catholics.

Some time later, in a letter to me of December 17, 1971, Card. William Conway, the Roman Catholic Primate of Ireland, confirmed that this was the situation: "The difficulty which the Protestant clergy experience and to which you refer in. . .your letter [of December 13], is well-known to us here and is a very real one. Some of these good men could lose half their congregation if they were seen to be too ecumenically minded. Some of them show great courage in resisting such pressures." One of these courageous ones was the ecumenically minded pastor I mentioned in the last paragraph, whose many years of service had won him respect and sturdy rootage in his pastorate.

Cardinal Conway had an experience, which his secretary narrated to me, that throws a rather lurid light upon the state of ecumenism in Northern Ireland. The cardinal had appeared on television together with Archbishop Simms, Primate of the Church of Ireland (Anglican), and Rt. Rev. J. L. M. Haire, Moderator of the Presbyterian Church. When Conway suggested that they end their discussion by saying the Our Father together, Simms agreed, Haire refused. He had run a great risk merely by appearing on television with the Catholic cardinal archbishop. He did not dare be seen praying with him!

In my initial meeting with the group brought together by Mr. Newe I proposed that Sodepax try to bridge this gap, of which they were all aware, by arranging a series of meetings between Roman Catholic and Protestant clergy. They unanimously approved. Cardinal Conway assured me of Catholic cooperation. In the same letter from which I quoted above, he wrote, "Certainly I feel sure that there will be little difficulty in having Catholic clergy take part in such meetings."

From Belfast I took the train to Dublin, where I attended a dinner with Sean McBride celebrating the opening of Fr. Michael Hurley's School of Ecumenism. The principal speaker was Erskine

Hamilton Childers, who two years later, after serving an uninter-
rupted thirty-five years as a member of Dail Eireann, was elected
the fourth president of Ireland. His father, Robert Erskine Childers,
was one of the heroes of the Irish struggle for independence and
a tragic victim of the civil war which followed. Principal secretary
of the Irish delegation to the London negotiations of 1921, he had
refused to accept the treaty which established an Irish Free State
at the cost of the separation of northern Ireland, the root of all the
troubles today. He joined the Republican side in the civil war and
was later captured by Free State forces in 1922, court-martialed,
and executed after shaking hands with each member of the firing
squad. At the Dublin dinner his son gave a moving account of his
last visit with his father in the prison cell on the eve of his
execution. His father's last words to him were an exhortation never
to let hatred take hold of his heart.

Back in Geneva I immediately wrote to Card. Jean Villot, the
Secretary of State, informing him of my activities. In reply he fully
approved and asked to be kept informed of future progress. I also
informed Dr. Blake, Max Kohnstamm, and Joe Gremillion.

Returning to Ireland I went to Armagh to see Cardinal
Conway. He was in Rome at the time, but before leaving had
instructed his acting secretary, Fr. John Lennon, S.J., to give me
whatever help he could. I learned from Father Lennon that the
apostolic nuncio in Dublin, Abp. Gaetano Alibrandi, had been
instructed by Cardinal Villot to give whatever support he could to
the Sodepax project and that he had communicated these instructions to Cardinal Conway.

Father Lennon gave me the names of five or six priests who,
he thought, could compile a list of clergy willing to participate in
the proposed program. From Armagh I drove to Derry (its original
name and still so called by Catholics, but known to Protestants as
Londonderry). Here Bp. Neil Farren offered full cooperation.

With a certain amount of trepidation, I approached Bp.
William J. Philbin, bishop of Down and Connor, to which diocese
the city of Belfast belongs. Although Mr. Newe had spoken highly
of Philbin's intellectual qualities, Fr. Desmond Wilson, one of his
diocesan priests, had drawn a rather negative portrait. Desmond
Wilson was the vicar at Saint John's Church on Falls Road, a heavily Catholic working-class neighborhood which had suffered much
from the violence. Close to the people, he had worked strenuously
for peace and reconciliation, not always with the bishop's approval. Several years later, discouraged by what he felt was lack

of support for his efforts, he resigned from the ministry of the priesthood.

The evening before my appointment with Bishop Philbin, the IRA planted a bomb in a pub on Shankill Road, which ran parallel to Falls Road through a heavily Protestant neighborhood. The bomb was set to go off at an hour when the pub was crowded with fans returning from a soccer game. More than twenty were killed and dozens wounded. The next morning en route to my appointment I had the taxi driver take me to the site of the tragedy. It was a scene of desolation, the pub a jumble of ruins.

The episcopal residence was in a neighborhood obviously peopled by the well-to-do, behind a wall and fronted by immaculately-kept lawns. A maid admitted me to the stately red-brick mansion and ushered me into the parlor. A few minutes later the bishop arrived, a small man attired in a knee-length morning coat and surrounded by four leaping and yelping poodles. I felt transported back to the mid nineteenth century and to the home of an Anglo-Irish landlord of the gentry class.

I mentioned the bombing of the previous evening and asked him if he intended to attend the funeral services for the victims. He did not. Such a gesture would be misunderstood. He had once gone to the Falls Road neighborhood and had been badly received, even in this Catholic area.

I explained to him the Sodepax proposal to set up dialogue between Catholic and Protestant clergy. I do not think he put much stock in its possibilities, but at least he did not, as I feared he might, forbid his priests to participate. In all of this, influenced no doubt by Desmond Wilson's view, I have probably been unfair to Bishop Philbin. In a letter of October 12 acknowledging a detailed report I had sent him of my activities, he wrote, "It is scarcely necessary for me to say how earnestly I hope that the painstaking efforts you have made and will be continuing to make in this worthy enterprise will have some constructive results."

Among the Protestant Church leaders whom I called upon to explain the Sodepax proposal and to enlist support were Abp. G. O. Simms, Primate of the Church of Ireland (Anglican); Principal J. M. L. Haire, Moderator of the Presbyterian Church; Rev. J. Weir, General Secretary of the same; Canon E. Elliott, pastor of Trinity Church; Rev. E. Gallagher, Methodist Church; Rev. N. Taggart, Organizing Secretary of the Irish Council of Churches. After returning to Geneva I despatched Roy Neehall, who was a Presbyterian pastor, to Belfast to meet with these same leaders, the purpose being to dissipate any suspicions they might have that the Sodepax initiative was a Roman Catholic scheme of some sort.

After assuring the support of these Catholic and Protestant Church leaders, I retained the services of two experts in conflict resolution. John Bayler was a graduate of the London School of Conflict Analysis, and Ron Wiener was a graduate in psychology from Louvain University. We agreed that they would organize on an experimental basis three small-group discussions to be held during November at Corrymeela, a conference center near Ballycastle in the extreme north of Ireland.

These activities necessitated several trips to Northern Ireland. On one of them, while waiting to board the plane in Geneva, I picked up *La Suisse*, the morning newspaper. A front-page story carried a report that the Wellington Park Hotel in Belfast had been destroyed by an IRA bomb the previous night. The Wellington Park Hotel was where I customarily stayed and where I had a reservation for this same evening. Upon arrival I discovered that the report had been exaggerated. The lobby and reservation area, the dining room, and a newly redecorated cocktail lounge had all indeed been destroyed. The wing where the living quarters were located had escaped.

It has been repeated time and again that the war in Northern Ireland is not a religious war. The bombing of the Wellington Park Hotel was a small bit of evidence in support of that claim. The owner of the hotel was a Roman Catholic whose teenage daughters attended the high school conducted by the Dominican sisters a few blocks away; this was where I would say Mass during my visits to Belfast. Many of the hotel employees were Catholics, including the lovely young Irish girl who was the receptionist. She described to me her frightening experience of the previous day when two young IRA men had walked into the lobby, deposited a package on a coffee table, and told her she had five minutes to evacuate the guests.

The IRA strategy was to paralyze the economy of Northern Ireland. The fairly small Wellington Park Hotel was a favorite stopping place for foreign business travelers and thus was part of the economy. As such it was a logical tactical target for the IRA, which evidently was indifferent to the religious affiliation of its victims.

Another small bit of evidence of the nondiscriminatory character of Northern Ireland violence was a letter of October 15, 1971, from Bp. Neil Farren of Derry:

Dear Father Dunne,
I replied a few days ago to your letter. Something strange
happened but it shows the conditions in which we are living.
My communication happened to be in a Mail Van. . .which was
hijacked. Evidently the letters were set on fire. It happened
that yours was only partly burned and was returned to me by
the Post Office officials. I thought that in the circumstances
you would like the original letter in spite of its dirt. Best
wishes. . .

While I was engaged in the activities in Ireland, October 1
came and went, and with it my mandate as general secretary of
Sodepax. I had no particular desire to return to the United States.
I find Europe a more interesting place to live and the lifestyle of
Europeans, generally speaking, preferable to that of Americans.
Consequently I had asked Father Arrupe for permission to find a
pied-à-terre in Europe. I hoped to have time to do some writing,
which perforce I had been unable to do for some years. Bp. Pierre
Mamie of the diocese of Fribourg, of which Geneva is a part, offered
me such a spot as chaplain of a Carmelite convent above the village
of Le Pâquier, where my duties would be limited to saying Mass for
the nuns and on Sundays adding a small homily; this suited me
fine. The incumbent chaplain had asked to be replaced because he
could not stand the solitude. I have never minded being alone. In
any case, as things turned out, I was not to be all that isolated.
Father Arrupe gave me permission to accept the appointment for
a year or two. I was to stay for thirteen years.

When I left Sodepax I agreed, upon Father Schütte's insistence, to continue as consultant until the Irish program was fully
launched. In this capacity I participated on November 17–18 in the
second of the small-group meetings arranged by Bayler and
Wiener. Corrymeela was a large barrack-type building on the
palisades above the beach and looking out over the North Sea. The
group met all afternoon Wednesday, again after supper, and all
day Thursday. Besides Bayley, Wiener, and me, the participants
included, on the Catholic side, Fr. Terence O'Keefe, a university
professor, and Fr. Brendan Murphy of the nearby city of Ballycastle, a former professor of religion in a teachers' college; on the
Protestant side, Canon Elliott, vicar of the Church of Ireland's
Trinity Church, Rev. Brown of the Presbyterian Church, Rev.
Loane, and Rev. Morrison of the Methodist Church, the former
from the Ardoyne and the latter from Derry.

In a letter of December 13, 1971, to Cardinal Conway, after describing the meeting, particularly a role-playing session which I thought especially fruitful, I remarked:

> It would be entirely unrealistic to expect that out of such meetings will come an immediate solution to the Irish problem. Ultimately that solution must be political. But no political solution will be effective in the long run unless that legacy of distrust and hatred handed down by fifty years of divisiveness and which has, in the wake of the events of the past several years, almost totally polarized the Catholic and Protestant communities, is dissipated. Nor will any political solution itself heal these wounds.
>
> It seems to me obvious that this is precisely where the role of the Church lies. It also seems to me clear that, if the divided communities are ever to learn to live together in peace and amity, the Catholic and Protestant clergy must first learn to do so themselves and develop the courage to demonstrate to their respective flocks that they have learned to do so.

Death of Father Schütte

While I was attending this Corrymeela meeting, tragedy struck Sodepax. Phoning from Geneva, Helen Carter, Mushakoji's secretary, told me that Father Schütte was dead. When I last saw him in the Sodepax office in Geneva on the eve of one of my trips to Northern Ireland, he told me that he was discouraged by Rome's failure to act upon the renewal of the Sodepax mandate. He added, although he did not explicitly connect the two, that for several weeks he had been deeply depressed.

Several years before, he had had a heart problem. Perhaps with this in mind, he was en route to the clinic on Monte Mario in Rome for a physical checkup when, only a block from the clinic, he blacked out. His Volkswagen swerved from the road and smashed into a tree, throwing him violently against the steering wheel. He was dead upon arrival at the hospital. Surprisingly, an autopsy revealed no sign of a heart attack which, it had been assumed, had accounted for his blacking out.

Back on the continent I accompanied the Sodepax staff to the Netherlands, where we attended his obsequies in the chapel of the motherhouse of the Society of the Divine Word, of which he had been the general superior and in whose cemetery he was laid to rest. Joe Gremillion and Max Kohnstamm each pronounced a eulogy at graveside. It was a melancholy voyage. Johann Schütte had been a warm personal friend and a staunch supporter of Sodepax.

Sodepax Cover Blown

On December 22, 1971, Bayler and Wiener, our conflict managers for the Irish program, came to Geneva and submitted their report of the meetings and recommendations for the future to me and the Sodepax staff. They recommended a year-long series of meetings and the employment of a full-time research officer to organize the meetings and, on a consultative basis, to chair the meetings of the Northern Ireland Research Institute which Bayler and Wiener were establishing. The estimated cost was 4,400 pounds—some ten or eleven thousand dollars—to be borne by Sodepax and the four main churches. Cardinal Conway for the Catholic bishops and Norman Taggart for the Irish Council of Churches indicated willingness to contribute a proportionate share.

Shortly thereafter some zealous soul in Rome, anxious to gain credit for the Holy See, blew Sodepax's cover, threatening the entire enterprise. The information came to me from Cardinal Conway who, in a postscript to his letter of January 10, remarked:

> I remember that your earlier reports laid a good deal of stress on the desire of the Protestant Churches that publicity in regard to these meetings should be avoided. You therefore may be interested in the enclosed newspaper cutting which appeared (with inch-high letters in a headline "Secret Vatican Peace Move") in "The Sunday Press," published in Dublin on 19th December. I am not worried about them at all, but as you well know, some Protestant Churchmen have good reason to be sensitive. Neither do I attach much importance to the expression "a Vatican source" since I know from experience that this term is applied to anyone attached even remotely to one of the many organizations there.

The article, accurately describing the nature of Sodepax, had said that it had been working for many months "behind the scenes" and it quoted "a Vatican source" as saying, "In a very unofficial way, you understand, Sodepax is trying very hard to get the Catholic and Protestant leaders of Northern Ireland together for talks."

In what I think was my final act as consultant I wrote to Monsignor Gremillion and Mr. Kohnstamm, with copies to Dr. Blake, Cardinal Villot, Bishop Torrella, and the Sodepax staff, complaining about this potentially disastrous leak. I reminded them that in the report of my first meeting with members of the clergy I had remarked "that, *provided it were done with no publicity*, an initiative by Sodepax. . .would be most welcome." (The emphasis was in the original document.) I also reminded them that in the same report I had warned that "it would not at all help this project to advertise in Northern Ireland that the Pope approved—quite the contrary." I concluded by saying:

> I do not know the identity of the Vatican source [it had to be someone in the Secretariat of State or in the Pontifical Commission Justice and Peace] but it bespeaks an enormous ignorance of Northern Ireland realities not to know that for broad sections of the Protestant, especially Presbyterian, community it is the kiss of death to identify any project with the Vatican. It is bad enough to identify it with the World Council of Churches which, as I have also pointed out in my previous reports, is held very much suspect in the same broad sections referred to above; it is to compound the error to add the ogre of the Vatican to the scene. I hope that the quoted Vatican source, out of zeal to burnish the image of the Holy See as peacemaker, has not extinguished the still small flame of hope enkindled by the Sodepax initiative.[2]

That small flame survived this gaffe only to be snuffed out in the emasculation of Sodepax which was in progress at this very moment.

Nineteen

Emasculation of Sodepax

When I left Sodepax at the end of September 1971, I had every reason to be confident of its future. Had there been any reasons for doubt, they would have been dissipated by an eloquent endorsement made by Card. Jan Willebrands at a dinner in Rome on September 23, 1971, in the presence of Abp. Giovanni Benelli. The dinner was to honor the termination of my service and of the first mandate of Sodepax. Since I was committed to negotiations in Northern Ireland at the time, I wired my regrets. In expressing his own regrets at my absence, Monsignor Gremillion sent me a copy of Cardinal Willebrands's speech. After noting that Sodepax had been established on an experimental basis three years earlier, the cardinal said:

> Should one not be astonished by the remarkable results which this initiative has produced? Sodepax has become a sign and a hope of Christian engagement in the promotion of social justice, of human development and of peace in the service of the entire human family. Sodepax is an ecumenical realization and *represents the best structure of collaboration in matters of international justice, development and peace between the World Council of Churches and the Catholic Church in the present state of our relations*. . .[Italics added]

After much more in the same tenor, the Cardinal said, "In concluding this brief discourse, I can assure you that the Secretariat for Unity firmly supports the demand for a renewed experimental mandate for Sodepax. . ."[1]

It is not surprising that I resigned my position as secretary general a week later fully confident that the future of Sodepax would be an enlargement of its past. Adding to this assurance were the many letters which came to me. Of particular importance, our relations having left much to be desired, was that of Monsignor Gremillion:

Dear George,
We were all disappointed that you did not come to our General Assembly for the discussion on *Sodepax*, and doubly disappointed that you could not accept our invitation to the dinner in your honor which we had planned. Your cable to that effect is acknowledged. I realize that your Peace Mission in Ireland had to take priority. But I renew the invitation; when you can come to Rome, please let me know, and we will get a few associates together for dinner. . .George, you really did a wonderful piece of work. Of course there were criticisms, in which I participated; to the degree that these caused pain, I am very sorry. However, on balance, the whole Sodepax enterprise, under your leadership, receives a very positive evaluation—from our Commission, from the Unity Secretariat and from myself.

Card. Maurice Roy, president of the Pontifical Commission Justice and Peace, wrote on November 6, 1971, expressing "deep gratitude and warm admiration for the manner in which you have filled your difficult role" and stating that "the overall evaluation after the first experimental period is strongly positive. . .And now we look forward to the second experimental period of three years. We will miss you. . ."

James Norris, a director of Catholic Relief Services, who as a lay auditor to Vatican Council II had astonished the assembled bishops by delivering a speech in Latin, wrote, "The effects of your work are being felt around the world, and it was obvious during the recent Synod that there is deep appreciation for the work of Sodepax which you so ably guided. . ."

Vittorino Veronese, intimate friend of Pope Paul VI, expressed similar sentiments, as did Baron Leon de Rosen, president of the European Association of Christian Businessmen. Fr. Pedro Arrupe, in a letter of September 30 authorizing me to accept Bishop Mamie's offer of my pied-à-terre in Le Pâquier, added, "The dedication and competency which you brought to your duties in Geneva have been a personal consolation to me and an honor to the Society."

All of these kudos, though addressed to me, were in fact an endorsement of Sodepax. Consequently, when an article in the August 15 issue of the *National Catholic Reporter* came tardily to my hands, I wrote a vigorous denial of its allegations that at the insistence of the Vatican I was to be removed against my will. I also corrected several other errors in the piece. My corrections were called into question in an interview published almost a year later, October 13, 1972, by the *National Catholic Reporter*, where Charles Elliott, although describing me as "a brilliant iconoclast, very much his own, not Rome's, man," opined that I had, under pressure from Rome not to rock the boat, done an about-face. This is not the case. The case quite simply is that in mid November 1971, I had no notion that Sodepax was in danger. Perhaps I would have defended the Vatican with less ardor had I known what was going on behind the scenes.

In fact, what was going on was a plot to emasculate Sodepax. Henri de Riedmatten's brag that he had warned Rome that Sodepax was becoming more important than the Justice and Peace commission was no idle boast. It had been heard and plans were being laid to make sure that the structure of Sodepax was so modified as to make this impossible in the future. My mistake was to have greatly underestimated the extent of de Riedmatten's influence in Rome.

I was aware that as Cardinal Benelli's man in Geneva he had considerable influence. I was also aware that he had served as secretary of the commission of experts which wrestled for four years on orders of Pope Paul VI with the problem of birth control. I had not realized that he was far more than a recording secretary. He had in fact been a member of the original six-man commission appointed by Pope John XXIII to advise him in the matter. As secretary of the far larger group, eventually numbering fifty-eight under Paul VI, he called and organized its meetings, often dictated its agenda, in certain cases named new members, wrote its reports, and throughout those four years hand-delivered those reports to both Paul VI and to Cardinal Ottaviani, the formidable head of the Congregation for the Doctrine of the Faith, formerly the Holy Office. This made him a familiar of all the cardinals who belonged to the Roman Curia and to many others outside the Curia. His influence in Rome reached far beyond anything I had imagined, and explains why even Cardinal Willebrands, although aware that he was a threat to both Sodepax and the ecumenical movement, was unable to do anything about it.[3]

In the months immediately following my departure, an increasing malaise took hold of the Sodepax staff. They were operating in a vacuum. Their mandate had expired. And still, despite repeated assurances that Rome intended to renew it, no affirmative action had been taken. No general secretary had been named. No one was in charge. In a letter of January 10, 1972, to Monsignor Gremillion, Dr. Kinhide Mushakoji complained sharply of the intolerable situation. Recalling the delay which had accompanied his own appointment to Sodepax, he observed that

> the bureaucratic inefficiency of the Curia is not new to me; but I must frankly say that as the only Roman Catholic staff of *Sodepax* since Father Dunne has retired, I have been more and more concerned about the terrible personal insecurity my colleagues experience because of this apparent lack of interest of my own Church in *Sodepax* or rather in ecumenical cooperation. I first tried to explain it, as I still try to believe it is, as a lack of bureaucratic efficiency, but this long delay does not easily allow such interpretation. Even if it was just inefficiency, I feel strongly that our brothers, my colleagues in *Sodepax* as well as the World Council, deserve some explanation or apology.[4]

Just a week before Mushakoji's letter, Vincent Cosmao, O.P., had written me: "it is evident that the Roman position is difficult to understand. Even Cardinal Willebrands, who is entirely devoted to Sodepax, told me that he is unable to understand the hesitancies of the Secretariat of State and of the Pope. It is in any case very sad to see paralyzed an initiative that was succeeding so well."

It is doubtful that Cardinal Willebrands was as ignorant of what was going on as these words suggest. He must have known that these "hesitancies" were due to a determination on the part of the Secretariat of State to clip the wings of Sodepax so that it could no longer fly. He had received a letter from Cardinal Villot which left little doubt that such was the intention. The "structure and way of working of Sodepax," wrote Villot, "were to be modified in such a way. . .that this organism of liaison could not become a third entity with a separate existence of its own."

This concern about Sodepax becoming a tertium quid—a third entity—was, as I have pointed out, a phony problem. Sodepax had never undertaken any program independently of or contrary to the wishes of either of its two constituent bodies; its structure precluded this. "The mission of Sodepax is not to relieve 'Justice and Peace' and the World Council of part of their responsibilities," continued Villot's letter, "but on the contrary to facilitate direct contact between the two partners each of whom operates in its own field of action."

Translated from the language peculiar to ecclesiastical doublespeak this means, "Do everything separately, but keep in close touch"; this was hardly in line with our maxim, "Do separately only what we cannot do together." This, as Dr. Mushakoji would presciently point out in his letter to Gremillion, would reduce Sodepax to the role of a switchboard.

"Sodepax will not assume the role of a representative of either of the constituent parties," again the words are Villot's, "nor will it act as their spokesman either to public opinion or international organizations or any other official body." The clear implication here is that Sodepax had been posing as spokesman for the parent bodies. I have pointed out how in the introduction to all of our publications I had taken pains to emphasize that we were in no sense speaking for either the Holy See or the World Council. The implication and the assumed need for corrective measures were both without foundation.

Both Cardinal Willebrands and Dr. Blake, unwittingly no doubt, had played into the hands of those who were hostile to Sodepax. In June 1971 they had cochaired a meeting of the Mixed Group in Stuttgart. I was unaware of this meeting, and was not informed of its results. I learned of it only when I received a copy of Villot's letter to Willebrands that was part of a packet of documents sent to me in January 1972 by a member of the Sodepax staff who felt that I should know what was happening. These documents shed light upon what was going on behind the scenes.

This meeting in Stuttgart had agreed to modifications in the Sodepax structure. And Cardinal Villot blandly shifted responsibility for his proposed restructuring to the Mixed Group: "This new form, *recommended by the Mixed Work Group* in its meeting of June 7 to 12 at Stuttgart, seems both opportune and necessary." (Italics added.)

That the evisceration proposed by Villot was not the same as the transmogrification envisaged at Stuttgart is indicated by Dr. Blake's reaction. He sent copies of Villot's letter to the two vice-presidents of the World Council and to several of his staff as well as to the Sodepax staff, one of whom, as I have said, sent it on to me; he also sent them his proposed reply and solicited their reactions. His reply accepted in general Villot's proposal but with several "assumptions" which amounted to modifications. Most important of these was the assumption that Sodepax would continue to supervise specific programs approved by both parent bodies. Another was that Sodepax would continue to publish the results of its consultations. These two assumptions could be interpreted as meaning that Sodepax would continue to operate as it had always operated.

The Secretariat of State was determined that if Sodepax continued it would not again overshadow the Pontifical Commission Justice and Peace. Dr. Blake, on the other hand, was unwilling that Sodepax continue as a mere switchboard through which the respective parties could keep each other informed. Three months of behind-the-scenes maneuvering ensued on both sides. This was the period of the intolerable situation which Dr. Mushakoji described in his letter to Gremillion.

Finally, in the last days of January 1972, a delegation consisting of Cardinal Willebrands, Bishop Torrella, Monsignor Gremillion, and Father Meeking arrived in Geneva to present what Gremillion said were "the maximum limits to which the Roman authorities would go." Roy Neehall took notes on the meeting with Dr. Blake and afterwards sent me a copy.

Apparently it had been previously agreed that the secretariat of Sodepax would be limited to a general secretary and his stenographer. The general secretary agreed upon was a Flemish priest, Joseph Spae, I.C.C.M., who after a brief missionary career in Mongolia had gone to Japan and during twenty-five years there had acquired a scholarly reputation by his studies in Buddhism and Shintoism.

The "maximum limits" now brought from Rome proposed to countermand this agreement. Instead Spae was to be appointed to the staff of the Pontifical Commission Justice and Peace with responsibility for collaboration with Sodepax and the World Council of Churches. There were to be no decision-making powers within the secretariat, which would be limited to an inspirational and liaison function—a kind of cheer-leader and messenger service! "Sodepax cannot go on the same way as before but can continue as an inspiration. . .The secretariat will keep the Sodepax dream alive, and will maintain a very small flame—the flame must be kept low and not turned up, with the possibility, in the future, of it becoming a larger flame"; thus Neehall summarized the tenor of the discussion.

At this point Cardinal Willebrands interjected, "To stop it completely would be a setback to ecumenical relations—keep the flame alive and after some time it may grow with more direct support and engagement on the part of Roman authorities." This was undoubtedly wishful thinking on the part of Willebrands. Only four months before he had described Sodepax as "a sign and a hope" and as "an ecumenical realization representing the best structure of collaboration in matters of international justice, development, and peace between the World Council and the Catholic Church. . ." Now he was being obliged by Roman authorities to preside at its evisceration. It must have been a painful experience.

In reaction to Gremillion's proposals Lucas Vischer, head of the Faith and Order division of the World Council, pointedly observed that this was not a renewal of Sodepax but something quite different, the effect of which was paralytic. Dr. Blake put up a feeble resistance which restored the agreement that Father Spae would be named general secretary, to which was added that he would be joined by an associate secretary.

Why did Blake not put up more of a fight? In the *National Catholic Reporter* interview which I cited above, Charles Elliott expressed a theory with which I agree: "Blake's great ambition is to have Rome join the WCC and although he did fight for Sodepax, he didn't want a major row on this issue if it might jeopardize his ambition to have Rome join the council—though there's no sign whatsoever that Rome will, in fact, join any time soon."

Immediately following this graveside ritual, the officers met with the Sodepax staff to break the news. The minutes of the meeting held on January 28 read like a scenario for a minicomedy: "The co-chairmen expressed gratitude to the staff for maintaining the central services of Sodepax during the past four months, and assured the staff of their continuing support."

The staff was then asked "to draft a short communique for public release stressing the element of hope and that the continuation of Sodepax in its new form will stimulate greater collaboration between the two parent bodies in matters pertaining to development, justice and peace. . ."

Then, having just assured them of their continuing support and ordered the preparation of an optimistic press release, they informed the staff that, with the exception of Brother Christophe, they were all fired. Christophe was retained as associate to Father Spae.

Roy Neehall was offered a job by Dr. Blake in CCPD as liaison with the Catholic Church in matters of development, justice, and peace. He accepted this for some months, but then returned to the Caribbean, where he became secretary general of the newly established Caribbean Council of Churches.

Charles Elliott was to "move as soon as may be convenient to him. . .to Norwich, England, to direct the *Poverty 2000* Research Programme." In the final negotiations Rome had refused to continue this as a Sodepax program. CPPD had agreed to take over its financing and sponsorship. Elliott did establish himself with his research staff at Norwich. Poverty 2000 was published several years later.

The press release expressing hope that the new form of Sodepax would "stimulate greater collaboration" became a set piece in the charade: Sodepax had not been diminished, but given a form which would make it work better. The other set piece was the statement, made with a straight face, that first the delay in coming to a decision and then the changes made in the structure of Sodepax had been due to financial problems. Monsignor Gremillion appears to have been the first to give currency to this canard. He was cited by Religious News Service in a release of February 2, 1972, as authority for the statement that "the agency was having difficulty trying to find sufficient funds for its work."

The truth of the matter was quite different: during the three months following the Nemi meeting the staff had put together a detailed three-year program to realize the general goals of *The New Vision*, the prospectus for the next three years. Largely through the efforts of Father Schütte, the funding for about eighty percent of this program had already been assured, chiefly from Catholic and Protestant German sources. From soundings taken of other sources, we were fully confident that the balance of our financial support would be forthcoming. The financing of Sodepax was not one of our worries when I left at the end of September. The program and staff were not cut because of budgetary limitations—as would repeatedly be implied. On the contrary, the budget was cut—from something under $400,000 to something under $70,000—in order to scuttle the program and decimate the staff. In none of the documents recording the Rome or Geneva discussions about Sodepax—copies of which, as I mentioned above, were sent to me—is finance mentioned as a problem.

The press was not fooled. The same Religious News Service press release mentioned above cites an unnamed "Vatican official" as saying that "conservatives in the Vatican and elsewhere, who never did approve the joint effort, are trying to use the lack of finances to sink Sodepax. . .There are some theological objections to the agency. . .they feel that they would rather the Catholic Church and the non-Catholic Churches paddle their own canoes in these dangerous streams [of development and peace]."

It quotes another "Vatican official closely associated with Sodepax" as saying: "I can tell you that just a few days ago the future of Sodepax looked pretty dim." A realistic appraisal would be that it had no future, a fact widely recorded in the world press.[5]

The most detailed and accurate analysis of what had happened was published by the International Documentation Center (IDOC) in Rome.[6] Following an eight-page summary of the history of Sodepax it concluded:

> The story of Sodepax over the first three years of its existence is but a reflection of the contemporary evolution of the Catholic Church. The days of Pope John XXIII, of the Vatican Council, are far behind us. Ecumenism still exists, but it has been canalized. Sodepax was a reality, "a unique instrument of collaboration," but it has been canalized as well. Instead of dynamism and an ongoing process of experimentation, Sodepax has to content itself with a rhythm that is imposed by the pace of higher authorities. Instead of the search for new styles and methods of work, it has to narrow itself in the old patterns of the institutional churches. It is not a third entity any more; perhaps it never was. It has lost its substance. The Sodepax experiment worked. It was an unique instrument of ecumenical collaboration; an instrument that was not static but an ongoing process. Sodepax aimed in its beginning at the highest church authorities, policy makers and experts. According to needs, it became more and more involved in the reality of its grassroots. The status of Sodepax was ambivalent from its beginnings. On the one hand it depended on the two parent bodies from which it derived its great impact. On the other hand it functioned and appeared as a separate unit. The crisis of Sodepax is a crisis of identification. The churches could not follow the dynamic, perhaps prophetic, pace of Sodepax, hence they could not recognize themselves in it. Sodepax does not exist anymore as a separate unit. . .Sodepax was reduced to a reference agency. One speaks in our days of the stand-still of renewal in the churches and one frequently hears the words "consolidation" and "normalization." The end of the Sodepax happening might well be the most significant example of "normalization" to date.

The article revealed an insider's familiarity with the story of Sodepax. And some assumed that I was the source. In a letter of April 16 to Dr. Blake, I made the following points:

1. I have expressed no opinions on the subject and supplied no information to the *IDOC*, the *London Observer*, or any other publication, communications media, or reporter.
2. Neither *IDOC* nor any other news service, publication, or reporter has been in touch with me nor I with them.
3. I first learned of the *IDOC* publication when I read about it in *La Liberté*, a small Fribourg daily newspaper which is my only regular contact with the "outside world."
4. I have since seen the *IDOC* report which in my judgment is a substantially accurate presentation of the facts and a fair, even restrained, evaluation of the same—but it is a report with which I had nothing to do.
5. I first learned of the *London Observer* story on the occasion of my last trip to Geneva. I am told that Frère Christophe, displaying deductive powers which I never suspected in him, identified me as the author because, describing what had been done to Sodepax, the story used the word "torpedoed," a word which I had recently employed in a brief note to Father Spae wishing him well in his efforts to refloat Sodepax. Assuming, as I think we may, that neither Father Spae nor Frère Christophe himself is the author of the article in question, I am afraid we must conclude that the word "torpedoed" so aptly describes what was done to Sodepax that it quite naturally suggested itself to the author as it had to me.[7]

Dr. Blake replied May 2 and denied responsibility for the rumors: "It never occurred to me to hold you responsible for the stories which appeared in *IDOC* and the *London Observer*. . .I agree with you that the *IDOC* publication was on the whole factual, although at the end some judgments were given which should not be given in a documentary service." It is worthy of notice that he did not take issue with the conclusions, but only with their appropriateness to a documentary service.

On February 10, 1972, Dr. Mushakoji wrote:

I am sending you some interesting documents about the end of the affair. These are CONFIDENTIAL. I am sending them not to ask you to publicize the case, because I think that even if we are at the end of a heroic period, there are people who will have to take up the burden after us and we should not make their job even more difficult than it is going to be, without the complication which may be caused by divulging the truth. I did hear, however, that you were planning to make a news release and also write a book for Father Cosmao, and I think it is preferable to give you this material so that you could base your declaration on good evidence. . .It is not a good thing to hide this crisis behind a facade, so I hope you will make a constructive rather than a destructive intervention.[8]

Father Cosmao had, indeed, written me just a week before: "The bad news which reaches me about *Sodepax* confirms my idea that it is absolutely necessary to do a thorough study and an evaluation of everything that has happened since the beginning. I continue to think that you are best qualified to make such a study, for which the Lebret Center [of which he was the director] is prepared to seek funding. . ."[9]

I did not intend to write a book for the reason suggested by Mushakoji himself. I did not want to make things more difficult for Father Spae. Had it not been for this I would have accepted Father Cosmao's proposition. Today Mushakoji's reservations do not hold. Sodepax no longer exists. I am thoroughly convinced that the long-range interests of the Church are not served by concealing the truth much less pandering to untruth. Yet this was what was being done and continued to be done by spokesmen for both of the constituent bodies.

Even Cardinal Willebrands joined the charade. In his report *Ecumenism in 1972* he mentioned that "many had the impression that the reduction of both personnel and budget reflected a decline in ecumenical collaboration itself." On the contrary, he wrote, "both reductions are due to the fact that the liaison character of Sodepax is now more strongly emphasized." Proof of this was supposed to be found in the fact that both he and Dr. Blake—for Rome and Geneva—would in the future favor meetings of Sodepax with their presence! Willebrands, desperately anxious to keep the now small flame flickering, may perhaps be excused this manifest manipulation of the truth.

What remained of Sodepax was, as Mushakoji had aptly labeled it, a facade, behind which was no more substance than in a Hollywood motion picture set. That facade sufficed to create an image. There is a mind-set in the Roman Curia to which the image, rather than the substance, is what imports. It would be unfair to say that it is not interested in peace or justice; but it is fair to say that it is more interested in assuring that the Church, and more precisely the Holy Father, is seen as interested. So with Sodepax. The substance had been destroyed, the facade or image had been retained. If someone wondered at the failure to join forces in the promotion of justice and peace, one could point to the image, as to a Hollywood set, and say: "But we do act together! There is Sodepax!" As real as Potemkin's palaces.

Sodepax had been effectively laid to rest. Sometime later Henri de Riedmatten was named a member of the Mixed Group to make sure that Sodepax did not like Lazarus come forth from the grave. He would see to it that there would not be another Sodepax.

In a gracious letter to me of February 23, 1972, Archbishop Benelli closed the chapter:

> Reverend Father,
> At the moment when the functions which you have exercised for the last three years at the head of the secretariat of *Sodepax* are being confided to Father Spae, the Holy Father has charged me to express to you his paternal gratitude for the services which you have rendered, with devotion and tact, to the work of ecumenical collaboration for the promotion of justice, development and peace.
> In this first experience of cooperation between the World Council of Churches and the Pontifical Commission Justice and Peace, you have known how to create, together with your collaborators, the climate of confidence and of dialogue which makes it possible today to prolong the enterprise.
> In joining myself to the testimony which the Holy Father insists upon giving you through my mediation—and of which the Pontifical medal accompanying this letter—is a visible sign, I beg you to accept with the assurance of my best wishes and my prayers, the expression of my respectful and devoted sentiments in Our Lord.

I was tempted to return the medal, but thought better of it. Instead I replied under date of March 17, 1972, expressing my gratitude to the Holy Father for the testimony he had rendered me and for the medal. I also thanked Benelli for his gracious words, but added:

> I regret that during the nearly four years that I have held this position I did not have direct contact with Your Excellency which might have given me the opportunity to communicate

frankly to you my views, formed in the experience of daily ecumenical collaboration, about the activities, the program, the structure and the future of Sodepax.

I do not conceal from Your Excellency that I have been very disappointed in the restructuring to which Sodepax has recently been subjected and that I do not understand what motives could have inspired these measures of reduction which, it seems to me, can with difficulty be reconciled with the positive conclusions of the evaluation made by the Pontifical Commission Justice and Peace and submitted to the Secretariat of State in March, 1971, and with the eulogy of His Eminence Cardinal Willebrands who, in a discourse pronounced at Rome on September 23, 1971, in qualifying the results accomplished as "astonishing," designated Sodepax as "a sign and a hope of Christian engagement for the promotion of social justice, development and peace in the service of the entire human family" and insisted that "its ecumenical character was authentic and efficacious."

Permit me to say in all frankness, and I trust you will not hold this to my blame, that had I had the occasion to advise Your Excellency and the Cardinal Secretary of State in the affair of Sodepax, the decisions taken would have been quite different. This in no way detracts from my personal gratitude for the kindness of your letter of February 23. Please accept, Excellency, my religious and respectful sentiments and the assurance of my high esteem.[10]

I expressed myself with less restraint in a letter of February 17, 1972, written to J. Ruiz-Gimenez, ambassador of Spain to the Holy See, who had been a participant in our Baden conference on peace.[11] He had offered, through Canon Moerman, to raise the question of Sodepax in his next scheduled audience with the pope. After narrating the events of the last several months and assuring him that he was free to make whatever use of the letter he wished, including showing it to the pope himself, I concluded: "Whether the Pope knows or does not know what his closest collaborators are doing, in either case I find this history crushing, scandalous and shameful. It is to betray at once the cause of peace, of development and of ecumenism, to which the Pope never tires of declaring his devotion." Obviously not the language of one seeking ecclesiastical advancement. I do not know whether Señor Ruiz-Gimenez showed the letter to Paul VI; probably not. He, unlike me, was a diplomat.

End of the affair, or almost. Father Spae carried on through his term. Upon his retirement he was succeeded by a brilliant young American Jesuit, Fr. John Lucal, S.J., one of the original Quiz Kids of radio fame. He kept the small flame flickering until it was finally blown out on December 31, 1980.

It had almost been snuffed out at the beginning of John Paul II's pontificate. Benelli was no longer in the Secretariat of State, but had been made archbishop of Florence. Gremillion had resigned and returned to the United States. He was succeeded by a French Jesuit, Roger Heckel, S.J., theretofore director of *Action Populaire* in Paris; en route to Rome he phoned me from Geneva and quizzed me about Sodepax. As secretary general of the Pontifical Commission Justice and Peace he is said to have "confined himself to a careful analysis of the Pope's teaching as an expression of the ongoing 'social doctrine' of the Church."[12] He was rewarded by the pope by being named bishop of Strasbourg but did not long survive his surprising ascension to the episcopal throne.

Heckel had not been interested in keeping the small flame of Sodepax alive. Early on he recommended to John Paul II that its demise be made official. John Paul II was persuaded, probably by Cardinal Willebrands, that to do this at the very outset of his pontificate would make a bad impression ecumenically. With the end of 1980 and the completion of Lucal's mandate, it was evidently felt that the frail structure could be dismantled without causing any ripples. So without fanfare the end was announced. Father Lucal left the Sodepax offices for the last time, bade good-by to the World Council of Churches, and moved into the International Labor Offices, where he succeeded Fr. Josef Joblin, S.J., retiring after twenty-five years as the representative of the Roman Catholic Church. Proving that they do not believe the maxim that you cannot fool all of the people all of the time, "Vatican spokespersons," according to Peter Hebblethwaite writing in the *National Catholic Reporter*, "explain that this does not mean the end of international ecumenical cooperation. On the contrary, new forms of collaboration are being studied."

A decade earlier the emasculation of Sodepax did not mean a weakening but, on the contrary, a strengthening. Now the final destruction of the facade that, like the famous front of the sixteenth-century Church of Saint Paul in Macao, had survived the shock of earthquake does not mean, as innocent people like you and I might think, an end but, on the contrary, a beginning. Doublespeak has replaced Latin as the lingua franca of the Church.

On the occasion of the first devastation, a cousin of mine, Finley Peter Dunne, Jr., whose father authored the famous

"Dooley Letters" and who himself, as secretary of The Temple of Understanding in Washington, D.C., is much experienced in the quest for peace, wrote me a thoughtful analysis of what happened to Sodepax:

> It seems to me that the history of *Sodepax* is a classic example of what often happens in great organizations such as Mother Church and the World Council. When a vibrant, new organism is introduced, and begins to score success after success a kind of rejection mechanism comes into play, as in the case of a transplanted heart or kidney. *Sodepax* is neither a part of the Church nor a bureau of the Council. Because it belongs to both, it therefore belongs to neither. If it generally fails in its programs, it may be forgiven but if it enjoys too great a success which it cannot completely share with the Church and Council, it becomes intolerable. This is particularly true when the spotlight of public applause shines on it, and other agencies turn to it directly for the help and counsel they need as has been the case with *Sodepax*.
>
> I am not inclined to attribute this rejection to human weakness as much as I would to the nature of human organization in which people do not act as much from personal motivations as from organizational motivations; and I think this is just as true in General Motors as it is in the Russian Government and in Church and Council.
>
> But there is something else. You know what *Sodepax* was able to accomplish and others also know it. More important is that it did accomplish so much in its short history and that it has opened up new portals of thought and new understanding in many places. . .

True enough, Peter; but we also know, and the thought haunts us through the years, all that remained to be done and could have been done had Sodepax been permitted to realize its potentials.

My former associate, Dr. Charles Elliott, has read this chapter and, in a letter of November 20, 1987, makes a criticism which, if I read it rightly, is not far different from that of Peter Dunne:

> I certainly warmly welcome an authoritative account from the inside of the sad history of *Sodepax*. . .It's splendid. If I have one reservation, I would put it like this: I think maybe you put too much emphasis on the personal failings of some of the key actors. . .and insufficient emphasis on the *structural* difficulties that *Sodepax* encountered. . .[13]

The criticism is no doubt justified. I have mentioned structures, but less so than individuals. One reason is that quite frankly I do not understand what seems an excessive concern with them. I have already stated that I never understood the repeated concern that Sodepax might become a tertium quid. In fact it was a tertium quid, but entirely subservient to its parent bodies. As long as it was helping to move those parent bodies closer, it was doing what it was supposed to do. So we thought.

Not everyone thought as we did. As the Religious News Service of February 2, 1972, had remarked, "There are some [who] would rather the Catholic Church and the non-Catholic Churches paddle their own canoes." In the end, preferring structures to substance, they prevailed.

I once asked a well known economist what caused inflation. His succinct reply: "People." If I were asked what caused the death of Sodepax, I would likely say: "People."

Twenty

Le Pâquier

The tiny village of Le Pâquier lies at the foot of Mt. Moléson, the highest peak in this part of Switzerland, which is to say in the prefecture of Gruyère. A short kilometer up a fairly steep road—a grade of twelve percent—is the convent of Carmel, since 1936 home to a community of discalced Carmelite nuns. The nearest town, consisting of some eight thousand people, is Bulle, five kilometers away. Thirty-two kilometers northeast is the city of Fribourg. One hundred and ten kilometers to the southwest is Geneva.

I first visited Le Pâquier in August 1971, at the invitation of Bp. Pierre Mamie of Fribourg, to meet the *mère prieure* or, as we say in English, the prioress. We met in the visitors' parlor, separated by a grille. Since Vatican II the severe rule of the Carmelites has been considerably relaxed, more in some convents than in others.

Here the grille remains, but the curtain is gone that would earlier have covered it. You can see the nun with whom you are conversing, which in former days was not the case. I recall the first time I gave a conference to a community of Carmelite nuns; it was in their convent in Santa Clara, California. The nuns were protected by a grille and concealed behind a curtain. It was an odd experience, somewhat like talking to a wall. This impression was, on the other hand, belied by the giggles from behind the curtain which constantly punctuated my remarks. I was surprised by this, because the subject of my talk—the intellectual apostolate in China—was, I thought, quite serious. I began to think I was the funniest fellow alive. The Carmelites are great gigglers. To any comic whose jokes are falling flat I recommend, as a confidence restorer, bringing one's act to a Carmelite convent.

The current prioress, Mother Marie Thérèse, was quite pleasant. My duties as chaplain would be minimal. They consisted in saying daily Mass, to which on Sundays, when a dozen or more people from nearby farms attended, I would be expected to add a modest homily. It would be quite a change from the busy life I had been leading for some years and would, I thought, leave me plenty of time for writing. It was just what I was looking for.

At this time there were twenty-six nuns in the convent, two of them novices and three of them *tourières*. The latter, in English known as "outside sisters," are not cloistered. They receive visitors, do the shopping, see that the chaplain is fed, take care of the chapel, and in general manage those things which cannot be handled by those behind cloistered walls. Of the twenty-six nuns then at Le Pâquier two were of French origin, two of Swiss-German origin, and the remainder of Swiss-French origin. The language of the house was French.

The prioress and I agreed that I would report for duty on November 1. I did not on the occasion of this visit inspect the chaplain's quarters. The priest whom I was to replace was in poor health and was resting, and I did not wish to disturb him. I expected the quarters to be modest and had no need to verify this. When I took over in November I found that this was indeed the case. The quarters consisted of a tiny bedroom, a bathroom, and a workroom or office from the window of which I looked out upon a picture-postcard scene.

A mile across the valley, crowning a hill which put it on the same level as me, was the Chateau Gruyère, standing against a backdrop of soaring mountain peaks. The Chateau Gruyère, dating from the eleventh century, was long the home of the Comtes de Gruyère, whose rule during a considerable part of the Middle Ages extended over much of the area between Lausanne and Fribourg. It is the second most famous Chateau in Switzerland and a major tourist attraction. Only the Chateau of Chilon is a greater tourist attraction; this is where the prisoner hymned in Byron's famous poem, a Benedictine abbot who had gone over to the Protestant side, was chained for years to a dungeon pillar.

I moved to Le Pâquier in November and, as I pointed out to the still extant Sodepax staff on the occasion of my first visit to Geneva, soon gave evidence of what a great loss in intelligence Sodepax had suffered with my retirement. I had brought with me my Fiat. The weather was windy, wintry, and colder than usual at this time of the year. There being no garage at the convent I was obliged to leave the car outside. I had a plastic cover to throw over the car, but was concerned that this was insufficient cover to protect the motor from freezing. Sr. Marie Gabrielle, one of the *tourières*, found in the attic several old, unusable rugs. These I carefully piled on the hood, weighting them down with a half dozen large rocks. Every time I left I painstakingly removed rocks, rugs, and plastic cover and upon return as painstakingly replaced them. I had been following this procedure for two weeks when, while driving down to the town of Bulle one day, a question suddenly appeared from nowhere, "Why are you taking such tender care of the baggage compartment?" In my vintage 1969 Fiat the motor was in the rear, the baggage compartment in front under the hood! The next year the Carmelites obligingly had a garage built to house my Fiat.

Until February 1972, as I have indicated, I was very much involved in the Sodepax enterprise in Northern Ireland, so I was often absent from Le Pâquier. Happily this did not inconvenience the Carmelites. The Canton of Fribourg, in which Le Pâquier is located, is one of the predominantly Catholic cantons of Switzerland, and there were a number of priests in the Gruyère area who stood ready at any time to say Mass in my stead for the Carmelites.

With the effective demise of Sodepax and the end of my Irish connection in February, I turned my attention to writing. Fr. William J. Byron, S.J., who was then president of the University of Scranton and is now president of the Catholic University of America, had asked me to write one of a series of paperbacks, *Topics in Moral Argument*, to be published by Paulist Press. I wrote a booklet, *The Right to Development*, which was published in 1974 as one of the series. I fondly dedicated it

To the Sodepixies
of
Happy Memory
for
Happy Memories.

Sodepixies was an affectionate tag for the associates and secretaries who had composed the late Sodepax staff.

My writing career was not of long duration. Not long after I had sent the manuscript of *The Right to Development* off to Bill Byron, I received a phone call from Georgetown University in Washington. Fr. Harold Bradley, S.J., who held the job that had once been mine, assistant to the president for international programs, was on the line. He wanted to discuss with me the possibility of my taking over the direction of Georgetown University's junior-year-abroad program at the University of Fribourg. I agreed to meet him in Fribourg a few days hence to talk about it.

Georgetown University had for many years maintained a program in Fribourg. Each year a number of students spent their junior year following courses at the University of Fribourg for which they received credit at Georgetown. The University of Fribourg did not maintain student housing facilities. There were, however, several privately operated student hostels in the city, most of them conducted by religious orders. The Georgetown students were housed in one of these, or rather, since Georgetown had recently become coeducational, in two of these. The boys were housed in Regina Mundi, which they shared with Marianist theological students from several countries. The girls were in another hostel, conducted by nuns.

Normally a Georgetown Jesuit would accompany the group to Fribourg. In the current year this had not been possible, so a young American Marianist student of theology had been put in charge. This had not worked out. The young Marianist was but a year or two older than the Georgetown students. He had difficulty persuading the boys to accommodate themselves to the rules of the house. Europeans have the curious idea that night is a time for sleep or study and therefore for quiet, contrary to the idea of American students that night is a time not for sleep, perhaps for study, but certainly for laughter and libation. Things had got a bit out of hand, and the superior of Regina Mundi had made it clear that in the future he would not accept any students from Georgetown.

Father Bradley had turned to me for help. He flew over from Washington, and we met at Regina Mundi. He wanted me to move into Fribourg and take charge. This I was unwilling to do. I thought I could handle the students without being visibly present in their midst seven days a week. I agreed to take over direction of the program upon condition that I remain in Le Pâquier, commuting to Fribourg two days each week. Meanwhile I had met with the superior of Regina Mundi and argued in favor of a second chance. He relented to the extent of agreeing to accept a maximum of six Georgetown students on a trial basis.

Father Bradley agreed to my conditions, and I took over the job of directing the Georgetown program. I took a room at Regina Mundi which served as my office. The number of students for whom I was responsible was not great, varying from a low of nine to a high of twenty-six, more girls than boys. But there was much to do.

First of all, there was the matter of housing. In time I was able to house all the students either in apartments of their own or with families, which was ideal from the point of view of language proficiency. I had been warned by pessimists that it would be impossible to find Swiss families willing to accept an American student. I found that it was possible, but not easy. Swiss families are understandably reluctant to disrupt the lifestyle which is theirs. American students are often reluctant to abandon the lifestyle to which they have been accustomed and to adapt themselves to the less tempestuous lifestyle of their hosts. But at the cost of much time and effort I found that, with occasional failures, the twain could meet.

The students arrived a month before the beginning of the winter semester. The intervening weeks were devoted to an orientation program. Before being accepted for the program they all had to pass written and oral language exams. Georgetown was pretty good at this, and no student ever arrived totally unprepared, as was sometimes the case in other programs. On the other hand, few arrived fully prepared to understand without difficulty lectures on economic, historical, philosophical, or whatever subjects, where the language of instruction was either French or German. Consequently the orientation program was designed to accustom the ear to the assault that would be loosed upon it the first day in class.

Beyond this my chief duties were as counselor, to advise them about the courses they should take; as registrar, to register them in the courses selected; as dean, to arrange with each of their professors to give them exams and grades at the end of the semester (European universities do not as a rule give semester exams or grades); as Georgetown's liaison, to transmit their grade sheets to Washington; as campus minister—spiritual father in the old days—to offer a shoulder to cry on; as prefect of discipline, to present a stern mien to the unruly. I seldom had to play the last role. One of my early discoveries was that the youth of today, contrary to the popular theme, are no worse, and in some ways probably better, than the youth of my and earlier generations. Perhaps the Georgetown students sent to me were the cream of the crop. In any case, I remember them with great affection and respect. They extended my youth.

From the above summary one may easily and correctly conclude that the two-day-a-week limit which I had made a condition of my employment was quickly breached. During the thirteen years that followed I averaged probably four to five days a week in Fribourg. In two of those years I took courses myself at the university, one in international money exchange—always a mystery to me—given by Prof. Gaston Gaudard, former *recteur magnifique* of the university; the other in international law—to see what changes had occurred since I had studied it at the University of Chicago more than forty years before under the renowned Dr. Quincy Wright—given by a future *recteur magnifique*, Prof. Augustin Macheret.

With so much of my time claimed by the Georgetown program I was unable to accomplish the writing I had hoped to do. I did manage to do the piece on Charlie Chaplin which I have already described. Two other articles, "Development—A Christian Concern?" and "Development—A Critique,"[1] had unforeseen consequences. Mr. Louis C. Fischer read them and wondered what he could do.

Horizons for Justice

Lou Fischer had been a football star at Ohio State and later played with the Baltimore Colts. With two of his Baltimore teammates, Alan ("the Horse") Ameche and Gino Marchetti, he established a chain of steak houses which made him a millionaire well before the age of forty. A retreat experience with the Spiritual Exercises of Saint Ignatius had kindled a fire and a desire to invest in treasures that do not rust.

Together with his business partners, he had already established a generous scholarship fund for black students at Saint Joseph's Prep in Philadelphia. He had also made a substantial contribution to the Gregorian University. Now he wanted to know what he could do about poverty in the underdeveloped world. He communicated with the provincial of the Jesuit Maryland Province and asked if he could meet with me to discuss possibilities. I first learned of his interest from Fr. Tony Zeits, S.J., an occasional golf partner when I was at Georgetown University and now the treasurer of the Maryland Province. This was followed by a letter from the provincial, Fr. James L. Connor, S.J., asking me to come to Baltimore armed with ideas for a meeting with Lou Fischer.

I had met Jim Connor while still with Sodepax. The chance meeting was in the Jesuit Curia in Rome and was a bit embarrassing for me though flattering to him. Struck by his youthful appearance I asked him if he were a scholastic and felt obliged to apologize for my imperceptiveness upon learning that he was Father Provincial of the Maryland Province.

For the meeting with Lou Fischer I prepared a concrete "proposal of aid to the third world." It was based upon several verifiable assumptions. The first was that "the most effective way to help the third world is to arouse public opinion at home to an awareness of the problem of underdevelopment and to quicken the public conscience to a sense of moral responsibility." Another was that, while experts had answers to the problem, lacking was the political will to put those answers to work. I cited in support Dr. Jan Tinbergen, Nobel Prize winner in economics and cochairman of the Sodepax Beirut conference and chairman of the United Nations Development Committee.

"The reason political will is lacking," I argued, "is that there is no strong pressure upon policy makers from an enlightened public opinion. . .To generate political will one must begin by forming public opinion. The task is therefore primarily one of education for justice."

I proposed to begin by educating the educators, and first of all Jesuits, who, regardless of the specific nature of their work, are primarily educators. Education is not limited to schools and classrooms. The reason I limited my proposal to the education of Jesuits was financial. "In the measure that increased funds make possible enlarging the program to include non-Jesuit educators, so much the better."

That Jesuits stood in need of education in the subject was, if my experience and observation could be trusted, beyond dispute. I recalled Fr. Art Falvey, S.J., who was regarded by many of his confreres as an oddball—and so he was—because of his stubborn determination to make the social encyclicals part of the learning experience of his students at Loyola High School in Los Angeles. I remembered when the offer of Fr. Wilfred Parsons, S.J., former editor of *America*, to teach a course in the social encyclicals at Georgetown University was politely refused because a place for it could not be found in the curriculum. And of course I had not forgotten the Jovian decree hurled by Zach Maher from his Olympian retreat in Poughkeepsie in reaction to my Alma retreat in 1943 that "social subjects have no place in the Spiritual Exercises of Saint Ignatius."

Most important of the assumptions upon which my proposal was based was "that the most effective way to educate the educator is to give him a living experience. It is one thing to read about poverty or to be told about it by a lecturer on development. It is quite another thing to see with one's own eyes the misery of the *favelas* of Rio or the slums of Lima and to listen to those personally affected." This was a conclusion drawn from my experience with the Peace Corps.

My proposal was that from each of the ten Jesuit provinces in the United States ten men be selected each summer to be sent in groups of twenty each to five underdeveloped countries for a six- to eight-week field experience. The countries suggested were Nicaragua, the Dominican Republic, Peru, Chile, and Mexico.

"In each of these countries," the proposal stated, "there is a Jesuit Center for Social Research, Training and Action which will be asked to organize and administer the program. The program will be designed to give participants the maximum possible exposure to the reality of poverty and of underdevelopment and the opportunity to hear what the people themselves, the poor, students, intellectuals, businessmen, labor leaders, think about the problem."

Included in the program would be as many weeks as possible actually living and working with poor families. In short, I envisaged it as a kind of mini-Peace Corps experience which in the space of ten years would profoundly affect the thinking of one thousand Jesuits, firing them with concern for the problems of underdevelopment and making each of them, whether in the classroom, the pulpit, the retreat director's desk, or wherever, an apostle of justice. That was my romantic imagination on the loose. Yet it did not seem unreal. "To educate the educators," I wrote, "has a radiating effect which cannot be matched merely by introducing a course on development into a college curriculum."

I told Fr. Harold Bradley, who chanced to be in Fribourg, about the demarche from Baltimore and outlined the proposal I intended to make. To my surprise, he informed me that while a member of the faculty of St. Louis University prior to coming to Georgetown he had organized substantially the same kind of program in Honduras for a group of St. Louis students. This conversation took place while I was driving him to Geneva, where he was booked for his return flight to Washington. He promised to send me photocopies of the evaluations written by participants in the program after their return to the States. These gave strong evidentiary support to the effectiveness of the kind of program I had in mind. I added excerpts from their evaluations to the proposal which I had prepared for presentation in Baltimore.

I flew to Washington in early April 1973. My ideas were presented, scrutinized, discussed, and debated at three major meetings. The day after my arrival I met with the Jesuit Conference staff, then an eight-man administrative group for the American provincials, enlarged for the occasion by the inclusion of Harold Bradley, Bill Ryan of the Center of Concern, Frank Ivern from Rome, and Jim Connor. I then flew to Boston to present my proposals to the mission and the formation directors of all the American provinces, who were meeting at the Weston Theological Center. A third meeting would follow in Baltimore.

Because I wore civilian clothes and a beret, which I was accustomed to wear in lieu of a hat, I was surprised when a young man, who identified himself as a Jesuit scholastic from Weston, picked me out of the throng heading for the bus depot at Logan Airport in Boston. I asked how he spotted me. He said that Fr. Jim Collins, who had phoned from Baltimore to ask him to meet me, had told him to watch for a man with grey hair who walked with a limp! That I walked with a limp was news to me, but watching my reflection in store windows I confirmed that it was true. Evidently the ligament in my thigh which had been torn in my tumble into the "wine cellar" in Fenffe, Belgium, had shortened the stride of my left leg, giving me a limp of which I had been unaware. To be identified as "the grey-haired man with a limp" made me feel like the title of a paperback spy story.

An incident peripheral to the main event but interesting to me occurred during the two days I spent at Weston. It was the discovery that twenty-eight years after the event the myth of my supposed dramatic defiance of the rector in St. Louis was still current. With this younger generation of Jesuits, however, it made me a kind of legendary hero. I wondered what dimensions my "heroic deed" would have assumed had I, as I had been tempted to do, dumped the contents of the soup tureen on the rector's head.

The meeting with Lou Fischer took place the following weekend at the provincial's residence in Baltimore. Besides Lou, Jim Connor, and myself, the participants were Tony Zeits, Jim Collins, and Hugh Kennedy of the provincial's staff and Bill Ryan and Peter Henriot of the Center of Concern. From Friday evening through Sunday morning we engaged in a wide-ranging discussion about the problem of underdevelopment and what should and could be done about it. Following another meeting with Bob Mitchell and Jim Connor, I returned to Switzerland, leaving further promotion of the program to them. On May 2, Jim Connor presented my proposed program to the American provincials gathered in Syracuse for their regular meeting. In a letter of May 22 he reported to me that "the Provincials accepted this proposal unanimously as their own and thereby took it on as an Assistancy-wide project."

Subsequently Harold Bradley was named as director and organizer, and coordinators were appointed in each province. The first Horizons for Justice group assembled at Georgetown University for a five-day orientation. The number of participants had been reduced to forty-four, the number of countries to four: Honduras, Peru, Mexico, and Nicaragua. The budget was established at $78,048, to which Lou Fischer made a substantial contribution. Lou also joined as a participant, becoming the eighth member of the group assigned to Peru. One of the eight was Fr. Donald Merrifield, president of Loyola Marymount University in Los Angeles. The policy established by the planning committee was to limit the program to Jesuits who had completed their formation and to encourage participation by administrators.

I came from Switzerland, at Harold Bradley's invitation, to take part in the orientation and to launch the first Horizons program. I was back again in August to join them in a debriefing session which followed their return from Latin America. For this we convened in a retreat house near Chicago. As the participants exchanged experiences over a period of several days and made plans to maintain contact in the future and to keep alive the flame that had been enkindled, it was plain to me that this initial experiment had produced the results we had hoped for. Without exception they had been deeply affected by their face-to-face confrontation with the third world. Whether the effects of their consciousness-raising would be permanent only time would tell.

In the course of the next few years evidence reached me more than once that the positive effects endured. In one case I learned through a news story that one of the participants played a leading role in a third world conference at Notre Dame and that in his remarks he credited his Horizons of Justice experience with opening his mind to a reality he had not hitherto perceived.

As I drove to St. Paul with Harold Bradley to attend a large-scale conference of mission directors at Saint Thomas College, I looked to the future of Horizons of Justice with great expectations.

San Francisco Symposium

The spring and summer of 1973 had been a busy time for me. Besides preparing for the 1973–74 Georgetown University program at Fribourg and the rather pressurized activities required in promoting and developing Horizons for Justice, I had a paper to prepare. Fr. Al Zabala, S.J., of the University of San Francisco, had asked me to present a paper at a week-long symposium on Ignatian spirituality and reform, which was scheduled for July 1973 as part of the summer school program. My paper was to be "The Missionary in China—Past, Present and Future." In its preparation I did considerable research, reading among other things the published works of Mao Tse-tung. I also wrote to Fr. Laszlo Ladany, S.J., in Hong Kong, who, as I remarked in my letter, "undoubtedly knows more about what is really going on behind the hermetically sealed Bamboo Curtain than anyone else." I asked him if he would share with me whatever thoughts he had on the subject of my paper.

Father Ladany had established a well-earned reputation as the most knowledgeable "China-watcher" in the world. A Hungarian Jesuit who, after nine years in the mission in the north of China, had been expelled by the triumphant Communist regime, he had established a listening- and watching-post in Hong Kong to keep track of what transpired in the country of his adoption. Reading every issue of the Ren Min Pao—the *People's Daily*—the official newspaper published in Peking, listening to the daily newscasts emanating not only from the capital but from regional radio stations as well, interviewing refugees as they fled to Hong Kong from the mainland, he regularly published his findings in a small periodical called *China News Analysis*. Probably every foreign office in the world and anyone concerned to know what was happening in China subscribed to his invaluable information sheet.

The events which were happening, particularly during the first decade of Communist rule, were shocking in the extreme. The degree of human suffering cannot be fully measured. Ladany came as close as anyone could to doing so. But in the process his own judgment, in my opinion, was affected. His mobilization of facts and usually his analysis were without fault. But occasionally, or so it seemed to me, his close-up view of communism as an unmitigated evil prevented him from making a dispassionate judgment.

His reply to my letter seemed implicitly to admit as much. He told me that he had been invited by Zabala to comment upon my paper at the San Francisco symposium. Although he did not say whether he intended to accept the invitation, I inferred that in any case he would not be sharing his views with me. He then went on to say:

> My trouble is that I am too close to the China scene, did not miss a page of the *People's Daily* since 1950 and meet too many people whose families are not particularly happy inside; and read their letters. Thus I find it difficult to share the joyful optimism, that is universal today; visitors saying that they know that everybody is happy, all love the Chairman [Mao Tse-tung], and all are better off than twenty years ago. My stubborn determination has always been to stand on the side of the people and not of the rulers; particularly those rulers who barred the way to others to enter Heaven (as the Lord said) and may find it difficult to enter themselves. . .

The paper I prepared for San Francisco was published by the World Lutheran Federation in Geneva and later in the year it appeared in the *Ampleforth Journal*. Meantime it stirred up a hornets' nest among the Jesuits in Taiwan. I was unaware of this until my arrival in California. Here I found awaiting me a letter from the provincial transmitting to me a letter from Fr. Michael Chu Li-teh, S.J., the provincial of the China Province in Taiwan, addressed to Father Zabala with a copy to him. His letter stated that my paper had been

> the subject of much discussion throughout our Province; unfortunately all of it adverse. Because the paper is not historically factual, is based on immature impressions and complete misinformation and misunderstanding of the FACTS of the Mao domination of the mainland of China, and an utterly unrealistic UTOPIAN view of the future, most of those who discussed the paper thought that because of its unfairness, the inaccuracies, and the ignorance on these matters of his audience, that we should suggest to you that the paper not be accepted by the Symposium committee.

After this rather sweeping and all-embracing condemnation of the paper, Father Chu, fearful that it was already too late to eliminate my paper from the symposium, made two alternative proposals:

So, we would request that in fairness to the subject matter, that you permit us to present another side of the picture in a paper which would be distributed with and published with Fr. Dunne's paper.

Further, in the interests of the Symposium itself we suggest that this paper be not the first on the program [it had been so listed on the printed program] but the last, so as not to devaluate the prestige of the Symposium.

Accompanying the letter were four criticisms of my paper prepared by Frs. James Thornton and Charles McCarthy (I had preached at their departure ceremony when they left California for China twenty-five years earlier), Father Ladany, whom I have already identified, and Fr. George Germain, who had been rector of the Aurora University in Shanghai during my years at Zikawei and until now a good friend. His was the longest of the critiques, running to twenty-nine pages, and the most severe, although none of the four fell short in that respect.

I was surprised not at their negative reaction but at its ferocity. They suffered from what I call the Taiwan syndrome: a deeply rooted bitterness, an absolute refusal to believe anything but the worst, a foreclosure against considering it possible that the Communist regime would perdure, an unwavering faith in an ultimate return to the mainland under the banners of the Kuomintang, and a feeling of betrayal by anyone who did not share these views. It is very similar to the mentality of White Russian exiles who found refuge in Paris and other metropolitan centers after the Bolshevik Revolution of 1917. I could empathize, but not agree.

I had not intended to read my paper at the symposium—it was much too long for that—but to read a précis of it. Now, confronted with this onslaught, I decided instead to discuss the criticisms, the authors of which, I argued, were "so convinced of the unmitigated evil of Mao Tse-tung and all his works that they read into anything short of unmitigated condemnation, whole-hearted approbation. Not to condemn is to canonize."

After examining the criticisms I summed up my position:

There is little likelihood that the Communist or Maoist system will disappear. If that is true, there is no future for the Church in China except by establishing a modus vivendi with that system. An examination of the record reveals evidence, however slight, that this possibility is not to be peremptorily dismissed. We should, therefore, be alert to every positive sign and ready to pursue every lead that points in the direction of rapprochement. It may be necessary to accept radical transformation of ecclesiastical structures and of methods of apostolate. However much we may nostalgically regret the disappearance of old and familiar forms we must not despair of finding new ways to carry the Good News to China.

In a word, I refuse to slam the door upon hope. If the door is to be slammed, let it be by them, not by us. And if they, as I am reminded by several of my critics, are moved by hatred, the appropriate Christian response is not hatred in return, but love. If this makes me sound naive, I am sorry, because it seems to me that love is the only thing that Christianity has to offer. If it cannot offer that, it has no future in China or indeed anywhere else.[2]

Two Jesuits came from Taiwan to respond to my paper. Fr. Yves Raguin, S.J., well qualified both as sinologist and philosopher, delivered a measured critique which I found unexceptionable. Unlike the critics I cited above, he seemed to have read my paper and, while having reservations about certain points, to have understood it. Fr. Michael Chu, S.J., the provincial of the China Province, was the other respondent. His observations were quite moderate and lacking entirely the anathematizing tenor of his letter of March 13 to Father Zabala demanding that my paper be excluded.

An amusing incident occurred during Father Chu's remarks. The background is this: Father Wei Tsing-hsin is a Chinese priest and historian long resident in Paris. He has written extensively on the history of relations between the Holy See and China. He had sent a copy of my article, which had been published by the World Lutheran Federation well before the San Francisco symposium, to Bp. Carlo van Melckebeke. The bishop, long of Mongolia and, since his expulsion by the Communists, Apostolic Visitor to the Chinese of the diaspora, was resident in Singapore. On March 13, 1973, the bishop wrote me: "I must tell you that in my opinion you have done an excellent work, objective, clairvoyant, sufficiently optimist. I agree with every paragraph of your text."

And he added an interesting observation: "Of the three men of the Vatican [apostolic delegates] in China, only the first, Costantini, was up to the measure of his task. The other two were *gaffeurs*—blunderers."[3]

I was astonished, to say the least, when, in the course of his remarks, Father Chu quoted from a letter he had received from

Bishop van Melckebeke deploring my criticism; he had told me he agreed with every paragraph of it! My only comment to the audience was that I felt as though I were at the Watergate hearings, which were in progress at the time, where truth was bandied about like a shuttlecock. I do not know what engendered this rather bizarre action on the part of the bishop. I had not solicited his support. In fact I did not know him, nor had ever heard of him until I received his unsolicited letter. Perhaps it was just his idea of being all things to all people. Or perhaps it was simply an idiosyncracy of old age, for the bishop was as old then as I am now.

Before, during, and after the session Fr. Jack Clifford, a California Jesuit, distributed mimeographed copies of Father Ladany's answer to my paper. For some reason this struck me as having a comic aspect, as though he had mounted a one-man counterdemonstration. I did not object. If anyone had a right to protest against Mao and all his works it was Jack Clifford, who had spent several years in a Chinese Communist prison subjected to interminable interrogations to which he never yielded an inch.

The unrelenting and uncompromising nature of his hatred—there is no other word for it—of communism is understandable. The same can be said of my other Jesuit critics in Taiwan. They, as he, had suffered in their flesh and in the flesh of their beloved Chinese friends and converts. That is impossible to forget. But sooner or later, if there is to be any future, the harsh edges of recollection have to be touched with forgiveness.

Cagayan de Oro

One Sunday in 1974, speaking to the Carmelite nuns at Mass through the grille which stood between us, I asked, "Would you pay $2,000 to hear me give a conference?" There was a general shaking of heads. "$1,500? $1,000? $500? $100? $50?" Each query brought the same negative response until I had reached the lowest offer: "Ten francs (less than two dollars then)?" The general shaking of heads had become unanimous.

The occasion of this jocular exchange had been an invitation I had received from Fr. Tom Matheson, S.J., to fly all the way to Cagayan de Oro in Mindanao, the Philippines, to read a paper at a three-day seminar he was organizing to convene December 6-9. The travel expenses of such a trip would amount to around $2,000, which I thought an outlandish price to pay for a single conference, the nuns obviously agreeing with me. (Since recently reading in the newspaper that Donald Regan, former chief of staff to Reagan's White House is charging, and getting, $20,000 for a single lecture, I have had second thoughts.)

Father Matheson was a Jesuit of singular achievement. Originally a member of the New York Province, he had been many years in the Philippines and was now a member of that province, where he had served as president of the Ateneo de Manila University. After that he had established near Cagayan de Oro in Mindanao, the largest of the islands, a school of agronomy of a unique sort. Here, young men and women from all over Asia were taught the most recent developments in agricultural productivity as well as leadership skills. They then returned to their own lands to organize village and countryside for development.

Father Matheson had been awarded the Magsaysay Prize for 1974. This was an award of $10,000 conferred annually upon the person adjudged to have made an outstanding contribution to the good of society. It had been established in honor of Ramon Magsaysay, the capable and popular president of the Philippines, whose tragic death in an airplane crash preluded all the woes which have followed including those of the Marcos dictatorship. Father Matheson used the prize money to finance a symposium on development. My paper was to be, at his request, on development and peace. I tried to persuade him, with the testimony of the nuns in support, that nothing I had to say was worth two thousand dollars. He refused to be persuaded, and so the advent of December saw me en route to Cagayan de Oro by way of Manila.

The symposium was interesting, the hospitality of Father Matheson, his faculty and students most enjoyable. A high point of the week was a typical Philippine dinner featuring a whole barbecued pig.

Whether Father Matheson felt that, in my case, the money was well spent, I do not know. My paper may have made him somewhat nervous. The dictatorship of Ferdinand Marcos was already installed. There was considerable bitterness because of his failure to implement the promised land reform. The beginnings of the armed rebellion, which has grown into the major problem with which Pres. Corazon Aquino is today confronted, had already broken surface. Among the participants at the symposium were several army officers. Revolution was one of the subjects which I discussed at some length. "If it is impossible to imagine Christ, gun in hand, urging his followers to man the barricades or to storm city hall," I said, "it is not difficult to imagine him, like Amos, thundering fierce warnings to the perpetrators of injustice: 'You serpents!. . .impostors!. . .You snakes and sons of snakes! How do you expect to escape from being condemned to hell?'" (Matthew 23)

It is unlikely that the army officers were pleased.

Twenty-one

China Revisited

C hina had been hermetically sealed for a quarter of a century. In the mid 1970s the first small signs of relaxation began to appear. A small number of foreigners were given a tour of a half dozen major cities under the guidance and control of the official government travel agency, the Liu Hsing She, which guidebooks commonly call CITS—the China International Travel Service. Among those who had successfully organized such a group was Fr. Al Stevenson, S.J., of the Jesuit California Province. Al had spent some years in Taiwan but had left there, out of sync with what I have called the Taiwan syndrome. He was as aware as others of the magnitude of the tragedy in China but preferred to look to the future rather than to brood over the past. After a stint in the Philippines and another as staff artist on *Jesuit Missions* magazine in New York, he joined the faculty of the University of San Francisco. When I heard that he was to lead another group to China in the summer of 1975, I wrote asking if I might join them.

Al was encouraging. He told me to send my curriculum vitae and passport, which he would submit together with those of the other applicants to the Chinese Embassy in Canada. In 1975 the United States still had no diplomatic relations with China, so one had to go to Ottawa for approval. I sent off a curriculum vitae. Although I thought it might militate against acceptance, I stated frankly that I was a Catholic priest, a Jesuit, and that I had spent four years in the Jesuit community at Zikawei. I had no desire to visit China under false pretenses.

I need not have worried. Although both Mao Tze-tung and the Gang of Four were still alive and in the saddle, major changes had already begun in the thought processes of Chinese officialdom. In due course I received word from Al that my application had been approved. The passports, however, had not yet been returned. Mine would be returned to me when I joined the group in Tokyo. The United States Embassy in Bern furnished me with a temporary passport without which I could not have got out of Switzerland or into Japan.

Sometime in July 1975—I have forgotten the exact date—I flew out of Geneva to Bangkok, where I spent several days with my old friend and colleague, Paul O'Brien, S.J., at the time superior of the Jesuits in Thailand. From there I flew via Korea Airlines to Seoul, where I stayed with my cousin, Fr. Michael Bransfield, M.M. From Seoul I flew to Tokyo, where I again enjoyed the hospitality of the Jesuit community at Sophia University.

In Tokyo I was joined by Father Stevenson and his group from San Francisco. They numbered some two dozen, all but four or five young graduates of the University of San Francisco. To our mutual surprise, it turned out that one of the less young, a graduate of the law school, had known me during the Hollywood strike days. She had been an active member of the Office Employees Union, belonging to the Conference of Studio Unions. She had been one of the hundreds arrested on the picket lines, hauled off to jail and charged with disturbing the peace. After the collapse of the CSU, she told me, she had worked for Robert Hutchins in Santa Barbara, on the staff of his Center for the Study of Democratic Institutions. It was he who had urged her to take up the study of law. We had much to reminisce about. From Tokyo we flew via CAAC, the Chinese national airline, to Peking.

Back in 1936, when I boarded the *Chichibu Maru* in Shanghai, I had promised myself that the first thing I would do upon my return to China would be to kneel down and kiss the soil. It never entered my mind that thirty-nine years would elapse before I set foot in China again. I had not forgotten the promise; but now, after so long a time and with all that had happened, the gesture was no longer appropriate. It would have been a meaningless act of grandstanding, especially since I was not here to stay. I filed it away with other unrealized dreams.

Night had fallen when we landed at Peking. We were met at the airport by the three guide-interpreters, two friendly and intelligent young men and an equally intelligent and charming young woman; they were to accompany us throughout our three-week tour of China. All three spoke English quite fluently and were skilled interpreters. They loaded us into buses and delivered us to the

Peace Hotel, where rooms had been reserved for us; this put us within easy walking distance of the great T'ian-an-men Square. My roommate was Paul Steidl-Meier, S.J., the third Jesuit in the group. Here and throughout the tour I said Mass each morning in my hotel room.

The Cultural Revolution had not yet ended but was in its second, or *p'i kung p'i lin*—criticize Confucius and Lin Piao—phase. The extreme violence which had cost thousands, perhaps hundreds of thousands, of lives and inflicted inestimable damage had wound down. The Red Guards, who were responsible for most of it, had been reined in. Nevertheless, I was surprised at the degree of freedom we enjoyed. The activities and the itinerary were scheduled for every day and were explained to us following our arrival at the Peace Hotel. We were naturally expected to accompany our guides on the scheduled round of visits to communes, schools, department stores, factories, etc., but this was not insisted upon. In fact, the schedule included a half day in which we were left to our own devices.

I was particularly interested in visiting the Immaculate Conception church or Nan Tang (south church). This church, the original of which had been built in the seventeenth century by Fr. Adam Schall, S.J., the famed Jesuit who had become a mandarin of the first class and director of the Imperial Bureau of Astronomy, was the only Catholic church still open in the whole of China. The advent of the Cultural Revolution had brought with it the complete suppression of religious activities of any kind. Not only Christian churches, Catholic and Protestant, but Buddhist, Taoist, and Confucian temples were closed by the Red Guards and damaged and desecrated as well. Alone excepted from this otherwise universal holocaust was the Nan Tang in Peking, and this at the insistence of European embassies, who demanded that their Roman Catholic staff members not be denied the opportunity to assist at Mass.

From my hotel window I spotted in the distance what unmistakably resembled a Church steeple. Not being familiar with Peking I thought this might be the Nan Tang. Very early one morning, long before the breakfast hour, I set out to see. It was a walk of perhaps forty-five minutes. It had obviously been a Catholic church, but it clearly was not the Nan Tang. The gate was heavily padlocked, and the church itself stood forlorn and neglected in the midst of unkempt grounds. The neighboring building, apparently once parochial property, perhaps a school, was occupied by the Romanian Embassy.

I resolved to devote a day, if necessary, to the search for the Nan Tang. Consequently, on the day scheduled for a visit to the Ming Tombs and the Great Wall, I told the head guide that I preferred to wander about Peking. Somewhat to my surprise, he raised no objection. Al Stevenson marked on the map the general area in which the Nan Tang was located, and after the others had set off by bus for the Great Wall I set out on foot west along Chang-an avenue, passing T'ian-an-men, the entrance to the Forbidden City, and then turning south at Xuan-wumen-wai, the first north-south thoroughfare I came to. I had gone perhaps two miles when fifty or so yards to my left I saw projecting above the surrounding roof tops what was without a doubt a church steeple.

This was indeed the Nan Tang, where on April 25, 1644, Adam Schall watched the Ch'ung-chen emperor, last of the Ming dynasty, ride by on horseback, fleeing from the hordes of Li Tzu-ch'eng who were pouring through the south gate, opened to them by the traitorous eunuch Ts'ao Hua-ch'un, who commanded this section of the city's defenses. Arrived back at his palace, the emperor ordered his empress to hang herself, his three sons to hide, and, to save her from falling into the hands of Li's soldiery, attempted to slay his daughter, who, warding off the saber blow, lost a hand and fled. The distraught emperor then climbed Mei Shan (Coal Hill) and hanged himself, bringing to an end the last genuine Chinese dynasty (1368–1644). The Ch'ing dynasty, which followed, was Manchu.

Before the end of May the combined forces of a Ming general, Wu San-kuei, and the Manchus inflicted a series of crushing defeats upon Li Tzu-ch'eng and his army of 200,000 men. Li fled, leaving in the capital a rear guard which fired the imperial palaces. From here Schall heard the roof of the Audience Hall crash in ruins as the flames destroyed its magnificent supporting columns:

> Many in the neighborhood took refuge in Schall's residence. Firebrands were hurled in from the street, incendiary arrows fired into the roof. Hot ashes and burning embers poured down. But the vigilance of the refugees saved the residence while everything else in the area was being devoured. A mob. . .tried to break into the mission compound. Schall seized a huge Japanese sword and planted himself inside the gate. The sight of this sturdy figure, made more impressive by a luxuriant beard which, wrote Schall, not without a certain note of satisfaction, would have sufficed to supply the whole mob with whiskers, unnerved the would-be looters who abandoned the attack.[1]

The scene passed before my eyes as I stood in this same gateway, looking at the priests' residence beyond a large and well tended courtyard and garden. To the right was the porter's lodge and beyond, the historic Nan Tang. Neither the rectory nor the church, to be sure, is the original building. This church dates from the late nineteenth century, its predecessor having been destroyed by fire.

The lodge was tended by an elderly Chinese to whom I identified myself. After thirty-nine years of disuse my Chinese was in a sorry state but not in utter ruin. I was still able to carry on an ordinary conversation. He confirmed that this was the Nan Tang. I asked about the attendance at Sunday Mass. He said that most of those who came were foreigners, but that a certain number were Chinese, Catholics like himself. According to him there were thirteen priests in the residence. When I asked if I might meet one of them, he replied that at the moment all were absent. I suspected that the priests were wary of receiving any foreigner unless he was armed with an authorization by the civil authorities and that the porter was instructed accordingly.

With the coming to power in 1950 of the Communist regime the practice of religion was subjected to severe trial, but not suppressed. All foreign bishops and priests were expelled from the country, many of them after imprisonment of from one to five years. Schools, hospitals, and other religious institutions were expropriated. Chou En-lai, the prime minister, announced that as a condition of survival both Protestant and Catholic churches must make themselves independent of foreign control in matters of finance, governance, and ministry, the so-called policy of Triple Autonomy. The structure of the Protestant churches presented no insuperable obstacle to the acceptance of these conditions. On the part of the Catholics, their ties to the papacy raised a serious question in the matter of governance; but at a meeting with Catholic leaders Chou En-lai stated that he was aware that they had a special tie to the pope, which they could maintain. Because of this many were of the opinion that the mandated policy was acceptable. Others, however, thought that this was but the first step in a move that would end in complete control of the Church. They appealed to Rome for a decision. Pius XII, through his representative in China, Abp. Antonio Riberi, informed the Church in China that the Triple Autonomy proposal was unacceptable.

The papal decision resulted in a serious division. A large majority of Catholics, both clergy and laity, obeyed the pope; Rome having spoken, the case was closed. A relatively small minority, however, including some priests and a few bishops, chose to accept Chou En-lai's conditions. These were permitted to continue to practice their faith. They formed what was called the Catholic Patriotic Association. The others, those who chose loyalty to the pope, for the most part refused to attend a Mass celebrated by a Patriotic Association priest. Many of them, including priests and bishops, were imprisoned.

The division was sealed in 1958. Most of the dioceses in China had been without a bishop for many years, all of the foreign bishops having been expelled long since. In 1958, following election by the clergy, Bishop Li Tao-nan of Puchi consecrated Fr. Tung Kuang-ch'ing, O.F.M., bishop of Hankow and Fr. Yuan Wen-hua bishop of Wuchang. The Holy Father had been notified by cable in the hope that he would sanction this procedure. There was clear precedent: in earlier ages bishops were chosen sometimes by the clergy, sometimes by the people, as in the case of St. Ambrose; even today the clergy of the diocese of Basle in Switzerland retain the privilege of electing their bishop. But the reaction of Pius XII dashed the hope that this process might prove acceptable in China. On June 29 he published an encyclical announcing that all three—Li, Tung, and Yuan—and any others who might resort to the same procedure were ipso facto excommunicated. A decree of the Holy Office (now the Congregation for the Doctrine of the Faith) of April 9, 1951, probably having in mind the situation in China, had decreed excommunication for any bishop who would confer and for those who would receive the episcopacy without authorization of the Roman Pontiff. I am told, however, that in the China case the participants fully expected to have in hand the sanction of the pope before proceeding with the consecration. I have also been told that following this they wrote a thirty-page letter in Latin to the pope explaining the situation and setting forth the reasons which, in their judgment, made such action imperative if the Church in China were to survive, but that they received no answer. I cannot verify either of these statements.

In any case this confirmed the division of China's Catholics, perhaps four million in number, into those who, affiliating with the Patriotic Association, were permitted to practice their faith and those who, refusing to do so, were denied this right and were often, especially in the case of the clergy, sentenced to long terms of imprisonment.

This remained the situation until 1966, when the fury of the Cultural Revolution spared neither "patriot" nor "loyalist." Every church in China, as I have said, was closed by the Red Guards, with the single exception of the Nan Tang, whose priests, perhaps thirteen in number, although affiliated with the Patriotic Association, were the only Catholic priests in the whole of China still allowed by the regime of Mao Tse-tung to celebrate the liturgy.

My genial interlocutor, the elderly porter in the gatekeeper's lodge, was an affiliate of the Patriotic Association. He was also, or so it seemed to me from our fairly extended conversation, no less a Catholic than I was. After giving him my card and asking him to deliver it to the vicar general, who, he had told me, was the pastor of the Nan Tang, I entered the church. It was immaculately kept and obviously in use. It was typical of the style before Vatican II— the main altar against the back wall, a statue of Jesus of the Sacred Heart on one side altar and of the Immaculate Virgin on the other, flowers on all three. The red glow of the sanctuary lamp, suspended from the ceiling, announced the Eucharistic presence in the tabernacle. Confessionals stood on both sides. Nothing had changed in the last twenty-five years. Neither the Communist triumph nor the Cultural Revolution nor Vatican Council II had made any visible mark here.

When I emerged from the church I found a younger porter on duty. The older man had finished his shift and gone home. His replacement was no less friendly. He too was affiliated with the Catholic Patriotic Association. And he too sounded no less Roman Catholic than his predecessor. I had the impression that the position of the pope in the ecclesiastical structure and their obligation as Catholics to profess loyalty to him is not something they deny, but something from which, because of the force of political circumstances, they for the moment prescind.

After taking leave of the Nan Tang, with all its historical memories, I worked my way back to the hotel through narrow residential side streets. I frequently stopped to chat with children at play and with adults squatting on their front doorstep. In no case did I encounter hostility, fear, or a reluctance to talk. I would discover in the course of our tour that this was so everywhere we went. From what I had been told by some who had been in China a few years earlier, this represented a change of considerable proportions. Although the Cultural Revolution had not yet been officially terminated, the Red Guards had been, as it were, returned to their barracks. Word had got about that foreigners were no longer to be regarded as *mo kuei*—foreign devils.

Chinese have often been described as a withdrawn, reserved people. Nothing is farther from the truth. They are by nature extroverts. It is true that finding themselves in a foreign environment which they, often with reason, sense to be a hostile environment, the Chinese will withdraw into themselves. This is a protective tactic which has given birth to the myth of the "inscrutable oriental." Actually, when free to be themselves, the Chinese are the most curious, interested, and friendly of people. During my China years, whenever I appeared on the balcony of our theologate at Zikawei to get a breath of air, within minutes a group of people would be gathered on the narrow strip of roadway that skirted the canal outside our walls, staring up at me. Their smiling faces evidenced not hostility but curiosity. Zikawei began where the tram from downtown Shanghai ended. Whenever I went downtown I took a book along to read. Second class was always crowded, standing room only. Soon I would find a chin resting on my shoulder. My neighbor was trying to see what I was reading. Again, not hostility or rudeness, but curiosity and friendly interest. This is a Chinese trait in which they are quite different from the Japanese.

Because I had known the pre-Mao China, I was frequently asked by my tour companions what changes I noted. I honestly had not noted any great changes. The man-drawn rickshaws were gone, replaced by pedicabs. That was an improvement. Everyone, male or female, dressed exactly alike—in blue or grey Mao-style cap, jacket, and trousers. The result was a general drabness throughout the city. That was not an improvement.

I was not familiar with Peking before communism and so was not qualified to make comparisons. However, I had read Simon Ley's complaint that much of the beauty of Peking had been destroyed in the demolition of the great city wall. That this was so I could easily believe. Although in his writings he encouraged respect for the cultural values of China's past, Mao's deeds often ran counter to his words. The campaign against the "four olds," featured in the Cultural Revolution, made many of the treasured legacies targets of its destructive fury. The ancient wall was destroyed with the idea of making Peking a modern city. The few broad avenues such as Ch'ang-an and modern buildings did not compensate aesthetically for the ancient city wall. Here and there a segment has been left standing.

As we were leaving Peking en route to the airport I suddenly spotted on top of one such segment a half dozen or more of the astronomical instruments which had been constructed in the seventeenth century by the Jesuits Adam Schall, Ferdinand Verbiest, and others for the Imperial Astronomical Observatory. There was no mistaking their identity. I had often seen photographs and illustrations of them. Fortunately, the destructive urge had not reached the Forbidden City. These extraordinarily beautiful imperial palaces, although in need of refurbishing after years of neglect, were still intact and visited daily by thousands of Chinese tourists who looked with awe, as did we, upon these magnificent monuments to China's imperial past. In one of them, now used as an exhibit hall for Chinese paintings, I made a surprising and, to me as a Jesuit, especially moving discovery.

Among the Jesuits who in the eighteenth century made their mark in China was Br. Giuseppe Castiglione, an artist of considerable talent; his Chinese name was Lang Shih-ning. It was he who introduced the notion of perspective, hitherto unknown in Chinese art. He became an artist attached to the imperial court. As I moved along examining the paintings I suddenly came upon one of the works of Brother Castiglione. Although he was especially renowned for his paintings of horses and—by order of the emperor—of dozens of imperial concubines, this was a beautiful still life of flowers. The card attached to it, as to all the exhibits, correctly identified him under his Chinese name. I excitedly called it to the attention of the woman from CITS, the government agency, who was in charge of the Peking phase of our tour. I had the impression that she was not unfamiliar with his name. I have recently been told by Fr. Jerry Martinson, S.J., director of the Kuangchi television center in Taipei, that every Chinese boy and girl in Taiwan who has been to high school is familiar with Castiglione's name and with that of Matteo Ricci, known as Li Ma-t'ou. They have read about them in their history books.

The summer palace of the notorious Empress Dowager Tzu-hsi, overlooking a lovely lake with a famous marble boat, had lost little of its beauty. A tree-lined pathway leads to the reception hall where on New Year's Day thousands of silken-clad mandarins of every rank approached on their knees to pay homage to Tzu-hsi; she would be seated upon the imperial throne which she had usurped from her nephew, whom she had imprisoned and later assassinated. So it was when I was born. Today it is very different. Instead of silk-gowned mandarins, the day we were there the pathway was crowded with thousands of ordinary Chinese, families on holiday, enjoying the imperial heritage which now was theirs. Among them were many Red Army soldiers on leave and, surprisingly, George Bush, newly appointed United States liaison to Peking, and his family.

One of the unexpected features of our visit to Peking was a guided tour of the astonishing air-raid shelter which runs for miles fifty feet or more beneath the surface of Peking. In one of the busiest sections of the city we entered what appeared to be an ordinary store where customers were examining bolts of cloth exhibited for sale. A button was pushed. The floor behind one of the counters receded into the wall, revealing a flight of stairs down which we descended into a well lighted tunnel below. For the next hour or more we were led through a labyrinth of tunnels, all paved and walled with brick. From time to time the winding tunnel opened into large areas designed to serve as storerooms, showers, infirmaries, and ventilators.

It is difficult to judge the full extent of this maze of tunnels, but we must have walked at least a mile. We were assured, and it was easy to believe, that ten thousand people could be accommodated in this shelter. We were also told that practice drills had demonstrated that all the people on the always-crowded street could enter this shelter by many entrances in five to six minutes. We were informed that similar shelters lie beneath a large part of Peking's surface and beneath the surface of other major cities. I recalled the reams of plans, the oceans of ink, and the welter of words about building air-raid shelters in the United States. This shelter had been constructed since 1969, with few words and much sweat.

We concluded our tour with a question-and-answer session in a large conference room, a part of the underground system. What emerged clearly from the comments was that it was the Soviet Union which was seen as the potential enemy and against which this defensive system has been built. Our Chinese hosts, in reference to the Korean War and to Vietnam, never hesitated to speak, quite candidly and in a matter-of-fact way, about American aggression and American imperialism. If the United States was not mentioned in connection with these preparations for defense, it was not out of a desire to spare the sensibilities of their American guests. It was rather because at that time the danger was seen to lie with the colossus to the north.

Our last night in Peking we had dinner in a restaurant whose specialty was Peking duck. Our host, Yueh Fei-heng, was the head of CITS. He was a tall, solidly built, handsome man of middle age. Before moving into the dining room we sipped tea and chatted with our genial host. He had evidently familiarized himself with the autobiographical sketch which I had submitted and knew who and what I was, for in the course of the conversation he suddenly looked directly at me and, smiling, remarked: "I understand that one of you lived in China before liberation. I welcome him back and trust that he will be pleased by the many changes he will undoubtedly notice."

I thanked him, recalled the traditional friendship which had existed between the Chinese and American people, regretted the rupture in relations which had divided us for twenty-five years, and expressed the hope that the welcome extended to us signified a rebirth of the ancient ties.

As is customary on such occasions and as ordinary courtesy requires, I ignored some pages of history in these remarks. The traditional friendship was indeed a fact, but it had on occasion been seriously blemished. I said nothing about the treatment accorded the thousands of Chinese laborers who helped build the first transcontinental railroad or the anti-Chinese riots in San Francisco in the nineteenth century, which most Americans but few Chinese have forgotten. I remember my first year in China in the city of Hsuchou, north of Nanking, together with Paul O'Brien, engaging two schoolboys in a conversation in which they challenged us about the San Francisco riots. I had forgotten them, or more probably had never heard about them. Neither did I mention the Boxer Rebellion of the nineteenth century, the siege of the foreign embassies in Peking, and the retaliatory looting and burning of imperial palaces by American and European soldiery. This was obviously not the time or place to invoke old grievances on either side, but to express new hope.

After this exchange of courtesies we moved to the dining room, where we enjoyed a delicious dinner of which Peking duck was the *pièce de résistance*. I should say that throughout the tour the meals we enjoyed supported the reputation of Chinese cuisine as one of the two or three best in the world.

The following morning we climbed aboard a CAAC DC-3 for the flight to Sian far to the west. At midday we landed at an isolated airport for lunch. It was really no more than an unpaved airstrip with a small lunchroom to serve China Airways passengers. I was reminded of my voyage as a child from Chicago to Los Angeles via the Santa Fe Railroad and of the Harvey Houses at which the train would stop long enough to allow the passengers to take a hasty meal.

Sian ("City of Western Peace," also known as Ch'ang-an, "Perpetual Peace") was the capital of China at the time of the T'ang dynasty (618–907), China's golden age. It was also for many centuries the terminus of the caravan trails from central Asia. It was here that the Jesuit brother Bento de Goes ended his remarkable two-year voyage with such a caravan in 1607, confirming Matteo Ricci's opinion, hotly disputed in Europe, that China and Marco Polo's Cathay were one and the same.

Every morning of our stay in Sian I left the hotel early in the morning, long before the breakfast hour, to wander through the streets. The Chinese are early risers. Here, as in Peking and later in Nanking, Shanghai, Canton, and Kweilin, seated with them on the curbstone, walking with them in the streets, I found them always ready and friendly conversationalists. Often I asked, "How are things today compared to the situation before liberation?"

I always received the same answer, "Much better."

When I asked in what way they were better, I always received substantially the same reply, "Today we have enough food to eat, clothes to wear, a roof over our heads, and a job."

One morning I fell in with two neatly dressed little girls on their way to school. They were neither embarrassed nor intimidated but laughingly invited me to accompany them to school; I did. There were some forty children, aged six to seven, already gathered in what appeared to be a preschool or kindergarten. My sudden appearance with my new-found little friends provoked much excitement among the children. Their two young women teachers welcomed me warmly as though I had been expected. Soon they had the children entertaining me with an improvised program of song and dance. It was a memorable experience and lives on as a heart-warming memory.

For me as a Jesuit, the highlight of the four or five days we spent in Sian was a visit to a museum containing the Forest of Steles, 1,095 stone monuments, some engraved with classic texts, most with Buddhist or Taoist texts. I was moving down row after row of these commemorative monuments, none of which particularly interested me; then, as I had stumbled upon the painting of Brother Castiglione in Peking, so now I suddenly found myself looking at the famous Nestorian monument of Sian, the discovery of which in 1624 was one of the most notable in the annals of archeology and one which added to the by no means meager stock of anti-Jesuit legends prevalent in certain European circles.

During the course of excavations in the subprefecture of Chowchih, some forty miles to the southwest of Sian, a monument was uncovered in 1625. This stele had been erected on February 4, 781. One of its inscriptions, carved in the stone, was a beautiful specimen of T'ang calligraphy; another was in Syriac. Although this was not immediately perceived, it revealed for the first time that Nestorian Christianity had entered China under the T'ang in the seventh century, that it had received the patronage of several emperors, and that it had enjoyed a period of considerable prosperity. Nestorian Christians took their name from Nestorius, the fifth-century bishop of Constantinople, who after a theological controversy was exiled to the East; his followers spread their version of Christianity into Asia.

The monument aroused great interest among the Chinese, who hold antiquities in the highest honor, and was brought to Sian by order of the prefect of the city. Scholars flocked to see it, but none was able to understand the meaning of the inscription. Probably the first Christian to see it was Chang Keng, a native of Fukien then living in Shansi. An old friend of Matteo Ricci, he had been baptized in 1621 by the Jesuit Giulio Aleni. Chang, suspecting that the inscription related to Christianity, made a copy and sent it to Li Chih-tsao, another of the late Father Ricci's scholar friends in Hangchow.

Li tells the story: "I was living in the country near Ling-chu when my friend Chang Keng of Chiyang had the goodness to send me a copy of the monument of the T'ang, saying: 'Recently in excavating at Changan it was discovered. It has for a title *Monument Eulogizing the Propagation in the Middle Kingdom of the Illustrious Religion.* One has not hitherto heard of this religion. Is it the same as the holy religion which Ricci came from the extremities of the Occident to preach?'"

Li and the Jesuits in Hangchow had no difficulty in recognizing that the "illustrious religion" was indeed Christianity. Although replete with nebulous phrases, obscured by expressions of Taoist and Buddhist tincture, the inscription contained clear references to many Christian doctrines. According to the inscription, a mission headed by the monk O-lo-pen had in 635 by the special favor of the reigning monarch made a "public and glorious" entrance to the capital; there was no doubt that was a Christian mission.

It could hardly have entered the minds of Li Chih-tsao or of the Jesuits that it had been a Nestorian mission, Nestorianism having long before faded into obscurity in Europe. They naturally tended at first to identify the "illustrious religion" of the monument with "the holy religion which Ricci came to preach." Nevertheless, they did not lose their critical sense. One must admire the scrupulously honest and scholarly caution with which they handled the subject. In their reports they made no extravagant claims.

One of the Jesuits, Manoel Dias, writing on March 1, 1626, to the general superior of the Society in Rome, announced the discovery: "There [in Sian] an ancient monument has been discovered which proves that there were once preachers of the Holy Gospel in China. . .It contains many equivocal expressions, a number of terms which are of pagan provenance and very difficult to understand, to say nothing of metaphors and literary allusions."

After a good translation of the opening passages of the inscription, he adds: "Father Trigault has been ordered to the spot to examine the stone, because the Doctors have omitted certain details which we must have. We hope that he will obtain an exact copy of the inscription. When we have received it we will send it immediately to Your Paternity." In this wise the Jesuits in China reacted to an epoch-making discovery.

Yet for the next two hundred and fifty years, the Jesuits were denounced as frauds and impostors by "scholarly" dilettantes in their homelands who saw in the Nestorian monument a gigantic Jesuit hoax. "A piece obviously faked," wrote Mathurin Veyssiere de Lacrozs in 1724. "A ridiculous fake. . .an absurd lie. . .a pious fraud," sneered Voltaire as he ridiculed the Jesuits in satirical verse which no doubt convulsed Paris salons in his day:

Ah! du moins Bonze que vous êtes
Puisque vous me voulez tromper,
Trompez-moi mieux que vous ne faites.

Roughly translated: Ah! Bonze (Monk) that you are, if you wish to fool me, fool me better than you do.

Ridicule was still the vogue as late as 1855, when Ernest Renan echoed the charges of fraud. He had the honesty eight years later to admit that he had been mistaken and that the objections to the authenticity of the monument had disappeared. Today its authenticity is universally recognized: research in dynastic records and archeological discoveries have confirmed the data given in the inscription itself.

The Jesuits in China were fully aware of the worth of the discovery. One of the objections which the Chinese had constantly raised to Christianity was its novelty. In China perhaps more than anywhere else in the world—Red Guards to the contrary notwithstanding—a high value attaches to what is old. With their sense of history the Chinese are little inclined to attribute importance to anything which has no roots in their past. The younger Manoel Dias (there were two) in his commentary on the monument describes the common experience of the missionaries,

"Visitors to the missionaries are wont to say: 'We have reason to be grateful for the teachings which you have brought to us from far off; but why were they not brought to our ancestors as well, why have they reached us so tardily? This is what we cannot understand. . .'"

In a brief account which he published in 1625 Li Chih-tsao refers to the same objection:

> For more than thirty years our scholars in China have been familiar with the doctrine and example of the learned men from the West. There is no one who has not proclaimed the excellence of this doctrine and held it in honor; nevertheless, many have still been skeptical because they regarded it as something new. Who could have believed it? Nine hundred and ninety years ago this doctrine was preached in China; amidst the constant vicissitudes of the world, the ever unchanging providence of God raised up wise men who knew no obstacle. Now this holy stone so providentially preserved has suddenly come to light. . .Buried for so many years, this treasure seems to have waited only the propitious moment.

My excitement and that of Alden Stevenson and Paul Steidl-Meier, who were with me, at coming unexpectedly upon this historic treasure probably rivaled that of Li Chih-tsao in 1625.[2]

The Sian Warriors

Twenty miles east of Sian is a famous resort. Several things make it famous: its hot springs, its early history, and its being the scene of Chiang Kai-shek's kidnapping in 1936 by one of his marshals, Chang Hsueh-liang.

Because of the natural hot springs which flow from the foot of Black Horse Hill, the Hsuan-tsung emperor (713–756) here built a summer palace for the lovely Yang Kuei-fei, his favorite concubine, whose beauty is celebrated in many a poem. During this emperor's reign the T'ang dynasty reached the apogee of its cultural brilliance, and his court attracted statesmen, artists, writers, among them the two most famous Chinese poets, Tu Fu and Li Po. Li Po wrote a hymn to Yang Kuei-fei's beauty, but this work was forthcoming, it is said, only after the emperor had stoked

Li's muse with copious draughts of wine. He was a notorious tippler who drowned while boating, legend has it, when he drunkenly leaned too far overboard in an effort to embrace the image of the moon reflected on the surface of the waters and fell in. Here the emperor was wont to dilly-dally the summer away with the beautiful Yang Kuei-fei until the romance, famed in China's folklore, ended with her tragic death in 755. She hanged herself to escape the vengeful wrath of mutinous soldiers.

I assume it remained imperial property until the advent of the republic in 1911. At some point it became a hot springs resort of no particular fame until suddenly, in 1936, it leaped into headlines around the world. The generalissimo, Chiang Kai-shek, had been kidnapped there by Chang Hsueh-liang!

Chang Tso-lin had been one of China's leading warlords, Manchuria his domain. He was assassinated by the Japanese in 1928. Hsueh-liang, his son, known chiefly as a playboy and opium addict, surprised everybody by stepping into his father's shoes. The Japanese conquest and establishment of the puppet state of Manchukuo in 1932 curtailed his career as warlord. Making the best of a bad situation he offered his services and his soldiers to Chiang Kai-shek; in return, he was given the rank of marshal in the Kuomintang armies. In 1935 Mao Tse-tung had arrived in Yenan, north of Sian, with one fourth of the original eighty thousand who had set out on the Long March, and here established his headquarters. The Japanese were threatening to declare the northern provinces an autonomous region, that is, under Japanese control. Chiang Kai-shek turned a deaf ear to the demand of an outraged public that he resist, arguing that he must first dispose of the Communists. He put Chang Hsueh-liang in command of the northwest sector headquartered at Sian with orders to attack and destroy the Communists. Chang and his troops, largely Manchus who bitterly resented Japanese occupation of their homeland, thought Chiang Kai-shek should come to terms with Mao Tse-tung and join the Communist forces with his in mutual resistance to the Japanese.

As Lincoln was concerned with the passivity of McClellan on the Potomac, Chiang Kai-shek was displeased with Chang's apparent foot-dragging. He flew to Sian to prod Chang into action against the Communists, and he established his headquarters at the once and soon-again-to-be famed hot springs.

The next morning Chiang Kai-shek was awakened by the sound of gunfire near at hand: Chang Hsueh-liang's troops were attacking his bodyguard. Chiang Kai-shek, still in his nightgown, climbed out a window and fled up a steep mountain path, taking refuge in a small pavilion. Chang's men quickly followed and took him prisoner, unharmed.

The marshal had no designs upon the generalissimo's life; it was a kidnapping, not an assassination. Chiang Kai-shek was offered his freedom in exchange for an agreement to make peace with the Communists and unite with them to resist the Japanese. Chou En-lai came and joined the negotiations. After several days, agreement was reached. Chiang Kai-shek called off his anti-Communist or, as he called them, "bandit extermination" campaigns and agreed to fight the Japanese. If Chou En-lai and Mao Tse-tung consented to the release of their principal enemy, it was because they recognized that he was the only symbol of national leadership around whom the people would rally to resist the Japanese.

On December 25 Chiang Kai-shek flew back to Nanking as the nation, which had been holding its breath all week, collectively sighed in relief. Oddly, as part of the bargain Chang Hsueh-liang returned with him to Nanking, where he was put under house arrest. When fourteen years later Chiang Kai-shek fled to Taiwan, he took Chiang Hsueh-liang with him; there he was kept under house arrest until he died. It would appear that the one who in the end paid the most to ransom the victim of this famous kidnapping was its successful architect.

This resort was on our tour schedule. We visited the bedroom from whose window Chiang Kai-shek had leaped in his nightgown the morning of the assault. The rest of the group climbed up the path to have a look at the pavilion where he had sought to hide; it was too steep for me. More interesting to me was the lovely chamber where is still preserved the sunken marble bath—or more probably jade; it is the color of jade—where centuries ago the beautiful royal concubine Yang Kuei-fei, attended by her maidservants, took her perfumed baths. I too took a bath, not in jade, to be sure, but in one of the dozen or more bath cabins where, for a nominal fee, one may bathe in the hot waters which from time immemorial have been flowing from the foot of Black Horse Hill.

Twenty miles away is the tomb of Ch'in Shih Huang-ti, the first and one of the greatest and cruelest of China's emperors. When he became ruler of the Kingdom of Ch'in at the age of thirteen, China was divided into nine feudal principalities. He conquered the other eight and established a central administration for the whole of China. His own Ch'in dynasty was of short duration (221–207 B.C.), but it created the empire of China which through many dynastic changes and more than one temporary relapse into disunity would endure until the fall of the Ch'ing and the advent of a republic in 1911.

Among Ch'in Shih's extraordinary accomplishments were the building of the Great Wall to protect the empire from the marauding barbarians from the north and the development of China's remarkable system of canals that serve both agriculture and transportation. Balancing his many achievements, however, is a record of foul misdeeds. He had a hatred of intellectuals more intense than that of Mao Tse-tung in our day. Mao was content to make them clean the latrines; Ch'in Shih buried them alive. He also ordered the burning of all books, excepting only those treating of technical subjects such as medicine.

Like most of us Emperor Ch'in Shih looked forward to death without relish. According to the great historian Ssu-ma Ch'ien, writing about 100 B.C., seven hundred thousand conscripts labored for thirty-six years to build a magnificent subterranean palace where Ch'in Shih hoped to spend eternity. It is his tomb, and it lies buried beneath a mound fifteen stories high known as Mount Li, twenty miles from Black Horse Hill.

No systematic excavation of Mount Li has been undertaken; it may well contain treasures of Chinese art and history beyond anything yet unearthed. But less than a mile distant and scarcely a year before our visit one of the most remarkable archeological discoveries of the century had been made, and systematic excavations were already well on the way.

In spring 1974, some farm workers who were digging a well stumbled upon a huge underground vault the size of a parade ground; it contained beautiful life-sized terra cotta statues of armed warriors, servants, and horses pulling manned war chariots. When we were there in 1975 after our visit to Black Horse Hill, hundreds of these astonishingly realistic figures had already been uncovered and were drawn up in battle array, "upright, intact, and poised, as if waiting for a command to attack."[3] They represented an elite imperial army buried there to guard the tomb of their master, Ch'in Shih Huang-ti. And there they were, still on the alert after the passage of 2,200 years. Experts estimate that when the entire three-acre site has been excavated the number will have increased to six thousand. (And indeed, when I returned five years later the number of statues on view had greatly increased.)

The substitution of terra cotta statues for human beings and live horses was a distinct step forward. In the China which preceded Ch'in Shih Huang-ti it had been the common practice to bury living beings, human and animal, to serve the deceased feudal ruler in the next world.

Return to Zikawei

From Sian we flew to Nanking. As we walked to the airport building we passed an enormous statue of Mao Tse-tung. "Na shih shema ren?" I asked the charming young woman who was one of our three interpreters—"Who is that?" She was visibly shocked by the question but took my little joke in good grace.

I was now on familiar ground. Familiar and at the same time unfamiliar. Here I noted many changes, some for the better. I noted even more change in Shanghai, our next stop, a short trip from Nanking.

Gone from Shanghai was the International Settlement and with it the turbaned Singh policemen, all well over six feet tall, who seemed to love nothing more than to belabor a Chinese rickshaw man about the shoulders with their rubber batons. Gone was the French Concession and the *poilus*, whose robust song used to accompany their cadenced morning march down Avenue Foch. Gone too was the British racetrack with its sign Chinese and Dogs Not Allowed, which had inspired a young Mao Tse-tung to dedicate his life to liberating China from all forms of foreign domination. Gone were many other once-familiar scenes and names. I think the only streets that retained their old names were Nanking Road and Bubbling Well Road. After an absence of almost forty years, my recollections were fogged. I could not find my way around as easily as I had expected.

I was determined to visit Zikawei, where I had spent four of the happiest years of my life. It was not on our schedule, so on the second day in Shanghai I told the chief guide that instead of accompanying the group that day I intended to visit Zikawei. He made no objections. Paul Steidl-Meier decided to come with me. I asked the hotel receptionist to call a taxi. She told us to take a seat while she did so. About five minutes later a young woman, perhaps thirty-five or forty years of age, entered the lobby and, after a glance at the receptionist who nodded in my direction, approached me. Evidently the receptionist had phoned the local office of CITS, which was only a few steps from the hotel.

"I understand you wish to visit Zikawei," she said. Then she asked why.

"Because I lived there forty years ago," I replied, "and I would like to see it again before I die."

"I will call a taxi and come with you," she said, speaking English perfectly.

"Oh, that is not necessary," I said. "I can find my way. I do not want to bother you."

"It is no bother at all," she replied quite pleasantly, but in a tone that left no doubt that willy-nilly we had a companion. And a very pleasant companion she proved to be, though very much in charge of our little tour.

Arrived in Zikawei, I asked if we might enter the buildings. She said that this was not permitted. However, she had no objections to Paul's taking pictures. He took a dozen or more, especially of the theologate in which I had spent three of my four years in China, and of the large church which the French Jesuits had named S. Ignace. I noted several uniformed soldiers lounging on the second floor balcony of our old theologate, which suggested that the Summa Theologica had been replaced by the Red Army manual of maneuvers.

As we left Zikawei our companion asked if we would like to see Bubbling Well Road. Here, at my request, she had the driver stop at a large bookstore where I bought a much-desired English-Chinese dictionary and Mao's famous Little Red Book.

I was determined to visit Zikawei without the inhibiting constraints of our pleasant companion. I had noted the number of the local bus. The following morning I left the hotel before others were astir. The bus depot was on the Bund, just a few blocks from the hotel. I took the bus to Zikawei.

Zikawei had originally been the estate of Hsu Kuang-ch'i (1562–1633), known in the local Shanghai dialect as Imperial Councilor Zi. He was an early convert to Christianity who had collaborated with Matteo Ricci in the writing of his books; he also helped other Jesuit missionaries in furthering their apostolic works, especially among Chinese intellectuals. In his later years he was a member of the Nei-k'o, or the state council, the highest governing body in imperial China. He was without doubt the most distinguished Catholic layman in the history of the Church in China.

When the Jesuits returned to China in the mid nineteenth century—the order had been allowed back in existence by Pius VII in 1814—they established themselves at Zikawei; when I was there in the 1930s, it was the largest Catholic mission center in the world. The church of S. Ignace, the largest Catholic church in China, dominated the complex of structures, which contained the theologate where Jesuits from all the missions in China studied theology in preparation for the priesthood; these represented thirteen nationalities. It also had a boys' high school and elementary school; a famous astronomical-meteorological observatory which every year saved millions of dollars in damages to shipping and other interests by warning of approaching hurricanes; a major and a minor seminary. In addition, it had a boys' orphanage, T'ou-se-wei, where the boys were educated and trained in crafts, especially printing and wood-carving. Directed by Jesuit brothers, this was the largest Catholic publishing house in China; and some of the wood carvings were much admired at the San Francisco World's Fair in 1915. All these institutions were run by the Jesuits of the Province of Paris.

On the other side of the broad canal that bordered the property were a girls' orphanage called Seng-mou Yuan, world-famed for its silk embroideries, and an excellent girls' high school and elementary school. These were directed by French nuns known as Auxiliatrices, in English called Helpers of the Holy Souls. There was also a convent of cloistered Carmelites, all but one of whom were Chinese; the exception was an American from Boston who, when asked what she would like for Christmas, replied "a can of Boston baked beans."

Besides these institutions there was the village itself, consisting of several thousand families, located behind the church of S. Ignace. Most of these had issued from the two orphanages. The nuns of Seng-mou Yuan and the brothers at T'ou-se-wei had for years collaborated in a boy-meets-girl program. When interest in marriage had bloomed in one of their respective charges they arranged for a series of get-acquainted meetings. If out of these flowered a mutual desire, a marriage was arranged. Often the couple then established their home in the village of Zikawei. Because of this, most of Zikawei's inhabitants were Catholic, and on Sundays and feast days the church of S. Ignace was crowded at every liturgical celebration. I have never forgotten the Mass on the Feast of All Souls, when it took a dozen priests more than half an hour to distribute communion. During the Mass little children, barely arrived at the walking age, freely wandered back and forth from their father on one side of the central aisle to their mother on the other, and up the aisle to crawl under the communion rail into the sanctuary. Entirely at home in the House of God—their home.

That was the Zikawei I had known. Most of it had gone. I spent the morning wandering about in search of memories. I found traces, to be sure, but that was all.

What struck me with greatest force was the disappearance of the central dividing canal, along whose banks had always been moored hundreds of sampans upon which families lived out their entire lives. Here they were born, here lived, and here died. There was now no canal, but instead a broad paved boulevard heavily traveled chiefly by trucks, buses, bicycles, and an occasional taxi.

Gone with the canal were the swarms of mosquitos which had been the bane of my life from May into October. Every morning before leaving for Mass and breakfast, I would close my window and light a coil of Chinese incense. When I returned I would sweep thousands of asphyxiated mosquitos into a pile an inch deep and a foot in circumference. It was an unending battle, for as long as the canal was there the mosquitos had limitless reserves to call upon. Now both were gone, and this could be chalked up as definitely a change for the better. Whether credit goes to the Kuomintang or to the Communist regime I do not know. Someone has told me that the transformation from canal to boulevard was accomplished before liberation. In any case, credit to whomever it is due!

Some buildings were easy to identify. The observatory was unchanged in appearance. Several automobiles standing in its parkway indicated that it was occupied. The gateman informed me that it was still maintained as a meteorological station by govern-ment-appointed scientists. Its astronomical component, he said, had been moved to the observatory formerly maintained by the Jesuits on the hill of Zosé.

The major seminary was now the headquarters of the local Communist party. I was unable to identify T'ou-se-wei, either because it had been totally transformed or because the new streets and new buildings, a theater, factories, office buildings, shops, etc., had replaced once-familiar landmarks. Seng-mou Yuan, the building, was still there, but not the institution. The building now served, I was told, as a residence for a small number of priests who had adhered to the Patriotic Association. Since the outbreak of the Cultural Revolution they had not been permitted publicly to exercise their priestly ministry. To support themselves they made umbrellas at the orders of the regime.

The three-story Jesuit residence was easy to find, separated from the theologate by a garden and a wide expanse of lawn where we used to play volleyball and basketball—in our soutanes, to be sure. Many memories lingered in this building. Here was the community chapel, where we assisted at daily Mass and where, at evening litanies, we disciplined ourselves not to duck when the bats came soaring down over our heads, up to the choir loft, around and back to where they lived behind the high altar. Here Paul O'Brien and I had lived during our first year in China studying Chinese. And here I had been summoned by the mission superior, Father LeFebvre, and shown the fateful telegram which had so drastically changed the course of my life: "General orders Dunne home immediately." Here too was the large library and invaluable archival material on the history of the mission. I hoped to find out if any of it was still there. I was stopped, however, when I started to enter the building, and was told that this was not permitted.

The great church of S. Ignace was a sorry sight. Its twin spires had been demolished by the Red Guards. The beautiful rose window had been smashed. The cobblestoned courtyard was littered with broken machinery and rubbish and was enclosed within a high wire fence. The church itself was apparently being used as a factory or warehouse. I started to pass through the opening in the fence but was stopped by the gatekeeper, who told me that I could not enter. I asked him how long he had been here. "Three years," he said.

"Well, I was here long before you. I lived here forty years ago and was often in this church," I argued.

"Pu yao chin—that makes no difference," he answered. "You have to have official permission."

I wandered through the streets of the village, exchanging a few words with those I met. One delightful old woman, who dated back to the days of footbinding, when women's feet were bound in cloth to keep them small and disformed, claimed that things were much better than in the old days; to support her claim she suddenly removed her denture and laughing triumphantly held it up for my inspection.

Small crowds would cluster around me. One woman invited me into her home, and several dozen others, of all ages, male and female, followed us. There was not room for all, and people overflowed into the narrow street. They could not have been friendlier. Our conversation was punctuated by laughter. I told them who I was, that I had lived here for four years forty years ago in the old theologate, and that I was a Jesuit. Evidently fearful that not all had understood, my hostess repeated: "T'a shih Iesu hui-ti—he is a Jesuit." It was clear that they knew what a Jesuit was.

Knowing that the village had been overwhelmingly Catholic forty years earlier, I looked about hoping to see a sign of affiliation. There was none. It was foolish to have expected one. As I have already remarked, Mao Tse-tung still lived, the Gang of Four was still in command, the Cultural Revolution had not run its course. Any crowd, even of fellow villagers, could contain informers. Publicly to identify oneself as a believer could have disastrous consequences.

A remarkable woman, Nien Cheng, has written an account of such consequences, describing in her *Life and Death in Shanghai* the sufferings she endured during seven years of imprisonment in solitary confinement.[4] The terrible prison experiences which Nien Cheng endured without yielding and, remarkably, without bitterness, others were still enduring as I walked the narrow streets of Zikawei. Among them were eleven Chinese Jesuits whom I had known, including four who had been classmates and close friends during the years I had spent here. They had already spent some twenty years in prison and would spend many more. I had given their names to our chief guide with the request that he obtain permission for me to visit them or, if that were not possible, that he find out where they were imprisoned so that I might write to them. The guide had been quite surprised by my request and wanted to know what crime they had committed. I assured him that they had committed no crime but were imprisoned solely because of their refusal to adhere to the Patriotic Association in violation of their conscientious convictions. This he found impossible to believe, insisting that in the People's Republic of China no one was imprisoned except for criminal conduct. He promised, nevertheless, to find out what he could about them. The day after my visit to Zikawei he sent word to me through Al Stevenson that he had been unable to get any information about them. I am sure that, probably under orders of his superiors at CITS, he did not try.

On another early morning sortie I went in search of the Sacred Heart Church on the other side of the Soochow Creek, which was only a few blocks from the hotel. It was in the rectory of this church that the California Jesuits had given me a farewell dinner thirty-nine years before. It was about half past five in the morning, but already, as on every other morning, thousands of people of both sexes and all ages, in groups of from ten to one hundred and more, were doing the ancient Chinese Tai-chi physical exercises, in parks, on sidewalks, in the streets, in every open space. This exercise ritual is a feature of life in most cities in China and, I am told, in Taiwan. Two more-than-middle-aged women laughingly challenged me to join them in the leg-stretching exercise they were performing against a wall. I tried, but the stretch was beyond the limits of my aging muscles. We shared a good laugh at my expense.

I did not remember the exact location of the church, but after wandering up and down streets in the Hongkew section of Shanghai I finally spotted over the roofs what had all the appearances of a small church spire, minus the cross. I headed in that direction. It was indeed Sacred Heart Church, but like the much larger S. Ignace it had been converted into some kind of factory or warehouse. Its small courtyard was littered with discarded machinery. The front gate was padlocked, but there was a gateman in the porter's lodge. I called him out and asked him to unlock the gate. He wanted to know why. I told him I wanted to look around. He was not unfriendly but said this was not permitted. I explained that this had formerly been a Catholic church, which he probably already knew, that I was a priest who had lived in China forty years ago, that the night of my long-lamented departure I had dined here with fellow Jesuits, and that I wanted to look inside to relive old memories. He seemed to find all of this very interesting but was not persuaded that it authorized him to let me in. "K'o-hsi-la," he sympathized; "too bad."

One thing that struck me forcibly in Shanghai—as it would later in Canton—was that everyone I met understood and spoke mandarin. This was far from the case forty years ago. Mandarin, the language used by the mandarin class in imperial days, had never achieved the status of a national language. In the large area of metropolitan Shanghai a substantially different dialect is spoken, and in two southern provinces the Cantonese dialect differs from mandarin about as much as English does from German. In addition to other dialects, there are countless patois. The Kuomintang had launched the effort to make mandarin a truly national language. With political control of the entire country, the Communist regime had evidently effectively realized the goal. Everyone to whom I spoke in my rusty mandarin, both in Shanghai and in Canton, answered in mandarin.

We visited many interesting places in Shanghai: the Children's Palace, where youngsters developed remarkable skills in vocal and instrumental music, ballet, calligraphy, and other arts; a theater featuring the breath-taking acrobatics at which the Chinese are particularly skilled; schools; and factories. We also visited a large residential compound in the Chapei section of Shanghai which, when I first saw it in 1932, was a vast area of rubble, the desolate product of naval gunfire by the Japanese the previous year. But for me, next to Zikawei, the highlight was our visit to Fu Tan University. For Fu Tan is, in a sense, both a child of—though born as it were out of wedlock—and a successor to the noted French Jesuit Chen Tan University, known in English as Aurora University.

Before arriving in China we had sent a list of places and institutions we would like to visit. Among them was a university. Why was Fu Tan chosen by the officials of the agency which arranged all tours? Was it sheer happenstance? Or was it a particularly delicate and quite Chinese gesture? I find it difficult to believe the former, and there is some evidence in support of the latter.

Our tour had begun in Peking, seat of famed universities both before and since the Communist takeover. In Nanking we had visited the Teachers' College, formerly the well-known American Protestant Ch'ing Ling Girls' College. But our university visit was saved for Shanghai. And why Fu Tan? There are other universities in Shanghai, notably Saint John's, which had been an American Protestant foundation.

I like to think that our visit to Fu Tan was not an accident but a deliberate choice on the part of the authorities who might have realized that it would be of particular interest to me, who they knew had spent four years at Zikawei, and to Al Stevenson and Paul Steidl-Meier because of its historical connection with the Jesuits.

Our visit began, as was customary in all our visitations, with a briefing session with a welcoming committee. Here the committee consisted of members of the Revolutionary Committee, faculty members, student leaders, and members of the workers' committee. The briefing was conducted by Mr. Chang, vice-chairman of the Revolutionary Committee, who began with a short history of the school. His account, although inadequate, was not inaccurate. He said briefly that Chen Tan (Aurora) University was a missionary university founded in 1902, and that in 1905 a group of "progressive teachers, who opposed the colonialist policies of the missionaries in charge, left Chen Tan and founded Fu Tan University."

The founder of Fu Tan was in fact Ma Hsiang-p'ei, co-founder of Chen Tan University. A brilliant Chinese Jesuit priest, he had serious differences with his French superiors. One of the differences, or so I was told by Stanislaus Shen, S.J., a friend and classmate at Zikawei, was about the reluctance of European superiors to appoint Chinese to positions of authority. Father Shen thought that this was what led Ma Hsiang-p'ei to leave the Society of Jesus and the Church. According to Fr. Georges Germain, S.J., former rector of Chen Tan University, this was not the case; Germain presented his interpretation in his critique of the paper I had prepared for the symposium at the University of San Francisco in 1974. Admitting the differences, Germain said that the real reason was related to the demands of celibacy. Given the character of Ma Hsiang-p'ei and the europeanism still dominant in missionary thinking in those early years of the twentieth century, it is possible that, while Germain is undoubtedly right, Shen was not entirely wrong. A disgruntled religious is more inclined to seek understanding and consolation elsewhere.

In any case, Ma Hsiang-p'ei quit the Jesuits. He founded Fu Tan University, which remained throughout the years a small school, never rivaling in importance its parent, Chen Tan. "Despite good will," remarked Vice-chairman Chang, "it did not have a bright future."

Its fortunes changed dramatically with the Communist triumph; apart from its medical school, which became the China Medical College, Chen Tan was taken over by Fu Tan. The death of Chen Tan gave new life to Fu Tan. As Chen Tan had unwittingly played a key role in the birth of Fu Tan, she unwillingly played a key role in her rebirth. By 1975 Fu Tan had grown to include thirteen departments, six of science, seven of liberal arts. Six thousand students were enrolled on campus, sixteen thousand others were taking correspondence courses. The library, which formerly housed 80,000 volumes, in 1975 boasted of 1,600,000. A large part of these additions consisted of the library of Chen Tan University. There was no mistaking whence they came. The library stamp was plain to be seen on each frontispiece: Chen Tan/ l'Université de l'Aurore.

The later history of Ma Hsiang-p'ei is interesting—and edifying. After founding Fu Tan University he went on to a brilliant career in public service, holding high office and becoming a nationally known figure especially admired by youth. Meanwhile he had married and raised a large family. He never lost his faith or, apparently, his affection for the Society of Jesus. In his old age, a widower, he returned to the Church and, in a sense, to the Society. In 1936, my last year at Zikawei, he was living in an apartment offered him by the Jesuits at the boys' orphanage. Ever the patriot, he emerged at the request of a national students' organization to deliver a nationwide radio speech rallying the youth of China to resist Japanese aggression. When the Japanese occupied Shanghai the following year, refusing to live on occupied soil, he left Zikawei. He died not long after in Vietnam.

Acupuncture Observed

Few things in our Shanghai visit exceeded in interest our observation of major surgery performed with only acupuncture as the anesthetic. I was particularly interested because I had had the very same surgery in Rome nineteen years earlier, the removal of a large part of my stomach because of a bleeding ulcer—but with more than acupuncture as anesthetic. The operation was performed at the Shanghai Medical College, formerly the Aurora University Medical Faculty.

First the director of the college briefed us; she was not a doctor but was flanked by two doctors prepared to answer our questions. She told us that acupuncture, although in use for hundreds of years as a curative for a large variety of ailments, was still in the experimental stage as an anesthetic. She assured us, however, that it was well advanced as an experiment, and she was quite confident that it would prove successful in the far-from-simple surgical operation we were about to witness. One of the doctors assured us that the patient, a young man, would be fully conscious the whole time and that, except for a slight sign of discomfort that might pass over his face at the moment that the excised section of ulcerated stomach was removed, it was unlikely that we would see any sign of pain.

We were then taken to the surgery where, seated in the student section, we looked directly down into the operating well below; the patient, stretched out on the surgical table, smiled up at us. Two surgeons, assisted by nurses, performed the operation. Seated at the patient's feet was an acupuncturist whose function it was from time to time to revolve the needle he had inserted into the patient's ankle. At the patient's side sat a second acupuncturist who controlled in like fashion a needle she had inserted into the left wrist. I was fascinated by the entire procedure; as I kept reminding myself, this was exactly what had been done to me years ago in Rome.

Everything proceeded exactly as foretold. The patient remained conscious throughout, usually smiling and occasionally flashing a broad grin up at us as though thoroughly enjoying himself. The only exception came, as predicted, when the surgeon finally removed and held up for us to see the excised section of the stomach. At that moment I observed a slight expression of distress, as from momentary nausea, pass over his face. As I glanced about, it appeared to me that the expression was less accentuated on his face than on that of several of my spectator comrades.

After visiting other sections of the college we were led back to the conference room for questions and answers. A few minutes later the doors opened and in was wheeled on a gurney our ever-smiling patient looking as fit as a fiddle and professing to feel the same way.

Canton

From Shanghai we flew south to Canton. I remember with greatest clarity three features of this visit.

The first was a two-day tour of the remarkable geological formations and extraordinary beauties of Kweilin in the western part of Guanghsi province. Not the least enjoyable part was the riverboat trip, during which we frequently passed groups of boy swimmers who greeted our passage with shouts and waving of hands. In the city of Kweilin, once part of the Maryknoll mission, it seemed as though almost the entire population turned out shortly after five o'clock every morning either to jog or to join with others in the Tai-chi exercises.

One morning I crossed a bridge to join a group on a tiny island in the middle of a small lake near the hotel. I endeavored clumsily to follow the leader. As in Shanghai and elsewhere, no one here seemed to take offense or to be surprised when I joined the ritual; in fact they seemed to be pleased. Afterwards I had a pleasant conversation with several of the participants.

A second memorable feature was a visit to the Catholic cathedral in Canton. I had spotted its spires from my hotel window. It was obviously some miles distant, but I identified the area on the map and from the desk clerk learned the number of the bus which would take me to that part of the city. I ventured forth, blithely mounted the bus and settled into my seat. A few minutes later, to my astonishment, the bus pulled into the end-of-the-line depot. Answering my protestations, the conductor explained that

I should have taken the bus in the opposite direction; she kindly put me aboard the proper bus and told the driver where I wished to go.

We had not been more than fifteen minutes on the road when the driver signaled to me that I had reached my destination. I had serious doubts but figured that she knew her business better than I did. I stopped two teenage girls, showed them my map and pointed out the area to which I wanted to go. They confirmed my doubts; there was still a long way to go. As we talked, an older woman stopped and asked if she could be of help. She said that she was going in that direction and invited me to accompany her. She spoke mandarin fluently and, with characteristic Chinese politesse which thinks courtesy more important than truth, complimented me upon my own mandarin. She was a pleasant companion and pointed out points of interest during our long walk. She even went a bit out of the way to show me where I could catch a pedicab to take me back to my hotel. Then she left me at the bridge which she was to cross to the other side of the Pearl River; the cathedral was a few blocks from here.

Like S. Ignace in Zikawei, the cathedral of Canton was a sorry sight. It had been turned into a factory of some sort. There was a paved approach, perhaps a hundred yards long, lined on both side with shops. I had a jovial conversation with an old man seated in the entrance to one of them. We joked about our respective ages. He found it hard to believe that I was seventy years old, probably because, unlike him, I had no whiskers. He confirmed that this had been a T'ian Chu tang—a Catholic church, but said there were no priests there since the Cultural Revolution. He did not know, or did not care to say, where they had gone.

The bishop of Canton, Dominic Tang, a Jesuit, had been in jail for some seventeen years, and it would be another five before he was released because of poor health. And even release from prison was not to bring him peace. For shortly after his release the local clergy in electing a bishop chose Bishop Tang, although he was not himself a member of the Patriotic Association. The latter raised no objection. The high hopes of reconciliation raised by this incident were soon dashed by what I regard as the ill-advised action of John Paul II. In 1981 he suddenly announced that he was raising Tang to the rank of archbishop. There was an immediate angry reaction in China by the regime and perforce by the Patriotic Association. It seemed a flaunting of the principle of "foreign governance" of the Church of China which, in view of the delicate circumstances of

Church-state relations at the time, was unnecessary. Tang, who had gone to Hong Kong for surgery, was not allowed to return to Canton and is still obliged to live abroad. A new election was held and another chosen to replace him as bishop of Canton. Someone should explain to the Vatican the handy Chinese phrase *man-man ti*—something like, "take it easy!"

The Red Army

The third major feature of our stay in Canton and the most interesting was our visit to a Red Army camp. Upon arriving in Canton from Shanghai, before leaving the airport, we had been given the customary briefing by the local representative of CITS, who would explain the schedule prepared for our stay in that area. We were asked, also the custom, if we had any criticisms or suggestions. Was there anything not scheduled that we would like to see?

Among the suggestions from the group was a visit to an army camp. I doubt that any of us seriously thought the request would be granted. Experience should have forewarned us against skepticism. With a single exception, everything we had asked to see during these weeks in Peking, Sian, Nanking, and Shanghai, we had seen.

When we returned from Kweilin we were presented with a revised schedule. Included was no mere cursory visit but an overnight stay in the camp of the 124th Division of the People's Liberation Army. By sheer happenstance, or so I suppose, the visit was scheduled to *begin* on July 3 and carry through July 4.

After a morning visit and lunch at a large rural commune, we continued by bus to the foot of Lo Fu Mountain, some hundred miles northeast of Canton. The condition of the road—some places still under construction, some places in need of repair—and the fairly heavy truck and bus traffic, precluded high speeds. It was a three-hour trip through the lush Kuangtung countryside, where teams of men, women, and often children busied themselves with the harvest and, aided by the ubiquitous water buffalo, with plowing the rice paddies.

At the entrance to the military reservation, a group of soldiers waved us on and then followed in their jeep. They evidently radioed ahead the news of our arrival, for when we pulled up a couple of miles further on in front of the divisional headquarters, a welcoming party was on hand. It included Chang Hsueh-i, the deputy political commissar of the 124th Division, and Wang Fu-jen, its deputy chief of staff, together with half a dozen other officers. And they greeted us with the applause to which we had become accustomed during our tour and to which we responded in kind.

That evening we were entertained at a sumptuous dinner by the officers who had greeted us plus two young army nurses. All the meals we had been served in China had been excellent; if there were a Chinese version of the Michelin Guide they would have rated three stars, and in two cases four. One fourth star would have to be given to the farewell dinner given us in Peking. The second would have to be conferred upon the dinner with the officers and nurses of the 124th Division. I proposed a toast—one among many—explaining the meaning of the Fourth of July to Americans and the extraordinary but hopeful significance of the fact that we should be celebrating its eve in a camp of the People's Liberation Army of the People's Republic of China.

The truly remarkable thing about this dinner was that, with the exception of the excellent beer and a liqueur much like the potent Mao-tai, everything served—fish, fowl, meat, vegetables, rice, fruit, sweets, and a pleasant wine—had been raised, processed, prepared, and cooked by the soldiers. The same was true of the less sumptuous but quite abundant and appetizing lunch the enlisted men of Company Four shared with us the following day. The camp of the 124th Division was, in fact, a large agricultural commune that the soldiers shared and worked with the peasants.

The Red Army is self-supporting. Obedient to a lesson it had learned and Mao had enjoined during its guerilla days, it does not live off the people. Rather, as a Mao slogan seen everywhere in China in 1975 enjoins upon all and sundry, it "serves the people."[5] I had seen soldiers in the north, like the university students and school children, helping with the harvest; thousands of them were at work in the fields every day gathering wheat side by side with the peasants. Others were laboring on construction jobs; at a school in Peking we saw them helping students build underground classrooms, a precaution against the genuinely feared possibility of an air attack from the north.

I am describing the Red Army of 1975, as I saw it. In recent years there have been extensive reforms in China, chiefly economic and social, but not without effects upon the political and military components. I relate what I saw in 1975; whether I would see the same today I do not know.

The 124th Division also had factories. We visited one of them the next morning and watched the manufacture of small electric batteries from the first step through the assembly line to the final step—packaging the finished products, which number eight thousand daily. This factory was staffed entirely by women; there was not a man on the premises. This in itself was not remarkable. What was remarkable was that the seventy-nine women who staffed the factory were all wives of officers on the divisional level. Shades of the Pentagon! The pleasant, intelligent, and obviously competent woman in charge was the wife of the deputy chief of staff. The wives of officers on the regimental and company levels also have their own factory where they manufacture pharmaceuticals.

After the factory, we visited the medical center, where we examined another of the peaceful pursuits of the Red Army—a beautiful garden, meticulously groomed, where the soldiers cultivate four hundred varieties of medicinal herbs, each plant tagged with both its popular and its scientific name. More than a few of them were familiar not as medicinal herbs but as decorative plants found in American homes. We were given a demonstration of the effectiveness of Chinese herbs. In its way, it was as startling as acupuncture.

We were shown a large cactus that looked no different from cacti seen in the deserts of California and Arizona. Its juice, the officer-guide said, was used by the army in the field to purify its drinking water. A soldier brought a large jar, perhaps eighteen inches deep and twelve inches wide; it was filled with dirty water, the color of the Yellow River. The soldier let fall into the water a few drops of the cactus juice, stirred it briefly, and then stood back. Soon, movement appeared in the water as the sand and dirt began to settle. In a matter of minutes, the bottom of the jar was covered to a depth of several inches with sand. The rest of the jar was filled with crystal clear water!

Near the garden was a laboratory and storeroom, where herbs are processed and converted into medicine. Many years before, I had resorted to Chinese herbs—just once! The herbalist had given me several packets of unpleasant-looking stuff with which, following his instructions, I brewed a horrid-looking and worse-tasting tea. I decided the cure was worse than the ailment and took the pledge against further indulgence in Chinese herbs. Here the herbs were processed into neutral-tasting pills and have lost their horror without losing their curative properties. The finished products, manufactured by soldiers, were displayed in row upon row of bottles, as in a pharmacy. In another nook of the laboratory, two soldiers were engaged in filling phials with medicinal liquid for hypodermic injection—another modern development in the use of herbs.

On July 4, as I have said, we lunched with the men of Company Four. As we entered the refectory two soldiers grabbed each of us and amidst an uproar of laughter and clapping of hands hauled us off to join them and their companions at table—two of us and six of them to a table.

These were peasant boys—eighteen to twenty-two years of age—open, cheerful, friendly, unspoiled. In the old China, the profession of soldiering was looked upon with disdain. In today's China, it enjoys high prestige. There are far more applicants than can be accepted. When a boy is accepted, I was told, his entire village celebrates the honor he has brought to it.

In one of our briefing sessions, the deputy political commissar, Chang Hsueh-i, remarked that there are not many armies like the People's Liberation Army of China. He might have gone further and said that there is no other army like it—an army that reclaims land from the sea, engages in water conservation projects, builds schoolrooms, plants rice, harvests wheat, grows vegetables, raises pigs, fowl and fish, cultivates orchards, tends medicinal herbs, manufactures pills, devotes its medical and hospital facilities in peacetime to the service of the local population. The officers of this army receive a wage equivalent to that of the average factory worker; their dress scarcely distinguishes them from the enlisted soldier; their wives organize and operate productive factories. I repeat—this is that army as I saw it in the 124th Division in 1975.

It is unique. But can it fight? After all, defending the country is one of the three tasks assigned to it by Mao Tse-tung. The other two are working with the people to build a socialist society and engaging in productive work.

Shortly after our arrival at the camp on July 3 we were given a demonstration of their competence in handling the tools of war. We climbed into our bus and followed several jeeploads of officers to the target range several kilometers away, where a company of soldiers stood at attention awaiting us. After we were seated in the large reviewing stand, the company marched briskly off the field, their perfectly cadenced step demonstrating that military precision does not require the highly polished boots of a United States marine on parade. It can be executed in tennis shoes or sneakers as well.

What followed was a sobering demonstration of precision targetry with rifles, heavy machine guns, mortars, and an armor-piercing antitank gun. First, targets were set up perhaps two hundred yards distant. Several squads of riflemen quick-stepped into position. At a command, they quickly ran up an embankment and threw themselves down in the prone position. Another command and they opened fire. Afterwards, another squad recovered the targets and brought them on the double to the reviewing stand for our inspection. Every bullet hole was plainly within the target circle.

The demonstration of heavy machine guns that followed was devastating. Every target dissolved in a burst of flame. The targets of the mortar fire were two chalk-marked circles high up the mountain side. The squads manning four mortars fired nine or ten rounds each. We watched the explosive bursts as the shells landed, every shell clearly within the target area.

In our group was a former American marine with three tours of duty in Vietnam on his record. His military career had ended when a shell from a Chinese mortar almost tore his arm off at the shoulder. He still carried shrapnel in his body. One piece worked its way painfully out his back during our tour of China. I asked him if he was impressed. "Good soldiers," was his laconic reply—high praise from a veteran marine.

The political instructor of Company Four summarized the history of his unit. In the civil war or, as it is known in China, the war of liberation, it took part in three hundred battles. In the Korean war it won a citation as the Sharp Knife Company because of its role in the campaign of January 1951, of which many Americans have bitter memories. As vanguard company it successfully broke through the thirty-eighth parallel—the demarcation line between North and South Korea. In eighteen hours of fighting in minus-thirty-degree weather, it advanced seventy-five kilometers, killed 250 of the enemy, took many prisoners, and captured a number of artillery pieces. Chang Hsueh-i listened silently to the narration by his younger subordinate officer. Through questioning, I later learned that Chang had been one of the commanders in that Korean action.

The enemy referred to were, of course, Americans. The history was narrated to us—also Americans—proudly, to be sure, but without any trace of animosity or hostility. I had the impression that since the collapse of the ill-advised, ill-starred, and ill-directed American adventure in Vietnam, the specter of the United States as a threat to China's part of the world had receded into the background.

One thing that struck me as curious in this narrative was the absence of any mention of Lin Piao. As I have mentioned, the leitmotif of the second phase of the Cultural Revolution, still in progress, was Criticize Lin Piao, Criticize Confucius. Of the many briefings we received during our tour I think this was the only one in which he was not mentioned, always with the disdain reserved for traitors. The explanation probably lay in the history of Company Four. It had participated in the campaign that ended in the destruction of the crack divisions which Chiang Kai-shek had sent north to Manchuria and in the capitulation of Peking. The commander of the Communist forces in that campaign and the author of its strategy had been Lin Piao. A lingering sense of loyalty inhibited the officers of Company Four. They were unwilling to join in the mandated criticism of Lin Piao.

I was tempted to ask how a man of such brilliant accomplishments for the revolution could in so short a time have come to be labeled a conspirator and traitor. But I had no doubt that the question would have embarrassed Chang Hsueh-i and would have been poor return for the hospitality which we had received. So I kept my question to myself.

As we climbed into our bus for our departure we were given a send-off by the men of Company Four as hearty as our welcome had been: "Hip-hip hooray, *i-lu p'ing-an*"—peace be with you on your way. As we headed back towards Canton I found myself hoping that the fresh-faced, engaging peasant boys with whom we had celebrated July the Fourth in the camp of the 124th Division of the People's Liberation Army would never know the horrors of war.

Taiwan

I intended to return to Switzerland by way of the United States with a stopover in Taiwan. The latter part of my plan ran into a snag in Hong Kong. In 1975 the policy of the Taiwan government was to refuse a visitor's visa to anyone who had first visited mainland China. I was aware of this, but I hoped to skirt the difficulty with the help of the temporary passport which, as I have narrated, was issued to me by the United States embassy in Bern. When applying for a visa at the Taiwanese consulate in Hong Kong, I presented this instead of my regular passport, which bore the telltale stamp of Communist China. The ruse failed. Noticing the legend Temporary, the consul asked to see my regular passport; and of course he immediately spotted the stamp of the People's Republic of China. There ensued a long but amiable argument. Knowing that exceptions were made to the general rule, I returned on each of several days to argue the point that one should be made in my case. Whether persuaded by my arguments or wearied by my perseverance, he finally gave way and I had my visa.

In Taipei I met some old Jesuit friends. Fr. Al O'Hara had entered the novitiate the same year as I and had come out to China the year after me. He had for twenty years or more been teaching sociology at the National University in Taipei. When Fr. Jim Thornton left for China with several other scholastics in 1937 I preached at his departure ceremony in Saint Ignatius Church in San Francisco. He had written one of the very critical responses to my paper "The China Missionary—Yesterday, Today, and Tomorrow." This, however, had not affected the warmth of our friendship. Especially moving for me was to see again, after almost forty years, Fr. Stanislaus Liu, S.J. He, like Stanislaus Shen, had been a close friend during my years at Zikawei. At the time of the Communist defeat of the Kuomintang armies in northern China in 1949 he was rector of the Jesuit technical university in Tientsin. He moved to Indonesia, where for many years he labored among the Chinese emigrants. He was now pastor of the Holy Family Church in Taipei.

I found very little curiosity among the Taiwan Jesuits about conditions on the mainland as I had seen them. I was asked if I thought the people were happy. I was not qualified, as I pointed out, to answer that question. Out of a population of probably more than 800,000,000 I had seen a few thousand and talked with a few dozen. All I could say was that, with a single exception, I had not seen anyone who looked unhappy. The exception was a sobbing woman being consoled by a friend. Whether the cause of her sorrow was party tyranny or the tyranny of a mother-in-law, I could not say.[6]

This answer was not satisfactory; what they wanted was a tale of horrors. They knew that horrors had existed; some of them had experienced them in their own person. Jim Thornton, for example, had spent several years in a Communist jail. That these horrors still existed in 1975, though on a somewhat diminished scale, is abundantly evidenced by Nien Cheng's book to which I have already referred, *Life and Death in Shanghai*. There was also the fact that Kung P'ing-mei, the bishop of Shanghai, the eleven Jesuits whom I had vainly tried to see, and probably others had been more than twenty years in prison. But I could only testify to what I had seen and heard in a brief tour of five cities. Since this left open the possibility that things, bad as they were, were not as bad as they thought them to be, the Jesuits in Taiwan were not interested. I was asked no more questions.

What had happened in China was a tragedy—millions of violent deaths, shattered institutions, wrenching social upheaval, unspeakable suffering. I shared this view with my confreres in Taiwan. I differed from them in my view of what had caused the tragedy. To me the remote cause lay in the whole history of the nineteenth and twentieth centuries; the immediate cause in the ineptitude, antidemocratic mind-set and corruption of Chiang Kai-shek, his C-C clique, and the Kuomintang Party which, aided and abetted by Japanese aggression, had made inevitable the triumph of Mao Tse-tung and his dedicated cohorts.

A Letter to Mao Tse-tung

After returning to Switzerland I wrote a letter to Mao Tze-tung in Chinese. I had sent him a postcard from Canton. There cannot possibly be any calligraphy in the world worse than mine, and I apologized for it to Mao, poet and calligrapher. In any case, it was legible, which is all one should expect of a clumsy foreigner (although Al Stevenson is an expert calligrapher). I mentioned my four years at Zikawei and acknowledged his extraordinary achievements, the luster of which was dimmed by the incarceration of prisoners of the faith. They were neither criminals nor subversives but staunch loyalists unwilling to disavow their faith. I wrote:

> I am not a young man. You, Mr. Chairman, are not a young man. We both are old men who, without a doubt, are soon to leave this world. Before you quit this world, please take these prisoners, some of whom have suffered the bitterness of a jail cell for more than twenty years, and set them free. This would

stand, among all the achievements of Mao Tze-tung's lifetime, high as a mountain, broad as the sea. It would win the plaudits of all the world.

I took the letter to the Chinese Embassy in Bern and asked that it be sent in the diplomatic pouch. The secretary took it in to the ambassador. After considerable delay he returned with the letter. He reported, with some embarrassment, that the ambassador regretted that he could not grant my request. The letter went off by ordinary post. Whether or not Mao saw it, I do not know. There was a chance that, just as a curiosity, it might have been passed on to him. In any event, a few months later Mao was dead. Perhaps the shock of my reminder that his death was imminent was responsible. Death is a quasi-taboo subject among the Chinese.

I sent a similar letter to Mao's successor, Hua Kuo-feng. Unlike Mao he did not quit this life; his career at the top was, however, short-lived. The scenes changed fast following Mao's death. Hua Kuo-feng, who was said to have been Mao's choice as his successor, in collusion with other party leaders, ended the dream of Chiang Ch'ing's, Mao's widow. She had expected that her late husband's mantle of power would fall upon her and during the last years of his life had, with her three close associates, been conspiring to this end. The dream ended when she and they—the Gang of Four—were put under arrest, later tried, and sentenced to life imprisonment, probably in a form of house arrest. Deng Hsiao-ping, for the second time, returned from banishment to center stage. Before long he had nudged Hua Kuo-feng aside and maneuvered himself into the position of power where he has remained ever since. In 1978, shortly after his return from the outer darkness, signs appeared of his intention to move China in a new direction. When I returned in 1982 for a second visit the signs were evident even to the superficial observer.

Twenty-two

China — A Last Farewell

I n August 1982, Fr. Richard Friedli, O.P., director of the missiological institute of the University of Fribourg, graciously allowed me to join a group of twenty-two people, mostly graduate students at the University of Fribourg, whom he was leading on a China tour. There were two young women from Marseilles; Dr. Jean Louis Golfin, a well known sinologist and professor at the University of Toulouse; two Indians, one of whom, Dr. Anand Nayak, was Father Friedli's assistant and the actual organizer of the tour; an African priest from Zaire, Fr. Kaseba Kulala, who was doing doctoral studies at the University of Fribourg; an Italian; and a Portuguese. The rest were Swiss. Our common language was French.

I had suffered a heart attack on January 17, 1979, followed by a hospital stay of two months—to the day. The doctor who had successfully seen me through this and whom I had been seeing every month since did not interpose an objection. And so, buoyed by the enthusiasm, intellectual sharpness, and youthful vigor of my companions, I flew out of Zurich on a bright August morning in 1982 for another, and no doubt last, visit to the land where a part of my heart had lain buried for nearly half a century. It was the longest of the many flights I have taken: Zurich-Paris-Copenhagen-Anchorage-Tokyo-Hong Kong.

We spent several days in Hong Kong, staying at the YMCA. I shared a room with two of the young men in our party in the old wing of the Y, which, unlike the new wing, did not seem to be air-conditioned. Three army cots were crammed into the room. The first time I climbed into mine, the head collapsed, leaving my feet above my head. I left the cot in the hallway and put the mattress on the floor.

I was not interested in sight-seeing, least of all, given my seventy-seven years, in seeing Hong Kong at night. The contrary, naturally, was true of my young companions. I retired early every night. They came in usually between two and three in the morning. All three of us awoke in the morning thoroughly bathed in sweat. We endured it without complaint because that was the way it was, as it had always been before air-conditioning was invented. On our third and last night my roommates came in around 3 A.M. One of them reached into the dark to turn on the light. He flicked a switch and—lo and behold!—waves of cool air poured down upon my sweat-drenched body. We had spent two days and well into the third night in that room without noticing that there were two switches, one for the lights, the other for the air-conditioning! We had a good laugh, at our own expense.

During our Hong Kong stay we had long question-and-answer sessions with the superior of the Jesuit residence in Kowloon, with the five or six priests who constituted the staff of the Holy Spirit Center, whose business was China Watching, and with the genial and ecumenical-minded Methodist pastor, Rev. Bud Carroll, director of a similar Protestant center. Although their assessments of the current situation of the Christian churches and their future prospects differed—the Jesuit being the least and Bud Carroll the most optimistic—all agreed that since the advent to power of Deng Hsiao-ping there had been a marked improvement.

That this improvement left much to be desired was attested by the cruel fate of the eleven Jesuits about whom I had attempted to obtain information during my visit in 1975. All were released during the years immediately following Deng's accession to power, after more than twenty-five years imprisonment. Although closely watched, they enjoyed up to three years of relative freedom. George Huang, for example, was allowed to live with his brother while teaching English in two schools. He said Mass and kept the Blessed Sacrament in a tabernacle between the headpiece of his bed and the wall.

Then in November 1981, they were suddenly arrested and sentenced to ten years either in jail or in labor camps. Given their age and the state of their health after the long years already spent as prisoners, this was equivalent to a death sentence. In fact two of them have since died, Francis Xavier Chu in a labor camp and Stanislaus Shen in the prison hospital in Shanghai. It is quite possible, even probable, that others too have died without word reaching me. When Vincent Chu was seized, he was known to have serious respiratory and cardiological problems. His sister-in-law apparently protested so vigorously that she was arrested with him, although later released.

There is a poignant story about the first arrest of Francis Xavier Chu in 1953. When the police arrived at Christ the King Church in Shanghai his elderly mother, who was with him, said, "Son, I have raised you for the Church."

He replied, "Mother, if I deny the Church, you should deny me."

"Yes, I will deny you," she answered. This mother of the Maccabees—four of her sons were imprisoned in 1953—was still living, blind, over ninety years old and as indomitable as ever, when he was rearrested and led away to his death. She belongs to the same old Catholic family as Bp. Simon Chu, one of the six Chinese bishops consecrated by Pius XI in 1926; this family traces its faith back to the days of Lazzaro Cattaneo, S.J., one of the companions of Matteo Ricci. The same is true of Vincent Chu.

What is the explanation of this sudden reversal of policy which contradicted the general tenor of the time, marked by the reopening of churches, the restoration of some ecclesiastical properties, the resumption of religious services? European newspapers attributed it to the alleged fact that Vincent Chu had been receiving frequent visits from foreigners and that these contacts caused concern to the regime, which had begun to restrict contacts between Chinese and foreigners.

More plausible is the explanation given by an Australian journalist in a long article which appeared in the Hong Kong edition of the *International Herald Tribune*.[1] He reported that the rearrests were due to the fact that Vincent Chu—the only one named—and presumably the others were urging Chinese Catholics in Shanghai not to attend Mass in the reopened churches because the celebrating priests belonged to the Patriotic Association, which was disloyal to the pope. This is quite possibly the case, for there is no doubt that this was their conviction attested to by nearly thirty years of imprisonment.

There was an additional reason in the case of Stanislaus Shen. Because of the suppression of all religious activities during the Cultural Revolution, many outside China wondered if the faith had survived. A sudden pilgrimage to the Marian shrine at Zosé, some twenty miles from Shanghai, gave an unexpected and spectacular answer. Some twelve thousand people participated, hundreds of them boat people who converged by sampan. There had been no announcement; communication had been by word of mouth, an effective and rapid mode of transmission long familiar to the Chinese.

The authorities were taken by surprise. They sent police, who vainly ordered the crowd to disperse. Their orders were ignored. The people remained over the weekend. They made the Stations of the Cross; although the stations had long since been destroyed by Red Guards, the people remembered the place of each one on the path up the hillside. They chanted their prayers and sang their hymns in the large basilica which crowns the Zosé hilltop. Conspicuous amid these activities was Stanislaus Shen, who had led a group of Christians from Shanghai and who must have been fully aware that he did so at the risk of being again imprisoned.

There is something special about the fierce loyalty of Stanislaus Shen to his Catholic faith, because he was more sensitive than most to the Europeanism which dominated the policy of the missionary Church in China throughout the nineteenth and well into the twentieth century. Chinese were deemed unsuited for positions of leadership which would have them exercising authority over Europeans. Before 1926 and Pius XI, there were no Chinese bishops or Chinese religious superiors. During my years at Zikawei (1932–36) Stanislaus, a close friend, often expressed his views on the subject. He resented every manifestation of Europeanism—foreign domination of the Church—and never hesitated to say so. I would have expected him to be among the first to identify with the Patriotic Association. On the contrary, resisting enormous pressure, he maintained to the end his allegiance to the pope as successor of Saint Peter at the price of spending one third of his life in prison. Stanislaus died in 1986 at the age of eighty-two.

The arrests in 1981 were a flagrant contradiction of the many other signs of a liberal swing in Peking's policy towards religion. Some theorized that the action reflected not Peking policy so much as the hostility of the head of the Shanghai office for religious affairs, who had held office since before the Cultural Revolution and had always been notoriously anti-Catholic. This was quite plausible. As is well known to historians, both in imperial China and in Kuomintang China, policies and orders emanating from the central government, supposedly all-powerful, were often ignored or even contradicted by local officials. There is some evidence that the same is true in Communist China. Deng Hsiao-ping's economic reform policies have been resisted and sometimes blocked by local and regional cadres.

In Hong Kong Bud Carroll told me that the previous year in Sianfu he had a conversation about the religious situation with a peasant who was tending his flock of sheep in the city square. The peasant, who was a Muslim, said, "In China we have religious liberty everywhere." He then smiled and added: "But policy and practice are not the same thing. Religious liberty is the policy. But practice is decided by the local official. Here in Sianfu the head of the religious bureau is a Han jen [non-Muslim as distinguished from Muslim Chinese] who hates the Hui [Muslim], and he gives us a lot of trouble."

Later in Shanghai, Willie Huang would tell me that in his opinion it was the handiwork of the local religious bureau chief. Willie Huang's brother George was one of those rearrested.

The new orientation of policy started by Deng Hsiao-ping in 1979 affected chiefly economic and social factors—reforms in the industrial and agricultural sectors. Our special interest, however, was in the extent to which the freedom of religious practice had benefited. At the request of Anand Nayak, the official Chinese travel office had constructed our entire tour with religion as its focus: visits to religious institutions, meetings with Church leaders and officials of the bureau of religious affairs, and other such activities.

We began with visits to several Buddhist temples in Canton and an excursion to the ancient Temple of the Ancestors in Foshan, seventeen miles distant. Foshan was a busy city as early as the T'ang Dynasty (618–907). In the eighteenth century, according to the Jesuits who described it in glowing terms, it numbered more than a million inhabitants, far more than today. It had become, beginning with the Sung Dynasty (960–1279), one of the major production centers in China of ceramics, textiles, and hardware. In the nineteenth century it lost its economic importance to Hong Kong and Canton. Today's craft trade specializes in paper lanterns and New Year's images.

The Zuci Miao, which dates from the Sung period (960–1279), is—or rather was—a Taoist temple. Today it is more a museum than a religious shrine; besides the large bronze statue of the Supreme Saviour of the Dark Sky and other religious artifacts, it houses the findings of excavations around Foshan. There were no monks in sight, Taoist or Buddhist. The guide who showed us through was a very articulate young woman. In response to a question she said that she herself had no religious belief. This was surprising in view of the ardent expertise with which she explained the religious significance of all the objects. Whether the large number of people who thronged the temple were drawn by religious belief or by the curiosity of museum visitors it is not possible to say. Nearby was a recently renovated Confucian temple, the cool simplicity of whose design and furnishings contrasted sharply with the rich exuberance of the Zuci Miao.

From Canton we flew directly to Peking. This time our guide-interpreters were two highly-intelligent and capable French-speaking young men, the leader probably in his thirties, the younger in his twenties.

Peking Again

As on my previous tour, I did not accompany the group on all of its scheduled rounds. I had a special project of my own. Before leaving for China I had been contacted by Father Schildknecht, an elderly priest of the Order of Bethlehem living in retirement in their motherhouse at Immensee, Switzerland. He had been a mission-ary in Tsitsihar, northeast China, from 1927 to 1949, when he was expelled by the Communists. He had heard that I was going to visit China and asked me, while in Peking, to try to locate a woman whom he had known years ago. She had left Tsitsihar as a young woman, he said, to study at Fu Jen University in Peking. There she had taken religious vows but had been forced by the Communists to marry and was then banished to Mongolia. He sent me two letters he had received from her since her recent return to Peking, giving her address.

And as before, I forewent a visit to the Great Wall with the group and dedicated myself to finding Madalena Liu. Although I had located on a map of Peking the area in which she lived, it was not easy. The taxi driver whose help I enlisted thought he could find it. He did find the neighborhood without difficulty, but then it was only after stopping to inquire at markets, a police station, and a post office and asking people in the street that we finally found the house itself. She was not at home. I explained to her teenage niece the purpose of my mission. She led me into the bedroom and introduced me to Madame Liu's husband, a genteel and alert old man, eighty-six years of age, ill and confined to bed. I asked him to have his wife phone me at the Peace Hotel where, as seven years earlier, I was staying. She did, and that afternoon came to see me. We had a long and interesting conversation, lasting several hours.

Her account differed in several important respects from that of Father Schildknecht. She had never taken religious vows but had belonged to a lay sodality. Nor had she been forced "out of necessity," as he had written, to marry. She had indeed left Tsitsihar as a young woman to study at Fu Jen University. After graduation she had stayed at the university for several years as assistant to one of her professors who had a doctorate in philosophy from Louvain University and was the dean of Fu Jen. During those years, despite an age differential of twenty years, they had fallen in love and married.

After the Communists occupied Peking in 1949, the rector of the university was imprisoned, and she and her husband were exiled to Inner Mongolia, where their only child, a boy, was born. She said, with particular insistence, that although he was born in Mongolia he had been conceived in Peking. They lived there for twenty-two years—"a hard life"—and only two years ago had been allowed to return to Peking.

Her husband, like herself, was a devout Catholic. He had taught school during the Mongolian years and received a pension from the government. She is a talented artist who supplements the family income with her artwork, such as silk paintings, mostly religious subjects like Nativity scenes, which she sends to friends in Europe who sell them for her. She presented me with an exquisitely carved artifact which serves me as pen and pencil holder.

In the course of our conversation an incident occurred which confirmed that the thaw initiated by Deng Hsiao-ping was far from total. We had been talking without any inhibitions for some time until I asked her, "Are there any Catholics in Peking who do not go to Mass because it is celebrated by a priest who belongs to the patriotic association?"

She put a finger to her lips while pointing with her other hand to the four walls of my room, a manner of saying, "Be careful, the room could be bugged." She then came to my side and whispered in my ear, "Hen toa"—many. The average tourist in China sees no signs of repression. But, as this and another incident, which occurred later in Shanghai, indicate, in 1982 Big Brother was still watching and listening and people were aware and fearful of it.

The following day I saw convincing evidence that the thaw, if not total, was nevertheless real. We attended Mass at the Nan Tang, the Church of the Immaculate Conception; this is the church I had visited seven years before, when it was the only Catholic church functioning in China, serving chiefly foreigners from various embassies. It was a Thursday. We had telephoned early in the morning and, in response to our question, were told that there was to be a Mass at 7 A.M. We arrived to find that it was a funeral Mass for a nun. That itself was quite a surprise, inasmuch as I did not think there were any nuns left in Peking. After the Mass one of the priests told me that when the Communists closed all convents and ordered the nuns to return to their homes, some twenty who had no homes to return to had formed a community and had been living together ever since. The deceased was one of these nuns. She was evidently well known and had many friends. There were at least four hundred people at the Mass, as many men as women, and by no means all old people.

The Mass was sung in Latin, with every detail of the ancient liturgy scrupulously observed. The entire congregation chanted prayers and sang the responses throughout. Following the Mass there was the final absolution. The coffin was on a dais just within the front entrance to the church. A male choir in the loft above sang in impeccable Latin the ancient liturgy, including the "Dies Irae."

After the Mass we had a long conversation with Father Lorenz and another priest, Fr. Anthony Liu, who had emerged from the rectory where, he said, Matteo Ricci had died. This was, indeed, the site, but not the original house in which Ricci had died on May 11, 1610. There were two other priests in our group, Fr. Richard Friedli, O.P., and Fr. Kaseba Kalala. I served as interpreter and was astonished at how my ability to speak Chinese returned. I had more difficulty understanding than speaking but always managed by asking my interlocutor to repeat more slowly what I had not understood. Both Father Lorenz and Father Liu were friendly and completely at ease with us. There was no constraint in their manner and no hesitancy in answering our questions. They told us that Tung Tang (the East Church) had been reopened, but not yet the Pei Tang (the North Church). The churches in Peking had traditionally been known by their geographical location in the city. There was no priest in residence at Tung Tang, where Mass was said only on Sundays by a priest from Nan Tang. There was a Marist brother who took care of the church and acted as sacristan.

My impression of both priests was altogether favorable. They seemed to me dedicated priests and the attitude of the people towards them strongly suggested that they shared the same opinion.

The conventional wisdom among Catholics in exile from China, especially among former missionaries, was that out of loyalty to the pope very few Catholics would attend a Mass said by a priest or bishop who belonged to the Patriotic Association. This was true in the first years after the division, and as Madame Liu had told me, there were perhaps many of whom it was still true. But what I had witnessed at Nan Tang this morning and would witness again in Sian and in Shanghai was evidence that there were many of whom it was no longer true. A Chinese nun, Thérèse Chu, herself one of the exiles, in a letter to me described what has happened:

> The difference is that, at that time [the fifties] a majority of Catholics were with the opposition whereas patriotic priests were a very small number. Now the situation has changed. People like my own relatives, who were not political to begin with, but who resisted the Patriotic Movement merely because they were told they would be excommunicated if they went to Mass, have now figured out that it would not be a mortal sin to worship in the church. With that understanding more people have come back.[2]

The following day a meeting with officials of the Bureau for Religious Affairs and a recently established Institute of Religious Studies was scheduled. I skipped this in favor of a visit with Madalena Liu to what had been Fu Jen University and to the former Jesuit language school, Chabanel House.

Fu Jen had been established in the late 1920s as a joint enterprise of all the American Benedictine monasteries. The structure of the Benedictine Order, in which each monastery is independent, is ill-suited to such an undertaking. Despite generous investment of resources, both men and money, the enterprise became an administrative nightmare. In the early 1930s the Benedictines turned it over to the fathers of the Society of the Divine Word. It was a flourishing institution when Madalena was a student there and her husband the dean.

In 1975 I had not succeeded in finding Fu Jen, which was, of course, no longer known by that name.[3] All my inquiries had been met by blank looks. This time, with Madame Liu with me, there was no problem.

The first thing to strike me was the faithful observance of traditional Chinese architectural design in all of the buildings. This reflected the influence of Archbishop Costantini, the exceptionally enlightened apostolic delegate to China in the 1920s, who had untiringly lobbied with Pius XI for the sinicization of the Church in China. In fact, not only its architecture but its very existence owed much to Costantini. He may be said to have been the first hierarch of prominence to have listened to the voice of Fr. Vincent Lebbe, who in 1920 had been hounded out of China by his superiors for incessantly arguing the cause of sinicization as against europeanization.

The institution still serves university purposes as a teachers college. It was evidently a holiday, for there were no students about. Madame Liu spoke to the elderly doorkeeper, who had no objections to our entering. We strolled through the entire building. The physical plant had not been well maintained. This was especially true of the gardens in back, which gave signs of once having been quite beautiful but were now badly overgrown with weeds and untended plants. Madame Liu pointed out to me what had been her husband's offices when he was dean. She also showed me the small bungalow in the middle of the gardens which had been the home of the rector, Fr. Harold Rigney, S.V.D. These were no doubt memory-filled moments for Madame Liu, but she made no complaints and expressed no bitterness. She did not mention it, but I was aware that it was from this bungalow that Father Rigney had been taken in chains by Communist soldiers in March 1949 to spend four years in jail, accused of being a CIA agent. He has described his harrowing experience in *Four Years in a Red Hell.*

Madame Liu always referred to her husband as the dean; actually he was probably the president. Under the Kuomintang the law required that the president of every university be a Chinese. The French Jesuits solved the problem by naming a Chinese scholar who understood and was sympathetic to their aims and content to hold the honor and perquisites of office while leaving control of policy in the hands of the Jesuit rector. Thus Fr. Georges Germain was rector, not president, of Aurora University in Shanghai. Unless I am mistaken part of the problem of the Benedictines at Fu Jen had been caused by a breakdown in this system.

After we completed our visit of Fu Jen, Madame Liu directed our taxi driver to Chabanel House. This was of particular interest

to me since I had had a little something to do with its establishment. When Paul O'Brien and I arrived in China in 1932, the
language program for newly arrived Jesuit missionaries was
virtually nil. Together with two French scholastics we had one
hour of class a day. Our teacher was Fr. Pasquale D'Elia, S.J.,
accomplished sinologist who would later achieve fame in the
scholarly world as Gregorian University professor and editor of the
massive three-volume *Fonti Ricciane*, the memoirs of Matteo Ricci.
The difficulty was that we were taught the rudiments of how to
read Chinese but not how to speak it.

Spoken and written Chinese are two different things. Of
course the spoken language can be written, that is, expressed in
characters. But all the Confucian classics and until our own day
anything deemed worthy of publication, including newspapers,
was written in a classical style known as *wen-li* which was not
spoken. To a considerable extent, this *wen-li* has its own vocabulary of words that are not used in the speech. It is also extremely
concise; and for one who is not yet its master, understanding it is
often a guessing game. This is the language to which Father D'Elia
introduced us, using the same text book that was used by Chinese
boys in the first grade. One could study *wen-li* for a year, the length
of time allotted, and at the end be unable to exchange the time of
day with a Chinese.

The French superiors had a rationale for the system then in
place; it was based upon the relative paucity of missionary
vocations. The decimation of World War I was a major factor in the
shrunken number of religious vocations for generations after.
Demand far outran supply, and it was necessary to put new
arrivals to work as soon as possible. Hence they could not be
allowed more than one year for language. If they were not
introduced to wen-li then, they probably never would learn to
read.

I recognized the problem but was convinced that this was not
an acceptable solution. Regardless of the imbalance between
supply and demand, the language program for all missionaries
had to be lengthened and improved. In correspondence with Fr.
Wlodimir Ledochowski, then the superior general of the Society of
Jesus, I argued the point at length, reminding him of the many
years Father Ricci had devoted to mastering language and literature. He did not need to be persuaded. Chabanel House was
established during my last year in China. From then until the
Communist takeover, every Jesuit newly arrived in China, regard-

less of provenance or destination, spent his first two years in Chabanel House following a professionally organized language program. The program is pursued today in Taiwan.

I had learned from Madame Liu that the government had recently restored the property to the Church. We had a friendly conversation with the gatekeeper and his wife, who occupied the porter's lodge. Chabanel House was a two-story building of considerable length running back from the street and facing a large open yard and garden. The ground floor now served as a kindergarten of some sort, as the large number of small children evidenced. The upper floor, the gatekeeper told us, was the office, probably chancery office, of Bp. Fu Tie-shan. I asked if we might see him. The gatekeeper said that he was ill and actually in the hospital, confirming what I had already been told by Fr. Anthony Liu at Nan Tang.

Madame Liu planned to take me the next morning to visit Tung Tang and Father Ricci's tomb. The latter was given to the Jesuits for that purpose by the emperor in 1610. It had become a Jesuit cemetery sheltering not only Ricci's tomb but those of Adam Schall, Ferdinand Verbiest, and other notables who had followed him. During the Cultural Revolution the Red Guards had smashed and scattered these tombs, but they had recently been completely restored.

Unfortunately I saw neither Tung Tang nor Ricci's tomb. Our schedule was suddenly changed, and we were leaving for Sian the next morning, not in the afternoon as expected. Madame Liu insisted, nevertheless, on coming to the hotel for a short final visit. At the end she knelt down and asked for absolution and blessing. It was an emotional moment for both of us. She then accompanied me to our airport bus, helping me with my bags. There we embraced in final farewell—another emotional moment.

We have kept in touch since. Her Christmas message of 1987 brought the news that her husband, one-time dean of Fu Jen University, noble Confucian and Christian gentleman, had left this world. May he rest in peace.

The Faith in Sian

Our first event in Sian was a two-hour meeting with the Catholic Bishop Chi. He was in prison from 1966, the first year of the Cultural Revolution, until 1979, when Deng Hsiao-ping's policy of relative relaxation began. He was elected bishop by the dozen or so priests belonging to the Patriotic Association in Sian after his release from prison.

His answers were interpreted from Chinese into French by one of our two guide-interpreters. Bishop Chi was a man who spoke freely and frankly. He said that there were some 5,000 practicing Catholics in Sian. He objected to the use of the term *patriotic Catholic Church*, insisting that there were not two Catholic Churches in China but one. The so-called *Patriotic Association* is simply an association within that one Church. He admitted, without hesitation, that there were some Catholics who did not approve of the policy of consecrating bishops without the sanction of Rome. But he thought they were mistaken in their attitude because, in his view, it was that policy alone which had enabled the Church to revive after the Cultural Revolution. He did not find fault with them and insisted that they belonged to the one Chinese Catholic Church, although not to its Patriotic Association. He told us that there were some sixty active Catholic bishops in China in 1982; hanging on his wall was a group photograph of a recent episcopal conference, which confirmed this number.

Bishop Chi was highly critical of Vatican policy towards China and the Church in China. He returned to the subject repeatedly, but it seemed to me significant that the object of his criticism was always the Vatican, never the pope. He mentioned Pope John Paul II several times and always sympathetically, reserving his harsh comments for "the Vatican." The distinction may be *sine fundamento in re*—a merely mental distinction—inasmuch as Vatican policies carry the stamp of papal approval. However, the fact that he made the distinction seemed to me strongly to suggest the desire to keep open the door to eventual reconciliation with the Holy See. By making "the Vatican" the scapegoat one can more easily be reconciled with the pope. He also mentioned sympathetically the visits to China of Cardinals Roger Etchegaray of Marseilles and Franz Koenig of Vienna.

Bishop Chi did not speak of his prison experience except in direct answer to questions. He then said that he was jailed in 1966 and released in 1979 and that he had never been told why he had been imprisoned. Asked what had enabled him to support the long prison years, he replied, "Staying close to Jesus Christ."

The church where we met the bishop had been closed during the Cultural Revolution, and a factory had been built around it so that the church was almost within the factory itself. As we emerged from our meeting, some twenty or more workers quit their work and came outside to talk to us. They were curious but friendly. They asked if we were Catholics, and one of them, to make sure we understood, made the sign of the cross. In answer to my question he said that he was not a Catholic, but it was evident that he was quite familiar and friendly with the Chinese priest who accompanied us. This priest, apparently the bishop's chief assistant and seemingly of about the same age, perhaps a bit older, was a gentle, quiet, priestly man who at Mass on the following Sunday served with finesse and natural dignity as master of ceremonies.

We attended this Mass. It was August 15, the feast of the Assumption of Mary. The church was packed to the doors. There were as many men as women, easily verified because they observed the old custom of men on one side and women on the other and both sides were equally crowded. From the beginning of the Mass to the end, the congregation chanted the ancient prayers, in perfect unison and with a vigor that made the rafters ring. They stopped only for the consecration and communion. It seemed to me remarkable that after all the years of suppression and without access to Mass or to the Blessed Sacrament, they remembered all the old prayers and chanted them as though they had been doing this every day.

There were many elderly, but the congregation by no means consisted only of old people. All ages were well represented, including small children. If there was a noticeable falling off it was in the late teens to early thirties; but even here there was not a total absence but simply a less conspicuous attendance. The same could probably be said of Mass attendance in many non-Communist countries of the world. I made two other noteworthy observations: throughout the Mass there was a constant stream of people going to confession and at communion seemingly the entire congregation received the Eucharist. If there were any who did not, they were not noticeable.

The Mass was not celebrated by Bishop Chi, who knelt in the sanctuary, but by Bp. Bernardin Tung Kuan-ching, O.F.M., of Wuhan. He was one of the first two bishops whose election by their clergy and subsequent consecration in 1958 led to the sad division in the China Church.[4] Bishop Tung said the Mass in Latin and followed the pre-Vatican II liturgy in every detail; and every detail was executed without any improvisation but with an air of devotion and dignity.

After the Mass we had a meeting with the two bishops. Bishop Tung impressed me as a very priestly man, intelligent but at the same time simple and humble. He spoke little, chiefly because every time a question was addressed to Bishop Tung the loquacious Bishop Chi jumped in to answer. The former accepted this with a smile. He did manage to get in a few words. He told us that he was a Franciscan and that his Christian name was Bernardin. He also said that the state of his diocese was comparable to that of Sian, with roughly the same number of Catholics and of priests. He did not speak of his excommunication except, in answer to a question, to admit that it had occurred. I had the distinct impression that he suffered at the recollection. Both bishops freely admitted that they accepted and cooperated with the regime. They regarded this as a patriotic duty. One of their criticisms of the Vatican was that it had over the years urged Catholics not to accept the regime. This resembled the situation of Catholics in France following the Revolution until Leo XIII abandoned this self-destructive policy. The bishops regarded this as antipatriotic and anti-China. At the same time, they insisted vigorously and unequivocally that they reject both atheism and Marxism. When asked what could be done to heal the breach in the Church, they replied, "Pray."

While the kind of ecumenical activities which had developed in the West since Vatican II were unknown in China, Bishop Chi said that he had good personal relations with the Protestant pastor and with the Muslim imam. Because of another meeting, Bishop Tung bade us good-by after some forty-five minutes; we continued with Bishop Chi for another half hour.

Bishop Chi insisted that since the end of the Cultural Revolution and the fall of the Gang of Four the policy in China, constitutionally guaranteed, was one of religious liberty. He freely admitted, however, that in practice there were many limitations to which they had to adjust. For example, the Church formerly could have schools to teach children the catechism; he was asked if he found the absence of such schools satisfactory. Without hesitation he replied that it was obviously not satisfactory, but that the Church had to adjust and find other means of teaching religion.

Sian has a large Muslim population, and we visited a large, centuries-old mosque in the heart of the Muslim quarter. The rest of the group had a question-and-answer session with the imam. I missed this because, before he arrived, I had wandered out to the street, where I found myself quickly surrounded by a crowd of all ages. They were all Muslims and, being also Chinese, were curious, good natured, and friendly. I had a great time asking them questions and responding to theirs. There was a good deal

On a return trip to China, Father Dunne took time to discuss the country's future and its past with the young and the old. Photos here and on page 475 by Alden Stevenson, S.J.

of laughter. I suspect that what they found amusing was less my wit than my peculiar pronunciation of Chinese. I took leave of them with regret, amid a general waving of hands as our bus pulled away.

Luoyang

Luoyang, in the province of Honan, was the only stop which had not figured in my tour in 1975. We arrived there by train. Luoyang, like Sian, has several times served both as a feudal and an imperial capital. King Wu, the second ruler of the Kingdom of Chou (c. 1122–249 B.C.), was the first to make it his capital. A few miles east of Luoyang, however, archeologists have recently unearthed the remains of a palace which they estimate to be thirty-seven hundred years old, which would take us all the way back to the previous Shang dynasty (1766–1122 B.C.).

In this same area is one of the most famous of Buddhist temples in China, the White Horse Temple. One of the first Buddhist temples was founded here about 61 B.C. Legend says that the Han emperor, Ming-ti, inspired by a dream of a golden Buddha, sent an emissary to India to bring back Buddhist scriptures. This emissary, Ch'in Ching, returned with two Indian Buddhist monks, Kasyapa-Matanga and Dharmaraksa, and with a troop of white horses bearing the Buddhist sutras. The emperor ordered the construction of the White Horse Temple. This may be said to have been the birthplace of Buddhism in China. It is now but one of many buildings which make up the Buddhist center.

We visited several Buddhist temples and monasteries, and in one of them—I cannot remember with certainty if it was here at the White Horse Temple or at another—we had an interesting discussion with the abbot of the Buddhist community. I find many contradictions in Buddhism. For example, Buddhists pray. They pray a great deal. Yet they do not believe in God. To whom do they pray? I put the question to the abbot. "To Buddha," he replied. But Buddha is not God. He is, or was, a man, Siddhartha or Sakyamuni, born around 563 B.C. How can he answer your prayers? Buddhists do not believe in an immortal soul, yet they pray for their beloved departed. How does one explain this seeming contradiction? I did not put these questions to the abbot because I did not wish to engage in a disputation which I knew from experience would shed no real light upon the subject.

A few miles from Luoyang is Lungmen—the Dragon Gate—famed for the thousands of Buddhist statues carved into the cliffs on each side of the River Yi. The rest of the group descended to the riverbank to visit them on foot. I was content to view them from the bridge which crosses the River Yi at this point. It is an extraordinary sight. According to one authority—I did not count them—there are in all "1352 caves, 750 niches, 39 small pagodas, 3608 inscriptions, and 97,306 statues, ranging from the tallest of 17.14 metres to the tiniest of 2 centimetres—all within an area of half a mile."[5] This prodigious work of sculpture was begun in the fifth century during the dynasty of the Northern Wei and completed four centuries later.

From Luoyang we took the train to Nanking. It was during this stage of our journey that I encountered the sole instance of hostility experienced in either of my visits to Communist China. There had been heavy floods in the province of Shansi. Several times our train was delayed for long stretches because of flooded tracks some miles ahead. One such delay, which lasted several hours, was at a moderate-sized town whose name I have forgotten. Vendors on the station quay were doing a land-office business selling flavored ices. It was July, which in China means hot. Among the vendors was a boy of eleven or twelve years. When I looked at him he glared at me. When I started to approach him he spat in my direction. Every time I glanced in his direction as I paced the quay he was staring at me with hate-filled eyes. I have never forgotten the malevolence of his expression. He had evidently been thoroughly brainwashed with hatred for foreign devils. Had he been born a century earlier he would probably have been a zealous member of the Boxer movement. I repeat, this was the only experience of its kind during my visits to China.

Because of the repeated delays caused by flood waters, this day trip became an overnight trip. We arrived in Nanking in the morning.

Nanking

While in Peking I had asked authorization to visit Zosé, which was not scheduled on our tour. Zosé was a property of the French Jesuits some twenty miles from Shanghai, rising several hundred feet above the surrounding plain and its network of canals. Halfway up the hill was a mission church and residence which for several weeks in the summertime served as summer villa for the scholastics. Crowning the summit was an astronomical observatory manned by the French Jesuits and a basilica erected in fulfillment of a promise made when the Shanghai mission stations were spared the violence of the Boxer Rebellion, which swept across China in 1900 taking the lives of some thirty thousand Christians. I explained that it was for nostalgic reasons alone, since having spent four summer vacations there with other Jesuit scholastics between 1932 and 1936 it held many happy memories for me. To my considerable surprise my request was readily granted. Since our itinerary called for less than two full days in Shanghai I suggested that I stay over an extra day. The official said this could not be arranged. He suggested instead, again to my surprise, that I leave Nanking a day ahead of schedule and go on to Shanghai alone. This I did.

Shanghai

With his customary efficiency our number-one guide made all the arrangements for me, getting the railroad ticket, calling a taxi whose driver he instructed to see that I got on the train (I told the driver not to wait, that I could manage myself), and phoning the Shanghai office of the official travel agency, known as CITS, to have me met at the station and taken to the hotel.

I had with me a packet of medicine for Fr. George Huang, S.J. George and his brother Willie—he prefers this to his formal name William—had become Catholics while students at the Marist High School in Shanghai. Later, after graduating from Aurora University, George entered the Society of Jesus in California. Normally he would have entered the Province of Paris, but because of his admiration for Fr. Frank Rouleau, who had been his English professor at the university, he asked to be received in the California Province. After completing the ten or more years of study which constitute the Jesuit formation process, he returned to Shanghai shortly before the Communist takeover. He soon found himself clapped into jail along with others who refused to join the Patriotic Association. There he remained for twenty-seven years. He was one of the eleven Jesuits about whom I had vainly sought information on my visit in 1975; with them he had been released following the relaxation introduced by Deng Hsiao-ping in 1979.

For two to three short years of freedom he lived with his brother Willie, saying Mass privately in the house and teaching English in two schools in Shanghai. He was one of those who in November 1981 had been rearrested. He was sent to a labor camp in the province of Anwei. His brother got word to Father Rouleau in Los Gatos, California, that George was in need of certain medicines which were not available in China, and Father Rouleau had sent the package of medicines to me. Fr. Alden Stevenson had supplied me with Willie Huang's address on Yu Yuan-lu—which I translate as Idiot's Garden Road! I expected to be queried about the contents of the package when entering China from Hong Kong; but Chinese customs officers had passed us through without examining our bags or asking questions.

After checking in at the hotel I got out my map of Shanghai, upon which I had marked the location of Willie Huang's house. It did not appear to be too far from my hotel, and I decided I could make it on foot. So shortly after arriving at the hotel I started out.

It was mid afternoon and mid summer, and anyone who knows Shanghai knows what that means. Furthermore, maps are deceiving. Yu Yuan-lu proved to be much farther than it appeared on the map. When I finally reached it I showed my map to a Chinese pedestrian, indicating the location of Willie's home. He advised me that it was too far to attempt on foot. Ignoring his advice, I attempted to make it, but failed. Less than halfway there I began to have warning signals of angina pectoris. I took a nitroglycerin tablet and returned, not without difficulty, to the hotel.

That evening around seven o'clock, which Alden had told me was the best time to call on Willie, I returned, but this time by taxi. Not wanting to lose the taxi lest I have to return on foot, which I knew I was not up to, I asked the driver to wait. What resulted, although it did not occur to me at the time, must have looked to the taxi driver like a scene from a spy movie. The house was protected by a stone wall. I rattled the large iron gate. After much rattling the gate opened, and Willie Huang appeared in the darkness which had already set in. I identified myself. Father Rouleau had informed him that I was coming. He and his wife, who had appeared, naturally wanted me to come in; but remembering the angina of the afternoon, I declined, handed him the package of medicine, gave him the name of the hotel, told him to phone me, and hurried back to the waiting taxi, whose bemused driver had witnessed the strange operation which had taken at most two minutes.

He must have reported it; he would have been delinquent had he not. This was a Friday evening. When Willie Huang came to the hotel on Sunday to take me by bus to his home for dinner he was questioned closely by the young woman at the reception desk before she called my room: what was his relationship with me? How did he know me? Had I appeared at his home on Friday evening?

Like all the young women and young men on the staff, she was very friendly; but as Willie Huang pointed out, they all work for CITS and undoubtedly are under orders to report suspicious looking incidents. My behavior Friday evening was nothing if not suspicious. When Willie brought me back after dinner Sunday we got off the bus a block from the hotel. Willie left me there, explaining that he did not want to be seen there again.

Saturday morning I took the bus alone to Zikawei. A young man from the hotel staff told me the number of the bus to take and kindly showed me where to get it—a half block from the hotel. I asked the conductor to tell me when we arrived at Zikawei, which she did. As I have already remarked, anyone familiar with the Zikawei of 1932 could not possibly recognize it in 1982; and it had changed even more since my visit in 1975. More modern buildings, including a large cinema, had been added.

The bus stop was some distance beyond the ancient Jesuit buildings. I had not noticed this. Upon descending from the bus I started to walk in the wrong direction. I had gone some distance, looking in vain for a familiar landmark, before I asked a Chinese fruit vendor for help. I told him that I was a Catholic and that I was looking for the Catholic church in Zikawei. With a smile he turned me around and headed me in the right direction.

I was astonished by the appearance of Saint Ignatius Church. I have described its wretched condition in 1975. The wire fence was gone. The area in front of the church had been cleaned up, all the debris removed. The shattered rose window had been replaced, the new window if anything more beautiful than the old. I was told that during the years of the Cultural Revolution, one of the priests, most of whom made umbrellas, had shown exceptional talent working with stained glass. It is perhaps he who made the new rose window. The two spires, destroyed by the Red Guards, were in process of being restored. The steel structures of both had been erected; because the masonry work was not yet completed the scaffolding was still in place. The interior of the church had been completely restored, cleaned, and renovated. The pews had been painted and varnished. A bishop's throne had been installed in the sanctuary, indicating that this was now the cathedral. The small garden area at the side of the church was carefully tended, and a modern restroom had been built.

I wandered about quite freely. I was able to approach, but not enter, the old theologate building. The new wing, which was under construction when I left in 1936, was occupied by the Shanghai branch of the Scientific and Historical Institute. I was told this by a young man who came out from what seemed to be a kind of porter's lodge to inquire what I wanted. Through a window of the new wing I could see that a meeting was in progress. Incidentally, it was here, as well as in a factory school, that George Huang had taught English during his two to three years of freedom. Over the wall I was able to point out to my interlocutor the room in which I had lived for three years, 1933–36. He was very interested in my account of what the building served for then and in what I was doing there, studying theology.

I crossed the boulevard and entered the ancient Seng-mou Yuan, the girls' orphanage, high school, and convent. It now served as residence for Bp. (Aloysius) Chang Chia-shu and a number of priests. The doorkeeper, to whom I identified myself and for whom I signed the guest book, was quite friendly, although I had trouble understanding his mandarin, which carried distinct traces of the Shanghai dialect. He told me that because of his age— eighty-nine years—the bishop did not receive visitors. Since our program called for a group meeting with the bishop that afternoon—or so I thought—I did not press the matter.

The afternoon meeting turned out to be quite a surprise. We were taken to a building not far from the Bund, the Shanghai waterfront. It was occupied by ecclesiastical offices and seemed familiar. We all thought that we were to meet with the Roman Catholic patriotic bishop, Aloysius Chang, S.J. When the bishop entered the conference room, I was astonished by his youthful appearance. He looked like a man in his sixties, perhaps, but certainly not in his late eighties. I had no reason, however, to question his identity and did not. He introduced his two companions, a priest, Father Yao, and a layman, both of whom served on his episcopal staff as researchers in the history of the Church in China. He answered our questions quite freely, occasionally asking one of his companions to reply. I asked him about Bp. Kung

P'ing-mei, who had been in prison for some thirty years. He replied that he had no recent information.

After some forty-five minutes of questions and answers, still not questioning his identity, I said to him: "I am a Jesuit, as you are also. A number of our Jesuit confreres, whom I knew fifty years ago and whom you know, after having spent many years in prison have recently been arrested again. What do you think can be done about this and what do you think can be done to end the division in the Church?"

With a smile he replied: "I cannot answer that. I am not a Roman Catholic."

"Aren't you Bishop Chang?" I asked.

"No, I am Bishop Cheng, the head of the Anglo-Catholic Church in Shanghai." He added that he had very good personal relations with Bishop Chang, but that he could not speak for him or for the Roman Catholic community.

The meeting continued, although everyone was surprised—and I was shocked—to discover that we were not talking to the man we thought we were. Father Yao gave a rather lengthy and accurate summary of the history of the Church in China, from the Nestorian appearance in the seventh century through the Franciscan effort in the thirteenth and the Jesuit arrival in the sixteenth to today, with special emphasis upon the foreign domination characteristic of the nineteenth and well into the twentieth century. It was all quite familiar to me, but probably not to the rest of the group. In any case, I had lost interest in the meeting.

At my first meeting with the group in Fribourg I had raised the question of a visit with Bishop Chang; and Dr. Anand Nayak had replied that, at his request, CITS had already arranged this. So I now wondered if we had been deceived. I later learned that this was not so; it was a case of mistaken identity for which no one was really at fault although Dr. Nayak was responsible. After my return to Switzerland he let me read the correspondence relating to arranging a meeting with Bishop Chang. What had happened was clear.

More than a year before the tour, Fr. Leon Trivière of the Foreign Mission Society of Paris, an old China hand and well-known writer about things Chinese, had recommended to Dr. Nayak that he try to arrange a meeting with Bishop Cheng, giving the bishop's address. Dr. Nayak had mistakenly assumed that this was the Roman Catholic Patriotic Association bishop of Shanghai. He wrote to Cheng and received a gracious reply expressing willingness to meet with the group. In making program arrangements he asked CITS to include, if possible, a meeting with Bishop Cheng. The agency did exactly as he asked. Still under the illusion that Cheng was Chang, Dr. Nayak was as surprised as anyone when in response to my question Cheng informed us that he was not a Roman Catholic!

The day before, I had noted on the schedule posted in the church at Zikawei that there were four Masses on Sunday, the principal one a high Mass at 9:30 A.M. Since I had been there, I led the group on the public bus. Afraid, nevertheless, that I might miss the stop I asked a young passenger if she would tell me when we reached Zikawei. I told her we wanted to go to the Catholic church. Again I noted the total lack of hostility. She said that she was not a Catholic herself, but that she could lead us directly there since she worked just across the street from the church.

We arrived just in time for the Mass. Although this was but one of four Masses, we found the church, which easily accommodates two thousand people, about eighty percent filled. Unlike in Sian, here the old custom of separating the sexes was no longer observed, but there seemed to me as many men as women. There were also many young people and children. And there was the same window-shaking chanting of prayers in perfect unison. At communion it seemed that the entire congregation received the Eucharist, distributed by the celebrant and another priest, both assistants in the parish. After the Mass there was solemn benediction of the Blessed Sacrament, during which a mixed choir of some forty voices sang beautifully the ancient Latin hymns.

To kneel in these same pews where I had so often knelt fifty years before and to find myself surrounded by hundreds of Chinese Catholics participating in the Eucharist, after years of persecution and closed churches, with the same fervor and devotion as those who had knelt there with me a half century earlier was a profoundly moving experience. I sobbed uncontrollably and without shame.

After Mass I met the pastor, Father Ai. We conversed for some twenty minutes, standing on the porch outside the side entrance. Throughout our conversation people old and young approached with rosaries, holy medals, and holy pictures which they asked him to bless. He told me that Bishop Chang, although in good health, is usually not available to visitors because of his advanced age. For this same reason, he said, the bishop did not preside at the 9:30 Mass this morning, though he sometimes did. He said that the life of the parish was flourishing, with three hundred conversions the previous year. Instruction classes were held after Mass on Sundays. As we spoke I saw fifteen or twenty people, men and women, enter the rectory, and when Father Ai left me it was to conduct their instruction class.

Father Ai told me that there were nine Catholic churches reopened in Shanghai and its environs. At Zosé, where part of the property had been returned to the Church (perhaps the part not returned was the astronomical observatory), a seminary with forty students and three priests was already in operation. The rector of the seminary, I later learned, was Fr. (Aloysius) Chin Lu-hsien, a Jesuit, who had done his doctoral studies in Cologne, Germany, and maintained regular correspondence with friends there, Jesuits and others. Father Chin had spent sixteen or more years in prison as a papal loyalist, followed by ten years in a labor camp in the north.[6] Following his release he was named superior of the seminary at Zosé, which is controlled by the Patriotic Association, and several years ago was named auxiliary bishop to the aged Bp. (Ignatius) Chang Chia-shu of Shanghai. Upon the death of the latter in 1988, he became bishop of Shanghai. Bp. Kung P'ing-mei remains, of course, the bishop recognized by Rome.

As he was about to take leave of me, Father Ai introduced me to a sister of Bp. Chang Chia-shu who had just emerged from the church. A gentle, fragile, smiling woman of eighty-six years, she was being helped by a younger woman. I accompanied them to the front gate. She said that her brother was in good health but remarked with a smile that he was even older than she was.

I had brought with me to give to Bishop Chang as a gift a missal which I had obtained a few years before in Taiwan. It contained the new liturgy of the Mass, with the four Eucharistic Prayers in facing columns of Chinese and Latin. In it I had written a message to the bishop, wishing him well and expressing the hope that the division in the Church would be healed before either of us left this world. I had hoped to present this to him at the flawed meeting of the previous day. This not having been possible, I returned to Zikawei after dinner on Sunday to make another effort. Again I went to Seng-mou Yuan, formerly the sisters' schools. There was a priest in the parlor apparently counseling two women; I interrupted their conversation and explained the purpose of my visit. The priest repeated what others had said, that the bishop was not receiving visitors, and told me to take my book to the priests in the rectory across the street. (Father Ai and his three assistants do not live in Seng-mou Yuan but have their own rectory attached to Saint Ignatius Cathedral. Unless my memory faults me, the old sacristy, which was very large, had been remodeled, and perhaps enlarged, to provide living quarters and several offices for the priests.)

I followed his advice. The priest on duty was the same who had celebrated the 9:30 Mass that morning, Fr. Joachim Liu. We had an extensive conversation. He, as had Father Ai that morning, inquired about Fr. Frank Rouleau, whom both remembered with affection. Father Rouleau had taught them ecclesiastical and mission history at the major seminary. Father Liu told me that he had entered the major seminary in 1936, the year I left China, after studying in the minor seminary, both located in Zikawei. He had been ordained in 1940, not by Bishop Haouisée, who was ill at the time, but by a bishop from another diocese. We talked about many Jesuits we both had known, among them my old rector and friend, Fr. Yves Henry.

Father Liu showed great interest in the missal and its new Eucharistic Prayers. He examined it at some length and promised that he would see that it reached Bishop Chang. I inquired about Bp. Kung P'ing-mei. He, as had Father Ai, said he had no recent information about him. I asked if he were still living. He assumed he was, because he felt sure that had he died he would have heard of it. Neither did he have any information about the eleven—the exact number was in dispute—Jesuits who had been reimprisoned the previous November.

Kung P'ing-mei was indeed still living. He would be released, probably because of his age, in 1986, after thirty-five or more years in prison. Still refusing to join the Patriotic Association, he resided until recently in quiet retirement with Bishops Chang and Chin in Zikawei. Since the death of Bishop Chang he has been permitted by the political authorities to come to the United States for medical treatment. As for the Jesuits, Frs. Francis Xavier Chu and Stanislaus Shen found their freedom in death several years ago. The others have been released. George Huang is again living with his brother; although not belonging to the Patriotic Association he maintains friendly relations with those who do. Until recently he taught a class in American history at the Zosé seminary; this was terminated, apparently because someone did not deem Lincoln's Gettysburg Address an appropriate subject to be committed to memory by Chinese seminarians. Vincent Chu has also been released, but remains severely limited in his contacts. Of the several other Jesuits I have no information, but presume that they too have benefited from the somewhat relaxed policy.

I asked Father Liu if they had received financial assistance from the government to renovate the church, especially to rebuild the two spires which must have been quite costly. He replied in the negative. The Catholic parishioners themselves were meeting all the expenses without outside help.

Despite my demurrer, Father Liu, in typical Chinese fashion, insisted upon accompanying me to the gate where we embraced in Christian and fraternal charity and bade each other a fond adieu.

I did not get to Zosé, as I had hoped. My visits with Willie Huang and to Zikawei had preempted all my free time. Our China tour was coming to an end. From Shanghai we flew to Canton and from Canton to Japan. A young Japanese Dominican priest in doctoral studies at the University of Fribourg had arranged a week's visit divided between Kyoto and Tokyo.

Japan—The Beauty and the Horror

Beautiful Kyoto, a city of Buddhist and Shinto temples and shrines galore, was the imperial capital of Japan from 794 until the Meiji restoration in 1868 and is still its cultural capital. In Kyoto we stayed in a kindergarten, thanks to the hospitality of the Japanese Dominican nuns who operated it. It was summer vacation, so the school was vacant. Everyone slept on mats except me, the men in one room, the women in another. Over my protests I was assigned the only bed in the school, in deference to my age. Everything else—dining tables, chairs, wash stands, even toilets—was tailored to the size of the small children for whom they were intended, which made for some excruciatingly funny experiences.

On our first day in Kyoto we met with the founder and staff of a new and small Japanese Christian sect. They were nice people, but I found the explanation of their doctrine boring; at the first opportunity, which was the lunch break, I ducked out.

I found extremely interesting, however, the liturgies which we witnessed in two Shinto temples. In one, an analogue of the Christian baptismal ceremony, a young Japanese couple proudly presented their infant to a priest for initiation into the Shinto religion. The symbolic meaning of the rites was lost on me, but not their beauty. The same must be said of the other ceremony we attended; somewhat analogous to our Mass, I assume it is the central act of worship in the Shinto liturgy. It was conducted by several Shinto priests assisted by half a dozen acolytes. If I did not understand its meaning, I thoroughly appreciated its grace and beauty. Afterwards we had tea, cookies, and conversation with one of the Shinto priests.

None of our experiences was more interesting than our visit to a large Zen Buddhist monastery, although I have no desire to repeat it. The monastery consisted of a great many temples and halls against a background of immaculate lawns, pebbled paths, lovely flowers, and graceful trees. We were met by a sophisticated Zen monk who was obviously well educated, keenly intelligent, and well informed on Catholic asceticism. He had, in fact, spent some months living with the Benedictine monks in a famous monastery in Germany.

After an explanatory tour of some of the buildings he took us to a lecture hall, where he summarized for us the history and characteristics of Zen Buddhism. He then took us to a meditation hall, where he proposed to lead us through a period of Zen meditation. Each of us was provided with a pillow upon which to sit Japanese fashion. This, of course, is not possible; any attempt to do so is agonizing, endurable but a few moments. Japanese sit on their insteps, their feet turned outward flat on the floor; they can do this because they have done it since they were infants, when their leg and foot bones were still malleable. It is because of this manner of sitting that many Japanese are a bit pigeon-toed and bow-legged. The best this westerner could do was to sit on his heels and the soles of his feet, while gritting his teeth.

Our genial mentor was aware of our limitations and allowed us to settle for a second-class Zen posture. He was more demanding when it came to the position of the hands, which is clearly defined, and of the spinal column, which must be maintained at all times as unbending as that of an English schoolmaster. To make sure that it was, our master from time to time arose from his pillow and, armed with what appeared to be a curtain rod, proceeded around the circle measuring the rigidity of our spinal columns.

We had not been assigned any special subject for meditation. Without any conscious choice I found myself meditating on the subject of pain as my seventy-seven-year-old arthritis-riddled body struggled to uphold the honor of Christian ascetics.

I thanked whatever Zen gods there be that our mentor had told us beforehand that while the normal meditation period was an hour he was cutting ours in half, out of consideration for our inexperience. Every once in a while a bell, like that of a clock, quietly broke the profound silence, bringing assurance that, however contrary to what seemed the fact, time was passing and the end approaching. When it arrived I struggled to suppress a huge sigh of relief—and had to be helped to my feet. I have never been very good at the meditation methods of Saint Ignatius. I was a total failure at the Zen. Nevertheless, the experience is something to look back upon, though not forward to. And our mentor was a gracious and brilliant gentleman.

Other interesting experiences in Kyoto included a group discussion with the young Catholic bishop, following the Mass which Father Kulala and I concelebrated with him. The most unforgettable, however, was a trip to Hiroshima. Though I should forget everything else, this I shall never forget.

We took the famous hundred-mile-an-hour train from Kyoto. En route we ran into a typhoon, whose shrieking winds and smashing torrents of rain threatened to sweep us off the track. It slowed us down to about thirty miles an hour, but we eventually reached Hiroshima.

The first event scheduled was a visit and lunch at a factory on the outskirts of the city. I skipped this in favor of a visit to the Jesuit high school, Hiroshima Gakuin, built after the war by the California Province with substantial fund-raising help from Fr. Tom Sullivan. The school, one of the elite of Japan, belongs to the Jesuit Japanese Province. Its staff, like the Japanese Province itself, is international. California Jesuits have been associated with it from the beginning. Its first rector, who supervised its construction, was Fr. Hilary Werts, S.J.

When I visited in 1982, there were two Californians on the staff, Fr. Glen Smith and Br. Francis Uyeda. It was Brother Uyeda who picked me up at the railroad station. After lunch with the Jesuit community, Father Smith drove me to the Museum of Horrors, where I was joined by the other members of our group. The wind had somewhat abated, but the rain was still torrential.

Museum of Horrors is not the name of the museum, but it might well be. Hiroshima in 1982 was a beautiful city. There were few traces of the frightful devastation which visited it and its anguished inhabitants thirty-seven years earlier. But gathered within this museum in abundance are grisly relics and photographs which recreate the agony of that day when demonic forces destroyed in an instant the myth that, unlike others, we of the West are a civilized people. We had managed to nurture that illusion despite Coventry, Amsterdam, Dresden, Hamburg, Warsaw, the firebombing of Tokyo, the Holocaust, and a thousand other mass massacres which forever live in infamy.

We clung to the illusion even after the hellish events of August 6 and August 9 in 1945. I myself, as I have recounted above, rang the bells of Our Lady of Sorrows Church in Santa Barbara with such euphoric joy that the bell-rope broke in my hands. Of course we did not know what we were doing and may therefore be forgiven as those who crucified Christ were forgiven. We thought we were celebrating the end of the horrors of war.

I do not think I really knew the extent of the horrors by which we had ended the war until my visit to the museum in Hiroshima. I don't think anyone but the utterly soulless could emerge from that museum without feeling forever branded with a mark of sorrow and shame. I left wishing that Ronald Reagan and his crowd together with Leonid Brezhnev and his crowd could be locked within and left there on bread and water until they had reached an agreement upon the elimination of nuclear weapons from their respective warhouses.

There is little more to tell about the Japanese phase of our tour. It was difficult to believe that exactly half a century had passed since I first saw Tokyo; that Tokyo had been almost totally obliterated by our fire bombs to be replaced, thanks to Japanese energy and ingenuity, by the modern and considerably western-ized Tokyo of today, one of the world's most populous cities.

One day the group took the train to Kamakura to spend the day with a well-known monk and exponent of Zen Buddhist doctrine. I abandoned the group at the last station before Kamakura, not because I feared a repetition of the bone-creaking experience in Kyoto but because I wanted to visit another elite Jesuit school, the Taisei Gakuin, with certain California connections. Its founder was Fr. George Voss, S.J., who spent the war years in California. Although a German citizen and a member of the Jesuit province of Japan, he was not interned but was allowed to minister to German soldiers in prisoner-of-war camps. Immediately after the war, he returned to Japan, where for a nominal sum he bought a large part of what had been the principal Japanese naval base at Shonan-taura and converted it into a high school. A few years later, the Japanese government negotiated a deal with Father Voss; in exchange for their former naval base they deeded to him a magnificent piece of property and several million dollars with which to build Taisei Gakuin.

I hoped to see again this brilliant educator, administrator, entrepreneur, and religious who had been my friend during the war years. I learned from Fr. Walter Brennan, S.J., the present rector and himself a member of the California Province, that Father Voss had suffered a stroke the previous year and, although now recovered, was living at Sophia University in Tokyo. I would see him there the following day.

After lunch Father Brennan drove me to Kamakura to the home of the Zen Buddhist monk, where I rejoined my traveling companions.

After a highly successful career as an architect this brilliant man had become an exponent of Zen Buddhism. He and his wife had established in their home a community of a dozen or more students of Zen among whom I discovered, somewhat to my surprise, were an American Maryknoll nun and a bearded, but young, Jesuit priest whose provenance and name I no longer remember. I arrived near the end of the dialogue which everyone evidently had greatly enjoyed.

One of the special events of this visit to Tokyo, no doubt my last, was a reunion with Naphasra—"Nappy" to her many friends—Javanguru and her husband Robert du Marais. She had been among the Georgetown students in the junior-year-abroad program at the University of Fribourg in 1972. Nappy's father was Thai, her mother Japanese, and she embodied the best qualities of both cultures. She had been raised in Japan and was a graduate of the famed Sacred Heart Academy, the college of choice of many of the leading families of Japan for the education of their daughters. One famed student of this academy is now the Empress Michiko, whose husband, Akihito, has succeeded his father, the Showa emperor Hirohito, to the Chrysanthemum Throne of Japan; as a student at Sacred Heart she probably little dreamed—or perhaps she did—of where destiny was leading her.

Nappy, who spoke impeccable French and English as well as Thai and Japanese, was a brilliant student. She was also in love. On a visit to Switzerland the previous summer she had met Robert du Marais, scion of a titled French family of Provence who was doing graduate studies in the highly ranked school of economics at the Swiss University of Galles. The attraction was reciprocal.

Although the French are far more immune than Americans to the virus of antimiscegenational bigotry, even they are not always predisposed to accept without resistance that East and West should meet in the marriage of one of the family. Robert spent the Christmas holidays of 1972 not in the family chateau in Reaumont, near Grenoble, but in Fribourg, near Nappy. The three of us shared a delicious Japanese dinner that Nappy prepared in her tiny student apartment. Nappy had been raised a Buddhist, but as a result of her long years in Catholic schools—Sacred Heart Academy, Georgetown University, and now Fribourg—was thoroughly familiar with things Catholic. I encouraged them in their *amour*, confident that once they had met Nappy, Baron and Baroness du Marais, Robert's parents, would prove as vulnerable to her charms as had Robert himself.

That is what happened. Over two years later, in February 1975, I found myself en route to Reaumont to preside at their marriage, scheduled to take place the next day in the village church. I stopped in Lausanne to pick up two of Nappy's former schoolmates at the Sacred Heart Academy in Tokyo, who were doing graduate work in Lausanne. One of them was the daughter of the first secretary in the Japanese embassy in Rome. The other was a Mitsubishi, a name as well known in the industrial and commercial world as that of Rothschild in the financial world. Both were charming companions.

We sighted the du Marais chateau some time before arriving at the village of Reaumont. Its walls, a watchtower at each of the four corners, enclose the entire top of a plateau which looms above the village. Within the walls is the chateau itself, looking much as it did six hundred years ago. Included in the list of those who have owned it at one time or another is a Prince-Archbishop of Vienna and a Dauphin of France. The last to own it before Baron du Marais was the Prince of Monaco. It had suffered badly when the fires of the French Revolution raged through the countryside, but the Prince of Monaco had it completely restored following the original architectural plans preserved in the archives. To medieval charm were added the comforts provided by plumbing and central heating.

I had forgotten that France was on daylight savings time; Switzerland was not. We were expected for lunch at 12 o'clock. We arrived at 1 o'clock. Luncheon had been put off from minute to minute, opinions differing about whether we would arrive or not.

The wise decision to wait no longer was made just before we drove into the courtyard. I was quite embarrassed by my failure to take account of the time change.

The only thing worse than being late for a dinner engagement is to forget it entirely. This too had happened to me years before, when I became so engrossed in listening to the radio account of the Joe Louis–Billy Conn fight that I completely forgot that I was to dine that evening at the home of a rather prominent lady who had expressed to Joe Rice, president of the Catholic Theatre Guild, the desire to meet the author of *Trial by Fire*. That, to be sure, was truly gross, a *faux pas* for which I could not expect to be forgiven. Nor was I. In the present instance, the gracious demeanor of Baron and Baroness du Marais easily covered my embarrassment and resolved my feeling of guilt.

Nappy's father had flown out from Tokyo for the wedding. He reinforced an impression formed during my first visit to Bangkok, confirmed in subsequent visits and by ever-smiling Nappy herself, that risibility is the centerpiece of the Thai character. I do not know if they are, but they seem to be the happiest people on earth. I think Aristotle says that it is risibility which sets the human apart from the merely animal. Perhaps the Thai are simply more human than the rest of us.

The wedding day was beautiful—cloudless blue skies, snow-clad French Alps towering above—but bitterly cold. The village church, crowded with several hundred friends, was an icebox. Nappy, lovely in her beautiful but far from thermal Japanese kimono, shivered uncontrollably. I brought my overcoat out from the sacristy to drape around her shoulders, but Robert waved me away impatiently. Perhaps, as he thought, the shivers were due as much to nervousness as to the cold.

The seriousness of the occasion was lightened by unexpected and amusing incidents. One of Robert's two brothers, seated in the second row, reached out to get his hand on one of his restless children. He reached too far. The wicker chair on which he was seated slid out from under him. He went crashing to the floor, his boy on top of him, amidst general hilarity.

Two other priests, friends of the family, assisted at the wedding. One of them gave an appropriate homily in French. I had been asked by Baron du Marais to speak in English, out of consideration for Nappy's father, who understood English but not French. I had scarcely begun when, like a clap of thunder, the church bells in the tower directly above my head began to toll. The sound was deafening. No one present knew how to stop it. The bells were controlled electrically and were set to announce to the countryside the arrival of noon time. There was nothing to do but wait out the bells which rang clangorously for fully five minutes, shouting the good news for miles around that midday had come. While my homily was put on hold, a quick-thinking young woman filled in by leading us all in singing commonly known carols. It cannot be said that we made the rafters ring; the bells had already seen to that. But we converted the solemnity of the liturgy into a freewheeling and joyous songfest. By the time the bells ceased, allowing us to get on to more serious business, everyone was in a near hilarious mood which carried on throughout the afternoon.

The afternoon featured a splendid dinner served to three hundred or more guests in the large library which occupied the fourth floor of the chateau. I had to leave in the midst of the festivities for the long drive back to Fribourg over icy roads.

I would return the following year to baptize the first baby, a little girl. Nappy and Robert lived in Versailles, but they brought their little girl home to be baptized in the village church which had witnessed their memorable wedding. I had something to do with the selection of her name. Nappy had written to me for advice; she knew that it was Catholic custom to select a name from the list of recognized saints. This imposed severe limitations because the number of Japanese names in the calendar of saints is not extensive. I told Nappy to forget the custom and to give her baby a real Japanese name. (This, I believe, is now generally done by Japanese Catholics.) The important thing was that she be a saint, not that she bear the name of one. Their baby had been born in August. I baptized her with the lovely Japanese name Natsuko, which means "Child of the Summer."

Several years later Robert was sent to Tokyo by his company for a year's initiation in the language, after which he was put in charge of its Asian office. So they were there in 1982 waiting for me, their number increased to four. Natsuko now had a little sister, Malia, both of them a blend of the beauty and grace of the several cultures which had formed them. Nappy and Robert had an apartment within two blocks of the Jesuits' Sophia University. We had a pleasantly nostalgic reunion. Afterwards they drove me through the maze of Tokyo's darkened streets to Risso-Kosei-Kai, where I was staying; there we said farewell.

This brought to an end what was without doubt my last visit to Japan and to the Orient. I returned to Switzerland, pausing in

Los Angeles for a visit with my sister and other remnants of the family, which then included a surviving brother, since gone, and an assortment of nieces, nephews, and grandnieces and grand-nephews.

I wrote a report of what I had observed in China, particularly as it related to the life of the Church. I tried to limit it to an objective statement of what I had seen and heard, with a minimum of commentary. It was not written for publication but chiefly for the eyes of the pope. Whether he read it or not, I do not know. I do know that he received it because it was placed in his hands by a mutual friend, Karolyn de Habicht.

I had known her husband, Mieczyslaw de Habicht, during my Sodepax days, when he was associate secretary of the Council of the Laity in Rome. His family, whose ancient roots were Swiss, had through intermarriage become Polish in the Middle Ages. In the pre-Communist era he had been in the Polish diplomatic service. His wife, Karolyn, was Dutch, highly intelligent and, like many Dutch, a gifted linguist. She and her husband were intimate friends of Card. Karol Wojtyla of Cracow. She and he shared the same patron saint, and every year on the feast of Saint Charles Borromeo she and her husband assisted at Wojtyla's Mass and afterwards breakfasted with him. After he was elected pope he had said to her, "Now that I am pope, you must come to Rome to celebrate our feast together." She and her husband, and after his death she alone, had done so, assisting at John Paul II's Mass in his private chapel and afterwards breakfasting with him.

Mme. de Habicht was a professor and director of the legal library in the faculty of law at the University of Fribourg. It was here that I had made her acquaintance. Aware of her scheduled rendezvous with the pope on the feast of Saint Charles Borromeo, November 4, I asked her if she would put my manuscript directly in his hands. She agreed to do so and, upon her return to Fribourg, assured me that she had done so. I sent a copy of the same report to Card. Agostino Casaroli, Secretary of State. In a gracious letter of thanks, he said that he and his staff had given serious attention to its contents. I also sent copies to Cardinals Koenig and Etchegaray, both of whom had recently visited mainland China. The latter, who was then the president of the conference of bishops of France but has since been called to Rome to head the Justice and Peace commission, expressed keen interest in the subject and sent me a copy of an interview which he had given to the French Catholic daily La Croix after his visit to China.

La Comedia E Finita—or Almost

There is not much more to record. In the summer of 1984 I flew to California to attend a general assembly of the California Province. The day after my arrival in Los Angeles an angiogram revealed that I now had two blockages of the coronary arteries. The next day an angioplasty, or "balloon" operation, was successful. In a few weeks I was ready to return to Switzerland. The provincial, Fr. Jack Clark, was of a different mind. He thought it was time that I come home. My widowed sister, Isabel, who has always strongly supported me although not necessarily always agreeing with me, lives here; so do her two married daughters, Pamela and Sheila. My mother and brothers are buried here. Nieces and nephews and their children abound. But these ties apart, this has long since ceased to be home to me. So I argued the case—not too strongly, however, being still mindful of obedience. In the end we struck a compromise. He agreed that I return to Switzerland to greet the Georgetown students who would be arriving at the end of September, get them settled, oversee their orientation program, see them launched on their program of studies at the university, make arrangements for the future of the program. I agreed that, these things attended to, I would retire to the quiet of the Jesuit infirmary, then under construction at Loyola Marymount University in Los Angeles.

This I did, arriving here on the eve of Thanksgiving Day 1984. It is perhaps fitting that here, where it all began, it should also end. The year 1986 was the sixtieth anniversary of my graduation from Loyola College, as it was then known, and of my entry into the Society of Jesus. At the commencement Fr. James Loughran, president of the university, conferred upon me an honorary degree, for what reason it is difficult to see. At the commencement in 1975, Fr. Don Merrifield, his predecessor, had conferred upon me a medal for distinguished leadership. There was a touch of irony on that occasion, for presiding at the commencement was Card. Timothy Manning—the man who, as a young auxiliary bishop, had said that I had "the makings of another Martin Luther." He was gracious to me, and I to him. He is a gracious man; and I don't live in the past.[7]

I am well into my eighty-fifth year. To the annoyance of my sister, I calculate age in the logical Chinese way; it seems obvious to the Chinese, as it does to me, that one's first birthday is the day one is born. When I survey from that high point the road traveled,

the milestones of which are indicated in these pages, I see little in the way of lasting accomplishment. It is largely a record of failure and frustration which contrasts sharply with the achievements of most of my contemporaries, five of whom share with me the patient ministrations of the nursing staff of the Arrupe Infirmary attached to the Jesuit community at Loyola Marymount University. Here we await from day to day the coming of Godot.

Chess is a fascinating game, but one I never mastered. When I sailed out of San Francisco Bay in 1932 I expected to spend the rest of my life in China. Father Ledochowski, then the general superior of the Society of Jesus, held firmly to the principle that a commitment to the missions was a commitment for life. I looked forward to ending that life in the anonymous obscurity of a Chinese village in inland China. Many decisions, some by me, others—notable among them the decision to recall me from China—made by others with no input from me, headed me in far different directions and bring me now as evening gathers back to where it all began.

I have no regrets. Remorse, of course, for my many sins, but no regrets. The sins have remained unrecorded here because they are of interest only to me and to God, who has, I hope, forgiven them, if not forgotten them. They remind me that I have a debt to pay and enable me to say in all honesty, whatever disappointments there have been, I got what was coming to me. One cannot ask for anything more.

FINIS

Notes

Notes to Chapter One

1. Letter to me of May 30, 1986.

2. Michael J. Dunne's privately published *A Family in Migration: The Dunnes from 1820 to 1914* gives an interesting account of the voyage.

3. Dennis Dunne was named vicar general of the diocese by Bishop O'Regan. The latter's successor, Bp. James Duggan, young and brilliant, showed signs of mental instability which Dunne, as chairman of a committee of priests, reported to Rome. Duggan in retaliation fired Dunne both as vicar general and as pastor and suspended his faculties as priest. Dunne died of a heart attack on December 23, 1868, refusing on his deathbed to retract his charges. The *Chicago Tribune* described the funeral services as "the most impressive ever witnessed in this city." Less than six months later Bishop Duggan was committed to a mental hospital where he spent the last ten years of his life. For the details of this sad story, see James Patrick Gaffey, M.A., *The Life of Patrick William Riordan, Second Archbishop of San Francisco, 1841-1914*, The Catholic University of America, 1965.

Note to Chapter Three

1. The original reads: "Le Christ, le Saint Sacrament, la messe, la sainte vierge, tout la reste c'est la blague." The term *la*

blague, for which I suggest "flummery," is nuanced. Many other things—"the rest"— serve a purpose in the history of salvation but are not essential to the faith.

Notes to Chapter Seven

1. *Studies in the Spirituality of Jesuits*, vol. XIII, no. 4 (September 1981).

2. Donald J. Kemper, *Catholic Integration in St. Louis, 1935-1947*, unpublished manuscript.

3. Today the preferred word is *blacks* or *Afro-Americans*. I generally use the word *Negroes* because it was the preferred word when the events here described occurred.

4. Letter of January 4, 1945, to Father Zuercher in the archives of the Missouri Province, located in St. Louis, hereinafter referred to as MARC.

5. Letter from Heithaus to Zuercher, December 18, 1944; in MARC.

6. Letter from Maher to Zuercher, January 4, 1945; in MARC.

7. Letter from Maher to provincials, May 3, 1945; in MARC.

8. To this point I have drawn heavily from the account of the desegregation of the university by William Bernard Faherty, S.J., "Breaking the Color Barrier," *Universitas* (Autumn 1987, St. Louis University), adding some details which, for understandable reasons, he has omitted, and making certain judgments for which he bears no responsibility.

9. Quoted in letter from Heithaus to Zuercher, December 18, 1944; in MARC.

10. Quoted in letter from Heithaus to Zuercher, December 18, 1944; in MARC.

11. Letter of January 28, 1944; MARC.

12. Letter of June 7, 1945; in MARC.

13. Commencement Report, May 16, 1945; in MARC.

14. Faherty, *op.cit.*, p. 20.

15. Letter from Maher to Zuercher, April 10, 1945; in MARC.

16. 32 C.2d 711;198P.2d 17.

17. Cf. *infra*, p. 234.

Notes to Chapter Eight

1. A member of the California Province. He had been doing graduate studies in history at St. Louis University and was an eyewitness to the events which I have described. He had become, like his brother Fr. Daniel McGloin, S.J., a close friend. After my departure, we maintained for some time a rather extensive correspondence in which we discussed the St. Louis episode and its aftermath. John preserved my letters throughout the years and upon hearing that I was writing my memoirs sent me the entire collection. They have proved an enormous help in reconstructing the events of those days and particularly problems relating to my failure to return to China.

2. This letter, dated September 19, 1945, is in the archives of the California Province of the Society of Jesus, Los Gatos, Calif., hereinafter designated as CARC.

3. Letter to John McGloin, S.J., November 12, 1945; in CARC.

4. "Quaeque latissimum influxum habere potuerit in vastissima Sinarum regione." Letter dated June 21, 1935; in CARC.

5. Letter of January 2, 1946; in CARC.

6. Letter of January 10, 1946; in CARC.

7. Following his term as ambassador Oscar Lange served as Poland's representative to the United Nations. Ultimately he returned to Poland and to the academic life. Thirty years later on a tour of inspection of a half dozen Georgetown University junior year programs in Europe, I visited the University of Warsaw in Poland. The Georgetown students were attending classes in a very modern building which, so a plaque in the library informed me, was the School of Statistical Economics, whose founder, now deceased, was Oscar Lange. When I told the professor who was my contact that Oscar Lange had been a friend of mine, I became an instant celebrity. Word quickly spread among the faculty, who insisted that they honor me with a special reception. Such was the measure of esteem in which they held Oscar Lange.

8. Barbara Tuchman, *Stilwell & the American Experience in China, 1911-1945* (Macmillan, 1971).

9. *Studies in the Spirituality of Jesuits*, vol. XI, no. 1 (January 1979).

10. "Socialism and socialism," *Commonweal*, November 23, 1945.

Notes to Chapter Nine

1. The story of the strike is told in my brochure *Hollywood Labor Dispute: A Study in Immorality* (Conference Publishing Company, 1950).

2. See *Nitti Tax Hearings*: Stenographic minutes before the tax court of the United States at Chicago, Ill, Sept. 27 to Oct. 4, 1948, in the matter of *Estate of Joseph Nitti, a minor, Annette Carvaretto Nitti, guardian, vs. Commissioner of Internal Revenue* (Docket nos. 8840, 8841, 8842). Faced with trial for evading taxes on his Hollywood loot, Frank Nitti committed suicide. Hence the trial against his estate.

3. In return for early release from the penitentiary, Browne and Bioff testified at the Nitti tax hearings, revealing from its beginning the details of the producers–crime syndicate collusion. Some years later, living under an assumed name (which I recall as Newton) in Phoenix, Bioff stepped on the

starter of his car one morning and was blown to smithereens. The hireling was thus paid by his former associates for singing like a canary. I too was living in Phoenix at the time and learned of his pyrotechnic demise when I saw the headlines of the afternoon paper when making my rounds at the Veterans Hospital.

4.   Dan Marshall was a devout Catholic and dedicated Christian. Early in his career he put his legal talents at the service of ethnic minorities. He founded the Catholic Interracial Council, which would be suppressed by Abp. (later Cardinal) James McIntyre shortly after his arrival of unhappy memory to take command of the Los Angeles archdiocese. Dan Marshall carried to the California Supreme Court the landmark case of *Perez v. Sharp*, 32c.2d 711, and won a decision which declared unconstitutional the long-standing antimiscegenation law. I collaborated modestly in Dan's preparation of the brief, which argued that the law violated the freedom of religion guaranteed by the First Amendment.

5.   We know of these meetings thanks to the fact that Victor Clarke, one of the producers' agents participating, had the happy habit of taking notes. These were produced only in the last days of the congressional hearings described below. They were reproduced in the report *Congressional investigation: Hearings before a subcommittee of the House Committee on Education and Labor, appointed to investigate jurisdictional disputes in the motion picture industry (80th Congress)*, Washington, D.C. Hereinafter known as the *Kearns Report*.

6.   The committee consisted of three vice-presidents of the AFL: William C. Doherty, Felix H. Knight, and William C. Birthright.

7.   See Kearns Report.

8.   *Ibid.*, p. 36.

9.   Pat Casey, about to retire after twenty-five years in charge of labor relations for all of the producers, one day near the end of the hearings asked me to meet him at the Wilshire Country Club. Taking me to a table well out of any earshot, and after eliciting from me a promise not to quote or cite him, he

informed me that my view of the strike as the planned strategy of the producers and the IATSE to destroy the CSU was correct. Why did he confide in me? Perhaps to ease his conscience. It was he who produced the incriminating notes mentioned above, in note 5—perhaps for the same reason.

10. Kearns Report.

11. Quoted by Nancy Schwartz, *Hollywood Writers' Wars* (Alfred Knopf, 1982), p. 299.

12. Gary Wills has made an interesting study of this phenomenon in his *Innocents at Home: Reagan's America* (Doubleday, 1987).

13. *Hollywood Labor Dispute*, p. 42.

Notes to Chapter Ten

1. Urban Nagle, O.P., *Behind the Mask* (Macmillan, 1951).

2. See *supra*, P. 136.

Notes to Chapter Eleven

1. See *supra*, p. 167.

2. See *supra*, pp. 152 ff.

3. These documents are in CARC.

4. See *supra*, p. 135.

5. See *supra*, pp. 159 ff.

Notes to Chapter Twelve

1. The text of this report is in CARC.

2. In CARC.

3.   In CARC.

4.   See *supra*, p. 101.

5.   This letter, fifteen pages in length, is also in CARC.

6.   "Superiores ne facile credant iis qui alicuius culpam deferunt, sed singula perquirant; in primis ipsum, qui defertur, audiant, ut se defendere possit; et si innocens reperiatur, deferens pro ratione culpae aut reprehendatur aut puniatur." Epitome, #219.

7.   A summary of the Jesuit Constitutions in fifty-three rules provided a digest of Jesuit ideals, attitudes and everyday procedures. The pertinent part of rule eleven is quoted in part below, note 9.

8.   The facts were these: when the FEPC bill was before the California legislature a committee waited on the archbishop and asked him to sign an endorsement of the bill. The archbishop tore up the prepared statement and wrote another and much stronger endorsement in his own hand. The endorsement spoke of the "necessity" of "FEPC legislation." Subsequently a group of racist-minded citizens formed a committee, which included a number of prominent Catholics, among them George Breslin, Frank Doherty, former president of the Chamber of Commerce, and Frank Montgomery, scion of an old Los Angeles family and Loyola alumnus, to defeat the bill. They brought pressure to bear upon the chancery office which, not daring openly to repudiate the archbishop, quietly spread word that he had not really endorsed the bill. I did not mention this to Bishop Manning nor the fact that I had in my possession a copy of the archbishop's handwritten endorsement.

9.   This rule, written by St. Ignatius of Loyola, reads as follows: "For as men of the world who follow the world love and very earnestly seek honors, distinctions, and the reputation of a great name among men, as the world teaches them; so they who are making progress in the spiritual life and are serious about following Christ our Lord love and warmly desire the very opposite—to be clothed, in fact, in the same garments and wear the same attire as our Lord, out of love and rever-

ence for him; and this to such an extent, that if it could be done without offence to his Divine Majesty, or sin on the part of their neighbor, they would wish to suffer abuse, injustice, false accusation and to be considered and treated as fools (without, however, giving occasion for such treatment), their whole desire being to resemble and in some way imitate our Creator and Lord Jesus Christ..."

Notes to Chapter Fourteen

1.   See *supra*, p. 97 (Parsons); 97–99 (Lafarge).

2.   See *supra*, pp. 122–123.

3.   The citation reads in part:
Alma Mater is grateful to all who honored her; today she in turn honors two of her faculty who by their own wisdom, dynamism, and sense of discovery, added lustre and meaning to the Anniversary theme: "Wisdom and Discovery for a Dynamic World." As a token of appreciation of their exemplary work and planning that brought to Alma Mater's halls many great thinkers, artists, writers, and public figures, to join in a fitting remembrance of a great past and a dedication to an even greater future, the President and the Board of Directors of Georgetown University are privileged to confer on the Reverend George H Dunne, S.J., and Dr. Riley Hughes the well deserved award of the John Carroll Medal of Merit for the year 1965.

4.   See *supra*, p. 123.

5.   This and the above quotes are from my article "This Was Montgomery," *America*, May 8, 1965.

6.   See my article, "How We Look to Others," *America*, June 17, 1961.

Notes to Chapter Fifteen

1.   *Great Rivers* (National Geographic Society, 1984), p. 299.

2.   See *supra*, p. 97.

Notes to Chapter Sixteen

1.   The proposed program:

On development: fourteen regional conferences, three each for Asia, Africa, Latin America; one each for the Middle East, East Europe, Caribbean, Pacific, North Atlantic; five international conferences. On peace: A European symposium; five regional conferences; in 1970 a World Conference similar to the Beirut Conference which I shall describe below. In addition to this there were provisions for working groups, ad-hoc groups, and educational programs for both Church-related and secular schools; projects for dialogue with Jews, Moslems, Hindi, Buddhists; employment of mass media, publications, research, etc. The total budget for all these activities, which were to depend upon the Geneva office of Sodepax, was estimated at $1,640,000.

Section II of the prospectus envisaged the development of a vast network of regional, national and local offices reaching to the level of parish, congregation, school and village organization, the grassroots of the world community. This was described as the "circulatory system" which from its center in Geneva would carry the findings of Sodepax into every corner of the world. The estimated budget for this part of the program was $15,350,000, which was to be the contribution of "the main circulatory system of the Churches."

2.   Among the many distinguished participants was Amb. Edwin Martin. As recounted earlier, it is he with whom I was lunching when word came of the assassination of Pres. John F. Kennedy.

3.   Charles Sherman, Liberian minister of finance, was one of fifteen cabinet members who, in the military coup which ten years later overthrew the Tubman government in Liberia, were tied to pillars on the beach and executed by a firing squad.

4.   Henri de Riedmatten, O.P., was at the time representative of the Holy See to the United Nations in Geneva. He would later

be named the first secretary of the newly established Cor Unum dicastery in the Roman Curia. He would also prove to be a bête noire of Sodepax.

5. Robert Bowie, formerly Assistant Secretary of State, was director of the Harvard Center for International Affairs.

6. All published Sodepax reports were printed by L'Imprimerie La Concorde, Lausanne. Copies are available at the Publications Department, Ecumenical Center, 150 Route de Ferney, 20, Geneva, Switzerland.

7. In the last days of November 1989 I received word of the unexpected death of Father Bransfield in Inchon, Korea. He was widely known and, outside of government circles, much beloved.

8. Gustavo Gutierrez, *A Theology of Liberation* (Orbis Books, 1973), p. xi, footnote.

Notes to Chapter Seventeen

1. The full text of this letter is in CARC.

2. The full text of this letter is in CARC.

3. Sodepax Publications:
   1. *World Development,* the Beirut Report. In English, French, German, Spanish, Italian, and Arabic.
   2. *World Development.* Published by Corpus Books. Contains both the report and the conference papers.
   3. *The Development Challenge.* The Montreal Report. In English, French, German, and Spanish.
   4. *In Search of a Theology of Development.* Papers of Cartigny conference.
   5. *Towards a Theology of Development.* An annotated bibliography of over 2000 titles in English, French, German, Spanish, Italian, and Portuguese.
   6. *Peace: The Desperate Imperative.* The Baden Report: In English, French, and German.
   7. *Partnership or Privilege?* An ecumenical reaction to the UN Second Development Decade.

8.   *Christian Reflections on the Second Development Decade.* A nontechnical version of *Partnership or Privilege?*
9.   *Money in a Village World.* An ecumenical critique of interests of the Third World in the IFM. In English.
10.   *Church—Communication—Development.* The Driebergen Report. In English.
11.   *Sodepax Brochure.* A prospectus. In English, French, German, and Japanese.

In addition, there were staff publications and papers, nine by me, nine by Neehall, eleven by Elliott, and five by Christophe.

Notes to Chapter Eighteen

1.   For a full account see my article "The Irish Sea of Troubles," *America*, March 4, 1972.

2.   In CARC.

Notes to Chapter Nineteen

1.   The text of this speech is in CARC.

2.   All these letters are in CARC.

3.   For a detailed account of de Riedmatten's activities as secretary of the birth control commission, see Robert Blair Kaiser, *The Politics of Sex and Religion* (Leaven Press, 1985). For the full list of members of this commission see *ibid.*, pp. 246-249.

4.   In CARC.

5.   The *London Observer* headlined its story "Vatican Diehards Kill World Poverty Scheme"; the *Washington Post*: "Vatican Conservatives Abort Plan to Tackle World Poverty;" the *Duluth News-Tribune*: "Antipoverty Bid Torpedoed at Vatican;" the *Toronto Star*: "Vatican Withdraws Support of Joint Anti-poverty Group." An editorial in the *Christian Century* remarked: "To those who have been following the fortunes of Sodepax over the past 12 months, this talk of strengthening

the Joint Commission must appear as ludicrous as it is misleading"; and: "Over the course of the centuries the Vatican has developed considerable skill in concealing truth by means of ambiguity, diversionary tactics and circumlocution. It will be a sad day when the WCC feels the need of similar skill, and it should resist the temptation to practice it, even when the cause is as good as unity with the church of Rome." The same editorial described my successor as "an elderly Belgian missionary priest from Japan." In a letter to the *Christian Century* I corrected this: "Apart from the fact that he is quite some years younger than I who—despite what some may think—am not a doddering old idiot, Fr. Spae has an established reputation among savants as a scholar in the field of Asiatic religions. He is the founder of the Oriens Institute for Religious Research in Tokyo and the author of several learned volumes in his field of interest—which may or may not relate to what were the chief interests of Sodepax during the first period of its history....Apart from this mild dissent, offered in justice to Fr. Spae, my only comment on the rest of your discerning editorial is: No comment." European newspapers in general carried the press release announcing the continuation of Sodepax. Some sources, such as the German *Evangelischer Pressedienst* and the Italian weekly *Nuovi Tempi,* said that the official press release had tried to conceal the truth that the activities of Sodepax had been drastically curtailed, its staff decimated, its structure totally altered.

6.   International Documentation Center (Rome, IDOC, no. 2, 1972).

7.   In CARC.

8.   In CARC.

9.   In CARC.

10. Benelli's letter to me and my reply, are both in CARC.

11. In CARC.

12. Peter Hebblethwaite, *op. cit.*, p. 98.

13. Both these letters—Finley Peter Dunne's and Charles Elliott's—are in CARC; Dr. Charles Elliott was recently named dean at Trinity College, Cambridge University.

Notes to Chapter Twenty

1. These appeared in *America*, July 2 and 9, 1972.

2. My paper in full is in CARC.

3 . In CARC

Notes to Chapter Twenty-One

1. George H. Dunne, S.J., *Generation of Giants* (Notre Dame University Press, 1962), pp. 321 ff.

2. See *idem*, pp. 193 ff.

3. *National Geographic*, April 1978, p. 440.

4. Nien Cheng, *Life and Death in Shanghai* (Grove Press, 1986); I recommend this remarkable account.

5. The bloody massacre in T'ian-an-men Square in June 1989 would hardly seem to conform to the image of an army which "serves the people." It is still composed, nevertheless, largely of unsophisticated boys fo peasant background. It will be recalled that in the days preceding the tragic affair, they were often seen on television in smiling, friendly exchanges with students. But they were told that the students were not "the people" but were counterrevolutionary "enemies of the people." Like military everywhere (Ollie North is a good example) they were disciplined to unquestioning obedience. This military mind-set is not peculiar to the Chinese. Our own military history is stained with episodes of ruthless massacres in obedience to orders: atrocities in the Philippines in the insurrection of 1898; German prisoners in World War II; My Lai in Vietnam. As for using violence against their own, T'ian-an-men differs in scale but not in kind from shameful

episodes in our own history: Chicago policemen in the mid thirties massacring striking workers outside the Inland Empire steel works; General MacArthur's troops driving thousands of unemployed veterans out of Washington at bayonet point after burning their tents and ramshackle hovels; national guardsmen gunning down students peacefully demonstrating at Kent State.

6.   The tyranny of mothers-in-law towards daughters-in-law is part of Chinese history and folklore.

Notes to Chapter Twenty-Two

1.   I do not know the date; I saw only a photocopy from which the date was missing.

2.   This letter is in CARC.

3.   The Catholic University of Fu Jen has been reestablished in Taipei, Taiwan.

4.   See *supra*, p. 404.

5.   Charles Meyer, *China Observed*, tr. Jean Joss (Gallery Books), p. 136.

6.   Since writing this I have learned that the authenticity of his prison experience is vigorously challenged by some of his former confreres in the priesthood. Unable either to affirm or to deny the validity of the challenge, I simply record it.

7.   Since this was written, Cardinal Manning, in retirement for some years, after a painful but mercifully brief illness, passed away on June 23, 1989, accompanied by signs of general affection and respect on the part of clergy and people.

Index